MySQL

New
Riders

New Riders Professional Library

MySQL

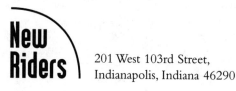

201 West 103rd Street,
Indianapolis, Indiana 46290

Paul DuBois

MySQL

Paul DuBois

International Standard Book Number: 0-7357-0921-1

Library of Congress Catalog Card Number: 99-067431

Printed in the United States of America

First Printing: *December, 1999*

04   03   02   01   7   6   5

Interpretation of the printing code: The rightmost double-digit number is the year of the book's printing; the rightmost single-digit number is the number of the book's printing. For example, the printing code 00-1 shows that the first printing of the book occurred in 2000.

Trademarks

Warning and Disclaimer

Publisher
David Dwyer

Executive Editor
Stephanie Wall

Acquisitions Editor
Katie Purdum

Product Marketing Manager
Stephanie Layton

Publicity Manager
Susan Petro

Managing Editor
Sarah Kearns

Development Editor
Leah Williams

Project Editor
John Rahm

Cover Designer
Aren Howell

Indexers
Cheryl Lenser
Tim Wright

Technical Reviewers
David Axmark
Vijay Chaugule
Chad Cunningham
Bill Gerrard
Jijo George John
Fred Read
Dr. Egon Schmid
Jani Tolonen
Michael "Monty" Widenius

Proofreader
Debra Neel

Compositors
Gina Rexrode
Wil Cruz

About the Author

Paul DuBois has been a network and database administrator for the past 15 years at the University of Wisconsin-Madison. He is the author of *Software Portability with imake* and *Using csh & tcsh* (O'Reilly & Associates, ISBNs 1-56592-226-3 and 1-56592-132-1, respectively), and is a contributor to the MySQL Reference Manual.

About the Reviewers

David Axmark has been working as a Software Consultant for over 15 years. Among the many projects he has worked on are a state-of-the-art market research system (CommonLISP+CLOS+MySQLs-ISAM), advanced business graphics (in 32k RAM), and a system to write working orders for a power company. He has written many lines of code in 6502 and Z80 assembler, BASIC, C, CommonLisp, (Bourne)-Shell, and Perl. His involvement with MySQL started some years before the first public release. David lives in Uppsala, Sweden with his plants and computers.

Vijay Chaugule is working as Senior Systems Administrator for a Bay Area company handling a large UNIX network. He has eight years of experience in systems and network management and has worked on a lot of commercial and GNU tools. He loves to write Perl scripts and to compile and install GNU software. He is currently using MySQL on a project for induscrafts.com.

Chad Cunningham is a Systems Developer for the Ohio State University Department of Mathematics, where he focuses on developing Web-based learning tools to augment traditional classroom instruction.

Bill Gerrard is the Vice-President of Technology at Daze Networks, Inc. in Huntington Beach, California. Daze Networks operates Internet services, including DigitalDaze.com virtual Web servers that give you complete control over your own MySQL database server and DNSCentral.com, which offers domain name registration, parking, Web forwarding, and email forwarding using MySQL as the back-end database.

Jijo George John is a Technical Lead in the software development division of the Chemical Analysis group of Hewlett Packard Company. He is experienced in developing system and application software for chemical instruments. He has worked on software close to the instruments/devices as well as large database applications. He is currently using MySQL on a project for induscrafts.com.

Fred Read has been running his own consultancy, ServaLan Systems Limited, for the past 14 years. ServaLan Systems specializes in producing Unix systems in the areas of Telecoms, databases, finance, and the Internet. He is currently working on a Telecoms switching system. For the last three years, he has also been running an Internet Service Provider (PremierISP) and a Web advertising business (PremierAds). He has been married to Helen for the past nine years. They have three children (two girls and a boy) and live in England.

Dr. Egon Schmid is with Six Offene Systeme GmbH in Leinfelden-Echterdingen, Germany, where he is part of the development team that develops sophisticated Web-based database solutions. He is also a member of the PHP Documentation Group. He co-authored the first PHP book in German.

Jani Tolonen is a Software Developer of MySQL. He is a 23-year-old student at Helsinki University of Technology, where he focuses on computer technology and software programming in many areas. Jani has been under the training of Michael "Monty" Widenius, the creator of MySQL, and is dedicated to its further development. Jani and Monty became very good friends incidentally: They were neighbors over ten years ago. Jani's work with MySQL began shortly after Monty started developing MySQL in 1995.

Michael "Monty" Widenius is a Swedish-speaking Finn who has been working with databases since 1978. He has been employed by and been part owner of TcX since 1981 and has written the whole part of UNIREG (the predecessor to MySQL) and most of the MySQL server. He studied physics at the Helsinki University of Technology, but when it comes to programming, he is mostly self taught. He has mainly been working in Basic, Assembler, C, LISP, Perl, SQL, C++ (in this order), but he is always willing to look at some new languages when he gets some time. He is married and has two children (a boy and a girl—Max and My), two turtles, one dog, and two snakes. Nowadays, most of his time goes into answering mails.

New Riders would like to thank Tomas Karlsson, Colin McKinnon, Sasha Pachev, Eric Savage, Derick H. Siddoway, and Bob Worthy for their contributions as well.

Contents

Foreword

When I was presented with the opportunity to technically review Paul's book, I didn't expect to also get stuck with the foreword. My opinion has always been that one should never let a programmer write a book, not even a book for programmers.

I may have a small talent for producing usable programming code, but fortunately Paul has a great talent for explaining things that a lot of users may find hard to grasp otherwise. Those of us who have been working on MySQL have put a great deal of effort into making it fast and easy to use, but MySQL has many different features, and most users will need information that can only be gathered by experience in order to utilize MySQL to its fullest. Over the past year, Paul has been working on the MySQL manual, and throughout this process, he has asked us many hundreds of questions on how MySQL works in an effort to understand everything. With this book, he now shares this knowledge with you. (You are of course also welcome to work on the MySQL online manual if you want, even if you now have the shortcut to understanding MySQL in your hands.)

The MySQL manual has always been regarded by us at TcX as a technical reference to MySQL. We have always had a need for a user manual that can communicate the technical concepts in a more relaxed way. We think this book will fill this gap nicely! One of the goals of MySQL is to be as compatible with older versions as possible. We are sure that in spite of the high developing pace of MySQL, most concepts in this book will hold true for a very long time.

As long as I still have your attention, I would like to take this opportunity to thank my wife, Carola, for the time she has let me spend on MySQL during the last three years. To my children, Max and My, for understanding that even if their father is working at home, he isn't always available. I also want to thank David for convincing me to write MySQL, and Allan Larson for giving me the opportunity to do so. I have had a lot of help from the current MySQL team: Jani Tolonen, Sinisa Milivojevic, Antti Halonen, and Tõnu Samuel. Last, but not least, I want to thank all of those people who have written APIs and client programs and submitted patches and nice bug reports, which have helped us make MySQL the success it is today.

Michael "Monty" Widenius
Helsingfors, 1999-11-14

Acknowledgments

This book benefited greatly from the comments, corrections, and criticisms provided by the technical reviewers: David Axmark, Vijay Chaugule, Chad Cunningham, Bill Gerrard, Jijo George John, Fred Read, Egon Schmid, and Jani Tolonen. Special thanks goes to Michael "Monty" Widenius, the principal MySQL developer, who not only reviewed the manuscript, but also fielded hundreds of questions that I sent his way during the course of writing the book. Naturally, any errors that remain are my own.

I'd also like to thank Tomas Karlsson, Colin McKinnon, Sasha Pachev, Eric Savage, Derick H. Siddoway, and Bob Worthy, who reviewed the initial proposal, and helped shape the book into its present form.

The staff at New Riders are responsible first for conceiving this book and then for turning my scribblings into the finished work you hold in your hands. Laurie Petrycki acted as Executive Editor. Katie Purdum, Acquisitions Editor, helped me get under way and took the heat when I missed deadlines. Leah Williams did double duty not only as Development Editor but as Copy Editor; she put in many, many late hours, especially in the final stages of the project. Cheryl Lenser and Tim Wright produced the index. John Rahm served as Project Editor. Debra Neel proofread the manuscript. Gina Rexrode and Wil Cruz, Compositors, laid out the book in the form you see now. My thanks to each of them.

Most of all, I want to express my appreciation to my wife, Karen, for putting up with another book, and for her understanding and patience as I disappeared, sometimes for days on end, into "the writing zone." Her support made the task easier on many occasions, and I am pleased to acknowledge her contribution; she helped me write every page.

Tell Us What You Think!

As the reader of this book, *you* are our most important critic and commentator. We value your opinion and want to know what we're doing right, what we could do better, what areas you'd like to see us publish in, and any other words of wisdom you're willing to pass our way.

As an Executive Editor at New Riders Publishing, I welcome your comments. You can fax, email, or write me directly to let me know what you did or didn't like about this book—as well as what we can do to make our books stronger.

Please note that I cannot help you with technical problems related to the topic of this book, and that due to the high volume of mail I receive, I might not be able to reply to every message.

When you write, please be sure to include this book's title and author, as well as your name and phone or fax number. I will carefully review your comments and share them with the author and editors who worked on the book.

Fax: 317-581-4663
Email: nrfeedback@newriders.com
Mail: Stephanie Wall
         Executive Editor
         New Riders Publishing
         201 West 103rd Street
         Indianapolis, IN 46290 USA

Introduction

A relational database management system (RDBMS) is an essential tool in many environments, from the more traditional uses in business, research, and education contexts, to newer applications, such as powering search engines on the Internet. However, despite the importance of a good database for managing and accessing information resources, many organizations have found them out of reach of their financial resources. Historically, database systems have been an expensive proposition, with vendors charging healthy fees both for software and for support, and because database engines often had substantial hardware requirements to run with any reasonable performance, the cost was even greater.

In recent years, the situation has changed, on both the hardware and software sides of the picture. Personal computers have become inexpensive but powerful, and a whole movement has sprung up to write high-performance operating systems for them that are available for the cost of an inexpensive CD, or even free over the Internet. These include several BSD UNIX derivatives (FreeBSD, NetBSD, OpenBSD) as well as various forms of Linux (RedHat, Caldera, LinuxPPC, to name a few).

Production of free operating systems to drive personal computers to their full capabilities has proceeded in concert with—and to a large extent has been made possible by—the development of freely available tools like gcc, the GNU C compiler. These efforts to make software available to anyone who wants it have resulted in what is now called the Open Source movement, and have produced many important pieces of software. The busiest FTP site in the world, ftp.cdrom.com, runs FreeBSD. Apache is the most widely used Web server on the Internet. Other Open Source successes are the Perl general-purpose scripting language and PHP, a language rapidly gaining in popularity due to the ease with which it allows dynamic Web pages to be written. These all stand in contrast to proprietary solutions that lock you into high-priced products from vendors that don't even provide source code.

Database software has become more accessible, too. Database systems such as Postgres and mSQL have become available for free or at low cost. More recently, commercial vendors such as Informix and Oracle have begun to offer their software at no cost for operating systems such as Linux. (However, these latter products generally come in binary-only form with no support, which lessens their usefulness.)

One of the newer entries into the no-to-low cost database arena is MySQL, a SQL client/server relational database management system originating from Scandinavia. MySQL includes an SQL server, client programs for accessing the server, administrative tools, and a programming interface for writing your own programs.

MySQL's roots begin in 1979, with the UNIREG database tool created by Michael "Monty" Widenius for the Swedish company TcX. In 1994, TcX began looking around for a SQL server for use in developing Web applications. They tested some commercial servers, but found all too slow for TcX's large tables. They also took a look at mSQL, but it lacked certain features TcX required. Consequently, Monty began developing a new server. The programming interface was explicitly designed to be similar to the one used by mSQL because several free tools were available for mSQL, and by using a similar interface, those same tools could be used for MySQL with a minimum of porting effort.

In 1995, David Axmark of Detron HB began to push for TcX to release MySQL on the Internet. David also worked on the documentation and on getting MySQL to build with the GNU `configure` utility. MySQL 3.11.1 was unleashed on the world in 1996 in the form of binary distributions for Linux and Solaris. Today, MySQL works on many more platforms and is available in both binary and source form.

MySQL is not an Open Source project because a license is necessary under certain conditions. Nevertheless, MySQL enjoys widespread popularity in the Open Source community because the licensing terms are not very restrictive. (In essence, MySQL is generally free unless you want to make money by selling it or by selling services that require it.)

MySQL's popularity isn't limited to the Open Source community. Yes, it runs on personal computers (indeed, much MySQL development takes place on inexpensive Linux systems). But MySQL is portable and runs on commercial operating systems (such as Solaris, Irix, and Windows) and on hardware all the way up to enterprise servers. Furthermore, its performance rivals any database system you care to put up against it, and it can handle large databases with millions of records.

MySQL lies squarely within the picture that now unfolds before us: freely available operating systems running on powerful but inexpensive hardware, putting substantial processing power and capabilities in the hands of more people than ever before, on a wider variety of systems than ever before. This lowering of the economic barriers to computing puts powerful database solutions within reach of more people and organizations than at any time in the past. For example, I use MySQL with Perl, Apache, and PHP on my G3 PowerBook running LinuxPPC. This allows me to carry my work with me anywhere. Total cost: the cost of the PowerBook.

Organizations that once could only dream of putting the power of a high-performance RDBMS to work for them now can do so for very little cost. Database use is increasing at the individual level, too. People who might never have considered using a database begin thinking of all kinds of uses for them once it's possible to obtain one easily—for example, storing and accessing the results of genealogical research, tracking and maintaining hobbyist collections (butterflies, stamps, baseball cards, etc.), helping to manage a startup business, or providing search capabilities for personal Web sites.

Why Choose MySQL?

If you're looking for a free or inexpensive database management system, several are available from which to choose: MySQL, mSQL, Postgres, one of the free-but-unsupported engines from commercial vendors, and so forth. When you compare MySQL with other database systems, think about what's most important to you. Performance; support; features (SQL conformance, extensions, etc.); licensing conditions and restrictions; and price all are factors to take into account. Given these considerations, MySQL has many attractive features to offer:

- **Speed.** MySQL is fast. The developers contend that MySQL is about the fastest database you can get. You can investigate this claim by visiting http://www.mysql.com/benchmark.html, a performance-comparison page on the MySQL Web site.

- **Ease of use.** MySQL is a high-performance but relatively simple database system and is much less complex to set up and administer than larger systems.

- **Cost.** MySQL is free for most in-house uses. See "Is MySQL Free?" later in this introduction.

- **Query language support.** MySQL understands SQL (Structured Query Language), the language of choice for all modern database systems. You can also access MySQL using applications that support ODBC (Open Database Connectivity), a database communications protocol developed by Microsoft.

- **Capability.** Many clients can connect to the server at the same time. Clients can use multiple databases simultaneously. You can access MySQL interactively using several interfaces that let you enter queries and view the results: command-line clients, Web browsers, or X Window System clients. In addition, a variety of programming interfaces is available for languages such as C, Perl, Java, PHP, and Python. Thus, you have the choice of using prepackaged client software or writing your own for custom applications.

- **Connectivity and security.** MySQL is fully networked, and databases can be accessed from anywhere on the Internet, so you can share your data with anyone, anywhere. But MySQL has access control so that people who shouldn't see your data can't.

- **Portability.** MySQL runs on many varieties of UNIX, as well as on other non-UNIX systems, such as Windows and OS/2. MySQL runs on hardware from home PCs to high-end servers.

- **Open distribution.** MySQL is easy to obtain; just use your Web browser. If you don't understand how something works or are curious about an algorithm, you can get the source code and poke around in it. If you don't like how something works, you can change it.

What about support? Good question; a database isn't much use if you can't get help for it. Naturally, I'd like to think this book is all the assistance you'll ever need. But, realistically, you'll have questions that I never thought of or didn't have room to cover. You'll find that other resources are available, and that MySQL has good support:

- MySQL includes an extensive Reference Manual (450 pages and growing).

- Technical support contracts are available from the MySQL developers, for those who prefer a formal arrangement.

- There is an active mailing list to which anyone may subscribe. The list has many helpful participants, including the MySQL developers. As a support resource, many people find it sufficient for their purposes.

The MySQL community, developers and non-developers alike, is very responsive. Answers to questions on the mailing list often arrive within minutes. When bugs are reported, the developers generally release a fix within days (sometimes within hours!), and fixes are immediately available over the Internet. Contrast this with the often-frustrating experience of navigating the Byzantine support channels of the big vendors. (You've been there? Me, too. I know which alternative I prefer when I have a question about a product. Being put on hold at a vendor's convenience has no appeal compared to being able to post a question to a mailing list and check for replies at my convenience.)

MySQL is an ideal candidate for evaluation if you are in the database-selection process. You can try MySQL with no risk or financial commitment. Yet, if you get stuck, you can use the mailing list to get help. An evaluation costs some of your time, but that's true no matter what database system you're considering—and it's a safe bet that your installation and setup time for MySQL will be less than for many other systems.

Already Running Another RDBMS?

If you're currently running another database system, should you convert to MySQL? Not necessarily. If you're happy with your current system, why bother to switch? But if you feel constrained by what you're using, you definitely should consider MySQL. Perhaps performance of your current system is a concern, or it's proprietary and you don't like being locked into it. Perhaps you'd like to run on hardware that's not supported by your current system, or your software is provided in binary-only format and you'd really prefer to have the source available. Or maybe it just costs too much! All of these are reasons to look into MySQL. Use this book to familiarize yourself with MySQL's capabilities, ask some questions on the MySQL mailing list, and you'll probably find the answers you need to make a decision.

If you are considering switching from another SQL database to MySQL, check out the comparison page on the MySQL Web site at `http://www.mysql.com/crash-me-choose.htmy`. Then check the chapters dealing with MySQL's data types and dialect of SQL. You may decide that the version of SQL supported by your current RDBMS is too different and that porting your applications would involve significant effort.

Part of your evaluation should be to try porting a few examples, of course, because it may turn out not to be as difficult as you think. It may not be that difficult even if your database is an older one that doesn't understand SQL. I recently converted a records management system from an RDBMS that wasn't SQL-based. There wasn't any language similarity at all to take advantage of, and some of the data types had no SQL equivalent. This project involved conversion of the network access methods and dozens of screen-based entry programs and canned queries. It took perhaps a month and a half of full-time effort. That's not bad.

Tools Provided with MySQL

The MySQL distribution includes the following tools:

- **A SQL server.** This is the engine that powers MySQL and provides access to your databases.

- **Client programs for accessing the server.** An interactive program allows you to enter queries directly and view the results, and several administrative and utility programs help you run your site. One utility allows you to control the server. Others let you import or export data, check access permissions, and more.

- **A client library for writing your own programs.** You can write clients in C because the library is in C, but the library also provides the basis for third-party bindings for other languages.

In addition to the software provided with MySQL itself, MySQL is used by many talented and capable people who like writing software to enhance their productivity and who are willing to make that software available. The result is that you have access to a variety of third-party tools that make MySQL easier to use or that extend its reach into areas such as Web site development.

Is MySQL Free?

MySQL is not an Open Source product but generally may be used for free. You should consult the MySQL Reference Manual for licensing specifics, but the basic principles are as follows:

- The client programs and the client-programming library are free, on all platforms.

- For UNIX and other non-Windows platforms, the MySQL server can be used freely unless you want to sell it or any software or services that require it. In that case, you should license the server. The idea is that if you're making money from MySQL, it's reasonable that the MySQL developers should see some of it. ($200 is a bargain for a professional RDBMS that's helping you make money, and there's lots of free software you can get to help you use it more effectively.)

- The Windows version of the MySQL server requires a license.

- Older versions of MySQL are available under the GNU Public License (GPL) and can be used for any purpose whatsoever without payment. MySQL 3.20.32a is available under the terms of the GPL.

Whether or not you need a server license, formal support can be obtained on a fee basis from the MySQL developers, and I'd encourage you to consider this. (Especially if you work for a company in which management frowns on any software for which no such agreement is in place.) Several levels of support are available, and, besides getting excellent assistance, you'll be helping further the development of MySQL and thus the entire MySQL community.

A Note on the Windows License

People sometimes ask, "How come I have to license the MySQL server just because I'm running Windows?" That's a reasonable question, and there's a reasonable answer. Consider the economics of the issue. To engage in software development, you need an operating system and some development tools, such as an editor and a compiler. With respect to these requirements, there is a fundamental difference between developing for UNIX and developing for Windows. Under UNIX, you can get pretty much everything you need for free:

- For the operating system, you have several choices, such as Linux or one of the free BSD variants, such as FreeBSD, NetBSD, and OpenBSD.

- For development tools, all of those operating systems come complete with editors such as vi and emacs and compilers such as gcc and egcs.

- When updates to the operating system or development tools are released, you can simply download them from the Internet or get an inexpensive CD. This is true even for major revisions.

On the other hand, it's fairly expensive to develop software on Windows:

- The operating system isn't free.

- Development tools such as the compiler aren't free.

- When updates to the operating system or tools are released, you pay again unless they are simply bug fix releases or minor incremental upgrades.

All of this means that while software development costs under UNIX are essentially zero, for Windows they can be considerable. The MySQL developers may like working on MySQL, but not so much that they want to pay for the privilege. The Windows development costs must be recovered somehow, and the license charge is the means by which that happens.

In addition, the developers have found that it takes much more time to develop for Windows than for UNIX. Because the developers' time is a fixed commodity, this is a cost that must be borne at the expense of the UNIX version (which is, after all, the primary MySQL deployment platform). The Windows license fee provides incentive to direct time and effort into the Windows port.

If you want to run Windows, but don't want to license the server, you still have some options:

- A shareware version of MySQL is available that you can try for evaluation purposes. This gives you 30 days to use the server, after which you may decide to license it after all.

- If you run the Windows server for educational use or for use in university or government research settings, you can ask the developers to waive the license fee.

- The client programs are free in any case, so if you can find someone who already runs a server and is willing to let you use it, you have complete access to MySQL's capabilities.

What You Can Expect from This Book

By reading this book, you'll learn how to use MySQL effectively so that you can get your work done more productively. You'll be able to figure out how to get your information into a database, and you'll learn how to formulate queries that give you the answers to the questions you want to ask of that data.

You don't need to be a programmer to understand or use SQL. This book will show you how it works. But there's more to understanding how to use a database properly than just knowing SQL syntax. This book emphasizes MySQL's unique capabilities and shows how to use them. Other books focus on SQL in general, or on the SQL dialect of some other RDBMS.

You'll also see how MySQL integrates with other tools. The book shows how to use MySQL with PHP or Perl to generate dynamic Web pages created from the result of database queries. You'll learn how to write your own programs that access MySQL databases. All of these enhance MySQL's capabilities to handle the requirements of your particular applications.

If you'll be responsible for administrating a MySQL installation, this book will tell you what your duties are and how to carry them out. You'll learn how to set up user accounts, perform database backups, and make sure your site is secure.

Road Map to This Book

This book is organized into four parts.

Part I: General MySQL Use

- **Introduction to MySQL and SQL.** Discusses how MySQL can be useful to you, and provides a general tutorial that introduces the interactive MySQL client program and covers the basics of SQL.

- **Working with Data in MySQL.** Discusses the column types that MySQL provides for describing your data, properties and limitations of each type, when and how to use them, how to choose between similar types, expression evaluation, and type conversion.

- **MySQL SQL Syntax and Use.** Every major RDBMS now available understands SQL, but every database engine implements a slightly different SQL dialect. This chapter discusses SQL with particular emphasis on those features that make MySQL distinctive. It also discusses features that are present in other databases but not in MySQL, and the workarounds that exist.

- **Query Optimization.** How to make your queries run more efficiently.

Part II: Using MySQL Programming Interfaces

- **Introduction to MySQL Programming.** Discusses some of the application programming interfaces available for MySQL and provides a general comparison of the APIs that the book covers in detail.

- **The MySQL C API.** How to write C programs using the API provided by the client library included in the MySQL distribution.

- **The Perl DBI API.** How to write Perl scripts using the DBI module. Covers standalone scripts and CGI scripts for Web site programming.

- **The PHP API.** How to use the PHP scripting language to write dynamic Web pages that access MySQL databases.

Part III: MySQL Administration

- **Introduction to MySQL Administration.** What the database administrator's duties are and what you should know to run a successful site.

- **The MySQL Data Directory.** An in-depth look at the organization and contents of the data directory, the area under which MySQL stores databases and status files.

- **General MySQL Administration.** How to make sure your server starts up and shuts down properly when your system does. Also includes instructions for setting up MySQL user accounts, and discusses log file maintenance, backup strategies, server tuning, and database backup and recovery strategies.

- **Security.** What you need to know to make your MySQL installation safe from intrusion, both from other users on the server host and from clients connecting over the network.

- **Database Maintenance and Repair.** How to reduce the likelihood of disaster through preventive maintenance and how to perform crash recovery if disaster strikes in spite of your preventive measures.

Part IV: Appendixes

- **Obtaining and Installing Software.** Where to get and how to install the major tools described in the book.

- **Column Type Reference.** Descriptions of MySQL's column types.

- **Operator and Function Reference.** Descriptions of the operators and functions that can be used to write expressions in SQL statements.

- **SQL Syntax Reference.** Descriptions of each SQL statement that MySQL understands.

- **MySQL Program Reference.** Descriptions of each program provided in the MySQL distribution.

- **C API Reference.** Descriptions of data types and functions in the MySQL C client library.

- **Perl DBI API Reference.** Descriptions of methods and attributes provided by the Perl DBI module.

- **PHP API Reference.** Descriptions of the functions that PHP provides for MySQL support.

- **Useful Third-Party Tools.** A brief overview of some of the tools available to help you use MySQL, such as data conversion and administrative utilities.

- **Internet Service Providers.** What to consider when choosing an ISP that provides MySQL access. What to consider when operating as an ISP providing MySQL services to customers.

How To Read This Book

Whichever part of the book you happen to be reading at any given time, it's best to try out the examples as you go along. If MySQL isn't installed on your system, you should install it or ask someone to do so for you. Then get the files needed to set up the sample database to which we'll be referring throughout the book. Appendix A, "Obtaining and Installing Software," says where you can obtain all this stuff and has instructions for installing it.

If you're a complete newcomer to MySQL or to SQL, begin with Chapter 1, "Introduction to MySQL and SQL." This provides you with a tutorial introduction that grounds you in basic MySQL and SQL concepts and brings you up to speed for the rest of the book. Then proceed to Chapter 2, "Working with Data in MySQL," and Chapter 3, "MySQL SQL Syntax and Use," to find out how to describe and manipulate your own data so that you can exploit MySQL's capabilities for your own applications.

If you already know some SQL, you should still read Chapters 2 and 3. SQL implementations vary, and you'll want to find out what makes MySQL's implementation distinctive in comparison to others with which you may be familiar.

If you have experience with MySQL but need more background on the details of performing particular tasks, use the book as a reference, looking up topics on a need-to-know basis.

If you're interested in writing your own programs to access MySQL databases, read the API chapters, beginning with Chapter 5, "Introduction to MySQL Programming." If you want to produce a Web-based front end to your databases for easier access to them, or, conversely, to provide a database back end for your Web site to enhance your site with dynamic content, check out Chapters 7, "The Perl DBI API," and 8, "The PHP API."

If you're evaluating MySQL to find out how it compares to your current RDBMS, several parts of the book will be useful. Read the data type and SQL syntax chapters in Part I to compare MySQL to the SQL that you're used to, the programming chapters in Part II if you have custom applications, and the administrative chapters in Part III to assess the level of administrative support a MySQL installation requires. This information is also useful if you're not currently using a database but are performing a comparative analysis of MySQL along with other database systems for the purpose of choosing one of them.

If you want access to MySQL and are seeking an Internet Service Provider (ISP) who offers it, see Appendix J, "Internet Service Providers," for some tips on how to choose one. This appendix also provides advice to service providers who want to provide MySQL to attract new customers or serve existing ones better.

Versions of Software Covered in This Book

As of this writing, the current stable release of MySQL is the 3.22 version series, and active development is taking place in the 3.23 series. This book covers them both. Where features are not present in earlier releases (including the 3.21 series), that is pointed out.

For the other major packages discussed here, any recent versions should be sufficient for the examples in this book. Current versions are:

Package	Version
Perl DBI	1.13
Perl MySQL DBI driver	1.22.xx (stable), 1.23.xx (beta)
PHP	3.0.12 (4.0 is on the horizon)
Apache	1.3.9
CGI.pm	2.56

All the software discussed in this book is available on the Internet. Appendix A provides instructions for getting MySQL, Perl DBI support, PHP, Apache, and CGI.pm onto your system. This appendix also contains instructions for obtaining the sample database that is used in examples throughout this book, as well as the example programs that are developed in the programming chapters.

Conventions Used in This Book

Typographical conventions used in this book are as follows:

Monospaced font indicates hostnames, filenames, directory names, commands, options, and Web sites.

Where commands are shown as you enter them, bold indicates the part you enter. The prompt indicates how the command is run:

%	Command is run as a regular UNIX user
#	Command is run as the root UNIX user
C:\>	Command is run under Windows

Italicized font in commands indicates where you should substitute a value of your own choosing.

In SQL statements, SQL keywords and function names are written in uppercase. Database, table, and column names are written in lowercase. In syntax descriptions, square brackets ([]) indicate optional information.

Additional Resources

This book aims to tell you virtually everything you'll need to know about MySQL. But if you have a question the book doesn't answer, where should you turn?

Useful resources include the Web sites for the software you need help with:

Package	Primary Web site
MySQL	http://www.mysql.com/doc.html
Perl DBI	http://www.symbolstone.org/technology/perl/DBI/
PHP	http://www.php.net/
Apache	http://www.apache.org/
CGI.pm	http://stein.cshl.org/WWW/software/CGI/

Using the Online MySQL Reference Manual

Be sure to check the online MySQL Reference Manual occasionally for information on the latest improvements to MySQL. The manual is updated continually as changes are made.

These sites contain pointers to various forms of information, such as reference manuals, frequently asked-question (FAQ) lists, and mailing lists:

- Reference manuals

  The primary documentation included with MySQL itself is the Reference Manual. It's available in several formats, including an online version.

  PHP's manual comes in several forms, too; however, the online version tends to be more complete than the print-format versions.

  The DBI module and its MySQL-specific driver are documented separately. The DBI document provides general concepts. The MySQL driver document discusses capabilities specific to MySQL.

- FAQs

  There are FAQs for DBI, PHP, and Apache.

- Mailing lists

  Several mailing lists centering around the software discussed in this book are available. It's a good idea to subscribe to the ones that deal with the tools you want to use. Please remember, though, that you should also learn how to use the archives for those lists that have them. When you're new to a tool, you will have many of the same questions that have been asked (and answered) a million times, and there is no reason to ask again when you can find the answer with a quick search of the archives.

  Instructions for subscribing to the mailing lists vary, but you can find information at the URLs shown here:

Package	Mailing List Instructions
MySQL	http://www.mysql.com/doc.html
Perl DBI	http://www.symbolstone.org/technology/perl/DBI/
PHP	http://www.php.net/support.php3
Apache	http://www.apache.org/foundation/mailinglists.html

- Ancillary Web sites

  Besides the official Web sites, some of the tools discussed here have ancillary sites that provide more information, such as sample source code or topical articles. Check for a "Links" area on the official site you're visiting.

I

General MySQL Use

1

Introduction to MySQL and SQL

T HIS CHAPTER PROVIDES AN INTRODUCTION to the MySQL relational database management system (RDBMS), and to the Structured Query Language (SQL) that MySQL understands. It lays out basic terms and concepts you should understand, describes the sample database we'll be using for examples throughout the book, and provides a tutorial that shows you how to use MySQL to create a database and interact with it.

Begin here if you are new to databases and perhaps uncertain whether or not you need one or can use one. You should also read the chapter if you don't know anything about MySQL or SQL and need an introductory guide to get started. Readers who have experience with MySQL or with database systems might want to skim through the material. However, everybody should read the section "A Sample Database" because it's best if you're familiar with the purpose and contents of the database that we'll be using repeatedly throughout the book.

How MySQL Can Help You

This section describes situations in which the MySQL database system is useful. This will give you an idea of the kinds of things MySQL can do and the ways in which it can help you. If you don't need to be convinced about the usefulness of a database system—perhaps because you've already got a problem in mind and just want to find out how to put MySQL to work helping you solve it—you can proceed to "A Sample Database."

A *database system* is essentially just a way to manage lists of information. The information can come from a variety of sources. For example, it can represent research data, business records, customer requests, sports statistics, sales reports, personal hobby information, personnel records, bug reports, or student grades. However, although database systems can deal with a wide range of information, you don't use such a system for its own sake. If a job is easy to do already, there's no reason to drag a database into it just to use one. A grocery list is a good example: You write down the items to get, cross them off as you do your shopping, and then throw the list away. It's highly unlikely that you'd use a database for this. Even if you have a palmtop computer, you'd probably use its notepad function for a grocery list, not its database capabilities.

The power of a database system comes in when the information you want to organize and manage becomes voluminous or complex so that your records become more burdensome than you care to deal with by hand. Databases can be used by large corporations processing millions of transactions a day, of course. But even small-scale operations involving a single person maintaining information of personal interest may require a database. It's not difficult to think of situations in which the use of a database can be beneficial because you needn't have huge amounts of information before that information becomes difficult to manage. Consider the following situations:

- Your carpentry business has several employees. You need to maintain employee and payroll records so that you know who you've paid and when, and you must summarize those records so that you can report earnings statements to the government for tax purposes. You also need to keep track of the jobs your company has been hired to do and which employees you've scheduled to work on each job.

- You run a network of automobile parts warehouses and need to be able to tell which ones have any given part in their inventory so that you can fill customer orders.

- As a toy seller, you're particularly subject to fad-dependent demand for items that you carry. You want to know what the current sales trajectory is for certain items so that you can estimate whether to increase inventory (for an item that's becoming more popular) or decrease it (so you're not stuck with a lot of stock for something that's no longer selling well).

- That pile of research data you've been collecting over the course of many years needs to be analyzed for publication, lest the dictum "publish or perish" become the epitaph for your career. You want to boil down large amounts of raw data to generate summary information, and to pull out selected subsets of observations for more detailed statistical analysis.

- You're a popular speaker who travels the country to many types of assemblies, such as graduations, business meetings, civic organizations, and political conventions. You give so many addresses that it's difficult to remember what you've spoken on at each place you've been, so you'd like to maintain records of your past talks and use them to help you plan future engagements. If you return to a place at which you've spoken before, you don't want to give a talk similar to one you've already delivered there, and a record of each place you've been would help you avoid repeats. You'd also like to note how well your talks are received. (Your address "Why I Love Cats" to the Metropolitan Kennel Club was something of a dud, and you don't want to make that mistake again the next time you're there.)

- You're a teacher who needs to keep track of grades and attendance. Each time you give a quiz or a test, you record every student's grade. It's easy enough to write down scores in a gradebook, but using the scores later is a tedious chore. You'd rather avoid sorting the scores for each test to determine the grading curve, and you'd really rather not add up each student's scores when you determine final grades at the end of the grading period. Counting each student's absences is no fun, either.

- The organization for which you are the secretary maintains a directory of members. (The organization could be anything—a professional society, a club, a repertory company, a symphony orchestra, or an athletic booster club.) You generate the directory in printed form each year for members, based on a word processor document that you edit as membership information changes.

  You're tired of maintaining the directory that way because it limits what you can do with it. It's difficult to sort the entries in different ways, and you can't easily select just certain parts of each entry (such as a list consisting only of names and phone numbers). Nor can you easily find a subset of members, such as those who need to renew their memberships soon—if you could, it would eliminate the job of looking through the entries each month to find those members who need to be sent renewal notices.

  Also, you'd really like to avoid doing all the directory editing yourself, but the society doesn't have much of a budget, and hiring someone is out of the question. You've heard about the "paperless office" that's supposed to result from electronic record-keeping, but you haven't seen any benefit from it. The membership records are electronic, but, ironically, aren't in a form that can be used easily for anything *except* generating paper by printing the directory!

These scenarios range from situations involving large amounts to relatively small amounts of information. They share the common characteristic of involving tasks that can be performed manually but that could be performed more efficiently by a database system.

What specific benefits should you expect to see from using a database system such as MySQL? It depends on your particular needs and requirements—and as seen in the preceding examples, those can vary quite a bit. Let's look at a type of situation that occurs frequently, and thus is fairly representative of database use.

Database management systems are often employed to handle tasks such as those for which people use filing cabinets. Indeed, a database is like a big filing cabinet in some ways, but one with a built-in filing system. There are some important advantages of electronically maintained records over records maintained by hand. For example, if you work in an office setting in which client records are maintained, here are some of the ways MySQL can help you:

- **Reduced record filing time.** You don't have to look through drawers in cabinets to figure out where to add a new record. You just hand it to the filing system and let it put the record in the right place for you.

- **Reduced record retrieval time.** When you're looking for records, you don't search through each one yourself to find the ones containing the information you want. Suppose you work in a dentist's office. If you want to send out reminders to all patients who haven't been in for their checkup in a while, you ask the filing system to find the appropriate records for you. Of course, you do this differently than if you were talking to another person. With a person, you'd say, "Please determine which patients haven't visited within the last 6 months." With a database, you utter a strange incantation:

  ```
  SELECT last_name, first_name, last_visit FROM patient
  WHERE last_visit < DATE_SUB(CURRENT_DATE,INTERVAL 6 MONTH)
  ```

  That can be pretty intimidating if you've never seen anything like it before, but the prospect of getting results in a second or two rather than spending an hour looking for it should be attractive. (In any case, you needn't worry. That odd-looking bit of gobbledygook won't look strange for long. In fact, you'll understand exactly what it means by the time you've finished this chapter.)

- **Flexible retrieval order.** You needn't retrieve records according to the fixed order in which you store them (by patient's last name, for example). You can tell the filing system to pull out records sorted in any order you like: by last name, insurance company name, date of last visit, and so forth.

- **Flexible output format.** After you've found the records in which you're interested, you don't have to copy the information manually. You can let the filing system generate a list for you. Sometimes you might just print the information. Other times you might want to use it in another program. (For example, after you generate the list of patients who are overdue on their dental visits, you might feed this information into a word processor that prints out notices that you can send to those patients.) Or you might be interested only in summary information, such as a count of the selected records. You don't have to count them yourself; the filing system can generate the summary for you.

- **Simultaneous multiple-user access to records.** With paper records, if two people want to look up a record at the same time, the second person needs to wait for the first one to put the record back. MySQL gives you multiple-user capability so that both can access the record simultaneously.

- **Remote access to and electronic transmission of records.** Paper records require you to be where the records are located, or someone has to make copies and send them to you. Electronic records open up the potential for remote access to the records or electronic transmission of them. If your dental group has associates in branch offices, those associates can access your records from their own locations. You don't need to send copies by courier. If someone who needs records doesn't have the same kind of database software you do but does have electronic mail, you can select the desired records and send their contents electronically.

If you've used database management systems before, you already know about the benefits just described, and you may be thinking about how to go beyond the usual "replace the filing cabinet" applications. Database systems are used now to provide services in ways that were not possible until relatively recently. The manner in which many organizations use a database in conjunction with a Web site is a good example.

Suppose your company has an inventory database that is used by the service desk staff when customers call to find out whether or not you have an item in stock and how much it costs. That's a relatively traditional use for a database. However, if your company puts up a Web site for customers to visit, you can provide an additional service: a search page that allows customers to determine item pricing and availability. This gives customers the information they want, and the way you provide it is by searching the inventory information stored in your database for the items in question—automatically. The customer gets the information immediately, without being put on hold listening to annoying canned music or being limited by the hours your service desk is open. And for every customer who uses your Web site, that's one less phone call that needs to be handled by a person on the service desk payroll. (Perhaps the Web site pays for itself this way.)

But you can put the database to even better use than that. Web-based inventory search requests can provide information not only to your customers, but to you as well. The queries tell you what customers are looking for, and the query results tell you whether or not you're able to satisfy their requests. To the extent you don't have what they want, you're probably losing business. So it makes sense to record information about inventory searches: what customers were looking for, and whether or not you had it in stock. Then you can use this information to adjust your inventory and provide better service to your customers.

Another recent application for databases is to serve up banner advertisements on Web pages. I don't like them any better than you do, but the fact remains that they are a popular application for MySQL, which can be used to store advertisements and retrieve them for display by a Web server. In addition, MySQL can perform the kind of record-keeping often associated with this activity by tracking which ads have been served, how many times they've been displayed, which sites accessed them, and so forth.

So how does MySQL work? The best way to find out is to try it for yourself, and for that we'll need a database to work with.

A Sample Database

This section describes the sample database we'll use throughout the rest of this book. It gives you a source of examples you can try out as you learn to put MySQL to work. We'll draw examples largely from two of the situations described previously:

- **The organizational secretary scenario.** We need something more definite than "an organization," so I'll make one up with these characteristics: It's composed of people drawn together through a common affinity for United States history (called, for lack of a better name, the US Historical League). The members maintain their affiliation by renewing their membership periodically on a dues-paying basis. Dues go toward the expenses incurred by the League, such as publication of a newsletter, "Chronicles of US Past." The League also operates a small Web site, but it hasn't been developed very much. Thus far, the site has been limited to basic information, such as what the League is about, who the officers are, and how people can join.

- **The grade-keeping scenario.** During the grading period, you administer quizzes and tests, record scores, and assign grades. Afterward, you determine final grades, which you turn in to the school office along with an attendance summary.

Now let's examine these situations more closely in terms of two requirements:

- You have to decide what you want to get out of the database—that is, what goals you want to accomplish.
- You have to figure out what you're going to put into the database—that is, what data you will keep track of.

Perhaps it seems backward to think about what comes out of the database before considering what goes in. After all, you must enter your data before you can retrieve it. But the way you use a database is driven by your goals, and those are more closely associated with what you want to get from your database than with what you put into it. You certainly aren't going to waste time and effort putting information into a database unless you're going to use it for something later.

The US Historical League

The initial situation for this scenario is that you as League secretary maintain the membership list using a word processing document. That works well for generating a printed directory but limits what else you can do with the information. You have the following objectives in mind:

- You want to be able to produce output from the directory in different formats, using only information appropriate to the application. One goal is to be able to generate the printed directory each year—a requirement the League has had in the past that you plan to continue to carry out. You can think of other uses for the information in the directory, too—for example, to provide the current member list for the program that's handed out at the League's annual banquet. These applications involve different sets of information. The printed directory uses the entire contents of each member's entry. For the banquet program, you need to pull out only member names (something that hasn't been easy using a word processor).

- You want to search the directory for members whose entries satisfy various criteria. For example, you want to know which members need to renew their memberships soon. Another application that involves searching arises from the list of keywords you maintain for each member. These keywords describe areas of US history in which each member is particularly interested (for example, the Civil War, the Depression, civil rights, or the life of Thomas Jefferson). Members sometimes ask you for a list of other members with interests similar to their own, and you'd like to be able to satisfy these requests.

- You want to put the directory online at the League's Web site. This would benefit both the members and yourself. If you could convert the directory to Web pages by some reasonably automated process, an online version of the directory could be kept up to date in a more timely fashion than the printed version. And if the online directory could be made searchable, members could look for information easily themselves. For example, a member who wants to know which other members are interested in the Civil War could find that out without waiting for you to perform the search, and you wouldn't need to find the time to do it yourself.

I'm well aware that a database is not the most exciting thing in the world, so I'm not about to make any wild claims that using a database stimulates creative thinking. Nevertheless, when you stop thinking of information as something you must wrestle with (as you do with your word processing document) and begin thinking of it as something you can manipulate relatively easily (as you hope to do with MySQL), it has a certain liberating effect on your ability to come up with new ways to use or present that information:

- If the information in the database can be moved to the Web site in the form of an online directory, you might be able to make information flow the other way. For example, if members could edit their own entries online to update the database, you wouldn't have to do all the editing yourself, and it would help make the information in the directory more accurate.

- If you stored email addresses in the database, you could use them to send email to members that haven't updated their entries in a while. The messages could show members the current contents of their entry, ask them to review it, and indicate how to make any needed modifications using the facilities provided on the Web site.

- A database might help you make the Web site more useful in ways not even related to the membership list. The League publishes a newsletter, "Chronicles of US Past," that has a children's section in each issue containing a history-based quiz. Some of the recent issues have focused on biographical facts about US presidents. The Web site could have a children's section, too, where the quizzes are put online. Perhaps this section could even be made interactive, by putting the information from which quizzes are drawn in the database and having the Web server query the database for questions to be presented on a random basis.

Well! At this point the number of uses for the database that you're coming up with may make you realize you may be getting a little carried away. After pausing to come back down to earth, you start asking some practical questions:

- **Isn't this a little ambitious?** Won't it be a lot of work to set this up? Anything's easier when you're just thinking about it and not doing it, of course, and I won't pretend that all of this will be trivial to implement. Nevertheless, by the end of this book you'll have done everything we've just outlined. Just keep one thing in mind: It's not necessary to do everything all at once. We'll break the job into pieces and tackle it a piece at a time.

- **Can MySQL do all these things?** No, it can't. For example, MySQL has no direct Web capabilities. But even though MySQL by itself cannot do everything we've discussed, other tools are available that work with MySQL to complement and extend its abilities.

  We'll use the Perl scripting language and the DBI (database interface) Perl module to write scripts that access MySQL databases. Perl has excellent text-processing capabilities, which allow for manipulation of query results in a highly flexible manner to produce output in a variety of formats. For example, we can use Perl to generate the directory in Rich Text Format (RTF), a format that can be read by all kinds of word processors.

  We'll also use PHP, another scripting language. PHP is particularly adapted to writing Web applications, and it works with databases. This allows you to run MySQL queries right from Web pages and to generate new pages that include the results of database queries. PHP works well with Apache (the most popular Web server in the world), making it easy to do things such as presenting a search form and displaying the results of the search.

  MySQL integrates well with these tools and gives you the flexibility to combine them in ways of your own, choosing to achieve the ends you have in mind.

You're not locked into some all-in-one suite's components that have highly touted "integration" capabilities but that actually work well only with each other.

- **And, finally, the big question—how much will all this cost?** The League has a limited budget, after all. This may surprise you, but it probably won't cost anything. If you're familiar with the usual ken of database systems, you know that they're generally pretty pricey. By contrast, MySQL is usually free. There are some circumstances under which you do need a license, but that's only $200 for an unlimited number of users. (See the Preface for general guidelines on licensing, and the MySQL Reference Manual for specific details.) The other tools we'll use (Perl, DBI, PHP, Apache) are free, so, all things considered, you can put together a useful system quite inexpensively.

The choice of operating system for developing the database is up to you. All the software we'll discuss runs under UNIX, and most of it runs under Windows. I recommend running MySQL and the other tools under UNIX. All of them had their origin in UNIX and were ported later to Windows, and they're more widely deployed under UNIX than under Windows. This means the Windows versions have had a shorter maturing period and have not been as thoroughly tested and used.

Now let's consider the other situation we'll be using the sample database for.

The Grade-Keeping Project

The initial scenario here is that as a teacher, you have grade-keeping responsibilities. You want to convert the grading process from a manual operation using a gradebook to an electronic representation using MySQL. In this case, what you want to get from a database is implicit in the way you use your gradebook now:

- For each quiz or test, you record the scores. For tests, you put the scores in order so that you can look at them and determine the cutoffs for each letter grade (A, B, C, D, and F).

- At the end of the grading period, you calculate each student's total score, then sort the totals and determine grades based on them. The totals might involve weighted calculations because you probably want to count tests more heavily than quizzes.

- You provide attendance information to the school office at the end of the grading period.

The objectives are to avoid manually sorting and summarizing scores and attendance records. In other words, you want MySQL to sort the scores and perform the calculations necessary to compute each student's total score and number of absences when the grading period ends. To achieve these goals, you'll need the list of students in the class, the scores for each quiz and test, and the dates on which students are absent.

How the Sample Database Applies to You

If you're not particularly interested in the Historical League or in grade-keeping, you may be wondering what any of this has to do with you. The answer is that these example scenarios aren't an end in themselves. They simply provide a vehicle by which to illustrate what you can do with MySQL and tools that are related to it.

With a little imagination, you'll see how example database queries apply to the particular problems you want to solve. Suppose you're working in that dentist's office to which we referred earlier. You won't see many dentistry-related queries in this book, but you will see that many of the queries you find here apply to your own interests. For example, determining which Historical League members need to renew their memberships soon is similar to determining which patients haven't visited the dentist for a while. Both are date-based queries, so once you learn to write the membership-renewal query, you can apply that skill to writing the delinquent-patient query in which you have a more immediate interest.

Basic Database Terminology

You may have noticed that you're already several pages into a database book and still haven't seen a whole bunch of jargon and technical terminology. In fact, I still haven't said anything at all about what "a database" actually looks like, even though we have a rough specification of how our sample database will be used. However, we're about to design that database, and then we'll begin implementing it, so we can't avoid terminology any longer. That's what this section is about. It describes some terms that come up throughout the book so that you'll be familiar with them. Fortunately, many relational database concepts are really quite simple. In fact, much of the appeal of relational databases stems from the simplicity of their foundational concepts.

Structural Terminology

Within the database world, MySQL is classified as a *relational database management system* (RDBMS). That phrase breaks down as follows:

- The database (the "DB" in RDBMS) is the repository for the information you want to store, structured in a simple, regular fashion:
    - The collection of data in a database is organized into tables.
    - Each table is organized into rows and columns.
    - Each row in a table is a record.
    - Records may contain several pieces of information; each column in a table corresponds to one of those pieces.
- The management system (the "MS") is the software that lets you use your data by allowing you to insert, retrieve, modify, or delete records.

- The word "relational" (the "R") indicates a particular kind of DBMS, one that is very good at relating (that is, matching up) information stored in one table to information stored in another by looking for elements common to each of them. The power of a relational DBMS lies in its ability to pull data from those tables conveniently and to join information from related tables to produce answers to questions that can't be answered from individual tables alone.

Here's an example that shows how a relational database organizes data into tables and relates the information from one table to another. Suppose you run a Web site that includes a banner-advertisement service. You contract with companies that want their ads displayed when people visit the pages on your site. Each time a visitor hits one of your pages, you serve the ad embedded in the page to the visitor's browser and assess the company a small fee. To represent this information, you maintain three tables (see Figure 1.1). One table, company, has columns for company name, number, address, and telephone number. Another table, ad, lists ad numbers, the number for the company that "owns" the ad, and the amount you charge per hit. The third table, hits, logs ad hits by ad number and the date on which the ad was served.

Some questions can be answered from this information using a single table. To determine the number of companies you have contracts with, you need count only the rows in the company table. Similarly, to determine the number of hits during a given time period, only the hit table need be examined. Other questions are more complex, and it's necessary to consult multiple tables to determine the answers. For example, to determine how many times each of the ads for Pickles, Inc. was served on July 14, you'd use all three tables as follows:

1. Look up the company name (Pickles, Inc.) in the company table to find the company number (14).

2. Use the company number to find matching records in the ad table so you can determine the associated ad numbers. There are two such ads, 48 and 101.

3. For each of the matched records in the ad table, use the ad number in the record to find matching records in the hit table that fall within the desired date range, then count the number of matches. There are three matches for ad 48 and two matches for ad 101.

Sounds complicated! But that's just the kind of thing at which relational database systems 'excel. The complexity is actually somewhat illusory because each of the steps just described really amounts to little more than a simple matching operation: You relate one table to another by matching values from one table's rows to values in another table's rows. This same simple operation can be exploited in various ways to answer all kinds of questions: How many different ads does each company have? Which company's ads are most popular? How much revenue does each ad generate? What is the total fee for each company for the current billing period?

Now you know enough relational database theory to understand the rest of the book, and we don't have to go into Third Normal Form, Entity-Relationship Diagrams, and all that kind of stuff. If you really want to know about such things, that's terrific, but you're in the wrong place to find out. I suggest you begin by reading some C.J. Date or E.F. Codd.

company table

company_name	company_num	address	phone
Big deal, Ltd.	13	14 Grand Blvd.	875-2934
Pickles, Inc.	14	59 Cucumber Dr.	884-2472
Real Roofing Co.	17	928 Shingles Rd.	882-4173
GigaFred & Son	23	2572 Family Ave.	847-4738

ad table

company_num	ad_num	hit_fee
14	48	0.01
23	49	0.02
17	52	0.01
13	55	0.03
23	62	0.02
23	63	0.01
23	64	0.02
13	77	0.03
23	99	0.03
14	101	0.01
13	102	0.01
17	119	0.02

hit table

ad_num	date
49	July 13
55	July 13
48	July 14
63	July 14
101	July 14
62	July 14
119	July 14
102	July 14
52	July 14
48	July 14
64	July 14
119	July 14
48	July 14
101	July 14
63	July 15
49	July 15
77	July 15
99	July 15

Figure 1.1   Banner advertisement tables.

Query Language Terminology

To communicate with MySQL, you use a language called SQL (Structured Query Language). SQL is today's standard database language, and all major database systems understand it. SQL includes many different kinds of statements, all designed to make it possible to interact with your database in interesting and useful ways.

As with any language, SQL may seem strange while you're first learning it. For example, to create a table, you need to tell MySQL what the table's structure should be. You and I might think of the table in terms of a diagram or picture, but MySQL doesn't, so you create the table by telling MySQL something like this:

```
CREATE TABLE company
(
    company_name CHAR(30),
    company_num INT,
    address CHAR(30),
    phone CHAR(12)
)
```

When you're new to SQL, statements like that can be somewhat imposing, but you don't need to be a programmer to learn how to use SQL effectively. As you gain familiarity with the language, you'll look at CREATE TABLE in a different light—as an ally that helps you describe your information, not as just a weird bit of gibberish.

MySQL Architecture Terminology

When you use MySQL, you're actually using two programs because MySQL operates using a client/server architecture:

- The database server is a program located on the machine where your data are stored. It listens for client requests coming in over the network and accesses database contents according to those requests to provide clients with the information they ask for.

- Clients are programs that connect to the database server and issue queries to tell it what information they want.

The MySQL distribution includes the server and several client programs. You use the clients according to the purposes you want to achieve. The one most commonly used is mysql, an interactive client that lets you issue queries and see the results. Other clients include mysqldump and mysqlimport, which dump table contents into a file and vice versa, and mysqladmin, which allows you to check on the status of the server and performs administrative tasks, such as telling the server to shut down. If you have applications for which the standard clients are unsuited, MySQL also provides a client-programming library so that you can write your own programs. The library is usable directly from C programs, and several other interfaces are available if you prefer a language other than C.

MySQL's client/server architecture has certain benefits:

- **The server provides concurrency control so that two users cannot modify the same record at the same time.** All client requests go through the server, so the server sorts out who gets to do what, and when. If multiple clients want to access the same table at the same time, they don't all have to find and negotiate with each other. They just send their requests to the server and let it take care of determining the order in which the requests will be performed.

- **You don't have to be logged in on the machine where your database is located.** MySQL understands how to work over the Internet, so you can run a client program from wherever you happen to be, and the client can connect to the server over the network. Distance isn't a factor; you can access the server from anywhere in the world. If the server is located on a computer in Australia, you can take your laptop computer on a trip to Iceland and still access your database.

Does that mean *anyone* can get at your data, just by connecting to the Internet? No. MySQL includes a flexible security system, so you can allow access only to people who should have it. And you can make sure those people are able to do only what they should. Perhaps Sally in the billing office should be able to read and update (modify) records, but Phil at the service desk should be able only to look at them. You can set their privileges accordingly. If you do want to run a self-contained system, just set the access privileges so that clients can connect only from the host on which the server is running.

A MySQL Tutorial

You have all the background you need now; it's time to put MySQL to work!

This section will help you familiarize yourself with MySQL by providing a tutorial for you to try out. As you work through the tutorial, you will create a sample database and the tables within it, then interact with the database by adding, retrieving, deleting, and modifying information. In addition, during the process of working with the sample database, you will learn the following things:

- How to communicate with a MySQL server using the mysql client program.
- The basics of the SQL language that MySQL understands. (If you already know SQL from having used some other RDBMS, it would be a good idea to skim through this tutorial to see whether or not MySQL's version of SQL differs from the version with which you are familiar.)

As noted in the previous section, MySQL operates using a client/server architecture in which the server runs on the machine containing the databases and clients connect to the server over a network. This tutorial is based largely on the use of the mysql client program. mysql reads SQL queries from you, sends them to the server to be executed, and displays the results so you can see what happened. mysql runs on all platforms supported by MySQL and provides the most direct means of interacting with the server, so it's the logical client to begin with.

Throughout this book, we'll use `samp_db` as the name of our sample database. However, you may need to use a different database name as you work through the examples. Someone else on your system may be using the name `samp_db` already, or your administrator may assign you a different database name. In either case, substitute the actual name of your database for `samp_db` whenever you see the latter in examples.

Table names can be used exactly as shown in the examples, even if multiple people on your system have their own sample databases. In MySQL, it doesn't matter if someone else uses the same table names. As long as each of you has your own database, MySQL will keep the names straight and prevent you from interfering with each other.

Preliminary Requirements

To try the examples in this tutorial, MySQL must be installed. In particular, you must have access to MySQL clients and to some MySQL server. The client programs must be located on your machine. You'll need at least `mysql`, and `mysqlimport` is useful as well. The server can be located on your machine, though that is not required. As long as you have permission to connect to it, the server can be located anywhere.

If the server does happen to be running on your machine, the client programs likely are installed as well, and you should be ready to go. If you need to get MySQL, see Appendix A, "Obtaining and Installing Software," for instructions. Either refer to that chapter (if you're installing MySQL yourself) or show it to your system administrator. If your network access comes through an Internet service provider (ISP), check whether or not your provider has MySQL. If your ISP doesn't offer MySQL service and won't install it, check Appendix J, "Internet Service Providers," for some advice on choosing a more suitable provider.

In addition to the MySQL software, you'll need permission to create the sample database and its tables. If you don't have permission, ask your MySQL administrator. The administrator can give you this permission by running `mysql` and issuing commands like these:

```
GRANT ALL ON samp_db.* TO paul@localhost IDENTIFIED BY "secret"
GRANT ALL ON samp_db.* TO paul@% IDENTIFIED BY "secret"
```

The Difference Between MySQL and `mysql`

To avoid confusion, I should point out that "MySQL" refers to the entire MySQL RDBMS and "mysql" is the name of a particular client program. They sound the same if you pronounce them, but they're distinguished here by capitalization and typeface differences.

Speaking of pronunciation, MySQL is pronounced "my-ess-queue-ell." We know this because the MySQL Reference Manual says so. On the other hand, SQL is pronounced "sequel" or "ess-queue-ell," depending on who you ask. I'm not going to take sides. Pronounce it how you like, but be prepared for the eventuality that you'll run into someone who will correct you and inform you of the "proper" pronunciation!

The first command gives `paul` complete access to the `samp_db` database and all tables in it when `paul` connects from `localhost` (the same host the server is running on). It also assigns a password of `secret`. The second command is similar but allows `paul` to connect from any host ('`%`' is a wildcard character). You could also substitute a specific hostname for '`%`' to allow `paul` to connect from just that host. (Such a `GRANT` statement may be necessary if your server allows anonymous access from `localhost`, due to the way the server searches the grant tables for matches to incoming connections.) More information on the `GRANT` statement and setting up MySQL user accounts may be found in Chapter 11, "General MySQL Administration."

Obtaining the Sample Database Distribution

This tutorial refers at certain points to files from the "sample database distribution." These are files containing queries or data that will help you set up the sample database. To get this distribution, see Appendix A. When you unpack the distribution, it will create a directory named `samp_db` containing the files you'll need. I recommend that you move into that directory whenever you're trying out examples pertaining to the sample database.

Establishing and Terminating Connections to the Server

To connect to your server, invoke the `mysql` program from your shell (that is, from your UNIX prompt, or from a DOS console under Windows). The command looks like this:

```
% mysql options
```

I use '`%`' throughout this book to indicate the shell prompt. That's one of the standard UNIX prompts; another is '`$`'. Under Windows, the prompt is something like '`C:\>`'.

The *options* part of the `mysql` command line may be empty, but more likely you'll have to issue a command something like this:

```
% mysql -h host_name -u user_name -p
```

You may not need to supply all those options when you invoke `mysql`; ask your MySQL administrator for the exact command to use. You'll probably need to specify at least a name and password.

When you're just starting to learn MySQL, you'll probably consider its security system to be an annoyance because it makes it harder to do what you want. (You must obtain permission to create and access a database, and you must specify your name and password whenever you connect to the server.) However, after you move beyond the sample database to entering and using your own records, your perspective will change radically. Then you'll appreciate that MySQL keeps other people from snooping through (or worse, destroying!) your stuff.

Here's what the options mean:

- -h *host_name* (alternate form: --host=*host_name*)

  The server host you want to connect to. If the server is running on the same machine that you are running mysql on, this option normally may be omitted.

- -u *user_name* (alternate form: --user=*user_name*)

  Your MySQL user name. If you're using UNIX and your MySQL username is the same as your login name, you can omit this option; mysql will use your login name as your MySQL name.

  Under Windows, the default user name is ODBC. This is not likely to be very useful. Either specify a name on the command line, or set a default in your environment by setting the USER variable. For example, I can use the following set command to specify a user name of paul:

  ```
  set USER=paul
  ```

- -p (alternate form: --password)

  This option tells mysql to prompt you for your MySQL password. Note: you can give your password on the command line by typing it as -p*your_password* (alternate form: --password=*your_password*). However, for security reasons, it's best not to do that. Specifying -p with no password following it tells mysql to prompt you for a password when it starts up. For example:

  ```
  % mysql -h host_name -u user_name -p
  Enter password:
  ```

  When you see Enter password:, type in your password. (It won't be echoed to the screen, in case someone's looking over your shoulder.) Note that your MySQL password is not necessarily the same as your UNIX or Windows password.

  If you omit the -p option entirely, mysql assumes you don't need one and doesn't prompt for it.

  Note: The -h and -u options are associated with the words that follow them, whether or not there is a space between the option and the following word. This is *not* true for -p. If you specify the password on the command line, there must be no space between -p and the password.

Example: Suppose my MySQL user name and password are paul and secret, and that I want to connect to the server that is running on the same machine that I'm logged in on. The mysql command to do this is:

```
% mysql -u paul -p
Enter password: ******
```

After I enter the command, mysql prints Enter password: to prompt for my password, and I type it in (the ****** indicates where I type secret).

If all goes well, mysql prints a greeting and a 'mysql>' prompt indicating that it is waiting for me to issue queries. The full startup sequence looks like this:

```
% mysql -u paul -p
Enter password: ******
Welcome to the MySQL monitor.  Commands end with ; or \g.
Your MySQL connection id is 1805 to server version: 3.22.25-log

Type 'help' for help.

mysql>
```

To connect to a server running on some other machine, I need to specify the host-name using -h. If that host is pit-viper.snake.net, the command looks like this:

```
% mysql -h pit-viper.snake.net -u paul -p
```

In most of the examples that follow that show a mysql command line, I'm going to leave out the -h, -u, and -p options for brevity. It's assumed that you'll supply whatever options are necessary.

There are ways to set up your account so you don't have to type in connection parameters each time you run mysql. This is discussed in "Tips for Interacting with mysql." You may want to skip ahead to that section right now to get an idea of some of the possibilities for making it easier to connect to the server.

After you establish a connection to the server, you can terminate your session any time by typing QUIT:

```
mysql> QUIT
Bye
```

You can also quit by typing Control-D, at least on UNIX.

Issuing Queries

After you're connected to the server, you're ready to issue queries. This section describes some general things you should know about interacting with mysql.

To enter a query in mysql, just type it in. At the end of the query, type a semicolon (';') and press Enter. The semicolon tells mysql that the query is complete. (You can also use '\g' to terminate queries if you prefer to type two characters rather than one.)

After you've entered a query, mysql sends it to the server to be executed. The server processes the query and sends the results back to mysql, which displays the result for you.

Here's an example of a simple query and the result:

```
mysql> SELECT NOW();
+---------------------+
| NOW()               |
+---------------------+
| 1999-07-24 11:02:36 |
+---------------------+
1 row in set (0.00 sec)
```

This tells me the current date and time. (The NOW( ) function is not so useful by itself, but it can be used in expressions—for example, to calculate the difference between the current date and another date.)

mysql also displays a count of the number of rows in the result. I usually will not show this count in examples.

Because mysql waits for the semicolon before sending the query to the server, you don't need to enter it on a single line. You can spread a query over several lines if you want:

```
mysql> SELECT NOW(),
    -> USER(),
    -> VERSION()
    -> ;
+---------------------+----------------+------------------+
| NOW()               | USER()         | VERSION()        |
+---------------------+----------------+------------------+
| 1999-07-24 11:06:16 | paul@localhost | 3.23.1-alpha-log |
+---------------------+----------------+------------------+
```

Note how the prompt changes from 'mysql' to '->' after you enter the first line of the query; this tells you that mysql thinks you're still entering the query. That's important feedback because if you forget the semicolon at the end of a query, the prompt helps you realize that mysql is still waiting for something. Otherwise, you'll be waiting, wondering why it's taking MySQL so long to execute your query, and mysql will be waiting, wondering why it's taking you so long to finish entering your query!

For the most part, it doesn't matter whether you enter queries using uppercase, lowercase, or mixed case. These queries are all equivalent:

```
SELECT USER()
select user()
SeLeCt UsEr()
```

The examples in this book use uppercase for SQL keywords and function names, and lowercase for database, table, and column names.

When you invoke a function in a query, there must be no space between the function name and the following parenthesis:

```
mysql> SELECT NOW();
+---------------------+
| NOW()               |
+---------------------+
| 1999-07-17 12:44:52 |
+---------------------+
mysql> SELECT NOW ();
ERROR 1064: You have an error in your SQL syntax near '()' at line 1
```

These two queries look similar, but the second one fails because the parenthesis doesn't immediately follow the function name.

If you've begun typing in a multiple-line query and decide you don't want to execute it, type '\c' to clear (cancel) it:

```
mysql> SELECT NOW(),
    -> VERSION(),
    -> \c
mysql>
```

Notice that the prompt changes back to 'mysql>' to indicate that mysql is ready for a new query.

You can store queries in a file and tell mysql to read queries from the file rather than waiting for you to type them in at the keyboard. Use your shell's input redirection facilities for this. For example, if I have queries stored in a file my_file.sql, I can execute its contents like this:

```
% mysql < my_file.sql
```

You can call the file whatever you want. I use the '.sql' suffix to indicate that the file contains SQL statements.

Executing mysql this way is something that will come up in "Adding New Records" when we enter data into the samp_db database. It's a lot more convenient to load a table by having mysql read INSERT statements from a file than to type in each statement manually.

The remainder of this tutorial shows many queries that you can try out for yourself. These are indicated by the 'mysql>' prompt before the query and the terminating semicolon after it, and such examples are usually accompanied by the output of the query. You should be able to type in these queries as shown, and the resulting output should be the same.

Queries that are shown without a prompt or the semicolon statement terminator are intended simply to illustrate a point, and you need not execute them. (You can try them out if you like, but if you do, remember to add a semicolon at the end.)

In later chapters of this book, I usually will not show the 'mysql>' prompt or the semicolon with SQL statements. The reason for this is that you can issue queries in contexts other than the mysql client program (for example, in Perl scripts or in PHP scripts), and in those contexts, no prompt appears and no semicolon is needed. I will indicate cases in which it is specifically intended that you enter a query in mysql.

Creating the Database

We'll begin by creating the samp_db sample database and the tables within it, populating its tables, and performing some simple queries on the data contained in those tables.

Using a database involves several steps:

1. Creating (initializing) the database
2. Creating the tables within the database
3. Interacting with the tables by inserting, retrieving, modifying, or deleting data

Retrieving existing data is easily the most common operation performed on a database. The next most common operations are inserting new data and updating or deleting existing data. Less frequent are table creation operations, and least frequent of all is database creation.

We're beginning from scratch, so we must begin with database creation, the least common thing, and work our way through table creation and insertion of our initial data before we get to where we can do the really common thing—retrieving data.

To create a new database, connect to the server using `mysql` and then issue a `CREATE DATABASE` statement that specifies the database name:

```
mysql> CREATE DATABASE samp_db;
```

You'll need to create the `samp_db` database before you can create any of the tables that will go in it or do anything with the contents of those tables.

Does creating the database make it the current (default) database? No, it doesn't, as you can see by executing the following query:

```
mysql> SELECT DATABASE();
+------------+
| DATABASE() |
+------------+
|            |
+------------+
```

To make `samp_db` current, issue a `USE` statement:

```
mysql> USE samp_db
```

`USE` is one of the few statements that require no terminating semicolon, although you can add it if you want. `HELP` is another, and if you issue a `HELP` statement, it will show you the full list of statements that don't need a semicolon.

After you issue the `USE` statement, `samp_db` is the default database:

```
mysql> SELECT DATABASE();
+------------+
| DATABASE() |
+------------+
| samp_db    |
+------------+
```

The other way to make a database current is to name it on the command line when you invoke `mysql`:

```
% mysql samp_db
```

That is, in fact, the usual way to name the database you want to use. If you need any connection parameters, specify them before the database name. For example, the following two commands allow me to connect to the `samp_db` database on the local host and on `pit-viper.snake.net`:

```
% mysql -u paul -p samp_db
% mysql -h pit-viper.snake.net -u paul -p samp_db
```

Unless specified otherwise, all the examples that follow assume that when you invoke mysql, you name the samp_db database on the command line to make it the current database. If you invoke mysql but forget to name the database on the command line, just issue a USE samp_db statement.

Creating Tables

In this section, we'll build the tables needed for the samp_db sample database. First, we'll consider the tables needed for the Historical League. Then we'll consider those needed for the grade-keeping project. This is the part where some database books start talking about Analysis and Design, Entity-Relationship Diagrams, Normalization Procedures, and other such stuff. There's a place for all that, but I prefer just to say we need to think a bit about what our database will look like: what tables it should contain, what the contents of each table should be, and some of the issues involved in deciding how to represent our data.

The choices made here about data representation are not absolute. In other situations, you might well elect to represent similar data in a different way, depending on the requirements of your applications and the uses to which you intend to put your data.

Tables for the Historical League

Table layout for the Historical League is pretty simple:

- **A president table.** This contains a descriptive record for each US president. We'll need this for the online quiz on the League Web site (the interactive analog to the printed quiz that appears in the children's section of the League's newsletter).
- **A member table.** This is used to maintain current information about each member of the League. It'll be used for creating printed and online versions of the member directory, sending automated membership renewal reminders, and so forth.

The president *Table*

The president table is simpler, so let's discuss it first. This table will contain some basic biographical information about each United States president:

- **Name.** Names can be represented in a table several ways. For example, we could have a single column containing the entire name, or separate columns for the first and last name. It's certainly simpler to use a single column, but that limits you in some ways:
  - If you enter the names with the first name first, you can't sort on last name.
  - If you enter the names with the last name first, you can't display them with the first name first.

- It's harder to search for names. For example, to search for a particular last name, you must use a pattern and look for names that match the pattern. This is less efficient and slower than looking for an exact last name.

Our `president` table will use separate columns for the first and last name to avoid these limitations.

The first name column will also hold the middle name or initial. This shouldn't break any sorting we might do because it's not likely we'll want to sort on middle name (or even first name). Name display should work properly, too, whether a name is printed in "Bush, George W." or in "George W. Bush" format. The middle name immediately follows the first name either way.

There is another slight complication. One president (Jimmy Carter) has a "Jr." at the end of his name. Where does that go? Depending on the format in which names are printed, this president's name is displayed as "James E. Carter, Jr.," or "Carter, James E., Jr." The "Jr." doesn't associate with either first or last name, so we'll create another column to hold a name suffix. This illustrates how even a single value can cause problems when you're trying to determine how to represent your data. It also shows why it's a good idea to know as much as possible about the type of data values you'll be working with before you put them in a database. If you have incomplete knowledge of what your data look like, you may have to change your table structure after you've already begun to use it. That's not necessarily a disaster, but in general it's something you want to avoid.

- **Birthplace (city and state).** Like the name, this too can be represented using a single column or multiple columns. It's simpler to use a single column, but as with the name, separate columns allow you to do some things you can't do easily otherwise. For example, it's easier to find records for presidents born in a particular state if city and state are listed separately.

- **Birth date and death date.** The only special problem here is that we can't require the death date to be filled in because some presidents are still alive. MySQL provides a special value `NULL` that means "no value"— we can use that in the death date column to mean "still alive."

The `member` *Table*

The `member` table for the Historical League membership list is similar to the `president` table in the sense that each record contains basic descriptive information for a single person. But each `member` record contains more columns:

- **Name.** We'll use the same three-column representation as for the `president` table: last name, first name (and middle if available), suffix.

- **ID number.** This is a unique value assigned to each member when a membership first begins. The League hasn't ever used ID numbers before, but now that the records are being made more systematic, it's a good time to start. (I am anticipating that you'll find MySQL beneficial and that you'll think of other ways to apply it to the League's records. When that happens, it'll be easier to associate records in the member table with other member-related tables you may create if you use numbers rather than names.)

- **Expiration date.** Members must renew their memberships periodically to avoid having them lapse. For some applications, you might use the date of the most recent renewal, but this is not suitable for the League's purposes. Memberships can be renewed for a variable number of years (typically one, two, three, or five years), and a date for the most recent renewal wouldn't tell you when the next renewal must take place. In addition, the League allows lifetime memberships. We could represent these with a date far in the future, but NULL seems more appropriate because "no value" logically corresponds to "never expires."

- **Email address.** For members that have email addresses, this will allow them to communicate with each other easily. For your purposes as League secretary, this will allow you to send out membership renewal notices electronically rather than by postal mail. This should be easier than going to the post office and less expensive, too. You'll also be able to use email to send members the current contents of their directory entries and ask them to update the information as necessary.

- **Postal address.** This is needed for contacting members that don't have email (or who don't respond to it). We'll use columns for street address, city, state, and Zip code. The street address column can double for box number for members that have an address such as P.O. Box 123 rather than 123 Elm St.

  I'm assuming that all League members live in the United States. For organizations with a membership that is international in scope, that assumption is an oversimplification, of course. If you want to deal with addresses from multiple countries, you'll run into some sticky issues having to do with the different address formats used for different countries. For example, Zip code is not an international standard, and some countries have provinces rather than states.

- **Phone number.** Like the address fields, this is useful for contacting members.

- **Special interest keywords.** Every member is assumed to be have a general interest in US history, but members probably also have some special areas of interest. This column records those interests. Members can use it to find other members with similar interests.

Creating the Tables

Now we're ready to create the Historical League tables. For this we use the CREATE TABLE statement, which has the following general form:

```
CREATE TABLE tbl_name ( column_specs )
```

tbl_name indicates the name you want to give the table. *column_specs* provides the specifications for the columns in the table, as well as any indexes (if you have any). Indexes make lookups faster; we'll discuss them further in Chapter 4, "Query Optimization."

The CREATE TABLE statement for the president table looks like this:

```
CREATE TABLE president
(
    last_name VARCHAR(15) NOT NULL,
    first_name VARCHAR(15) NOT NULL,
    suffix VARCHAR(5) NULL,
    city VARCHAR(20) NOT NULL,
    state VARCHAR(2) NOT NULL,
    birth DATE NOT NULL,
    death DATE NULL
)
```

If you want to type that statement in yourself, invoke mysql, making samp_db the current database:

```
% mysql samp_db
```

Then enter the CREATE TABLE statement as just shown. (Remember to add a semicolon at the end or mysql won't know where the end of the statement is.)

To create the president table by using a prewritten description file from the sample database distribution (see "Obtaining the Sample Database Distribution"), run this command from the shell:

```
% mysql samp_db < create_president.sql
```

Whichever way you invoke mysql, specify any connection parameters you may need (hostname, username, or password) on the command line preceding the database name.

Each column specification in the CREATE TABLE statement consists of the column name, the type (the kind of values the column will hold), and possibly some column attributes.

The two column types used in the president table are VARCHAR and DATE. VARCHAR(*n*) means the column contains variable-length character (string) values, with a maximum length of *n* characters each. You choose the value of *n* according to how long you expect your values to be. state is declared as VARCHAR(2); that's all we need if states are entered using their two-character abbreviations. The other string-valued columns need to be wider to accommodate longer values.

The other column type we've used is DATE. This type indicates, not surprisingly, that the column holds date values. However, what may be surprising to you is that dates are represented with the year first. The standard format is "YYYY-MM-DD" (for example, "1999-07-18"). This is the ANSI SQL standard for date representation.

The only column attributes we're using for the president table are NULL (values can be missing) and NOT NULL (values must be filled in). Most columns are NOT NULL, because we'll always have a value for them. The two columns that can have NULL values are suffix (most names don't have one), and death (some presidents are still alive, so there is no date of death).

The CREATE TABLE statement for the member table looks like this:

```
CREATE TABLE member
(
    last_name VARCHAR(20) NOT NULL,
    first_name VARCHAR(20) NOT NULL,
    suffix VARCHAR(5) NULL,
    expiration DATE NULL DEFAULT "0000-00-00",
    email VARCHAR(100) NULL,
    street VARCHAR(50) NULL,
    city VARCHAR(50) NULL,
    state VARCHAR(2) NULL,
    zip VARCHAR(10) NULL,
    phone VARCHAR(20) NULL,
    interests VARCHAR(255) NULL
)
```

Type that statement into mysql or execute the following shell command:

```
% mysql samp_db < create_member.sql
```

In terms of column types, the member table is not very interesting: every column except one is created as a variable-length string. The exception, expiration, is a DATE. The expiration value has a default value of "0000-00-00", which is a non-NULL value that means no legal date has been entered. The reason for this is that expiration can be NULL to indicate that a member has a lifetime membership. However, because the column can be NULL, that becomes the default value unless you specify a different default. If you created a new member record but forgot to specify the expiration date, the member would become a lifetime member! By using a default value of "0000-00-00", we avoid this problem. It also gives us a value we can search for periodically to find records for which the expiration date was never properly entered.

Note that I've "forgotten" to put in a column for the membership ID number. That's because I need an excuse to use the ALTER TABLE statement later on, and leaving out this column provides that excuse.

Let's make sure that MySQL created the tables as we expect. In mysql, issue the following query:

```
mysql> DESCRIBE president;
+------------+-------------+------+-----+------------+-------+
| Field      | Type        | Null | Key | Default    | Extra |
+------------+-------------+------+-----+------------+-------+
| last_name  | varchar(15) |      |     |            |       |
| first_name | varchar(15) |      |     |            |       |
| suffix     | varchar(5)  | YES  |     | NULL       |       |
| city       | varchar(20) |      |     |            |       |
| state      | char(2)     |      |     |            |       |
| birth      | date        |      |     | 0000-00-00 |       |
| death      | date        | YES  |     | NULL       |       |
+------------+-------------+------+-----+------------+-------+
```

As of MySQL 3.23, the output includes another column showing access privilege information. I've not shown it here, as it makes the lines too long to show easily.

The output looks pretty much as we'd expect, except that the information for the `state` column says its type is `CHAR(2)`. That's odd; wasn't it declared as `VARCHAR(2)`? Yes, it was, but MySQL has silently changed the type from `VARCHAR` to `CHAR`. The reason for this has to do with efficiency of storage space for short character columns, which I won't go into here. If you want the details, check the discussion of the `ALTER TABLE` statement in Chapter 3, "MySQL SQL Syntax and Use," provides the details. For our purposes here, there is no difference between the two types.

If you issue a `DESCRIBE member` query, `mysql` will show you similar information for the `member` table.

`DESCRIBE` is useful when you forget the name of a column in a table, need to know the column type, need to know how wide the column is, and so forth. It's also useful for finding out the order in which MySQL stores columns in table rows. That order is important when you use `INSERT` or `LOAD DATA` statements that expect column values to be listed in the default column order.

`DESCRIBE` may be abbreviated as `DESC`, or, if you prefer to type more rather than less, `SHOW COLUMNS FROM tbl_name` is a synonym for `DESCRIBE tbl_name`.

What if you forget the names of your tables? Then you can use `SHOW TABLES`. For the `samp_db` database, with the two tables we've created so far, the output looks like this:

```
mysql> SHOW TABLES;
+-------------------+
| Tables_in_samp_db |
+-------------------+
| member            |
| president         |
+-------------------+
```

If you can't even remember the name of your database, invoke `mysql` without specifying a database name on the command line, then issue a `SHOW DATABASES` query:

```
mysql> SHOW DATABASES;
+-----------+
| Database  |
+-----------+
| menagerie |
| mysql     |
| samp_db   |
| test      |
+-----------+
```

The list of databases varies from server to server, but you should see at least `samp_db` and `mysql`; the latter database holds the grant tables that control MySQL access privileges.

The DESCRIBE and SHOW queries have command-line equivalents that you can use from the shell:

% **mysqlshow**	List all databases, like SHOW DATABASES
% **mysqlshow** *db_name*	List tables in given database, like SHOW TABLES
% **mysqlshow** *db_name tbl_name*	List columns in given table, like *DESCRIBE tbl_name*

Tables for the Grade-Keeping Project

To see what tables we need for the grade-keeping project, let's look at how you might write down scores when you use a paper-based gradebook. Figure 1.2 shows a page from your gradebook. The main body of this page is a matrix for recording scores. There is also other information necessary for making sense of the scores. Student names and ID numbers are listed down the side of the matrix. (For simplicity, only four students are shown.) Along the top of the matrix, you put down the dates when you give quizzes and tests. The figure shows that you've given quizzes on September 3, 6, 16, and 23, and tests on September 9 and October 1.

To keep track of this kind of information using a database, we need a score table. What should records in this table contain? That's easy. For each row, we need student name, the date of the quiz or test, and the score. Figure 1.3 shows how some of the scores from the gradebook look when represented in a table like this. (Dates are written the way MySQL represents them, in "YYYY-MM-DD" format.)

students		scores						
		Q	Q	T	Q	Q	T	
ID	name	9/3	9/6	9/9	9/16	9/23	10/1	...
1	Billy	14	10	73	14	15	67	...
2	Missy	17	10	68	17	14	73	...
3	Johnny	15	10	78	12	17	82	...
4	Jenny	14	13	85	13	19	79	...
...	...	...	...	...	...	...	...	...

Figure 1.2 Example gradebook.

score table

name	date	score
Billy	1999-09-23	15
Missy	1999-09-23	14
Johnny	1999-09-23	17
Jenny	1999-09-23	19
Billy	1999-10-01	67
Missy	1999-10-01	73
Johnny	1999-10-01	82
Jenny	1999-10-01	79

Figure 1.3 Initial score table layout.

However, there seems to be a problem with setting up the table in this way. It appears to leave out some information. For example, looking at the records in Figure 1.3, we can't tell whether scores are for a quiz or a test. It could be important to know score types when determining final grades if quizzes and tests are weighted differently. We might try to infer the type from the range of scores on a given date (quizzes usually are worth fewer points than a test), but that's ugly because it relies on inference and not something explicit in the data.

It's possible to distinguish scores by recording the type in each record, for example, by adding a column to the score table that contains 'T' or 'Q' for each row to indicate "test" or "quiz," as in Figure 1.4. This has the advantage of making the type of score explicit in the data. The disadvantage is that this information is somewhat redundant. Observe that for all records with a given date, the score type column always has the same value. The scores for September 23 all have a type of 'Q', and the scores for October 1 all have a type of 'T'. This is unappealing. If we record a set of scores for a quiz or test this way, not only will we be putting in the same date for each new record in the set, we'll be putting in the same score type over and over again. Ugh. Who wants to enter all that redundant information?

Let's try an alternative representation. Instead of recording score types in the score table, we'll figure them out from the dates. We can keep a list of dates and use it to keep track of what kind of "grade event" (quiz or test) occurred on each date. Then we can determine whether any given score was from a quiz or a test by combining it with the information in our event list: Just match the date in the score table record with the date in the event table to get the event type. Figure 1.5 shows this table layout and demonstrates how the association works for a score table record with a date of September 23. By matching the record with the corresponding record in the event table, we see that the score is from a quiz.

score table

name	date	score	type
Billy	1999-09-23	15	Q
Missy	1999-09-23	14	Q
Johnny	1999-09-23	17	Q
Jenny	1999-09-23	19	Q
Billy	1999-10-01	67	T
Missy	1999-10-01	73	T
Johnny	1999-10-01	82	T
Jenny	1999-10-01	79	T

Figure 1.4   score table layout, revised to include score type.

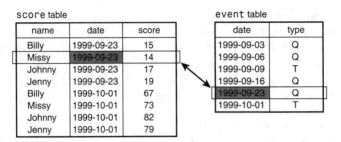

Figure 1.5 score and event table, linked on date.

This is much better than trying to infer the score type based on some guess; instead, we're deriving the type directly from data recorded explicitly in our database. It's also preferable to recording score types in the score table because we must record each type only once.

However, if you're like me, when you first hear about this kind of thing (combining information from multiple tables), you think, "Yeah, that's a cute idea, but isn't it a lot of work to do all that looking up all the time; doesn't it just make things more complicated?"

In a way, you're right. Keeping two lists of records *is* more complicated than keeping one list. But take another look at your gradebook (see Figure 1.2). Aren't you *already* keeping two sets of records? Consider these facts:

- You keep track of scores using the cells in the score matrix, where each cell is indexed by student name and date (down the side and along the top of the matrix). This represents one set of records; it's analogous to the contents of the score table.

- How do you know what kind of event each date represents? You've written a little 'T' or 'Q' above the date! Thus, you're also keeping track of the association between date and score type along the top of the matrix. This represents a second set of records; it's analogous to the event table contents.

In other words, even though you may not think about it as such, you're really not doing anything different with the gradebook than what I'm proposing to do by keeping information in two tables. The only real difference is that the two kinds of information aren't so explicitly separated in the gradebook.

The page in the gradebook illustrates something about the way we think of information, and about the difficulty of figuring out how to put information in a database: We tend to integrate different kinds of information and interpret them as a whole. Databases don't work like that, which is one reason they sometimes seem artificial and unnatural. Our natural tendency to unify information makes it quite difficult sometimes even to realize when we have multiple types of data instead of just one. Because of this, you may find it a challenge to "think as a database thinks" about how your data should be represented.

One requirement imposed on the `event` table by the layout shown in Figure 1.5 is that the dates be unique because the date is used to link together records from the `score` and `event` tables. In other words, you cannot give two quizzes on the same day, or a quiz and a test. If you do, you'll have two sets of records in the `score` table and two records in the `event` table, all with the same date, and you won't be able to tell how to match `score` records with `event` records.

That's a problem that will never come up if there is never more than one grade event per day, but is it really valid to assume that will never happen? It might seem so; after all, you don't consider yourself sadistic enough to give a quiz and a test on the same day. But I hope you'll pardon me if I'm skeptical. I've often heard people claim about their data, "That odd case will never occur." Then it turns out the odd case *does* occur on occasion, and usually you have to redesign your tables to fix problems that the odd case causes.

It's better to think about the possible problems in advance and anticipate how to handle them. So, let's suppose you might need to record two sets of scores for the same day sometimes. How can we handle that? As it turns out, this problem isn't so difficult to solve. With a minor change to the way we lay out our data, multiple events on a given date won't cause trouble:

1. Add a column to the `event` table and use it to assign a unique number to each record in the table. In effect, this gives each event its own ID number, so we'll call this the `event_id` column. (If this seems like an odd thing to do, consider that your gradebook in Figure 1.2 already has this property: The event ID is just like the column number in your gradebook score matrix. The number might not be written down explicitly there and labeled "event ID," but that's what it is.)

2. When you put scores in the `score` table, record the event ID rather than the date.

The result of these changes is shown in Figure 1.6. Now you link together the `score` and `event` tables using the event ID rather than the date, and you use the `event` table to determine not just the type of each score, but also the date on which it occurred. Also, it's no longer the date that must be unique in the `event` table, it's the event ID. This means you can have a dozen tests and quizzes on the same day, and you'll be able to keep them straight in your records. (No doubt your students will be thrilled to hear this.)

Unfortunately, from a human standpoint, the table layout in Figure 1.6 seems less satisfactory than the previous ones. The `score` table is more abstract because it contains fewer columns with a readily apparent meaning. The table layout shown earlier in Figure 1.4 was easy to look at it and understand because the `score` table had columns for both dates and score types. The current `score` table shown in Figure 1.6 has columns for neither. This seems highly removed from anything we can think about easily. Who wants to look at a `score` table that has "event IDs" in it? That just doesn't mean much to us.

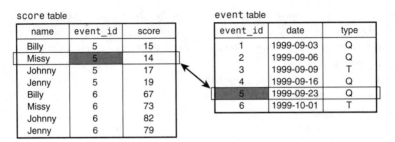

Figure 1.6   score and event tables, linked on event ID.

At this point you reach a crossroads. You're intrigued by the possibility of being able to perform grade-keeping electronically and not having to do all kinds of tedious manual calculations when assigning grades. But after considering how you actually would represent score information in a database, you're put off by how abstract and disconnected the representation seems to make that information.

This leads naturally to a question: "Would it be better not to use a database at all? Maybe MySQL isn't for me." As you might guess, I will answer that question in the negative because otherwise this book will come to a quick end. But when you're thinking about how to do a job, it's not a bad idea to consider various alternatives and to ask whether you're better off using a database system, such as MySQL, or something else, such as a spreadsheet:

- The gradebook has rows and columns, and so does a spreadsheet. This makes the gradebook and a spreadsheet conceptually and visually very similar.
- A spreadsheet can perform calculations, so you could total up each student's scores using a calculation field. It might be a little tricky to weight quizzes and tests differently, but you could do it.

On the other hand, if you want to look at just part of your data (quizzes only or tests only, for example), perform comparisons such as boys versus girls, or display summary information in a flexible way, it's a different story. A spreadsheet doesn't work so well, whereas relational database systems perform those operations easily.

Another point to consider is that the abstract and disconnected nature of your data as represented in a relational database is not really that big of a deal, anyway. You have to think about that representation when setting up the database so that you don't lay out your data in a way that doesn't make sense for what you want to do with it. However, after you determine the representation, you're going to rely on the database engine to pull together and present your data in a way that is meaningful to you. You're not going to look at it as a bunch of disconnected pieces.

For example, when you retrieve scores from the score table, you don't want to see event IDs; you want to see dates. That's not a problem. The database will look up dates from the event table based on the event ID and show them to you. You may also want to see whether the scores are for tests or quizzes. That's not a problem, either. The database will look up score types the same way—using event ID. Remember, that's what a relational database system like MySQL is good at: relating one thing to another to pull out information from multiple sources to present you with what you really want to see. In the case of our grade-keeping data, MySQL does the thinking about pulling information together using event IDs so that you don't have to.

Now, just to provide a little advance preview of how you'd tell MySQL to do this relating of one thing to another, suppose you want to see the scores for September 23, 1999. The query to pull out scores for an event given on a particular date looks like this:

```
SELECT score.name, event.date, score.score, event.type
FROM score, event
WHERE event.date = "1999-09-23"
AND score.event_id = event.event_id
```

Pretty scary, huh? This query retrieves the student name, the date, score, and the type of score by joining (relating) `score` table records to `event` table records. The result looks like this:

```
+--------+------------+-------+------+
| name   | date       | score | type |
+--------+------------+-------+------+
| Billy  | 1999-09-23 |    15 | Q    |
| Missy  | 1999-09-23 |    14 | Q    |
| Johnny | 1999-09-23 |    17 | Q    |
| Jenny  | 1999-09-23 |    19 | Q    |
+--------+------------+-------+------+
```

Notice anything familiar about the format of that information? You should; it's the same as the table layout shown in Figure 1.4! And you don't need to know the event ID to get this result. You specify the date you're interested in and let MySQL figure out which score records go with that date. If you've been wondering whether all the abstraction and disconnectedness loses us anything when it comes to getting information out of the database in a form that's meaningful to us, it doesn't.

Of course, after looking at that query, you might be wondering something else, too. Namely, it looks kind of long and complicated; isn't writing something like that a lot of work to go to just to find the scores for a given date? Yes, it is. However, there are ways to avoid typing several lines of SQL each time you want to issue a query. Generally, you figure out once how to perform a query such as that one and then you store it so that you can repeat it easily as necessary. We'll see how to do this in "Tips for Interacting with `mysql`."

I've actually jumped the gun a little bit in showing you that query. It is, believe it or not, a little simpler than the one we're really going to use to pull out scores. The reason for this is that we need to make one more change to our table layout. Instead of recording student name in the `score` table, we'll use a unique student ID. (That is, we'll use the value from the "ID" column of your gradebook rather than from the "Name" column.) Then we create another table called `student` that contains `name` and `student_id` columns (Figure 1.7).

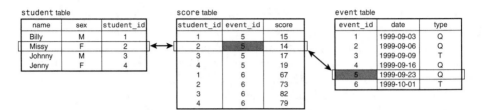

Figure 1.7   student, score, and event tables, linked on student ID and event ID.

Why make this modification? For one thing, there might be two students with the same name. Using a unique student ID number helps you tell their scores apart. (This is exactly analogous to the way you can tell scores apart for a test and quiz given on the same day by using a unique event ID rather than the date.)

After making this change to the table layout, the query we'll actually use to pull out scores for a given date becomes a little more complex:

```
SELECT student.name, event.date, score.score, event.type
FROM event, score, student
WHERE event.date = "1999-09-23"
AND event.event_id = score.event_id
AND score.student_id = student.student_id
```

If you're concerned because you don't find the meaning of that query immediately obvious, don't be. Most people wouldn't. We'll see the query again after we get further along into this tutorial, but the difference between now and later is that later you'll understand it. And, no, I'm not kidding.

You'll note from Figure 1.7 that I added something to the student table that wasn't in your gradebook: It contains a column for sex. This will allow for simple things like counting the number of boys and girls in the class or more complex things like comparing scores for boys and girls.

We're almost done with the tables for the grade-keeping project. We need just one more table to record absences for attendance purposes. Its contents are relatively straightforward: a student ID number and a date (see Figure 1.8). Each row in the table indicates that the given student was absent on the given date. At the end of the grading period, we'll call on MySQL's counting abilities to summarize the table's contents to tell us how many times each student was absent.

absence table

student_id	date
2	1999-09-02
4	1999-09-15
2	1999-09-20

Figure 1.8   absence table.

We're ready to create our grade-keeping tables now that we know what they should look like.

The CREATE TABLE statement for the student table looks like this:

```
CREATE TABLE student
(
    name VARCHAR(20) NOT NULL,
    sex ENUM('F','M') NOT NULL,
    student_id INT UNSIGNED NOT NULL AUTO_INCREMENT PRIMARY KEY
)
```

Type that statement into mysql or execute the following shell command:

```
% mysql samp_db < create_student.sql
```

The CREATE TABLE statement creates a table named student with three columns: name, sex, and student_id.

name is a variable-length string column that can hold up to 20 characters. This name representation is simpler than the one used for the Historical League tables; it uses a single column rather than separate first name and last name columns. That's because I know in advance that no grade-keeping query examples will need to do anything that would work better with separate columns. (Yes, that's cheating. I admit it.)

sex represents whether a student is a boy or a girl. It's an ENUM (enumeration) column, which means it can take on only one of the values explicitly listed in the column specification: 'F' or 'M' for female or male. ENUM is useful when you have a restricted set of values that a column can hold. We could have used CHAR(1) instead, but ENUM makes it more explicit what the column values can be. If you issue a DESCRIBE *tbl_name* statement for a table that contains an ENUM column, MySQL will show you exactly what the possible values are.

By the way, values in an ENUM column need not be just a single character. The type column could have been declared as something like ENUM('female','male') instead.

student_id is an integer column that will contain unique student ID numbers. Normally, you'd probably get ID numbers for your students from a central source, such as the school office, but we'll just make them up. The student_id column declaration has several parts, even though it just contains numbers:

- INT signifies that the column holds integers (values with no fractional part).

- UNSIGNED disallows negative numbers.

- NOT NULL means that the column value must be filled in. (No student can be without an ID number.)

- AUTO_INCREMENT is a special attribute in MySQL. It works like this: If the value for the student_id column is missing (or NULL) when you create a new student table record, MySQL automatically generates a unique number that is one greater than the maximum value currently in the column. We'll use this fact when we load the student table, by specifying values only for the name and sex columns and letting MySQL generate the student_id column value for us.

- PRIMARY KEY means that the column is indexed for fast lookups and that each value in the column must be unique. This prevents us from using the same ID twice by mistake, which is a desirable property for student ID numbers. (Not only that, but MySQL requires that every AUTO_INCREMENT column have a unique index.)

If you don't understand that stuff about AUTO_INCREMENT and PRIMARY KEY, just think of them as giving us a magic way of generating ID numbers for each student. It doesn't particularly matter what the values are, as long as they're unique.

Note: If you really were going to get student ID numbers from the office (and not generate them automatically), you could declare the student_id column the same way, except that you'd leave out the AUTO_INCREMENT attribute.

The event table looks like this:

```
CREATE TABLE event
(
    date DATE NOT NULL,
    type ENUM('T','Q') NOT NULL,
    event_id INT UNSIGNED NOT NULL AUTO_INCREMENT PRIMARY KEY
)
```

Type that statement into mysql or execute the following shell command:

```
% mysql samp_db < create_event.sql
```

All the columns are declared as NOT NULL because none of them can be missing.

The date column holds a standard MySQL DATE value, in "YYYY-MM-DD" (year-first) format.

type represents score type. Like sex in the student table, type is an enumeration column. The allowable values are 'T' and 'Q', representing "test" and "quiz."

event_id is an AUTO_INCREMENT column, similar to student_id in the student table. Using AUTO_INCREMENT allows us to generate unique event ID values easily. As with the student_id column in the student table, the particular values are less important than that they be unique.

The score table looks like this:

```
CREATE TABLE score
(
    student_id INT UNSIGNED NOT NULL,
    event_id INT UNSIGNED NOT NULL,
    score INT NOT NULL,
    PRIMARY KEY (event_id, student_id)
)
```

Type that statement into mysql or execute the following shell command:

```
% mysql samp_db < create_score.sql
```

score is an INT (integer) column. That is, I'm assuming score values are always integers. If you wanted to allow scores such as 58.5 that have a fractional part, you'd use one of the floating-point column types such as FLOAT or DECIMAL instead.

The `student_id` and `event_id` columns are integers representing which student and event each score is for. By using them to link to the `student` and `event` tables, we'll be able to tell the student name and event date. We've also made the combination of the two columns a `PRIMARY KEY`. This ensures that we won't have duplicate scores for a student for a given quiz or test. Also, it'll be easier to change a score later. For example, when a score is entered incorrectly, we can clobber the old record when we put in the new records by using MySQL's `REPLACE` statement. It's not necessary to do a `DELETE` coupled with an `INSERT`; MySQL does it for us.

Note that it's the combination of `event_id` and `student_id` that is unique. In the `score` table, neither value is unique by itself. There will be multiple score records for each `event_id` value (one per student), and multiple records for each `student_id` value (one for each quiz and test).

The `absence` table for attendance looks like this:

```
CREATE TABLE absence
(
    student_id INT UNSIGNED NOT NULL,
    date DATE NOT NULL,
    PRIMARY KEY (student_id, date)
)
```

Type that statement into `mysql` or execute the following shell command:

```
% mysql samp_db < create_absence.sql
```

The `student_id` and `date` columns are both declared as `NOT NULL` to disallow missing values. We make the combination of the two columns a primary key so that we don't accidentally create duplicate records. After all, it's not fair to count a student absent twice on the same day!

Adding New Records

At this point, our database and its tables have been created, and in the next section, "Retrieving Information," we'll see how to pull data out of the database. But first, we need to put some records into the tables.

There are several ways to add data to a database. You can insert records into a table manually by issuing `INSERT` statements. You can also add records by reading them from a file, either as raw data values that you load using the `LOAD DATA` statement or the `mysqlimport` utility, or in the form of pre-written `INSERT` statements that you feed to `mysql`.

This section demonstrates each method of inserting records into your tables. What you should do is play with the various methods to see how they work. Then go to the end of the section and run the commands you find there to clear out the tables and reload them. By doing so, you'll make sure the tables contain the same records that I was working with while writing the next section, and you'll get the same results.

Let's start adding records by using INSERT, a SQL statement for which you specify the table into which you want to insert a row of data and the values to put in the row. The INSERT statement has several forms:

- You can specify values for all the columns:

    ```
    INSERT INTO tbl_name VALUES(value1,value2,...)
    ```

    For example:

    ```
    mysql> INSERT INTO student VALUES('Kyle','M',NULL);
    mysql> INSERT INTO event VALUES("1999-9-3","Q",NULL);
    ```

    The word INTO is optional as of MySQL 3.22.5. (This is true for the other forms of INSERT as well.) The VALUES list must contain a value for each column in the table, in the order that the columns are stored in the table. (Normally, this is the order in which the columns were specified when the table was created. Use DESCRIBE tbl_name to find out the order if you're not sure what it is.)

    You can quote string and date values in MySQL using either single or double quotes. The NULL values in the preceding example are for the AUTO_INCREMENT columns in the student and event tables. (Inserting a "missing value" causes the next student_id or event_id number to be generated.)

    MySQL versions from 3.22.5 up allow you to insert several rows into a table with a single INSERT statement by specifying multiple value lists:

    ```
    INSERT INTO tbl_name VALUES(...),(...),...
    ```

    For example:

    ```
    mysql> INSERT INTO student VALUES('Abby','F',NULL),("Kyle","M",NULL);
    ```

    This involves less typing than multiple INSERT statements, and also is more efficient for the server to execute.

- You can name the columns to which you want to assign values, then list the values. This is useful when you want to create a record for which only a few columns need to be set up initially.

    ```
    INSERT INTO tbl_name (col_name1,col_name2,...) VALUES(value1,value2,...)
    ```

    For example:

    ```
    mysql> INSERT INTO member (last_name,first_name) VALUES('Stein','Waldo');
    ```

    As of MySQL 3.22.5, this form of INSERT allows multiple value lists, too:

    ```
    mysql> INSERT INTO student (name,sex) VALUES('Abby','F'),("Kyle","M");
    ```

    Any column not named in the column list is assigned a default value.

- As of MySQL 3.22.10, you can name columns and values in col_name=value form.

    ```
    INSERT INTO tbl_name SET col_name1=value1, col_name2=value2, ...
    ```

    For example:

    ```
    mysql> INSERT INTO member SET last_name='Stein',first_name='Waldo';
    ```

Any column not named in the SET clause is assigned a default value.

You cannot insert multiple rows using this form of INSERT.

Another method for loading records into a table is to read the data values directly from a file. You can load records this way with the LOAD DATA statement or with the mysqlimport utility.

The LOAD DATA statement acts as a bulk loader that reads data from a file. Use it from within mysql:

```
mysql> LOAD DATA LOCAL INFILE "member.txt" INTO TABLE member;
```

This statement reads the contents of the data file member.txt located in your current directory on the client host and sends it to the server to be loaded into the member table.

LOAD DATA LOCAL won't work if your MySQL is older than version 3.22.15 because that's when the capability of reading files from the client was added to LOAD DATA. (Without the LOCAL keyword, the file must be located on the server host and you need a server access privilege that most MySQL users don't have.)

By default, the LOAD DATA statement assumes that column values are separated by tabs and that lines end with newlines. It also assumes that the values are present in the order that columns are stored in the table. It's possible to read files in other formats or to specify a different column order. See the entry for LOAD DATA in Appendix D, "SQL Syntax Reference" for more details.

The mysqlimport utility acts as a command line interface to LOAD DATA. You invoke mysqlimport from the shell, and it generates a LOAD DATA statement for you:

```
% mysqlimport --local samp_db member.txt
```

mysqlimport generates a LOAD DATA statement for you that causes member.txt file to be loaded into the member table. This won't work if your MySQL is older than version 3.22.15 because the --local option requires LOAD DATA LOCAL. As with mysql, if you need to specify connection parameters, indicate them on the command line preceding the database name.

mysqlimport derives the table name from the name of the data file. (It uses everything up to the first period of the filename as the table name.) For example, member.txt would be loaded into the member table, and president.txt would be loaded into the president table. If you have multiple files that you want to load into a single table, choose the filenames carefully or mysqlimport won't use the correct table name. With names like member1.txt and member2.txt, mysqlimport would think the table names are member1 and member2. You could, however, use names like member.1.txt and member.2.txt, or member.txt1 and member.txt2.

After you have tried these record-adding methods, you should clear out the tables and reload them so that their contents are the same as what the next section assumes.

From your shell, execute the following commands:

```
% mysql samp_db < insert_president.sql
% mysql samp_db < insert_member.sql
% mysql samp_db < insert_student.sql
% mysql samp_db < insert_score.sql
% mysql samp_db < insert_event.sql
% mysql samp_db < insert_absence.sql
```

Each file contains a DELETE statement to delete any records you may have inserted into the table, followed by a set of INSERT statements to reinitialize the table contents. If you don't want to type those commands individually, try this:

```
% cat insert_*.sql | mysql samp_db
```

Retrieving Information

Our tables are created and loaded with data now, so let's see what we can do with that data. The SELECT statement allows you to retrieve and display information from your tables, in as general or specific a manner as you like. You can display the entire contents of a table:

```
SELECT * FROM president
```

Or you can select as little as a single column of a single row:

```
SELECT birth FROM president WHERE last_name = "Eisenhower"
```

The SELECT statement has several clauses (parts), which you combine as necessary to retrieve the information in which you're interested. Each of these clauses can be simple or complex, so SELECT statements as a whole can be simple or complex. However, you may rest assured that you won't find any page-long queries that take an hour to figure out in this book. (When I see arm-length queries in something I'm reading, I generally skip right over them, and I'm guessing you do the same.)

The general form of SELECT is:

```
SELECT what to select
FROM table or tables
WHERE conditions that data must satisfy
```

Remember that SQL is a free-format language, so when you write your own SELECT queries, you need not put line breaks in the same places I do.

To write a SELECT statement, specify what you want to retrieve and then some optional clauses. The clauses just shown (FROM, WHERE) are the ones most commonly used, although others can be specified as well, such as GROUP BY, ORDER BY, and LIMIT.

The FROM clause is usually present, but it need not be if you're not selecting data from tables. For example, the following query simply displays the values of some expressions that can be calculated without reference to any table, so no FROM is required:

```
mysql> SELECT 2+2, "Hello, world", VERSION();
+-----+--------------+-------------------+
| 2+2 | Hello, world | VERSION()         |
+-----+--------------+-------------------+
|   4 | Hello, world | 3.23.0-alpha-log  |
+-----+--------------+-------------------+
```

When you do use a FROM clause to specify a table from which to retrieve data, the most "generic" form of SELECT is to retrieve everything. To do this, use '*', which is shorthand for "all columns." The following query retrieves all rows from the student table and displays them:

```
mysql> SELECT * FROM student;
+-----------+-----+------------+
| name      | sex | student_id |
+-----------+-----+------------+
| Megan     | F   |          1 |
| Joseph    | M   |          2 |
| Kyle      | M   |          3 |
| Katie     | F   |          4 |
...
```

The columns are returned in the order that MySQL stores them in the table. This is the same order in which the columns are listed when you issue a DESCRIBE student statement. (The '...' at the end of the example indicates that the query returns more rows than are shown.)

You can explicitly name the column or columns you want to see. To select just student names, do this:

```
mysql> SELECT name FROM student;
+-----------+
| name      |
+-----------+
| Megan     |
| Joseph    |
| Kyle      |
| Katie     |
...
```

If you name more than one column, separate them with commas. The following statement is equivalent to SELECT * FROM student, but each column is named explicitly:

```
mysql> SELECT name, sex, student_id FROM student;
+-----------+-----+------------+
| name      | sex | student_id |
+-----------+-----+------------+
| Megan     | F   |          1 |
| Joseph    | M   |          2 |
| Kyle      | M   |          3 |
| Katie     | F   |          4 |
...
```

You can name columns in any order:

```
SELECT name, student_id FROM student
SELECT student_id, name FROM student
```

You can even name a column more than once if you like, although generally that's kind of pointless.

Column names are not case sensitive in MySQL. The following queries are equivalent:

```
SELECT name, student_id FROM student
SELECT NAME, STUDENT_ID FROM student
SELECT nAmE, sTuDeNt_Id FROM student
```

Database and table names may be case sensitive; it depends on the file system used on the server host. A server running on UNIX treats database and table names as case sensitive because UNIX filenames are case sensitive. Windows filenames are not case sensitive, so a server running on Windows does not treat database and table names as case sensitive.

MySQL allows you to select columns from more than one table at a time. We'll get to this in "Retrieving Information from Multiple Tables."

Specifying Retrieval Criteria

To restrict the set of records retrieved by the SELECT statement, use a WHERE clause that specifies criteria for selecting rows. You can select rows by looking for column values that satisfy various criteria.

You can look for numeric values:

```
mysql> SELECT * FROM score WHERE score > 95;
+------------+----------+-------+
| student_id | event_id | score |
+------------+----------+-------+
|          5 |        3 |    97 |
|         18 |        3 |    96 |
|          1 |        6 |   100 |
|          5 |        6 |    97 |
|         11 |        6 |    98 |
|         16 |        6 |    98 |
+------------+----------+-------+
```

Alternatively, you can look for string values. (Note that string comparisons normally are not case sensitive.)

```
mysql> SELECT last_name, first_name FROM president
    -> WHERE last_name="ROOSEVELT";
+-----------+-------------+
| last_name | first_name  |
+-----------+-------------+
| Roosevelt | Theodore    |
| Roosevelt | Franklin D. |
+-----------+-------------+
```

```
mysql> SELECT last_name, first_name FROM president
    -> WHERE last_name="roosevelt";
+-----------+------------+
| last_name | first_name |
+-----------+------------+
| Roosevelt | Theodore   |
| Roosevelt | Franklin D.|
+-----------+------------+
```

Or you could look for date values:

```
mysql> SELECT last_name, first_name, birth FROM president
    -> WHERE birth < "1750-1-1";
+------------+------------+------------+
| last_name  | first_name | birth      |
+------------+------------+------------+
| Washington | George     | 1732-02-22 |
| Adams      | John       | 1735-10-30 |
| Jefferson  | Thomas     | 1743-04-13 |
+------------+------------+------------+
```

Or you can search for a combination of values:

```
mysql> SELECT last_name, first_name, birth, state FROM president
    -> WHERE birth < "1750-1-1" AND (state="VA" OR state="MA");
+------------+------------+------------+-------+
| last_name  | first_name | birth      | state |
+------------+------------+------------+-------+
| Washington | George     | 1732-02-22 | VA    |
| Adams      | John       | 1735-10-30 | MA    |
| Jefferson  | Thomas     | 1743-04-13 | VA    |
+------------+------------+------------+-------+
```

Expressions in WHERE clauses can use arithmetic operators, as in Table 1.1, comparison operators, as in Table 1.2, and logical operators, as in Table 1.3. You can also use parentheses to group parts of an expression. Operations can be performed using constants, table columns, and function calls. We will have occasion to use several of MySQL's functions in queries throughout this tutorial, but there are far too many to show here. See Appendix C, "Operator and Function Reference," for a complete list.

Table 1.1 **Arithmetic Operators**

Operator	Meaning
+	Addition
-	Subtraction
*	Multiplication
/	Division

Table 1.2   **Comparison Operators**

Operator	Meaning
<	Less than
<=	Less than or equal to
=	Equal to
!= or <>	Not equal to
>=	Greater than or equal to
>	Greater than

Table 1.3   **Logical Operators**

Operator	Meaning
AND	Logical AND
OR	Logical OR
NOT	Logical negation

When you're formulating a query that requires logical operators, take care not to confuse the meaning of the logical AND operator with the way we use "and" in everyday speech. Suppose you want to find "presidents born in Virginia and presidents born in Massachusetts." Note how that is phrased using "and"—do you therefore write the query as follows?:

```
SELECT last_name, first_name, state FROM president
WHERE state="VA" AND state="MA"
```

No, because what that query means is "Select presidents who were born both in Virginia and in Massachusetts," which makes no sense. In English, you might express the query using "and," but in SQL, you connect the two conditions with OR:

```
mysql> SELECT last_name, first_name, state FROM president
    -> WHERE state="VA" OR state="MA";
+------------+-------------+-------+
| last_name  | first_name  | state |
+------------+-------------+-------+
| Washington | George      | VA    |
| Adams      | John        | MA    |
| Jefferson  | Thomas      | VA    |
| Madison    | James       | VA    |
| Monroe     | James       | VA    |
| Adams      | John Quincy | MA    |
| Harrison   | William H.  | VA    |
| Tyler      | John        | VA    |
| Taylor     | Zachary     | VA    |
| Wilson     | Woodrow     | VA    |
| Kennedy    | John F      | MA    |
| Bush       | George W.   | MA    |
+------------+-------------+-------+
```

This is something to be aware of, not just when formulating your own queries, but also when writing queries for other people. It's best to listen carefully as they describe what they want to retrieve, but you don't necessarily want to transcribe their descriptions into SQL using the same logical operators. For the example just described, the proper English equivalent for the query is "Select presidents who were born either in Virginia or in Massachusetts."

The NULL Value

The NULL value is special; because it means "no value," you can't assess it against known values the way you can assess two known values against each other. If you attempt to use NULL with the usual arithmetic comparison operators, the result is undefined:

```
mysql> SELECT NULL < 0, NULL = 0, NULL != 0, NULL > 0;
+----------+----------+-----------+----------+
| NULL < 0 | NULL = 0 | NULL != 0 | NULL > 0 |
+----------+----------+-----------+----------+
|     NULL |     NULL |      NULL |     NULL |
+----------+----------+-----------+----------+
```

In fact, you can't even compare NULL against itself because the result of comparing two unknown values cannot be known:

```
mysql> SELECT NULL = NULL, NULL != NULL;
+-------------+--------------+
| NULL = NULL | NULL != NULL |
+-------------+--------------+
|        NULL |         NULL |
+-------------+--------------+
```

To perform searches for NULL values, you must use a special syntax. Instead of using = or != to test for equality or inequality, use IS NULL or IS NOT NULL.

For example, because we have represented the death date for living presidents as NULL, you can find them like this:

```
mysql> SELECT last_name, first_name FROM president WHERE death IS NULL;
+-----------+------------+
| last_name | first_name |
+-----------+------------+
| Ford      | Gerald R   |
| Carter    | James E.   |
| Reagan    | Ronald W.  |
| Bush      | George W.  |
| Clinton   | William J. |
+-----------+------------+
```

To find names that have a suffix part, use IS NOT NULL:

```
mysql> SELECT last_name, first_name, suffix
    -> FROM president WHERE suffix IS NOT NULL;
+-----------+------------+--------+
| last_name | first_name | suffix |
+-----------+------------+--------+
| Carter    | James E.   | Jr.    |
+-----------+------------+--------+
```

MySQL 3.23 and up has a special MySQL-specific '<=>' comparison operator that is true even for NULL-to-NULL comparisons. The preceding two queries can be rewritten to use this operator as follows:

```
mysql> SELECT last_name, first_name FROM president WHERE death <=> NULL;
+-----------+------------+
| last_name | first_name |
+-----------+------------+
| Ford      | Gerald R   |
| Carter    | James E.   |
| Reagan    | Ronald W.  |
| Bush      | George W.  |
| Clinton   | William J. |
+-----------+------------+
mysql> SELECT last_name, first_name, suffix
    -> FROM president WHERE NOT (suffix <=> NULL);
+-----------+------------+--------+
| last_name | first_name | suffix |
+-----------+------------+--------+
| Carter    | James E.   | Jr.    |
+-----------+------------+--------+
```

Sorting Query Results

Sometimes people notice that if you issue a SELECT * FROM *tbl_name* query on a table after loading an initial data set into it, the rows are retrieved in the same order in which they were inserted. You can't count on that always being true. If you delete and insert rows after loading the table initially, you'll find that changes the order in which the server returns the table's rows. (Deleting records puts "holes" of unused space in the table, which MySQL tries to fill later when you insert new records.)

By default, when you select rows, the server makes no guarantees about the order in which rows will be returned. To sort rows, use an ORDER BY clause:

```
mysql> SELECT last_name, first_name FROM president
    -> ORDER BY last_name;
+-----------+--------------+
| last_name | first_name   |
+-----------+--------------+
| Adams     | John         |
| Adams     | John Quincy  |
| Arthur    | Chester A.   |
| Buchanan  | James        |
...
```

You can specify whether to sort a column in ascending or descending order by using the `ASC` or `DESC` keywords after column names in the `ORDER BY` clause. For example, to sort president names by reverse (descending) name order, use `DESC` like this:

```
mysql> SELECT last_name, first_name FROM president
    -> ORDER BY last_name DESC;
+------------+-------------+
| last_name  | first_name  |
+------------+-------------+
| Wilson     | Woodrow     |
| Washington | George      |
| Van Buren  | Martin      |
| Tyler      | John        |
...
```

Ascending order is the default if you specify neither `ASC` nor `DESC` for a column name in an `ORDER BY` clause.

If you sort a column that may contain `NULL` values, any `NULL` values appear at the beginning of the column, or at the end if you sort in descending order.

Query output can be sorted on multiple columns, and each column can be sorted in ascending or descending order independently of any other. The following query retrieves rows from the `president` table, sorts them by reverse state of birth, and by last name within each state:

```
mysql> SELECT last_name, first_name, state FROM president
    -> ORDER BY state DESC, last_name ASC;
+------------+-------------+-------+
| last_name  | first_name  | state |
+------------+-------------+-------+
| Arthur     | Chester A.  | VT    |
| Coolidge   | Calvin      | VT    |
| Harrison   | William H.  | VA    |
| Jefferson  | Thomas      | VA    |
| Madison    | James       | VA    |
| Monroe     | James       | VA    |
| Taylor     | Zachary     | VA    |
| Tyler      | John        | VA    |
| Washington | George      | VA    |
| Wilson     | Woodrow     | VA    |
| Eisenhower | Dwight D.   | TX    |
| Johnson    | Lyndon B.   | TX    |
...
```

Limiting Query Results

When a query returns many rows, but you want to see only a few of them, the `LIMIT` clause is useful, especially in conjunction with `ORDER BY`. MySQL allows you to limit the output of a query to the first *n* rows of the result that would otherwise be returned. The following query selects the five presidents who were born first:

```
mysql> SELECT last_name, first_name, birth FROM president
    -> ORDER BY birth LIMIT 5;
+------------+------------+------------+
| last_name  | first_name | birth      |
+------------+------------+------------+
| Washington | George     | 1732-02-22 |
| Adams      | John       | 1735-10-30 |
| Jefferson  | Thomas     | 1743-04-13 |
| Madison    | James      | 1751-03-16 |
| Monroe     | James      | 1758-04-28 |
+------------+------------+------------+
```

If you sort in reverse order, using ORDER BY birth DESC, you'd get the five most recently born presidents instead.

LIMIT also allows you to pull a section of records out of the middle of a result set. To do this, you must specify two values. The first value is the number of the initial record in the result set that you want to see. (The first record is numbered 0, not 1.) The second value indicates the number of records to return. The following query is similar to the previous one but returns five records beginning with the eleventh row of the result:

```
mysql> SELECT last_name, first_name, birth FROM president
    -> ORDER BY birth LIMIT 10, 5;
+------------+------------+------------+
| last_name  | first_name | birth      |
+------------+------------+------------+
| Tyler      | John       | 1790-03-29 |
| Buchanan   | James      | 1791-04-23 |
| Polk       | James K.   | 1795-11-02 |
| Fillmore   | Millard    | 1800-01-07 |
| Pierce     | Franklin   | 1804-11-23 |
+------------+------------+------------+
```

As of MySQL 3.23.2, you can order query results according to a formula. For example, to pull a randomly selected record from the president table, use ORDER BY RAND() in conjunction with LIMIT:

```
mysql> SELECT last_name, first_name FROM president
    -> ORDER BY RAND() LIMIT 1;
+------------+------------+
| last_name  | first_name |
+------------+------------+
| McKinley   | William    |
+------------+------------+
```

Calculating and Naming Output Column Values

Most of the preceding queries have produced output by retrieving values from tables. MySQL also allows you to calculate an output column value as the result of an expression. Expressions can be simple or complex. The following query evaluates a

simple expression (a constant) and a more complex expression involving several arithmetic operations and a couple of function calls:

```
mysql> SELECT 17, FORMAT(SQRT(3*3+4*4),0);
+----+------------------------+
| 17 | FORMAT(SQRT(3*3+4*4),0) |
+----+------------------------+
| 17 | 5                      |
+----+------------------------+
```

Expressions may also refer to table columns:

```
mysql> SELECT CONCAT(first_name," ",last_name),CONCAT(city,", ",state)
    -> FROM president;
+---------------------------------+-------------------------+
| CONCAT(first_name," ",last_name) | CONCAT(city,", ",state) |
+---------------------------------+-------------------------+
| George Washington               | Wakefield, VA           |
| John Adams                      | Braintree, MA           |
| Thomas Jefferson                | Albemarle County, VA    |
| James Madison                   | Port Conway, VA         |
...
```

This query formats president names as a single string by concatenating first and last
names separated by a space and formats birthplaces as the birth cities and states separated by a comma.

When you use an expression to calculate a column value, the expression is used for
the column heading. That can lead to a very wide column if the expression is long (as
the preceding query illustrates). To deal with this, the column can be assigned a name
for the heading, using the AS *name* construct. Such names are called column aliases. The
output from the previous query can be made more meaningful like this:

```
mysql> SELECT CONCAT(first_name," ",last_name) AS Name,
    -> CONCAT(city,", ",state) As Birthplace
    -> FROM president;
+--------------------+-------------------------+
| Name               | Birthplace              |
+--------------------+-------------------------+
| George Washington  | Wakefield, VA           |
| John Adams         | Braintree, MA           |
| Thomas Jefferson   | Albemarle County, VA    |
| James Madison      | Port Conway, VA         |
...
```

If the column alias contains spaces, you'll need to put it in quotes:

```
mysql> SELECT CONCAT(first_name," ",last_name) AS "President Name",
    -> CONCAT(city,", ",state) As "Place of Birth"
    -> FROM president;
```

```
+----------------------+----------------------------+
| President Name       | Place of Birth             |
+----------------------+----------------------------+
| George Washington    | Wakefield, VA              |
| John Adams           | Braintree, MA              |
| Thomas Jefferson     | Albemarle County, VA       |
| James Madison        | Port Conway, VA            |
...
```

Working With Dates

The principal thing to keep in mind when it comes to dates in MySQL is that they are always represented with the year first. July 27, 1999 is represented as `"1999-07-27"`. It is *not* represented as `"07-27-1999"` or as `"27-07-1999"`, as you might be more used to writing.

MySQL provides several ways to perform operations on dates. Some of the things you can do are as follows:

- Sort by date. (We've seen this several times already.)
- Look for particular dates or a range of dates.
- Extract parts of a date value, such as the year, month, or day.
- Calculate the difference between dates.
- Compute a date by adding or subtracting an interval from another date.

Some examples of these operations follow.

To look for particular dates, either by exact value or compared to another value, compare a DATE column to the value you're interested in:

```
mysql> SELECT * FROM event WHERE date = "1999-10-01";
+------------+------+----------+
| date       | type | event_id |
+------------+------+----------+
| 1999-10-01 | T    |        6 |
+------------+------+----------+
mysql> SELECT last_name, first_name, death
    -> FROM president
    -> WHERE death >= "1970-01-01" AND death < "1980-01-01";
+-----------+------------+------------+
| last_name | first_name | death      |
+-----------+------------+------------+
| Truman    | Harry S.   | 1972-12-26 |
| Johnson   | Lyndon B.  | 1973-01-22 |
+-----------+------------+------------+
```

To test or retrieve parts of dates, you can use functions such as YEAR(), MONTH(), or DAYOFMONTH(). For example, I can find presidents who were born in the same month that I was (March) by looking for dates with a month value of 3:

```
mysql> SELECT last_name, first_name, birth
    -> FROM president WHERE MONTH(birth) = 3;
```

```
+-----------+------------+------------+
| last_name | first_name | birth      |
+-----------+------------+------------+
| Madison   | James      | 1751-03-16 |
| Jackson   | Andrew     | 1767-03-15 |
| Tyler     | John       | 1790-03-29 |
| Cleveland | Grover     | 1837-03-18 |
+-----------+------------+------------+
```

The query can also be written in terms of the month name:

```
mysql> SELECT last_name, first_name, birth
    -> FROM president WHERE MONTHNAME(birth) = "March";
+-----------+------------+------------+
| last_name | first_name | birth      |
+-----------+------------+------------+
| Madison   | James      | 1751-03-16 |
| Jackson   | Andrew     | 1767-03-15 |
| Tyler     | John       | 1790-03-29 |
| Cleveland | Grover     | 1837-03-18 |
+-----------+------------+------------+
```

To be more specific—down to the day—I can combine tests for MONTH() and DAYOFMONTH() to find presidents born on my birthday:

```
mysql> SELECT last_name, first_name, birth
    -> FROM president WHERE MONTH(birth) = 3 AND DAYOFMONTH(birth) = 29;
+-----------+------------+------------+
| last_name | first_name | birth      |
+-----------+------------+------------+
| Tyler     | John       | 1790-03-29 |
+-----------+------------+------------+
```

This is the kind of query you'd use to generate one of those "these people have birthdays today" lists such as you see in the Entertainment section of your newspaper. However, you don't have to plug in a specific day the way the previous query did. To check for presidents born today, no matter what day of the year today is, compare their birthdays to the value of CURRENT_DATE:

```
SELECT last_name, first_name, birth
FROM president WHERE MONTH(birth) = MONTH(CURRENT_DATE)
AND DAYOFMONTH(birth) = DAYOFMONTH(CURRENT_DATE)
```

You can subtract one date from another. This allows you to find the interval between dates, which is useful for determining ages. For example, to determine which presidents lived the longest, subtract the birth date from the death date. To do this, convert birth and death to days using the TO_DAYS() function, take the difference, and divide by 365 to yield approximate age in years:

```
mysql> SELECT last_name, first_name, birth, death,
    -> FLOOR((TO_DAYS(death) - TO_DAYS(birth))/365) AS age
    -> FROM president WHERE death IS NOT NULL
    -> ORDER BY age DESC LIMIT 5;
```

```
+-----------+------------+------------+------------+------+
| last_name | first_name | birth      | death      | age  |
+-----------+------------+------------+------------+------+
| Adams     | John       | 1735-10-30 | 1826-07-04 |  90  |
| Hoover    | Herbert C. | 1874-08-10 | 1964-10-20 |  90  |
| Truman    | Harry S.   | 1884-05-08 | 1972-12-26 |  88  |
| Madison   | James      | 1751-03-16 | 1836-06-28 |  85  |
| Jefferson | Thomas     | 1743-04-13 | 1826-07-04 |  83  |
+-----------+------------+------------+------------+------+
```

The FLOOR() function used in this query chops off any fractional part from the age to produce an integer.

Taking the difference between dates is also useful for determining how far dates are from some reference date. That's how you can tell which Historical League members need to renew their memberships soon. Compute the difference between their expiration dates and the current date, and if it's less than some threshold value, a renewal will soon be needed. The following query finds memberships that are due for renewal within 60 days:

```
SELECT last_name, first_name, expiration FROM member
WHERE (TO_DAYS(expiration) - TO_DAYS(CURRENT_DATE)) < 60
```

As of MySQL 3.22, you can use DATE_ADD() or DATE_SUB() to calculate one date from another. These functions take a date and an interval and produce a new date. For example:

```
mysql> SELECT DATE_ADD("1970-1-1", INTERVAL 10 YEAR);
+----------------------------------------+
| DATE_ADD("1970-1-1", INTERVAL 10 YEAR) |
+----------------------------------------+
| 1980-01-01                             |
+----------------------------------------+
mysql> SELECT DATE_SUB("1970-1-1", INTERVAL 10 YEAR);
+----------------------------------------+
| DATE_SUB("1970-1-1", INTERVAL 10 YEAR) |
+----------------------------------------+
| 1960-01-01                             |
+----------------------------------------+
```

A query shown earlier in this section selected presidents who died during the 1970s, using literal dates for the endpoints of the selection range. That query can be rewritten to use a literal starting date and an ending date calculated from the starting date and an interval:

```
mysql> SELECT last_name, first_name, death
    -> FROM president
    -> WHERE death >= "1970-1-1"
    -> AND death < DATE_ADD("1970-1-1", INTERVAL 10 YEAR);
+-----------+------------+------------+
| last_name | first_name | death      |
+-----------+------------+------------+
| Truman    | Harry S.   | 1972-12-26 |
| Johnson   | Lyndon B.  | 1973-01-22 |
+-----------+------------+------------+
```

The membership-renewal query can be written in terms of `DATE_ADD()`:

```
SELECT last_name, first_name, expiration FROM member
WHERE expiration < DATE_ADD(CURRENT_DATE, INTERVAL 60 DAY)
```

Earlier in this chapter, a query was presented for determining which of a dentist's patients haven't been in for their checkups in a while:

```
SELECT last_name, first_name, last_visit FROM patient
WHERE last_visit < DATE_SUB(CURRENT_DATE,INTERVAL 6 MONTH)
```

This query may not have meant much to you then. Is it more meaningful now?

Pattern Matching

MySQL allows you to look for values that match a pattern. In this way, you can select records without supplying an exact value. To perform a pattern matching operation, you use special operators (`LIKE` and `NOT LIKE`), and you specify a string containing wild card characters. The character '_' matches any single character, and '%' matches any sequence of characters (including an empty sequence). Pattern matches using `LIKE` or `NOT LIKE` are not case sensitive.

This pattern matches last names that begin with 'W' or 'w':

```
mysql> SELECT last_name, first_name FROM president
    -> WHERE last_name LIKE "W%";
+------------+------------+
| last_name  | first_name |
+------------+------------+
| Washington | George     |
| Wilson     | Woodrow    |
+------------+------------+
```

This pattern match is erroneous:

```
mysql> SELECT last_name, first_name FROM president
    -> WHERE last_name = "W%";
Empty set (0.00 sec)
```

The query demonstrates a common error, which is to use a pattern with an arithmetic comparison operator. The only way for such a comparison to succeed is for the column to contain exactly the string "W%" or "w%".

This pattern matches last names that contain 'W' or 'w' anywhere in the name:

```
mysql> SELECT last_name, first_name FROM president
    -> WHERE last_name LIKE "%W%";
+------------+------------+
| last_name  | first_name |
+------------+------------+
| Washington | George     |
| Wilson     | Woodrow    |
| Eisenhower | Dwight D.  |
+------------+------------+
```

This pattern matches last names that contain exactly four characters:

```
mysql> SELECT last_name, first_name FROM president
    -> WHERE last_name LIKE "____";
+-----------+-----------+
| last_name | first_name |
+-----------+-----------+
| Polk      | James K.   |
| Taft      | William H. |
| Ford      | Gerald R.  |
| Bush      | George W.  |
+-----------+-----------+
```

MySQL also provides another form of pattern matching based on extended regular expressions. Regular expressions are described in the discussion of the REGEXP operator in Appendix C.

Generating Summaries

One of the most useful things MySQL can do for you is to boil down lots of raw data and summarize it. MySQL becomes a powerful ally when you learn to use it to generate summaries because that is an especially tedious, time-consuming, error-prone activity when done manually.

One simple form of summarizing is to determine which unique values are present in a set of values. Use the DISTINCT keyword to remove duplicate rows from a result. For example, the different states in which presidents have been born can be found like this:

```
mysql> SELECT DISTINCT state FROM president ORDER BY state;
+-------+
| state |
+-------+
| AR    |
| CA    |
| GA    |
| IA    |
| IL    |
| KY    |
| MA    |
| MO    |
| NC    |
| NE    |
| NH    |
| NJ    |
| NY    |
| OH    |
| PA    |
| SC    |
| TX    |
| VA    |
| VT    |
+-------+
```

Another form of summarizing involves counting, using—you guessed it—the COUNT() function. If you use COUNT(*), it tells you the number of rows selected by your query. If a query has no WHERE clause, COUNT(*) tells you the number of rows in your table. The following query shows how many US presidents there have been:

```
mysql> SELECT COUNT(*) FROM president;
+----------+
| COUNT(*) |
+----------+
|       41 |
+----------+
```

If a query does have a WHERE clause, COUNT(*) tells you how many rows the clause selects. This query shows how many quizzes you have given to your class so far:

```
mysql> SELECT COUNT(*) FROM event WHERE type = 'Q';
+----------+
| COUNT(*) |
+----------+
|        4 |
+----------+
```

COUNT(*) counts every row selected. By contrast, COUNT(col_name) counts only non-NULL values. The following query demonstrates these differences:

```
mysql> SELECT COUNT(*),COUNT(suffix),COUNT(death) FROM president;
+----------+---------------+--------------+
| COUNT(*) | COUNT(suffix) | COUNT(death) |
+----------+---------------+--------------+
|       41 |             1 |           36 |
+----------+---------------+--------------+
```

This shows that there have been 41 presidents in all, that only one of them has a name suffix, and that most presidents are no longer living.

As of MySQL 3.23.2, you can combine COUNT() with DISTINCT to count the number of distinct values in a result. For example, to count the number of different states in which presidents have been born, do this:

```
mysql> SELECT COUNT(DISTINCT state) FROM president;
+-----------------------+
| COUNT(DISTINCT state) |
+-----------------------+
|                    19 |
+-----------------------+
```

You can break down counts by individual values in the summarized column. For example, you may know the overall number of students in your class as a result of running this query:

```
mysql> SELECT COUNT(*) FROM student;
+----------+
| COUNT(*) |
+----------+
|       31 |
+----------+
```

But how many students are boys and how many are girls? One way to find out is by asking for a count for each sex separately:

```
mysql> SELECT COUNT(*) FROM student WHERE sex='f';
+----------+
| COUNT(*) |
+----------+
|       15 |
+----------+
mysql> SELECT COUNT(*) FROM student WHERE sex='m';
+----------+
| COUNT(*) |
+----------+
|       16 |
+----------+
```

However, although this approach works, it's tedious and not really very well suited for columns that might have several different values. Consider how you'd determine the number of presidents born in each state this way. You'd have to find out which states are represented so as not to miss any (SELECT DISTINCT state FROM president), then run a SELECT COUNT(*) query for each state. That is clearly something you don't want to do.

Fortunately, MySQL can count, using a single query, how many times each distinct value occurs in a column: For our student list, we can count boys and girls like this:

```
mysql> SELECT sex, COUNT(*) FROM student GROUP BY sex;
+-----+----------+
| sex | COUNT(*) |
+-----+----------+
| F   |       15 |
| M   |       16 |
+-----+----------+
```

The same form of query tells us how many presidents were born in each state:

```
mysql> SELECT state, COUNT(*) FROM president GROUP BY state;
+-------+----------+
| state | COUNT(*) |
+-------+----------+
| AR    |        1 |
| CA    |        1 |
| GA    |        1 |
| IA    |        1 |
| IL    |        1 |
| KY    |        1 |
| MA    |        4 |
| MO    |        1 |
| NC    |        2 |
| NE    |        1 |
| NH    |        1 |
| NJ    |        1 |
| NY    |        4 |
| OH    |        7 |
| PA    |        1 |
| SC    |        1 |
```

```
| TX    |        2 |
| VA    |        8 |
| VT    |        2 |
+-------+----------+
```

When you count values this way, the GROUP BY clause is necessary; it tells MySQL how to cluster values before counting them. You'll just get an error if you omit it.

The use of COUNT(*) with GROUP BY to count values has a number of advantages over counting occurrences of each distinct column value individually:

- You don't have to know in advance what values are present in the column you're summarizing.
- You need only a single query, not several.
- You get all the results with a single query, so you can sort the output.

The first two advantages are important for expressing queries more easily. The third advantage is important because it affords you flexibility in displaying your results. When you use a GROUP BY clause, the results are sorted on the columns you group by, but you can use ORDER BY to sort in a different order. For example, if you want number of presidents grouped by state of birth, but sorted with the most well-represented states first, you can use an ORDER BY clause as follows:

```
mysql> SELECT state, COUNT(*) AS count FROM president
    -> GROUP BY state ORDER BY count DESC;
+-------+-------+
| state | count |
+-------+-------+
| VA    |     8 |
| OH    |     7 |
| MA    |     4 |
| NY    |     4 |
| NC    |     2 |
| VT    |     2 |
| TX    |     2 |
| SC    |     1 |
| NH    |     1 |
| PA    |     1 |
| KY    |     1 |
| NJ    |     1 |
| IA    |     1 |
| MO    |     1 |
| CA    |     1 |
| NE    |     1 |
| GA    |     1 |
| IL    |     1 |
| AR    |     1 |
+-------+-------+
```

When the column you want to sort by is determined by calculation, you can give the column an alias and refer to the alias in the ORDER BY clause. The preceding query demonstrates this; the COUNT(*) column is aliased as count. Another way to refer to such a column is by its position in the output. The previous query could have been written like this instead:

```
SELECT state, COUNT(*) FROM president
GROUP BY state ORDER BY 2 DESC
```

I don't find that referring to columns by position is very readable. If you add, remove, or reorder output columns, you must remember to check the ORDER BY clause and fix the column number if it has changed. Aliases don't have this problem.

If you want to use GROUP BY with a calculated column, you should refer to it using an alias or column position, just as with ORDER BY. The following query determines how many presidents were born in each month of the year:

```
mysql> SELECT MONTH(birth) as Month, MONTHNAME(birth) as Name,
    -> COUNT(*) AS count
    -> FROM president GROUP BY Name ORDER BY Month;
+-------+-----------+-------+
| Month | Name      | count |
+-------+-----------+-------+
|     1 | January   |     4 |
|     2 | February  |     4 |
|     3 | March     |     4 |
|     4 | April     |     4 |
|     5 | May       |     2 |
|     6 | June      |     1 |
|     7 | July      |     3 |
|     8 | August    |     4 |
|     9 | September |     1 |
|    10 | October   |     6 |
|    11 | November  |     5 |
|    12 | December  |     3 |
+-------+-----------+-------+
```

Using column positions, the query would be written like this:

```
SELECT MONTH(birth), MONTHNAME(birth), COUNT(*)
FROM president GROUP BY 2 ORDER BY 1;
```

COUNT() may be combined with ORDER BY and LIMIT to find, for example, the four most well-represented states in the president table:

```
mysql> SELECT state, COUNT(*) AS count FROM president
    -> GROUP BY state ORDER BY count DESC LIMIT 4;
+-------+-------+
| state | count |
+-------+-------+
| VA    |     8 |
| OH    |     7 |
| MA    |     4 |
| NY    |     4 |
+-------+-------+
```

If you don't want to limit query output with a LIMIT clause, but rather by looking for particular values of COUNT(), use a HAVING clause. The following query will tell you which states are represented by two or more presidents:

```
mysql> SELECT state, COUNT(*) AS count FROM president
    -> GROUP BY state HAVING count > 1 ORDER BY count DESC;
+-------+-------+
| state | count |
+-------+-------+
| VA    |     8 |
| OH    |     7 |
| MA    |     4 |
| NY    |     4 |
| NC    |     2 |
| VT    |     2 |
| TX    |     2 |
+-------+-------+
```

More generally, this is the type of query to run when you want to find duplicated values in a column.

HAVING is similar to WHERE, but it's applied after the query results have been selected and used to narrow down the results actually sent by the server to the client.

There are summary functions other than COUNT(). The MIN(), MAX(), SUM(), and AVG() functions are useful for determining the minimum, maximum, total, and average values in a column. You can even use them all at the same time. The following query shows various numeric characteristics for each quiz and test you've given. It also shows how many scores go into computing each of the values. (Some students may have been absent and are not counted.)

```
mysql> SELECT
    -> event_id,
    -> MIN(score) AS minimum,
    -> MAX(score) AS maximum,
    -> MAX(score)-MIN(score)+1 AS range,
    -> SUM(score) AS total,
    -> AVG(score) AS average,
    -> COUNT(score) AS count
    -> FROM score
    -> GROUP BY event_id;
+----------+---------+---------+-------+-------+---------+-------+
| event_id | minimum | maximum | range | total | average | count |
+----------+---------+---------+-------+-------+---------+-------+
|        1 |       9 |      20 |    12 |   439 | 15.1379 |    29 |
|        2 |       8 |      19 |    12 |   425 | 14.1667 |    30 |
|        3 |      60 |      97 |    38 |  2425 | 78.2258 |    31 |
|        4 |       7 |      20 |    14 |   379 | 14.0370 |    27 |
|        5 |       8 |      20 |    13 |   383 | 14.1852 |    27 |
|        6 |      62 |     100 |    39 |  2325 | 80.1724 |    29 |
+----------+---------+---------+-------+-------+---------+-------+
```

This information might be more meaningful if you knew whether the values were from quizzes or tests, of course. However, to produce that information, we need to consult the event table as well; we'll revisit this query in "Retrieving Information from Multiple Tables."

Summary functions are fun to play with because they're so powerful, but it's easy to get carried away with them. Consider this query:

```
mysql> SELECT
    -> state AS State,
    -> AVG((TO_DAYS(death)-TO_DAYS(birth))/365) AS Age
    -> FROM president WHERE death IS NOT NULL
    -> GROUP BY state ORDER BY Age;
+-------+-----------+
| State | Age       |
+-------+-----------+
| KY    | 56.208219 |
| VT    | 58.852055 |
| NC    | 60.141096 |
| OH    | 62.866145 |
| NH    | 64.917808 |
| NY    | 69.342466 |
| NJ    | 71.315068 |
| TX    | 71.476712 |
| MA    | 72.642009 |
| VA    | 72.822945 |
| PA    | 77.158904 |
| SC    | 78.284932 |
| CA    | 81.336986 |
| MO    | 88.693151 |
| IA    | 90.254795 |
+-------+-----------+
```

The query selects presidents who have died, groups them by date of birth, figures out their age at time of death, computes the average age (per state), and then sorts the results by average age. In other words, the query determines, for non-living presidents, the average age of death by state of birth.

And what does that demonstrate? It shows only that you can write the query. It certainly doesn't show that the query is worth writing. Not all things you can do with a database are equally meaningful; nevertheless, people sometimes go query-happy when they find out what they can do with their database. This may account for the rise of increasingly esoteric (and pointless) statistics on televised sporting events over the last few years. The sports statisticians can use their databases to figure out everything you'd ever want to know about a team, and also everything you'd *never* want to know. Do you really care which third-string quarterback holds the record for most interceptions on third down when his team is leading by more than 14 points with the ball inside the 15-yard line and less than three minutes remaining on the clock in the second quarter?

Retrieving Information from Multiple Tables

The queries we've written so far have pulled data from a single table. Now we get to the interesting part. I've mentioned before that the power of a relational DBMS lies in its ability to relate one thing to another because that allows you to combine information from multiple tables to answer questions that can't be answered from individual tables alone. This section describes how to write queries that do that.

When you select information from multiple tables, you're performing an operation called a *join*. That's because you're producing a result by joining the information from one table to the information in another. This is done by matching up common values in the tables.

Let's work through an example. Earlier, in "Tables for the Grade-Keeping Project," a query to retrieve quiz or test scores for a given date was presented without explanation. Now it's time for the explanation. The query actually involves a three-way join, so we'll work up to it in two steps.

In the first step, we construct a query to select scores for a given date as follows:

```
mysql> SELECT student_id, date, score, type
    -> FROM event, score
    -> WHERE date = "1999-09-23"
    -> AND event.event_id = score.event_id;
+------------+------------+-------+------+
| student_id | date       | score | type |
+------------+------------+-------+------+
|          1 | 1999-09-23 |    15 | Q    |
|          2 | 1999-09-23 |    12 | Q    |
|          3 | 1999-09-23 |    11 | Q    |
|          5 | 1999-09-23 |    13 | Q    |
|          6 | 1999-09-23 |    18 | Q    |
...
```

The query works by finding the event record with the given date and then uses the event ID in that record to locate scores with the same event ID. For each matching event record and score record combination, the student ID, score, date, and event type are displayed.

The query differs from others we have written in two important respects:

- The FROM clause names more than one table because we're retrieving data from more than one table:

    FROM event, score

- The WHERE clause specifies that the event and score tables are joined by matching up the event_id values in each table:

    WHERE ... event.event_id = score.event_id

Notice how we refer to the columns using *tbl_name.col_name* syntax so that MySQL knows which tables we're referring to. (event_id occurs in both tables, so it's ambiguous if used without a table name to qualify it.)

The other columns in the query (date, score, type) can be used without a table qualifier because they appear in only one of the tables and thus are unambiguous. However, I generally prefer to qualify every column in a join to make it clearer which table each column is part of. In fully qualified form, the query looks like this:

```
SELECT score.student_id, event.date, score.score, event.type
FROM event, score
WHERE event.date = "1999-09-23"
AND event.event_id = score.event_id
```

I will use the fully qualified form from now on.

In the second step, we complete the query by using the student table to display student names. (Output of the query from the first step shows us the student_id field, but names are more meaningful.) Name display is accomplished using the fact that the score and student tables both have student_id columns allowing the records in them to be linked. The resulting query looks like this:

```
mysql> SELECT student.name, event.date, score.score, event.type
    -> FROM event, score, student
    -> WHERE event.date = "1999-09-23"
    -> AND event.event_id = score.event_id
    -> AND score.student_id = student.student_id;
+--------+------------+-------+------+
| name   | date       | score | type |
+--------+------------+-------+------+
| Megan  | 1999-09-23 |    15 | Q    |
| Joseph | 1999-09-23 |    12 | Q    |
| Kyle   | 1999-09-23 |    11 | Q    |
| Abby   | 1999-09-23 |    13 | Q    |
| Nathan | 1999-09-23 |    18 | Q    |
...
```

This query differs from the previous one as follows:

- The student table is added to the FROM clause because it is used in addition to the event and score tables.
- The student_id column is ambiguous now, so it must be qualified as score.student_id or student.student_id to make it clear which table to use. (This is true even if you prefer writing joins that don't fully qualify every column reference.)
- The WHERE clause has an additional term specifying that score table records are matched against student table records based on student ID:
  ```
  WHERE ... score.student_id = student.student_id
  ```
- The query displays the student name rather than the student ID. (You could display both if you wanted to, of course.)

With this query, you can plug in any date and get back the scores for that date, complete with student names and the score type. You don't have to know anything about student IDs or event IDs. MySQL takes care of figuring out the relevant ID values and using them to match up table rows, automatically.

Another task the grade-keeping project involves is summarizing student absences. Absences are recorded by student ID and date in the `absence` table. To get student names (not just IDs), we need to join the `absence` table to the `student` table, based on the `student_id` value. The following query lists student ID number and name along with a count of absences:

```
mysql> SELECT student.student_id, student.name,
    -> COUNT(absence.date) as absences
    -> FROM student, absence
    -> WHERE student.student_id = absence.student_id
    -> GROUP BY student.student_id;
+------------+-------+----------+
| student_id | name  | absences |
+------------+-------+----------+
|          3 | Kyle  |        1 |
|          5 | Abby  |        1 |
|         10 | Peter |        2 |
|         17 | Will  |        1 |
|         20 | Avery |        1 |
+------------+-------+----------+
```

Note: Although I'm supplying a qualifier in the GROUP BY clause, it isn't strictly necessary for this query. GROUP BY refers to columns in the selection list (on the first two lines of the query). There is only one column named `student_id` there, so MySQL knows which column you mean. This is also true for columns named in ORDER BY clauses.

The output produced by the query is fine if we want to know only which students had absences. But if we turn in this list to the school office, they may say, "What about the other students? We want a value for each student." That's a slightly different question. It means we want to know the number of absences, even for students that had none. Because the question is different, the query is different as well.

To answer the question, we can use LEFT JOIN rather than associating student ID in the WHERE clause. LEFT JOIN tells MySQL to produce a row of output for each row selected from the table named first in the join (that is, the table named to the left of the LEFT JOIN keywords). By naming the `student` table first, we'll get output for every student, even those who are not represented in the `absence` table. The query looks like this:

```
mysql> SELECT student.student_id, student.name,
    -> COUNT(absence.date) as absences
    -> FROM student LEFT JOIN absence
    -> ON student.student_id = absence.student_id
    -> GROUP BY student.student_id;
```

```
+------------+----------+----------+
| student_id | name     | absences |
+------------+----------+----------+
|          1 | Megan    |        0 |
|          2 | Joseph   |        0 |
|          3 | Kyle     |        1 |
|          4 | Katie    |        0 |
|          5 | Abby     |        1 |
|          6 | Nathan   |        0 |
|          7 | Liesl    |        0 |
...
```

Earlier, in "Generating Summaries," we ran a query that produced a numeric characterization of the data in the score table. Output from that query listed event ID but did not include score date or type, because we didn't know then how to join the score table to the event table to get score dates and types. Now we do. The following query is similar to one we ran earlier, but shows the date and type for scores rather than simply the numeric event ID:

```
mysql> SELECT
    -> event.date,event.type,
    -> MIN(score.score) AS minimum,
    -> MAX(score.score) AS maximum,
    -> MAX(score.score)-MIN(score.score)+1 AS range,
    -> SUM(score.score) AS total,
    -> AVG(score.score) AS average,
    -> COUNT(score.score) AS count
    -> FROM score, event
    -> WHERE score.event_id = event.event_id
    -> GROUP BY event.date;
```

date	type	minimum	maximum	range	total	average	count
1999-09-03	Q	9	20	12	439	15.1379	29
1999-09-06	Q	8	19	12	425	14.1667	30
1999-09-09	T	60	97	38	2425	78.2258	31
1999-09-16	Q	7	20	14	379	14.0370	27
1999-09-23	Q	8	20	13	383	14.1852	27
1999-10-01	T	62	100	39	2325	80.1724	29

You can use functions such as COUNT() and AVG() to produce a summary over multiple columns, even if the columns come from different tables. The following query determines the number of scores and the average score for each combination of event date and student sex:

```
mysql> SELECT event.date, student.sex,
    -> COUNT(score) AS count, AVG(score) As average
    -> FROM event, score, student
    -> WHERE event.event_id = score.event_id
    -> AND score.student_id = student.student_id
    -> GROUP BY event.date, student.sex;
```

```
+------------+-----+-------+---------+
| date       | sex | count | average |
+------------+-----+-------+---------+
| 1999-09-03 | F   |    14 | 14.6429 |
| 1999-09-03 | M   |    15 | 15.6000 |
| 1999-09-06 | F   |    14 | 14.7143 |
| 1999-09-06 | M   |    16 | 13.6875 |
| 1999-09-09 | F   |    15 | 77.4000 |
| 1999-09-09 | M   |    16 | 79.0000 |
| 1999-09-16 | F   |    13 | 15.3077 |
| 1999-09-16 | M   |    14 | 12.8571 |
| 1999-09-23 | F   |    12 | 14.0833 |
| 1999-09-23 | M   |    15 | 14.2667 |
| 1999-10-01 | F   |    14 | 77.7857 |
| 1999-10-01 | M   |    15 | 82.4000 |
+------------+-----+-------+---------+
```

We can use a similar query to perform one of the grade-keeping project tasks: computing the total score per student at the end of the semester. The query looks like this:

```
SELECT student.student_id, student.name,
SUM(score.score) AS total, COUNT(score.score) AS n
FROM event, score, student
WHERE event.event_id = score.event_id
AND score.student_id = student.student_id
GROUP BY score.student_id
ORDER BY total
```

There is no requirement that a join be performed using two different tables. It might seem odd at first, but you can join a table to itself. For example, you can determine whether any presidents were born in the same city by checking each president's birthplace against every other president's birthplace:

```
mysql> SELECT p1.last_name, p1.first_name, p1.city, p1.state
    -> FROM president AS p1, president AS p2
    -> WHERE p1.city = p2.city AND p1.state = p2.state
    -> AND (p1.last_name != p2.last_name OR p1.first_name != p2.first_name)
    -> ORDER BY state, city, last_name;
+-----------+-------------+-----------+-------+
| last_name | first_name  | city      | state |
+-----------+-------------+-----------+-------+
| Adams     | John Quincy | Braintree | MA    |
| Adams     | John        | Braintree | MA    |
+-----------+-------------+-----------+-------+
```

There are two tricky things about this query:

- We need to refer to two instances of the same table, so we create table aliases (p1, p2) and use them to disambiguate references to the table's columns.

- Every president's record matches itself, but we don't want to see that in the output. The second line of the WHERE clause disallows matches of a record to itself by making sure the records being compared are for different presidents.

A similar query finds presidents who were born on the same day. Birth dates cannot be compared directly because that would miss presidents who were born in different years. Instead, we use MONTH() and DAYOFMONTH() to compare month and day of the birth date:

```
mysql> SELECT p1.last_name, p1.first_name, p1.birth
    -> FROM president AS p1, president AS p2
    -> WHERE MONTH(p1.birth) = MONTH(p2.birth)
    -> AND DAYOFMONTH(p1.birth) = DAYOFMONTH(p2.birth)
    -> AND (p1.last_name != p2.last_name OR p1.first_name != p2.first_name)
    -> ORDER BY p1.last_name;
+-----------+------------+------------+
| last_name | first_name | birth      |
+-----------+------------+------------+
| Harding   | Warren G.  | 1865-11-02 |
| Polk      | James K.   | 1795-11-02 |
+-----------+------------+------------+
```

Using DAYOFYEAR() rather than the combination of MONTH() and DAYOFMONTH() would result in a simpler query, but it would produce incorrect results when comparing dates from leap years to dates from non-leap years.

The joins performed thus far combined information from tables that have some meaningful logical relationship, but only you know the meaningfulness of that relationship. MySQL doesn't know (or care) whether or not the joined tables have anything to do with each other. For instance, you can join the event table to the president table to find out whether or not you gave any quizzes or tests on a president's birthday:

```
mysql> SELECT president.last_name, president.first_name,
    -> president.birth, event.type
    -> FROM president, event
    -> WHERE MONTH(president.birth) = MONTH(event.date)
    -> AND DAYOFMONTH(president.birth) = DAYOFMONTH(event.date);
+-----------+------------+------------+------+
| last_name | first_name | birth      | type |
+-----------+------------+------------+------+
| Carter    | James E.   | 1924-10-01 | T    |
+-----------+------------+------------+------+
```

It turns out you did. But so what? This illustrates that MySQL will happily crank out results, whether they make any sense or not. Just because you're using a computer, it doesn't automatically mean that results from a query are useful or worthwhile. Fortunately or unfortunately, we still must think about what we're doing.

Deleting or Updating Existing Records

Sometimes you want to get rid of records or change their contents. The DELETE and UPDATE statements let you do this.

The DELETE statement has this form:

```
DELETE FROM tbl_name WHERE which records to delete
```

The WHERE clause specifies which records should be deleted. It's optional, but if you leave it out, all records are deleted. That means the simplest DELETE statement is also the most dangerous:

```
DELETE FROM tbl_name
```

This query wipes out the table's contents entirely. *Be careful with this!*

To delete specific records, use the WHERE clause to select the records in which you're interested. This is similar to the WHERE clause in a SELECT statement. For example, to delete from the president table all presidents born in Ohio, use this query:

```
mysql> DELETE FROM president WHERE state="OH";
Query OK, 7 rows affected (0.00 sec)
```

One limitation of the WHERE clause for DELETE is that you can refer only to columns of the table from which you're deleting records.

Before issuing a DELETE statement, it's often a good idea to test the WHERE clause by using it with a SELECT statement to make sure you'll actually delete the records you intend (and *only* those records). Suppose you want to delete the record for Teddy Roosevelt. Would the following query do the job?

```
DELETE FROM president WHERE last_name="Roosevelt"
```

Yes, in the sense that it would delete the record you have in mind. No, in the sense that it also would delete the record for Franklin Roosevelt. It's safer to check the WHERE clause first, like this:

```
mysql> SELECT last_name, first_name FROM president
    -> WHERE last_name="Roosevelt";
+-----------+------------+
| last_name | first_name |
+-----------+------------+
| Roosevelt | Theodore   |
| Roosevelt | Franklin D.|
+-----------+------------+
```

From that you can see the need to be more specific:

```
mysql> SELECT last_name, first_name FROM president
    -> WHERE last_name="Roosevelt" AND first_name="Theodore";
+-----------+------------+
| last_name | first_name |
+-----------+------------+
| Roosevelt | Theodore   |
+-----------+------------+
```

Now we know the proper WHERE clause to select the desired record, so the DELETE query can be constructed correctly:

```
mysql> DELETE FROM president
    -> WHERE last_name="Roosevelt" AND first_name="Theodore";
```

This seems like a lot of work to delete a record, doesn't it? Better safe than sorry! (This is the type of situation in which you'll want to minimize typing through the use of copy and paste or input line-editing techniques. See "Tips for Interacting With `mysql`" for more information.)

To modify existing records, use UPDATE, which has this form:

```
UPDATE tbl_name SET which columns to change
WHERE which records to update
```

The WHERE clause is just as for DELETE. It's optional, so if you don't specify one, *every record in the table is updated.* The following query changes the name of each of your students to "George":

```
mysql> UPDATE student SET name="George";
```

Obviously, you must be careful with queries like that.

Usually you'll be more specific with the records you're updating. Suppose you recently added a new member to the Historical League but filled in only a few columns of his entry:

```
mysql> INSERT member (last_name,first_name)
    -> VALUES('York','Jerome');
```

Then you realize you forgot to set his membership expiration date. You can fix that as follows:

```
mysql> UPDATE member
    -> SET expiration='2001-7-20'
    -> WHERE last_name='York' AND first_name='Jerome';
```

You can update multiple columns at the same time. The following statement updates Jerome's email and postal addresses:

```
mysql> UPDATE member
    -> SET email='jeromey@aol.com',street='123 Elm St',city='Anytown',
    -> state='NY',zip='01003'
    -> WHERE last_name='York' AND first_name='Jerome';
```

You can also "unset" a column by setting its value to NULL (assuming the column allows NULL values). If at some point in the future Jerome later decides to pay the big membership renewal fee that allows him to become a lifetime member, you can mark his record that way by setting his expiration date to NULL ("never expires"):

```
mysql> UPDATE member
    -> SET expiration=NULL
    -> WHERE last_name='York' AND first_name='Jerome';
```

With UPDATE, just as for DELETE, it's not a bad idea to test a WHERE clause using a SELECT statement to make sure you're choosing the right records to update. If your selection criteria are too narrow or too broad, you'll update too few or too many records.

If you've tried the queries in this section, you'll have deleted and modified records in the `samp_db` tables. Before proceeding to the next section you should undo those changes. Do that by reloading the tables using the instructions at the end of the section "Adding New Records."

Altering the Structure of Tables

Remember how we created the Historical League member table without a membership number column so that I'd have an excuse to use the ALTER TABLE statement? It's time to do that. With ALTER TABLE, you can rename tables, add or drop columns, change column types, and more. The only example I'll show here is how to add a new column. See Chapter 3 for more details about what ALTER TABLE is capable of.

The primary consideration when adding a membership number column to the member table is that the values should be unique to avoid confusion between entries. An AUTO_INCREMENT column is useful here because then we can let MySQL generate unique numbers for us automatically when we add new members. In a CREATE TABLE statement, the specification for such a column would look like this:

```
member_id INT UNSIGNED NOT NULL AUTO_INCREMENT PRIMARY KEY
```

For ALTER TABLE, the syntax is similar. Run this query to add the column:

```
mysql> ALTER TABLE member
    -> ADD member_id INT UNSIGNED NOT NULL AUTO_INCREMENT PRIMARY KEY;
```

Now that we have a new column to hold membership numbers, how do we assign numbers to the existing records in the member table? That's easy—MySQL has already done it! When you add a column to a table, MySQL initializes column values with the default value. In the case of an AUTO_INCREMENT column, this causes a new sequence number to be generated for each row.

Tips for Interacting with mysql

This section discusses how to interact with the mysql client program more efficiently and with less typing. It describes how to connect to the server more easily and how to enter queries without typing each one from scratch.

Simplifying the Connection Process

It's likely that you need to specify connection parameters such as hostname, username, or password when you invoke mysql. That's a lot of typing just to run a program, and it gets tiresome very quickly. There are several ways to make it easier to connect by minimizing the amount of typing you do:

- Use an option file to store connection parameters.
- Repeat commands by taking advantage of your shell's command history capabilities.
- Define a mysql command line shortcut using a shell alias or script.

Using an Option File

As of version 3.22, MySQL allows you to store connection parameters in an option file. Then you don't have to type the parameters each time you run mysql; they are used just as if you had entered them on the command line. The parameters are also used by other MySQL clients, such as `mysqlimport`. That means an option file reduces typing when you use those programs, too.

To use the option file method of specifying connection parameters, create a file named `~/.my.cnf` (that is, a file named `.my.cnf` in your home directory). An option file is a plain text file, so you can create it using any text editor. The file's contents look something like this:

```
[client]
host=serverhost
user=yourname
password=yourpass
```

The `[client]` line signals the beginning of the client option group; any lines following it are read by MySQL client programs to obtain option values, through the end of the file or until a different parameter group begins. Replace *serverhost*, *yourname*, and *yourpass* with the hostname, username, and password that you specify when you connect to the server. For me, `.my.cnf` looks like this:

```
[client]
host=pit-viper.snake.net
user=paul
password=secret
```

Only the `[client]` line is required. The lines that define parameter values are optional; you can specify just the ones you want. For example, if your MySQL username is the same as your UNIX login name, there is no need to include a `user` line.

After you create the `.my.cnf` file, set its access mode to a restrictive value to make sure no one else can read it:

```
% chmod 600 .my.cnf
```

Under Windows, the option file contents are the same, although the name is different (`C:\my.cnf`), and you don't invoke the `chmod` command.

Because option files were not added to MySQL until version 3.22, you can't use them with earlier releases. In particular, you cannot use an option file under Windows with the clients that come with the shareware MySQL distribution because that's based on MySQL 3.21. Option files work fine with the registered Windows version of MySQL, or you can get newer option file-aware clients from the MySQL Web site.

More information on option files may be found in Appendix E, "MySQL Program Reference."

Using Your Shell's Command History

Shells such as `csh`, `tcsh`, and `bash` remember your commands in a history list and allow you to repeat commands from that list. If you use such a shell, your history list can help you avoid typing entire commands. For example, if you've recently invoked `mysql`, you can execute it again like this:

```
% !my
```

The '!' character tells your shell to search through your command history to find the most recent command that begins with 'my' and reissue it as though you'd typed it again yourself. Some shells also allow you to move up and down through your history list using the up-arrow and down-arrow keys (or perhaps Ctrl-P and Ctrl-N). You can select the command you want this way and then press Enter to execute it. tcsh and bash have this facility, and other shells may as well. Check the documentation for your shell to find out more about using your history list.

Using Shell Aliases and Scripts

If your shell provides an alias facility, you can set up command shortcuts that allow you to invoke a long command by typing a short name. For example, in csh or tcsh, you can use the alias command to set up an alias named samp_db, such as this:

```
alias samp_db 'mysql -h pit-viper.snake.net -u paul -p samp_db'
```

The syntax for bash is slightly different:

```
alias samp_db='mysql -h pit-viper.snake.net -u paul -p samp_db'
```

Defining an alias makes these two commands equivalent:

```
samp_db
mysql -h pit-viper.snake.net -u paul -p samp_db
```

Clearly, the first is easier to type than the second. To make the alias take effect each time you log in, put the alias command in one of your shell's startup files (for example, .cshrc for csh, or .bash_profile for bash).

Another form of shortcut is to create a shell script that executes mysql for you with the proper options. In UNIX, a script file that is equivalent to the samp_db alias just shown looks like this:

```
#! /bin/sh
exec mysql -h pit-viper.snake.net -u paul -p samp_db
```

If I name the script samp_db and make it executable (with chmod +x samp_db), I can type samp_db to run mysql and connect to my database.

Under Windows, a batch file can be used to do the same thing. Name the file samp_db.bat and put a line like this in it:

```
mysql -h pit-viper.snake.net -u paul -p samp_db
```

This batch file can be run either by typing samp_db at the prompt in a DOS console or by double-clicking its Windows icon.

If you access multiple databases or connect to multiple hosts, you can define several aliases or scripts, each of which invokes mysql with different options.

Issuing Queries with Less Typing

mysql is an extremely useful program for interacting with your database, but its interface is most suitable for short, single-line queries. mysql itself doesn't care whether or not a query spreads across multiple lines, of course, but long queries aren't much fun to type. Nor it is very entertaining to enter a query, even a short one, only to discover that you must retype it because it has a syntax error.

There are several techniques you can use to avoid needless typing and retyping:

- Use mysql's input line-editing facility.
- Use copy and paste.
- Run mysql in batch mode.
- Avoid typing INSERT statements by using existing data to create new records.

Using mysql's Input Line Editor

mysql has the GNU Readline library built in to allow input line editing. You can manipulate the line you're currently entering, or you can recall previous input lines and re-enter them, either as is or after further modification. This is convenient when you're entering a line and spot a typo; you can back up within the line to correct the problem before pressing Enter. If you enter a query that has a mistake in it, you can recall the query and edit it to fix the problem, then resubmit it. (This is easiest if you type the entire query on one line.)

Some of the editing sequences you will find useful are shown in Table 1.4, but there are many input editing commands available besides those shown in the table. You should be able to find an online version of the Readline manual by consulting your favorite Internet search engine. The manual is also included in the Readline distribution, available from the GNU project Web site at http://www.gnu.org/.

Table 1.4   mysql **Input Editing Commands**

Key Sequence	Meaning
Up arrow, Ctrl-P	Recall previous line
Down arrow, Ctrl-N	Recall next line
Left arrow, Ctrl-B	Move cursor left (backward)
Right arrow, Ctrl-F	Move cursor right (forward)
Escape Ctrl-B	Move backward one word
Escape Ctrl-F	Move forward one word
Ctrl-A	Move cursor to beginning of line
Ctrl-E	Move cursor to end of line
Ctrl-D	Delete character under cursor
Delete	Delete character to left of cursor
Escape D	Delete word
Escape Backspace	Delete word to left of cursor
Ctrl-K	Erase everything from cursor to end of line
Ctrl-_	Undo last change; may be repeated

The following example describes a simple use for input editing. Suppose you've entered this query while using mysql:

```
mysql> SHOW COLUMNS FROM persident;
```

If you notice that you've misspelled "president" as "persident" before pressing Enter, press left arrow or Ctrl-B a few times to move the cursor left until it's on the 's'. Then press Delete twice to erase the 'er', type 're' to fix the error, and press Enter to issue the query. If you press Enter before you notice the misspelling, that's not a problem. After mysql displays its error message, press up arrow or Ctrl-P to recall the line, then edit it as just described.

Input line editing is not available in the Windows version of mysql, but you can obtain the free cygwin_32 client distribution from the MySQL Web site. The mysqlc program in that distribution is like mysql, but understands input line editing commands.

Using Copy and Paste to Issue Queries

If you work in a windowing environment, you can save the text of queries that you find useful in a file and use copy and paste operations to issue those queries easily. Simply follow this procedure:

1. Invoke mysql in a Telnet window or a DOS console window.

2. Open the file containing your queries in a document window. (For example, I use BBEdit under Mac OS, and vi in an xterm window under the X Window System in UNIX.)

3. To execute a query stored in your file, select it and copy it. Then switch to your Telnet window or DOS console and paste the query into mysql.

The procedure sounds cumbersome when written out, but it's an easy way to enter queries quickly and with no typing when you're actually using it.

This technique also allows you to edit your queries in the document window, and it allows you to construct new queries by copying and pasting pieces of existing queries. For example, if you often select rows from a particular table, but like to view the output sorted in different ways, you can keep a list of different ORDER BY clauses in your document window, then copy and paste the one you want to use for any particular query.

You can use copy and paste in the other direction, too (from Telnet to your query file). When you enter lines in mysql, they are saved in a file named .mysql_history in your home directory. If you manually enter a query that you want to save for further reference, quit mysql, open .mysql_history in an editor, and then copy and paste the query from .mysql_history into your query file.

Running `mysql` in Batch Mode

It's not necessary to run `mysql` interactively. `mysql` can read input from a file in non-interactive (batch) mode. This is useful for queries that you run periodically because you certainly don't want to retype such a query every time you run it. It's easier to put it into a file once, then have `mysql` execute the contents of the file as needed.

Suppose you have a query that finds Historical League members who have an interest in a particular area of US history by looking in the `interests` column of the `member` table. For example, to find members with an interest in the Great Depression, the query could be written like this (note the semicolon at the end so that `mysql` can tell where it ends):

```
SELECT last_name, first_name, email, interests FROM member
WHERE interests LIKE "%depression%"
ORDER BY last_name, first_name;
```

Put the query in a file `interests.sql`, then run it by feeding it to `mysql` like this:

```
% mysql samp_db < interests.sql
```

By default, `mysql` produces output in tab-delimited format when run in batch mode. If you want the same kind of tabular ("boxed") output you get when you run `mysql` interactively, use the `-t` option:

```
% mysql -t samp_db < interests.sql
```

If you want to save the output, redirect it to a file:

```
% mysql -t samp_db < interests.sql > output_file
```

To use the query to find members with an interest in Thomas Jefferson, you could edit the query file to change `depression` to `Jefferson` and then run `mysql` again. That works okay as long as you don't use the query very often. If you do, a better method is needed. One way to make the query more flexible is to put it in a shell script that takes an argument from the script command line and uses it to change the text of the query. That parameterizes the query so that you can specify the interest keyword when you run the script. To see how this works, write a little shell script, `interests.sh`:

```
#! /bin/sh
if [ $# -ne 1 ]; then echo "Please specify one keyword"; exit; fi
mysql -t samp_db <<QUERY_INPUT
SELECT last_name, first_name, email, interests FROM member
WHERE interests LIKE "%$1%"
ORDER BY last_name, first_name;
QUERY_INPUT
```

The second line makes sure there is one keyword on the command line; it prints a short message and exits otherwise. Everything between `<<QUERY_INPUT` and the final `QUERY_INPUT` line becomes the input to `mysql`. Within the text of the query, the shell replaces the reference to `$1` with the keyword from the command line. (In shell scripts, `$1`, `$2`, ... refer to the command arguments.) This causes the query to reflect whatever keyword you specify on the command line when you run the script.

Before you can run the script, you must make it executable:

```
% chmod +x interests.sh
```

Now you don't need to edit the script each time you run it. Just tell it what you're looking for on the command line:

```
% interests.sh depression
% interests.sh Jefferson
```

Creating New Records Using Existing Data

It's possible to add new records into a table a row at a time with INSERT, but after creating a few records by typing INSERT statements manually, most people are convinced there must be a better way. One alternative is to use a file that contains data values only and then load records from the file using the LOAD DATA statement or the mysqlimport utility.

Often, you can create the data file using data that already exist in some other format. Your information might be contained in a spreadsheet, or perhaps it's in some other database and you'd like to transfer it to MySQL. To keep this discussion simple, I'll assume you have data in a spreadsheet on your desktop microcomputer.

To transfer spreadsheet data from your desktop microcomputer to a file in your UNIX account, you can use copy and paste in conjunction with Telnet. Here's how:

1. Open a Telnet connection to your UNIX account. Under Mac OS, you can use an application such as BetterTelnet or NCSA Telnet. Under Windows, you can use its standard Telnet program.

2. Open the spreadsheet, select the block of data you want to transfer, and copy it.

3. In the Telnet window, type the following command to begin capturing data in the file data.txt:

   ```
   % cat > data.txt
   ```

   The cat command waits for input.

4. Paste the data you copied from the spreadsheet into the Telnet window. cat thinks you're typing in the information yourself and dutifully writes it to the data.txt file.

5. After all the pasted data have been written to the file, press Enter if the cursor ends up at the end of a data line rather than at the beginning of a new line. Then press Ctrl-D to signal "end of file." cat stops waiting for input and closes the file.

You now have a file data.txt containing the block of data you selected in your spreadsheet, and it's ready to be loaded into your database with LOAD DATA or mysqlimport.

Copy and paste is a quick and easy way to transfer data into a UNIX file, but it's most appropriate for smaller data sets. Larger amounts of data may exceed the limits of your system's copy buffer. In such cases, it might be better to save the spreadsheet in plain text format (tab delimited). Then you can transfer the file from your microcomputer to your UNIX account using FTP. Transfer the file in text mode (rather than in binary or image mode) so that line endings get converted to UNIX line endings.

(UNIX uses linefeeds, Mac OS uses carriage returns, and Windows uses carriage return/linefeed pairs.) You can tell LOAD DATA or mysqlimport what kind of line endings to expect, but under UNIX it's easier to work with the file if it contains linefeeds.

After transferring the file, it's a good idea to check whether or not it has blank lines at the end. If so, you should delete them, or they'll turn into blank or malformed records when you load the file into the database.

Files saved as plain text from a spreadsheet may have quotes surrounding values that contain spaces. To strip the quotes when you load the file into your database, use the FIELDS ENCLOSED BY clause for LOAD DATA or the --fields-enclosed-by option for mysqlimport. See the entry for LOAD DATA in Appendix D for more details.

Where to Now?

You know quite a bit about using MySQL now. You can set up a database and create tables. You can put records into those tables, retrieve them in various ways, change them, or delete them. But there's still a lot to know about MySQL—the tutorial in this chapter only scratches the surface. You can see this by considering the state of our example database. We've created it and its tables and populated them with some initial data. During the process we've seen how to write some of the queries we need for answering questions about the information in the database. But much remains to be done.

For example, we have no convenient interactive way to enter new score records for the grade-keeping project or new member entries for the Historical League directory. We have no convenient way to edit existing records. And we still can't generate the printed or online forms of the League directory. These tasks and others will be revisited in the upcoming chapters, particularly in Chapters 7, "The Perl DBI API," and 8, "The PHP API."

Where you go next in this book depends on what you're interested in. If you want to see how to finish the job we've started with our Historical League and grade-keeping projects, Part II covers MySQL programming. If you're going to serve as the MySQL administrator for your site, Part III of this book deals with administrative tasks. However, I recommend acquiring additional general background in using MySQL first, by reading the remaining chapters in Part I. These chapters discuss how MySQL handles data, provide further information on the syntax and use of query statements, and show how to make your queries run faster. A good grounding in these topics will stand you in good stead no matter the context in which you use MySQL—whether you're running mysql, writing your own programs, or acting as a database administrator.

2

Working with Data in MySQL

VIRTUALLY EVERYTHING YOU DO IN MySQL involves data in some way or another because the purpose of a database management system is, by definition, to manage data. Even a simple SELECT 1 statement involves expression evaluation to produce an integer data value.

Every data value in MySQL has a type. For example, 37.4 is a number, and "abc" is a string. Sometimes data types are explicit, as when you issue a CREATE TABLE statement that specifies the type for each column you declare as part of the table:

```
CREATE TABLE my_table
(
    int_col INT,        /* integer-valued column */
    str_col CHAR(20),   /* string-valued column */
    date_col DATE       /* date-valued column */
)
```

Other times data types are implicit, such as when you refer to literal values in an expression, pass values to a function, or use the value returned from that function:

```
INSERT INTO my_table (int_col,str_col,date_col)
VALUES(14,CONCAT("a","b"),19990115)
```

This INSERT statement performs the following operations, all of which involve data types:

- It assigns the integer value 14 to the integer column int_col.
- It passes the string values "a" and "b" to the CONCAT() function. CONCAT() returns the string value "ab", which is assigned to the string column str_col.
- It assigns the integer value 19990115 to the date column date_col. The assignment involves a type mismatch, so MySQL converts the integer 19990115 to the date "1999-01-15"; this illustrates that MySQL performs automatic type conversion.

To use MySQL effectively, it's essential to understand how MySQL handles data. This chapter describes the types of data that MySQL can handle, and discusses the issues involved in working with those types:

- The general kinds of values MySQL can represent, including the NULL value.
- The specific data types MySQL provides for table columns, and the properties that characterize each column type. Some of MySQL's column types are fairly generic, such as the CHAR string type. Others, such as AUTO_INCREMENT integer types and the TIMESTAMP date type, behave in special ways that you should understand to avoid being surprised.
- Choosing column types appropriately for your tables. It's important to know how to pick the best type for your purposes when you build a table, and when to choose one type over another when several related types might be applicable to the kind of values you want to store.
- MySQL's rules for expression evaluation. MySQL provides a wide range of operators and functions that you can use in expressions to retrieve, display, and manipulate data. The rules for expression evaluation include the rules governing type conversion, when a value of one type is used in a context requiring a value of another type.

  It's important to understand when type conversion happens and how it works; some conversions don't make sense and result in meaningless values. Assigning the string "13" to an integer column results in the value 13, but assigning the string "abc" to that column results in the value 0 because "abc" doesn't look like a number. Worse, if you perform a comparison without knowing the conversion rules, you can do considerable damage, such as updating or deleting every row in a table when you intend to affect only a few rows.

Two appendixes provide additional information about MySQL's column types, operators, and functions. These are Appendix B, "Column Type Reference," and Appendix C, "Operator and Function Reference."

MySQL Data Types

MySQL knows about several data types—that is, general categories in which values can be represented.

Numeric Values

Numbers are values such as 48 or 193.62. MySQL understands numbers specified as integers (with no fractional part) or floating-point values (with a fractional part). Integers may be specified in decimal or hexadecimal format.

An integer consists of a sequence of digits. An integer specified in hexadecimal form consists of '0x' followed by one or more hexadecimal digits ('0' through '9' and 'a' through 'f'). For example, 0x0a is 10 decimal, and 0xffff is 65535 decimal. Non-numeric hex digits may be specified in uppercase or lowercase, but the leading '0x' cannot be given as '0X'. That is, 0x0a and 0x0A are legal, but 0X0a and 0X0A are not.

A floating-point number consists of a sequence of digits, a decimal point, and another sequence of digits. One sequence of digits or the other may be empty, but not both.

MySQL understands scientific notation. This is indicated by immediately following an integer or floating-point number with 'e' or 'E', a sign character ('+' or '-'), and an integer exponent. 1.34E+12 and 43.27e-1 are numbers in legal scientific notation. On the other hand, 1.34E12 is *not* legal because the sign character is missing before the exponent. Hexadecimal numbers cannot be used in scientific notation: The 'e' that begins the exponent part is also a legal hex digit and thus would be ambiguous.

Numbers may be preceded by a minus sign ('-') to indicate a negative value.

String (Character) Values

Strings are values such as "Madison, Wisconsin", or "patient shows improvement". You can use either single or double quotes to surround a string value.

Several escape sequences are recognized within strings and can be used to indicate special characters, as shown in Table 2.1. Each sequence begins with a backslash character ('\') to signify a temporary escape from the usual rules for character interpretation. Note that a NUL byte is not the same as the NULL value; NUL is a zero-valued byte, NULL is the absence of a value.

Table 2.1   **String Escape Sequences**

Sequence	Meaning
\0	NUL (ASCII 0)
\'	Single quote
\"	Double quote
\b	Backspace

continues

Table 2.1 **Continued**

Sequence	Meaning
\n	Newline
\r	Carriage return
\t	Tab
\\	Backslash

To include a quote character within a string, you can do one of three things:

- Double the quote character if the string is quoted using the same character:
  ```
  'I can''t'
  "He said, ""I told you so."""
  ```

- Quote the string with the other quote character; in this case, you do not double the quote characters within the string:
  ```
  "I can't"
  'He said, "I told you so."'
  ```

- Escape the quote character with a backslash; this works regardless of the quote characters used to quote the string:

  ```
  'I can\'t'
  "I can\'t"
  "He said, \"I told you so.\""
  'He said, \"I told you so.\"'
  ```

In string contexts, hexadecimal constants may be used to specify string values. The syntax is as described earlier for numeric values, but pairs of hexadecimal digits are interpreted as ASCII codes and converted to characters. The result is used as a string. For example, when interpreted as a string, `0x616263` is `"abc"`.

Date and Time (Temporal) Values

Dates and times are values such as `"1999-06-17"` or `"12:30:43"`. MySQL also understands combined date/time values, such as `"1999-06-17 12:30:43"`. Take special note of the fact that MySQL represents dates in year–month–day order. This often surprises newcomers to MySQL, although this format is the ANSI SQL standard. You can display date values any way you like using the `DATE_FORMAT()` function, but the default display format lists the year first, and input values *must* be specified with the year first.

The `NULL` Value

`NULL` is something of a "typeless" value. Generally, it's used to mean "no value," "unknown value," "missing value," "out of range," "none of the above," and so forth. You can insert `NULL` values into tables, retrieve them from tables, and test whether or not a value is `NULL`. You can't perform arithmetic on `NULL` values. (If you try, the result is `NULL`.)

MySQL Column Types

Each table in a database is made up of one or more columns. When you create a table using a CREATE TABLE statement, you specify a type for each column. A column type is more specific than a data type, which is just a general category such as "number" or "string." A column type precisely characterizes the kind of values a given table column may contain, such as SMALLINT or VARCHAR(32).

MySQL's column types are the means by which you describe what kinds of values a table's columns contain, which in turn determines how MySQL treats those values. For example, if you have numeric values, you can store them using a numeric or a string column type, but MySQL will treat the values somewhat differently depending on how you store them. Each column type has several characteristics:

- What kind of values you can store in it
- How much space values take up, and whether the values are fixed-length (all values of the type taking the same amount of space) or variable-length (the amount of space depending on the particular value being stored)
- How values of the type are compared and sorted
- Whether or not the type allows NULL values
- Whether or not the type can be indexed

We'll survey MySQL's column types briefly to get a broad overview, then discuss in more detail the properties that characterize each type.

Overview of Column Types

MySQL provides column types for values from all the general data type categories except the NULL value. NULL spans all types in the sense that whether or not a column may contain NULL values is treated as a type attribute.

MySQL has column types for both integer and floating-point numeric values, as shown in Table 2.2. Integer columns can be signed or unsigned. A special attribute allows integer column values to be generated automatically, which is useful in applications that require unique sequence or identification numbers.

Table 2.2 **Numeric Column Types**

Type Name	Meaning
TINYINT	A very small integer
SMALLINT	A small integer
MEDIUMINT	A medium-sized integer
INT	A standard integer
BIGINT	A large integer

continues

Table 2.2 **Continued**

Type Name	Meaning
FLOAT	A single-precision floating-point number
DOUBLE	A double-precision floating-point number
DECIMAL	A floating-point number, represented as a string

MySQL string column types are shown in Table 2.3. Strings can hold anything, even arbitrary binary data such as images or sounds. Strings can be compared according to whether or not they are case sensitive. In addition, you can perform pattern matching on strings. (Actually, in MySQL you can perform pattern matching on any column type, but it's most often done with string types.)

Table 2.3 **String Column Types**

Type Name	Meaning
CHAR	A fixed-length character string
VARCHAR	A variable-length character string
TINYBLOB	A very small BLOB (binary large object)
BLOB	A small BLOB
MEDIUMBLOB	A medium-sized BLOB
LONGBLOB	A large BLOB
TINYTEXT	A very small text string
TEXT	A small text string
MEDIUMTEXT	A medium-sized text string
LONGTEXT	A large text string
ENUM	An enumeration; columns may be assigned one enumeration member
SET	A set; columns may be assigned multiple set members

MySQL date and types are shown in Table 2.4. For temporal values, MySQL provides types for dates (either with or without a time), times, and timestamps (a special type that allows you to track when changes were last made to a record). There is also a type for efficiently representing year values when you don't need an entire date.

Table 2.4 **Date and Time Column Types**

Type Name	Meaning
DATE	A date value, in "*YYYY-MM-DD*" format
TIME	A time value, in "*hh:mm:ss*" format
DATETIME	A date and time value, in "*YYYY-MM-DD hh:mm:ss*" format
TIMESTAMP	A timestamp value, in *YYYYMMDDhhmmss* format
YEAR	A year value, in *YYYY* format

To create a table, you issue a CREATE TABLE statement and specify a list of the columns that make up the table. Each column has a name and a type, and various attributes may be associated with each type. Here's an example that creates a table my_table with three columns named f, c, and i:

```
CREATE TABLE my_table
(
    f FLOAT(10,4),
    c CHAR(15) NOT NULL DEFAULT "none",
    i TINYINT UNSIGNED NULL
)
```

The syntax for declaring a column is as follows:

```
col_name col_type [col_attributes] [general_attributes]
```

The name of the column is given by col_name. Column names may be up to 64 characters long, and may consist of alphanumeric characters, as well as the underscore and dollar sign characters ('_' and '$'). A column name may begin with any character that is legal in a name, including a digit. A name may not consist entirely of digits, however, because that would make it indistinguishable from a number. Words such as SELECT, DELETE, and CREATE are reserved and cannot be used as column names. However, function names (words such as POS and MIN) are not reserved and may be used.

The column type col_type indicates the specific kind of values the column can hold. The type specifier may also indicate the maximum length of the values you store in the column. For some types, you specify the length explicitly as a number. For others, the length is implied by the type name. For example, CHAR(10) specifies an explicit length of 10 characters, whereas TINYBLOB values have an implicit maximum length of 255 characters. Some of the type specifiers allow you to indicate a maximum display width (how many characters to use for displaying values). Floating-point types allow the number of decimal places to be specified, so you can control how precise values are.

Following the column type, you may specify optional type-specific attributes as well as more general attributes. The attributes function as type modifiers. They cause MySQL to change the way it treats column values in some way:

- The type-specific attributes that are allowable depend on the column type you choose. For example, UNSIGNED is allowable only for integer types, and BINARY is allowable only for CHAR and VARCHAR.

- The general attributes may be given for any column type, with a few exceptions. You may specify NULL or NOT NULL to indicate whether or not a column can hold NULL values. You may also specify DEFAULT def_value to indicate that a column should be assigned the value def_value when a new row is created without explicitly specifying the column's value. The value of def_value must be a constant; it cannot be an expression or refer to other columns. You cannot specify a default value for BLOB or TEXT columns.

If multiple column-specific attributes are given, they may be specified in any order as long as they follow the column type and precede any general attributes. Similarly, if multiple general attributes are given, they may be specified in any order as long as they follow the column type and any column-specific attributes that may be present.

The rest of this section discusses each of MySQL's column types to show the syntax for declaring the type and the properties that characterize it, such as its range and storage requirements. The type specifications are shown as you use them in CREATE TABLE statements. Optional information is indicated by square brackets ([ ]). For example, the syntax MEDIUMINT[(M)] indicates that the maximum display width, specified as (M), is optional. On the other hand, for CHAR(M), the lack of brackets indicates that (M) is required.

Numeric Column Types

MySQL's numeric column types fall into two general classifications:

- **Integer types.** For numbers that have no fractional part, such as 1, 43, -3, 0, or -798432. You can use integer columns for data represented by whole numbers, such as weight to the nearest pound, height to the nearest inch, number of stars in a galaxy, number of people in a household, or number of bacteria in a petri dish.

- **Floating-point types.** For numbers that may have a fractional part, such as 3.14159, -.00273, -4.78, or 39.3E+4. You can use floating-point column types for values that may have a fractional part or that are extremely large or small. Some types of data you might represent as floating-point values are average crop yield; distances; money values, such as item cost or salary; unemployment rates; or stock prices. Integer values may be assigned to floating-point columns. They are treated as floating-point values with a fractional part of zero.

The name and range of each numeric type are shown in Table 2.5. The amount of storage required for values of each type is shown in Table 2.6.

The CREATE TABLE Statement

The examples used throughout this chapter use CREATE TABLE extensively. The statement should be reasonably familiar to you since we used it in the tutorial section of Chapter 1, "Introduction to MySQL and SQL." See also the entry for CREATE TABLE in Appendix D, "SQL Syntax Reference."

Table 2.5   **Numeric Column Type Ranges**

Type Specification	Range
TINYINT[(M)]	Signed values: -128 to 127 (-2^7 to 2^7-1) Unsigned values: 0 to 255 (0 to 2^8-1)
SMALLINT[(M)]	Signed values: -32768 to 32767 (-2^{15} to $2^{15}-1$) Unsigned values: 0 to 65535 (0 to $2^{16}-1$)
MEDIUMINT[(M)]	Signed values: -8388608 to 8388607 (-2^{23} to $2^{23}-1$) Unsigned values: 0 to 16777215 (0 to $2^{24}-1$)
INT[(M)]	Signed values: -2147683648 to 2147483647 (-2^{31} to $2^{31}-1$) Unsigned values: 0 to 4294967295 (0 to $2^{32}-1$)
BIGINT[(M)]	Signed values: -9223372036854775808 to 9223372036854775807 (-2^{63} to $2^{63}-1$) Unsigned values: 0 to 18446744073709551615 (0 to $2^{64}-1$)
FLOAT[(M,D)], FLOAT(4)	Minimum non-zero values: $\pm1.175494351\text{E}-38$ Maximum non-zerovalues: $\pm3.402823466\text{E}+38$
DOUBLE[(M,D)], FLOAT(8)	Minimum non-zero values: $\pm2.2250738585072014\text{E}-308$ Maximum non-zero values: $\pm1.7976931348623157\text{E}+308$
DECIMAL(M,D)	Varies; range depends on M and D

Table 2.6   **Numeric Column Type Storage Requirements**

Type Specification	Storage Required
TINYINT[(M)]	1 byte
SMALLINT[(M)]	2 bytes
MEDIUMINT[(M)]	3 bytes
INT[(M)]	4 bytes
BIGINT[(M)]	8 bytes
FLOAT[(M,D)], FLOAT(4)	4 bytes
DOUBLE[(M,D)], FLOAT(8)	8 bytes
DECIMAL(M,D)	M bytes (MySQL < 3.23), M+2 bytes (MySQL ≥ 3.23)

MySQL provides five integer types: TINYINT, SMALLINT, MEDIUMINT, INT, and BIGINT. INTEGER is a synonym for INT. These types vary in the range of values they can represent. Integer columns can be declared as UNSIGNED to disallow negative values; this shifts the range for the column upward to begin at 0. The types also vary in the amount of storage required. Types with a larger range require more storage.

MySQL provides three floating-point types: FLOAT, DOUBLE, and DECIMAL. Unlike integer types, floating-point types cannot be UNSIGNED, and their range is different from integer types in the sense that there is not only a maximum value the type can represent, but there is also a minimum non-zero value. The minimum values provide a measure of how precise the type is, which is often important for recording scientific data. (There are, of course, corresponding negative maximum and minimum values.)

DOUBLE PRECISION[(M,D)] and REAL[(M,D)] are synonyms for DOUBLE[(M,D)]. NUMERIC(M,D) is a synonym for DECIMAL(M,D). FLOAT(4) and FLOAT(8) are provided for ODBC compatibility. Prior to MySQL 3.23, they are synonyms for FLOAT(10,2) and DOUBLE(16,4). From MySQL 3.23 on, FLOAT(4) and FLOAT(8) have their own behavior, described shortly below.

When you choose a numeric type, consider the range of values you need to represent and choose the smallest type that will cover the range. Choosing a larger type wastes space, leading to tables that are unnecessarily large and that cannot be processed as efficiently as if you had chosen a smaller type. For integer values, TINYINT is the best if the range of values in your data is small, such as a person's age or number of siblings. MEDIUMINT can represent millions of values and can be used for many more types of values, at some additional cost in storage space. BIGINT has the largest range of all but requires twice as much storage as the next smallest integer type (INT) and should be used only when really necessary. For floating-point values, DOUBLE takes twice as much space as FLOAT. Unless you need exceptionally high precision or an extremely large range of values, you can probably represent your data at half the storage cost by using FLOAT.

When you declare an integer column, you can specify an optional display size M. If given, M should be an integer from 1 to 255. It represents the number of characters used to display values for the column. For example, MEDIUMINT(4) specifies a MEDIUMINT column with a display width of 4. If you declare an integer column without an explicit width, a default width is assigned. The defaults are the lengths of the "longest" values for each type. If the printable representation of a particular value requires more than M characters, the full value is displayed; values are not chopped to fit within M characters.

For each floating-point type, you may specify a maximum display size M and the number of decimal places D. The value of M should be from 1 to 255. The value of D may be from 0 to 30, but should be no more than M−2. (If you're more familiar with ODBC terms, M and D correspond to the ODBC concepts of "precision" and "scale.") M and D are optional for FLOAT and DOUBLE, but required for DECIMAL.

Where M and D are optional, default values are used if they are omitted. The following statement creates a table to illustrate the default values of M and D for numeric column types (DECIMAL is not included because M and D are not optional for that type):

```
CREATE TABLE my_table
(
    itiny TINYINT, itiny_u TINYINT UNSIGNED,
    ismall SMALLINT, ismall_u SMALLINT UNSIGNED,
```

```
    imedium MEDIUMINT, imedium_u MEDIUMINT UNSIGNED,
    ireg INT, ireg_u INT UNSIGNED,
    ibig BIGINT, ibig_u BIGINT UNSIGNED,
    fp_single FLOAT, fp_double DOUBLE
)
```

If you issue a DESCRIBE my_table statement after creating the table, the Field and Type columns of the output look like this:[1]

```
+-----------+-----------------------+
¦ Field     ¦ Type                  ¦
+-----------+-----------------------+
¦ itiny     ¦ tinyint(4)            ¦
¦ itiny_u   ¦ tinyint(3) unsigned   ¦
¦ ismall    ¦ smallint(6)           ¦
¦ ismall_u  ¦ smallint(5) unsigned  ¦
¦ imedium   ¦ mediumint(9)          ¦
¦ imedium_u ¦ mediumint(8) unsigned ¦
¦ ireg      ¦ int(11)               ¦
¦ ireg_u    ¦ int(10) unsigned      ¦
¦ ibig      ¦ bigint(20)            ¦
¦ ibig_u    ¦ bigint(20) unsigned   ¦
¦ fp_single ¦ float(10,2)           ¦
¦ fp_double ¦ double(16,4)          ¦
+-----------+-----------------------+
```

Every numeric column has a range of values determined by the column's type. If you attempt to insert a value that lies outside the column's range, truncation occurs: MySQL clips the value to the appropriate endpoint of the range and uses the result. No truncation occurs when values are retrieved.

Value truncation occurs according to the range of the column type, not the display width. For example, a SMALLINT(3) column has a display width of 3 and a range from -32768 to 32767. The value 12345 is wider than the display width but within the range of the column, so it is inserted without clipping and retrieved as 12345. The value 99999 is outside the range, so it is clipped to 32767 when inserted. Subsequent retrievals retrieve the value 32767.

In general, values assigned to a floating-point column are rounded to the number of decimals indicated by the column specification. If you store 1.23456 in a FLOAT(8,1) column, the result is 1.2. If you store the same value in a FLOAT(8,4) column, the result is 1.2346. This means you should declare floating-point columns with a sufficient number of decimals to give you values as precise as you require. If you need accuracy to thousandths, don't declare a type with only two decimal places.

[1] The display width for BIGINT will be 21 (not 20) if you run this query using a version of MySQL older than 3.23, due to a minor glitch.

The exception to this handling of floating-point values is that in MySQL 3.23, the behavior of FLOAT(4) and FLOAT(8) changed. These two types are now single-precision (4-byte) and double-precision (8-byte) types that are true floating-point types in the sense that values are stored as given, within the limits imposed by your hardware.

The DECIMAL type differs from FLOAT and DOUBLE in that DECIMAL values are actually stored as strings. The maximum possible range for DECIMAL is the same as for DOUBLE, but the effective range is determined by the values of M and D. If you vary M and hold D fixed, the range becomes larger as M becomes larger. This is illustrated by the first three rows of Table 2.7. If you hold M fixed and vary D, the range becomes smaller as D becomes larger (though the precision increases). This is shown by the last three rows of Table 2.7.

Table 2.7 **How M and D Affect the Range of DECIMAL(M,D)**

Type Specification	Range (for MySQL < 3.23)	Range (for MySQL≥3.23)
DECIMAL(4,1)	-9.9 to 99.9	-999.9 to 9999.9
DECIMAL(5,1)	-99.9 to 999.9	-9999.9 to 99999.9
DECIMAL(6,1)	-999.9 to 9999.9	-99999.9 to 999999.9
DECIMAL(6,2)	-99.99 to 999.99	-9999.99 to 99999.99
DECIMAL(6,3)	-9.999 to 99.999	-999.999 to 9999.999

The range for a given DECIMAL type depends on your version of MySQL. For versions of MySQL prior to 3.23, DECIMAL(M,D) columns are stored using M bytes per value, and the sign character (if needed) and decimal point are included in the M bytes. Thus, for a type DECIMAL(5,2), the range is −9.99 to 99.99 because those cover all the possible 5-character values.

As of MySQL 3.23, DECIMAL values are handled according to the ANSI specification, which states that a type of DECIMAL(M,D) must be able to represent any value with M digits and D decimal places. For example, DECIMAL(5,2) must be able to represent values from −999.99 to 999.99. The sign character and decimal point must still be stored, so DECIMAL values from MySQL 3.23 and up use M+2 bytes. For DECIMAL(5,2), 7 bytes are needed for the "longest" value (−999.99). At the positive end of the range, the sign byte is not needed to hold a sign character, so MySQL uses it to extend the range beyond that required by the ANSI specification. For DECIMAL(5,2), the maximum value can be 9999.99 because 7 bytes are available.

In short, the range for DECIMAL(M,D) in MySQL 3.23 and up is equivalent to the range for DECIMAL(M+2,D) in earlier versions.

In all versions of MySQL, if D is 0 for a DECIMAL column, the decimal point is not stored. The effect of this is to extend the range of the column by an extra order of magnitude because the byte normally used to store the decimal point can be used for another digit.

Numeric Column Type Attributes

The ZEROFILL attribute may be specified for all numeric types. It causes displayed values for the column to be padded with leading zeros to the display width. You can use ZEROFILL when you want to make sure column values always display using a given number of digits. Actually, it's more accurate to say "a given *minimum* number of digits" because values wider than the display width are displayed in full without being chopped. You can see this by issuing the following statements:

```
CREATE TABLE my_table (my_zerofill INT(5) ZEROFILL)
INSERT INTO my_table VALUES(1),(100),(10000),(1000000)
SELECT my_zerofill FROM my_table
```

The output from the SELECT statement is as follows. Note that the final value, which is wider than the column's display width, is displayed in full:

```
+-------------+
| my_zerofill |
+-------------+
|       00001 |
|       00100 |
|       10000 |
|     1000000 |
+-------------+
```

Two other attributes may be specified for integer column types only:

- **AUTO_INCREMENT.** Use the AUTO_INCREMENT attribute when you want to generate unique identifiers or values in a series. AUTO_INCREMENT values normally begin at 1 and increase by 1 per row. When you insert NULL into an AUTO_INCREMENT column, MySQL inserts a value one greater than the current maximum value in that column. You may have at most one AUTO_INCREMENT column in a table.

  For any column that you want to use with AUTO_INCREMENT, the column should be declared NOT NULL, and it should be declared as a PRIMARY KEY or as a UNIQUE key. For example, you can declare such a column in any of the following ways:

  ```
  CREATE TABLE ai (i INT AUTO_INCREMENT NOT NULL PRIMARY KEY)
  CREATE TABLE ai (i INT AUTO_INCREMENT NOT NULL, PRIMARY KEY (i))
  CREATE TABLE ai (i INT AUTO_INCREMENT NOT NULL, UNIQUE (i))
  ```

  The behavior of AUTO_INCREMENT is discussed further in "Working With Sequences."

- **UNSIGNED.** This attribute disallows negative values. Making a column UNSIGNED doesn't change the size of the underlying data type's range; it just shifts the range upward. Consider this table specification:

  ```
  CREATE TABLE my_table
  (
      itiny TINYINT,
      itiny_u TINYINT UNSIGNED
  )
  ```

itiny and `itiny_u` are both `TINYINT` columns with a range of 256 values, but the range of `itiny` is -128 to 127, whereas the range of `itiny_u` is 0 to 255.

`UNSIGNED` is useful for columns into which you plan to store data that don't take on negative values, such as population counts or attendance figures. If you use a regular, signed column for such values, you use only half of the column type's range. By making the column `UNSIGNED`, you effectively double your range. If you use the column for sequence numbers, it will take twice as long to run out of values if you make it `UNSIGNED`.

Following the attributes just described, which are specific to numeric columns, you may also specify the general attributes `NULL` or `NOT NULL`. If you do not specify `NULL` or `NOT NULL`, the default is `NULL`. You may also specify a default value using the `DEFAULT` attribute. If you do not specify a default value, one is chosen automatically. For all numeric column types, the default is `NULL` for columns that may contain `NULL`, and `0` otherwise.

The following example creates a table with three `INT` columns, having default values of -1, 1, and `NULL`:

```
CREATE TABLE t
(
    i1 INT DEFAULT -1,
    i2 INT DEFAULT 1,
    i3 INT DEFAULT NULL
)
```

Working With Sequences

Many applications need to use unique numbers for identification purposes. The requirement for unique values occurs in a number of contexts: membership numbers, sample or lot numbering, customer IDs, bug report or trouble ticket tags, and so forth.

MySQL's mechanism for providing unique numbers is through `AUTO_INCREMENT` columns. These allow you to generate sequential numbers automatically. Unfortunately, `AUTO_INCREMENT` is also sometimes poorly understood, a phenomenon perhaps compounded by the changes that were made to `AUTO_INCREMENT` in MySQL 3.23. This section describes how `AUTO_INCREMENT` columns behave so that you can use them effectively without running into the traps that sometimes surprise people. It also describes how you can generate sequences without using an `AUTO_INCREMENT` column.

AUTO_INCREMENT *for MySQL Versions up to 3.23*

For versions of MySQL up to 3.23, `AUTO_INCREMENT` columns behave as follows:

- Inserting `NULL` into an `AUTO_INCREMENT` column causes MySQL to automatically generate the next sequence number and insert that value into the column instead. `AUTO_INCREMENT` sequences begin at 1, so the first record inserted into the table gets a sequence column value of 1, and subsequent records get values of 2, 3, and so forth. In general, each automatically generated value will be one more than the current maximum value stored in the column.

- Inserting 0 into an AUTO_INCREMENT column is like inserting NULL into the column. Inserting a row without specifying a value for the AUTO_INCREMENT column also is like inserting NULL.

- If you insert a record and explicitly specify a value for the AUTO_INCREMENT column, one of two things will occur. If a record already exists with that value, an error occurs because values in AUTO_INCREMENT columns must be unique. If a record does not exist with that value, the record is inserted and, if the value in the column is the new largest value, the sequence continues with the next value after that for subsequent rows. In other words, you can "bump up" the counter by inserting a record with a sequence value greater than the current counter value.

  Bumping up the counter can result in gaps in the sequence, but you can also exploit this behavior to your advantage. Suppose you create a table with an AUTO_INCREMENT column, but you want a sequence to begin at 1000 rather than at 1. You can achieve this one of two ways. First, you can insert the first record with an explicit sequence value of 1000, then insert subsequent records by inserting NULL into the AUTO_INCREMENT column. Second, you can insert a fake record with a value of 999 in the AUTO_INCREMENT column. The first real record you insert after that will get a sequence number of 1000, after which you can delete the fake record.

- If you insert an illegal value into an AUTO_INCREMENT column, do not expect anything useful to happen. The result is unpredictable.

- If you delete the record containing the largest value in an AUTO_INCREMENT column, that value is reused the next time you generate a new value. If you delete all the records in the table, all values are reused: The sequence begins over, starting with 1.

- REPLACE statements work normally.

- UPDATE statements work using rules similar to those that apply to inserting new records. If you update an AUTO_INCREMENT column to NULL or 0, it is updated to the next sequence number. If you attempt to update the column to a value that already exists, an error occurs (unless you happen to be setting the column to the value that it already has). If you update the column to a value larger than any existing column value, the sequence continues with the next number after that for subsequent records.

- The value of the most recent automatically generated sequence number is available by calling the LAST_INSERT_ID() function. This allows you to reference the AUTO_INCREMENT value in other statements without knowing what the value is. LAST_INSERT_ID() is tied to AUTO_INCREMENT values generated during the current server session; it is not affected by AUTO_INCREMENT activity associated with other clients. If no AUTO_INCREMENT value has been generated during the current session, LAST_INSERT_ID() returns 0.

It's extremely useful to be able to generate sequence numbers automatically. However, the behavior just described has two shortcomings. First, the reuse of sequence values when records at the top of the sequence are deleted makes it harder to generate a monotonic (strictly increasing) set of values for applications that may delete records as well as insert them. Second, the means by which you begin a sequence at a value higher than 1 are clumsy.

AUTO_INCREMENT *for MySQL Versions 3.23 and up*

MySQL 3.23 introduced the following changes to AUTO_INCREMENT behavior to deal with the concerns just noted:

- The values in an automatically generated series are strictly increasing and are not reused. If the maximum value is 143 and you delete the record containing that value, MySQL still generates the next value as 144.
- You can specify the initial sequence number explicitly when you create the table. The following example creates a table with an AUTO_INCREMENT column seq that begins at 1,000,000:

```
CREATE TABLE my_table
    (seq INT UNSIGNED AUTO_INCREMENT NOT NULL PRIMARY KEY)
    AUTO_INCREMENT = 1000000
```

When a table has multiple columns (as most tables do), there is no ambiguity about which column the terminating AUTO_INCREMENT = 1000000 clause applies to because you can have only one AUTO_INCREMENT column per table.

Issues to Consider with AUTO_INCREMENT

You should keep the following points in mind to avoid being surprised when you use AUTO_INCREMENT columns:

- AUTO_INCREMENT is not a column type; it's a column type attribute. Furthermore, AUTO_INCREMENT is an attribute intended for use only with integer types. Versions of MySQL earlier than 3.23 are lax in enforcing this constraint and will let you declare a column type such as CHAR with the AUTO_INCREMENT attribute. However, only the integer types work correctly as AUTO_INCREMENT columns.
- The primary purpose of the AUTO_INCREMENT mechanism is to allow you to generate a sequence of positive integers, and it's best if you stick to using AUTO_INCREMENT columns that way. For this reason, you should declare AUTO_INCREMENT columns to be UNSIGNED. This also has the advantage of giving you twice as many sequence numbers before you hit the upper end of the column type's range.

It is possible under some circumstances to generate sequences of negative values using an `AUTO_INCREMENT` column, but I don't recommend it. If you're determined to try it, make sure to perform adequate testing, and retest if you upgrade to a different version of MySQL. My own experiments indicate somewhat inconsistent behavior between versions with regard to negative sequences.

■ Don't be fooled into thinking that adding `AUTO_INCREMENT` to a column declaration is a magic way of getting an unlimited sequence of numbers. It's not; `AUTO_INCREMENT` sequences are bound by the range of the underlying column type. For example, if you use a `TINYINT UNSIGNED` column, the maximum sequence number is 255. When you reach that limit, your application will begin to fail with "duplicate key" errors.

■ MySQL 3.23 introduced the new `AUTO_INCREMENT` behaviors of not reusing sequence numbers and allowing you to specify an initial sequence number in the `CREATE TABLE` statement. These behaviors are undone if you delete all records in the table using a `DELETE` statement of the following form:

```
DELETE FROM tbl_name
```

In this case, the sequence starts over from 1 rather than continuing in strictly increasing order. The sequence starts over even if your `CREATE TABLE` statement specifies an initial sequence number explicitly. This occurs due to the way MySQL optimizes `DELETE` statements that empty a table entirely: It re-creates the data and index files from scratch rather than deleting each record, and that causes all sequence number information to be lost. If you want to delete all records but preserve the sequence information, you can suppress the optimization and force MySQL to perform a row-by-row delete operation instead, like this:

```
DELETE FROM tbl_name WHERE 1 > 0
```

What can you do to maintain a strictly increasing series if you have a version of MySQL older than 3.23? One solution is to maintain a separate table that you use only for generating `AUTO_INCREMENT` values, and from which you never delete records. That way, the values in the table are never reused. When you need to generate a new record in your main table, first insert a `NULL` into the sequence number table. Then insert the record into your main table using the value of `LAST_INSERT_ID()` for the column that you want to contain a sequence number:

```
INSERT INTO ai_tbl SET ai_col = NULL
INSERT INTO main_tbl SET id=LAST_INSERT_ID() ...
```

Suppose you want to write an application that generates `AUTO_INCREMENT` values, but you want the sequence to start with 100 rather than 1. Suppose also that you want it to be portable to all versions of MySQL. How can you accomplish this?

If portability is a goal, you can't rely on the capability that MySQL 3.23 provides for specifying the initial sequence number in the `CREATE TABLE` statement. Instead, when you want to insert a record, first check whether or not the table is empty by issuing the following statement:

```
SELECT COUNT(*) FROM tbl_name
```

This is an extra step, but it doesn't cost you much because SELECT COUNT(*) with no WHERE clause is optimized to return quickly. If the table is empty, insert the record and explicitly specify a value of 100 for the sequence number column. If the table isn't empty, simply specify NULL for the sequence number column value and let MySQL generate the next number automatically.

This approach allows you to insert records with sequence numbers of 100, 101, and so on, and it works whether or not MySQL allows the initial sequence value to be specified. This approach does not work if you require sequence numbers to be strictly increasing even when records are deleted from the table. In that case, you can combine this method with the technique described earlier of using a secondary table for nothing else but to generate sequence numbers for use in your main table.

Why might you want to begin a sequence with a value higher than 1? One reason is to make sequence numbers all have the same number of digits. If you're generating customer ID numbers, and you expect never to have more than a million customers, you could begin the series at 1,000,000. You'll be able to add well over a million customer records before the digit count for customer ID values changes.

Another way to force sequence numbers to be a certain width is to use a ZEROFILL column, of course. That can present problems, depending on the context in which you use your data. For example, if you manipulate sequence numbers with leading zeros in Perl or PHP scripts, you have to be careful to use them only as strings; if they get converted to numbers, the leading zeros will be lost. The following short Perl script illustrates the perils of dealing with numbers like this:

```perl
#! /usr/bin/perl
$s = "00010";   # create "number" with leading zeroes
print "$s\n";
$s++;           # use Perl's intelligent increment
print "$s\n";
$s += 1;        # use $s in a numeric context
print "$s\n";
```

When executed, the script prints the following output:

00010 Okay

00011 Okay

12   Oops!

Perl's '++' autoincrement operator is smart and can create sequence values from either strings or numbers, but '+=' operates on numbers only. In the output just displayed, you can see that '+=' causes a string-to-number conversion and the leading zeroes in the value of $s are lost.

Other reasons for not beginning a sequence at 1 might have nothing to do with technical considerations. For example, if you were assigning membership numbers, you might want to begin a sequence at a number higher than 1 to forestall political squabbling over who gets to be member number 1 by making sure there isn't any such number. Hey, it happens. Sad, but true.

Generating Sequences Without AUTO_INCREMENT

Another method for generating sequence numbers doesn't use an AUTO_INCREMENT column at all. Instead, it uses the variant form of the LAST_INSERT_ID() function that takes an argument. (This form was introduced in MySQL 3.22.9.) If you insert or update a column using LAST_INSERT_ID(*expr*), the next call to LAST_INSERT_ID() with no argument will return the value of *expr*. In other words, *expr* is treated as though it had been generated by the AUTO_INCREMENT mechanism. This allows you to generate a sequence number and then use it in a later statement within the client session, without having the value be affected by other clients.

One way to use this strategy is to create a single-row table containing a value that is updated each time you want the next value in the sequence. For example, you can create the table like this:

```
CREATE TABLE seq_table (seq INT UNSIGNED NOT NULL)
INSERT INTO seq_table VALUES(0)
```

These statements create the table seq_table and initialize it with a single row containing a seq value of 0. To use the table, generate the next sequence number like this:

```
UPDATE seq_table SET seq = LAST_INSERT_ID(seq+1)
```

This statement retrieves the current value of the seq column and increments it by 1 to produce the next value in the sequence. Generating the new value using LAST_INSERT_ID(seq+1) causes it to be treated as though it were an AUTO_INCREMENT value, and the value can be retrieved in a later statement by calling LAST_INSERT_ID() without an argument. This works even if some other client has generated another sequence number in the meantime because LAST_INSERT_ID() is client-specific.

You can also use this method if you want to generate sequence values that increment by a value other than 1, or that are negative. For example, the following two statements could be used to generate a sequence of numbers that increase by 100 each time or a sequence of negative numbers:

```
UPDATE seq_table SET seq = LAST_INSERT_ID(seq+100)
UPDATE seq_table SET seq = LAST_INSERT_ID(seq-1)
```

You can also use this method to generate a sequence that begins at an arbitrary value by setting the seq column to an appropriate initial value.

For an application of this sequence-generation method for multiple counters, see "Setting Up a Counter Table" in Chapter 3, "MySQL SQL Syntax and Use."

String Column Types

MySQL provides several string types to hold character data. Strings are often used for values like these:

```
"N. Bertram, et al."
"Pencils (no. 2 lead)"
"123 Elm St."
"Monograph Series IX"
```

But strings are actually "generic" types in a sense because you can use them to represent any value. For example, you can use string types to hold binary data, such as images or sounds, or output from `gzip`, should you wish to store compressed data.

For all string types, values that are too long are chopped to fit. But string types range from very small to very large, with the largest type able to hold nearly 4GB of data, so you should be able to find something long enough to avoid truncation of your information.[2]

Table 2.8 shows the types provided by MySQL for declaring string-valued columns, and the maximum size and storage requirements of each type. For variable-length column types, the amount of storage taken by a value varies from row to row, and depends on the length of the values actually stored in the column. This length is represented by L in the table.

The extra bytes required in addition to L are the number of bytes needed to store the length of the value. MySQL handles variable-length values by storing both the content of the value and its length. These extra bytes are treated as an unsigned integer. Notice the correspondence between a variable-length type's maximum length, the number of extra bytes required for that type, and the range of the unsigned integer type that uses the same number of bytes. For example, `MEDIUMBLOB` values may be up to $2^{24}-1$ bytes long and require 3 bytes to record the result. The 3-byte integer type `MEDIUMINT` has a maximum unsigned value of $2^{24}-1$. That's not a coincidence.

Table 2.8 **String Column Types**

Type Specification	Maximum Size	Storage Required
`CHAR(M)`	M bytes	M bytes
`VARCHAR(M)`	M bytes	$L+1$ bytes
`TINYBLOB`, `TINYTEXT`	2^8-1 bytes	$L+1$ bytes
`BLOB`, `TEXT`	$2^{16}-1$ bytes	$L+2$ bytes
`MEDIUMBLOB`, `MEDIUMTEXT`	$2^{24}-1$ bytes	$L+3$ bytes
`LONGBLOB`, `LONGTEXT`	$2^{32}-1$ bytes	$L+4$ bytes
`ENUM("value1","value2",...)`	65535 members	1 or 2 bytes
`SET("value1","value2",...)`	64 members	1, 2, 3, 4, or 8 bytes

[2] Due to limitations imposed by the maximum packet size of the client/server communication protocol, the effective limit on column values is 24MB.

CHAR and VARCHAR **Column Types**

CHAR and VARCHAR are the most commonly used string types. The difference between them is that CHAR is a fixed-length type and VARCHAR is a variable-length type. Values in a CHAR(M) column each take M bytes; shorter values are right-padded with spaces when they are stored. (Trailing spaces are stripped off on retrieval, however.) Values in a VARCHAR(M) column are stored using only as many bytes as necessary, plus one byte to record the length.[3]

If your values don't vary much in length, CHAR is a better choice than VARCHAR because tables with fixed-length rows can be processed more efficiently than tables with variable-length rows. If your values are all the same length, VARCHAR will actually use more space due to the extra byte used to record the length of values.

Prior to MySQL 3.23, CHAR and VARCHAR columns may be declared with a maximum length M from 1 to 255. Beginning with MySQL 3.23, CHAR(0) is also legal. CHAR(0) is useful as a placeholder when you want to declare a column but don't want to allocate space for it if you're not sure yet how wide to make it. You can use ALTER TABLE to widen the column later. A CHAR(0) column may also be used to represent on/off values if you allow it to be NULL. Values in such a column may have two values, NULL and the empty string. A CHAR(0) column takes very little storage space in the table—only a single bit.

With a few limited exceptions, you can't mix CHAR and VARCHAR within the same table. MySQL will even change columns from one type to another, depending on the circumstances. (This is something that other databases do not do.) The principles that apply are as follows:

- Tables with fixed-length rows are processed more easily than tables with variable-length rows. (The reasons for this are discussed in the section "Choosing Column Types.")

- Table rows are fixed-length only if all the columns in the table are fixed-length types. If even a single column has a variable length, table rows become variable-length as well.

- Because the performance advantages of fixed-length rows are lost when the row becomes variable-length, any fixed-length columns may as well be converted to variable-length equivalents when that will save space.

What this means is that if you have VARCHAR columns in a table, you cannot also have CHAR columns; MySQL silently converts them to VARCHAR. Suppose you create a table like this:

```
CREATE TABLE my_table
(
    c1 CHAR(10),
    c2 VARCHAR(10)
)
```

---

[3] Trailing spaces are stripped when values are stored; this differs from the ANSI SQL standard for VARCHAR values.

If you issue a DESCRIBE my_table query, the output looks like this:

```
+-------+-------------+------+-----+---------+-------+
| Field | Type        | Null | Key | Default | Extra |
+-------+-------------+------+-----+---------+-------+
| c1    | varchar(10) | YES  |     | NULL    |       |
| c2    | varchar(10) | YES  |     | NULL    |       |
+-------+-------------+------+-----+---------+-------+
```

Notice that the presence of the VARCHAR column causes MySQL to convert c1 to
VARCHAR as well. If you try using ALTER TABLE to convert c1 to CHAR, it won't work. The
only way to convert a VARCHAR column to CHAR is to convert all VARCHAR columns in
the table at the same time:

```
ALTER TABLE my_table MODIFY c1 CHAR(10), MODIFY c2 CHAR(10)
```

The BLOB and TEXT column types are variable-length like VARCHAR, but they have no
fixed-length equivalent, so you cannot use CHAR columns in the same table as BLOB or
TEXT columns. Any CHAR column will be converted to VARCHAR.

The exception to non-mixing of fixed-length and variable-length columns is that
CHAR columns shorter than four characters are not converted to VARCHAR. For example,
MySQL will not change the CHAR column in the following table to VARCHAR:

```
CREATE TABLE my_table
(
    c1 CHAR(2),
    c2 VARCHAR(10)
)
```

The reason columns shorter than four characters are not converted is that, on average,
any savings you might gain by not storing trailing spaces are offset by the extra byte
needed in a VARCHAR column to record the length of each value. In fact, if *all* your
columns are short, MySQL will convert any that you declare as VARCHAR to CHAR.
MySQL does this because the conversion won't increase storage requirements on average and will improve performance by making table rows fixed-length. If you create a
table with the following specification, the VARCHAR columns are all silently changed to
CHAR:

```
CREATE TABLE my_table
(
    c1 VARCHAR(1),
    c2 VARCHAR(2),
    c3 VARCHAR(3)
)
```

You can see that the columns are changed by examining the output of DESCRIBE my_table:

```
+-------+---------+------+-----+---------+-------+
| Field | Type    | Null | Key | Default | Extra |
+-------+---------+------+-----+---------+-------+
| c1    | char(1) | YES  |     | NULL    |       |
| c2    | char(2) | YES  |     | NULL    |       |
| c3    | char(3) | YES  |     | NULL    |       |
+-------+---------+------+-----+---------+-------+
```

BLOB and TEXT Column Types

A "BLOB" is a binary large object—basically, a container that can hold anything you want to toss into it, and that you can make about as big as you want. In MySQL, the BLOB type is really a family of types (TINYBLOB, BLOB, MEDIUMBLOB, LONGBLOB), which are identical except in the maximum amount of information they can hold (see Table 2.8). MySQL also has a family of TEXT types (TINYTEXT, TEXT, MEDIUMTEXT, LONGTEXT). These are identical to the corresponding BLOB types in all respects except that for comparison and sorting purposes, BLOB values are case sensitive and TEXT values are not. BLOB and TEXT columns are useful for storing data that may grow very large or that may vary widely in size from row to row. Some examples are word-processing documents, images and sounds, compound data, and news articles.

BLOB or TEXT columns can be indexed from MySQL 3.23.2 on, although you must specify a prefix size to be used for the index to avoid creating index entries that might be huge and thereby defeat any benefits to be gained by that index. Besides, you generally don't perform searches by looking through a BLOB or TEXT column anyway because such columns often contain binary data (such as images). It's more common to use other columns in the table to record some sort of identifying information about the BLOB or TEXT values and use those to determine which rows you want.

BLOB or TEXT columns may require special care:

- Due to the typical large variation in the size of BLOB and TEXT values, tables containing them are subject to high rates of fragmentation if many deletes and updates are done. You'll want to run OPTIMIZE TABLE periodically to reduce fragmentation and maintain good performance. See Chapter 4, "Query Optimization," for more information.

- If you're using very large values, you may need to tune the server to increase the value of the max_allowed_packet parameter. See Chapter 11, "General MySQL Administration," for more information. You will also need to increase the packet size for any client that wishes to use very large values. Appendix E, "MySQL Program Reference," describes how to do this for the mysql and mysqldump clients.

ENUM and SET Column Types

ENUM and SET are special string types for which column values must be chosen from a fixed set of strings. The primary difference between them is that ENUM column values must consist of exactly one member of the set of values whereas SET column values may contain any or all members of the set. In other words, ENUM is used for values that are mutually exclusive, whereas SET allows multiple choices from a list of values.

The ENUM column type defines an enumeration. ENUM columns may be assigned values consisting of exactly one member chosen from a list of values specified at table-creation time. An enumeration may have up to 65,536 members (one of which is reserved by MySQL). Enumerations are commonly used to represent category values. For example, values in a column declared as ENUM("N","Y") can be either "N" or "Y". Or you can use ENUM for such things as answers to multiple-choice questions in a survey or questionnaire, or available sizes or colors for a product:

```
employees ENUM("less than 100","100-500","501-1500","more than 1500")
color ENUM("red","green","blue","black")
size ENUM("S","M","L","XL","XXL")
```

If you are processing selections from Web pages, you can use an ENUM to represent the option that a visitor to your site chooses from a set of mutually exclusive radio buttons on a page. For example, if you run an online pizza ordering service, an ENUM can be used to represent the type of crust a customer orders:

```
crust ENUM("thin","regular","pan style")
```

If enumeration categories represent counts, it's important to choose your categories properly when you create the enumeration. For example, when recording white blood cell counts from a laboratory test, you may group the counts into categories like this:

```
wbc ENUM("0-100","101-300",">300")
```

When a test result comes in as an exact count, you record the value in terms of the category into which the count falls. But you cannot recover the original count if you decide you want to convert the column from a category-based ENUM to an integer column based on exact count.

The SET type is similar to ENUM in the sense that when you create a SET column, you specify a list of legal set members. But unlike ENUM, each column value may consist of any number of members from the set. The set may have up to 64 members. You can use a SET when you have a fixed set of values that are not mutually exclusive, as they are in an ENUM column. For example, you might use a SET to represent options available for an automobile:

```
SET("luggage rack","cruise control","air conditioning","sun roof")
```

Then particular SET values would represent those options actually ordered by customers:

```
SET("cruise control,sun roof")
SET("luggage rack,air conditioning")
```

```
SET("luggage rack,cruise control,air conditioning")
SET("air conditioning")
SET("")
```

The empty string means the customer ordered no options. This is a legal SET value.

SET column values are represented as a single string. If a value consists of multiple set members, the members are separated in the string by commas. Obviously, this means you shouldn't use a string containing a comma as a SET member.

Other uses for SET columns might be for representing information such as patient diagnoses or results from selections on Web pages. For a diagnosis, there may be a standard list of symptoms to ask a patient about, and the patient might exhibit any or all of them. For your online pizza service, the Web page for ordering could have a set of check boxes for ingredients that a customer wants on a pizza, and several might be chosen.

The way you declare the legal value list for an ENUM or SET column is significant in several ways:

- The list determines the possible legal values for the column, as has already been discussed.

- You can insert ENUM or SET values in any lettercase, but the lettercase of the strings specified in the column declaration determines the lettercase of column values when they are retrieved later. For example, if you have an ENUM("Y","N") column and you store "y" and "n" in it, the values are displayed as "Y" and "N" when you retrieve them. This does not affect comparison or sorting behavior because ENUM and SET columns are not case sensitive.

- The order of values in an ENUM declaration is the order used for sorting. The order of values in a SET declaration also determines sort order, although the relationship is more complicated because column values may contain multiple set members.

- The order of values in a SET declaration determines the order in which substrings appear when SET column values consisting of multiple set members are displayed.

ENUM and SET are classified as string types because enumeration and set members are specified as strings when you create columns of these types. However, the members are stored internally as numbers and you can operate on them as such. This means that ENUM and SET types are more efficient than other string types because they often can be handled using numeric operations rather than string operations. It also means that ENUM and SET values can be used in either string or numeric contexts.

ENUM members in the column declaration are numbered sequentially beginning with 1. (0 is used by MySQL for the error member, which is represented in string form by the empty string.) The number of enumeration values determines the storage size of an ENUM column. One byte can represent 256 values, two bytes can represent

65,536 values. (Compare this to the ranges of the one-byte and two-byte integer types TINYINT UNSIGNED and SMALLLINT UNSIGNED.) Thus, the maximum number of enumeration members is 65,536 (counting the error member) and the storage size depends on whether or not there are more than 256 members. You can specify a maximum of 65,535 (not 65,536) members in the ENUM declaration because MySQL reserves a spot for the error member as an implicit member of every enumeration. When you assign an illegal value to an ENUM column, MySQL assigns the error member instead.

Here is an example you can try using the mysql client. It shows the numeric ordering of enumeration members and also demonstrates that the NULL value has no number in the ordering:

```
mysql> CREATE TABLE e_table (e ENUM("jane","fred","will","marcia"));
mysql> INSERT INTO e_table
VALUES("jane"),("fred"),("will"),("marcia"),(""),(NULL);
mysql> SELECT e, e+0, e+1, e*3 FROM e_table;
+--------+------+------+------+
| e      | e+0  | e+1  | e*3  |
+--------+------+------+------+
| jane   |    1 |    2 |    3 |
| fred   |    2 |    3 |    6 |
| will   |    3 |    4 |    9 |
| marcia |    4 |    5 |   12 |
|        |    0 |    1 |    0 |
| NULL   | NULL | NULL | NULL |
+--------+------+------+------+
```

You can operate on ENUM members either by name or number:

```
mysql> SELECT e FROM e_table WHERE e="will";
+------+
| e    |
+------+
| will |
+------+
mysql> SELECT e FROM e_table WHERE e=3;
+------+
| e    |
+------+
| will |
+------+
```

It is possible to declare the empty string as a legal enumeration member. It will be assigned a non-zero numeric value, just as would be any other member listed in the declaration. However, using an empty string may cause some confusion because that string is also used for the error member that has a numeric value of 0. In the following example, assigning the illegal enumeration value "x" to the ENUM column causes the error member to be assigned. This is distinguishable from the empty string member only when retrieved in numeric form:

```
mysql> CREATE TABLE t (e ENUM("a","","b"));
mysql> INSERT INTO t VALUES("a"),(""),("b"),("x");
mysql> SELECT e, e+0 FROM t;
+------+------+
| e    | e+0  |
+------+------+
| a    |    1 |
|      |    2 |
| b    |    3 |
|      |    0 |
+------+------+
```

The numeric representation of SET columns is a little different than for ENUM columns. Set members are not numbered sequentially. Instead, each member corresponds to an individual bit in the SET value. The first set member corresponds to bit 0, the second member corresponds to bit 1, and so on. A numeric SET value of 0 corresponds to the empty string. SET members are maintained as bit values. Eight set values per byte can be stored this way, so the storage size for a SET column is determined by the number of set members, up to a maximum of 64 members. SET values take 1, 2, 3, 4, or 8 bytes for set sizes of 1 to 8, 9 to 16, 17 to 24, 25 to 32, and 33 to 64.

The representation of a SET as a set of bits is what allows a SET value to consist of multiple set members. Any combination of bits can be turned on in the value, so the value may consist of any combination of the strings in the SET declaration that correspond to those bits.

Here's an example that shows the relationship between the string and numeric forms of a SET column; the numeric value is displayed in both decimal and binary form:

```
mysql> CREATE TABLE s_table (s SET("jane","fred","will","marcia"));
mysql> INSERT INTO s_table
VALUES("jane"),("fred"),("will"),("marcia"),(""),(NULL);
mysql> SELECT s, s+0, BIN(s+0) FROM s_table;
+--------+------+---------+
| s      | s+0  | BIN(s+0)|
+--------+------+---------+
| jane   |    1 | 1       |
| fred   |    2 | 10      |
| will   |    4 | 100     |
| marcia |    8 | 1000    |
|        |    0 | 0       |
| NULL   | NULL | NULL    |
+--------+------+---------+
```

If you assign to a SET column a value containing substrings that are not listed as set members, those strings drop out and the column is assigned a value consisting of the remaining substrings. When you assign values to SET columns, the substrings don't need to be listed in the same order that you used when you declared the column.

However, when you retrieve the value later, members will be listed in declaration order. Suppose you declare a SET column to represent furniture items using the following declaration:

```
SET("table","lamp","chair")
```

If you assign a value of "chair,couch,table" to this column, two things happen. First, "couch" drops out because it's not a member of the set. Second, when you retrieve the value later, it appears as "table,chair". This occurs because MySQL determines which bits correspond to each substring of the value to be assigned and turns them on in the stored value. "couch" corresponds to no bit and is ignored. On retrieval, MySQL constructs the string value from the numeric value by scanning the bits in order, which automatically reorders the substrings to the order used when the column was declared. This behavior also means that if you specify a set member more than once in a value, it will appear only once when you retrieve the value. If you assign "lamp,lamp,lamp" to a SET column, it will be simply "lamp" when retrieved.

The fact that MySQL reorders members in a SET value means that if you search for values using a string, you must list members in the proper order. If you insert "chair,table" and then search for "chair,table" you won't find the record; you must look for it as "table,chair".

Sorting and indexing of ENUM and SET columns is done according to the internal (numeric) values of column values. The following example might appear to be incorrect otherwise because the values are not sorted in alphanumeric order:

```
mysql> SELECT e FROM e_table ORDER BY e;
+---------+
| e       |
+---------+
| NULL    |
|         |
|         |
| jane    |
| fred    |
| will    |
| marcia  |
+---------+
```

The NULL value sorts before other values (or after, for a descending sort).

You can exploit the ENUM sorting order if you have a fixed set of values and you want them to sort in a particular order. Make the column an ENUM when you create the table and list the enumeration values in the column declaration in the order that you want them to be sorted.

For cases where you want an ENUM to sort in regular lexicographic order, you can convert the column to a non-ENUM string by using CONCAT() and sorting the result:

```
mysql> SELECT CONCAT(e) as e_str FROM e_table ORDER BY e_str;
+---------+
¦ e_str ¦
+---------+
¦ NULL    ¦
¦         ¦
¦ fred    ¦
¦ jane    ¦
¦ marcia  ¦
¦ will    ¦
+---------+
```

String Column Type Attributes

The BINARY attribute may be specified for the CHAR and VARCHAR types to cause column values to be treated as binary strings (that is, case sensitive in comparison and sorting operations).

The general attributes NULL or NOT NULL may be specified for any of the string types. If you don't specify either of them, NULL is the default. However, declaring a string column as NOT NULL does not prevent entry of an empty string. An empty value is different than a missing value, so don't make the mistake of thinking that you can force a string column to contain non-empty values by declaring it NOT NULL. If you require string values to be non-empty, that is a constraint you must enforce within your own applications.

You may also specify a default value using the DEFAULT attribute for all string column types except the BLOB and TEXT types. If you don't specify a default value, one is chosen automatically. The default is NULL for columns that may contain NULL. For columns that may not contain NULL, the default is the empty string except for ENUM, where the default is the first enumeration member. (For SET, the default when the column cannot contain NULL is actually the empty set, but that is equivalent to the empty string.)

Date and Time Column Types

MySQL provides several column types for temporal values: DATE, DATETIME, TIME, TIMESTAMP, and YEAR. Table 2.9 shows the types provided by MySQL for declaring columns that hold date and time values and the range of legal values for each type. The YEAR type was introduced in MySQL 3.22. The others have been present in all versions of MySQL. The storage requirements for each type are shown in Table 2.10.

Table 2.9   **Date and Time Column Types**

Type Specification	Range
DATE	"1000-01-01" to "9999-12-31"
TIME	"-838:59:59" to "838:59:59"
DATETIME	"1000-01-01 00:00:00" to "9999-12-31 23:59:59"
TIMESTAMP[(M)]	19700101000000 to sometime in the year 2037
YEAR[(M)]	1901 to 2155

Table 2.10 **Date and Time Column Type Storage Requirements**

Type Specification	Storage Required
DATE	3 bytes (4 bytes prior to MySQL 3.22)
TIME	3 bytes
DATETIME	8 bytes
TIMESTAMP	4 bytes
YEAR	1 byte

Each date and time type has a "zero" value that is stored when you insert a value that is illegal for the type, as shown in Table 2.11. This value is also the default value for date and time columns that are declared NOT NULL.

Table 2.11 **Date and Time Type "Zero" Values**

Type Specification	Zero Value
DATE	"0000-00-00"
TIME	"00:00:00"
DATETIME	"0000-00-00 00:00:00"
TIMESTAMP	00000000000000
YEAR	0000

MySQL always represents dates with the year first, in accordance with the ANSI specification. For example, December 3, 1999 is represented as "1999-12-03". MySQL does allow some leeway in the way it allows input dates to be specified. For example, it will convert two-digit year values to four digits, and you need not supply a leading zero digit for month and day values that are less than 10. However, you must specify the year first. Formats that you may be more used to, such as "12/3/99" or "3/12/99", will be interpreted incorrectly. The date interpretation rules MySQL uses are discussed further in "Working with Date and Time Columns."

Time values are returned in the time zone local to the server; MySQL doesn't make any time zone adjustments for the values that it returns to the client.

DATE, TIME, and DATETIME Column Types

The DATE, TIME, and DATETIME types hold date, time, and combined date and time values. The formats are "YYYY-MM-DD", "hh:mm:ss", and "YYYY-MM-DD hh:mm:ss". For the DATETIME type, the date and time parts are both required; if you assign a DATE value to a DATETIME column, MySQL automatically adds a time part of "00:00:00".

MySQL treats the time in DATETIME and TIME values slightly differently. For DATETIME, the time part represents a time of day. A TIME value, on the other hand, represents elapsed time (that's why the range is so great and why negative values are allowed). The rightmost part of the value is taken to indicate seconds, so if you insert a "short" (not fully qualified) time value, such as "12:30", into a TIME column, the value stored is "00:12:30". That is, it's interpreted as "12 minutes, 30 seconds." You can use TIME columns to represent time of day if you like, but keep this conversion rule in mind to avoid problems. To insert a value of "12 hours, 30 minutes," you must specify it as "12:30:00".

TIMESTAMP **Column Type**

TIMESTAMP columns represent values in *YYYYMMDDhhmmss* format, with a range from 19700101000000 to sometime in the year 2037. The range is tied to UNIX time, where the first day of 1970 is "day zero," also known as "the epoch." The beginning of 1970 determines the lower end of the TIMESTAMP range. The upper end of the range corresponds to the four-byte limit on UNIX time, which can represent values into the year 2037.[4]

The TIMESTAMP type is so called because it has the special property of recording when a record is created or modified. If you insert a NULL into a TIMESTAMP column, the column value is set automatically to the current date and time. This also happens if you create or update a row but assign no explicit value to the column. However, only the first TIMESTAMP column in a row is treated this way, and even for the first TIMESTAMP column, you can defeat timestamping by inserting an explicit date and time value into the column rather than NULL.

A TIMESTAMP column declaration may include a specification for a maximum display width *M*. Table 2.12 shows the display formats for the allowed values of *M*. If *M* is omitted from a TIMESTAMP declaration or has a value of 0 or greater than 14, the column is treated as TIMESTAMP(14). Odd values of *M* in the range from 1 to 13 are treated as the next higher even number.

Table 2.12 TIMESTAMP **Display Formats**

Type Specification	Display Format
TIMESTAMP(14)	*YYYYMMDDhhmmss*
TIMESTAMP(12)	*YYYYMMDDhhmm*
TIMESTAMP(10)	*YYMMDDhhmm*
TIMESTAMP(8)	*YYYYMMDD*
TIMESTAMP(6)	*YYMMDD*
TIMESTAMP(4)	*YYMM*
TIMESTAMP(2)	*YY*

[4] The upper limit on TIMESTAMP values will increase as operating systems are modified to extend the upper range of UNIX time values. This is something that must be addressed at the system library level. MySQL will take advantage of these changes as they are made.

The display width for TIMESTAMP columns has nothing to do with storage size or with the values stored internally. TIMESTAMP values are always stored in 4 bytes and used in calculations to full 14-digit precision, regardless of the display width. To see this, suppose you declare a table as follows, then insert some rows into it and retrieve them:

```
CREATE TABLE my_table
(
    ts TIMESTAMP(8),
    i INT
)
INSERT INTO my_table VALUES(19990801120000,3)
INSERT INTO my_table VALUES(19990801120001,2)
INSERT INTO my_table VALUES(19990801120002,1)
INSERT INTO my_table VALUES(19990801120003,0)
SELECT * FROM my_table ORDER BY ts, i
```

The output from the SELECT statement looks like this:

```
+----------+-----+
| ts       | i   |
+----------+-----+
| 19990801 |  3  |
| 19990801 |  2  |
| 19990801 |  1  |
| 19990801 |  0  |
+----------+-----+
```

On the face of it, the rows appear to be sorted in the wrong order—the values in the first column are all the same, so it seems the sort should order the rows according to the values in the second column. This apparently anomalous result is due to the fact that MySQL is sorting based on the full 14-digit values inserted into the TIMESTAMP column.

MySQL has no column type that can be set to the current date and time when the record is created and that remains immutable thereafter. If you want to achieve that, you can do it two ways:

- Use a TIMESTAMP column. When a record is first created, set the column to NULL to initialize it to the current date and time:

  ```
  INSERT INTO tbl_name (ts_col, ...) VALUES(NULL, ...)
  ```

  Whenever you update the record thereafter, explicitly set the column to the value it already has. Assigning an explicit value defeats the timestamping mechanism because it prevents the column's value from being automatically updated:

  ```
  UPDATE tbl_name SET ts_col=ts_col WHERE ...
  ```

- Use a DATETIME column. When you create a record, initialize the column to NOW():

  ```
  INSERT INTO tbl_name (dt_col, ...) VALUES(NOW(), ...)
  ```

Whenever you update the record thereafter, leave the column alone:

```
UPDATE tbl_name SET /* anything BUT dt_col here */ WHERE ...
```

If you want to use TIMESTAMP columns to maintain both a time-created value and a last-modified value, you can do so by using one TIMESTAMP for the time-modified value, and a second TIMESTAMP for the time-created value. Make sure the time-modified column is the first TIMESTAMP, so that it's set when the record is created or changed. Make the time-created column the second TIMESTAMP, and initialize it to NOW() when you create new records. That way its value will reflect the record creation time and will not change after that.

YEAR Column Type

YEAR is a one-byte column type used for efficient representation of year values. It has a range of 1901 to 2155. You can use the YEAR type when you want to store date information but only need the year part of the date, such as year of birth, year of election to office, and so forth. When you do not need a full date value, YEAR is much more space-efficient than other date types.

A YEAR column declaration may include a specification for a display width M, which should be either 4 or 2. If M is omitted from a YEAR declaration, the default is 4.

TINYINT has the same storage size as YEAR (one byte), but not the same range. To cover the same range of years as YEAR by using an integer type, you would need a SMALLINT, which takes twice as much space. If the range of years you need to represent coincides with the range of the YEAR type, YEAR is more space-efficient than SMALLINT. Another advantage of YEAR over an integer column is that MySQL will convert two-digit values into four-digit values for you using MySQL's usual year-guessing rules. For example, 97 and 14 become 1997 and 2014. However, be aware that inserting the numeric value 00 will result in the value 0000 being stored, not 2000. If you want a value of zero to convert to 2000, you must specify it as a string "00".

Date and Time Column Type Attributes

There are no attributes that are specific to the date and time column types. The general attributes NULL or NOT NULL may be specified for any of the date and time types. If you don't specify either of them, NULL is the default. You may also specify a default value using the DEFAULT attribute. If you don't specify a default value, one is chosen automatically. The default is NULL for columns that may contain NULL. Otherwise, the default is the "zero" value for the type.

Working with Date and Time Columns

MySQL tries to interpret date and time values in a variety of formats. DATE values may be specified in any of the following formats, including both string and numeric forms. Table 2.13 shows the allowable formats for each of the date and time types.

Table 2.13   **Date and Time Type Input Formats**

Type	Allowable Formats
`DATETIME`, `TIMESTAMP`	`"YYYY-MM-DD hh:mm:ss"`
	`"YY-MM-DD hh:mm:ss"`
	`"YYYYMMDDhhmmss"`
	`"YYMMDDhhmmss"`
	`YYYYMMDDhhmmss`
	`YYMMDDhhmmss`
`DATE`	`"YYYY-MM-DD"`
	`"YY-MM-DD"`
	`"YYYYMMDD"`
	`"YYMMDD"`
	`YYYYMMDD`
	`YYMMDD`
`TIME`	`"hh:mm:ss"`
	`"hhmmss"`
	`hhmmss`
`YEAR`	`"YYYY"`
	`"YY"`
	`YYYY`
	`YY`

Formats that have two digits for the year value are interpreted using the rules described in "Interpretation of Ambiguous Year Values." For string formats that include delimiter characters, you don't have to use '-' for dates and ':' for times. Any punctuation character may be used as the delimiter. Interpretation of values depends on context, not on the delimiter. For example, although times are typically specified using a delimiter of ':', MySQL won't interpret a value containing ':' as a time in a context where a date is expected. In addition, for the string formats that include delimiters, you need not specify two digits for month, day, hour, minute, or second values that are less than 10. The following are all equivalent:

```
"2012-02-03 05:04:09"
"2012-2-03 05:04:09"
"2012-2-3 05:04:09"
"2012-2-3 5:04:09"
"2012-2-3 5:4:09"
"2012-2-3 5:4:9"
```

Note that values with leading zeroes may be interpreted differently depending on whether they are specified as strings or numbers. The string `"001231"` will be seen as a six-digit value and interpreted as `"2000-12-31"` for a DATE, as `"2000-12-31 00:00:00"` for a DATETIME. On the other hand, the number `001231` will be seen as `1231` after the parser gets done with it and then the interpretation becomes problematic. This is a case where it's best to supply a string value, or else use a fully qualified value if you are using numbers (that is, `20001231` for DATE and `200012310000` for DATETIME).

In general, you may freely assign values between the DATE, DATETIME, and TIMESTAMP types, although there are certain restrictions to keep in mind:

- If you assign a DATETIME or TIMESTAMP value to a DATE, the time part is discarded.
- If you assign a DATE value to a DATETIME or TIMESTAMP, the time part of the resulting value is set to zero.
- The types have different ranges. In particular, TIMESTAMP has a more limited range (1970 to 2037), so, for example, you cannot assign a pre-1970 DATETIME value to a TIMESTAMP and expect reasonable results. Nor can you assign values that are well in the future to a TIMESTAMP.

MySQL provides many functions for working with date and time values. See Appendix C for more information.

Interpretation of Ambiguous Year Values

For all date and time types that include a year part (DATE, DATETIME TIMESTAMP, YEAR), MySQL handles values that contain two-digit years by converting them to four-digit years. This conversion is performed according to the following rules:[5]

- Year values from 00 to 69 become 2000 to 2069
- Year values from 70 to 99 become 1970 to 1999

You can see the effect of these rules most easily by assigning different two-digit values into a YEAR column and then retrieving the results. This will also demonstrate something you should take note of:

```
mysql> CREATE TABLE y_table (y YEAR);
mysql> INSERT INTO y_table VALUES(68),(69),(99), (00);
mysql> SELECT * FROM y_table;
+------+
| y    |
+------+
| 2068 |
| 1969 |
| 1999 |
| 0000 |
+------+
```

---

[5] In MySQL 4.0, the rules will change slightly in that 69 will be converted to 1969 rather than to 2069. This is according to the rules specified by the X/Open UNIX standard.

Notice that 00 was converted to 0000, not to 2000. That's because 0 is a perfectly legal value for the YEAR type; if you insert a numeric zero, that's what you get. To get 2000, insert the string "0" or "00". You can make sure MySQL sees a string and not a number by inserting YEAR values using CONCAT(). This function returns a string result uniformly regardless of whether its argument is a string or a number.

In any case, keep in mind that the rules for converting two-digit to four-digit year values provide only a reasonable guess. There is no way for MySQL to be certain about the meaning of a two-digit year when the century is unspecified. If MySQL's conversion rules don't produce the values that you want, the solution is obvious: Provide unambiguous data with four-digit years.

Choosing Column Types

The previous section describes the various MySQL column types from which you can choose and the general properties of those types, such as the kind of values they may contain, how much storage space they take, and so on. But how do you actually decide which types to use when you create a table? This section discusses issues to consider that will help you choose.

The most "generic" column types are the string types. You can store anything in them because numbers and dates can be represented in string form. So why not just declare all your columns as strings and be done with it? Let's consider a simple example. Suppose you have values that look like numbers. You can represent these as strings, but should you? What happens if you do?

For one thing, you'll probably use more space, because numbers can be stored more efficiently than strings. You'll also notice some differences in query results due to the different ways that numbers and strings are handled. For example, the sort order for numbers is not the same as for strings. The number 2 is less than the number 11, but the string "2" is lexicographically greater than the string "11". You can work around this by using the column in a numeric context like this:

```
SELECT col_name + 0 as num ... ORDER BY num
```

Is MySQL Year-2000 Safe?

MySQL itself is year-2000 safe because it stores dates internally with four-digit years, but it's your responsibility to provide data that result in the proper values being stored in the first place. The real problem with two-digit year interpretation comes not from MySQL, but from the human desire to take a shortcut and enter ambiguous data. If you're willing to take the risk, go ahead. It's your risk to take, and MySQL's guessing rules are adequate for many situations. Just be aware that there are times when you really do need to enter four digits. For example, to enter birth and death dates into the president table that lists US presidents back into the 1700s, four-digit year values are in order. Values in these columns span several centuries, so letting MySQL guess the century from a two-digit year is definitely the wrong thing to do.

Adding zero to the column forces a numeric sort, but is that a reasonable thing to do? In general, probably not. Causing MySQL to treat the column as a number rather than a string has a couple of significant implications. It forces a string-to-number conversion for each column value, which is inefficient. Also, turning the column into a calculation prevents MySQL from using any index on the column, which slows down the query further. Neither of these performance degradations will occur if you store the values as numbers in the first place. The simple choice of using one representation rather than another has implications for storage requirements, query handling, and processing performance.

The preceding example illustrates that several issues come into play when you choose column types. The following list gives a quick rundown on factors to think about when picking a type for a column.

- **What kind of values will the column hold?** Numbers? Strings? Dates? This is an obvious question, but you must ask it. You can represent any type of value as a string, but as we've just seen, it's likely that you'll get better performance if you use other more appropriate types for numeric values. (This is also true for date and time values.) However, assessing the type of values you're working with isn't necessarily trivial, particularly when it's someone else's data. It's especially important to ask what kind of values the column will hold if you're setting up a table for someone else, and you must be sure to ask enough questions to get sufficient information for making a good decision.

- **Do your values lie within some particular range?** If they are integers, will they always be non-negative? If so, you can use UNSIGNED. If they are strings, will they always be chosen from among a fixed set of values? If so, you may find ENUM or SET a useful type.

  There is a tradeoff between the range of a type and the amount of storage it uses. How "big" of a type do you need? For numbers, you can choose small types with a limited range of values, or large types, which are essentially unlimited. For strings, you can make them short or long, and you wouldn't choose CHAR(255) if all the values you want to store contain fewer than 10 characters.

- **What are the performance and efficiency issues?** Some types can be processed more efficiently than others. Numeric operations generally can be performed more quickly than string operations. Short strings can be compared more quickly than long strings, and also involve less disk overhead. Performance is better for fixed-length types than for variable-length types.

- **How do you want your values to be compared?** For strings, comparisons can be case sensitive or not case sensitive. You choices here also affect sorting, which is based on comparisons.

- **Do you plan to index a column?** If you do, it affects your choice of column type because some versions of MySQL do not allow you to index certain types, such as BLOB and TEXT. Also, some versions of MySQL require that an indexed column be declared as NOT NULL, which affects your ability to use NULL values.

Now let's consider each of these issues in more detail. But before we do, allow me to point something out: You want to make the best column type choices you can when you create a table, but if you make a choice that turns out to be non-optimal, it's not the end of the world. You can use ALTER TABLE to change the type to a better one. This can be as simple as changing a SMALLINT to MEDIUMINT after finding out your data contain values larger than you originally thought. Or it can be more complex, such as changing a CHAR to an ENUM with a specific set of allowed values. In MySQL 3.23 and up, you can use PROCEDURE ANALYSE() to obtain information about your table's columns, such as the minimum and maximum values as well as a suggested optimal type to cover the range of values in a column. This may help you determine that a smaller type can be used, which can improve the performance of queries that involve the table and reduce the amount of space required for table storage.

What Kind of Values Will the Column Hold?

The first thing you think of when you're trying to decide on a column type is the kind of values the column will be used for because this has the most obvious implications for the type you choose. In general, you do the obvious thing: You store numbers in numeric columns, strings in string columns, and dates and times in date and time columns. If your numbers have a fractional part, you use a floating-point column type rather than an integer type, and so on. But sometimes there are exceptions. The principle here is that you need to understand the nature of your data to be able to choose the type in an informed manner. If you're going to store your own data, you probably have a good idea of how to characterize it. On the other hand, if others ask you to set up a table for them, it's sometimes a different story. It may not be so easy to know just what you're working with. Be sure to ask enough questions to find out what kind of values the table really should contain.

Suppose you're told a column is needed to record "amount of precipitation." Is that a number? Or is it "mostly" numeric—that is, typically but not always coded as a number? For example, when you watch the news on television, the weather report generally includes a measure of precipitation. Sometimes this is a number (as in "0.25 inches of rain"), but sometimes it's "trace" of precipitation, meaning "not much at all." That's fine for the weather report, but what does it mean for storage in a database? You either need to quantify "trace" as a number so that you can use a numeric column type to record precipitation amounts, or you need to use a string so that you can record the word "trace." Or you could come up with some more complicated arrangement, using a number column and a string column where you fill in one column and leave the other one NULL. It should be obvious that you want to avoid that option, if possible; it makes the table harder to understand and it makes query-writing much more difficult.

I would probably try to store all rows in numeric form, then convert them as necessary for display purposes. For example, if any non-zero amount of precipitation less than .01 inches is considered a trace amount, you could display values from the column like this:

```
SELECT IF(precip>0 AND precip<.01,"trace",precip) FROM ...
```

For monetary calculations, you're working with values that have dollars and cents parts. These look like floating-point values, but `FLOAT` and `DOUBLE` are subject to round-ing error and may not be suitable except for records in which you need only approxi-mate accuracy. Because people tend to be touchy about their money, it's more likely you need a type that affords perfect accuracy. You have a couple of choices:

- You can represent money as a `DECIMAL(M,2)` type, choosing *M* as the maximum width appropriate for the range of values you need. This gives you floating point values with two decimal places of accuracy. The advantage of `DECIMAL` is that val-ues are represented as strings and are not subject to roundoff error. The disad-vantage is that string operations are less efficient than operations on values represented internally as numbers.

- You can represent all monetary values internally as cents using an integer type. The advantage is that calculations are done internally using integers, which is very fast. The disadvantage is that you will need to convert values on input or output by multiplying or dividing by 100.

Some values are obviously numeric but you must determine whether to use a floating-point or integer type. You should ask what your units are and what accuracy you require. Is whole-unit accuracy sufficient or do you need to represent fractional units? This may help you distinguish between integer and floating-point column types. For example, if you're representing weights, you can use an integer column if you record values to the nearest pound. You'd use a floating-point column if you want to record fractional units. In some cases, you might even use multiple fields—for exam-ple, if you want to record weight in terms of pounds and ounces.

Height is another numeric type of information for which there are several repre-sentational possibilities:

- **A string such as `"6-2"` for a value like "6 feet, 2 inches".** This has the advantage of having a form that's easy to look at and understand (certainly more so than "74 inches"), but it's difficult to use this kind of value for mathematical operations such as summation or averaging.

- **One numeric field for feet, another for inches.** This would be a little eas-ier to work with for numerical operations, but two fields are more difficult to use than one.

- **One numeric field representing inches.** This is easiest for a database to work with, but least meaningful for humans. But remember that you don't have to present values in the same format that you use to work with them. You can reformat values for meaningful display using MySQL's many functions. That means this might be the best way to represent height.

If you need to store date information, do the values include a time? That is, will they *ever* need to include a time? MySQL doesn't provide a date type that has an optional time part: DATE never has a time, and DATETIME must have a time. If the time really is optional, use a DATE column to record the date, and a separate TIME column to record the time. Then allow the TIME column to be NULL and interpret that as "no time":

```
CREATE TABLE my_table
(
    date DATE NOT NULL,
    time TIME NULL
)
```

One type of situation in which it's especially important to determine whether or not you need a time value occurs when you're joining two tables with a master-detail relationship that are "linked" based on date information.

Suppose you're conducting research involving subjects who come in to your office to be tested. Following a standard initial set of tests, you may run several additional tests that same day, with the choice of tests varying according to the results of the initial tests. You might represent this information using a master-detail relationship, in which the subject identification information and the standard initial tests are stored in a master record and any additional tests are stored as rows in a secondary detail table. Then you link together the two tables based on subject ID and the date on which the tests are given.

The question you must answer in this situation is whether you can use just the date or whether you need both date and time. This depends on whether or not a subject may go through the testing procedure more than once during the same day. If so, record the time (say, the time that the procedure begins), either using a DATETIME column or separate DATE and TIME columns that both must be filled in. Without the time value, you will not be able to associate a subject's detail records with the proper master records if the subject is tested twice in a day.

I've heard people claim "I don't need a time; I will never test a subject twice on the same day." Sometimes they're correct, but I have also seen some of these same people turn up later wondering how to prevent detail records from being mixed up with the wrong master record after entering data for subjects who were tested multiple times in a day. Sorry, then it's too late!

Sometimes you can deal with this problem by retrofitting a TIME column into the tables. Unfortunately, it's difficult to fix existing records unless you have some independent data source, such as the original paper records. Otherwise, you have no way to disambiguate detail records to associate them to the proper master record. Even if you have an independent source of information, this is very messy and likely to cause problems for applications you've already written to use the tables. It's best to explain the issues to the table owners and make sure you've got a good characterization of the data values before creating their tables.

Sometimes you may have incomplete data, and this will influence your choice of column types. You may be collecting birth and death dates for genealogical research, and sometimes all you can find out is the year someone was born or died, but not the exact date. If you use a DATE column, you can't enter a date unless you have the full date. If you want to be able to record whatever information you have, even if it's incomplete, you may have to keep separate year, month, and day fields. Then you can enter such parts of the date as you have and leave the rest NULL. Another possibility is available in MySQL 3.23 and up, which allows the day or month and day parts of DATE values to be 0. Such "fuzzy" dates can be used to represent incomplete date values.

Do Your Values Lie Within Some Particular Range?

If you've decided on general category from which to pick a type for a column, thinking about the range of values you want to represent will help you narrow down your choices to a particular type within that category. Suppose you want to store integer values. The range of your values determine the types you can use. If you need values in the range from 0 to 1000, you can use anything from a SMALLINT up to a BIGINT. If your values range up to 2 million, you can't use SMALLINT, and your choices range from MEDIUMINT to BIGINT. Then you need to pick one type from among the possibilities.

You could, of course, simply use the largest type for the kind of value you want to store (BIGINT for the examples in the previous paragraph). Generally, however, you should use the smallest type that is large enough for your purposes. By doing so, you'll minimize the amount of storage used by your tables, and they will give you better performance because smaller columns usually can be processed more quickly than larger ones.

If you don't know the range of values you'll need to be able to represent, you either must guess or use BIGINT to accommodate the worst possible case. (Remember that if you guess and use a type that turns out to be too small, all is not lost; you can use ALTER TABLE later to make the column bigger.)

In Chapter 1, we created a score table for the grade-keeping project that had a score column for recording quiz and test scores. The table was created using INT in order to keep the discussion simpler, but you can see now that if scores are in the range from 0 to 100, a better choice would be TINYINT UNSIGNED, because that would use less storage.

The range of values in your data also affects the attributes you can use with your column type. If values are never negative, you can use UNSIGNED; otherwise, you can't.

String types don't have a "range" in the same way numeric columns do, but they have a length, and the maximum length you need affects the column types you can use. If your strings are shorter than 256 characters, you can use CHAR, VARCHAR, TINYTEXT, or TINYBLOB. If you want longer strings, you can use a TEXT or BLOB type, but CHAR and VARCHAR are no longer options.

For string columns that you will use to represent a fixed set of values, you might consider using an ENUM or SET column type. These can be good choices because they are represented internally as numbers. Operations on them are performed numerically, so they are more efficient than other string types. They can also be more compact than other string types, which saves space.

When characterizing the range of values you have to deal with, the best terms are "always" and "never" (as in "always less than 1000" or "never negative"), because they allow you to constrain your column type choices more tightly. But be wary of using these terms when they're not really justified. Be especially wary if you're consulting with other people about their data and they start throwing around those two terms. When people say "always" or "never," be sure they really mean it. Sometimes people say their data always have a particular characteristic when they really mean "almost always."

For example, suppose you're designing a table for some people and they tell you, "Our test scores are always 0 to 100." Based on that statement, you choose TINYINT and you make it UNSIGNED because the values are always non-negative. Then you find out that the people who code the data for entry into the database sometimes use −1 to mean "student was absent due to illness." Oops. They didn't tell you that. It may be acceptable to use NULL to represent such values, but if not, you'll have to record a −1, and then you can't use an UNSIGNED column. (ALTER TABLE to the rescue!)

Sometimes decisions about these types of cases can be made more easily by asking a simple question: Are there *ever* exceptions? If an exceptional case *ever* occurs, even just once, you must allow for it. You will find that people who talk to you about designing a database invariably think that if exceptions don't occur very often, they don't matter. When you're creating a table, you can't think that way. The question you need to ask isn't how often do exceptions occur, but do exceptions occur? If they do, you must allow for them.

What Are the Performance and Efficiency Issues?

Your choice of column type can influence query performance in several ways. If you keep the general guidelines discussed in the following sections in mind, you'll be able to choose types that will help MySQL process your tables more efficiently.

Numeric Versus String Operations

Numeric operations are generally faster than string operations. Consider comparison operations. Numbers can be compared in a single operation. String comparisons may involve several byte-by-byte comparisons, more so as the strings become longer.

If a string column has a limited number of values, use an ENUM or SET type to get the advantages of numeric operations. These types are represented internally as numbers and can be processed more efficiently.

Consider alternative representations for strings. Sometimes you can improve performance by representing string values as numbers. For example, to represent IP numbers in dotted-quad notation, such as 192.168.0.4, you might use a string. But as an alternative, you could convert the IP numbers to integer form by storing each part of the dotted-quad form in one byte of a four-byte INT UNSIGNED type. This would both save space and speed lookups. On the other hand, representing IP numbers as INT values would make it difficult to perform pattern matches such as you might do if you wanted to look for numbers in a given subnet. So you cannot consider only space issues; you must decide which representation is more appropriate based on what you want to do with the values.

Smaller Types Versus Bigger Types

Smaller types can be processed more quickly than larger types. For one thing, they take less space and involve less overhead for disk activity. For strings, processing time is in direct relationship to string length.

In general, smaller tables are faster because query processing involves less disk I/O. For columns that use fixed-size types, choose the smallest type that will hold the required range of values. For example, don't use BIGINT if MEDIUMINT will do. Don't use DOUBLE if you only need FLOAT precision. For variable-size types, you may still be able to save space. A BLOB uses 2 bytes to record the length of the value, a LONGBLOB uses 4 bytes. If you're storing values that are never as long as 64KB, using BLOB saves you 2 bytes per value. (Similar considerations apply for TEXT types, of course.)

Fixed-Length Versus Variable-Length Types

In general, fixed-length types can be processed more quickly than variable-length types:

- With variable-length columns, you get more fragmentation of a table on which you perform many deletes or updates due to the differing sizes of the records. You'll need to run OPTIMIZE TABLE periodically to maintain performance. This is not an issue with fixed-length rows.

- Tables with fixed-length rows are easier to reconstruct if you have a table crash because the beginning of each record can be determined. This is not true with variable-length rows. This is not a performance issue with respect to query processing, but it can certainly speed up the table repair process.

If you have variable-length columns in your table, converting them to fixed-length columns will improve performance because fixed-length records are easier to process. Before you attempt to do this, though, consider the following:

- Using fixed-length columns involves a tradeoff. They're faster, but they take more space. CHAR(n) columns always take n bytes per value (even empty ones) because values are padded with trailing spaces when stored in the table. VARCHAR(n) columns take less space because only as much space is allocated as is necessary to store each value, plus one byte per value to record the length. Thus, if you are choosing between CHAR and VARCHAR columns, the tradeoff is one of time versus space. If speed is your primary concern, use CHAR columns to get the performance benefits of fixed-length columns. If space is at a premium, use VARCHAR columns.

- You cannot convert just one variable-length column; you must convert them all. And you must convert them all at the same time using a single ALTER TABLE statement, or the attempt will have no effect.

- Sometimes you cannot use a fixed-length type, even if you want to. There is no fixed-length type for strings longer than 255 characters, for example.

Indexable Types

Indexes speed up queries, so choose types you can index. See "Indexing Issues" for more information.

NULL Versus NOT NULL Types

If you declare a column NOT NULL, it can be handled more quickly because MySQL doesn't have to check the column's values during query processing to see whether or not they are NULL. It also saves one bit per row in the table.

Avoiding NULL in columns can make your queries simpler because you don't have to think about NULL as a special case. Simpler queries generally are processed more quickly.

The performance guidelines just presented sometimes conflict. For example, a fixed-length row containing CHAR columns will be faster than a variable-length row containing VARCHAR columns in terms of MySQL being able to locate rows. On the other hand, it will also take up more space, so you incur additional disk activity. From that point of view, VARCHAR may be faster. As a rule of thumb, you can assume that fixed-length rows will improve performance even though more space is used. For an especially critical application, you may wish to implement a table both ways and run some tests to determine which alternative actually is better for your particular application.

How Do You Want Your Values to be Compared?

You can cause string types to be compared and sorted in case-sensitive or not case-sensitive fashion by the way you declare them. Table 2.14 shows each type that is not case sensitive and the equivalent case-sensitive type. Some types (CHAR, VARCHAR) are binary or not binary according to the presence or absence of the keyword BINARY in the column declaration. The "binary-ness" of other types (BLOB, TEXT) is implicit in the type name.

Table 2.14 **Case Sensitivity of String Types**

Non-Binary Type (not case sensitive)	Binary Type (case sensitive)
CHAR(*M*)	CHAR(*M*) BINARY
VARCHAR(*M*)	VARCHAR(*M*) BINARY
TINYTEXT	TINYBLOB
TEXT	BLOB
MEDIUMTEXT	MEDIUMBLOB
LONGTEXT	LONGBLOB

Note that the binary (case-sensitive) types differ from the corresponding non-binary (not case-sensitive) types only in their comparison and sorting behavior. Any string type may contain any kind of data. In particular, the TEXT types can hold binary data just fine, despite the "TEXT" in the column type names.

If you want to use a column for both case-sensitive and not case-sensitive comparisons, use a non-binary type. Then, whenever you want a case-sensitive comparison, use the BINARY keyword to force a string to be treated as a binary string value. For example, if my_col is a CHAR column, you can compare it different ways:

```
my_col = "ABC"             Not case sensitive
BINARY my_col = "ABC"      Case sensitive
my_col = BINARY "ABC"      Case sensitive
```

If you have string values that you want to sort in some non-lexicographic order, consider using an ENUM column. Sorting of ENUM values occurs according to the order in which you list the enumeration values in the column declaration, so you can make those values sort in any order you want.

Do You Plan to Index a Column?

Indexes allow MySQL to process queries more efficiently. Choosing indexes is a topic covered in more detail in Chapter 4, but a general principle is that columns you commonly use in WHERE clauses to select rows are good candidates for indexing.

If you want to index a column or include it in a multiple-column index, there may be constraints on the types you can choose. In releases of MySQL earlier than 3.23.2, indexed columns must be declared NOT NULL, and you cannot index BLOB or TEXT types. These restrictions were lifted in MySQL 3.23.2, but if you're using an earlier version and cannot or do not want to upgrade, you must operate within those restrictions. However, you may be able to work around them in the following cases:

- If you can designate some value as special, you might be able to treat it as though it means the same thing as NULL. For a DATE column, you might designate

"`0000-00-00`" to mean "no date." In a string column, you might designate that the empty string means "missing value." In a numeric column, you might use −1 if the column normally would hold only non-negative values.

- You cannot index `BLOB` or `TEXT` types, but if your strings do not exceed 255 characters, use the equivalent `VARCHAR` column type and index that. You can use `VARCHAR(255) BINARY` for `BLOB` values and `VARCHAR(255)` for `TEXT` values.

Inter-Relatedness of Column Type Choice Issues

You can't always consider the issues involved in choosing column types as though they are independent of one another. For example, range is related to storage size for numeric types; as you increase the range, you require more storage, which affects performance. As another example, consider the implications of choosing to use `AUTO_INCREMENT` to create a column for holding unique sequence numbers. That single choice has several consequences, which involve column type, indexing, and use of `NULL`:

- `AUTO_INCREMENT` is a column attribute that should be used only with integer types. That immediately limits your choices to `TINYINT` through `BIGINT`.
- `AUTO_INCREMENT` columns should be indexed so that the current maximum sequence number can be ascertained quickly without a full scan of the table. Furthermore, to prevent sequence numbers from being reused, the index must be unique. This means you must declare the column as a `PRIMARY KEY` or as a `UNIQUE` index.
- If your version of MySQL is older than 3.23.2, indexed columns cannot contain `NULL` values, so you must declare the column `NOT NULL`.

All of this means you cannot just declare an `AUTO_INCREMENT` column like this:

```
my_col arbitrary_type AUTO_INCREMENT
```

You declare it like this:

```
my_col integer_type AUTO_INCREMENT NOT NULL PRIMARY KEY
```

Or like this:

```
my_col integer_type AUTO_INCREMENT NOT NULL, UNIQUE(my_col)
```

An additional consequence of using `AUTO_INCREMENT` is that since it is intended for generating a sequence of positive values, you may as well declare an `AUTO_INCREMENT` column as `UNSIGNED`:

```
my_col integer_type UNSIGNED AUTO_INCREMENT NOT NULL PRIMARY KEY
my_col integer_type UNSIGNED AUTO_INCREMENT NOT NULL, UNIQUE(my_col)
```

Expression Evaluation and Type Conversion

MySQL allows you to write expressions that include constants, function calls, and references to table columns. These values may be combined using different kinds of operators, such as arithmetic or comparison operators, and terms of an expression may be grouped with parentheses.

Expressions occur most commonly in the column selection list and WHERE clause of SELECT statements:

```
SELECT
    CONCAT(last_name, ", ", first_name),
    (TO_DAYS(death) - TO_DAYS(birth) / 365)
FROM president
WHERE
    birth > "1900-1-1" AND DEATH IS NOT NULL
```

Each column selected represents an expression, as does the content of the WHERE clause. Expressions also occur in the WHERE clause of DELETE and UPDATE statements, the VALUES() clause of INSERT statements, and so forth.

When MySQL encounters an expression, it evaluates it to produce a result. For example, (4*3)/(4-2) evaluates to the value 6. Expression evaluation may involve type conversion. For example, MySQL converts the number 960821 into a date "1996-08-21" when the number is used in a context requiring a date value.

This section discusses how you can write expressions in MySQL, and what the rules are that govern the various kinds of type conversions that MySQL performs during the process of expression evaluation. Each of MySQL's operators is listed here, but MySQL has so many functions that only a few are touched on. However, every operator and function is described further in Appendix C.

Writing Expressions

An expression can be as simple as a single constant:

0	Numeric constant
"abc"	String constant

Expressions can use function calls. Some functions take arguments (values inside the parentheses), and some do not. Multiple arguments should be separated by commas. When you invoke a function, there may be spaces around arguments, but there must be no space between the function name and the opening parenthesis:

NOW()	Function with no arguments
STRCMP("abc","def")	Function with two arguments
STRCMP("abc", "def")	Spaces around arguments are legal
STRCMP ("abc","def")	Space after function name is illegal

If there is a space after the function name, the MySQL parser may interpret the function name as a column name. (Function names are not reserved words and you can use them for column names if you want.) The usual result is a syntax error.

You can use table column values in expressions. In the simplest case, when the table to which a column belongs is clear from context, a column reference may be given simply as the column name. Only one table is named in each of the following SELECT statements, so the column references are unambiguous:

```
SELECT last_name, first_name FROM president
SELECT last_name, first_name FROM member
```

If it's not clear which table should be used, column names may be preceded by the table name. If it's not even clear which database should be used, the table name may be preceded by the database name. You can also use these more-specific forms in unambiguous contexts if you simply want to be more explicit:

```
SELECT
    president.last_name, president.first_name,
    member.last_name, member.first_name
FROM president, member
WHERE president.last_name = member.last_name

SELECT samp_db.student.name FROM samp_db.student
```

Finally, you can combine all these kinds of values to form more complex expressions.

Operator Types

MySQL includes several kinds of operators that may be used to combine terms of expressions. Arithmetic operators, listed in Table 2.15, include the usual addition, subtraction, multiplication, and division operators, as well as the modulo operator. Arithmetic is performed using BIGINT (64-bit) integer values for '+', '-', and '*' when both operands are integers, as well as for '/' and '%' when the operation is performed in a context where the result is expected to be an integer. Be aware that if an operation involves large values such that the result exceeds 64-bit range, you will get unpredictable results.

Table 2.15   **Arithmetic Operators**

Operator	Syntax	Meaning
+	a + b	Addition; sum of operands
-	a - b	Subtraction; difference of operands
-	-a	Unary minus; negation of operand
*	a * b	Multiplication; product of operands
/	a / b	Division; quotient of operands
%	a % b	Modulo; remainder after division of operands

Logical operators, shown in Table 2.16, evaluate expressions to determine whether they are true (non-zero) or false (zero). MySQL includes the C-style '&&', '||', and '!' operators as alternative forms of AND, OR, and NOT. Note in particular the '||' operator; ANSI SQL specifies || as the string concatenation operator, but in MySQL it signifies a logical OR operation. If you execute the following query, expecting it to perform string concatenation, you may be surprised to discover that it returns the number 0:

```
SELECT "abc" || "def"                          → 0
```

"abc" and "def" are converted to integers for the operation, and both turn into 0. In MySQL, you must use CONCAT("abc","def") to perform string concatenation.

Table 2.16 **Logical Operators**

Operator	Syntax	Meaning
AND, &&	a AND B, a && b	Logical intersection; true if both operands are true
OR, ||	a OR B, a || b	Logical union; true if either operand is true
NOT, !	NOT a, !a	Logical negation; true if operand is false

Bit operators, shown in Table 2.17, perform bitwise intersection and union, where each bit of the result is evaluated as the logical AND or OR of the corresponding bits of the operands. You can also perform bit shifts left or right. Bit operations are performed using BIGINT (64-bit) integer values.

Table 2.17 **Bit Operators**

Operator	Syntax	Meaning
&	a & b	Bitwise AND (intersection); each bit of result is set if corresponding bits of both operands are set
|	a | b	Bitwise OR (union); each bit of result is set if corresponding bit of either operand is set
<<	a << b	Left shift of a by b bit positions
>>	a >> b	Right shift of a by b bit positions

Comparison operators, shown in Table 2.18, include operators for testing relative magnitude or lexicographic ordering of numbers and strings, as well as operators for performing pattern matching and for testing NULL values. The '<=>' operator is MySQL-specific and was introduced in MySQL 3.23.

Table 2.18   **Comparison Operators**

Operator	Syntax	Meaning
=	a = b	True if operands are equal
!=, <>	a != b, a <> b	True if operands are not equal
<	a < b	True if a is less than b
<=	a <= b	True if a is less than or equal to b
>=	a >= b	True if a is greater than or equal to b
>	a > b	True if a is greater than b
IN	a IN (b1, b2, ...)	True if a is equal to any of b1, b2, ...
BETWEEN	a BETWEEN b AND c	True if a is between the values of b and c, inclusive
LIKE	a LIKE b	SQL pattern match; true if a matches b
NOT LIKE	a NOT LIKE b	SQL pattern match; true if a does not match b
REGEXP	a REGEXP b	Extended regular expression match; true if a matches b
NOT REGEXP	a NOT REGEXP b	Extended regular expression match; true if a does not match b
<=>	a <=> b	True if operands are equal (even if NULL)
IS NULL	a IS NULL	True if operand is NULL
IS NOT NULL	a IS NOT NULL	True if operand is not NULL

The BINARY operator is available as of MySQL 3.23 and may be used to cast (convert) a string to a binary string so that it is case sensitive in comparisons. The first of the following comparisons is not case sensitive, but the second and third ones are:

```
"abc" = "Abc"                      → 1
BINARY "abc" = "Abc"               → 0
"abc" = BINARY "Abc"               → 0
```

There is no corresponding NOT BINARY cast. If you expect to use a column both in case-sensitive and in not case-sensitive contexts, use a column type that is not case sensitive and use BINARY for those comparisons that you want to be case sensitive.

Comparisons are always case sensitive for columns that you declare using a binary string type (CHAR BINARY, VARCHAR BINARY, and the BLOB types). To achieve a comparison that is not case sensitive for such a column type, use UPPER() or LOWER() to convert both operands to the same case:

```
UPPER(col_name) < UPPER("Smith")
LOWER(col_name) < LOWER("Smith")
```

For string comparisons that are not case sensitive, it is possible that multiple characters will be considered equivalent, depending on your character set. For example 'E' and 'É' might be treated the same for comparison and ordering operations. Binary (case sensitive) comparisons are done using the ASCII values of the characters.

Pattern matching allows you to look for values without having to specify an exact literal value. MySQL provides SQL pattern matching using the `LIKE` operator and the wildcard characters '%' (match any sequence of characters) and '_' (match any single character). MySQL also provides pattern matching based on the `REGEXP` operator and extended regular expressions that are similar to those used in UNIX programs such as `grep`, `sed`, and `vi`. You must use one of these pattern-matching operators to perform a pattern match; you cannot use '='. To reverse the sense of a pattern match, use `NOT LIKE` or `NOT REGEXP`.

The two types of pattern matching differ in important respects besides the use of different operators and pattern characters:

- `LIKE` is not case sensitive unless at least one operand is a binary string. `REGEXP` is case sensitive.[6]

- SQL patterns match only if the entire string is matched. Regular expressions match if the pattern is found anywhere in the string.

Patterns used with the `LIKE` operator may include the '%' and '_' wildcard characters. For example, the pattern `"Frank%"` matches any string that begins with `"Frank"`:

```
"Franklin" LIKE "Frank%"                      → 1
"Frankfurter" LIKE "Frank%"                   → 1
```

The wildcard character '%' matches any sequence of characters, including the empty sequence, so `"Frank%"` matches `"Frank"`:

```
"Frank" LIKE "Frank%"                         → 1
```

This also means the pattern `"%"` matches any string, including the empty string. However, `"%"` will not match `NULL`. In fact, any pattern match with a `NULL` operand fails:

```
"Frank" LIKE NULL                             → NULL
NULL LIKE "Frank%"                            → NULL
```

MySQL's `LIKE` operator is not case sensitive, unless one of its operands is a binary string. Thus, `"Frank%"` matches both of the strings `"Frankly"` and `"frankly"` by default, but matches only one of them in a binary comparison:

```
"Frankly" LIKE "Frank%"                       → 1
"frankly" LIKE "Frank%"                       → 1
BINARY "Frankly" LIKE "Frank%"                → 1
BINARY "frankly" LIKE "Frank%"                → 0
```

This differs from the ANSI SQL `LIKE` operator, which is case sensitive.

---

[6] As of MySQL 3.23.4, `REGEXP` is not case sensitive unless at least one operand is a binary string.

The wildcard character may be specified anywhere in the pattern. `"%bert"` matches `"Englebert"`, `"Bert"`, and `"Albert"`. `"%bert%"` matches all of those strings, and also strings like `"Berthold"`, `"Bertram"`, and `"Alberta"`.

The other wildcard character allowed with LIKE is '`_`', which matches any single character. `"___"` matches any string of exactly three characters. `"c_t"` matches `"cat"`, `"cot"`, `"cut"`, and even `"c_t"` (because '`_`' matches itself).

To turn off the special meaning of '`%`' or '`_`', to match literal instances of these characters, precede them by a backslash ('`\%`' or '`\_`'):

```
"abc" LIKE "a%c"                              → 1
"abc" LIKE "a\%c"                             → 0
"a%c" LIKE "a\%c"                             → 1
```

MySQL's other form of pattern matching uses regular expressions. The operator is REGEXP rather than LIKE. (RLIKE is a synonym for REGEXP.) The most common regular expression pattern characters are as follows:

'`.`' matches any single character:

```
"abc" REGEXP "a.c"                            → 1
```

'`[...]`' matches any character between the square brackets. You can specify a range of characters by listing the endpoints of the range separated by a dash '`-`'. To negate the sense of the class (to match any character not listed), specify '`^`' as the first character of the class:

```
"abc" REGEXP "[a-z]"                          → 1
"abc" REGEXP "[^a-z]"                         → 0
```

'`*`' means "match any number of the previous thing," so that, for example, '`x*`' matches any number of '`x`' characters:

```
"abcdef" REGEXP "a.*f"                        → 1
"abc" REGEXP "[0-9]*abc"                      → 1
"abc" REGEXP "[0-9][0-9]*"                    → 0
```

"Any number" includes zero instances, which is why the second expression succeeds. '`^pat`' and '`pat$`' anchor a pattern match so that the pattern *pat* matches only when it occurs at the beginning or end of a string, and '`^pat$`' matches only if *pat* matches the entire string:

```
"abc" REGEXP "b"                              → 1
"abc" REGEXP "^b"                             → 0
"abc" REGEXP "b$"                             → 0
"abc" REGEXP "^abc$"                          → 1
"abcd" REGEXP "^abc$"                         → 0
```

The REGEXP pattern can be taken from a table column, although this will be slower than a constant pattern if the column contains several different values. The pattern must be examined and converted to internal form each time the column value changes.

MySQL's regular expression matching has other special pattern characters as well. See Appendix C for more information.

Operator Precedence

When MySQL evaluates an expression, it looks at the operators to determine the order in which it should group the terms of the expression. Some operators have higher precedence; that is, they are "stronger" than others in the sense that they are evaluated earlier than others. For example, multiplication and division have higher precedence than addition and subtraction. The following two expressions are equivalent because '*' and '/' are evaluated before '+' and '-':

```
1 + 2 * 3 - 4 / 5                               → 6.2
1 + 6 - .8                                      → 6.2
```

Operator precedence is shown in the following list, from highest precedence to lowest. Operators listed on the same line have the same precedence. Operators at a higher precedence level are evaluated before operators at a lower precedence level.

```
BINARY
NOT  !
- (unary minus)
*  /  %
+  -
<<  >>
&
|
<  <=  =  <=>  !=  <>  >=  >  IN  IS  LIKE  REGEXP  RLIKE
BETWEEN
AND  &&
OR  ||
```

You can use parentheses to override the precedence of operators and change the order in which expression terms are evaluated:

```
1 + 2 * 3 - 4 / 5                               → 6.2
(1 + 2) * (3 - 4) / 5                           → -0.6
```

NULL Values in Expressions

Take care when you use the NULL value in expressions because the result may not always be what you expect. The following guidelines will help you avoid surprises.

If you supply NULL as an operand to any arithmetic or bit operator, the result is NULL:

```
1 + NULL                                        → NULL
1 | NULL                                        → NULL
```

If you use NULL with a logical operator, the NULL is considered false:

```
1 AND NULL                                      → 0
1 OR NULL                                       → 1
0 AND NULL                                      → 0
0 OR NULL                                       → 0
```

NULL as an operand to any comparison operator produces a NULL result, except for the '<=>', IS NULL, and IS NOT NULL operators, which are intended specifically for dealing with NULL values:

1 = NULL	→ NULL
NULL = NULL	→ NULL
1 <=> NULL	→ 0
NULL <=> NULL	→ 1
1 IS NULL	→ 0
NULL IS NULL	→ 1

Functions generally return NULL if given NULL arguments, except for those functions designed to deal with NULL arguments. For example, IFNULL() is able to handle NULL arguments and returns true or false appropriately. STRCMP() expects non-NULL arguments; if it discovers you've passed it a NULL argument, it returns NULL rather than true or false.

In sorting operations, NULL values group together. NULL sorts ahead of all non-NULL values (including the empty string) for an ascending sort and after all non-NULL values for a descending sort.

Type Conversion

MySQL performs extensive type conversion automatically according to the kind of operation you're performing, whenever a value of one type is used in a context that requires a value of another type. Type conversion may occur for any of the following reasons:

- Conversion of operands to a type appropriate for evaluation of an operator
- Conversion of a function argument to a type expected by the function
- Conversion of a value for assignment into a table column that has a different type

The following expression involves type conversion. It consists of the addition operator '+' and two operands, 1 and "2":

```
1 + "2"
```

The operands are of different types (number and string), so MySQL converts one of them to make them the same type. But which one should it change? In this case, '+' is a numeric operator, so MySQL wants the operands to be numbers and converts the string "2" to the number 2. Then it evaluates the expression to produce the result 3. Here's another example. The CONCAT() function concatenates strings to produce a longer string as a result. To do this, it interprets its arguments as strings, no matter what type they are. If you pass it a bunch of numbers, CONCAT() will convert them to strings, then return their concatenation:

CONCAT(1,2,3)	→ "123"

If the call to CONCAT() is part of a larger expression, further type conversion may take place. Consider the following expression and its result:

```
REPEAT('X',CONCAT(1,2,3)/10)                    → "XXXXXXXXXXXX"
```

CONCAT(1,2,3) produces the string "123". The expression "123"/10 is converted to 123/10 because division is an arithmetic operator. The result of this expression would be 12.3 in floating-point context, but REPEAT() expects an integer repeat count, so an integer division is performed to produce 12. Then REPEAT('X',12) produces a string result of 12 'X' characters.

A general principle to keep in mind is that MySQL attempts to convert values to the type required by an expression rather than generating an error. Depending on the context, it will convert values of each of the three general categories (numbers, strings, or dates and times) to values in any of the other categories. However, values can't always be converted from one type to another. If a value to be converted into a given type doesn't look like a legal value for that type, the conversion fails. Conversion to numbers of things like "abc" that don't look like numbers results in a value of 0. Conversion to date or time types of things that don't look like a date or time result in the "zero" value for the type. For example, converting the string "abc" to a date results in the "zero" date "0000-00-00". On the other hand, any value can be treated as a string, so generally it's not a problem to convert a value to a string.

MySQL also performs more minor type conversions. If you use a floating-point value in an integer context, the value is converted (with rounding). Conversion in the other direction works as well; an integer can be used without problem as a floating-point number.

Hexadecimal constants are treated as strings unless the context clearly indicates a number. In string contexts, each pair of hexidecimal digits is converted to a character and the result is used as a string. The following examples illustrate how this works:

```
0x61                                            → "a"
0x61 + 0                                        → 97
CONCAT(0x61)                                    → "a"
CONCAT(0x61 + 0)                                → "97"
```

The same interpretative principle applies in comparisons; a hexadecimal constant is treated as a string unless it is compared to a number:

```
10 = 0x0a                                       → 1
10 = 0x09                                       → 0
"\n" = 0x0a                                      → 1
"\n" = 0x0a + 0                                  → 0
("\n" = 0x0a) + 0                                → 1
```

Some operators force conversion of the operands to the type expected by the operator, no matter what the type of the operands is. Arithmetic operators are an example of this; they expect numbers, and the operands are converted accordingly:

```
3 + 4                                           → 7
"3" + 4                                          → 7
"3" + "4"                                        → 7
```

It's not enough for a string simply to contain a number somewhere. MySQL doesn't look all through the string hoping to find a number; it looks only at the beginning. If a string has no leading numeric part, the conversion result is 0.

```
"1973-2-4" + 0                              → 1973
"12:14:01" + 0                              → 12
"23-skidoo" + 0                             → 23
"-23-skidoo" + 0                            → -23
"carbon-14" + 0                             → 0
```

Be aware that MySQL's string-to-number conversion rule has changed as of version 3.23. Prior to that version, numeric-looking strings were converted to integer values, with rounding. From 3.23 on, they are converted to floating-point values:

```
"-428.9" + 0                                → -429 (MySQL < 3.23)
"-428.9" + 0                                → -428.9 (MySQL ≥ 3.23)
```

The logical and bit operators are even stricter than the arithmetic operators. They want the operators to be not only numeric, but to be integers, and type conversion is performed accordingly. This means that a floating-point number such as 0.3 is not considered true, even though it's non-zero; that's because when it's converted to an integer, the result is 0. In the following expressions, the operands are not considered true until they have a value of at least 1.

```
0.3 OR .04                                  → 0
1.3 OR .04                                  → 1
0.3 AND .04                                 → 0
1.3 AND .04                                 → 0
1.3 AND 1.04                                → 1
```

This type of conversion also occurs with the IF() function, which expects the first argument to be an integer. To test floating-point values properly, it's best to use an explicit comparison. Otherwise, values less than 1 will be considered false:

```
IF(1.3,"non-zero","zero")                   → "non-zero"
IF(0.3,"non-zero","zero")                   → "zero"
IF(0.3>0,"non-zero","zero")                 → "non-zero"
```

Pattern matching operators expect to operate on strings. This means you can use MySQL's pattern matching operators on numbers because it will convert them to strings in the attempt to find a match!

```
12345 LIKE "1%"                             → 1
12345 REGEXP "1.*5"                         → 1
```

The magnitude comparison operators ('<', '<=', '=', and so on) are context sensitive; that is, they are evaluated according to the types of their operands. The following expression compares the operands numerically because they are both numbers:

```
2 < 11                                      → 1
```

This expression involves a string (lexicographic) comparison because both operands are strings:

```
"2" < "11"                                    → 0
```

In the following comparisons, the types are mixed, so MySQL compares them as numbers. As a result, both expressions are true:

```
"2" < 11                                      → 1
2 < "11"                                      → 1
```

In comparisons, MySQL converts operands as necessary according to the following rules:

- Other than for the '<=>' operator, comparisons involving NULL values evaluate as NULL. ('<=>' is like '=', except that NULL <=> NULL is true.)

- If both operands are strings, they are compared lexicographically as strings. String comparisons are performed using the character set in force on the server.

- If both operands are integers, they are compared numerically as integers.

- Hexadecimal constants that are not compared to a number are compared as binary strings.

- If either operand is a TIMESTAMP or DATETIME value and the other is a constant, the operands are compared as TIMESTAMP values. This is done to make comparisons work better for ODBC applications.

- Otherwise, the operands are compared numerically as floating-point values. Note that this includes the case of comparing a string and a number. The string is converted to a number, which results in a value of 0 if the string doesn't look like a number. For example, "14.3" converts to 14.3, but "L4.3" converts to 0.

Date and Time Interpretation Rules

MySQL freely converts strings and numbers to date and time values as demanded by context in an expression, and vice versa. Date and time values are converted to numbers in numeric context; numbers are converted to dates or times in date or time contexts. This conversion to a date or time value happens when you assign a value to a date or time column or when a function requires a date or time value. In comparisons, the general rule is that date and time values are compared as strings.

If the table my_table contains a DATE column date_col, the following statements are equivalent:

```
INSERT INTO my_table SET date_col = "1997-04-13"
INSERT INTO my_table SET date_col = "19970413"
INSERT INTO my_table SET date_col = 19970413
```

In the following examples, the argument to the TO_DAYS() function is interpreted as the same value for all three expressions:

```
TO_DAYS("1997-04-10")                          → 729489
TO_DAYS("19970410")                            → 729489
TO_DAYS(19970410)                              → 729489
```

Testing and Forcing Type Conversion

To see how type conversion will be handled in an expression, use the mysql program to issue a SELECT query that evaluates the expression:

```
mysql> SELECT 0x41, 0x41 + 0;
+-------+----------+
| 0x41  | 0x41 + 0 |
+-------+----------+
| A     |       65 |
+-------+----------+
```

As you might imagine, I did quite a bit of that sort of thing while writing this chapter!

Testing expression evaluation is especially important for statements such as DELETE or UPDATE that modify records because you want to be sure you're affecting only the intended rows. One way to check an expression is to run a preliminary SELECT statement with the same WHERE clause that you're going to use with the DELETE or UPDATE statement to verify that the clause selects the proper rows. Suppose the table my_table has a CHAR column char_col containing these values:

```
"abc"
"def"
"00"
"ghi"
"jkl"
"00"
"mno"
```

Given these values, what is the effect of the following query?

```
DELETE FROM my_table WHERE char_col = 00
```

The *intended* effect is probably to delete the two rows containing the value "00". The actual effect is to delete all the rows—an unpleasant surprise. This happens as a consequence of MySQL's comparison rules. char_col is a string column, but 00 is not quoted, so it is treated as a number. By MySQL's comparison rules, a comparison involving a string and a number is evaluated as a comparison of two numbers. As the DELETE query is performed, each value of char_col is converted to a number and compared to 0: "00" converts to 0, but so do all the strings that don't look like numbers. Therefore, the WHERE clause is true for every row, and the DELETE statement empties the table. Obviously, this is a case where it would have been prudent to test the

WHERE clause with a SELECT statement prior to executing the DELETE, because that would have shown you that too many rows are selected by the expression:

```
mysql> SELECT char_col FROM my_table WHERE char_col = 00;
+----------+
¦ char_col ¦
+----------+
¦ "abc"    ¦
¦ "def"    ¦
¦ "00"     ¦
¦ "ghi"    ¦
¦ "jkl"    ¦
¦ "00"     ¦
¦ "mno"    ¦
+----------+
```

When you're uncertain about the way a value will be used, you may want to exploit MySQL's expression evaluation mechanism to force conversion of a value to a particular type:

- Add +0 or +0.0 to a term to force conversion to a numeric value:

0x65	→ "e"
0x65 + 0	→ 101
0x65 + 0.0	→ 101.0

- Use CONCAT() to turn a value into a string:

14	→ 14
CONCAT(14)	→ "14"

- Use ASCII() to get the ASCII value of a character:

"A"	→ "A"
ASCII("A")	→ 65

- Use DATE_ADD() to force a string or number to be treated as a date:

19990101	→ 19990101
DATE_ADD(19990101, INTERVAL 0 DAY)	→ "1999-01-01"
"19990101"	→ "19990101"
DATE_ADD("19990101", INTERVAL 0 DAY)	→ "1999-01-01"

Conversion of Out-of-Range or Illegal Values

The basic principle is this: Garbage in, garbage out. If you don't verify your data first before storing it, you may not like what you get. Having said that, here are some general principles that describe MySQL's handling of out-of-range or otherwise improper values:

- For numeric or TIME columns, values that are outside the legal range are clipped to the nearest endpoint of the range and the resulting value is stored.

- For string columns other than ENUM or SET, strings that are too long are truncated to fit the maximum length of the column. Assignments to an ENUM or SET column depend on the values that are listed as legal when the column is declared. If you assign to an ENUM column a value that is not listed as an enumeration member, the error member is assigned instead (that is, the empty string that corresponds to the zero-valued member). If you assign to a SET column a value containing substrings that are not listed as set members, those strings drop out and the column is assigned a value consisting of the remaining members.

- For date or time columns, illegal values are converted to the appropriate "zero" value for the type (see Table 2.11). For date and time columns other than TIME, values that are outside the range for a type may be converted to the "zero" value, to NULL, or to some other value. (In other words, the results are unpredictable.)

These conversions are reported as warnings for ALTER TABLE, LOAD DATA, UPDATE, and multiple-row INSERT statements. In the mysql client, this information is displayed in the status line that is reported for a query. In a programming language, you may be able to get this information by some other means. If you're using the MySQL C API, you can call the mysql_info() function. With the Perl DBI API, you can use the mysql_info attribute of your database connection. The information provided is a count of the number of warnings. To see which rows were changed, you can issue a SELECT ... INTO OUTFILE query and compare the result to the original rows.

3

MySQL SQL Syntax and Use

Fluency with SQL is necessary in order to communicate with the MySQL server. For example, when you use a program such as the `mysql` client, it functions primarily as a means for you to send SQL statements to the server to be executed. But you must also know SQL if you write programs that use the MySQL interface provided by your programming language because you'll still communicate with the server by sending SQL statements to it.

Chapter 1, "Introduction to MySQL and SQL," presented a tutorial introduction to many of MySQL's capabilities. This chapter builds on that material to go into more detail on several areas of SQL implemented by MySQL. It discusses how to refer to elements of databases, including the rules for naming and what case sensitivity constraints apply. It also describes many of the more important SQL statements, such as those for creating and destroying databases, tables, and indexes; statements for retrieving data using joins; and statements that provide information about your databases and tables. The discussion highlights some of the extensions that MySQL provides to standard SQL.

What's Present and What's Missing in MySQL?

MySQL's SQL statements may be grouped into several broad categories, as shown in Figure 3.1. In this chapter, we'll cover statements in the first four categories shown in this figure. Some of the MySQL utilities provide what is essentially a command line interface to certain SQL statements. For example, `mysqlshow` is an interface to the `SHOW COLUMNS` statement. Where appropriate, those equivalencies are described in this chapter, too.

Of the statements not covered here, several are discussed in other chapters. For example, the `GRANT` and `REVOKE` statements for setting up user privileges are dealt with in Chapter 11, "General MySQL Administration." The invocation syntax for all statements is listed in Appendix D, "SQL Syntax Reference." In addition, you should consult the MySQL Reference Manual for additional information, especially for changes made in recent versions of MySQL.

The final section of the chapter describes what MySQL does *not* include—that is, what features it lacks. These are capabilities found in some other databases but not in MySQL. Such features include subselects, transactions, referential integrity, triggers, stored procedures, and views. Do these omissions mean that MySQL isn't a "real" database system? Some people think so, but in response I'll simply observe that the lack of these capabilities in MySQL hasn't stopped large numbers of people from using it. That's probably because for many applications, lack of those features doesn't matter. For other cases, methods exist for working around a missing feature. Lack of cascading delete, for example, means you may need to issue an extra query in your applications when you delete records from a table. Lack of transaction support may not matter to you if you find it sufficient to use MySQL's ability to group statements for uninterrupted execution by surrounding them with `LOCK TABLES` and `UNLOCK TABLES` statements.

(The real issue here isn't generally lack of transactions; it's the lack of automatic rollback to cancel all of the statements if any of them fail. If you have applications with requirements such as the need to perform complex financial transactions involving several interlocking statements that must be executed as a group or not at all, then you may want to consider a database with commit/rollback capabilities, such as Postgres.) Some features are missing simply because they haven't been implemented yet. For example, subselects are not present in MySQL as I write, but are scheduled to be included in version 3.24, which may be out by the time you read this.

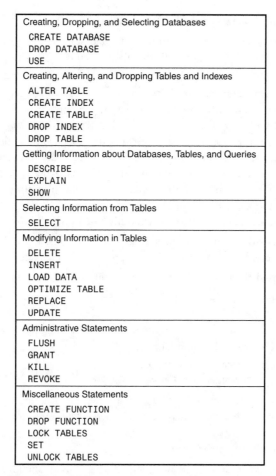

Creating, Dropping, and Selecting Databases
```
CREATE DATABASE
DROP DATABASE
USE
```

Creating, Altering, and Dropping Tables and Indexes
```
ALTER TABLE
CREATE INDEX
CREATE TABLE
DROP INDEX
DROP TABLE
```

Getting Information about Databases, Tables, and Queries
```
DESCRIBE
EXPLAIN
SHOW
```

Selecting Information from Tables
```
SELECT
```

Modifying Information in Tables
```
DELETE
INSERT
LOAD DATA
OPTIMIZE TABLE
REPLACE
UPDATE
```

Administrative Statements
```
FLUSH
GRANT
KILL
REVOKE
```

Miscellaneous Statements
```
CREATE FUNCTION
DROP FUNCTION
LOCK TABLES
SET
UNLOCK TABLES
```

Figure 3.1 SQL statements supported by MySQL.

MySQL Naming Rules

Almost every SQL statement refers in some way to a database or its constituent elements. This section describes the syntax rules for referring to databases, tables, columns, indexes, and aliases. Names are subject to case sensitivity considerations, which are described as well.

Referring to Elements of Databases

When you use names to refer to elements of databases, you are constrained by the characters you can use and the length that names can be. The form of names also depends on the context in which you use them:

- **Legal characters in names.** Names may consist of any alphanumeric characters in the character set used by the server, plus the characters '_' and '$'. Names may start with any character that is legal in a name, including a digit. However, a name may not consist solely of digits because that would make it indistinguishable from a number. The ability that MySQL provides to begin a name with a number is unusual. If you use such a name, be particularly careful of names containing an 'E' or 'e' because those characters can lead to ambiguous expressions. 23e + 14 means column 23e plus 14, but what about 23e+14? Does it mean the same thing, or is it a number in scientific notation?

- **Name length.** Names for databases, tables, columns, and indexes may be up to 64 characters long. Alias names may be up to 256 characters long.

- **Name qualifiers.** To refer to a database, just specify its name:

  ```
  USE db_name
  SHOW TABLES FROM db_name
  ```

  To refer to a table, you have two choices. A fully qualified table name consists of a database name and a table name:

  ```
  SHOW TABLES FROM db_name.tbl_name
  SELECT * FROM db_name.tbl_name
  ```

  A table name by itself refers to a table in the default (current) database. If samp_db is the default database, the following statements are equivalent:

  ```
  SELECT * FROM member
  SELECT * FROM samp_db.member
  ```

  To refer to a column, there are three choices: fully qualified, partially qualified, and unqualified. A fully qualified name (written as *db_name.tbl_name.col_name*) is completely specified. A partially qualified name (written as *tbl_name.col_name*) refers to a column in the named table. An unqualified name (written simply as *col_name*) refers to whatever table is indicated by the surrounding context. The following two queries refer to the same column names, but the context supplied by the FROM clauses indicates which tables to select the columns from:

  ```
  SELECT last_name, first_name FROM president
  SELECT last_name, first_name FROM members
  ```

It's usually unnecessary to supply fully qualified names, although it's always legal to do so if you like. If you select a database with a USE statement, that database becomes the default database and is implicit in every unqualified table reference. If you're using a SELECT statement that refers to only one table, that table is implicit for every column reference in the statement. It's necessary to qualify names only when a table or database cannot be determined from context. Here are some situations in which ambiguity arises:

- *Queries that refer to tables from multiple databases.* Any table not in the default database must be referenced using the *db_name.tbl_name* form to let MySQL know which database to look in to find the table.

- *Queries that select a column from multiple tables,* where more than one table contains a column with that name.

Case Sensitivity in SQL Statements

Case sensitivity rules in SQL statements vary for different parts of the statement, and also depend on what you referring to and the operating system on which the server is running:

- **SQL keywords and function names.** Keywords and function names are not case sensitive. They may be given in any lettercase. The following statements are equivalent:

```
SELECT NOW()
select now()
sElEcT nOw()
```

- **Database and table names.** Databases and tables in MySQL correspond to directories and files in the underlying file system on the server host. As a result, case sensitivity of database and table names depends on the way the operating system on that host treats filenames. A server running on UNIX treats database and table names as case sensitive because UNIX filenames are case sensitive. Windows filenames are not case sensitive, so a server running on Windows does not treat database and table names as case sensitive.

  You should be aware of this characteristic if you create a database on a UNIX server that you might someday move to a Windows server: If you create two tables named abc and ABC, they would not be distinguishable on a Windows machine. One way to avoid having this become an issue is to pick a given lettercase (for example, lowercase) and always create databases and tables using names in that lettercase. Then case of names won't be an issue if you move a database to a different server.

- **Column and index names.** Column and index names are not case sensitive in MySQL. The following queries are equivalent:

```
SELECT name FROM student
SELECT NAME FROM student
SELECT nAmE FROM student
```

- **Alias names.** Aliases are case sensitive. You can specify an alias in any lettercase (upper, lower, or mixed), but you must refer to it elsewhere in the query using the same case.

Regardless of whether or not a database, table, or alias name is case sensitive, you must refer to a given name from any of those categories using the same lettercase throughout a query. That is not true for SQL keywords; function names; or column and index names; which may be referred to in varying lettercase style throughout a query. Naturally, the query will be more readable if you use a consistent lettercase rather than "ransom note" style (SelECt NamE FrOm ...).

Creating, Dropping, and Selecting Databases

MySQL provides three database-level statements: CREATE DATABASE for creating databases, DROP DATABASE for removing them, and USE for selecting a default database.

The CREATE DATABASE Statement

Creating a database is easy; just name it in a CREATE DATABASE statement:

```
CREATE DATABASE db_name
```

The constraints are that the name must be legal, the database must not already exist, and you must have sufficient privileges to create it.

The DROP DATABASE Statement

Dropping a database is just as easy as creating one, assuming you have sufficient privileges:

```
DROP DATABASE db_name
```

However, the DROP DATABASE statement is not something you should use with wild abandon. It removes the database and all tables within it. After you drop a database, it's gone forever. In other words, don't try out this statement just to see how it works. If your administrator has been performing database backups regularly, you may be able to get the database back. But I can guarantee that no administrator will be sympathetic if you say, "Uh, I was just playing around with DROP DATABASE to see what would happen, and, uh...can you restore my database for me?"

Note that a database is represented by a directory under the data directory. If you have put non-table files in that directory, they are not deleted by the DROP DATABASE statement. In that case, the database directory itself is not removed, either.

The USE Statement

The USE statement selects a database to make it the default (current) database for a given connection to the server:

```
USE db_name
```

You must have some access privilege for the database or you cannot select it. It's not actually necessary to select a database to use the tables in it because you can refer to its tables using *db_name.tbl_name* form. However, it's much more convenient to refer to tables without having to specify a database qualifier.

Selecting a default database doesn't mean it must be the default for the duration of the connection. You can issue any number of USE statements to switch back and forth among databases as often as you like, as long as you have access privileges to use them. Selecting a database also doesn't limit you to using tables only from that database. You can still refer to tables in other databases by qualifying table names with a database name.

When a connection to the server terminates, any notion by the server of what the default database was disappears. That is, if you connect to the server again, it doesn't remember what database you had selected previously. In fact, that's not even an idea that makes any sense, given that MySQL is multi-threaded and can handle multiple connections from a given user, which can connect and disconnect in any order. In this environment, it's not clear what the meaning of "the previously selected database" might be.

Creating, Dropping, Indexing, and Altering Tables

MySQL allows you to create tables, drop (remove) them, and change their structure using the CREATE TABLE, DROP TABLE, and ALTER TABLE statements. For each of these statements, there are MySQL-specific extensions that make them more useful. The CREATE INDEX and DROP INDEX statements allow you to add or remove indexes on existing tables.

The CREATE TABLE Statement

Tables are created with CREATE TABLE. The full syntax for this statement is pretty horrendous because there are so many optional clauses, but in practice this statement is usually fairly simple to use. For example, all of the CREATE TABLE statements that we used in Chapter 1 are reasonably uncomplicated.

Ironically, much of this additional complexity comes from clauses that MySQL parses and then throws away! You can see this complexity by referring to Appendix D. Take a look at the entry for CREATE TABLE and notice how much of the statement syntax is devoted to the REFERENCES, CONSTRAINT, and CHECK clauses. Those clauses concern foreign keys, referential integrity, and input value restriction. MySQL doesn't support these features, but it parses the syntax to make it easier to use table definitions that you've created in other database systems. (You can use that code more easily with less editing.) If you're writing your own table descriptions from scratch, you can completely forget about having to deal with those clauses. I won't say another word about them in this section.

The `CREATE TABLE` specifies, at a minimum, the table name and a list of the columns in it. For example:

```
CREATE TABLE my_table
(
    name CHAR(20),
    age INT NOT NULL,
    weight INT,
    sex ENUM('F','M')
)
```

In addition to the columns that make up a table, you can specify how the table should be indexed when you create it. Another option is to leave the table unindexed when you create it and add the indexes later. That's a good strategy if you plan to populate the table with a lot of data before you begin using it for queries. Updating indexes as you insert each row is much slower than loading the data into an unindexed table and creating the indexes afterward.

We have already covered the basic syntax for the `CREATE TABLE` statement in Chapter 1 and discussed how to describe the column types in Chapter 2, "Working with Data in MySQL." I assume you've read those chapters, so we won't repeat the material here. Instead, for the remainder of this section, we'll deal with some important extensions to the `CREATE TABLE` statement that were introduced in MySQL 3.23 and that give you a lot of flexibility in how you construct tables:

- Table storage-type specifiers
- Creation of a table only if it doesn't already exist
- Temporary tables that are dropped automatically when the client session ends
- The capability to create a table simply by selecting the data you want it to contain

Table Storage-Type Specifiers

Prior to MySQL 3.23, all user-created tables used the ISAM storage method. In MySQL 3.23, you can explicitly create tables in any of three types by specifying `TYPE = type` after the column list part of the `CREATE TABLE` statement. `type` can be `MYISAM`, `ISAM`, or `HEAP`. For example:

```
CREATE TABLE my_tbl (i INT, c CHAR(20)) TYPE = HEAP
```

You can convert tables from one type to another with `ALTER TABLE`:

```
ALTER TABLE my_tbl TYPE = ISAM
ALTER TABLE my_tbl TYPE = MYISAM
ALTER TABLE my_tbl TYPE = HEAP
```

It may not be a good idea to convert a table to type HEAP, however, if you expect the table to last beyond server shutdown. HEAP tables are held in memory and disappear when the server exits.

The general characteristics of these three table types are as follows:

- **MyISAM Tables.** The MyISAM storage format is the default table type in MySQL as of version 3.23:

  - Files can be larger than for the ISAM storage method if your operating system itself allows larger files.

  - Data are stored in machine-independent format with the low byte first. This means you can copy tables from one machine to another, even if they have different architectures.

  - Numeric index values take less storage space because they are stored with the high byte first. Index values tend to vary faster in the low-order bytes, so high-order bytes are more subject to compression.

  - `AUTO_INCREMENT` handling is better than for ISAM tables. The details of this are discussed in Chapter 2 in the section "Working with Sequences."

  - Several indexing constraints have been relaxed. For example, you can index columns that contain `NULL` values, and you can index `BLOB` and `TEXT` types.

  - For improved table integrity checking, each table has a flag that is set when the table is checked by `myisamchk`. You can use `myisamchk —fast` to skip checks on tables that haven't been modified since the previous check, which makes this administrative task quicker. Tables also have a flag indicating whether a table was closed properly. If the server shuts down abnormally or the machine crashes, the flag can be used to detect tables that need to be checked at server startup time.

- **ISAM Tables.** The ISAM storage format is the older format used prior to MySQL 3.23 but still available currently. In general, MyISAM tables are preferable to ISAM tables because they have fewer limitations. Support for ISAM tables will likely fade as this storage format is supplanted by the MyISAM table format.

- **HEAP Tables.** The HEAP storage format creates in-memory tables that use fixed-length rows, which makes them very fast. It also means they are temporary in the sense that they disappear when the server terminates. However, in contrast to temporary tables created with `CREATE TEMPORARY TABLE`, HEAP tables are visible to other clients. Several constraints apply to HEAP tables that do not apply to MyISAM or ISAM tables:

  - Indexes are used only for '=' and '<=>' comparisons.

  - You cannot have `NULL` values in indexed columns.

- `BLOB` and `TEXT` columns cannot be used.
- `AUTO_INCREMENT` columns cannot be used.

Provisional Table Creation

To create a table only if it doesn't already exist, use `CREATE TABLE IF NOT EXISTS`. You can use this for an application that makes no assumptions about whether tables that it needs have been set up in advance and simply attempts to create the tables as a matter of course. The `IF NOT EXISTS` modifier is particularly useful for scripts that you run as batch jobs with `mysql`. In this context, a regular `CREATE TABLE` statement doesn't work very well. The first time the job runs, the tables are created, but the second time an error occurs because the tables already exist. If you use `IF NOT EXISTS`, there is no problem. The first time the job runs, the tables are created, as before. For second and subsequent times, table creation attempts fail, but no error is generated. This allows the job to continue processing as if the attempt had succeeded.

Temporary Tables

You can use `CREATE TEMPORARY TABLE` to create temporary tables that disappear automatically when your session ends. This is handy because you don't have to bother issuing a `DROP TABLE` statement explicitly to get rid of the table, and the table doesn't hang around if your session terminates abnormally. For example, if you have a canned query in a file that you run with `mysql` and you decide not to wait for it to finish, you can kill the script in the middle with impunity and the server will remove any temporary tables.

In older versions of MySQL, there are no true temporary tables, except in the sense that you consider them temporary in your own mind. For applications that need such a table, you must remember to drop it yourself. If you forget to drop it, or an error occurs in the client causing it to exit early, the temporary table hangs around until someone notices and removes it.

A temporary table is visible only to the client that creates the table. The name can be the same as that of an existing permanent table. This is not an error, nor does the existing permanent table get clobbered. Suppose you create a temporary table in the `samp_db` database named `member`. The original `member` table becomes hidden (inaccessible), and references to `member` refer to the temporary table. If you issue a `DROP TABLE member` statement, the temporary table is removed and the original `member` table "reappears." If you simply disconnect from the server without dropping the temporary table, the server automatically drops it for you. The next time you connect, the original `member` table is visible again.

The name-hiding mechanism works only to one level. That is, you cannot create two temporary tables with the same name.

Creating Tables from SELECT Results

One of the key concepts of relational databases is that everything is represented as a table of rows and columns, and the result of every SELECT is also a table of rows and columns. In many cases, the "table" that results from a SELECT is just an image of rows and columns that scroll off the top of your display as you continue working. Prior to MySQL 3.23, if you wanted to save the results of a SELECT in a table for use in further queries, you had to make special arrangements:

1. Run a DESCRIBE or SHOW COLUMNS query to determine the types of the columns in the tables from which you want to capture information.

2. Create a table, explicitly specifying the names and types of the columns that you just looked up.

3. After creating the table, issue an INSERT ... SELECT query to retrieve the results and insert them into the table.

In MySQL 3.23, that has all changed. The CREATE TABLE ... SELECT statement eliminates all that ugly messing around and makes it possible to cause a new table to spring into existence on the fly using the result of an arbitrary SELECT query. You can do this in a single step without having to know or specify the data types of the columns you're retrieving. This makes it exceptionally easy to create a table fully populated with the data you're interested in, ready to be used in further queries.

You can copy a table by selecting its entire contents (no WHERE clause), or create an empty copy by adding a WHERE clause that always fails:

```
CREATE TABLE new_tbl_name SELECT * FROM tbl_name
CREATE TABLE new_tbl_name SELECT * FROM tbl_name WHERE 1 = 0
```

Creating an empty copy is useful if you want to load a data file into the original file using LOAD DATA, but you're not sure if you have the options for specifying the data format quite right. You don't want to end up with malformed records in the original table if you don't get the options right the first time! Using an empty copy of the original table allows you to experiment with the LOAD DATA options for specifying column and line delimiters until you're satisfied your input data are being interpreted properly. After you're satisfied, you can load the data into the original table.

You can combine CREATE TEMPORARY TABLE with SELECT to create a temporary table as a copy of itself:

```
CREATE TEMPORARY TABLE my_tbl SELECT * FROM my_tbl
```

That allows you to modify the contents of my_tbl without affecting the original. This is useful when you want to try out some queries that modify the contents of the table without changing the original table. To use pre-written scripts that use the original table name, you don't need to edit them to refer to a different table; just add the CREATE TEMPORARY TABLE statement to the beginning of the script. The script will create a temporary copy and operate on the copy, and the server will delete the copy when the script finishes.

To create a table as an empty copy of itself, use a `WHERE 0` clause in conjunction with `CREATE TEMPORARY ... SELECT`:

```
CREATE TEMPORARY TABLE my_tbl SELECT FROM my_tbl WHERE 1 = 0
```

However, there are several caveats to consider when creating tables on the fly. When you create a table by selecting data into it, the column names are taken from the columns that you are selecting. If a column is calculated as the result of an expression, the "name" of the column is the text of the expression. An expression isn't a legal column name. You can see this by running the following query in `mysql`:

```
mysql> CREATE TABLE my_tbl SELECT 1;
ERROR 1166 at line 1: Incorrect column name '1'
```

To make this work, provide a column alias to give the column a legal name:

```
mysql> CREATE TABLE my_tbl SELECT 1 AS my_col;
Query OK, 1 row affected (0.01 sec)
```

A related snag occurs if you select columns from different tables that have the same name. Suppose tables `t1` and `t2` both have a column `c` and you want to create a table from all combinations of rows in both tables. You can provide aliases to specify unique column names in the new table:

```
CREATE TABLE t3 SELECT t1.c AS c1, t2.c AS c2 FROM t1, t2;
```

Creating a table by selecting data into it does not automatically copy any indexes from the original table.

The DROP TABLE Statement

Dropping a table is much easier than creating it because you don't have to specify anything about its contents; you just have to name it:

```
DROP TABLE tbl_name
```

MySQL extends the `DROP TABLE` statement in some useful ways. First, you can drop several tables by specifying them all on the same statement:

```
DROP TABLE tbl_name1, tbl_name2, ...
```

Second, if you're not sure whether or not a table exists, but you want to drop it if it does, you can add `IF EXISTS` to the statement. This causes MySQL not to complain or issue an error if the table or tables named in the statement don't exist:

```
DROP TABLE IF EXISTS tbl_name
```

`IF EXISTS` is useful in scripts that you use with the `mysql` client because `mysql`, by default, exits when an error occurs, and it is an error to try to remove a table that doesn't exist. For example, you might have a setup script that creates tables that you use as the basis for further processing in other scripts. In this situation, you want to make sure the setup script has a clean slate when it begins. If you use a regular `DROP TABLE` at the beginning of the script, it would fail the first time because the tables have never been created. If you use IF EXISTS, there is no problem. If the tables are there, they are dropped; if not, the script continues anyway.

Creating and Dropping Indexes

Indexes are the primary means of speeding up access to the contents of your tables, particularly for queries that involve joins on multiple tables. This is an important enough topic that Chapter 4, "Query Optimization," discusses why you use indexes, how they work, and how best to take advantage of them to optimize your queries. In this section, we'll cover the characteristics of indexes and the syntax you use for creating and dropping them.

Characteristics of Indexes

MySQL provides quite a bit of flexibility in the way you can construct indexes. You can index single columns or combinations of columns. You can also have more than one index on a table if you want to be able to look up a value quickly from different columns of a table. If a column is a string type other than ENUM or SET, you may elect to index only the leftmost *n* characters of the column. If the column is mostly unique within the first *n* characters, you usually won't sacrifice performance, and may well improve it: Indexing a column prefix rather than the entire column can make an index much smaller and faster to access.

There are also some constraints on index creation, though these have tended to lessen as MySQL development continues. The following table shows some of the differences between ISAM and MyISAM tables in terms of indexing capabilities:

Index Characteristic	ISAM Tables	MyISAM Tables
NULL values	Not allowed	Allowed
BLOB and TEXT columns	Cannot be indexed	Can be indexed
Indexes per table	16	32
Columns per index	16	16
Maximum index row size	256 bytes	500 bytes

You can see from the table that for ISAM tables, an indexed column must be declared NOT NULL, and you cannot index BLOB or TEXT columns. The MyISAM table type removes these constraints on index creation, and relaxes some of the others. One implication of these differences in index characteristics for the two-table types is that, depending on your version of MySQL, you may simply not be able to index certain columns. For example, you can use only ISAM tables if your MySQL is older than 3.23, which means you can't index a column if you want it to be able to contain NULL values.

If you have MySQL 3.23 or later, you may have older tables that were originally created as ISAM tables. You can easily convert them to MyISAM storage format using ALTER TABLE, which allows you to take advantage of some of the newer indexing features:

```
ALTER TABLE tbl_name TYPE = MYISAM
```

Creating Indexes

You can create indexes for a new table when you use CREATE TABLE, or you can add indexes to existing tables with CREATE INDEX or ALTER TABLE. CREATE INDEX was introduced in MySQL 3.22, but you can use ALTER TABLE if your version of MySQL is older than that. (MySQL currently maps CREATE INDEX onto ALTER TABLE internally.)

You can specify that the index may or may not contain duplicate values. If it cannot, the index should be created as a PRIMARY KEY or a UNIQUE index. For a single-column unique index, this ensures that the column contains no duplicate values. For a multiple-column unique index, it ensures that no combination of values is duplicated.

A PRIMARY KEY and a UNIQUE index are very similar. In fact, a PRIMARY KEY is just a UNIQUE index with the name PRIMARY. This means that a table may contain only one PRIMARY KEY because you can't have two indexes with the same name. You can place multiple UNIQUE indexes on a table, although it's somewhat unusual to do so.

To add an index to an existing table, you can use ALTER TABLE or CREATE INDEX. ALTER TABLE is the more versatile of the two because you can use it to create a regular index, a UNIQUE index, or a PRIMARY KEY:

```
ALTER TABLE tbl_name ADD INDEX index_name (column_list)
ALTER TABLE tbl_name ADD UNIQUE index_name (column_list)
ALTER TABLE tbl_name ADD PRIMARY KEY (column_list)
```

tbl_name is the name of the table to add the index to, and column_list indicates which column or columns should be indexed. If the index consists of more than one column, separate the names by commas. The index name index_name is optional, so you can leave it out and MySQL will pick a name based on the name of the first indexed column. ALTER TABLE allows you to specify multiple table alterations in a single statement, so you can create several indexes at the same time.

CREATE INDEX can add a regular or UNIQUE index to a table:

```
CREATE UNIQUE INDEX index_name ON tbl_name (column_list)
CREATE INDEX index_name ON tbl_name (column_list)
```

tbl_name, index_name, and column_list have the same meaning as for ALTER TABLE. The index name is not optional, though. You cannot create a PRIMARY KEY with CREATE INDEX.

To create an index for a new table when you issue a CREATE TABLE statement, you use syntax similar to that for ALTER TABLE, but you specify the index-creation clauses in the part of the statement where you declare the table columns:

```
CREATE TABLE tbl_name
(
    ...
    INDEX index_name (column_list),
    UNIQUE index_name (column_list),
    PRIMARY KEY (column_list),
    ...
)
```

As for ALTER TABLE, the index name is optional for INDEX and UNIQUE and MySQL will pick a name if you leave it out.

As a special case, you can create a single-column PRIMARY KEY by adding PRIMARY KEY to the end of the column declaration:

```
CREATE TABLE my_tbl
(
    i INT NOT NULL PRIMARY KEY
)
```

That statement is equivalent to the following one:

```
CREATE TABLE my_tbl
(
    i INT NOT NULL,
    PRIMARY KEY (i)
)
```

Each of the preceding table-creation examples have specified NOT NULL for the indexed columns. If you have ISAM tables, that's a requirement because you cannot index columns that may contain NULL values. If you have MyISAM tables, indexed columns may be NULL, as long as the index is not a PRIMARY KEY.

If you index a prefix of a string column (the leftmost n characters of column values), the syntax for naming the column in a column_list specifier is col_name(n) rather than simply col_name. For example, the first of the following statements creates a table with two CHAR columns and an index that uses both columns. The second statement is similar, but it indexes a prefix of each column:

```
CREATE TABLE my_tbl
(
    name CHAR(30),
    address CHAR(60),
    INDEX (name,address)
)

CREATE TABLE my_tbl
(
    name CHAR(30),
    address CHAR(60),
    INDEX (name(10),address(20))
)
```

In some circumstances, you may find it necessary to index a column prefix. For example, the length of index rows has an upper bound, so you may need to use prefixes if the length of the indexed columns exceeds that bound. Prefixes are also necessary for BLOB or TEXT columns in MyISAM table indexes.

Indexing a prefix of a column constrains changes you can make to the column later; you cannot shorten the column to a length less than the prefix length without dropping the index and re-creating it using a shorter prefix.

Dropping Indexes

You can drop indexes using either the DROP INDEX or ALTER TABLE statements. Like the CREATE INDEX statement, DROP INDEX currently is handled internally as an ALTER TABLE statement and was introduced in MySQL 3.22. The syntax for index-dropping statements looks like this:

```
DROP INDEX index_name ON tbl_name
ALTER TABLE tbl_name DROP INDEX index_name
ALTER TABLE tbl_name DROP PRIMARY KEY
```

The first two of these statements are equivalent. The third is used only for dropping a PRIMARY KEY; in this case, no index name is needed because a table may have only one such key. If no index was created explicitly as a PRIMARY KEY but the table has one or more UNIQUE indexes, MySQL drops the first of them.

Indexes may be affected if you drop columns from a table. If you drop a column that is a part of an index, the column is removed from the index as well. If all columns that make up an index are dropped, the entire index is dropped.

The ALTER TABLE Statement

ALTER TABLE is a versatile statement in MySQL, and you can use it to do many things. We've already seen several of its capabilities (for creating and dropping indexes and for converting tables from one storage format to another). In this section, we'll cover some of its other talents. The full syntax for ALTER TABLE is described in Appendix D.

ALTER TABLE is useful when you find that the structure of a table no longer reflects what you want to do with it. You may want to use the table to record additional information, or perhaps it contains information that has become superfluous. Maybe existing columns are too small, or perhaps you've declared them larger than it turns out you need and you'd like to make them smaller to save space and improve query performance. Or maybe you just typed in the table's name incorrectly when you issued the CREATE TABLE statement. Here are some examples:

- You're running a Web-based questionnaire, and you store the results from each submitted questionnaire as a record in a table. Then you decide to modify the questionnaire to add some additional questions. You must add some columns to the table to accommodate the new questions.

- You're running a research project. You assign case numbers to research records using an AUTO_INCREMENT column. You didn't expect your funding to last long enough to generate more than about 50,000 records, so you made the column type UNSIGNED SMALLINT, which holds a maximum of 65,535 unique values. However, the funding for the project was renewed, and it looks like you may generate another 50,000 records. You need to make the type bigger to accommodate more case numbers.

- Size changes can go the other way, too. Maybe you created a CHAR(255) column but now recognize that no value in the table is more than 100 characters long. You can shorten the column to save space.

The syntax for ALTER TABLE looks like this:

```
ALTER TABLE tbl_name action, ...
```

Each *action* specifies a modification you want to make to the table. MySQL extends the ALTER TABLE statement by allowing you to specify multiple actions, separated by commas. This is useful for cutting down on typing, but a more important reason for this extension is that it's impossible to change tables from variable-length rows to fixed-length rows unless you can change all the VARCHAR columns to CHAR at the same time.

The following examples show some of the capabilities of ALTER TABLE.

- **Renaming a table.** This is easy; just specify the old name and the new name:

  ```
  ALTER TABLE tbl_name RENAME AS new_tbl_name
  ```

  In MySQL 3.23, which has temporary tables, renaming a temporary table to a name that already exists in the database hides the original table for as long as the temporary table exists. This is analogous to the way that a table is hidden by creating a temporary table with the same name.

- **Changing a column type.** To change a column type, you can use either a CHANGE or MODIFY clause. Suppose the column in a table my_tbl is SMALLINT UNSIGNED and you want to change it to MEDIUMINT UNSIGNED. Do so using either of the following commands:

  ```
  ALTER TABLE my_tbl MODIFY i MEDIUMINT UNSIGNED
  ALTER TABLE my_tbl CHANGE i i MEDIUMINT UNSIGNED
  ```

  Why is the column named twice in the command that uses CHANGE? Because one thing that CHANGE can do that MODIFY cannot is to rename the column in addition to changing the type. If you had wanted to rename i to j at the same time you changed the type, you'd do so like this:

  ```
  ALTER TABLE my_tbl CHANGE i j MEDIUMINT UNSIGNED
  ```

  The important thing is that you name the column you want to change and then specify a complete column declaration, which includes the column name. You still need to include the name in the declaration, even if it's the same as the old name.

An important reason for changing column types is to improve query efficiency for joins that compare columns from two tables. A comparison is quicker when the columns are both the same type. Suppose you're running a query like this:

```
SELECT ... FROM t1, t2 WHERE t1.name = t2.name
```

If t1.name is CHAR(10) and t2.name is CHAR(15), the query won't run as quickly as if they were both CHAR(15). You can make them the same by changing t1.name using either of these commands:

```
ALTER TABLE t1 MODIFY name CHAR(15)
ALTER TABLE t1 CHANGE name name CHAR(15)
```

For versions of MySQL prior to 3.23, it's essential that joined columns be of the same type, or indexes cannot be used for the comparison. For version 3.23 or above, indexes can be used for dissimilar types, but the query will still be faster if the types are identical.

- **Converting a table from variable-length rows to fixed-length rows.**
  Suppose you have a table chartbl with VARCHAR columns that you want to convert into CHAR columns to see what kind of performance improvements you get. (Tables with fixed-length rows generally can be processed more quickly than tables with variable-length rows.) The table was created like this:

  ```
  CREATE TABLE chartbl (name VARCHAR(40), address VARCHAR(80))
  ```

  The problem here is that you need to change the columns all at once in the same ALTER TABLE statement. You can't do them one at a time or the attempt will be ineffective. If you run DESCRIBE chartbl, you'll find that the columns are still defined as VARCHAR! The reason is that if you change a single column at a time, MySQL notices that the table still contains variable-length columns and reconverts the changed column back to VARCHAR to save space. To deal with this, change all the VARCHAR columns at the same time:

  ```
  ALTER TABLE chartbl MODIFY name CHAR(40), MODIFY address CHAR(80)
  ```

  Now DESCRIBE will show that the table contains CHAR columns. It's exactly this type of operation that makes it important that ALTER TABLE support multiple actions in the same statement.

  There is a caveat to be aware of when you want to convert a table like this: The presence of BLOB or TEXT columns in the table will defeat any attempt to convert a table to fixed-length row format. The presence of even one variable-length column in a table causes it to have variable-length rows, and these column types have no fixed-length equivalent.

- **Converting a table from fixed-length rows to variable-length rows.**
  Okay, so chartbl is faster with fixed-length rows, but it takes more space than you'd like, so you decide to convert it back to its original form to save space. Converting a table in this direction is much easier. You only need to make one CHAR column to VARCHAR and MySQL will convert the other CHAR columns

automatically. To convert the `chartbl` table, either of the following statements will do:

```
ALTER TABLE chartbl MODIFY name VARCHAR(40)
ALTER TABLE chartbl MODIFY address VARCHAR(80)
```

- **Converting a table type.** If you have upgraded from a pre-3.23 version of MySQL to 3.23 or later, you may have older tables that were created as ISAM tables. If you want to create them to MyISAM format, do so as follows:

```
ALTER TABLE tbl_name TYPE = MYISAM
```

Why would you do this? One reason, as already discussed in "Creating and Dropping Indexes," is that the MyISAM storage format has some indexing features that the ISAM format does not, such as the ability to index `NULL` values and `BLOB` and `TEXT` column types. Another reason is that MyISAM tables are machine independent, so you can move them to other machines by copying table files directly, even if the machines have different hardware architectures. This is discussed further in the section "Backing Up and Copying Databases" in Chapter 11.

Getting Information about Databases and Tables

MySQL provides several statements for getting information about databases and the tables in them. These statements are helpful for keeping track of the contents of your databases and for reminding yourself about the structure of your tables. You can also use them as an aid to using `ALTER TABLE`; it's easier to figure out how to specify a change to a column when you can find out how the column is defined currently.

The `SHOW` statement can be used to obtain information about several aspects of your databases and tables:

`SHOW DATABASES`	List databases on server
`SHOW TABLES`	List tables in current database
`SHOW TABLES FROM db_name`	List tables in named database
`SHOW COLUMNS FROM tbl_name`	Display information about columns in named table
`SHOW INDEX FROM tbl_name`	Display information about indexes in named table
`SHOW TABLE STATUS`	Display descriptive information about tables in default database
`SHOW TABLE STATUS FROM db_name`	Display descriptive information about tables in named database

The `DESCRIBE tbl_name` and `EXPLAIN tbl_name` statements are synonymous with `SHOW COLUMNS FROM tbl_name`.

The `mysqlshow` command provides some of the same information as the `SHOW` statement, which allows you to get database and table information from the shell:

% **mysqlshow**	List databases on server
% **mysqlshow** *db_name*	List tables in named database
% **mysqlshow** *db_name* *tbl_name*	Display information about columns in named table
% **mysqlshow --keys** *db_name* *tbl_name*	Display information about indexes in named table
% **mysqlshow --status** *db_name*	Display descriptive information about tables in named database

The `mysqldump` utility allows you to see the structure of your tables in the form of a `CREATE TABLE` statement. (In comparison with the `SHOW COLUMNS` statement, I find the output from the `mysqldump` command easier to read, and the output shows indexes on the table as well.) But if you use `mysqldump`, make sure to invoke it with the `--no-data` option so that you don't get swamped with your table's data!

    % **mysqldump --no-data** *db_name* *tbl_name*

For both `mysqlshow` and `mysqldump`, you can specify the usual options, such as `--host`, to connect to a server on a different host.

Retrieving Records

It does no good to put records in a database unless you retrieve them eventually and do something with them. That's the purpose of the `SELECT` statement: to help you get at your data. `SELECT` is probably the most commonly used statement in the SQL language, but it can also be the trickiest; the constraints you use to choose rows can be arbitrarily complex and can involve comparisons between columns in many tables.

The basic syntax of the `SELECT` statement looks like this:

SELECT *selection_list*	What columns to select
FROM *table_list*	Where to select rows from
WHERE *primary_constraint*	What conditions rows must satisfy
GROUP BY *grouping_columns*	How to group results
ORDER BY *sorting_columns*	How to sort results
HAVING *secondary_constraint*	Secondary conditions rows must satisfy
LIMIT *count*	Limit on results

Everything in this syntax is optional except the word `SELECT` and the *selection_list* part that specifies what you want to retrieve. Some databases require the `FROM` clause as well. MySQL does not, which allows you to evaluate expressions without referring to any tables:

```
SELECT SQRT(POW(3,2)+POW(4,2))
```

In Chapter 1, we devoted quite a bit of attention to SELECT, concentrating primarily on the column selection list and the WHERE, GROUP BY, ORDER BY, HAVING, and LIMIT clauses. In this chapter, we'll concentrate on the aspect of SELECT that is perhaps the most confusing—the join. We'll discuss the types of join MySQL supports, what they mean, and how to specify them. This should help you employ MySQL more effectively, because in many cases, the real problem of figuring out how to write a query is determining the proper way to join tables together. You may also want to take a look at the section "Solutions Miscellany" that appears later in this chapter. There you'll find solutions to several SQL problems, most of which involve SELECT in some capacity or another.

One problem with using SELECT is that when you first encounter a new type of problem, it's not always easy to see how to write a SELECT query to solve it. However, after you figure it out, you can use that experience when you run across similar problems in the future. SELECT is probably the statement for which past experience plays the largest role in being able to use it effectively, simply because of the sheer variety of ways you can use it.

As you gain experience, you'll be able to apply it more easily to new problems, and you'll find yourself thinking things like, "Oh, yes, that's one of those LEFT JOIN things," or, "Aha, that's a three-way join restricted by the common pairs of key columns." (I'm a little reluctant to point that out, actually. You may find it encouraging to hear that experience helps you. On the other hand, you may find it scary to consider that you could wind up thinking in terms like that!)

In the next few sections, which demonstrate how to use the forms of join operations that MySQL supports, most of the examples use the following two tables. They're small, which makes them simple enough that the effect of each type of join can be seen readily:

```
table t1:          table t2:
+------+------+     +------+------+
| i1   | c1   |     | i2   | c2   |
+------+------+     +------+------+
|    1 | a    |     |    2 | c    |
|    2 | b    |     |    3 | b    |
|    3 | c    |     |    4 | a    |
+------+------+     +------+------+
```

The Trivial Join

The simplest join is the trivial join, in which only one table is named. In this case, rows are selected from the named table:

```
SELECT * FROM t1
+------+------+
| i1   | c1   |
+------+------+
|    1 | a    |
|    2 | b    |
|    3 | c    |
+------+------+
```

Some authors don't consider this form of SELECT a join at all, and use the term only for SELECT statements that retrieve records from two or more tables. I suppose it's a matter of perspective.

The Full Join

If multiple tables are named, with the names separated by commas, a full join is done. For example, if you join two tables, each row from the first table is combined with each row in the second table:

```
SELECT t1.*, t2.* FROM t1, t2
+------+------+------+------+
| i1   | c1   | i2   | c2   |
+------+------+------+------+
|    1 | a    |    2 | c    |
|    2 | b    |    2 | c    |
|    3 | c    |    2 | c    |
|    1 | a    |    3 | b    |
|    2 | b    |    3 | b    |
|    3 | c    |    3 | b    |
|    1 | a    |    4 | a    |
|    2 | b    |    4 | a    |
|    3 | c    |    4 | a    |
+------+------+------+------+
```

A full join is also called a cross join because each row of each table is crossed with each row in every other table to produce all possible combinations. This is also known as the cartesian product. Joining tables this way has the potential to produce a very large number of rows because the possible row count is the product of the number of rows in each table. A full join between three tables that contain 100, 200, and 300 rows, respectively, could return 100 x 200 x 300 = 6 million rows. That's a lot of rows, even though the individual tables are small. In cases like this, normally a WHERE clause will be used to reduce the result set to a more manageable size!

If you add a condition in the WHERE clause causing tables to be matched on the values of certain columns, the join becomes what is known as an equi-join, because you're selecting only rows with equal values in the specified columns:

```
SELECT t1.*, t2.* FROM t1, t2 WHERE t1.i1 = t2.i2
+------+------+------+------+
¦ i1   ¦ c1   ¦ i2   ¦ c2   ¦
+------+------+------+------+
¦    2 ¦ b    ¦    2 ¦ c    ¦
¦    3 ¦ c    ¦    3 ¦ b    ¦
+------+------+------+------+
```

The JOIN, CROSS JOIN, and INNER JOIN join types are equivalent to the ',' join operator.

A STRAIGHT_JOIN is like a full join but the tables are joined in the order named in the FROM clause. Normally, the MySQL optimizer considers itself free to rearrange the order of tables in a full join to retrieve rows more quickly. On occasion, the optimizer will make a non-optimal choice, which you can override using the STRAIGHT_JOIN keyword.

STRAIGHT_JOIN can be specified at two points in a SELECT statement. You can specify it between the SELECT keyword and the selection list to have a global effect on all full joins in the statement, or you can specify it in the FROM clause. The following two statements are equivalent:

```
SELECT STRAIGHT_JOIN ... FROM table1, table2, table3 ...
SELECT ... FROM table1 STRAIGHT_JOIN table2 STRAIGHT_JOIN table3 ...
```

Qualifying Column References

References to table columns throughout a SELECT statement must be unambiguously resolvable to a single table named in the FROM clause . If only one table is named, there is no ambiguity because all columns must be columns of that table. If multiple tables are named, any column name that appears in only one table is similarly unambiguous. However, if the column name appears in multiple tables, references to the column must be qualified by the table name using tbl_name.col_name syntax to specify which table you mean. If a table my_tbl1 contains columns a and b, and a table my_tbl2 contains columns b and c, references to columns a or c are unambiguous, but references to b must be qualified as either my_tbl1.b or my_tbl2.b:

```
SELECT a, my_tbl1.b, my_tbl2.b, c FROM my_tbl1, my_tbl2 ...
```

In some cases, a table name qualifier is not sufficient to resolve a column reference. For example, if you're using a table multiple times in a query, it doesn't help to qualify a column name with the table name. In this case, table aliases are useful for communicating your intent. You can assign an alias to any instance of the table and refer to columns from that instance as alias_name.col_name. The following query joins a table to itself, but assigns an alias to one instance of the table to allow column references to be specified unambiguously:

```
SELECT my_tbl.col1, m.col2
    FROM my_tbl, my_tbl AS m
    WHERE my_tbl.col1 > m.col1
```

The Left Join

An equi-join shows only rows where a match can be found in both tables. A left join shows matches, too, but it also shows rows in the left table that do *not* have a match in the right table. Any columns selected from the right table for such rows are displayed as NULL. The way this works is that each row is selected from the left table. If there is a matching row in the right table, that row is selected. If there is no match, a row is still selected, but it's a "fake" row in which all the columns have been set to NULL. In other words, a LEFT JOIN forces the result set to contain a row for every row in the left side table, whether or not there is a match for it in the right side table. Matching is done according to the columns named in an ON or USING() clause. You can use ON whether or not the columns you're joining on have the same name:

```
SELECT t1.*, t2.* FROM t1 LEFT JOIN t2 ON t1.i1 = t2.i2
```

```
+------+------+------+------+
| i1   | c1   | i2   | c2   |
+------+------+------+------+
|    1 | a    | NULL | NULL |
|    2 | b    |    2 | c    |
|    3 | c    |    3 | b    |
+------+------+------+------+
```

The USING() clause is similar to ON, but the name of the joined column or columns must be the same in each table. The following query joins my_tbl1.b to my_tbl2.b:

```
SELECT my_tbl1.*, my_tbl2.* FROM my_tbl1 LEFT JOIN my_tbl2 USING (b)
```

LEFT JOIN is especially useful when you want to find only those rows in the left side table that do not appear in the right side table. You do this by adding a WHERE clause that looks for rows in the right table that have NULL values:

```
SELECT t1.*, t2.* FROM t1 LEFT JOIN t2 ON t1.i1 = t2.i2 WHERE t2.i2 IS NULL
+------+------+------+------+
| i1   | c1   | i2   | c2   |
+------+------+------+------+
|    1 | a    | NULL | NULL |
+------+------+------+------+
```

Normally, you won't bother selecting the columns that are NULL because they are of no interest. What you're really after are the unmatched columns in the left table:

```
SELECT t1.* FROM t1 LEFT JOIN t2 ON t1.i1 = t2.i2 WHERE t2.i2 IS NULL
+------+------+
| i1   | c1   |
+------+------+
|    1 | a    |
+------+------+
```

One thing to watch out for with LEFT JOIN is that if the columns that you're joining on are not declared as NOT NULL, you may get extraneous rows in the result.

LEFT JOIN has a few synonyms and variants. LEFT OUTER JOIN is a synonym for LEFT JOIN. There is also an ODBC notation for LEFT JOIN that is accepted by MySQL (the 'oj' means "outer join"):

```
{ oj tbl_name LEFT OUTER JOIN tbl_name ON join_expr }
```

NATURAL LEFT JOIN is similar to LEFT JOIN; it performs a LEFT JOIN, matching all columns that have the same name in the left side and right side tables.

Some databases have a corresponding RIGHT JOIN; MySQL does not have this yet.

Writing Comments

MySQL allows you to intersperse comments with your SQL code. This can be useful for documenting queries that you store in files. You can write comments in two ways. Anything from a '#' character to the end of a line is considered a comment. C-style comments are allowed as well. That is, anything between '/*' and '*/' beginning and ending markers is considered a comment. C-style comments may span multiple lines:

```
# this is a single line comment
/* this is also a single line comment */
/* this, however,
   is a multiple line
   comment
*/
```

As of MySQL 3.23, you can "hide" MySQL-specific keywords in C-style comments by beginning the comment with '/*!' rather than with '/*'. MySQL looks inside this special type of comment and uses the keywords, but other database servers will ignore them as part of the comment. This helps you write code that takes advantage of MySQL-specific functions when executed by MySQL but that can be used with other database servers without modification. The following two statements are equivalent for database servers other than MySQL, but MySQL will perform an INSERT DELAYED operation for the second:

```
INSERT INTO absence (student_id,date) VALUES(13,"1999-09-28")
INSERT /*! DELAYED */ INTO absence (student_id,date) VALUES(13,"1999-09-28")
```

As of MySQL 3.23.3, in addition to the comment styles just described, you can begin a comment with two dashes and a space ('--'); everything from the dashes to the end of the line is treated as a comment. Some other databases use the double dash to begin a comment. MySQL allows this but requires the space as an aid for disambiguation.

Statements with expressions like 5--7 might be taken as containing a comment beginning otherwise. It's not likely you'd write such an expression as 5-- 7, so this is a useful heuristic. Still, it is only a heuristic, and it's probably better to use one of the other comment styles, and stick to double dashes only in code that you're porting from other databases.

Solutions Miscellany

This section is something of a grab bag; it shows how to write queries that solve various kinds of problems. For the most part, these are solutions to problems that I've seen come up on the mailing list. (With thanks to people on the list who've contributed many of these answers.)

Rewriting Subselects as Joins

MySQL will have subselects as of version 3.24. Lack of this feature is one of the more-often lamented omissions in MySQL, but something many people seem not to realize is that queries written using subselects often can be rephrased in terms of a join. In fact, even when MySQL gets subselects, it wouldn't be a bad idea to examine queries that you may be inclined to write in terms of them: It's often more efficient to use a join rather than a subselect.

Rewriting Subselects that Select Matching Values

Here's an example query containing a subselect; it selects scores from the score table for all tests (that is, it ignores quiz scores):

```
SELECT * FROM score
WHERE event_id IN (SELECT event_id FROM event WHERE type = "T")
```

The same query can be written without a subselect by converting it to a simple join:

```
SELECT score.* FROM score, event
WHERE score.event_id = event.event_id AND event.type = "T"
```

As another example, the following example selects scores for female students:

```
SELECT * from score
WHERE student_id IN (SELECT student_id FROM student WHERE sex = "F")
```

This can be converted to a join as follows:

```
SELECT score.* FROM score, student
WHERE score.student_id = student.student_id AND student.sex = "F"
```

There is a pattern here. The subselect queries follow this form:

```
SELECT * FROM table1
WHERE column1 IN (SELECT column2 FROM table2a WHERE column2b = value)
```

Such queries can be converted to a join using this form:

```
SELECT table1.* FROM table1, table2
WHERE table1.column1 = table2.column2a AND table2.column2b = value
```

Rewriting Subselects that Select Non-Matching Values

Another common type of subselect query searches for values in one table that are *not* present in another table. As we've seen before, the "which values are not present" type of problem is a clue that a LEFT JOIN may be helpful. Here's a query with a subselect that tests for the absence of values in a table (it finds those students with perfect attendance):

```
SELECT * FROM student
WHERE student_id NOT IN (SELECT student_id FROM absence)
```

This query may be rewritten using a LEFT JOIN as follows:

```
SELECT student.*
FROM student LEFT JOIN absence ON student.student_id = absence.student_id
WHERE absence.student_id IS NULL
```

In general terms, the subselect query form is as follows:

```
SELECT * FROM table1
WHERE column1 NOT EXISTS (SELECT column2 FROM table2)
```

A query having that form may be rewritten like this:

```
SELECT table1.*
FROM table1 LEFT JOIN table2 ON table1.column1 = table2.column2
WHERE table2.column2 IS NULL
```

This assumes that table2.column2 is declared as NOT NULL.

Checking for Values Not Present in a Table

We've already seen in the section "Retrieving Records" that when you want to know which values in one table are not present in another table, you use a LEFT JOIN on the two tables and look for rows in which NULL is selected from the second table. A simple situation was shown there using these two tables:

```
table t1:          table t2:
+------+------+     +------+------+
|  i1  |  c1  |     |  i2  |  c2  |
+------+------+     +------+------+
|    1 |  a   |     |    2 |  c   |
|    2 |  b   |     |    3 |  b   |
|    3 |  c   |     |    4 |  a   |
+------+------+     +------+------+
```

The LEFT JOIN to find all t1.i1 values that are not present in the t2.i2 column is as follows:

```
SELECT t1.* FROM t1 LEFT JOIN t2 ON t1.i1 = t2.i2 WHERE t2.i2 IS NULL
+------+------+
|  i1  |  c1  |
+------+------+
|    1 |  a   |
+------+------+
```

Now let's consider a more difficult version of the "Which values are missing?" question. For the grade-keeping project, first mentioned in Chapter 1, we have a student table listing students, an event table listing the grade events that have occurred, and a score table listing scores for each student for each grade event. However, if a student was ill on the day of some quiz or test, the score table wouldn't have any score for the student for that event, so a makeup quiz or test should be given. How do we find these missing records so that we can make sure those students take the makeup?

The problem is to determine which students have no score for a grade event for each grade event. Another way to say this is that we want to find out which combinations of student and event are not represented in the score table. This "which values are not present" wording is a tip-off that we want a LEFT JOIN. The join isn't as simple as in the previous example, though, because we aren't just looking for values that are not present in a single column; we're looking for a two-column combination.

The combinations we want are all the student/event combinations, which are produced by crossing the student table with the event table:

```
FROM student, event
```

Then we take the result of that join and perform a LEFT JOIN with the score table to find the matches:

```
FROM student, event
     LEFT JOIN score ON student.student_id = score.student.id
                    AND event.event_id = score.event_id
```

Note that the ON clause allows the rows in the score table to be joined according to matches in different tables. That's the key for solving this problem. The LEFT JOIN forces a row to be generated for each row produced by the cross join of the student and event tables, even when there is no corresponding score table record. The result set rows for these missing score records can be identified by the fact that the columns from the score table will all be NULL. We can select these records in the WHERE clause. Any column from the score table will do, but because we're looking for missing scores, it's probably conceptually clearest to test the score column:

```
WHERE score.score IS NULL
```

We can put the results in order using an ORDER BY clause. The two most logical orderings are by student and by event. I'll choose the first:

```
ORDER BY student.student_id, event.event_id
```

Now all we need to do is name the columns we want to see in the output, and we're done. Here is the final query:

```
SELECT
    student.name, student.student_id,
    event.date, event.event_id, event.type
FROM
    student, event
    LEFT JOIN score ON student.student_id = score.student_id
                   AND event.event_id = score.event_id
WHERE
    score.score IS NULL
ORDER BY
    student.student_id, event.event_id
```

Running the query produces these results:

```
+-----------+------------+------------+----------+------+
| name      | student_id | date       | event_id | type |
+-----------+------------+------------+----------+------+
| Megan     |          1 | 1999-09-16 |        4 | Q    |
| Joseph    |          2 | 1999-09-03 |        1 | Q    |
| Katie     |          4 | 1999-09-23 |        5 | Q    |
| Devri     |         13 | 1999-09-03 |        1 | Q    |
| Devri     |         13 | 1999-10-01 |        6 | T    |
| Will      |         17 | 1999-09-16 |        4 | Q    |
| Avery     |         20 | 1999-09-06 |        2 | Q    |
| Gregory   |         23 | 1999-10-01 |        6 | T    |
| Sarah     |         24 | 1999-09-23 |        5 | Q    |
| Carter    |         27 | 1999-09-16 |        4 | Q    |
| Carter    |         27 | 1999-09-23 |        5 | Q    |
| Gabrielle |         29 | 1999-09-16 |        4 | Q    |
| Grace     |         30 | 1999-09-23 |        5 | Q    |
+-----------+------------+------------+----------+------+
```

Here's a subtle point. The output lists the student IDs and the event IDs. The student_id column appears in both the student and score tables, so at first you might think that the selection list could name either student.student_id or score.student_id. That's not the case because the entire basis for being able to find the records we're interested in is that all the score table fields are returned as NULL. Selecting score.student_id would produce only a column of NULL values in the output. Similar reasoning applies to the event_id column, which appears in both the event and score tables.

Performing a UNION Operation

If you want to create a result set by selecting records from multiple tables that have the same structure, you can do that in some database systems using some kind of UNION statement. MySQL doesn't have UNION (at least not until MySQL 3.24), but you can work around this difficulty a couple of ways. Following are two possible solutions:

- Perform multiple SELECT queries, one on each table. This works if you don't care about the order of the rows you're selecting.

- Select rows from each table into a temporary holding table. Then select the contents of that table. This allows you to sort the rows as you like. In MySQL 3.23 and up, you can handle this problem easily by allowing the server to create the holding table for you. Also, you can make the table a temporary table so that it will be dropped automatically when your session with the server terminates.

  In the following code, we drop the table explicitly to allow the server to free resources associated with it. This is a good idea if the client session will continue to perform further queries. We also use a HEAP (in-memory) table for faster performance.

```
CREATE TEMPORARY TABLE hold_tbl TYPE=HEAP SELECT ... FROM table1 WHERE ...
INSERT INTO hold_tbl SELECT ... FROM table2 WHERE ...
INSERT INTO hold_tbl SELECT ... FROM table3 WHERE ...

...

SELECT * FROM hold_tbl ORDER BY ...
DROP TABLE hold_tbl
```

For versions of MySQL older than 3.23, the idea is similar, except that you must explicitly declare the columns in the *hold_tbl* table yourself, and the DROP TABLE at the end is mandatory to prevent the table from continuing to exist beyond the life of the client session:

```
CREATE TABLE hold_tbl (column1 ..., column2 ..., ...)
SELECT ... FROM table1 WHERE ...
INSERT INTO hold_tbl SELECT ... FROM table1 WHERE ...
INSERT INTO hold_tbl SELECT ... FROM table2 WHERE ...
INSERT INTO hold_tbl SELECT ... FROM table3 WHERE ...
SELECT * FROM hold_tbl ORDER BY ...
DROP TABLE hold_tbl
```

Adding a Sequence Number Column

If you use ALTER TABLE to add an AUTO_INCREMENT column, the column is filled in automatically with sequence numbers. The following set of statements in a mysql session shows how this works by creating a table, putting some data in it, and then adding an AUTO_INCREMENT column:

```
mysql> CREATE TABLE t (c CHAR(10));
mysql> INSERT INTO t VALUES("a"),("b"),("c");
mysql> SELECT * FROM t;
+------+
| c    |
+------+
| a    |
| b    |
| c    |
+------+
mysql> ALTER TABLE t ADD i INT AUTO_INCREMENT NOT NULL PRIMARY KEY;
mysql> SELECT * FROM t;
+------+---+
| c    | i |
+------+---+
| a    | 1 |
| b    | 2 |
| c    | 3 |
+------+---+
```

Sequencing or Resequencing an Existing Column

If you have a numeric column, you can sequence it (or resequence it if it was sequenced but you've deleted rows and you want to renumber the values to be contiguous) like this:

```
ALTER TABLE t MODIFY i INT NULL
UPDATE t SET i = NULL
ALTER TABLE t MODIFY i INT UNSIGNED AUTO_INCREMENT NOT NULL PRIMARY KEY
```

But an easier way to do this is simply to drop the column and add it again as an AUTO_INCREMENT column. ALTER TABLE allows multiple actions to be specified, so this can all be done in a single statement:

```
ALTER TABLE t
    DROP i,
    ADD i INT UNSIGNED AUTO_INCREMENT NOT NULL PRIMARY KEY
```

Sorting in Unusual Orders

Suppose you have a table representing personnel for a sports organization, such as a football team: You want to sort output by personnel position so that it comes out in a particular order, such as the following: coaches, assistant coaches, quarterbacks, running backs, receivers, linemen, and so forth. Define the column as an ENUM and list the enumeration elements in the order that you want to see them. Sort operations on that column will automatically come out in the order you specify.

Setting Up a Counter Table

In "Working With Sequences" in Chapter 2, we showed how to generate a sequence using LAST_INSERT_ID(*expr*). The example there illustrated how to set up a count using a table with a single row. That's okay for a single counter, but if you want several counters, that method leads to needless multiplication of tables. Suppose you have a Web site and you want to put some "this page has been accessed *nnn* times" counters in several pages. You probably don't want to set up a separate counter table for every page that has a counter.

One way to avoid creating multiple counter tables is to create a single table with two columns. One column holds a counter value; the other holds a counter name. We can still use the LAST_INSERT_ID() function, but we'll determine which row it applies to using the counter name. The table looks like this:

```
CREATE TABLE counter
(
    count INT UNSIGNED,
    name varchar(255) NOT NULL PRIMARY KEY
)
```

The name is a string so that we can call a counter whatever we want, and we make it a PRIMARY KEY to prevent duplicate names. This assumes that applications using the table agree on the names they'll be using. For our Web counters, we can ensure uniqueness of counter names simply by using the pathname of each page within the document tree as its counter name. For example, to set up a new counter for the site's home page, do this:

```
INSERT INTO counter (name) VALUES("index.html")
```

That initializes the counter called "index.html" with a value of zero. To generate the next sequence value, increment the count in the proper row of the table, then retrieve it using LAST_INSERT_ID():

```
UPDATE counter
    SET count = LAST_INSERT_ID(count+1)
    WHERE name = "index.html"
SELECT LAST_INSERT_ID()
```

An alternative approach would be to increment the counter without using LAST_INSERT_ID(), like this:

```
UPDATE counter SET count = count+1 WHERE name = "index.html"
SELECT count FROM counter WHERE name = "index.html"
```

However, that doesn't work correctly if another client increments the counter after you issue the UPDATE and before you issue the SELECT. You could solve that problem by putting LOCK TABLES and UNLOCK TABLES around the two statements to block other clients while you're using the counter. But the LAST_INSERT_ID() method accomplishes the same thing more easily. Because its value is client-specific, you always get the value you inserted, not the one from some other client, and you don't have to complicate the code with locks to keep other clients out.

Checking for Table Existence

It's sometimes useful to be able to tell from within an application whether or not a given table exists. To do this, you can use either of the following statements:

```
SELECT COUNT(*) FROM tbl_name
SELECT * FROM tbl_name WHERE 1=0
```

Each statement succeeds if the table exists, and fails if it doesn't. They are good queries for this kind of test. They execute very quickly, so you're not using a lot of time to run them. This strategy is most suitable for application programs that you write because you can test the success or failure of the query and take action accordingly. It's not especially useful in a batch script that you run from mysql because you can't do anything if an error occurs except terminate (or ignore the error, but then there's obviously no point in running the query at all).

Features that MySQL Does Not Support

This section describes features that are found in some other databases that MySQL does not support. It covers what's missing, and it shows how to work around these omissions where possible. In general, features are missing from MySQL because they have negative performance implications. Several of the items in this list are on the developers' To Do list, for implementation as time permits, and assuming a way can be found to do so without sacrificing their primary goal of good performance.

- **Subselects.** A subselect is a SELECT nested inside another SELECT, such as in the following query:

```
SELECT * FROM score
WHERE event_id IN (SELECT event_id FROM event WHERE type = "T")
```

Subselects are scheduled to appear in MySQL 3.24, at which point they will become a non-omission. Until then, many queries that are written using subselects can be written as joins instead. See the section "Rewriting Subselects as Joins."

- **Transactions and commit/rollback.** A transaction is a set of SQL statements that are executed as a unit without interruption by other clients. Commit/rollback capability allows you to state that the statements must be executed as a unit or not at all. That is, if any statement in the transaction fails, any statements executed up to that point are undone.

MySQL automatically performs locking for single SQL statements to keep clients from interfering with each other. (For example, two clients cannot write to the same table simultaneously.) In addition, you can use LOCK TABLES and UNLOCK TABLES to group statements as a unit, which allows you to perform operations for which single-statement concurrency control isn't sufficient. The transaction-related issues for MySQL are that it will not group the statements automatically for you, and you cannot perform rollback on the statements if one of them fails.

To see how transactions are useful, suppose you're in the garment sales business and you update inventory levels whenever one of your salesmen makes a sale. The following example demonstrates the kind of problem that can occur when multiple salesmen are updating the database simultaneously (assuming the initial shirt inventory level is 47):

t1 Salesman 1 sells three shirts

t2 Salesman 1 retrieves current shirt count (47):

```
SELECT quantity FROM inventory WHERE item = "shirt"
```

t3 Salesman 2 sells two shirts

t4 Salesman 2 retrieves current shirt count (47):

```
SELECT quantity FROM inventory WHERE item = "shirt"
```

t5 Salesman 1 computes new inventory level as 47–3=44 and sets shirt count to 44:

```
UPDATE inventory SET quantity = 44 WHERE item = "shirt"
```

t6 Salesman 2 computes new inventory level as 47–2=45 and sets shirt count to 45:

```
UPDATE inventory SET quantity = 45 WHERE item = "shirt"
```

At the end of this sequence of events, you've sold five shirts (that's good), but the inventory level says 45 rather than 42 (that's bad). The problem is that if you look up the inventory level in one statement and update the value in another statement, you have a multiple-statement transaction. The action taken in the second statement is dependent on the value retrieved in the first. But if separate transactions occur during overlapping time frames, the statements from each transaction intertwine and interfere with each other. In a transactional database, each salesman's statements can be executed as a transaction and Salesman 2's statements wouldn't execute until those for Salesmen 1 had completed. In MySQL, you can achieve the same effect in two ways:

- **Workaround 1: Execute a group of statements as a unit.** You can group together statements and execute them as an atomic unit by surrounding them with LOCK TABLES and UNLOCK TABLES: Lock all the tables that you need to use, issue your queries, and release the locks. This prevents anyone else from using the tables while you have them locked. Using table locking, the inventory situation looks like this:

  t1 Salesman 1 sells three shirts

  t2 Salesman 1 acquires a lock and retrieves current shirt count (47):

  ```
  LOCK TABLES inventory WRITE
  SELECT quantity FROM inventory WHERE item = "shirt"
  ```

  t3 Salesman 2 sells two shirts

  t4 Salesman 2 tries to acquire a lock; this will block because Salesman 1 already holds a lock:

  ```
  LOCK TABLES inventory WRITE
  ```

  t5 Salesman 1 computes new inventory level as 47-3=44, sets shirt count to 44, and releases the lock:

  ```
  UPDATE inventory SET quantity = 44 WHERE item = "shirt"
  UNLOCK TABLES
  ```

  t6 Now the request for a lock by Salesman 2 succeeds. Salesman 2 retrieves current shirt count (44):

  ```
  SELECT quantity FROM inventory WHERE item = "shirt"
  ```

  t7 Salesman 2 computes new inventory level as 44-2=42, sets shirt count to 42, and releases the lock:

  ```
  UPDATE inventory SET quantity = 42 WHERE item = "shirt"
  UNLOCK TABLES
  ```

Now the statements from the two transactions don't get mixed up and the inventory level is set properly. We use a WRITE lock here because we need to modify the inventory table. If you are only reading tables, you can use a READ lock instead. This lets other clients read the tables while you're using them, but prevents clients from writing to them.

In the example just shown, Salesman 2 probably wouldn't notice any difference in speed because the transactions are short and would execute quickly. However, as a general rule, you want to avoid locking tables for a long time.

If you're using multiple tables, you must lock all of them before you execute the grouped queries. If you only read from a particular table, however, you need only a read lock on it, not a write lock. Suppose you have a set of queries in which you want to make some changes to an inventory table, and you also need to read some data from a customer table. In this case, you need a write lock on the inventory table and a read lock on the customer table:

```
LOCK TABLES inventory WRITE, customer READ
...
UNLOCK TABLES
```

This requires you to lock and unlock your tables yourself. A database system with transaction support would do so automatically. However, the aspect of grouping statements for execution as a unit is the same as in transactional databases.

- **Workaround 2: Use relative updates, not absolute updates.** The second way around the problem of statements from multiple transactions getting mixed up is to eliminate the dependency between statements. Though that isn't always possible, it is for our inventory example. For the inventory updating method used with Workaround 1, the transaction involves looking up the current inventory level, computing the new value based on the number of shirts sold, and then updating the level to the new value. It's possible to do this in one step simply by updating the shirt count relative to its current value:

    t1   Salesman 1 sells three shirts

    t2   Salesman 1 decrements shirt count by three:

    ```
    UPDATE inventory SET quantity = quantity - 3 WHERE item =
    "shirt"
    ```

    t3   Salesman 2 sells two shirts

    t4   Salesman 2 decrements shirt count by two:

    ```
    UPDATE inventory SET quantity = quantity - 2 WHERE item =
    "shirt"
    ```

As you can see, this involves no need for multiple-statement transactions at all and thus no need to lock tables to simulate transactional capability. If the types of transactions you've been using are similar to this, you may be able to get by without transactions at all.

The preceding example shows how to avoid the "need" for transactions for a specific situation. This is not to say that there aren't other situations where you really do need transactions. The typical example of this involves a financial transfer where money from one account is placed into another account. Suppose Bill writes a check to Bob for $100.00 and Bob cashes the check. Bill's account should be decremented by $100.00 and Bob's account incremented by the same amount:

```
UPDATE account SET balance = balance - 100 WHERE name = "Bill"
UPDATE account SET balance = balance + 100 WHERE name = "Bob"
```

If a crash occurs between the two statements, the transaction is incomplete. A database system with true transactions and commit/rollback capability would be able to handle this situation. (At least that's the theory. You may still have to figure out which transactions weren't entered and re-issue them, but at least you don't have half-transactions to worry about.) In MySQL, you can figure out the state of transactions at crash time by examining the update log, although this may require some manual examination of the log.

- **Foreign keys and referential integrity.** A foreign key allows you to declare that a key in one table is related to a key in another, and referential integrity allows you to place constraints on what may be done to the table containing the foreign key. For example, the `score` table in our `samp_db` sample database contains a `student_id` column, which we use to relate score records to students in the `student` table. `score.student_id` would be declared a foreign key in databases supporting that concept, and we would impose a constraint on it such that no score record could be entered for a student that does not exist in the `student` table. In addition, we could allow cascading deletion such that if a student were deleted from the `student` table, any score records for the student would automatically be deleted from the `score` table.

Foreign keys help maintain the consistency of your data, and they provide a certain measure of convenience. The reasons MySQL doesn't support them are due primarily to certain negative effects of foreign keys on database performance and maintenance. (The MySQL Reference Manual details a whole list of such reasons.) Note that this view of foreign keys is a bit different than you will find in some other database literature, where you often find them described in terms such as "essential." The MySQL developers don't subscribe to that view. If you do, it might be best to consider other databases to provide foreign key support. For example, if your data have particularly complex relationships, you may not want to be responsible for implementing these dependencies in your applications (even if, as is often the case, this amounts to little more than adding a few extra `DELETE` statements).

MySQL doesn't support foreign keys, except to the extent that it parses `FOREIGN KEY` clauses in `CREATE TABLE` statements. (This helps make it easier to port SQL code from other databases to MySQL.) MySQL doesn't enforce foreign keys as a constraint, nor does it provide cascading delete capability.

The constraints that foreign keys are used to enforce are often not difficult to implement through application logic. Sometimes, it's simply a matter of how you approach the data entry process. For example, for inserting new records into our `score` table, it's unlikely that you'd insert scores for non-existent students. Clearly, the way you'd enter a set of scores would be to start with a list of students from the `student` table, and then for each one, take the score and use the student's ID number to generate a new `score` table record. With this procedure, there isn't any possibility of entering a record for a student that doesn't exist. You wouldn't just invent a score record to put in the `score` table.

To achieve the effect of cascading on `DELETE`, you must implement this with your own application logic, too. Suppose you want to delete student number 13. This also implies you want to delete any score records for that student. In a database that supports cascading deletes, you would delete the `student` table record and any `scores` table records with this statement:

```
DELETE FROM student WHERE student_id = 13
```

The records in the `score` for student 13 are automatically deleted. In MySQL, you perform the secondary deletion yourself with an explicit `DELETE` statement:

```
DELETE FROM student WHERE student_id = 13
DELETE FROM score WHERE student_id = 13
```

- **Stored procedures and triggers.** A stored procedure is SQL code that is compiled and stored in the server. It can be referred to later without having to be sent from the client and parsed again. You can also make changes to a procedure to affect any client applications that use it. Trigger capability allows a stored procedure to be activated when some event occurs, such as a record being deleted from a table. For example, you might do this if you wanted to regenerate some complex summary of which the record was a part to keep the summary up to date. A stored procedure language is on the MySQL to-do list.

- **Views.** A *view* is a logical entity that acts like a table but is not one. It provides a way to look at columns from different tables as though they're all part of the same table. Views are sometimes called virtual tables. Views are on the MySQL to-do list.

- **Record-level privileges and locking.** MySQL supports various levels of privileges, from global privileges down to database, table, and column privileges. It does not support record-level privileges. However, you can use the `GET_LOCK()` and `RELEASE_LOCK()` functions in your applications to implement cooperative record locks. The procedure for this is described in the entry for `GET_LOCK()` in Appendix C, "Operator and Function Reference."

- **'--' as a comment.** This comment style is not supported because it's an ambiguous construct, although as of MySQL 3.23.3, a comment beginning with two dashes and a space is accepted. See the section "Writing Comments" for more information.

4

Query Optimization

THE WORLD OF RELATIONAL DATABASE THEORY is a world dominated by tables and sets, and operations on tables and sets. A *database* is a set of tables, and a *table* is a set of rows and columns. When you issue a SELECT query to retrieve rows from a table, you get back another set of rows and columns. These are abstract notions that make no reference to the underlying representation a database system uses to operate on the data in your tables. Another abstraction is that operations on tables happen all at once; queries are conceptualized as set operations and there is no concept of time in set theory.

The real world, of course, is quite different. Database management systems implement abstract concepts but do so on real hardware bound by real physical constraints. As a result, queries take time—sometimes an annoyingly long time. And we, being impatient creatures, don't like to wait, so we leave the abstract world of instantaneous mathematical operations on sets and look around for ways to speed up our queries. Fortunately, there are several techniques for doing so. We index tables to allow the database server to look up rows more quickly. We consider how to write queries to take advantage of those indexes to the fullest extent. We write queries to affect the server's scheduling mechanism so that queries arriving from multiple clients cooperate better. We think about what's going on with the underlying hardware and how we can work around its physical constraints to improve performance.

These are the kinds of issues that this chapter focuses on, with the goal of assisting you in optimizing the performance of your database system so that it processes your queries as quickly as possible. MySQL is already quite fast, but even the fastest database can run queries more quickly if you help it do so.

Using Indexing

We'll discuss indexing first because it's the most important tool you have for speeding up your queries. There are other techniques available to you, too, but generally the one thing that will make the most difference is the proper use of indexes. On the MySQL mailing list, people often ask for help in making a query run faster. In a surprisingly large number of cases, there are no indexes on the tables in question, and adding indexes often solves the problem immediately. It doesn't always work like that because optimization isn't always simple. Nevertheless, if you don't use indexes, then in many cases you're just wasting your time trying to improve performance by other means. Use indexing first to get the biggest performance boost and then see what other techniques might be helpful.

This section describes what an index is, how it improves query performance, when indexes may degrade performance, and how to choose indexes for your tables. In the next section, we'll discuss MySQL's query optimizer. It's good to have some understanding of the optimizer in addition to knowing how to create indexes because then you'll be better able to take advantage of the indexes you create. Certain ways of writing queries actually prevent your indexes from being useful, and generally you'll want to avoid having that happen. (Not always, though. Sometimes you'll want to override the optimizer's behavior. We'll cover some of these cases, too.)

Benefits of Indexing

Let's consider how an index works by beginning with a table that has no indexes. An unindexed table is simply an unordered collection of rows. For example, Figure 4.1 shows the ad table that we first saw in Chapter 1, "Introduction to MySQL and SQL." There are no indexes on this table, so if we're looking for the rows for a particular company, we must examine each row in the table to see if it matches the desired value. This involves a full table scan, which is slow, as well as tremendously inefficient if the table contains only a few records matching the search criteria.

Figure 4.2 shows the same table, but with the addition of an index on the company_num column in the ad table. The index contains an entry for each row in the ad table, but the index entries are sorted on company_num value. Now, instead of searching through the table row by row looking for items that match, we can use the index. Suppose we're looking for all rows for company 13. We begin scanning the index and find three rows for that company. Then we reach the row for company 14, a value higher than the one we're looking for. Index values are sorted, so when we read the record containing 14, we know we won't find any more matches and can quit looking. If we were looking for a value that doesn't occur until some point midway into the index table, there are positioning algorithms for finding the first matching index entry without doing a linear scan of the table (for example, a binary search). That way, we can quickly position to the first matching value and save a lot of time in the search. Databases use various techniques for positioning to index values quickly, but it's not so important here what those techniques are. What's important is that they work and that indexing is a good thing.

You may be asking why we don't just sort the data file and dispense with the index file? Wouldn't that produce the same type of improvement in search speed? You're right, it would—if you had a single index. But you might want a second index, and you can't sort the data file two different ways at once. (For example, you might want one index on customer names and another on customer ID numbers or phone numbers.) Using indexes as entities separate from the data file solves the problem and allows multiple indexes to be created. In addition, rows in the index are generally shorter than data rows. When you insert or delete new values, it's easier to move around shorter index values to maintain the sort order than to move around the longer data rows.

ad table

company_num	ad_num	hit_fee
14	48	0.01
23	49	0.02
17	52	0.01
13	55	0.03
23	62	0.02
23	63	0.01
23	64	0.02
13	77	0.03
23	99	0.03
14	101	0.01
13	102	0.01
17	119	0.02

Figure 4.1 Unindexed ad table.

index		company_num	ad_num	hit_fee
13		14	48	0.01
13		23	49	0.02
13		17	52	0.01
14		13	55	0.03
14		23	62	0.02
17		23	63	0.01
17		23	64	0.02
23		13	77	0.03
23		23	99	0.03
23		14	101	0.01
23		13	102	0.01
23		17	119	0.02

Figure 4.2 Indexed ad table.

The example corresponds to the way MySQL indexes tables. A table's data rows are kept in a data file, and index values are kept in an index file. You can have more than one index on a table; if you do, they're all stored in the same index file. Each index in the index file consists of a sorted array of key records that are used for fast access into the data file.

The preceding discussion describes the benefit of an index in the context of single-table queries, where the use of an index speeds searches significantly by eliminating the need for full table scans. However, indexes are even more valuable when you're running queries involving joins on multiple tables. In a single-table query, the number of values you need to examine per column is the number of rows in the table. In a multiple-table query, the number of possible combinations skyrockets because it's the product of the number of rows in the tables.

Suppose you have three unindexed tables, t1, t2, and t3, each containing a column c1, c2, and c3, respectively, and each consisting of 1000 rows that contain the numbers 1 through 1000. (This example is contrived, of course. It's simple to make a point; nevertheless, the problems it will illustrate are real.) A query to find all combinations of table rows in which the values are equal looks like this:

```
SELECT c1, c2, c3
FROM t1, t2, t3
WHERE c1 = c2 AND c1 = c3
```

The result of this query should be 1000 rows, each containing three equal values. If we process the query in the absence of indexes, we have no idea which rows contain which values. Consequently, we must try all combinations to find the ones that match the WHERE clause. The number of possible combinations is 1000 x 1000 x 1000 (1 billion!), which is a million times more than the number of matches. That's a lot of wasted effort, and this query is likely to be very slow, even for a database such as MySQL that is very fast. And that is with only 1000 rows per table. What happens when you have tables with millions of rows? You can see that this quickly leads to very poor performance. If we index each table, we can speed things up considerably because indexing allows the query to be processed like this:

1. Select the first row from table t1 and see what value the row contains.

2. Using the index on table t2, go directly to the row that matches the value from t1. Similarly, using the index on table t3, go directly to the row that matches the value from t1.

3. Proceed to the next row of table t1 and repeat the preceding procedure until all rows in t1 have been examined.

In this case, we're still performing a full scan of table t1, but we're able to do indexed lookups on t2 and t3 to pull out rows from those tables directly. The query runs about a million times faster this way—literally.

MySQL uses indexes as just described to speed up searches for rows matching terms of a WHERE clause or rows that match rows in other tables when performing joins. It also uses indexes to improve the performance of other types of operations:

- The smallest or largest value for an indexed column can be found quickly without examining every row when you use the MIN() or MAX() functions.

- MySQL can often use indexes to perform sorting operations quickly for ORDER BY clauses.

- Sometimes MySQL can avoid reading the data file entirely. Suppose you're selecting values from an indexed numeric column, and you're not selecting other columns from the table. In this case, by reading an index value, you've already got the value you'd get by reading the data file. There's no reason to read values twice, so the data file need not even be consulted.

Disadvantages of Indexing

In general, if MySQL can figure out how to use an index to process a query more quickly, it will. This means that, for the most part, if you don't index your tables, you're hurting yourself. You can see that I'm painting a rosy picture of the benefits of indexing. Are there disadvantages? Yes, there are. In practice, these drawbacks tend to be outweighed by the advantages, but you should know what they are.

First, the index file takes up disk space. If you have lots of indexes, the index file may reach the maximum file size more quickly than the data file. Second, indexes speed up retrievals but slow down inserts and deletes, as well as updates of values in indexed columns (that is, most operations involving writing) because a write affects not only the data row, but often the indexes as well. The more indexes a table has, the greater the average performance degradation for write operations. In the section "Loading Data Efficiently," we'll go into more detail about this performance problem and what you can do about it.

Choosing Indexes

The syntax for creating indexes was covered in the section "Creating and Dropping Indexes" of Chapter 3, "MySQL SQL Syntax and Use." I assume here that you've read that section. But knowing syntax doesn't in itself help you determine how your tables should be indexed. That requires some thought about the way you use your tables. This section gives some guidelines on how to identify and select candidate columns for indexing:

- **Index columns that you search for, not columns you select.** In other words, the best candidate columns for indexing are the columns that appear in your WHERE clause or columns named in join clauses, not columns that appear in the selection list following the SELECT keyword:

```
SELECT
    col_a                              ← not a candidate
FROM
    tbl1 LEFT JOIN tbl2
    ON tbl1.col_b = tbl2.col_c         ← candidates
WHERE
    col_d = expr                       ← a candidate
```

The columns that you select and the columns you use in the WHERE clause might be the same, of course. The point is that appearance of a column in the selection list is not a good indicator that it should be indexed.

Columns that appear in join clauses or in expressions of the form *col1* = *col2* are especially good candidates for indexing. col_b and col_c in the query just shown are examples of this. If MySQL can optimize a query using joined columns, it cuts down the potential table-row combinations quite a bit by eliminating full table scans.

- **Use unique indexes.** Consider the spread of values in a column. Indexes work best for columns with unique values, and most poorly with columns that have many duplicate values. For example, if a column contains ages and has several different values, an index will differentiate rows readily. An index will not help as much if a column is used to record sex and contains only the two values "M" and "F" (whichever value you search for, you're still going to get about half of the rows).

- **Use short indexes.** If you're indexing a string column, specify a prefix length whenever it's reasonable to do so. For example, if you have a CHAR(200) column, don't index the entire column if most values are unique within the first 10 or 20 characters. Indexing the first 10 or 20 characters will save a lot of space in the index, and probably will make your queries faster as well. A smaller index involves less disk I/O, and shorter values can be compared more quickly. More importantly, with shorter key values, blocks in the index cache hold more key values, so MySQL can hold more keys in memory at once. This improves the likelihood of locating rows without reading additional blocks from the index. (You want to use some common sense, of course. Indexing just the first character from a column isn't likely to be that helpful because there won't be very many distinct values in the index.)

- **Take advantage of leftmost prefixes.** When you create an *n*-column index, you actually create *n* indexes that MySQL can use. A multiple-column index serves as several indexes because any leftmost set of columns in the index can be used to match rows. Such a set is called a leftmost prefix.[1]

---

[1] This is different than indexing a prefix of a column, which is using the first *n* characters of the column for index values.

Suppose you have a table with an index on columns named `state`, `city`, and `zip`. Rows in the index are sorted in `state/city/zip` order, so they're automatically sorted on `state/city` order and `state` order as well. This means that MySQL can take advantage of the index even if you specify only `state` values in a query, or only `state` and `city` values. Thus, the index can be used to search the following combinations of columns:

```
state, city, zip
state, city
state
```

MySQL cannot use the index for searches that don't involve a leftmost prefix. For example, if you search by `city` or by `zip`, the index isn't used. If you're searching for a given state and a particular zip code (columns 1 and 3 of the index), the index can't be used for the combination of values. However, MySQL can narrow the search using the index to find rows that match the state.

- **Don't over-index.** Don't index everything in sight based on the assumption "the more, the better." That's a mistake. Every additional index takes extra disk space and hurts performance of write operations, as has already been mentioned. Indexes must be updated and possibly reorganized when you modify the contents of your tables, and the more indexes you have, the longer this takes. If you have an index that is rarely or never used, you're slowing down table modifications unnecessarily. In addition, MySQL considers indexes when generating an execution plan for retrievals. Creating extra indexes creates more work for the query optimizer. It's also possible (if unlikely) that MySQL will fail to choose the best index to use when you have too many indexes. Maintaining only the indexes you need helps the query optimizer avoid making such mistakes.

  If you're thinking about adding an index to a table that is already indexed, consider whether or not the index you're thinking about adding is a leftmost prefix of an existing multiple-column index. If so, don't bother adding the index because, in effect, you already have it.

- **Consider the type of comparisons you perform on a column.** Indexes are used for '<', '<=', '=', '>=', '>', and `BETWEEN` operations. Indexes are also used for `LIKE` operations, when the pattern has a literal prefix. If you use a column only for other kinds of operations, such as `STRCMP()`, there is no value in indexing it.

The MySQL Query Optimizer

When you issue a query to select rows, MySQL analyzes it to see if it can take advantage of any optimizations that will allow it to process the query more quickly. In this section, we'll look at how the query optimizer works. For additional information, consult the chapter "Getting Maximum Performance from MySQL" in the MySQL Reference Manual. That chapter describes various optimization measures that MySQL takes. Information is added to the chapter from time to time because the MySQL developers keep making the optimizer smarter, and it's worth revisiting the chapter occasionally to see if there are any new tricks you can use. (The online MySQL manual at `http://www.mysql.com/` is continually updated.)

The MySQL query optimizer takes advantage of indexes, of course, but it also uses other information. For example, if you issue the following query, MySQL will execute it very quickly, no matter how large the table is:

```
SELECT * FROM tbl_name WHERE 1 = 0
```

In this case, MySQL looks at the WHERE clause, realizes that no rows can possibly satisfy the query, and doesn't even bother to search the table. You can see this with the EXPLAIN statement, which tells MySQL to display some information about how it would execute a SELECT query without actually executing it. To use EXPLAIN, just put the word EXPLAIN in front of the SELECT statement:

```
EXPLAIN SELECT * FROM tbl_name WHERE 1 = 0
```

The output from EXPLAIN is:

```
+------------------+
| Comment          |
+------------------+
| Impossible WHERE |
+------------------+
```

Normally, EXPLAIN returns more information than that, including information about the indexes that will be used to scan tables, the types of joins that will be used, and estimates of the number of rows that will need to be scanned from each table.

How the Optimizer Works

The MySQL query optimizer has several goals, but its primary aims are to use indexes whenever possible and to use the most restrictive index in order to eliminate as many rows as possible as soon as possible. That may sound backward, because *your* goal in issuing a SELECT statement is to find rows, not to reject them. The reason the optimizer works this way is that the faster it can eliminate rows from consideration, the more quickly the rows that do match your criteria can be found. Queries can be processed more quickly if the most restrictive tests can be done first. Suppose you have a query that tests two columns, each of which has an index on it:

```
WHERE col1 = "some value" AND col2 = "some other value"
```

Suppose also that the test on col1 matches 900 rows, the test on col2 matches 300 rows, and that both tests succeed on 30 rows. If you test col1 first, you have to examine 900 rows to find the 30 that also match the col2 value. That's 870 failed tests. If you test col2 first, you have to examine only 300 rows to find the 30 that also match the col1 value. That's 270 failed tests, which involve less computation and less disk I/O.

You can help the optimizer use indexes by using the following guidelines:

- **Compare columns that have the same type.** When you use indexed columns in comparisons, use columns that are of the same type. For example, CHAR(10) is considered the same as CHAR(10) or VARCHAR(10) but different than CHAR(12) or VARCHAR(12). INT is different than BIGINT. Using columns of the same type is a requirement in MySQL versions prior to 3.23, or indexes on the columns will not be used. From version 3.23 and up, this is not strictly necessary, but identical column types will still give you better performance than dissimilar types. If the columns you're comparing are of different types, you can use ALTER TABLE to modify one of them so that the types match.

- **Try to make indexed columns stand alone in comparisons.** If you use a column in a function call or in an arithmetic expression, MySQL can't use the index because it must compute the value of the expression for every row. Sometimes this is unavoidable, but many times you can rewrite a query to get the indexed column by itself.

The following WHERE clauses illustrate how this works. In the first line, the optimizer will simplify the expression 4/2 to the value 2, then use an index on my_col to quickly find values less than 2. In the second expression, MySQL must retrieve the value of my_col for each row, multiply by 2, and then compare the result to 4. No index can be used because each value in the column must be retrieved so that the expression on the left side of the comparison can be evaluated:

```
WHERE my_col < 4 / 2
WHERE my_col * 2 < 4
```

Let's consider another example. Suppose you have an indexed column date_col. If you issue a query such as the following, the index isn't used:

```
SELECT * FROM my_tbl WHERE YEAR(date_col) < 1990
```

The expression doesn't compare an indexed column to 1990; it compares a value calculated from the column value, and that value must be computed for each row. As a result, the index on date_col cannot be used. What's the fix? Just use a literal date, and the index on *date_col* will be used:

```
WHERE date_col < "1990-01-01"
```

But suppose you don't have a specific date. You might be interested instead in finding records that have a date that lies within a certain number of days from today. There are several ways to write a query like this—not all of which are equally good. Three possibilities are as follows:

```
WHERE TO_DAYS(date_col) - TO_DAYS(CURRENT_DATE) < cutoff
WHERE TO_DAYS(date_col) < cutoff + TO_DAYS(CURRENT_DATE)
WHERE date_col < DATE_ADD(CURRENT_DATE, INTERVAL cutoff DAY)
```

For the first line, no index is used because the column must be retrieved for each row so that the value of TO_DAYS(date_col) can be computed. The second line is better. Both *cutoff* and TO_DAYS(CURRENT_DATE) are constants, so the right hand side of the comparison can be calculated by the optimizer once before processing the query, rather than once per row. But the date_col column still appears in a function call, so the index isn't used. The third line is the way to go. Again, the right-hand side of the comparison can be computed once as a constant before executing the query, but now the value is a date. That value can be compared directly to date_col values, which no longer need to be converted to days. In this case, the index can be used.

- **Don't use wildcards at the beginning of a LIKE pattern.** Sometimes people search for strings using a WHERE clause of the following form:

    ```
    WHERE col_name LIKE "%string%"
    ```

    That's the correct thing to do if you want to find *string* no matter where it occurs in the column. But don't put '%' on both sides of the string simply out of habit. If you're really looking for the string only when it occurs at the beginning of the column, leave out the first '%'. For example, if you're looking in a column containing last names for names that begin with "Mac", write the WHERE clause like this:

    ```
    WHERE last_name LIKE "Mac%"
    ```

    The optimizer looks at the literal initial part of the pattern and uses the index to find rows that match as though you'd written the following expression, which is in a form that allows an index on last_name to be used:

    ```
    WHERE last_name >= "Mac" AND last_name < "Mad"
    ```

    This optimization does not apply to pattern matches that use the REGEXP operator.

- **Help the optimizer make better estimates about index effectiveness.** By default, when you are comparing values in indexed columns to a constant, the optimizer assumes that key values are distributed evenly within the index. The optimizer will also do a quick check of the index to estimate how many entries will be used when determining whether or not the index should be used for constant comparisons. You can provide the optimizer with better information by using the --analyze option with myisamchk or isamchk to analyze key value distribution. Use myisamchk for MyISAM tables and isamchk for ISAM tables. To perform key analysis, you must be able to log in on the MySQL server host, and you must have write access to the table files.

- **Use EXPLAIN to verify optimizer operation.** Check to see that indexes are being used in your query to reject rows quickly. If not, you might try using STRAIGHT_JOIN to force a join to be done using tables in a particular order. Run the query different ways to see; MySQL may have some good reason not to use indexes in the order you think is best.

- **Test alternate forms of queries, but run them more than once.** When testing alternate forms of a query, run it several times each way. If you run a query just once each of two different ways, you'll often find that the second query is faster just because information from the first query is still in the disk cache and need not actually be read from the disk. You should also try to run queries when the system load is relatively stable to avoid effects due to other activities on your system.

Overriding Optimization

It may sound odd, but there are times when you want to defeat MySQL's optimization techniques. Some of these circumstances are described in this section:

- **To force MySQL to delete table contents slowly.** When you need to empty a table completely, it's fastest to delete its entire contents using a `DELETE` statement with no `WHERE` clause:

  ```
  DELETE FROM tbl_name
  ```

  MySQL optimizes this special case of `DELETE`; it simply re-creates empty data and index files from scratch using the table description in the table information file. This optimization makes the `DELETE` operation extremely fast because MySQL doesn't have to delete each row individually. However, it has some effects that may be undesirable under certain circumstances:

  - MySQL reports the number of rows affected as zero, even when the table wasn't empty. Most of the time that doesn't matter (though it can be puzzling if you don't expect it), but for applications that really want to know the true number of rows, this is not appropriate.

  - If the table contains an `AUTO_INCREMENT` column, sequence numbering for the column is reset to start over at 1. This is true even for the `AUTO_INCREMENT` handling improvements introduced in MySQL 3.23 and discussed in the section "Working With Sequences" in Chapter 2, "Working with Data in MySQL."

  You can "unoptimize" a `DELETE` statement by adding a `WHERE 1>0` clause:

  ```
  DELETE FROM tbl_name WHERE 1 > 0
  ```

  This forces MySQL to do a row-by-row deletion. The query executes much more slowly, but it will return the true number of rows deleted. It will also preserve the current `AUTO_INCREMENT` sequence numbering, although only for MyISAM tables (available in MySQL 3.23 and above). For ISAM tables, the sequence is still reset, unfortunately.

- **To avoid an endless update loop.** If you update a column that is indexed, it's possible for the rows that are updated to be updated endlessly if the column is used in the `WHERE` clause and the update moves the index value into the part of the range that hasn't been processed yet. Suppose the table `my_tbl` has an integer column `key_col` that is indexed. Queries such as the following can cause problems:

```
UPDATE my_tbl SET key_col = key_col+1 WHERE key_col > 0;
```

The solution for this is to use `key_col` in an expression in the `WHERE` clause so that MySQL can't use the index:

```
UPDATE my_tbl SET key_col = key_col+1 WHERE key_col+0 > 0;
```

Actually, there is another solution: Upgrade to MySQL 3.23.2 or newer, which fixes this problem.

- **To retrieve results in random order.** As of MySQL 3.23.2, you can use `ORDER BY RAND()` to sort results randomly. Another technique, which is useful for older versions of MySQL, is to select a column of random numbers and sort on that column. However, if you write the query as follows, the optimizer defeats your intent:

  ```
  SELECT ..., RAND() as rand_col FROM ... ORDER BY rand_col
  ```

  The problem here is that MySQL sees that the column is a function call, thinks that the value of the column will be a constant, and optimizes the `ORDER BY` clause right out of the query! You can fool the optimizer by referring to a table column in the expression. For example, if your table has a column named `age`, you can write the query like this:

  ```
  SELECT ..., age*0+RAND() as rand_col FROM ... ORDER BY rand_col
  ```

- **To override the optimizer's table join order.** Use `STRAIGHT_JOIN` to force the optimizer to use tables in a particular order. If you do this, you should order the tables so that the first table is the one from which the smallest number of rows will be chosen. (If you are not sure which table this is, put the table with the most rows first.) In other words, try to order the tables to cause the most restrictive selection to come first. Queries perform better the earlier you can narrow the possible candidate rows. Make sure to try the query both ways; there may be some reason the optimizer isn't joining tables the way you think it should, and `STRAIGHT_JOIN` may not actually help.

Column Type Choices and Query Efficiency

This section provides some guidelines for choosing your columns that can help queries run more quickly:[2]

---

[2] In this discussion, "`BLOB` types" should be read as meaning both `BLOB` and `TEXT` types.

- **Use fixed-length columns rather than variable-length columns.** This is especially true for tables that are modified often and therefore more subject to fragmentation. For example, make all character columns CHAR rather than VARCHAR. The tradeoff is that your table will use more space, but if you can afford the extra space, fixed-length rows can be processed more quickly than variable-length rows.

- **Don't use longer columns when shorter ones will do.** If you are using fixed-length CHAR columns, don't make them unnecessarily long. If the longest value you store in a column is 40 characters, don't declare it as CHAR(255); declare it as CHAR(40). If you can use MEDIUMINT rather than BIGINT, your table will be smaller (less disk I/O), and values can be processed more quickly in computations.

- **Declare columns to be NOT NULL.** This gives you faster processing and requires less storage. It will also simplify queries sometimes because you don't need to check for NULL as a special case.

- **Consider using ENUM columns.** If you have a string column that contains only a limited number of distinct values, consider converting it to an ENUM column. ENUM values can be processed quickly because they are represented as numeric values internally.

- **Use PROCEDURE ANALYSE().** If you have MySQL 3.23 or newer, run PROCEDURE ANALYSE() to see what it tells you about the columns in your table:

```
SELECT * FROM tbl_name PROCEDURE ANALYSE()
SELECT * FROM tbl_name PROCEDURE ANALYSE(16,256)
```

One column of the output is a suggestion for the optimal column type for each of the columns in your table. The second example tells PROCEDURE ANALYSE() not to suggest ENUM types that contain more than 16 values or that take more than 256 bytes (you can change the values as you like). Without such restrictions, the output may be very long; ENUM declarations are often difficult to read.

Based on the output from PROCEDURE ANALYSE(), you may find that your table can be changed to take advantage of a more efficient type. Use ALTER TABLE if you want to change a column type.

- **Pack data into a BLOB.** Using a BLOB to store data that you pack and unpack in your application may allow you to get everything with a single retrieval operation rather than with several. This can also be helpful for data that are not easy to represent in a standard table structure, or that change over time. In the discussion of the ALTER TABLE statement in Chapter 3, one of the examples dealt with a table being used to hold results from the fields in a Web-based questionnaire. That example discussed how you could use ALTER TABLE to add columns to the table whenever you add questions to the questionnaire.

Another way to approach this problem is to have the application program that processes the Web form pack the data into some kind of data structure, then insert it into a single `BLOB` column. This adds application overhead for encoding the data (and decoding it later when you retrieve records from the table), but simplifies the table structure, and obviates the need to change the table structure when you change your questionnaire.

On the other hand, `BLOB` values can cause their own problems, especially if you do a lot of `DELETE` or `UPDATE` operations. Deleting a `BLOB` may leave a large hole in the table that will be filled in later with a record or records of probably different sizes.

- **Use `OPTIMIZE TABLE` for tables that are subject to fragmentation.** Tables that are modified a great deal, particularly those that contain variable-length columns, are subject to fragmentation. Fragmentation is bad because it leads to unused space in the disk blocks used to store your table. Over time, you must read more blocks to get the valid rows, and performance is reduced. This is true for any table with variable-length rows, but is particularly acute for `BLOB` columns because they can vary so much in size. Use of `OPTIMIZE TABLE` on a regular basis helps keep performance on the table from degrading.

- **Use a synthetic index.** Synthetic index columns can sometimes be helpful. One technique is to create a hash value based on other columns and store it in a separate column. Then you can find rows by searching for hash values. This is good only for exact-match queries. (Hash values are useless for range searches with operators such as '<' or '>='). Hash values can be generated in MySQL 3.23 and up by using the `MD5()` function.

  A hash index can be particularly useful with `BLOB` columns. For one thing, you cannot index these types prior to MySQL 3.23.2. But even with 3.23.2 or later, it may be quicker to find `BLOB` values using a hash as an identifier value than by searching the `BLOB` column itself.

- **Avoid retrieving large `BLOB` or `TEXT` values unless you must.** For example, a `SELECT *` query isn't a good idea unless you're sure the `WHERE` clause is going to restrict the results to just the rows you want. Otherwise, you may be pulling potentially very large `BLOB` values over the network for no purpose. This is another case where `BLOB` identifier information stored in another column can be useful. You can search that column to determine the row or rows you want and then retrieve the `BLOB` value from the qualifying rows.

- **Segregate `BLOB` values into a separate table.** Under some circumstances, it may make sense to move `BLOB` columns out of a table into a secondary table, if that allows you to convert the table to fixed-length row format for the remaining columns. This will reduce fragmentation in the primary table and also allow you to take advantage of the performance benefits of having fixed-length rows.

Loading Data Efficiently

Most of the time you'll probably be concerned about optimizing SELECT queries, because they are the most common type of query and because it's not always straightforward to figure out how to optimize them. By comparison, loading data into your database is straightforward. Nevertheless, there are strategies you can use to improve the efficiency of data-loading operations. The basic principles are as follows:

- Bulk loading is faster than single-row loading because the index cache need not be flushed after each record is loaded; it can be flushed at the end of the batch of records.

- Loading is faster when a table has no indexes than when it is indexed. If there are indexes, not only must the record be added to the data file, but also each index must be modified to reflect the addition of the new record.

- Shorter SQL statements are faster than longer statements because they involve less parsing on the part of the server and because they can be sent over the network from the client to the server more quickly.

Some of these factors may seem minor (the last one in particular), but if you're loading a lot of data, even small efficiencies make a difference. We can use the preceding general principles to draw several practical conclusions about how to load data most quickly:

- LOAD DATA (all forms) is more efficient than INSERT because it loads rows in bulk. Index flushing takes place less often, and the server needs to parse and interpret one statement, not several.

- LOAD DATA is more efficient than LOAD DATA LOCAL. With LOAD DATA, the file must be located on the server and you must have the FILE privilege, but the server can read the file directly from disk. With LOAD DATA LOCAL, the client reads the file and sends it over the network to the server, which is slower.

- If you must use INSERT, use the form that allows multiple rows to be specified in a single statement:

  ```
  INSERT INTO tbl_name VALUES(...),(...),...
  ```

  The more rows you can specify in the statement, the better. This reduces the total number of statements you need and minimizes the amount of index flushing.

  If you use mysqldump to generate database backup files, use the --extended-insert option so that the dump file contains multiple-row INSERT statements. You can also use --opt (optimize), which turns on the --extended-insert option. Conversely, avoid using the --complete-insert option with mysqldump; the resulting INSERT statements will be for single rows and will be longer and require more parsing than will statements generated without --complete-insert.

- Use the compressed client/server protocol to reduce the amount of data going over the network. For most MySQL clients, this can be specified using the `--compress` command line option. Generally, this should only be used on slow networks because compression uses quite a bit of processor time.

- Let MySQL insert default values for you; don't specify columns in `INSERT` statements that will be assigned the default value anyway. On average, your statements will be shorter, reducing the number of characters sent over the network to the server. In addition, because the statements contain fewer values, the server does less parsing and value conversion.

- If a table is indexed, you can lessen indexing overhead by using batched inserts (`LOAD DATA` or multiple-row `INSERT` statements). These minimize the impact of index updating because the index needs flushing only after all rows have been processed, rather than after each row.

- If you need to load a lot of data into a new table to populate it, it's faster to create the table without indexes, load the data, and then create the indexes. It's faster to create the indexes all at once rather than to modify them for each row.

- It may be faster to load data into an indexed table if you drop or deactivate the indexes before loading and rebuild or reactivate them afterward.

If you want to use the strategy of dropping or deactivating indexes for data loading, be prepared to do some experimentation to find out if it is worthwhile. (If you're loading a small amount of data into a large table, building the indexes may well take longer than loading the data.)

You can drop and rebuild indexes with `DROP INDEX` and `CREATE INDEX`. An alternative approach is to deactivate and reactivate the indexes by using `myisamchk` or `isamchk`. This requires that you have an account on the MySQL server host and you have write access to the table files. To deactivate a table's indexes, move into the appropriate database directory and run one of the following commands:

```
% myisamchk --keys-used=0 tbl_name
% isamchk --keys-used=0 tbl_name
```

Use `myisamchk` for MyISAM tables that have an index file with an `.MYI` extension and `isamchk` for ISAM tables that have an index file with a `.ISM` extension. After loading the table with data, reactivate the indexes:

```
% myisamchk --recover --quick --keys-used=n tbl_name
% isamchk --recover --quick --keys-used=n tbl_name
```

n is the number of indexes the table has. You can determine this value by invoking the appropriate utility with the `--description` option:

```
% myisamchk --description tbl_name
% isamchk --description tbl_name
```

If you decide to use index deactivation and activation, you should use the table repair locking protocol described in Chapter 13, "Database Maintenance and Repair," to keep the server from changing the table at the same time that you are. (You're not repairing the table, but you are modifying it like the table repair procedure does, so the same locking protocol is appropriate.)

The preceding data-loading principles also apply to mixed-query environments involving clients performing different kinds of operations. For example, you generally want to avoid long-running SELECT queries on tables that are updated frequently. This causes a lot of contention and poor performance for the writers. A possible way around this, if your writes are mostly INSERT operations, is to add new records to a temporary table and then add those records to the main table periodically. This is not a viable strategy if you need to be able to access new records immediately, but if you can afford to leave them inaccessible for a short time, use of the temporary table will help you two ways. First, it reduces contention with SELECT queries that are taking place on the main table, so they execute more quickly. Second, it takes less time overall to load a batch of records from the temporary table into the main table than it would to load the records individually; the index cache need be flushed only at the end of each batch, rather than after each individual row.

One application for this strategy is when you're logging Web page accesses from your Web server into a MySQL database. In this case, it's probably not a high priority to make sure the entries get into the main table right away.

Another strategy for reducing index flushing is to use the DELAYED_KEY_WRITE table creation option for MyISAM tables if your data are such that it's not absolutely essential that every single record be inserted in the event of abnormal system shutdown. (This might be the case if you're using MySQL for some sort of logging.) The option causes the index cache to be flushed only occasionally rather than after each insert.

If you want to use delayed index flushing on a server-wide basis, start mysqld with the --delayed-key-write option. In this case, index block writes are delayed until blocks must be flushed to make room for other index values, until a flush-tables command has been executed, or until the indexed table is closed.

Scheduling and Locking Issues

The previous sections have focused primarily on making individual queries faster. MySQL also allows you to affect the scheduling priorities of statements, which may allow queries arriving from several clients to cooperate better so that individual clients aren't locked out for a long time. Changing the priorities can also ensure that particular kinds of queries are processed more quickly. We'll look first at MySQL's default scheduling policy and then see what options are available to you for influencing this policy. For the purposes of this discussion, a client performing a retrieval (a SELECT) is a reader. A client performing an operation that modifies a table (DELETE, INSERT, REPLACE, or UPDATE) is a writer.

MySQL's basic scheduling policy can be summed up like this:

- Write requests should be processed in the order in which they arrive.
- Writes have higher priority than reads.

The scheduling policy is implemented with the aid of table locks. Whenever a client accesses a table, a lock for it must be acquired first. It's possible to do this explicitly with LOCK TABLES, but normally the server's lock manager acquires locks as necessary automatically. When the client is finished with a table, the lock on it can be released. An explicitly acquired lock is released with UNLOCK TABLES, but here too the server automatically releases locks that it has acquired.

A client performing a write operation must have a lock for exclusive access to the table. The table is in an inconsistent state while the operation is in progress because the data record is being deleted, added, or changed, and any indexes on the table may need to be updated to match. Allowing other clients to access the table while the table is in flux causes problems. It's clearly a bad thing to allow two clients to write to the table at the same time because that would quickly corrupt the table into an unusable mess. But it's not good to allow a client to read from an in-flux table, either, because the table might be changing right at the spot being read, and the results would be inaccurate.

A client performing a read operation must have a lock to prevent other clients from writing to the table so that the table doesn't change while the table is being read. The lock need not provide exclusive access for reading, however. The lock can allow other clients to read the table at the same time. Reading doesn't change the table, so there is no reason readers should prevent each other from accessing the table.

MySQL allows you to influence its scheduling policy by means of several query modifiers. One of these is the LOW_PRIORITY keyword for DELETE, INSERT, LOAD DATA, REPLACE, and UPDATE statements. Another is the HIGH_PRIORITY keyword for SELECT statements. The third is the DELAYED keyword for INSERT and REPLACE statements.

The LOW_PRIORITY keyword affects scheduling as follows. Normally, if a write operation for a table arrives while the table is being read, the writer blocks until the reader is done because once a query has begun it will not be interrupted. If another read request arrives while the writer is waiting, the reader blocks, too, because the default scheduling policy is that writers have higher priority than readers. When the first reader finishes, the writer proceeds, and when the writer finishes, the second reader proceeds.

If the write request is a LOW_PRIORITY request, the write is not considered to have a higher priority than reads. In this case, if a second read request arrives while the writer is waiting, the second reader is allowed to slip in ahead of the writer. Only when there are no more readers is the writer is allowed to proceed. One implication of this scheduling modification is that, theoretically, it's possible for LOW_PRIORITY writes to be blocked forever. As long as additional read requests arrive while previous ones are still in progress, the new requests will be allowed to get in ahead of the LOW_PRIORITY write.

The HIGH_PRIORITY keyword for SELECT queries is similar. It allows a SELECT to slip in ahead of a waiting write, even if the write has normal priority.

The DELAYED modifier for INSERT acts as follows. When an INSERT DELAYED request arrives for a table, the server puts the rows in a queue and returns a status to the client immediately so that the client can proceed even before the rows have been inserted. If readers are reading from the table, the rows in the queue are held. When there are no readers, the server begins inserting the rows in the delayed-row queue. Every now and then, the server pauses to see whether any new read requests have arrived and are waiting. If so, the delayed-row queue is suspended and the readers are allowed to proceed. When there are no readers left, the server begins inserting delayed rows again. This process continues until the queue is empty.

The scheduling modifiers did not appear in MySQL all at once. The following table lists these modifiers and the version of MySQL in which they appeared. You can use this to determine what capabilities your version of MySQL has.

Statement Type	Version of Initial Appearance
DELETE LOW_PRIORITY	3.22.5
INSERT LOW_PRIORITY	3.22.5
INSERT DELAYED	3.22.15
LOAD DATA LOW_PRIORITY	3.23.0
LOCK TABLES ... LOW_PRIORITY	3.22.8
REPLACE LOW_PRIORITY	3.22.5
REPLACE DELAYED	3.22.15
SELECT ... HIGH_PRIORITY	3.22.9
UPDATE LOW_PRIORITY	3.22.5
SET SQL_LOW_PRIORITY_UPDATES	3.22.5

Client-Side Effects of INSERT DELAYED

INSERT DELAYED is useful if other clients may be running lengthy SELECT statements and you don't want to block waiting for completion of the insertion. The client issuing the INSERT DELAYED can proceed more quickly because the server simply queues the row to be inserted.

You should be aware of certain other differences between normal INSERT and INSERT DELAYED behavior, however. The client gets back an error if the INSERT statement contains a syntax error, but other information that would normally be available is not. For example, you can't rely on getting the AUTO_INCREMENT value when the statement returns. You also won't get a count for the number of duplicates on unique indexes. This happens because the insert operation returns a status before the operation actually has been completed. Another implication is that if rows from INSERT DELAYED statements are queued while waiting to be inserted and the server crashes or is killed (with kill -9), the rows are lost. This is not true for a normal TERM kill; in that case, the server inserts the rows before exiting.

Optimization for Administrators

The previous sections have described optimizations that can be performed by ordinary MySQL users in terms of table creation and indexing operations, and in terms of how you write queries. But there are also optimizations that can be performed only by MySQL and system administrators who have control of the MySQL server or the machine on which it runs. Some server parameters pertain directly to query processing and may be tuned, and certain hardware configuration issues have a direct effect on query processing speed.

Server Parameters

The server has several parameters (variables) that you can change to affect its operation. A general discussion of server parameter tuning is given in Chapter 11, "General MySQL Administration," but a few of these parameters are related primarily to query processing and merit brief mention here:

- delayed_queue_size

  This determines the number of rows from INSERT DELAYED statements that will be queued before clients performing additional INSERT DELAYED statements get blocked. Increasing this value allows the server to accept more rows from this type of request so that clients can proceed without blocking.

- key_buffer_size

  This is the size of the buffer used to hold index blocks. If you have the memory, increasing this value should improve index creation and modification time. Larger values allow MySQL to hold more index blocks in memory at once, which increases the likelihood of finding key values in memory without having to read a new block from disk.

In MySQL 3.23 and up, if you increase the key buffer size, you might also want to start the server using the --init-file option. This allows you to specify a file of SQL statements to be executed when the server starts up. If you have read-only tables that you'd like to have held in memory, you can copy them to HEAP tables for very fast index lookups.

Hardware Issues

You can use your hardware more effectively to improve server performance:

- **Install more memory into your machine.** This enables you to increase the server's cache and buffer sizes. This allows the server to use information held in memory more often and with less need to fetch information from disk.

- **Reconfigure your system to remove all disk swap devices if you have enough RAM to do all swapping into a memory file system.** Otherwise, some systems will continue to swap to disk even if you have sufficient RAM for swapping.

- **Add faster disks to improve I/O latency.** Seek time is typically the primary determinant of performance here. It's slow to move the heads laterally; once the heads are positioned, reading blocks off the track is fast by comparison.

- **Try to redistribute disk activity across physical devices.** For example, if you can store your two busiest databases on separate physical drives, do so. Note that using different partitions on the same physical device isn't sufficient. That won't help you because they'll still contend for the same physical resource (disk heads). The procedure for moving databases is described in Chapter 10, "The MySQL Data Directory."

  Before you relocate data to a different device, make sure you understand your system's load characteristics. If there's some other major activity already taking place on a particular physical device, putting a database there may actually make performance worse. For example, you may not realize any overall benefit if you process a lot of Web traffic and move a database onto the device where your Web server document tree is located. (If you have only a single drive, you can't perform much disk activity redistribution, of course.)

- **When you build MySQL, configure it to use static libraries rather than shared libraries.** Dynamic binaries that use shared libraries save on disk space, but static binaries are faster. (However, you cannot use static binaries if you want to load user-defined functions because the UDF mechanism relies on dynamic linking.)

II

Using MySQL
Programming Interfaces

5

Introduction to MySQL Programming

I N THIS PART OF THE BOOK, WE'LL DISCUSS what you need to know to write your own programs that access MySQL databases. MySQL comes with a set of utility programs. For example, `mysqldump` exports the contents and structure definitions of tables, `mysqlimport` loads data files into tables, `mysqladmin` performs administrative operations, and `mysql` lets you interact with the server to execute arbitrary queries. Each of the standard MySQL utilities is intended as a small, focused program with a specific, limited function. This is true even for `mysql`, which is more flexible than the other utilities in the sense that you can use it to execute any number of different queries: It's designed with the single purpose of allowing you to issue SQL queries directly to the server and view the results.

This limited nature of the MySQL clients is not a flaw—it's by design. The programs are general-purpose utilities; they are not intended to anticipate all possible requirements you might have. The MySQL developers do not subscribe to the philosophy of writing huge, bloated programs that try to do everything you might possibly want to do (and thus end up including lots of code for many things you don't care at all about). Nevertheless, applications sometimes have requirements that cannot be handled by the capabilities of the standard clients. To deal with these cases, MySQL provides a client-programming library. This allows you to write your own programs and provides you with the flexibility to satisfy whatever specialized requirements your applications may have. By giving you access to the MySQL server, the client library opens up possibilities limited only by your own imagination.

What specific capabilities do you gain by writing your own programs? Let's examine this question in comparison to the capabilities of the `mysql` client and its no-frills interface to the MySQL server:

- **You can customize input handling.** With `mysql`, you enter raw SQL statements. With your own programs, you can provide input methods for the user that are more intuitive and easier to use. The program can eliminate the need for the user to know SQL—or even to be aware of the role of the database in the task being performed.

  Input collection can be something as rudimentary as a prompt- and value-reading loop for a command-line style interface or something as sophisticated as a screen-based entry form implemented using a screen management package such as `curses` or S-Lang, an X window using Tcl/Tk, or a Web browser form.

  For most people, it's a lot easier to specify search parameters by filling in a form than by issuing a `SELECT` statement. For example, a realtor looking for houses in a certain price range, style, or location just wants to enter search parameters into a form and get back the qualifying offerings with a minimum of fuss. For entering new records or updating existing records, similar considerations apply. A keyboard operator in a data entry department shouldn't need to know the SQL syntax for `INSERT`, `REPLACE`, or `UPDATE`.

  An additional reason to interpose an input-collection layer between the end user and the MySQL server is that you can validate input provided by the user. For example, you can check dates to make sure they conform to the format that MySQL expects, or you can require certain fields to be filled in.

- **You can customize your output.** `mysql` output is essentially unformatted; you have a choice of tab-delimited or tabular style. If you want nicer-looking output, you must format it yourself. This might range from something as simple as printing "Missing" rather than `NULL` to more complex report-generation requirements. Consider the following report:

```
State  City       Sales
.............................
AZ     Mesa        $94,384.24
       Phoenix     $17,328.28
       ...........................
       subtotal   $117,712.52
.............................
CA     Los Angeles $118,198.18
       Oakland     $38,838.36
       ...........................
       Subtotal   $157,036.54
=============================
       TOTAL       $274,749.06
```

This report includes several specialized elements:

- Customized headers.
- Suppression of repeating values in the `State` column so that the values are printed only when they change.
- Subtotal and total calculations.
- Formatting of numbers, such as `94384.24`, to print as dollar amounts, such as `$94,384.24`.

For some types of tasks, you may not even want any output. Perhaps you're simply retrieving information to calculate a result that you insert back into another database table. You may even want the output to go somewhere other than to the user running the query. For example, if you're extracting names and email addresses to feed automatically into a process that generates form letters for bulk email, your program produces output. But the output consists of the messages that go to the mail recipients, not to the person running the program.

- **You can work around constraints imposed by the nature of SQL itself.** SQL is not a procedural language with a set of flow control structures, such as conditionals, loops, and subroutines. SQL scripts consist of a set of statements executed one at a time from beginning to end, with minimal error checking.

If you execute a file of SQL queries using `mysql` in batch mode, `mysql` either quits after the first error, or, if you specify the `--force` option, executes all the queries indiscriminately, no matter how many errors occur. A program can provide flow control around statements so that you can selectively adapt to the success or failure of queries. You can make execution of one query contingent on the success or failure of another or make decisions about what to do next based on the result of a previous query.

SQL has very limited persistence across statements, and this carries into `mysql`. It's difficult to use the results from one query and apply them to another or to tie together the results of multiple queries. `LAST_INSERT_ID()` can be used to get the `AUTO_INCREMENT` value that was most recently generated by a prior statement, but that's about it.

More generally, it can be difficult to retrieve a set of records, then use each one as the basis for a complex series of further operations. For example, retrieving a list of customers and then looking up a detailed credit history for each one may involve several queries per customer. In certain cases, you may want to produce an invoice for which you need to associate the invoice header with information on the customer and on each item ordered. `mysql` is unsuitable for these kinds of tasks, both because you may need several queries that depend on the results of previous queries and because the tasks exceed `mysql`'s formatting capabilities.

In general, a tool other than `mysql` is needed for tasks that involve master-detail relationships and have complex output-formatting requirements. A program provides the "glue" that links queries together and allows you to use the output from one query as the input to another.

- **You can integrate MySQL into any application.** Many programs stand to benefit by exploiting the ability of a database to provide information. An application that needs to verify a customer number or check whether or not an item is present in inventory can do so by issuing a quick query. A Web application that lets a client ask for all books by a certain author can look them up in a database and then present the results to the client's browser.

  It's possible to achieve a kind of rudimentary "integration" by using a shell script that invokes `mysql` with an input file containing SQL statements, then postprocessing the output using other UNIX utilities. But that can become ugly, especially as your task becomes more involved. It also may produce a sense of "it-works-but-feels-wrong" as the application grows by accretion into a messy patchwork. In addition, the process-creation overhead of a shell script that runs other commands may be more than you wish to incur. It can be more effective to interact with the MySQL server directly, extracting exactly the information you want as you need it at each phase of your application's execution.

With respect to our `samp_db` sample database that we set up in Chapter 1, "Introduction to MySQL and SQL," we enumerated several goals there that require us to write programs to interact with the MySQL server. Some of these goals are shown in the following list:

- Format the Historical League directory for printing
- Allow for presentation and search of the directory online
- Send membership renewal notices by email
- Easily enter scores into the gradebook using a Web browser

One area that we'll consider in some detail is integrating MySQL's capabilities into a Web environment. MySQL provides no direct support for Web applications, but by combining MySQL with appropriate tools, your databases can be accessed easily over the Web. You can specify queries using your Web server and report the results to a client's browser.

There are two complementary perspectives on the marriage of MySQL and the Web:

- Your main interest is your database, and you want to use the Web as a tool to gain easier access to your data. The place of a database in such a scenario is explicit and obvious because it's the focus of your interest. For example, you can write Web pages that allow you to see what tables your database contains, what each one's structure is, and what its contents are. You're using your Web server to enhance your access to MySQL. This is the point of view a MySQL administrator probably would take.

- Your primary interest may be your Web site, and you may want to use MySQL as a tool for making your site's content more valuable to the people who visit it. For example, if you run a message board or discussion list for visitors to the site, you can use MySQL to keep track of the messages. In this case, the role of the database is more subtle, and visitors may not even be aware that it plays a part in the services you have to offer. You're using MySQL to enhance the capabilities of your Web server. This is the point of view a Web site developer probably would take.

These perspectives are not mutually exclusive. For example, in the Historical League scenario, we want to use the Web as a means for members to gain easy access to the contents of the membership directory by making entries available online. That is a use of the Web to provide access to the database. At the same time, the League's Web site is somewhat underdeveloped, so adding directory content to the site increases the site's value to members. That is a use of the database to enhance the services provided at the site.

No matter how you view the integration of MySQL with the Web, the implementation is similar. You connect your Web site front end to your MySQL back end, using the Web server as an intermediary. The Web server sends a query from the user to the MySQL server, retrieves the query results, and then conveys them to the client for viewing in a browser.

You don't have to put your data online, of course, but often there are benefits to doing so, particularly in comparison with accessing your data via the standard MySQL client programs:

- People accessing your data through the Web can use the browser they prefer, on the type of platform they prefer. They're not limited to systems that the MySQL client programs run on. No matter how widespread the MySQL clients are, Web browsers are more so.

- A Web interface can be made simpler to use than a standalone command-line MySQL client.

- A Web interface can be customized to the requirements of a particular application. The MySQL clients are general-purpose tools with a fixed interface.

- Dynamic Web pages extend MySQL's capabilities to do things that are difficult or impossible to do using the MySQL clients. For example, you can't really put together an application that incorporates a shopping cart using just MySQL clients.

Any programming language can be used to write Web-based applications, but some are more suitable than others. We'll see this in "Choosing an API."

APIs Available for MySQL

To facilitate application development, MySQL provides a client library written in the
C programming language that allows you to access MySQL databases from within any
C program. The client library implements an application programming interface (API)
that defines how client programs establish and carry out communications with the
server.

However, you are not limited to using C to write MySQL programs. Many other
language processors are either written in C themselves or have the capability of using
C libraries, so the MySQL client library provides the means whereby MySQL bindings for these languages can be built on top of the C API. This gives you many choices
for writing applications that talk to the MySQL server. Client APIs exist for Perl, PHP,
Java, Python, C++, Tcl, and others. Check the MySQL Reference Manual or the
MySQL Web site for an up-to-date list because new language APIs are added from
time to time.

Each language binding defines its own interface, specifying the rules for accessing
MySQL. There is insufficient space here to discuss each of the APIs available for
MySQL, so we'll concentrate on three of the most popular:

- **The C client library API.** This is the primary programming interface to
  MySQL.

- **The DBI (Database Interface) API for the Perl general purpose scripting language.** DBI is implemented as a Perl module that interfaces with other
  modules at the DBD (Database Driver) level, each of which provides access to a
  specific type of database engine. (The particular DBD module on which we'll
  concentrate is the one that provides MySQL support, of course.) The most common uses of DBI with MySQL are for writing standalone clients to be invoked
  from the command line and for scripts intended to be invoked by a Web server
  to provide Web access to MySQL.

- **The PHP API.** PHP is a scripting language that provides a convenient way of
  embedding programs in Web pages. Such a page is processed by PHP before
  being sent to the client, which allows the script to generate dynamic content,
  such as including the result of a MySQL query in the page. "PHP" originally
  meant Personal Home Page, but PHP has grown far beyond its original humble
  beginnings. The PHP Web site now uses the name to stand for "PHP: Hypertext
  Preprocessor," which is self-referential in the same manner as GNU ("GNU's
  Not UNIX").

Consider Building on the Work of Others

When the standard MySQL clients are insufficient for your needs, you need not always write your own
programs. Other people already have been busy writing programs, many of which are freely available.
See Appendix I, "Useful Third-Party Tools," for some examples. You just might find a few that can save
you some work.

Each of these three APIs is described in detail in its own chapter. The present chapter provides a comparative overview of the APIs to describe their general characteristics and to give you an idea why you might choose one over another for particular applications.

There's no reason to consider yourself locked into a single API, of course. Get to know each API and arm yourself with the knowledge that enables you to choose wisely. If you have a large project with several components, you might use multiple APIs and write some parts in one language and other parts in another language, depending on which one is most appropriate for each piece of the job. You may also find it instructive to implement an application several ways if you have time. This gives you direct experience with different APIs as they apply to your own applications.

If you need to get the software necessary for using any of the APIs that you'd like to try, see Appendix A, "Obtaining and Installing Software," for instructions.

The C API

The C API is used within the context of compiled C programs. It's a client library that provides the lowest level interface available for talking to the MySQL server—giving you the capabilities you need for establishing a connection to and conversing with the server.

Predecessors of DBI and PHP

The Perl predecessor to DBI is the Mysqlperl module, Mysql.pm. This module is no longer supported and should not be used for new MySQL development. For one thing, Mysqlperl is MySQL-dependent, whereas DBI is not. If you write Perl applications for MySQL and then decide you want to use them with another database engine, it's easier to port DBI scripts than Mysqlperl scripts because they are less dependent on a particular database engine.

If you obtain a Perl script for accessing MySQL and discover that it's written for Mysqlperl rather than for DBI, you can still use DBI. DBI can be built to include Mysqlperl emulation support, so it's not necessary to install both packages.

The predecessor to PHP 3 is PHP/FI 2.0 (FI stands for "form interpreter"). Like Mysqlperl, PHP/FI is obsolete and I won't discuss it further.

The Origin of the MySQL C API

If you have experience writing programs for the mSQL RDBMS, you'll notice that the MySQL C API is similar to the corresponding C API for mSQL. When the MySQL developers began implementing their SQL engine, a number of useful free utilities were available for mSQL. To make it possible to port those mSQL utilities to MySQL with minimum difficulty, the MySQL API was designed deliberately to be similar to the mSQL API. (MySQL even comes with a `msql2mysql` script that does simple textual substitution of mSQL API function names to the corresponding MySQL names. This operation is relatively trivial, yet actually takes care of much of the work involved in converting a mSQL program for use with MySQL.)

The C clients provided in the MySQL distribution are based on this API. The C client library also serves as the basis for the MySQL bindings for other languages, with the exception of the Java APIs. For example, the MySQL-specific driver for the Perl DBI module and the PHP code are both made MySQL-aware by linking in the code for the MySQL C client library. (This process is illustrated by the DBI and PHP installation instructions in Appendix A.)

The Perl DBI API

The DBI API is used within the context of applications written for the Perl scripting language. This API is the most highly architected of the three APIs we're considering, because it tries to work with as many databases as possible, while at the same time hiding as many database-specific details as possible from the script writer.

DBI is implemented via Perl modules that use a two-level architecture (see Figure 5.1):

- **The DBI (database interface) level.** Provides the interface for client scripts. This level provides an abstraction that does not refer to specific database engines.

- **The DBD (database driver) level.** Support for various database engines is provided at this level by drivers that are engine specific.

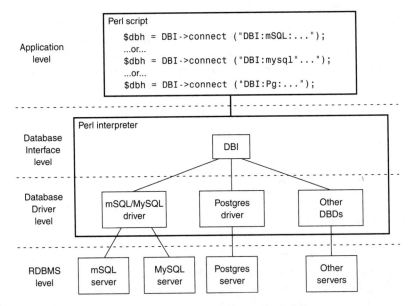

Figure 5.1 DBI architecture.

MySQL support for DBI is provided by the `Msql-Mysql-modules` distribution. This module operates at the DBD level. As you can tell from the distribution name and also from Figure 5.1, it's possible for a driver to provide support for more than one RDBMS. `Msql-Mysql-modules` was written originally for mSQL, then extended for MySQL later. This reflects the similarity of the C APIs for mSQL and for MySQL. Since the MySQL C API was designed to be similar to the mSQL C API, it made sense to extend the mSQL DBD (which uses the mSQL C API) to work with MySQL.

The DBI architecture allows you to write applications in relatively generic fashion. When you write a DBI script, you use a standard set of calls. The DBI layer invokes the proper driver at the DBD level to handle your requests, and the driver handles the specific issues involved in communicating with the particular database server you want to use. The DBD level passes data returned from the server back up to the DBI layer, which presents the data to your application. The form of the data is consistent no matter what database the data originated from.

The result is an interface that from the application writer's point of view hides differences between database engines, yet works with a wide variety of engines—as many as there are drivers for. DBI provides a consistent client interface that increases portability by allowing you to access each database in a uniform fashion.

The one necessarily database-specific aspect of script writing occurs when you open a database. You indicate which driver to use when you establish the connection. For example, to use a MySQL database, you connect like this:

```
$dbh = DBI->connect ("DBI:mysql:...");
```

To use Postgres or mSQL instead, you connect like this:

```
$dbh = DBI->connect ("DBI:Pg:...");
$dbh = DBI->connect ("DBI:mSQL:...");
```

After you've made the connection, you don't need to make any specific reference to the driver. Let DBI and the driver work out database-specific details.

That's the theory, anyway. However, at least two factors work against DBI script portability:

- SQL implementations differ betweeen RDBMS engines, and it's perfectly possible to write SQL for one engine that another will not understand. If your SQL is reasonably generic, your scripts will be correspondingly portable between engines. If your SQL is engine dependent, your scripts will be, too. For example, if you use the MySQL-specific SHOW TABLES statement, your script won't work with other databases.

- DBD modules often provide engine-specific types of information to allow script writers to use particular features of particular database systems. For example, the MySQL DBD provides a way to access properties of the columns in a query result such as the maximum length of each column, whether or not columns are numeric, and so forth. These properties don't necessarily have any analog in other databases. DBD-specific features are antithetical to portability, and by using them, you make it difficult to use a script written for MySQL with other database systems.[1]

Despite the potential of these two factors for making your scripts database specific, the DBI mechanism for providing database access in an abstract fashion is a reasonable means of achieving portability. It's up to you to decide how much you want to take advantage of it.

The PHP API

Like Perl, PHP is a scripting language. Unlike Perl, PHP is designed less as a general-purpose language than as a language for writing Web applications. The PHP API is used primarily as a means of embedding executable scripts into Web pages. This makes it easy for Web developers to write pages with dynamically generated content. When a client browser sends a request for a PHP page to a Web server, PHP executes any script it finds in the page and replaces it with the script's output. The result is sent to the browser. This allows the page that actually appears in the browser to differ according to the circumstances under which the page is requested. For example, when the following short PHP script is embedded in a Web page, it displays the IP address of the host that requested the page:

```
<?php echo $REMOTE_ADDR; ?>
```

As a less trivial and more interesting application, you can use a script to provide up-to-the-minute information to visitors based on the contents of your database. The following example shows a simple script such as might be used at the Historical League Web site. The script issues a query to determine the current League membership count and reports it to the person visiting the site (If an error occurs, the script simply doesn't report any count.):

```
<HTML>
<HEAD>
<TITLE>US Historical League</TITLE>
</HEAD>
<BODY>
```

The Meaning of DBI and DBD

Although the DBI level is database independent and the DBD level is database dependent, that isn't what "DBI" and "DBD" stand for. They mean "database interface" and "database driver."

[1] Nevertheless, you will discover that in Chapter 7, "The Perl DBI API," I make little effort to avoid MySQL-specific constructs provided by the MySQL DBD. That's because you should know what those constructs are so that you can decide for yourself whether or not to use them.

```
<P>Welcome to the US Historical League Website.
<?php
$link = @mysql_pconnect ("pit-viper.snake.net", "paul", "secret")
    or exit ();
mysql_select_db ("samp_db")
    or exit ();
$result = mysql_query ("SELECT COUNT(*) FROM member")
    or exit ();
if ($row = mysql_fetch_array ($result))
    echo "<P>The League currently has " . $row[0] . " members";
mysql_free_result ($result);
?>
</BODY></HTML>
```

PHP scripts typically look like HTML pages with scripts embedded inside the '<?php'
and '?>' tags. A page can contain several scripts. This provides an extremely flexible
approach to script development. For example, if you like, you can write a normal
HTML page to build the general page framework, then add script content later.

PHP makes no effort to unify the interface to different database engines the way
DBI does. Instead, the interface to each engine looks much like the interface for the
corresponding C library implementing the low-level API for that engine. For example,
the names of the PHP functions that you use to access MySQL from within PHP
scripts are very similar to the names of the functions in the MySQL C client library.

Choosing an API

This section provides general guidelines to help you choose an API for various types
of applications. It compares the capabilities of the C, DBI, and PHP APIs to give you
some idea of their relative strengths and weaknesses, and to indicate when you might
choose one over another.

I should probably point out first that I am not advocating any one of these languages over the others. I use them all, although I do have my preferences. You will
have your own preferences, too, as did my reviewers. In fact, one reviewer felt that I
should emphasize the importance of C for MySQL programming to a much greater
extent, while another thought I should come down much harder on C programming
and discourage its use! You'll have to weigh the factors discussed in this section and
come to your own conclusions.

A number of considerations can enter in to your assessment of which API to
choose for a particular task:

- **Intended execution environment.** The context in which you expect the
  application to be used.

- **Performance.** How efficiently applications perform when written in the API
  language.

- **Ease of development.** How convenient the API and its language make application writing.

- **Portability.** Whether or not the application will be used for database systems other than MySQL.

Each of these factors is examined further in the following discussion. Be aware that some of the factors interact. For example, you may want an application that performs well, but it can be just as important to use a language that lets you develop the application quickly even if it doesn't perform quite as efficiently.

Execution Environment

When you write an application, you generally have some idea of the environment in which it will be used. For example, it might be a report generator program that you invoke from the shell, or an accounts payable summary program that runs as a cron job at the end of each month. Commands run from the shell or from cron generally stand on their own and require little from the execution environment. On the other hand, you might be writing an application intended to be invoked by a Web server. Such a program may expect to be able to extract very specific types of information from its execution environment: What browser is the client using? What parameters were entered into a mailing list subscription request form? Did the client supply the correct password for accessing our personnel information?

Each API language varies in its suitability for writing applications in these differing environments:

- C is a general-purpose language, so in principle you can use it for anything. In practice, C tends to be used more often for standalone programs rather than for Web programming. One reason is probably that it isn't as easy in C as in Perl or in PHP to perform text processing and memory management, and those tend to be heavily used in Web applications.

- Perl, like C, is suitable for writing standalone programs. However, it also happens that Perl is quite useful for Web site development—for example, by using the CGI.pm module. This makes Perl a handy language for writing applications that link MySQL with the Web. Such an application can interface to the Web via the CGI.pm module and interact with MySQL using DBI.

- PHP is intended by design for writing Web applications, so that's obviously the environment to which it is best suited. Furthermore, database access is one of PHP's biggest strengths, so it's a natural choice for Web applications that perform MySQL-related tasks. It's possible to use PHP as a standalone interpreter (for example, to execute scripts from the shell), but it's not used that way very often.

Given these considerations, C and Perl are the most likely candidate languages if you're writing a standalone application. For Web applications, Perl and PHP are most suitable. If you need to write both types of applications, but don't know any of these languages and want to learn as few as possible, Perl might be your best option.

Performance

All other things being equal, we generally prefer to have our applications run as quickly as possible. However, the actual importance of performance tends to be related to the frequency with which a program is used. For a program that you run once a month as a cron job during the night, performance may not matter that much. If you run a program several times a second on a heavily used Web site, every bit of inefficiency you can eliminate can make a big difference. In the latter case, performance plays a significant role in the usefulness and appeal of your site. A slow site is annoying for users, no matter what the site is about, and if you depend on the site as a source of income, decreased performance translates directly into reduced revenue. You cannot service as many connections at a time, and disgusted visitors simply give up and go elsewhere.

Performance assessment is a complex issue. The best indicator of how well your application will perform when written for a particular API is to write it under that API and test it. And the best comparative test is to implement it multiple times under different APIs to see how the versions stack up against each other. Of course, that's not how things usually work. More often, you just want to get your program written. Once it's working, you can think about tuning it if it needs to run faster, use less memory, or has some other aspect that needs to be improved in some other way. But there are at least two factors that you can count on as affecting performance in a relatively consistent way:

- Compiled programs execute more quickly than interpreted scripts.
- For interpreted languages used in a Web context, performance is better when the interpreter is invoked as a module that is part of the Web server itself rather than as a separate process.

Compiled Versus Interpreted Languages

As a general principle, compiled applications are more efficient, use less memory, and execute more quickly than an equivalent version of the program written in a scripting language. This is due to the overhead involved with the language interpreter that executes the scripts. Because C is compiled and Perl and PHP are interpreted, C programs generally will run faster than Perl or PHP scripts.

For a heavily used program, C is often the best choice. The `mysql` command-line client included in the MySQL distribution is a good example of this.

There are, of course, factors that tend to diminish this clear distinction. For one thing, writing in C generally gives you a faster program, but it's quite possible to write inefficient C programs. Writing a program in a compiled language is no automatic passport to better performance. It's still necessary to think about what you're doing. In addition, the difference between compiled and interpreted programs is lessened if a scripted application spends most of its time executing code in the MySQL client library routines that are linked into the interpreter engine.

Standalone Versus Module Versions of Language Interpreters

For Web-based applications, script language interpreters are usually used in one of two forms—at least for Apache, which is the Web server we'll be using when we write Web applications:

- You can arrange for Apache to invoke the interpreter as a separate process. When Apache needs to run a Perl or PHP script, it starts up the corresponding program and tells it to execute the script. In this case, Apache uses the interpreters as CGI programs—that is, it communicates with them using the Common Gateway Interface (CGI) protocol.

- The interpreter can be used as a module that is linked in directly to the Apache binary and that runs as part of the Apache process itself. In Apache terms, the Perl and PHP interpreters take the form of the `mod_perl` and `mod_php3` modules.

Perl and PHP advocates will debate the speed advantages of their favorite interpreter, but all agree that the form in which the interpreter runs is a much bigger factor than the languages themselves. Either interpreter runs much faster as a module than as a standalone CGI application.

With a standalone application, it's necessary to start up the interpreter each time a script is to be executed, so you incur a significant penalty in process-creation overhead. When used as a module within an already running Apache process, an interpreter's capabilities can be accessed from your Web pages instantly. This dramatically improves performance by reducing overhead and translates directly into an increased capacity to handle incoming requests and to dispatch them quickly.

The standalone interpreter startup penalty typically results in at least an order of magnitude poorer performance than the module interpreter. Interpreter startup cost is particularly significant when you consider that Web page serving typically involves quick transactions with light processing rather than substantial ones with a lot of processing. If you spend a lot of time just starting up and not very much actually executing the script, you're wasting most of your resources. It's like spending most of the day getting ready for work, arriving at 4 o'clock, and then going home at 5.

You might wonder why there are any savings with the module versions of the interpreters because you must still start up Apache. The reason is that when Apache starts up, it immediately spawns a pool of child processes to be used to handle incoming requests. When a request arrives that involves execution of a script, there is already an Apache process ready and waiting to handle it. Also, each instance of Apache services multiple requests, so the process startup cost is incurred only once per set of requests, not once per request.

When Perl and PHP are installed in module form (as `mod_perl` and `mod_php3`), which performs better? That is subject to debate, but the following guidelines generally apply:

- Perl converts the script to an internally compiled form; PHP does not. Thus, once the script has been parsed, Perl is likely to execute it somewhat faster, particularly for loops with a large number of iterations.

- `mod_perl` can perform script caching for increased performance on scripts that are executed repeatedly. If a script is in the cache, Perl is faster to begin executing the script because it need not be parsed again. Otherwise, PHP starts executing the script more quickly.

- `mod_perl` has a bigger memory footprint than PHP; Apache processes are larger with `mod_perl` linked in than with `mod_php3`. PHP was designed under the assumptions that it must live cooperatively within another process and that it might be activated and deactivated multiple times within the life of that process. Perl was designed to be run from the command line as a standalone program, not as a language meant to be embedded in a Web server process. This probably contributes to its larger memory footprint; as a module, Perl simply isn't running in its natural environment. Other factors that contribute to the larger footprint are script caching and additional Perl modules that scripts use. In both cases, more code is brought into memory and remains there for the life of the Apache process.

Whatever advantages Perl may have over PHP in script execution speed may be eliminated by PHP 4. PHP 4 is like PHP 3 in terms of its capabilities and interface, but it incorporates Zend, a higher-performance interpreter engine.

In any case, all of these factors result only in percentage-point performance differences between the module versions of Perl and PHP. The most important thing is to avoid the standalone interpreters whenever possible, whichever language you choose.

The standalone version of an interpreter does have one advantage over its module counterpart, in that you can arrange for it to run under a different user ID. The module versions always run under the same user ID as the Web server, which is typically an account with minimal privileges for security reasons. That doesn't work very well for scripts that require specific privileges (for example, if you need to be able to read or write protected files). You can combine the module and standalone approaches if you like: Use the module version by default and the standalone version for situations in which scripts need to run with the privileges of a particular user.

Reducing the Memory Requirements of `mod_perl`

There are techniques that allow you to enable only certain Apache processes for `mod_perl`. That way, you incur the extra memory overhead only for those processes that execute Perl scripts. The `mod_perl` area of the Apache Web site has a good discussion of various strategies from which to choose. (See `http://perl.apache.org/guide/` for more information.)

What this adds up to is that, whether you choose Perl or PHP, you should try to use it from an Apache module rather than by invoking a separate interpreter process. Reserve use of the standalone interpreter only for those cases that cannot be handled by the module, such as scripts that require special privileges. For these instances, you can process your script by using Apache's suEXEC mechanism to start up the interpreter under a given user ID.

Development Time

The factors just described affect the performance of your applications, but raw execution efficiency may not be your only goal. Your own time is important, too, as is ease of programming, so another factor to consider in choosing an API for MySQL programming is how quickly you can develop your applications. If you can write a Perl script in half the time it takes to develop the equivalent C program, you may prefer to use the Perl DBI API rather than the C API, even if the resulting application doesn't run quite as fast. It's often reasonable to be less concerned about a program's execution time than about the time you spend writing it, particularly for applications that aren't executed frequently. An hour of your time is worth a lot more than an hour of machine time!

Generally, scripting languages allow you to get a program going more quickly, especially for working out a prototype of the finished application. At least two factors contribute to this.

First, scripting languages tend to provide more high-level constructs. This allows you to think at a higher level of abstraction so that you can think about what you want to do rather than about the details involved in doing it. For example, Perl's associative arrays (hashes) are a great time saver for maintaining data with a key/value relationship (such as student ID/student name pairs). C has no such construct. If you wanted to implement such a thing in C, you would need to write code to handle many low-level details involving issues such as memory management and string manipulation, and you would need to debug it. This takes time.

Second, the development cycle has fewer steps for scripting languages. With C, you go through the usual edit-compile-test cycle as you're developing your application. Every time you modify the program, you must recompile it before testing. With Perl and PHP, the development cycle is simply edit-test because you can run a script immediately after each modification with no compiling. On the other hand, the compiler enforces more constraints on your program in the form of stricter type checking. The need for greater discipline imposed by the compiler can help you avoid bugs that you would not catch as easily in looser languages, such as Perl and PHP. If you misspell a variable name in C, the compiler will warn you. PHP will not, and Perl won't unless you ask it to. These tighter constraints can be especially valuable as your applications become larger and more difficult to maintain.

In general, the tradeoff is the usual one between compiled and interpreted languages for development time versus performance: Do you want to develop the program using a compiled language so that it will execute more quickly when it runs, but spend more time writing it? Or do you want to write the program as a script so that you can get it running in the least amount of time, even at the cost of some execution speed?

It's also possible to combine the two approaches. Write a script as a "first draft" to quickly develop an application prototype to test out your logic and make sure the algorithms are appropriate. If the program proves useful and is executed frequently enough that performance becomes a concern, you can recode it as a compiled application. This gives you the best of both worlds: quick prototyping for initial development of the application, and the best performance for the final product.

In a strict sense, the Perl DBI and PHP APIs give you no capabilities that are not already present in the C client library. This is because both of those APIs gain access to MySQL by having the MySQL C library linked into the Perl and PHP interpreters. However, the environment in which MySQL capabilities are embedded is very different for C than for Perl or PHP. Consider some of the types of things you'll need to do as you interact with the MySQL server and ask how much each API language will help you do them. Here are some examples:

- **Memory management.** In C, you find yourself working with `malloc()` and `free()` for any tasks involving dynamically allocated data structures. Perl and PHP handle that for you. For example, arrays grow in size automatically and dynamic-length strings can be used without ever thinking about memory management.

- **Text manipulation.** Perl has the most highly developed capabilities in this area, and PHP runs a close second. C is very rudimentary by comparison.

Of course, in C you can write your own libraries to encapsulate tasks such as memory management and text processing into functions that make the job easier. But then you still have to debug them, and you want your algorithms to be efficient, too. In both respects, it's a fair bet that the algorithms in Perl and PHP for these things are generally well debugged and reasonably efficient, since they've had the benefit of being examined by many pairs of eyes. You can save your time by taking advantage of the time that others have already put into the job. (On the other hand, if the interpreter does happen to have a bug, you may simply have to live with it until the problem is fixed. When you write in C, you have a finer level of control over the behavior of your program.)

The languages differ in how "safe" they are. The C API provides the lowest-level interface to the server and enforces the least policy. In this sense, it provides the least amount of safety net. If you execute API functions out of order, you may be lucky and get an "out-of-sync" error, or you may be unlucky and have your program crash. Perl and PHP both protect you pretty well. Your script fails if you don't do things in the proper order, but the interpreter doesn't crash. Another fertile source of crashing bugs in C programs is the use of dynamically allocated memory and pointers associated with them. Perl and PHP handle memory management for you, so your scripts are much less likely to die from memory management bugs.

Development time is affected by the amount of external support that is available for a language. C external support is available in the form of wrapper libraries that encapsulate MySQL C API functions into routines that are easier to use. Libraries that do this are available for both C and C++. Perl undoubtedly has the largest number of add-ons, in the form of Perl modules (these are similar in concept to Apache modules). There is even an infrastructure in place designed to make it easy to locate and obtain these modules (the CPAN, or Comprehensive Perl Archive Network). Using Perl modules, you gain access to all kinds of functions without writing a line of code. Want to write a script that generates a report from a database, then mail it to someone as an attachment? Just get one of the MIME modules and you have instant attachment-generation capability.

PHP doesn't have the same amount of external support (which isn't surprising because it's a newer language). Perhaps the best known add-on is the PHP Base Library (PHPLIB). Suppose you're writing a Web application that needs to restrict access to certain Web pages to authorized users only, based on some sort of name and password mechanism. You can write support for that in any language, but if you use the PHP Base library (PHPLIB), you don't have to spend your time reinventing the wheel. PHPLIB provides authentication and also allows you to track authorized users through a session (a succession of page hits from a given client treated as parts of a single logical visit). You can also assign permissions to users, which allows you to do things like defining administrative users that have more privileges.

Portability

The question of portability has to do with how easily a program written to access the MySQL engine can be modified to use a different engine. This may be something you don't care about. However, unless you can predict the future, saying "I'll never use this program with any database other than MySQL" might be a little risky: Suppose you get a different job and want to use your old programs, but your new employer uses a different database system?

If portability is a priority, you should consider the clear differences between APIs:

- DBI provides the most portable API because database independence is an explicit DBI design goal.
- PHP is less portable because it doesn't provide the same sort of uniform interface to various database engines that DBI does. The PHP function calls for each supported database tend to resemble those in the corresponding underlying C API. There is some smoothing of differences, but at a minimum, you'll need to change the names of the database-related functions you invoke. You may also have to revise your application's logic a bit as well because the interfaces for the various databases don't all work quite the same way.

- The C API provides the least portability between databases. By its very nature it is designed and intended specifically for MySQL.

Portability in the form of database independence is especially important when you need to access multiple database systems within the same application. This can involve simple tasks such as moving data from one RDBMS to another, or more complex undertakings, such as generating a report based on information from a number of database systems.

DBI and PHP both provide support for accessing multiple database engines, so you can easily connect simultaneously to servers for different databases, even on different hosts. However, DBI and PHP differ in their suitability for tasks that retrieve and process data from multiple disparate database systems. DBI is preferable because you use a single set of access calls, no matter which databases you're using. Suppose you want to transfer data between MySQL, mSQL, and Postgres databases. With DBI, the only necessary difference in how you use the three databases is the `DBI->connect()` call used to connect to each server. With PHP, you'd have a more complicated script incorporating three sets of read calls and three sets of write calls.

An extreme case of the multiple–database application is the `crash-me` script in the MySQL distribution that tests the capabilities of many different database servers. This script is written using DBI, which is the obvious choice for such an application because you can access every database the same way.

6

The MySQL C API

MYSQL PROVIDES A CLIENT LIBRARY WRITTEN in the C programming language that you can use to write client programs that access MySQL databases. This library defines an application programming interface that includes the following facilities:

- Connection management routines to establish and terminate a session with a server.
- Routines to construct queries, send them to the server, and process the results.
- Status- and error-reporting functions for determining the exact reason for an error when other C API calls fail.

This chapter shows how to use the client library to write your own programs. Some of the goals we'll keep in mind are consistency with existing client programs in the MySQL distribution, as well as modularity and reusability of the code. I assume you know something about programming in C, but I've tried not to assume you're an expert.

The chapter develops a series of client programs in a rough progression from very simple to more complex. The first part of this progression develops the framework for a client skeleton that does nothing but connect to and disconnect from the server. The reason for this is that although MySQL client programs are written for different purposes, they all have one thing in common: They establish a connection to the server.

We'll build the skeleton in steps:

1. Write some bare-bones connection and disconnection code (`client1`).
2. Add error checking (`client2`).
3. Make the connection code modular and reusable (`client3`).
4. Add the ability to get connection parameters (host, user, password) at runtime (`client4`).

This framework is reasonably generic, and you can use it as the basis for any number of client programs. After developing it, we'll pause to consider how to handle various kinds of queries. Initially, we'll discuss how to handle specific hardcoded SQL statements, then develop code that can be used to process arbitrary statements. After that, we'll add our query-processing code to our client framework to develop another program (`client5`) that's similar to the `mysql` client.

We'll also consider (and solve) some common problems, such as, "How can I get information about the structure of my tables" and "How can I insert images in my database?"

This chapter discusses functions and data types from the client library only as they are needed. For a comprehensive listing of all functions and types, see Appendix F, "C API Reference." You can use that appendix as a reference for further background on any part of the client library you're trying to use.

The example programs are available online for downloading so you can try them directly without typing them in yourself. See Appendix A, "Obtaining and Installing Software," for instructions.

Where to Find Examples

A common question on the MySQL mailing list is "Where can I find some examples of clients written in C?" The answer, of course, is "right here in this book!" But something many people seem not to consider is that the MySQL distribution contains several client programs (`mysql`, `mysqladmin`, and `mysqldump`, for example), most of which are written in C. Because the distribution is readily available in source form, MySQL itself provides you with quite a bit of example client code. Therefore, if you haven't already done so, grab a source distribution sometime and take a look at the programs in the `client` directory. The MySQL client programs are in the public domain and you may freely borrow code from them for your own programs.

Between the examples provided in this chapter and the client programs included in the MySQL distribution, you may be able to find something similar to what you want to do when writing your own programs. If you do, you may be able to reuse code by copying an existing program and modifying it. You should read this chapter to gain an understanding of how the client library works. Remember, however, that you don't always need to write everything yourself from the ground up. (You'll notice that code reusability is one of the goals in our discussion of writing programs in this chapter.) If you can avoid a lot of work by building on what someone else has already done, so much the better.

General Procedure for Building Client Programs

This section describes the steps involved in compiling and linking a program that uses the MySQL client library. The commands to build clients vary somewhat from system to system, and you may need to modify the commands shown here a bit. However, the description is general and you should be able to apply it to almost any client program you write.

Basic System Requirements

When you write a MySQL client program in C, you'll need a C compiler, obviously. The examples shown here use `gcc`. You'll also need the following in addition to your own source files:

- The MySQL header files
- The MySQL client library

The MySQL header files and client library constitute client programming support. They may be installed on your system already. Otherwise, you need to obtain them. If MySQL was installed from a source or binary distribution, client programming support should have been installed as part of that process. If MySQL was installed from RPM files, this support won't be present unless you installed the developer RPM. If you need to install the MySQL header files and library, see Appendix A.

Compiling and Linking the Client

To compile and link a client program, you must specify where the MySQL header files and client library are located because they usually are not installed in locations that the compiler and linker search by default. For the following example, suppose the header file and client library locations are `/usr/local/include/mysql` and `/usr/local/lib/mysql`.

To tell the compiler how to find the MySQL header files, pass it a `-I/usr/local/include/mysql` argument when you compile a source file into an object file. For example, you might use a command like this:

```
% gcc -c -I/usr/local/include/mysql myclient.c
```

To tell the linker where to find the client library and what its name is, pass `-L/usr/local/lib/mysql` and `-lmysqlclient` arguments when you link the object file to produce an executable binary, as follows:

```
% gcc -o myclient myclient.o -L/usr/local/lib/mysql -lmysqlclient
```

If your client consists of multiple files, name all the object files on the link command. If the link step results in an error having to do with not being able to find the `floor()` function, link in the math library by adding `-lm` to the end of the command:

```
% gcc -o myclient myclient.o -L/usr/local/lib/mysql -lmysqlclient -lm
```

You might need to add other libraries as well. For example, you'll probably need `-lsocket -lnsl` on Solaris.

If you don't use `make` to build programs, I suggest you learn how so that you won't have to type a lot of program-building commands manually. Suppose you have a client program, `myclient`, comprising two source files, `main.c` and `aux.c`, and a header file, `myclient.h`. A simple `Makefile` to build this program might look like this:

```
CC = gcc
INCLUDES = -I/usr/local/include/mysql
LIBS = -L/usr/local/lib/mysql -lmysqlclient

all: myclient

main.o: main.c myclient.h
    $(CC) -c $(INCLUDES) main.c
aux.o: aux.c myclient.h
    $(CC) -c $(INCLUDES) aux.c

myclient: main.o aux.o
    $(CC) -o myclient main.o aux.o $(LIBS)

clean:
    rm -f myclient main.o aux.o
```

If your system is one for which you need to link in the math library, change the value of `LIBS` to add `-lm` to the end:

```
LIBS = -L/usr/local/lib/mysql -lmysqlclient -lm
```

If you need other libraries, such as `-lsocket` and `-lnsl`, add those to `LIBS`, too.

Using the `Makefile`, you can rebuild your program whenever you modify any of the source files simply by typing "`make`". That's easier and less error prone than typing a long `gcc` command.

Client 1—Connecting to the Server

Our first MySQL client program is about as simple as can be: It connects to a server, disconnects, and exits. That's not very useful in itself, but you have to know how to do it because before you can really do anything with a MySQL database, you must be connected to a server. This is such a common operation that code you develop to establish a connection is code you'll use in every client program you write. Besides, this task gives us something simple to start with. We can flesh out the client later to do something more useful.

The source for our first client program, client1, consists of a single file, client1.c:

```
/* client1.c */

#include <stdio.h>
#include <mysql.h>

#define def_host_name   NULL /* host to connect to (default = localhost) */
#define def_user_name   NULL /* user name (default = your login name) */
#define def_password    NULL /* password (default = none) */
#define def_db_name     NULL /* database to use (default = none) */

MYSQL    *conn;                 /* pointer to connection handler */

int
main (int argc, char *argv[])
{

    conn = mysql_init (NULL);
    mysql_real_connect (
              conn,             /* pointer to connection handler */
              def_host_name,    /* host to connect to */
              def_user_name,    /* user name */
              def_password,     /* password */
              def_db_name,      /* database to use */
              0,                /* port (use default) */
              NULL,             /* socket (use default) */
              0);               /* flags (none) */
    mysql_close (conn);
    exit (0);
}
```

The source file begins by including stdio.h and mysql.h. MySQL clients may include other header files, but generally these two are the bare minimum.

The defaults for the hostname, username, password, and database name are hard-wired into the code to keep things simple. Later we'll parameterize these values so you can specify them in option files or on the command line.

The main() function of the program establishes and terminates the connection to the server. Making a connection is a two-step process:

1. Call mysql_init() to obtain a connection handler. The MYSQL data type is a structure containing information about a connection. Variables of this type are called connection handlers. When you pass NULL to mysql_init(), it allocates a MYSQL variable, initializes it, and returns a pointer to it.

2. Call mysql_real_connect() to establish a connection to the server. mysql_real_connect() takes about a zillion parameters:

   - A pointer to the connection handler. This should not be NULL; it should be the value returned by mysql_init().

- The server host. If you specify NULL or the host "localhost", the client connects to the server running on the local host using a UNIX socket. If you specify a hostname or host IP address, the client connects to the named host using a TCP/IP connection.

  On Windows, the behavior is similar, except that TCP/IP connections are used instead of UNIX sockets. (On Windows NT, the connection is attempted using a named pipe before TCP/IP if the host is NULL.)

- The username and password. If the name is NULL, the client library sends your login name to the server. If the password is NULL, no password is sent.

- The port number and socket file. These are specified as 0 and NULL, to tell the client library to use its default values. By leaving the port and socket unspecified, the defaults are determined according to the host you wish to connect to. The details on this are given in the description of `mysql_real_connect()` in Appendix F.

- The flags value. This is 0 because we aren't using any special connection options. The options that are available for this parameter are discussed in more detail in the entry for `mysql_real_connect()` in Appendix F.

To terminate the connection, pass a pointer to the connection handler to `mysql_close()`. A connection handler that is allocated automatically by `mysql_init()` is de-allocated automatically when you pass it to `mysql_close()` to terminate the connection.

To try out `client1`, compile and link it using the instructions given earlier in the chapter for building client programs, then run it:

```
% client1
```

The program connects to the server, disconnects, and exits. Not very exciting, but it's a start. However, it's *just* a start, because there are two significant shortcomings:

- The client does no error checking, so you don't really know whether or not it actually works!
- The connection parameters (hostname, username, etc.) are hardwired into the source code. It would be better to allow the user to override them by specifying the parameters in an option file or on the command line.

Neither of these problems is difficult to deal with. We'll address them both in the next few sections.

Client 2—Adding Error Checking

Our second client will be like the first one, but it will be modified to take into account the possibility of errors occurring. It seems to be fairly common in programming texts to say "Error checking is left as an exercise for the reader," probably because checking for errors is—let's face it—such a bore. Nevertheless, I prefer to promote the view that MySQL client programs should test for error conditions and respond to them appropriately. The client library calls that return status values do so for a reason, and you ignore them at your peril. You end up trying to track down obscure problems that occur in your programs due to failure to check for errors, users of your programs wonder why those programs behave erratically, or both.

Consider our program, `client1`. How do you know whether or not it really connected to the server? You could find out by looking in the server log for `Connect` and `Quit` events corresponding to the time at which you ran the program:

```
990516 21:52:14      20 Connect     paul@localhost on
                     20 Quit
```

Alternatively, you might see an `Access denied` message instead:

```
990516 22:01:47      21 Connect     Access denied for user: 'paul@localhost'
                                     (Using password: NO)
```

This message indicates that no connection was established at all. Unfortunately, `client1` doesn't tell us which of these outcomes occurred. In fact, it can't. It doesn't perform any error checking, so it doesn't even know itself what happened. In any case, you certainly shouldn't have to look in the log to find out whether or not you were able to connect to the server! Let's fix that right away.

Routines in the MySQL client library that return a value generally indicate success or failure in one of two ways:

- Pointer-valued functions return a non-`NULL` pointer for success and `NULL` for failure. (`NULL` in this context means "a C `NULL` pointer," not "a MySQL `NULL` column value.")

  Of the client library routines we've used so far, `mysql_init()` and `mysql_real_connect()` both return a pointer to the connection handler to indicate success and `NULL` to indicate failure.

- Integer-valued functions commonly return `0` for success and non-zero for failure. It's important not to test for specific non-zero values, such as `-1`. There is no guarantee that a client library function returns any particular value when it fails. On occasion, you may see older code that tests a return value incorrectly like this:

  ```
  if (mysql_XXX() == -1)       /* this test is incorrect */
      fprintf (stderr, "something bad happened\n");
  ```

This test might work, and it might not. The MySQL API doesn't specify that any non-zero error return will be a particular value, other than that it (obviously) isn't zero. The test should be written either like this:

```
if (mysql_XXX())                /* this test is correct */
    fprintf (stderr, "something bad happened\n");
```

or like this:

```
if (mysql_XXX() != 0)            /* this test is correct */
    fprintf (stderr, "something bad happened\n");
```

The two tests are equivalent. If you look through the source code for MySQL itself, you'll find that generally it uses the first form of the test, which is shorter to write.

Not every API call returns a value. The other client routine we've used, `mysql_close()`, is one that does not. (How could it fail? And if it did, so what? You were done with the connection, anyway.)

When a client library call fails and you need more information about the failure, two calls in the API are useful. `mysql_error()` returns a string containing an error message, and `mysql_errno()` returns a numeric error code. You should call them right after an error occurs because if you issue another API call that returns a status, any error information you get from `mysql_error()` or `mysql_errno()` will apply to the later call instead.

Generally, the user of a program will find the error string more enlightening than the error code. If you report only one of the two, I suggest it be the string. For completeness, the examples in this chapter report both values.

Taking the preceding discussion into account, we'll write our second client, `client2`. It is similar to `client1`, but with proper error-checking code added. The source file, `client2.c`, looks like this:

```
/* client2.c */

#include <stdio.h>
#include <mysql.h>

#define def_host_name   NULL /* host to connect to (default = localhost) */
#define def_user_name   NULL /* user name (default = your login name) */
#define def_password    NULL /* password (default = none) */
#define def_db_name     NULL /* database to use (default = none) */

MYSQL   *conn;                      /* pointer to connection handler */

int
main (int argc, char *argv[])
{
    conn = mysql_init (NULL);
    if (conn == NULL)
    {
        fprintf (stderr, "mysql_init() failed (probably out of memory)\n");
        exit (1);
    }
```

```
       if (mysql_real_connect (
                   conn,            /* pointer to connection handler */
                   def_host_name,   /* host to connect to */
                   def_user_name,   /* user name */
                   def_password,    /* password */
                   def_db_name,     /* database to use */
                   0,               /* port (use default) */
                   NULL,            /* socket (use default) */
                   0)               /* flags (none) */
             == NULL)
       {
           fprintf (stderr, "mysql_real_connect() failed:\nError %u (%s)\n",
                           mysql_errno (conn), mysql_error (conn));
           exit (1);
       }
       mysql_close (conn);
       exit (0);
   }
```

The error-checking logic is based on the fact that both `mysql_init()` and
`mysql_real_connect()` return NULL if they fail. Note that although the program checks
the return value of `mysql_init()`, no error-reporting function is called if it fails. That's
because the connection handler cannot be assumed to contain any meaningful information when `mysql_init()` fails. By contrast, if `mysql_real_connect()` fails, the connection handler doesn't reflect a valid connection, but does contain error information
that can be passed to the error-reporting functions. (Don't pass the handler to any
other client routines, though! Because they generally assume a valid connection, your
program may crash.)

Compile and link `client2`, and then try running it:

```
% client2
```

If `client2` produces no output (as just shown), it connected successfully. On the other
hand, you might see something like this:

```
% client2
mysql_real_connect() failed:
Error 1045 (Access denied for user: 'paul@localhost' (Using password: NO))
```

This output indicates no connection was established, and lets you know why. It also
means that our first program, `client1`, never successfully connected to the server,
either! (After all, `client1` used the same connection parameters.) We didn't know it
then because `client1` didn't bother to check for errors. `client2` does check, so it can
tell us when something goes wrong. That's why you should always test API function
return values.

Answers to questions on the MySQL mailing list often have to do with error
checking. Typical questions are "Why does my program crash when it issues this
query?" or "How come my query doesn't return anything?" In many cases, the program in question didn't check whether or not the connection was established successfully before issuing the query or didn't check to make sure the server successfully
executed the query before trying to retrieve the results. Don't make the mistake of
assuming that every client library call succeeds.

The rest of the examples in this chapter perform error checking, and you should, too. It might seem like more work, but in the long run it's really less because you spend less time tracking down subtle problems. I'll also take this approach of checking for errors in Chapters 7, "The Perl DBI API," and 8, "The PHP API."

Now, suppose you did see an Access denied message when you ran the client2 program. How can you fix the problem? One possibility is to change the #define lines for the hostname, username, and password to values that allow you to access your server. That might be beneficial, in the sense that at least you'd be able to make a connection. But the values would still be hardcoded into your program. I recommend against that approach, especially for the password value. You might think that the password becomes hidden when you compile your program into binary form, but it's not hidden at all if someone can run strings on the program. (Not to mention the fact that anyone with read access to your source file can get the password with no work at all.)

We'll deal with the access problem in the section "Client 4—Getting Connection Parameters at Runtime." First, I want to show some other ways of writing your connection code.

Client 3—Making the Connection Code Modular

For our third client, client3, we will make the connection and disconnection code more modular by encapsulating it into functions do_connect() and do_disconnect(), which can be used easily by multiple client programs. This provides an alternative to embedding the connection code literally into your main() function. That's a good idea anyway for any code that's stereotypical across applications. Put it in a function that you can access from multiple programs rather than writing it out in each one. If you fix a bug in or make an improvement to the function, you can change it once and all the programs that use the function can be fixed or take advantage of the improvement just by being recompiled. Also, some client programs are written such that they may connect and disconnect several times during the course of their execution. It's a lot easier to write such a client if you make the code modular by putting your setup and teardown machinery in connect and disconnect functions.

The encapsulation strategy works like this:

1. Split out common code into wrapper functions in a separate source file, common.c.
2. Provide a header file, common.h, containing prototypes for the common routines.
3. Include common.h in client source files that use the common routines.
4. Compile the common source into an object file.
5. Link that common object file into your client program.

With that strategy in mind, let's construct do_connect() and do_disconnect().

do_connect() replaces the calls to mysql_init() and mysql_real_connect(), as well as the error-printing code. You call it just like mysql_real_connect(), except that you don't pass any connection handler. Instead, do_connect() allocates and initializes the handler itself, then returns a pointer to it after connecting. If do_connect() fails, it returns NULL after printing an error message. (That way, any program that calls do_connect() and gets a NULL return value can simply exit without worrying about printing a message itself.)

do_disconnect() takes a pointer to the connection handler and calls mysql_close().

Here is the code for common.c:

```c
#include <stdio.h>
#include <mysql.h>
#include "common.h"

MYSQL *
do_connect (char *host_name, char *user_name, char *password, char *db_name,
            unsigned int port_num, char *socket_name, unsigned int flags)
{
MYSQL   *conn;  /* pointer to connection handler */

    conn = mysql_init (NULL);   /* allocate, initialize connection handler */
    if (conn == NULL)
    {
        fprintf (stderr, "mysql_init() failed\n");
        return (NULL);
    }
    if (mysql_real_connect (conn, host_name, user_name, password,
                        db_name, port_num, socket_name, flags) == NULL)
    {
        fprintf (stderr, "mysql_real_connect() failed:\nError %u (%s)\n",
                        mysql_errno (conn), mysql_error (conn));
        return (NULL);
    }
    return (conn);              /* connection is established */
}

void
do_disconnect (MYSQL *conn)
{
    mysql_close (conn);
}
```

common.h declares the prototypes for the routines in common.c:

```c
MYSQL *
do_connect (char *host_name, char *user_name, char *password, char *db_name,
            unsigned int port_num, char *socket_name, unsigned int flags);
void
do_disconnect (MYSQL *conn);
```

To access the common routines, include `common.h` in your source files. Note that
`common.c` includes `common.h` as well. That way, you get a compiler warning immediately if the function definitions in `common.c` don't match the declarations in the header
file. Also, if you change a calling sequence in `common.c` without making the corresponding change to `common.h`, the compiler will warn you when you recompile
`common.c`.

It's reasonable to ask why anyone would invent a wrapper function,
`do_disconnect()`, that does so little. It's true that `do_disconnect()` and `mysql_close()`
are equivalent. But suppose sometime down the road you decide there is some additional cleanup you'd like to perform whenever you disconnect. By calling a wrapper
function that you have complete control over, you can modify the wrapper to do what
you like and the change takes effect uniformly for any disconnect operation you do.
You can't do this if you invoke `mysql_close()` directly.

Earlier, I asserted that it's beneficial to modularize commonly used code by encapsulating it in a function that can be used by multiple programs, or from multiple places
within a single program. The preceding paragraph gives one reason why, and the following two examples provide some additional justification.

- **Example 1.** In versions of MySQL prior to the 3.22 series, the
  `mysql_real_connect()` call was slightly different than it is now: There was no
  database name parameter. If you want to use `do_connect()` with an older
  MySQL client library, it won't work. However, it's possible to modify
  `do_connect()` so that it will work on pre-3.22 installations. This means that
  by modifying `do_connect()`, you can increase the portability of all programs
  that use it. If you embed the connect code literally in every client, you must
  modify each of them individually.

  To fix `do_connect()` so that it can deal with the older form of
  `mysql_real_connect()`, use the `MYSQL_VERSION_ID` macro that contains
  the current MySQL version number. The modified `do_connect()` tests the
  value of `MYSQL_VERSION_ID` and uses the proper form of `mysql_real_connect()`:

```
MYSQL *
do_connect (char *host_name, char *user_name, char *password, char *db_name,
            unsigned int port_num, char *socket_name, unsigned int flags)
{
MYSQL   *conn;  /* pointer to connection handler */

    conn = mysql_init (NULL);   /* allocate, initialize connection handler */
    if (conn == NULL)
    {
        fprintf (stderr, "mysql_init() failed\n");
        return (NULL);
    }
#if defined(MYSQL_VERSION_ID) && MYSQL_VERSION_ID >= 32200  /* 3.22 and up */
    if (mysql_real_connect (conn, host_name, user_name, password,
```

```
                        db_name, port_num, socket_name, flags) == NULL)
    {
        fprintf (stderr, "mysql_real_connect() failed:\nError %u (%s)\n",
                        mysql_errno (conn), mysql_error (conn));
        return (NULL);
    }
#else                                   /* pre-3.22 */
    if (mysql_real_connect (conn, host_name, user_name, password,
                    port_num, socket_name, flags) == NULL)
    {
        fprintf (stderr, "mysql_real_connect() failed:\nError %u (%s)\n",
                        mysql_errno (conn), mysql_error (conn));
        return (NULL);
    }
    if (db_name != NULL)        /* simulate effect of db_name parameter */
    {
        if (mysql_select_db (conn, db_name) != 0)
        {
            fprintf (stderr, "mysql_select_db() failed:\nError %u (%s)\n",
                        mysql_errno (conn), mysql_error (conn));
            mysql_close (conn);
            return (NULL);
        }
    }
#endif
    return (conn);              /* connection is established */
}
```

The modified version of do_connect() is identical to the previous version in all
respects except two:

- It doesn't pass a db_name parameter to the older form of
  mysql_real_connect() because that version has no such parameter.

- If the database name is non-NULL, do_connect() calls mysql_select_db()
  to make the named database current. (This simulates the effect of the
  missing db_name parameter). If the database cannot be selected,
  do_connect() prints an error message, closes the connection, and returns
  NULL to indicate failure.

- **Example 2.** This example builds on the changes made to do_connect() for the
  first example. Those changes result in three sets of calls to the error functions
  mysql_errno() and mysql_error(), and it's really tiresome write those out each
  time the code needs to squawk about a problem. Besides, the error printing
  code is visually noisy and difficult to read. It's easier to read something like this:

  ```
  print_error (conn, "mysql_real_connect() failed");
  ```

So let's encapsulate error printing in a `print_error()` function. We can write it to do something sensible even if `conn` is `NULL`. That way, we can use `print_error()` if the `mysql_init()` call fails, and we don't have a mix of calls (some to `fprintf()` and some to `print_error()`).

I can hear someone in the back row objecting: "Well, you don't really *have* to call both error functions every time you want to report an error, so you're making your code difficult to read on purpose just so your encapsulation example looks better. And you wouldn't really write out all that error-printing code anyway; you'd write it once, then use copy and paste when you need it again." Those are valid points, but I would address the objections like this:

- Even if you use copy and paste, it's easier to do so with shorter sections of code.

- Whether or not you prefer to invoke both error functions each time you report an error, writing out all the error-reporting code the long way leads to the temptation to take shortcuts and be inconsistent when you do report errors. Putting the error-reporting code in a wrapper function that's easy to invoke lessens this temptation and improves coding consistency.

- If you ever do decide to modify the format of your error messages, it's a lot easier if you only need to make the change one place, rather than throughout your program. Or, if you decide to write error messages to a log file instead of (or in addition to) writing them to `stderr`, it's easier if you only have to change `print_error()`. This approach is less error prone and, again, lessens the temptation to do the job halfway and be inconsistent.

- If you use a debugger when testing your programs, putting a breakpoint in the error-reporting function is a convenient way to have the program break to the debugger when it detects an error condition.

Here's our error-reporting function `print_error()`:

```
void
print_error (MYSQL *conn, char *message)
{
    fprintf (stderr, "%s\n", message);
    if (conn != NULL)
    {
        fprintf (stderr, "Error %u (%s)\n",
                mysql_errno (conn), mysql_error (conn));
    }
}
```

print_error() is in common.c, so we add a prototype for it to common.h:

```
void
print_error (MYSQL *conn, char *message);
```

Now do_connect() can be modified to use print_error():

```
MYSQL *
do_connect (char *host_name, char *user_name, char *password, char *db_name,
            unsigned int port_num, char *socket_name, unsigned int flags)
{
MYSQL   *conn;  /* pointer to connection handler */

    conn = mysql_init (NULL);  /* allocate, initialize connection handler */
    if (conn == NULL)
    {
        print_error (NULL, "mysql_init() failed (probably out of memory)");
        return (NULL);
    }
#if defined(MYSQL_VERSION_ID) && MYSQL_VERSION_ID >= 32200  /* 3.22 and up
*/
    if (mysql_real_connect (conn, host_name, user_name, password,
                    db_name, port_num, socket_name, flags) == NULL)
    {
        print_error (conn, "mysql_real_connect() failed");
        return (NULL);
    }
#else                           /* pre-3.22 */
    if (mysql_real_connect (conn, host_name, user_name, password,
                    port_num, socket_name, flags) == NULL)
    {
        print_error (conn, "mysql_real_connect() failed");
        return (NULL);
    }
    if (db_name != NULL)        /* simulate effect of db_name parameter */
    {
        if (mysql_select_db (conn, db_name) != 0)
        {
            print_error (conn, "mysql_select_db() failed");
            mysql_close (conn);
            return (NULL);
        }
    }
#endif
    return (conn);              /* connection is established */
}
```

Our main source file, client3.c, is like client2.c, but has all the embedded connect and disconnect code removed and replaced with calls to the wrapper functions. It looks like this:

```
/* client3.c */

#include <stdio.h>
#include <mysql.h>
#include "common.h"

#define def_host_name    NULL /* host to connect to (default = localhost) */
#define def_user_name    NULL /* user name (default = your login name) */
#define def_password     NULL /* password (default = none) */
#define def_port_num     0    /* use default port */
#define def_socket_name  NULL /* use default socket name */
#define def_db_name      NULL /* database to use (default = none) */

MYSQL   *conn;  /* pointer to connection handler */

int
main (int argc, char *argv[])
{
    conn = do_connect (def_host_name, def_user_name, def_password, def_db_name,
                              def_port_num, def_socket_name, 0);
    if (conn == NULL)
        exit (1);

    /* do the real work here */

    do_disconnect (conn);
    exit (0);
}
```

Client 4—Getting Connection Parameters at Runtime

Okay, now that we have our easily modifiable and bullet-proof-in-case-an-error-occurs connection code, we're ready to figure out how to do something smarter than using NULL connection parameters—like letting the user specify those values at runtime.

The previous client, client3, still has a significant shortcoming in that the connection parameters are hardwired in. To change any of those values, you have to edit the source file and recompile it. That's not very convenient, especially if you intend to make your program available for other people to use.

One common way to specify connection parameters at runtime is by using command line options. The programs in the MySQL distribution accept connection parameters in either of two forms, as shown in Table 6.1.

Table 6.1   **Standard MySQL Command-Line Options**

Parameter	Short Form	Long Form
Hostname	`-h host_name`	`--host=host_name`
Username	`-u user_name`	`--user=user_name`
Password	`-p or -pyour_password`	`--password or` `--password=your_password`
Port number	`-P port_num`	`--port=port_num`
Socket name	`-S socket_name`	`--socket=socket_name`

For consistency with the standard MySQL clients, our client will accept those same formats. It's easy to do this because the client library includes a function to perform option parsing.

In addition, our client will have the ability to extract information from option files. This allows you to put connection parameters in `~/.my.cnf` (that is, the `.my.cnf` file in your home directory) so that you don't have to specify them on the command line. The client library makes it easy to check for MySQL option files and pull any relevant values from them. By adding only a few lines of code to your program, you can make it option file-aware, and you don't have to reinvent the wheel by writing your own code to do it. Option file syntax is described in Appendix E, "MySQL Program Reference."

Accessing Option File Contents

To read option files for connection parameter values, use the `load_defaults()` function. `load_defaults()` looks for option files, parses their contents for any option groups in which you're interested, and rewrites your program's argument vector (the `argv[]` array) to put information from those groups in the form of command line options at the beginning of `argv[]`. That way, the options appear to have been specified on the command line. Therefore, when you parse the command options, you get the connection parameters as part of your normal option-parsing loop. The options are added to the beginning of `argv[]` rather than at the end so that if connection parameters really are specified on the command line, they occur later than (and thus override) any options added by `load_defaults()`.

Here's a little program, `show_argv`, that shows how to use `load_defaults()` and illustrates how doing so modifies your argument vector:

```
/* show_argv.c */

#include <stdio.h>
#include <mysql.h>

char *groups[] = { "client", NULL };

int
```

continues

continued

```
main (int argc, char *argv[])
{
int i;

    my_init ();

    printf ("Original argument vector:\n");
    for (i = 0; i < argc; i++)
        printf ("arg %d: %s\n", i, argv[i]);

    load_defaults ("my", groups, &argc, &argv);

    printf ("Modified argument vector:\n");
    for (i = 0; i < argc; i++)
        printf ("arg %d: %s\n", i, argv[i]);

    exit (0);
}
```

The option file-processing code involves the following:

- groups[] is a character string array indicating which option file groups you are interested in. For client programs, you always specify as least "client" (for the [client] group). The last element of the array must be NULL.

- my_init() is an initialization routine that performs some setup operations required by load_defaults()

- load_defaults() takes four arguments: the prefix of your option files (this should always be "my"), the array listing the option groups in which you're interested, and the addresses of your program's argument count and vector. Don't pass the values of the count and vector. Pass their addresses instead because load_defaults() needs to change their values. Note in particular that although argv is a pointer, you still pass &argv, that pointer's address.

show_argv prints its arguments twice—first as you specified them on the command line, then as they were modified by load_defaults(). To see the effect of load_defaults(), make sure you have a .my.cnf file in your home directory with some settings specified for the [client] group. Suppose .my.cnf looks like this:

```
[client]
user=paul
password=secret
host=some_host
```

If this is the case, then executing show_argv produces output like this:

```
% show_argv a b
Original argument vector:
arg 0: show_argv
arg 1: a
arg 2: b
Modified argument vector:
```

```
arg 0: show_argv
arg 1: --user=paul
arg 2: --password=secret
arg 3: --host=some_host
arg 4: a
arg 5: b
```

It's possible that you'll see some options in the output from show_argv that were not on the command line or in your ~/.my.cnf file. If so, they were probably specified in a system-wide option file. load_defaults() actually looks for /etc/my.cnf and the my.cnf file in the MySQL data directory before reading .my.cnf in your home directory. (On Windows, load_defaults() searches for C:\my.cnf, C:\mysql\data\my.cnf, and the my.ini file in your Windows system directory.)

Client programs that use load_defaults() almost always specify "client" in the options group list (so that they get any general client settings from option files), but you can also ask for values that are specific to your own program. Just change the following:

```
char *groups[] = { "client", NULL };
```

to this:

```
char *groups[] = { "show_argv", "client", NULL };
```

Then you can add a [show_argv] group to your ~/.my.cnf file:

```
[client]
user=paul
password=secret
host=some_host

[show_argv]
host=other_host
```

With these changes, invoking show_argv again has a different result, as follows:

```
% show_argv a b
Original argument vector:
arg 0: show_argv
arg 1: a
arg 2: b
Modified argument vector:
arg 0: show_argv
arg 1: --user=paul
arg 2: --password=secret
arg 3: --host=some_host
arg 4: --host=other_host
arg 5: a
arg 6: b
```

The order in which option values appear in the argument array is determined by the order in which they are listed in your option file, not the order in which your option groups are listed in the groups[] array. This means you'll probably want to specify program-specific groups after the [client] group in your option file. That way, if you specify an option in both groups, the program-specific value will take precedence. You can see this in the example just shown: The host option was specified in both the [client] and [show_argv] groups, but because the [show_argv] group appears last in the option file, its host setting appears later in the argument vector and takes precedence.

load_defaults() does not pick up values from your environment settings. If you want to use the values of environment variables such as MYSQL_TCP_PORT or MYSQL_UNIX_PORT, you must manage that yourself using getenv(). I'm not going to add that capability to our clients, but here's an example showing how to check the values of a couple of the standard MySQL-related environment variables:

```
extern char *getenv();
char *p;
int port_num;
char *socket_name;

if ((p = getenv ("MYSQL_TCP_PORT")) != NULL)
    port_num = atoi (p);
if ((p = getenv ("MYSQL_UNIX_PORT")) != NULL)
    socket_name = p;
```

In the standard MySQL clients, environment variables' values have lower precedence than values specified in option files or on the command line. If you check environment variables and want to be consistent with that convention, check the environment before (not after) calling load_defaults() or processing command line options.

Parsing Command-Line Arguments

We can get all the connection parameters into the argument vector now, but we need a way to parse the vector. The getopt_long() function is designed for this.

getopt_long() is built into the MySQL client library, so you have access to it whenever you link in that library. In your source file, you need to include the getopt.h header file. You can copy this header file from the include directory of the MySQL source distribution into the directory where you're developing your client program.

---

load_defaults() and Security

You may be wondering about the process-snooping implications of having load_defaults() putting the text of passwords in your argument list because programs such as ps can display argument lists for arbitrary processes. There is no problem because ps displays the original argv[] contents. Any password argument created by load_defaults() points to an area that it allocates for itself. That area is not part of the original vector, so ps never sees it.

On the other hand, a password that is specified on the command line *does* show up in ps, unless you take care to wipe it out. The section "Parsing Command-Line Arguments" shows how to do that.

The following program, show_param, uses load_defaults() to read option files, then calls getopt_long() to parse the argument vector. show_param illustrates what happens at each phase of argument processing by performing the following actions:

1. Sets up default values for the hostname, username, and password.

2. Prints the original connection parameter and argument vector values.

3. Calls load_defaults() to rewrite the argument vector to reflect option file contents, then prints the resulting vector.

4. Calls getopt_long() to process the argument vector, then prints the resulting parameter values and whatever is left in the argument vector.

show_param allows you to experiment with various ways of specifying connection parameters (whether in option files or on the command line), and to see the result by showing you what values would be used to make a connection. show_param is useful for getting a feel for what will happen in our next client program, when we actually hook up this parameter-processing code to our connection function, do_connect().

Here's what show_param.c looks like:

```c
/* show_param.c */

#include <stdio.h>
#include <stdlib.h> /* needed for atoi() */
#include "getopt.h"

char *groups[] = { "client", NULL };

struct option long_options[] =
{
    {"host",     required_argument, NULL, 'h'},
    {"user",     required_argument, NULL, 'u'},
    {"password", optional_argument, NULL, 'p'},
    {"port",     required_argument, NULL, 'P'},
    {"socket",   required_argument, NULL, 'S'},
    { 0, 0, 0, 0 }
};

int
main (int argc, char *argv[])
{
char *host_name = NULL;
char *user_name = NULL;
char *password = NULL;
unsigned int port_num = 0;
char *socket_name = NULL;
int i;
int c, option_index;
```

continues

continued

```
my_init ();

printf ("Original connection parameters:\n");
printf ("host name: %s\n", host_name ? host_name : "(null)");
printf ("user name: %s\n", user_name ? user_name : "(null)");
printf ("password: %s\n", password ? password : "(null)");
printf ("port number: %u\n", port_num);
printf ("socket name: %s\n", socket_name ? socket_name : "(null)");

printf ("Original argument vector:\n");
for (i = 0; i < argc; i++)
    printf ("arg %d: %s\n", i, argv[i]);

load_defaults ("my", groups, &argc, &argv);

printf ("Modified argument vector after load_defaults():\n");
for (i = 0; i < argc; i++)
    printf ("arg %d: %s\n", i, argv[i]);

while ((c = getopt_long (argc, argv, "h:p::u:P:S:", long_options,
                &option_index)) != EOF)
{
    switch (c)
    {
    case 'h':
        host_name = optarg;
        break;
    case 'u':
        user_name = optarg;
        break;
    case 'p':
        password = optarg;
        break;
    case 'P':
        port_num = (unsigned int) atoi (optarg);
        break;
    case 'S':
        socket_name = optarg;
        break;
    }
}

argc -= optind; /* advance past the arguments that were processed */
argv += optind; /* by getopt_long() */

printf ("Connection parameters after getopt_long():\n");
printf ("host name: %s\n", host_name ? host_name : "(null)");
printf ("user name: %s\n", user_name ? user_name : "(null)");
printf ("password: %s\n", password ? password : "(null)");
printf ("port number: %u\n", port_num);
printf ("socket name: %s\n", socket_name ? socket_name : "(null)");
```

```
        printf ("Argument vector after getopt_long():\n");
        for (i = 0; i < argc; i++)
            printf ("arg %d: %s\n", i, argv[i]);

        exit (0);
    }
```

To process the argument vector, show_argv uses getopt_long(), which you typically call in a loop:

```
    while ((c = getopt_long (argc, argv, "h:p::u:P:S:", long_options,
                    &option_index)) != EOF)
    {
        /* process option */
    }
```

The first two arguments to getopt_long() are your program's argument count and vector. The third argument lists the option letters you want to recognize. These are the short-name forms of your program's options. Option letters may be followed by a colon, a double colon, or no colon to indicate that the option must be followed, may be followed, or is not followed by an option value. The fourth argument, long_options, is a pointer to an array of option structures, each of which specifies information for an option you want your program to understand. Its purpose is similar to the options string in the third argument. The four elements of each long_options[] structure are as follows:

- **The option's long name.**

- **A value for the option.** The value can be required_argument, optional_argument, or no_argument indicating whether the option must be followed, may be followed, or is not followed by an option value. (These serve the same purpose as the colon, double colon, or no colon in the options string third argument.)

- **A flag argument.** You can use this to store a pointer to a variable. If the option is found, getopt_long() stores the value specified by the fourth argument into the variable. If the flag is NULL, getopt_long() instead sets the optarg variable to point to any value following the option, and returns the option's short name. Our long_options[] array specifies NULL for all options. That way, getopt_long() returns each argument as it is encountered so that we can process it in the switch statement.

- **The option's short (single-character) name.** The short names specified in the long_options[] array *must* match the letters used in the options string that you pass as the third argument to getopt_long() or your program will not process command-line arguments properly.

The `long_options[]` array must be terminated by a structure with all elements set to 0.

The fifth argument to `getopt_long()` is a pointer to an `int` variable. `getopt_long()` stores into this variable the index of the `long_options[]` structure that corresponds to the option last encountered. (`show_param` doesn't do anything with this value.)

Note that the password option (specified as `--password` or as `-p`) may take an optional value. That is, you may specify it as `--password` or `--password=your_pass` if you use the long-option form, or as `-p` or `-pyour_pass` if you use the short-option form. The optional nature of the password value is indicated by the double colon after the "p" in the options string, and by `optional_argument` in the `long_options[]` array. MySQL clients typically allow you to omit the password value on the command line, then prompt you for it. This allows you to avoid giving the password on the command line, which keeps people from seeing your password via process snooping. When we write our next client, `client4`, we'll add this password-checking behavior to it.

Here is a sample invocation of `show_param` and the resulting output (assuming that `~/.my.cnf` still has the same contents as for the `show_argv` example):

```
% show_param -h yet_another_host x
Original connection parameters:
host name: (null)
user name: (null)
password: (null)
port number: 0
socket name: (null)
Original argument vector:
arg 0: show_param
arg 1: -h
arg 2: yet_another_host
arg 3: x
Modified argument vector after load_defaults():
arg 0: show_param
arg 1: --user=paul
arg 2: --password=secret
arg 3: --host=some_host
arg 4: -h
arg 5: yet_another_host
arg 6: x
Connection parameters after getopt_long():
host name: yet_another_host
user name: paul
password: secret
port number: 0
socket name: (null)
Argument vector after getopt_long():
arg 0: x
```

The output shows that the hostname is picked up from the command line (overriding the value in the option file), and that the username and password come from the option file. getopt_long() correctly parses options whether specified in short-option form (-h host_name) or in long-option form (--user=paul, --password=secret).

Now let's strip out the stuff that's purely illustrative of how the option-handling routines work and use the remainder as a basis for a client that connects to a server according to any options that are provided in an option file or on the command line. The resulting source file, client4.c, looks like this:

```
/* client4.c */

#include <stdio.h>
#include <stdlib.h> /* for atoi() */
#include <mysql.h>
#include "common.h"
#include "getopt.h"

#define def_host_name    NULL /* host to connect to (default = localhost) */
#define def_user_name    NULL /* user name (default = your login name) */
#define def_password     NULL /* password (default = none) */
#define def_port_num     0    /* use default port */
#define def_socket_name  NULL /* use default socket name */
#define def_db_name      NULL /* database to use (default = none) */

char *groups[] = { "client", NULL };

struct option long_options[] =
{
    {"host",     required_argument, NULL, 'h'},
    {"user",     required_argument, NULL, 'u'},
    {"password", optional_argument, NULL, 'p'},
    {"port",     required_argument, NULL, 'P'},
    {"socket",   required_argument, NULL, 'S'},
    { 0, 0, 0, 0 }
};

MYSQL    *conn;  /* pointer to connection handler */

int
main (int argc, char *argv[])
{
char *host_name = def_host_name;
char *user_name = def_user_name;
char *password = def_password;
unsigned int port_num = def_port_num;
char *socket_name = def_socket_name;
char *db_name = def_db_name;
char     passbuf[100];
int ask_password = 0;
int c, option_index=0;
int i;

    my_init ();
```

continues

continued

```
load_defaults ("my", groups, &argc, &argv);

while ((c = getopt_long (argc, argv, "h:p::u:P:S:", long_options,
                &option_index)) != EOF)
{
    switch (c)
    {
    case 'h':
        host_name = optarg;
        break;
    case 'u':
        user_name = optarg;
        break;
    case 'p':
        if (!optarg)          /* no value given */
            ask_password = 1;
        else                  /* copy password, wipe out original */
        {
                (void) strncpy (passbuf, optarg, sizeof(passbuf)-1);
                passbuf[sizeof(passbuf)-1] = '\0';
                password = passbuf;
                while (*optarg)
                    *optarg++ = ' ';
        }
        break;
    case 'P':
        port_num = (unsigned int) atoi (optarg);
        break;
    case 'S':
        socket_name = optarg;
        break;
    }
}

argc -= optind; /* advance past the arguments that were processed */
argv += optind; /* by getopt_long() */

if (argc > 0)
{
    db_name = argv[0];
    --argc; ++argv;
}

if (ask_password)
    password = get_tty_password (NULL);

conn = do_connect (host_name, user_name, password, db_name,
                                port_num, socket_name, 0);
if (conn == NULL)
    exit (1);
```

```
    /* do the real work here */

    do_disconnect (conn);
    exit (0);
}
```

Compared to the programs `client1`, `client2`, and `client3` that we developed earlier, `client4` does a few things we haven't seen before:

- It allows the database name to be specified on the command line, following the options that are parsed by `getopt_long()`. This is consistent with the behavior of the standard clients in the MySQL distribution.

- It wipes out any password value in the argument vector after making a copy of it. This is to minimize the time window during which a password specified on the command line is visible to `ps` or to other system status programs. (The window is *minimized*, not eliminated. Specifying passwords on the command line still is a security risk.)

- If a password option was given without a value, the client prompts the user for a password using `get_tty_password()`. This is a utility routine in the client library that prompts for a password without echoing it on the screen. (The client library is full of goodies like this. It's instructive to read through the source of the MySQL client programs because you find out about these routines and how to use them.) You may ask, "Why not just call `getpass()`?" The answer is that not all systems have that function – Windows, for example. `get_tty_password()` is portable across systems because it's configured to adjust to system idiosyncrasies.

`client4` responds according to the options you specify. Assume there is no option file to complicate matters. If you invoke `client4` with no arguments, it connects to `localhost` and passes your UNIX login name and no password to the server. If instead you invoke `client4`, as shown here, then it prompts for a password (there is no password value immediately following `-p`), connects to `some_host`, and passes the username `some_user` to the server as well as the password you type in:

```
% client4 -h some_host -u some_user -p some_db
```

`client4` also passes the database name `some_db` to `do_connect()` to make that the current database. If there is an option file, its contents are processed and used to modify the connection parameters accordingly.

Earlier, we went on a code-encapsulation binge, creating wrapper functions for disconnecting to and disconnecting from the server. It's reasonable to ask whether or not to put option-parsing stuff in a wrapper function, too. That's possible, I suppose, but I'm not going to do it. Option-parsing code isn't as consistent across programs as connection code: Programs often support other options in addition to the standard ones we've just looked for, and different programs are likely to support different sets of additional options. That makes it difficult to write a function that standardizes the option-processing loop. Also, unlike connection establishment, which a program may wish to do multiple times during the course of its execution (and thus is a good candidate for encapsulation), option parsing is typically done just once at the beginning of the program.

The work we've done so far accomplishes something that's necessary for every MySQL client: connecting to the server using appropriate parameters. You need to know how to connect, of course. But now you do know how, and the details of that process are implemented by the client skeleton (`client4.c`), so you no longer need to think about them. That means you can concentrate on what you're really interested in—being able to access the content of your databases. All the real action for your application will take place between the `do_connect()` and `do_disconnect()` calls, but what we have now serves as a basic framework that you can use for many different clients. To write a new program, just do this:

1. Make a copy of `client4.c`.

2. Modify the option-processing loop, if you accept additional options other than the standard ones that `client4.c` knows about.

3. Add your own application-specific code between the connect and disconnect calls.

And you're done.

The point of going through the discipline of constructing the client program skeleton was to come up with something that you can use easily to set up and tear down a connection so that you could focus on what you really want to do. Now you're free to do that, demonstrating the principle that from discipline comes freedom.

Processing Queries

Now that we know how to begin and end a conversation with the server, it's time to see how to conduct the conversation while it's going on. This section shows how to communicate with the server to process queries.

Each query you run involves the following steps:

1. **Construct the query.** The way you do this depends on the contents of the query—in particular, whether or not it contains binary data.

2. **Issue the query by sending it to the server for execution.**

3. **Process the query result.** This depends on what type of query you issued. For example, a `SELECT` statement returns rows of data for you to process. An `INSERT` statement does not.

One factor to consider in constructing queries is which function to use for sending them to the server. The more general query-issuing routine is `mysql_real_query()`. With this routine, you provide the query as a counted string (a string plus a length). You must keep track of the length of your query string and pass that to `mysql_real_query()`, along with the string itself. Because the query is a counted string, its contents may be anything, including binary data or null bytes. The query is not treated as a null-terminated string.

The other query-issuing function, `mysql_query()`, is more restrictive in what it allows in the query string but often is easier to use. Queries that you pass to `mysql_query()` should be null-terminated strings, which means they cannot contain null bytes in the text of the query. (The presence of null bytes within the query causes it to be interpreted erroneously as shorter than it really is.) Generally speaking, if your query can contain arbitrary binary data, it might contain null bytes, so you shouldn't use `mysql_query()`. On the other hand, when you are working with null-terminated strings, you have the luxury of constructing queries using standard C library string functions that you're probably already familiar with, such as `strcpy()` and `sprintf()`.

Another factor to consider in constructing queries is whether or not you need to perform any character-escaping operations. You do if you want to construct queries using values that contain binary data or other troublesome characters, such as quotes or backslashes. This is discussed in "Encoding Problematic Data in Queries."

A simple outline of query handling looks like this:

```
if (mysql_query (conn, query) != 0)
{
    /* failure; report error */
}
else
{
    /* success; find out what effect the query had */
}
```

`mysql_query()` and `mysql_real_query()` both return zero for queries that succeed and non-zero for failure. To say that a query "succeeded" means the server accepted it as legal and was able to execute it. It does not indicate anything about the effect of the query. For example, it does not indicate that a SELECT query selected any rows or that a DELETE statement deleted any rows. Checking what effect the query actually had involves additional processing.

A query may fail for a variety of reasons. Some common causes include the following:

- It contains a syntax error.
- It's semantically illegal—for example, a query that refers to a non-existent column of a table.
- You don't have sufficient privileges to access the data referenced by the query.

Queries may be grouped into two broad categories: those that do not return a result and those that do. Queries for statements such as INSERT, DELETE, and UPDATE fall into the "no result returned" category. They don't return any rows, even for queries that modify your database. The only information you get back is a count of the number of rows affected.

Queries for statements such as SELECT and SHOW fall into the "result returned" category; after all, the purpose of issuing those statements is to get something back. The set of rows produced by a query that returns data is called the result set. This is represented in MySQL by the MYSQL_RES data type, a structure that contains the data values for the rows, and also metadata about the values (such as the column names and data value lengths). An empty result set (that is, one that contains zero rows) is distinct from "no result."

Handling Queries That Return No Result Set

To process a query that does not return a result set, issue the query with mysql_query() or mysql_real_query(). If the query succeeds, you can find out how many rows were inserted, deleted, or updated by calling mysql_affected_rows().

The following example shows how to handle a query that returns no result set:

```
if (mysql_query (conn, "INSERT INTO my_tbl SET name = 'My Name'") != 0)
{
    print_error ("INSERT statement failed");
}
else
{
    printf ("INSERT statement succeeded: %lu rows affected\n",
            (unsigned long) mysql_affected_rows (conn));
}
```

Note how the result of mysql_affected_rows() is cast to unsigned long for printing. This function returns a value of type my_ulonglong, but attempting to print a value of that type directly does not work on some systems. (For example, I have observed it to work under FreeBSD but to fail under Solaris.) Casting the value to unsigned long and using a print format of '%lu' solves the problem. The same consideration applies to any other functions that return my_ulonglong values, such as mysql_num_rows() and mysql_insert_id(). If you want your client programs to be portable across different systems, keep this in mind.

mysql_affected_rows() returns the number of rows affected by the query, but the meaning of "rows affected" depends on the type of query. For INSERT, REPLACE, or DELETE, it is the number of rows inserted, replaced, or deleted. For UPDATE, it is the number of rows updated, which means the number of rows that MySQL actually modified. MySQL does not update a row if its contents are the same as what you're updating it to. This means that although a row might be selected for updating (by the WHERE clause of the UPDATE statement), it might not actually be changed.

This meaning of "rows affected" for UPDATE actually is something of a controversial point because some people want it to mean "rows matched"—that is, the number of rows selected for updating, even if the update operation doesn't actually change their values. If your application requires such a meaning, you can get this behavior by asking for it when you connect to the server. Pass a flags value of CLIENT_FOUND_ROWS to mysql_real_connect(). You can pass CLIENT_FOUND_ROWS as the flags argument to do_connect(), too; it will pass along the value to mysql_real_connect().

Handling Queries That Return a Result Set

Queries that return data do so in the form of a result set that you deal with after issuing the query by calling `mysql_query()` or `mysql_real_query()`. It's important to realize that in MySQL, `SELECT` is not the only statement that returns rows. `SHOW`, `DESCRIBE`, and `EXPLAIN` do so as well. For all of these statements, you must perform additional row-handling processing after you issue the query.

Handling a result set involves these steps:

- **Generate the result set by calling `mysql_store_result()` or `mysql_use_result()`.** These functions return a `MYSQL_RES` pointer for success or `NULL` for failure. Later, we'll go over the differences between `mysql_store_result()` and `mysql_use_result()`, as well as the conditions under which you would choose one over the other. For now, our examples use `mysql_store_result()`, which returns the rows from the server immediately and stores them in the client.

- **Call `mysql_fetch_row()` for each row of the result set.** This function returns a `MYSQL_ROW` value, which is a pointer to an array of strings representing the values for each column in the row. What you do with the row depends on your application. You might simply print the column values, perform some statistical calculation on them, or do something else altogether. `mysql_fetch_row()` returns `NULL` when there are no more rows left in the result set.

- **When you are done with the result set, call `mysql_free_result()` to deallocate the memory it uses.** If you neglect to do this, your application will leak memory. (It's especially important to dispose of result sets properly for long-running applications; otherwise, you will notice your system slowly being taken over by processes that consume ever-increasing amounts of system resources.)

The following example outlines how to process a query that returns a result set:

```
MYSQL_RES *res_set;

if (mysql_query (conn, "SHOW TABLES FROM mysql") != 0)
    print_error (conn, "mysql_query() failed");
else
{
    res_set = mysql_store_result (conn);    /* generate result set */
    if (res_set == NULL)
            print_error (conn, "mysql_store_result() failed");
    else
    {
        /* process result set, then deallocate it */
        process_result_set (conn, res_set);
        mysql_free_result (res_set);
    }
}
```

We cheated a little here by calling a function `process_result_set()` to handle each row. We haven't defined that function yet, so we need to do so. Generally, result set–handling functions are based on a loop that looks like this:

```
MYSQL_ROW row;

while ((row = mysql_fetch_row (res_set)) != NULL)
{
    /* do something with row contents */
}
```

The `MYSQL_ROW` return value from `mysql_fetch_row()` is a pointer to an array of values, so accessing each value is simply a matter of accessing `row[i]`, where `i` ranges from `0` to the number of columns in the row minus one.

There are several important points about the `MYSQL_ROW` data type to note:

- `MYSQL_ROW` is a pointer type, so you declare variables of that type as `MYSQL_ROW row`, not as `MYSQL_ROW *row`.

- The strings in a `MYSQL_ROW` array are null-terminated. However, if a column may contain binary data, it may contain null bytes, so you should not treat the value as a null-terminated string. Get the column length to find out how long the column value is.

- Values for all data types, even numeric types, are returned as strings. If you want to treat a value as a number, you must convert the string yourself.

- `NULL` values are represented by `NULL` pointers in the `MYSQL_ROW` array. Unless you have declared a column `NOT NULL`, you should always check whether or not values for that column are `NULL` pointers.

Your applications can do whatever they like with the contents of each row. For purposes of illustration, let's just print the rows with column values separated by tabs. To do that, we need an additional function, `mysql_num_fields()`, from the client library; this function tells us how many values (columns) the row contains.

Here's the code for `process_result_set()`:

```
void
process_result_set (MYSQL *conn, MYSQL_RES *res_set)
{
MYSQL_ROW     row;
unsigned int  i;

    while ((row = mysql_fetch_row (res_set)) != NULL)
    {
        for (i = 0; i < mysql_num_fields (res_set); i++)
        {
            if (i > 0)
                fputc ('\t', stdout);
            printf ("%s", row[i] != NULL ? row[i] : "NULL");
```

```
            }
            fputc ('\n', stdout);
    }
    if (mysql_errno (conn) != 0)
            print_error (conn, "mysql_fetch_row() failed");
    else
            printf ("%lu rows returned\n", (unsigned long) mysql_num_rows (res_set));
}
```

process_result_set() prints each row in tab-delimited format (displaying NULL values as the word "NULL"), followed by a count of the number of rows retrieved. That count is available by calling mysql_num_rows(). Like mysql_affected_rows(), mysql_num_rows() returns a my_ulonglong value, so cast that value to unsigned long and use a '%lu' format to print it.

The row-fetching loop is followed by an error test. If you create the result set with mysql_store_result(), a NULL return value from mysql_fetch_row() always means "no more rows." However, if you create the result set with mysql_use_result(), a NULL return value from mysql_fetch_row() can mean "no more rows" or that an error occurred. The test simply allows process_result_set() to detect errors, no matter how you create your result set.

This version of process_result_set() takes a rather minimalist approach to printing column values, an approach that has certain shortcomings. For example, suppose you execute this query:

```
SELECT last_name, first_name, city, state FROM president
```

You will receive the following output:

```
Adams      John       Braintree    MA
Adams      John Quincy Braintree    MA
Arthur     Chester A.  Fairfield    VT
Buchanan   James       Mercersburg PA
Bush       George W.   Milton  MA
Carter     James E. Jr Plains  GA
Cleveland  Grover     Caldwell     NJ
...
```

We could make the output prettier by providing information such as column labels and making the values line up vertically. To do that, we need the labels, and we need to know the widest value in each column. That information is available, but not as part of the column data values—it's part of the result set's metadata (data about the data). After we generalize our query handler a bit, we'll write a nicer display formatter in the section "Using Result Set Metadata."

Printing Binary Data

Column values that contain binary data that may include null bytes will not print properly using the '%s' printf() format specifier; printf() expects a null-terminated string and will print the column value only up to the first null byte. For binary data, it's best to use the column length so that you can print the full value. You could use fwrite() or putc(), for example.

A General Purpose Query Handler

The preceding query-handling examples were written using knowledge of whether or not the statement should return any data. That was possible because the queries were hardwired into the code: We used an INSERT statement, which does not return a result set, and a SHOW TABLES statement, which does.

However, you don't always know what kind of statement the query represents. For example, if you execute a query that you read from the keyboard or from a file, it might be any arbitrary statement. You won't know ahead of time whether or not to expect it to return rows. What then? You certainly don't want to try to parse the query to determine what kind of statement it is. That's not as simple as it might seem, anyway. It's not sufficient to look at the first word because the query might begin with a comment, as follows:

```
/* comment */ SELECT ...
```

Fortunately, you don't have to know the query type in advance to be able to handle it properly. The MySQL C API makes it possible to write a general purpose query handler that correctly processes any kind of statement, whether or not it returns a result set.

Before writing the code for the query handler, let's outline how this works:

- Issue the query. If it fails, we're done.
- If the query succeeds, call mysql_store_result() to retrieve the rows from the server and create a result set.
- If mysql_store_result() fails, it could be that the query does not return a result set, or that an error occurred while trying to retrieve the set. You can distinguish between these outcomes by passing the connection handler to mysql_field_count() and checking its value, as follows:
    - If mysql_field_count() is non-zero, it indicates an error: The query should have returned a result set but didn't. This can happen for various reasons. For example, the result set may have been too large and memory allocation failed, or a network outage between the client and the server may have occurred while fetching rows.

        A slight complication to this procedure is that mysql_field_count() doesn't exist prior to MySQL 3.22.24. In earlier versions, you use mysql_num_fields() instead. To write programs that work with any version of MySQL, include the following code fragment in any file that calls mysql_field_count():

        ```
        #if !defined(MYSQL_VERSION_ID) || MYSQL_VERSION_ID<32224
        #define mysql_field_count mysql_num_fields
        #endif
        ```

        This causes any calls to mysql_field_count() to be treated as calls to mysql_num_fields() for versions of MySQL earlier than 3.22.24.

- If `mysql_field_count()` returns 0, it means the query returned no result set. (This indicates the query was a statement such as INSERT, DELETE, or UPDATE).

- If `mysql_store_result()` succeeds, the query returned a result set. Process the rows by calling `mysql_fetch_row()` until it returns NULL.

The following listing shows a function that processes any query, given a connection handler and a null-terminated query string:

```c
#if !defined(MYSQL_VERSION_ID) || MYSQL_VERSION_ID<32224
#define mysql_field_count mysql_num_fields
#endif

void
process_query (MYSQL *conn, char *query)
{
MYSQL_RES *res_set;
unsigned int field_count;

    if (mysql_query (conn, query) != 0) /* the query failed */
    {
        print_error (conn, "process_query() failed");
        return;
    }

    /* the query succeeded; determine whether or not it returns data */

    res_set = mysql_store_result (conn);
    if (res_set == NULL)     /* no result set was returned */
    {
        /*
         * does the lack of a result set mean that an error
         * occurred or that no result set was returned?
         */
        if (mysql_field_count (conn) > 0)
        {
            /*
             * a result set was expected, but mysql_store_result()
             * did not return one; this means an error occurred
             */
            print_error (conn, "Problem processing result set");
        }
        else
        {
            /*
             * no result set was returned; query returned no data
             * (it was not a SELECT, SHOW, DESCRIBE, or EXPLAIN),
             * so just report number of rows affected by query
             */
            printf ("%lu rows affected\n",
                        (unsigned long) mysql_affected_rows (conn));
```

continues

continued

```
        }
    }
    else    /* a result set was returned */
    {
        /* process rows, then free the result set */
        process_result_set (conn, res_set);
        mysql_free_result (res_set);
    }
}
```

Alternative Approaches to Query Processing

The version of process_query() just shown has these three properties:

- It uses mysql_query() to issue the query.
- It uses mysql_store_query() to retrieve the result set.
- When no result set is obtained, it uses mysql_field_count() to distinguish occurrence of an error from a result set not being expected.

Alternative approaches are possible for all three of these aspects of query handling:

- You can use a counted query string and mysql_real_query() rather than a null-terminated query string and mysql_query().
- You can create the result set by calling mysql_use_result() rather than mysql_store_result().
- You can call mysql_error() rather than mysql_field_count() to determine whether result set retrieval failed or whether there was simply no set to retrieve.

Any or all of these approaches can be used instead of those used in process_query(). Here is a process_real_query() function that is analogous to process_query() but that uses all three alternatives:

```
void
process_real_query (MYSQL *conn, char *query, unsigned int len)
{
MYSQL_RES *res_set;
unsigned int field_count;

    if (mysql_real_query (conn, query, len) != 0)   /* the query failed */
    {
        print_error (conn, "process_real_query () failed");
        return;
    }

    /* the query succeeded; determine whether or not it returns data */

    res_set = mysql_use_result (conn);
    if (res_set == NULL)    /* no result set was returned */
    {
```

```
        /*
         * does the lack of a result set mean that an error
         * occurred or that no result set was returned?
         */
        if (mysql_errno (conn) != 0) /* an error occurred */
            print_error (conn, "Problem processing result set");
        else
        {
            /*
             * no result set was returned; query returned no data
             * (it was not a SELECT, SHOW, DESCRIBE, or EXPLAIN),
             * so just report number of rows affected by query
             */
            printf ("%lu rows affected\n",
                        (unsigned long) mysql_affected_rows (conn));
        }
    }
    else    /* a result set was returned */
    {
        /* process rows, then free the result set */
        process_result_set (conn, res_set);
        mysql_free_result (res_set);
    }
}
```

A Comparison of mysql_store_result() and mysql_use_result()

The mysql_store_result() and mysql_use_result() functions are similar in that both take a connection handler argument and return a result set. However, the differences between them actually are quite extensive. The primary difference between the two functions lies in the way rows of the result set are retrieved from the server. mysql_store_result() retrieves all the rows immediately when you call it. mysql_use_result() initiates the retrieval but doesn't actually get any of the rows. Instead, it assumes you will call mysql_fetch_row() to retrieve the records later. These differing approaches to row retrieval give rise to all other differences between the two functions. This section compares them so you'll know how to choose the one that's most appropriate for a given application.

When mysql_store_result() retrieves a result set from the server, it fetches the rows, allocates memory for them, and stores them in the client. Subsequent calls to mysql_fetch_row() never return an error because they simply pull a row out of a data structure that already holds the result set. A NULL return from mysql_fetch_row() always means you've reached the end of the result set.

By contrast, mysql_use_result() doesn't retrieve any rows itself. Instead, it simply initiates a row-by-row retrieval, which you must complete yourself by calling mysql_fetch_row() for each row. In this case, although a NULL return from mysql_fetch_row() normally still means the end of the result set has been reached, it's also possible that an error occurred while communicating with the server. You can distinguish the two outcomes by calling mysql_errno() or mysql_error().

mysql_store_result() has higher memory and processing requirements than does mysql_use_result() because the entire result set is maintained in the client. The overhead for memory allocation and data structure setup is greater, and a client that retrieves large result sets runs the risk of running out of memory. If you're going to retrieve a lot of rows at once, you may want to use mysql_use_result() instead.

mysql_use_result() has lower memory requirements because only enough space to handle a single row at a time need be allocated. This can be faster because you're not setting up as complex a data structure for the result set. On the other hand, mysql_use_result() places a greater burden on the server, which must hold rows of the result set until the client sees fit to retrieve all of them. This makes mysql_use_result() a poor choice for certain types of clients:

- Interactive clients that advance from row to row at the request of the user. (You don't want the server having to wait to send the next row just because the user decides to take a coffee break.)

- Clients that do a lot of processing between row retrievals.

In both of these types of situations, the client fails to retrieve all rows in the result set quickly. This ties up the server and can have a negative impact on other clients because tables from which you retrieve data are read-locked for the duration of the query. Any clients that are trying to update those tables or insert rows into them are blocked.

Offsetting the additional memory requirements incurred by mysql_store_result() are certain benefits of having access to the entire result set at once. All rows of the set are available, so you have random access into them: The mysql_data_seek(), mysql_row_seek(), and mysql_row_tell() functions allow you to access rows in any order you want. With mysql_use_result(), you can access rows only in the order in which they are retrieved by mysql_fetch_row(). If you intend to process rows in any order other than sequentially as they are returned from the server, you must use mysql_store_result() instead. For example, if you have an application that allows the user to browse back and forth among the rows selected by a query, you'd be best served by using mysql_store_result().

With mysql_store_result(), you can obtain certain types of column information that are unavailable when you use mysql_use_result(). The number of rows in the result set is obtained by calling mysql_num_rows(). The maximum widths of the values in each column are stored in the max_width member of the MYSQL_FIELD column information structures. With mysql_use_result(), mysql_num_rows() doesn't return the correct value until you've fetched all the rows, and max_width is unavailable because it can be calculated only after every row's data have been seen.

Because mysql_use_result() does less work than mysql_store_result(), it imposes a requirement that mysql_store_result() does not: The client *must* call mysql_fetch_row() for every row in the result set. Otherwise, any remaining records in the set become part of the next query's result set and an "out of sync" error occurs. This does not happen with `mysql_store_result()` because when that function returns, all rows have already been fetched. In fact, with `mysql_store_result()`, you need not call `mysql_fetch_row()` yourself at all. This can be useful for queries for which all that you're interested in is whether you got a non-empty result, not what the result contains. For example, to find out whether or not a table `my_tbl` exists, you can execute this query:

```
SHOW TABLES LIKE "my_tbl"
```

If, after calling `mysql_store_result()`, the value of `mysql_num_rows()` is non-zero, the table exists. `mysql_fetch_row()` need not be called. (You still need to call `mysql_free_result()`, of course.)

If you want to provide maximum flexibility, give users the option of selecting either result set processing method. `mysql` and `mysqldump` are two programs that do this. They use `mysql_store_result()` by default but switch to `mysql_use_result()` if you specify the `--quick` option.

Using Result Set Metadata

Result sets contain not only the column values for data rows but also information about the data. This information is called the result set metadata, which includes:

- The number of rows and columns in the result set, available by calling `mysql_num_rows()` and `mysql_num_fields()`.
- The length of each column value in a row, available by calling `mysql_fetch_lengths()`.
- Information about each column, such as the column name and type, the maximum width of each column's values, and the table the column comes from. This information is stored in `MYSQL_FIELD` structures, which typically are obtained by calling `mysql_fetch_field()`. Appendix F describes the `MYSQL_FIELD` structure in detail and lists all functions that provide access to column information.

Metadata availability is partially dependent on your result set processing method. As indicated in the previous section, if you want to use the row count or maximum column length values, you must create the result set with `mysql_store_result()`, not with `mysql_use_result()`.

Result set metadata is helpful for making decisions about how to process result set data:

- The column name and width information is useful for producing nicely formatted output that has column titles and lines up vertically.
- You use the column count to determine how many times to iterate through a loop that processes successive column values for data rows. You can use the row or column counts if you need to allocate data structures that depend on knowing the number of rows or columns in the result set.

- You can determine the data type of a column. This allows you to tell whether a column represents a number, whether it may contain binary data, and so forth.

Earlier, in the section "Handling Queries That Return Data," we wrote a version of `process_result_set()` that printed columns from result set rows in tab-delimited format. That's good for certain purposes (such as when you want to import the data into a spreadsheet), but it's not a nice display format for visual inspection or for printouts. Recall that our earlier version of `process_result_set()` produced output like this:

```
Adams    John     Braintree   MA
Adams    John Quincy Braintree   MA
Arthur   Chester A.  Fairfield   VT
Buchanan    James    Mercersburg PA
Bush     George W.   Milton  MA
Carter   James E. Jr Plains   GA
Cleveland    Grover  Caldwell    NJ
...
```

Let's make some changes to `process_result_set()` to produce tabular output by titling and "boxing" each column. The revised version will display those same results in a format that's easier to look at:

```
+-------------+---------------+-------------+-------+
| last_name   | first_name    | city        | state |
+-------------+---------------+-------------+-------+
| Adams       | John          | Braintree   | MA    |
| Adams       | John Quincy   | Braintree   | MA    |
| Arthur      | Chester A.    | Fairfield   | VT    |
| Buchanan    | James         | Mercersburg | PA    |
| Bush        | George W.     | Milton      | MA    |
| Carter      | James E., Jr. | Plains      | GA    |
| Cleveland   | Grover        | Caldwell    | NJ    |
| ...         | ...           | ...         | ...   |
+-------------+---------------+-------------+-------+
```

The general outline of the display algorithm is as follows:

1. Determine the display width of each column.
2. Print a row of boxed column labels (delimited by vertical bars and preceded and followed by rows of dashes).
3. Print the values in each row of the result set, with each column boxed (delimited by vertical bars) and lined up vertically. In addition, print numbers right justified and print the word "NULL" for NULL values.
4. At the end, print a count of the number of rows retrieved.

This exercise provides a good demonstration of the use of result set metadata. To display output as just described, we need to know quite a number of things about the result set other than just the values of the data contained in the rows.

You may be thinking to yourself, "Hmm, that description sounds suspiciously similar to the way mysql displays its output." Yes, it does, and you're welcome to compare the source for mysql to the code we end up with for the revised process_result_set(). They're not the same, and you may find it instructive to compare two approaches to the same problem.

First, we need to determine the display width of each column. The following listing shows how to do this. Observe that the calculations are based entirely on the result set metadata, and they make no reference whatsoever to the row values:

```
MYSQL_FIELD    *field;
unsigned int   i, col_len;

/* determine column display widths */
mysql_field_seek (res_set, 0);
for (i = 0; i < mysql_num_fields (res_set); i++)
{
    field = mysql_fetch_field (res_set);
    col_len = strlen (field->name);
    if (col_len < field->max_length)
        col_len = field->max_length;
    if (col_len < 4 && !IS_NOT_NULL (field->flags))
        col_len = 4;    /* 4 = length of the word "NULL" */
    field->max_length = col_len;    /* reset column info */
}
```

Column widths are calculated by iterating through the MYSQL_FIELD structures for the columns in the result set. We position to the first structure by calling mysql_fetch_seek(). Subsequent calls to mysql_fetch_field() return pointers to the structures for successive columns. The width of a column for display purposes is the maximum of three values, each of which depends on metadata in the column information structure:

- The length of field->name, the column title.
- field->max_length, the length of the longest data value in the column.
- The length of the string "NULL" if the column can contain NULL values. field->flags indicates whether or not the column can contain NULL.

Notice that after the display width for a column is known, we assign that value to max_length, which is a member of a structure that we obtain from the client library. Is that allowable, or should the contents of the MYSQL_FIELD structure be considered read-only? Normally, I would say "read-only," but some of the client programs in the MySQL distribution change the max_length value in a similar way, so I assume it's okay. (If you prefer an alternative approach that doesn't modify max_length, allocate an array of unsigned int values and store the calculated widths in that array.)

The display width calculations involve one caveat. Recall that `max_length` has no meaning when you create a result set using `mysql_use_result()`. Because we need `max_length` to determine the display width of the column values, proper operation of the algorithm requires that the result set be generated using `mysql_store_result()`.[1]

Once we know the column widths, we're ready to print. Titles are easy to handle; for a given column, we simply use the column information structure pointed to by `field` and print the `name` member, using the width calculated earlier:

```
printf (" %-*s |", field->max_length, field->name);
```

For the data, we loop through the rows in the result set, printing column values for the current row during each iteration. Printing column values from the row is a bit tricky because a value might be NULL, or it might represent a number (in which case we print it right justified). Column values are printed as follows, where row[i] holds the data value and field points to the column information:

```
if (row[i] == NULL)
    printf (" %-*s |", field->max_length, "NULL");
else if (IS_NUM (field->type))
    printf (" %*s |", field->max_length, row[i]);
else
    printf (" %-*s |", field->max_length, row[i]);
```

The value of the `IS_NUM()` macro is true if the column type indicated by `field->type` is a numeric type such as INT, FLOAT, or DECIMAL.

The final code to display the result set looks like this. Note that because we're printing lines of dashes multiple times, code to do that is encapsulated into its own function, `print_dashes()`:

```
void
print_dashes (MYSQL_RES *res_set)
{
MYSQL_FIELD    *field;
unsigned int   i, j;

    mysql_field_seek (res_set, 0);
    fputc ('+', stdout);
    for (i = 0; i < mysql_num_fields (res_set); i++)
    {
        field = mysql_fetch_field (res_set);
        for (j = 0; j < field->max_length + 2; j++)
            fputc ('-', stdout);
        fputc ('+', stdout);
    }
    fputc ('\n', stdout);
}
```

[1] The `length` member of the `MYSQL_FIELD` structure tells you the maximum length that column values can be. This may be a useful workaround if you're using `mysql_use_result()` rather than `mysql_store_result()`.

```
void
process_result_set (MYSQL *conn, MYSQL_RES *res_set)
{
MYSQL_FIELD    *field;
MYSQL_ROW      row;
unsigned int   i, col_len;

    /* determine column display widths */
    mysql_field_seek (res_set, 0);
    for (i = 0; i < mysql_num_fields (res_set); i++)
    {
        field = mysql_fetch_field (res_set);
        col_len = strlen (field->name);
        if (col_len < field->max_length)
            col_len = field->max_length;
        if (col_len < 4 && !IS_NOT_NULL (field->flags))
            col_len = 4;    /* 4 = length of the word "NULL" */
        field->max_length = col_len;    /* reset column info */
    }

    print_dashes (res_set);
    fputc ('|', stdout);
    mysql_field_seek (res_set, 0);
    for (i = 0; i < mysql_num_fields (res_set); i++)
    {
        field = mysql_fetch_field (res_set);
        printf (" %-*s |", field->max_length, field->name);
    }
    fputc ('\n', stdout);
    print_dashes (res_set);

    while ((row = mysql_fetch_row (res_set)) != NULL)
    {
        mysql_field_seek (res_set, 0);
        fputc ('|', stdout);
        for (i = 0; i < mysql_num_fields (res_set); i++)
        {
            field = mysql_fetch_field (res_set);
            if (row[i] == NULL)
                printf (" %-*s |", field->max_length, "NULL");
            else if (IS_NUM (field->type))
                printf (" %*s |", field->max_length, row[i]);
            else
                printf (" %-*s |", field->max_length, row[i]);
        }
        fputc ('\n', stdout);
    }
    print_dashes (res_set);
    printf ("%lu rows returned\n", (unsigned long) mysql_num_rows (res_set));
}
```

The MySQL client library provides several ways of accessing the column information structures. For example, the code in the preceding example accesses these structures several times using loops of the following general form:

```
mysql_field_seek (res_set, 0);
for (i = 0; i < mysql_num_fields (res_set); i++)
{
    field = mysql_fetch_field (res_set);
    ...
}
```

However, the `mysql_field_seek()` / `mysql_fetch_field()` combination is only one way of getting `MYSQL_FIELD` structures. See the entries for the `mysql_fetch_fields()` and `mysql_fetch_field_direct()` functions in Appendix F for other ways of getting column information structures.

Client 5—An Interactive Query Program

Let's put together much of what we've developed so far and use it to write a simple interactive client. It lets you enter queries, executes them using our general purpose query handler `process_query()`, and displays the results using the `process_result_set()` display formatter developed in the preceding section.

`client5` will be similar in some ways to `mysql`, although of course not with as many features. There are several restrictions on what `client5` will allow as input:

- Each input line must contain a single complete query.

- Queries should not be terminated by a semicolon or by '\g'.

- Commands such as `quit` are not recognized; instead, use Control-D to terminate the program.

It turns out that `client5` is almost completely trivial to write (fewer than 10 lines of new code). Almost everything we need is provided by our client program skeleton (`client4.c`) and by other code that we have written already. The only thing we need to add is a loop that collects input lines and executes them.

To construct `client5`, begin by copying the client skeleton `client4.c` to `client5.c`. Then add to that the code for `process_query()`, `process_result_set()`, and `print_dashes()`. Finally, in `client5.c`, look for the line in `main()` that says the following:

```
/* do the real work here */
```

Then replace it with this while loop:

```
while (1)
{
char    buf[1024];
    fprintf (stderr, "query> ");                        /* print prompt */
    if (fgets (buf, sizeof (buf), stdin) == NULL)       /* read query */
```

```
        break;
    process_query (conn, buf);                          /* execute query */
}
```

Compile `client5.c` to produce `client5.o`, link `client5.o` with `common.o` and the client library to produce `client5`, and you're done! You have an interactive MySQL client program that can execute any query and display the results.

Miscellaneous Topics

This section covers several subjects that didn't fit very well into the progression as we went from `client1` to `client5`:

- Using result set data to calculate a result, after using result set metadata to help verify that the data are suitable for your calculations.
- How to deal with data that are troublesome to insert into queries.
- How to work with image data.
- How to get information about the structure of your tables.
- Common MySQL programming mistakes and how to avoid them.

Performing Calculations on Result Sets

So far we've concentrated on using result set metadata primarily for printing row data, but clearly there will be times when you need to do something with your data besides print it. For example, you can compute statistical information based on the data values, using the metadata to make sure the data conform to requirements you want them to satisfy. What type of requirements? For starters, you'd probably want to verify that a column on which you're planning to perform numeric computations actually contains numbers!

The following listing shows a simple function, `summary_stats()`, that takes a result set and a column index and produces summary statistics for the values in the column. The function also reports the number of missing values, which it detects by checking for `NULL` values. These calculations involve two requirements that the data must satisfy, so `summary_stats()` verifies them using the result set metadata:

- The specified column must exist (that is, the column index must be within range of the number of columns in the result set).
- The column must contain numeric values.

If these conditions do not hold, `summary_stats()` simply prints an error message and returns. The code is as follows:

```
void
summary_stats (MYSQL_RES *res_set, unsigned int col_num)
{
```

continues

continued

```
MYSQL_FIELD     *field;
MYSQL_ROW       row;
unsigned int    n, missing;
double  val, sum, sum_squares, var;

    /* verify data requirements */
    if (mysql_num_fields (res_set) < col_num)
    {
        print_error (NULL, "illegal column number");
        return;
    }
    mysql_field_seek (res_set, 0);
    field = mysql_fetch_field (res_set);
    if (!IS_NUM (field->type))
    {
        print_error (NULL, "column is not numeric");
        return;
    }

    /* calculate summary statistics */

    n = 0;
    missing = 0;
    sum = 0;
    sum_squares = 0;

    mysql_data_seek (res_set, 0);
    while ((row = mysql_fetch_row (res_set)) != NULL)
    {
        if (row[col_num] == NULL)
            missing++;
        else
        {
            n++;
            val = atof (row[col_num]);  /* convert string to number */
            sum += val;
            sum_squares += val * val;
        }
    }
    if (n == 0)
        printf ("No observations\n");
    else
    {
        printf ("Number of observations: %lu\n", n);
        printf ("Missing observations: %lu\n", missing);
        printf ("Sum: %g\n", sum);
        printf ("Mean: %g\n", sum / n);
        printf ("Sum of squares: %g\n", sum_squares);
        var = ((n * sum_squares) - (sum * sum)) / (n * (n - 1));
```

```
        printf ("Variance: %g\n", var);
        printf ("Standard deviation: %g\n", sqrt (var));
    }
}
```

Note the call to `mysql_data_seek()` that precedes the `mysql_fetch_row()` loop. It's there to allow you to call `summary_stats()` multiple times for the same result set (in case you want to calculate statistics on several columns). Each time `summary_stats()` is invoked, it "rewinds" to the beginning of the result set. (This assumes that you create the result set with `mysql_store_result()`. If you create it with `mysql_use_result()`, you can only process rows in order, and you can process them only once.)

`summary_stats()` is a relatively simple function, but it should give you an idea of how you could program more complex calculations, such as a least-squares regression on two columns or standard statistics such as a *t*-test.

Encoding Problematic Data in Queries

Data values containing quotes, nulls, or backslashes, if inserted literally into a query, can cause problems when you try to execute the query. The following discussion describes the nature of the difficulty and how to solve it.

Suppose you want to construct a SELECT query based on the contents of the null-terminated string pointed to by `name`:

```
char query[1024];
```

```
sprintf (query, "SELECT * FROM my_tbl WHERE name='%s'", name);
```

If the value of `name` is something like `"O'Malley, Brian"`, the resulting query is illegal because a quote appears inside a quoted string:

```
SELECT * FROM my_tbl WHERE name='O'Malley, Brian'
```

You need to treat the quote specially so that the server doesn't interpret it as the end of the name. One way to do this is to double the quote within the string. That is the ANSI SQL convention. MySQL understands that convention, and also allows the quote to be preceded by a backslash:

```
SELECT * FROM my_tbl WHERE name='O''Malley, Brian'
SELECT * FROM my_tbl WHERE name='O\'Malley, Brian'
```

Another problematic situation involves the use of arbitrary binary data in a query. This happens, for example, in applications that store images in a database. Because a binary value may contain any character, it cannot be considered safe to put into a query as is.

To deal with this problem, use `mysql_escape_string()`, which encodes special characters to make them usable in quoted strings. Characters that `mysql_escape_string()` considers special are the null character, single quote, double quote, backslash, newline, carriage return, and Control-Z. (The last one occurs in Windows contexts.)

When should you use `mysql_escape_string()`? The safest answer is "always." However, if you're sure of the form of your data and know that it's okay—perhaps because you have performed some prior validation check on it—you need not encode it. For example, if you are working with strings that you know represent legal phone numbers consisting entirely of digits and dashes, you don't need to call `mysql_escape_string()`. Otherwise, you probably should.

`mysql_escape_string()` encodes problematic characters by turning them into 2-character sequences that begin with a backslash. For example, a null byte becomes '\0', where the '0' is a printable ASCII zero, not a null. Backslash, single quote, and double quote become '\\', '\'', and '\"'.

To use `mysql_escape_string()`, invoke it like this:

```
to_len = mysql_escape_string (to_str, from_str, from_len);
```

`mysql_escape_string()` encodes `from_str` and writes the result into `to_str`, It also adds a terminating null, which is convenient because you can use the resulting string with functions such as `strcpy()` and `strlen()`.

`from_str` points to a char buffer containing the string to be encoded. This string may contain anything, including binary data. `to_str` points to an existing char buffer where you want the encoded string to be written; *do not* pass an uninitialized or NULL pointer, expecting `mysql_escape_string()` to allocate space for you. The length of the buffer pointed to by `to_str` must be at least `(from_len*2)+1` bytes long. (It's possible that every character in `from_str` will need encoding with 2 characters; the extra byte is for the terminating null.)

`from_len` and `to_len` are `unsigned int` values. `from_len` indicates the length of the data in `from_str`; it's necessary to provide the length because `from_str` may contain null bytes and cannot be treated as a null-terminated string. `to_len`, the return value from `mysql_escape_string()`, is the actual length of the resulting encoded string, not counting the terminating null.

When `mysql_escape_string()` returns, the encoded result in `to_str` can be treated as a null-terminated string because any nulls in `from_str` are encoded as the printable '\0' sequence.

To rewrite the SELECT-constructing code so that it works even for values of names that contain quotes, we could do something like this:

```
char query[1024], *p;

p = strcpy (query, "SELECT * FROM my_tbl WHERE name='");
p += strlen (p);
p += mysql_escape_string (p, name, strlen (name));
p = strcpy (p, "'");
```

Yes, that's ugly. If you want to simplify it a bit, at the cost of using a second buffer, do this instead:

```
char query[1024], buf[1024];

(void) mysql_escape_string (buf, name, strlen (name));
sprintf (query, "SELECT * FROM my_tbl WHERE name='%s'", buf);
```

Working With Image Data

One of the jobs for which `mysql_escape_string()` is essential involves loading image data into a table. This section shows how to do it. (The discussion applies to any other form of binary data as well.)

Suppose you want to read images from files and store them in a table, along with a unique identifier. The `BLOB` type is a good choice for binary data, so you could use a table specification like this:

```
CREATE TABLE images
(
    image_id INT NOT NULL PRIMARY KEY,
    image_data BLOB
)
```

To actually get an image from a file into the `images` table, the following function, `load_image()`, does the job, given an identifier number and a pointer to an open file containing the image data:

```
int
load_image (MYSQL *conn, int id, FILE *f)
{
char            query[1024*100], buf[1024*10], *p;
unsigned int    from_len;
int             status;

    sprintf (query, "INSERT INTO images VALUES (%d,'", id);
    p = query + strlen (query);
    while ((from_len = fread (buf, 1, sizeof (buf), f)) > 0)
    {
        /* don't overrun end of query buffer! */
        if (p + (2*from_len) + 3 > query + sizeof (query))
        {
            print_error (NULL, "image too big");
            return (1);
        }
        p += mysql_escape_string (p, buf, from_len);
    }
    (void) strcpy (p, "')");
    status = mysql_query (conn, query);
    return (status);
}
```

`load_image()` doesn't allocate a very large query buffer (100K), so it works only for relatively small images. In a real-world application, you might allocate the buffer dynamically based on the size of the image file.

Handling image data (or any binary data) that you get back out of a database isn't nearly as much of a problem as putting it in to begin with because the data values are available in raw form in the `MYSQL_ROW` variable, and the lengths are available by calling `mysql_fetch_lengths()`. Just be sure to treat the values as counted strings, not as null-terminated strings.

Getting Table Information

MySQL allows you to get information about the structure of your tables, using either of these queries (which are equivalent):

```
DESCRIBE tbl_name
SHOW FIELDS FROM tbl_name
```

Both statements are like `SELECT` in that they return a result set. To find out about the columns in the table, all you need to do is process the rows in the result to pull out the information you want. For example, if you issue a `DESCRIBE images` statement from the `mysql` client, it returns this information:

```
+------------+----------+------+-----+----------+-------+
| Field      | Type     | Null | Key | Default  | Extra |
+------------+----------+------+-----+----------+-------+
| image_id   | int(11)  |      | PRI | 0        |       |
| image_data | blob     | YES  |     | NULL     |       |
+------------+----------+------+-----+----------+-------+
```

If you execute the same query from your own client, you get the same information (without the boxes).

If you want information only about a single column, use this query instead:

```
SHOW FIELDS FROM tbl_name LIKE "col_name"
```

The query will return the same columns, but only one row (or no rows if the column doesn't exist).

Client Programming Mistakes To Avoid

This section discusses some common MySQL C API programming errors and how to avoid them. (These problems seem to crop up periodically on the MySQL mailing list; I didn't make them up.)

Mistake 1—Using Uninitialized Connection Handler Pointers

In the examples shown in this chapter, we've called `mysql_init()` by passing a `NULL` argument to it. This tells `mysql_init()` to allocate and initialize a `MYSQL` structure and return a pointer to it. Another approach is to pass a pointer to an existing `MYSQL` structure. In this case, `mysql_init()` will initialize that structure and return a pointer to it without allocating the structure itself. If you want to use this second approach, be aware that it can lead to certain subtle problems. The following discussion points out some problems to watch out for.

If you pass a pointer to `mysql_init()`, it should actually point to something. Consider this piece of code:

```
main ()
{
MYSQL    *conn;
    mysql_init (conn);
    ...
}
```

The problem is that `mysql_init()` receives a pointer, but that pointer doesn't point anywhere sensible. `conn` is a local variable and thus is uninitialized storage that can point anywhere when `main()` begins execution. That means `mysql_init()` will use the pointer and scribble on some random area of memory. If you're lucky, `conn` will point outside your program's address space and the system will terminate it immediately so that you'll realize that the problem occurs early in your code. If you're not so lucky, `conn` will point into some data that you don't use until later in your program, and you won't notice a problem until your program actually tries to use that data. In that case, your problem will appear to occur much farther into the execution of your program than where it actually originates and may be much more difficult to track down.

Here's a similar piece of problematic code:

```
MYSQL    *conn;

main ()
{
    mysql_init (conn);
    mysql_real_connect (conn, ...)
    mysql_query(conn, "SHOW DATABASES");
    ...
}
```

In this case `conn` is a global variable, so it's initialized to `0` (that is, `NULL`) before the program starts up. `mysql_init()` sees a `NULL` argument, so it initializes and allocates a new connection handler. Unfortunately, `conn` is still `NULL` because no value is ever assigned to it. As soon as you pass `conn` to a MySQL C API function that requires a non-`NULL` connection handler, your program will crash. The fix for both pieces of code is to make sure `conn` has a sensible value. For example, you can initialize it to the address of an already-allocated MYSQL structure:

```
MYSQL conn_struct, *conn = &conn_struct;
...
mysql_init (conn);
```

However, the recommended (and easier!) solution is simply to pass NULL explicitly to mysql_init(), let that function allocate the MYSQL structure for you, and assign conn the return value:

```
MYSQL *conn;
...
conn = mysql_init (NULL);
```

In any case, don't forget to test the return value of mysql_init() to make sure it's not NULL.

Mistake 2—Failing to Test for a Valid Result Set

Remember to check the status of calls from which you expect to get a result set. This code doesn't do that:

```
MYSQL_RES *res_set;
MYSQL_ROW row;

res_set = mysql_store_result (conn);
while ((row = mysql_fetch_row (res_set)) != NULL)
{
    /* process row */
}
```

Unfortunately, if mysql_store_result() fails, res_set is NULL, and the while loop shouldn't even be executed. Test the return value of functions that return result sets to make sure you actually have something to work with.

Mistake 3—Failing to Account for NULL Column Values

Don't forget to check whether or not column values in the MYSQL_ROW array returned by mysql_fetch_row() are NULL pointers. The following code crashes on some machines if row[i] is NULL:

```
for (i = 0; i < mysql_num_fields (res_set); i++)
{
    if (i > 0)
        fputc ('\t', stdout);
    printf ("%s", row[i]);
}
fputc ('\n', stdout);
```

The worst part about this mistake is that some versions of printf() are forgiving and print "(null)" for NULL pointers, which allows you to get away with not fixing the problem. If you give your program to a friend who has a less-forgiving printf(), the program crashes and your friend concludes you're a lousy programmer. The loop should be written like this instead:

```
for (i = 0; i < mysql_num_fields (res_set); i++)
{
    if (i > 0)
        fputc ('\t', stdout);
```

```
    printf ("%s", row[i] != NULL ? row[i] : "NULL");
  }
  fputc ('\n', stdout);
```

The only time you need not check whether or not a column value is NULL is when you have already determined from the column's information structure that IS_NOT_NULL() is true.

Mistake 4—Passing Nonsensical Result Buffers

Client library functions that expect you to supply buffers generally want them to really exist. This code violates that principle:

```
char *from_str = "some string";
char *to_str;
unsigned int len;

len = mysql_escape_string (to_str, from_str, strlen (from_str));
```

What's the problem? to_str must point to an existing buffer. In this example, it doesn't—it points to some random location. Don't pass an uninitialized pointer as the to_str argument to mysql_escape_string() unless you want it to stomp merrily all over some random piece of memory.

7

The Perl DBI API

THIS CHAPTER DESCRIBES HOW TO USE THE Perl DBI interface to MySQL. It does not discuss DBI philosophy or architecture. For information about those aspects of DBI (particularly in comparison with the C and PHP APIs), see Chapter 5, "Introduction to MySQL Programming."

The examples in this chapter draw on our sample database, samp_db, using the tables needed for the grade-keeping project and for the Historical League. To get the most from the chapter, it's best if you know something about Perl. If you don't, you may be able to get along and write your own scripts simply by copying the sample code you see here. But you would probably find a good Perl book a worthwhile investment. One such book is *Programming Perl, Second Edition* by Wall, Christiansen, Schwartz, and Potter (O'Reilly, 1996).

DBI is currently at version 1.13, though most of the discussion here applies to earlier 1.xx versions as well. Features described here that are not present in earlier versions are noted.

DBI for MySQL requires a version of Perl at least as recent as 5.004_05. You must also install the Msql-Mysql-modules and Data-Dumper Perl modules, as well as the MySQL C client library and header files. If you plan to write Web-based DBI scripts, you'll probably want to use the CGI.pm module. In this chapter, that module is used in conjunction with the Apache Web server. If you need to obtain any of these packages, see Appendix A, "Obtaining and Installing Software." Instructions for obtaining the example scripts developed in this chapter are also given in that appendix. You can download the scripts to avoid typing them in yourself.

For the most part, this chapter describes Perl DBI methods and variables only as they are needed for the discussion here. For a more comprehensive listing of all methods and variables, see Appendix G, "Perl DBI API Reference." You can use that appendix as a reference for further background on any part of DBI that you're trying to use. Online documentation is available by running the following commands:

```
% perldoc DBI
% perldoc DBI::FAQ
% perldoc DBD::mysql
```

At the database driver (DBD) level, the driver for MySQL is built on top of the MySQL C client library, and therefore shares some of its characteristics. See Chapter 6, "The MySQL C API," for more information about that library.

Perl Script Characteristics

Perl scripts are just text files, and you can create them using any text editor. All Perl scripts in this chapter follow the UNIX convention of using a first line that begins with '#!', followed by the pathname of the program to use for executing the script. The line I use is as follows:

```
#! /usr/bin/perl
```

You'll need to modify the '#!' line if the pathname to Perl is different on your system, such as `/usr/local/bin/perl5` or `/opt/bin/perl`. Otherwise, Perl scripts won't run properly on your system.

I include a space after the '#!' because some systems interpret '#! /' as a 4-byte magic number, ignore the line if the space is missing, and thus treat the script as a shell script.

Under UNIX, a Perl script should be made executable so that you can run it just by typing its name. To make a script file executable, change its file mode as follows:

```
% chmod +x script_name
```

If you're using ActiveState Perl under Windows, you don't make scripts executable. Instead, you run a script like this:

```
C:\> perl script_name
```

Perl DBI Basics

This section provides background information for DBI—the information you'll need for writing your own scripts and for understanding scripts written by others. If you're already familiar with DBI, you may want to skip directly to the section "Putting DBI to Work."

DBI Data Types

In some ways, using the Perl DBI API is similar to using the C client library described in Chapter 6. When you use the C client library, you call functions and access MySQL-related data primarily by means of pointers to structures or to arrays. When you use the DBI API, you also call functions and use pointers to structures, except that functions are called *methods*, pointers are called *references*, pointer variables are called *handles*, and the structures that handles point to are called *objects*.

DBI uses several kinds of handles. These tend to be referred to in DBI documentation by the conventional names shown in Table 7.1. The way you use these handles will become clear as we go along. Several conventional names for non-handle variables are used as well (see Table 7.2). We don't actually use every one of these variable names in this chapter, but it's useful to know them when you read DBI scripts written by other people.

Table 7.1 **Conventional Perl DBI Handle Variable Names**

Name	Meaning
$dbh	A handle to a database object
$sth	A handle to a statement (query) object
$fh	A handle to an open file
$h	A "generic" handle; the meaning depends on context

Table 7.2 **Conventional Perl DBI Non-Handle Variable Names**

Name	Meaning
$rc	The return code from operations that return true or false
$rv	The return value from operations that return an integer
$rows	The return value from operations that return a row count
@ary	An array (list) representing a row of values returned by a query

A Simple DBI Script

Let's start with a simple script, dump_members, that illustrates several standard concepts in DBI programming, such as connecting to and disconnecting from the MySQL server, issuing queries, and retrieving data. This script produces as output the Historical League's member list in tab-delimited format. The format is not so interesting in itself; at this point, it's more important see how to use DBI than to produce pretty output.

dump_members looks like this:

```
#! /usr/bin/perl

# dump_members - dump Historical League's membership list

use DBI;
use strict;

my ($dsn) = "DBI:mysql:samp_db:localhost"; # data source name
my ($user_name) = "paul";  # user name
my ($password) = "secret"; # password
my ($dbh, $sth);           # database and statement handles
my (@ary);                 # array for rows returned by query

# connect to database
$dbh = DBI->connect ($dsn, $user_name, $password, { RaiseError => 1 });

# issue query
$sth = $dbh->prepare ("SELECT last_name, first_name, suffix, email,"
    . "street, city, state, zip, phone FROM member ORDER BY last_name");
$sth->execute ();

# read results of query, then clean up
while (@ary = $sth->fetchrow_array ())
{
    print join ("\t", @ary), "\n";
}
$sth->finish ();

$dbh->disconnect ();
exit (0);
```

To try out the script for yourself, either download it (see Appendix A), or create it using a text editor and then make it executable so that you can run it. You'll probably need to change at least some of the connection parameters (hostname, database name, username, password), of course. That will be true of other DBI scripts in this chapter as well. By default, the permissions on the downloadable scripts for this chapter are set so they are readable only by you. I suggest you leave them that way if you put your own MySQL username and password into them so that others can't read the values. Later, in "Specifying Connection Parameters," we'll see how to get parameters from an option file instead of putting them directly in the script.

Now let's go through the script a piece at a time. The first line contains the standard where-to-find-Perl indicator:

```
#! /usr/bin/perl
```

This line is part of every script we'll discuss in this chapter; I won't mention it further.

It's a good idea to include in a script at least a minimal description of its purpose, so the next line is a comment to give anyone who looks at the script a clue about what it does:

```
# dump_members - dump Historical League's membership list
```

Text from a '#' character to the end of a line is considered a comment. It's a worthwhile practice to sprinkle comments throughout your scripts that explain how they work.

Next we have a couple of use lines:

```
use DBI;
use strict;
```

use DBI tells the Perl interpreter that it needs to pull in the DBI module. Without this line, an error occurs as soon as you try to do anything DBI-related in the script. You don't have to indicate which DBD-level module you want, though. DBI activates the right one for you when you connect to your database.

use strict tells Perl to require you to declare variables before using them. You can write scripts without putting in a use strict line, but it's useful for catching mistakes, so I recommend you always include it. For example, with strict mode turned on, if you declare a variable $my_var but then later refer to it erroneously as $mv_var, you'll get the following message when you run the script:

```
Global symbol "$mv_var" requires explicit package name at line n
```

When you see that, you think, "What? $mv_var? I never used any variable with that name!" Then you look at line *n* of your script, see what the problem is, and fix it. Without strict mode, Perl won't squawk about $mv_var; it simply creates a new variable by that name with a value of undef (undefined), uses it without complaint, and you're left to wonder why your script doesn't work.

Because we're operating in strict mode, we'll declare the variables the script uses:

```
my ($dsn) = "DBI:mysql:samp_db:localhost"; # data source name
my ($user_name) = "paul";  # user name
my ($password) = "secret"; # password
my ($dbh, $sth);           # database and statement handles
my (@ary);                 # array for rows returned by query
```

Now we're ready to connect to the database:

```
# connect to database
$dbh = DBI->connect ($dsn, $user_name, $password, { RaiseError => 1 });
```

The connect() call is invoked as DBI->connect() because it's a method of the DBI class. You don't really have to know what that means; it's just a little object-oriented jargon to make your head hurt. (If you do want to know, it means that connect() is a function that "belongs" to DBI.) connect() takes several arguments:

- **The data source.** (Often called a data source name, or DSN.) Data source formats are determined by the requirements of the particular DBD module you want to use. For the MySQL driver, allowable formats include either of the following:

```
"DBI:mysql:db_name"
"DBI:mysql:db_name:host_name"
```

For the first format, the hostname defaults to `localhost`. (There actually are other allowable data source formats, which we'll discuss later in "Specifying Connection Parameters.") The capitalization of "`DBI`" doesn't matter, but "`mysql`" must be lowercase.

- **Your username and password.**

- **An optional argument indicating additional connection attributes.** This controls DBI's error-handling behavior, and the weird-looking construct we've specified enables the `RaiseError` attribute. This causes DBI to check for database-related errors and to print a message and exit whenever it detects one. (That's why you don't see error-checking code anywhere in the `dump_members` script; DBI handles it all.) The section "Handling Errors" covers alternate methods of responding to errors.

If the `connect()` call succeeds, it returns a database handle, which we assign to `$dbh`. (If `connect()` fails, it normally returns `undef`. However, because we enabled `RaiseError` in our script, `connect()` won't return; instead, DBI will print an error message and exit if an error occurs.)

After connecting to the database, `dump_members` issues a `SELECT` query to retrieve the membership list, then executes a loop to process each of the rows returned. These rows constitute the result set.

To perform a `SELECT`, you prepare it first, then execute it:

```
# issue query
$sth = $dbh->prepare ("SELECT last_name, first_name, suffix, email,"
    . "street, city, state, zip, phone FROM member ORDER BY last_name");
$sth->execute ();
```

`prepare()` is called using the database handle; it passes the SQL statement to the driver for preprocessing before execution. Some drivers actually do something with the statement at this point. Others just remember it until you invoke `execute()` to cause the statement to be performed. The return value from `prepare()` is a statement handle, `$sth`, or `undef` if an error occurs. The statement handle is used for all further processing related to the statement.

Notice that the query is specified with no terminating semicolon. You no doubt have the habit (developed through long hours of interaction with the `mysql` program), of terminating SQL statements with a ';' character. However, it's best to break yourself of that habit when using DBI because semicolons often cause queries to fail with syntax errors. The same applies to adding '\g' to queries—don't.

When you invoke a method without passing it any arguments, you can leave off the parentheses. These two calls are equivalent:

```
$sth->execute ();
$sth->execute;
```

I prefer to include the parentheses because it makes the call look less like a variable reference to me. Your preference may be different.

After you call `execute()`, the rows of the membership list can be processed. In the `dump_members` script, the row-fetching loop simply prints the contents of each row:

```
# read results of query, then clean up
while (@ary = $sth->fetchrow_array ())
{
    print join ("\t", @ary), "\n";
}
$sth->finish ();
```

`fetchrow_array()` returns an array containing the column values of the current row and an empty array when there are no more rows. Thus, the loop fetches successive rows returned by the SELECT statement and prints each one with tabs between column values. NULL values in the database are returned as `undef` values to the Perl script, but these print as empty strings, not as the word "NULL".

Note that the tab and newline characters (represented as '\t' and '\n') are enclosed in double quotes. In Perl, escape sequences are interpreted only when they occur within double quotes, not within single quotes. If single quotes had been used, the output would be full of literal instances of the strings "\t" and "\n".

After the row-fetching loop terminates, the call to `finish()` tells DBI that the statement handle is no longer needed and that any temporary resources allocated to it can be freed. It is not actually necessary to call `finish()` unless you have fetched only part of the result set (whether by design or because some problem occurred). However, `finish()` is always safe after a fetch loop and I find it's easier just to call it and be done with it than to write the logic required to distinguish between when `finish()` is necessary and when it's superfluous.

Having printed the membership list, we're done, so we can disconnect from the server and exit:

```
$dbh->disconnect ();
exit (0);
```

`dump_members` illustrates a number of concepts that are common to most DBI programs, and you could probably start writing your own DBI programs without knowing anything more. For example, to write out the contents of some other table, all you'd need to do is change the text of the SELECT statement that is passed to the `prepare()` method. And in fact, if you want to see some applications of this technique, you can skip ahead immediately to the part of the section "Putting DBI To Work" that discusses how to generate the member list for the Historical League annual banquet program and the League's printed directory. However, DBI provides many other useful capabilities. The next sections cover some of these in more detail so that you can see how to do more than run a simple SELECT statement in your Perl scripts.

Handling Errors

dump_members turned on the RaiseError error-handling attribute when it invoked the connect() method so that errors would automatically terminate the script with an error message. It's possible to handle errors in other ways. For example, you can check for errors yourself rather than having DBI do it.

To see how to control DBI's error-handling behavior, let's take a closer look at the connect() call's final argument. The two relevant attributes are RaiseError and PrintError:

- If RaiseError is enabled (set to a non-zero value), DBI calls die() to print a message and to exit if an error occurs in a DBI method.
- If PrintError is enabled, DBI calls warn() to print a message when a DBI error occurs, but the script continues executing.

By default, RaiseError is disabled and PrintError is enabled. In this case, if the connect() call fails, DBI prints a message but continues executing. Thus, with the default error-handling behavior that you get if you omit the fourth argument to connect(), you might check for errors like this:

```
$dbh = DBI->connect ($dsn, $user_name, $password)
    or exit (1);
```

If an error occurs, connect() returns undef to indicate failure, and that triggers the call to exit(). You don't have to print an error message because DBI already will have printed one.

If you explicitly specify the default values for the error-checking attributes, the call to connect() looks like this:

```
$dbh = DBI->connect ($dsn, $user_name, $password,
                { RaiseError => 0, PrintError => 1})
    or exit (1);
```

That's more work to write out, but it's also more obvious to the casual reader what the error-handling behavior is.

If you want to check for errors yourself and print your own messages, disable both RaiseError and PrintError:

```
$dbh = DBI->connect ($dsn, $user_name, $password,
                { RaiseError => 0, PrintError => 0})
    or die "Could not connect to server: $DBI::err ($DBI::errstr)\n";
```

The variables $DBI::err and $DBI::errstr, used in the die() call just shown, are useful for constructing error messages. They contain the MySQL error code and error string, much like the C API functions `mysql_errno()` and `mysql_error()`.

If you simply want DBI to handle errors for you so that you don't have to check for them yourself, enable `RaiseError`:

```
$dbh = DBI->connect ($dsn, $user_name, $password, { RaiseError => 1 });
```

This is by far the easiest approach, and the one that `dump_members` took. Enabling `RaiseError` may not be appropriate if you want to execute some sort of cleanup code of your own when the script exits, although in this case you may be able to do what you want by redefining the `$SIG{__DIE__}` handler.

Another reason you might want to avoid enabling the `RaiseError` attribute is that DBI prints technical information in its messages, like this:

```
disconnect(DBI::db=HASH(0x197aae4)) invalidates 1 active statement. Either
destroy statement handles or call finish on them before disconnecting.
```

That's good information for a programmer, but it might not be the kind of thing you want to present to the everyday user. In that case, it can be better to check for errors yourself so that you can display messages that are more meaningful to the people you expect to be using the script. Or you might consider redefining the `$SIG{__DIE__}` handler here, too. That may be useful because it allows you to enable `RaiseError` to simplify error handling but replace the default error messages that DBI presents with your own messages. To provide your own `__DIE__` handler, do something like the following before executing any DBI calls:

```
$SIG{__DIE__} = sub { die "Sorry, an error occurred\n"; };
```

You can also declare a subroutine in the usual fashion and set the handler value using a reference to the subroutine:

```
sub die_handler
{
    die "Sorry, an error occurred\n";
}

$SIG{__DIE__} = \&die_handler;
```

As an alternative to passing error-handling attributes literally in the `connect()` call, you can define them using a hash and pass a reference to the hash. Some people find that breaking out the attribute settings this way makes scripts easier to read and edit, but functionally both approaches are the same. Here's an example that shows how to use an attribute hash:

```
%attr =
(
    PrintError => 0,
    RaiseError => 0
);
$dbh = DBI->connect ($dsn, $user_name, $password, \%attr)
    or die "Could not connect to server: $DBI::err ($DBI::errstr)\n";
```

The following script dump_members2 illustrates how you might write a script when you want to check for errors yourself and print your own messages. dump_members2 processes the same query as dump_members, but explicitly disables PrintError and RaiseError and then tests the result of every DBI call. When an error occurs, the script invokes the subroutine bail_out() to print a message and the contents of $DBI::err and $DBI::errstr before exiting:

```perl
#! /usr/bin/perl

# dump_members2 - dump Historical League's membership list

use DBI;
use strict;

my ($dsn) = "DBI:mysql:samp_db:localhost"; # data source name
my ($user_name) = "paul";  # user name
my ($password) = "secret"; # password
my ($dbh, $sth);           # database and statement handles
my (@ary);                 # array for rows returned by query
my (%attr) =               # error-handling attributes
(
    PrintError => 0,
    RaiseError => 0
);

# connect to database
$dbh = DBI->connect ($dsn, $user_name, $password, \%attr)
    or bail_out ("Cannot connect to database");

# issue query
$sth = $dbh->prepare ("SELECT last_name, first_name, suffix, email,"
    . "street, city, state, zip, phone FROM member ORDER BY last_name")
    or bail_out ("Cannot prepare query");
$sth->execute ()
    or bail_out ("Cannot execute query");

# read results of query
while (@ary = $sth->fetchrow_array ())
{
    print join ("\t", @ary), "\n";
}
$DBI::err == 0
    or bail_out ("Error during retrieval");

# clean up
$sth->finish ()
    or bail_out ("Cannot finish query");
```

```
$dbh->disconnect ()
    or bail_out ("Cannot disconnect from database");
exit (0);

# bail_out() subroutine - print error code and string, then exit

sub bail_out
{
my ($message) = shift;

    die "$message\nError $DBI::err ($DBI::errstr)\n";
}
```

bail_out() is similar to the print_error() function we used for writing C programs in Chapter 6, except that bail_out() exits rather than returning to the caller. bail_out() saves you the trouble of writing out the names of $DBI::err and $DBI::errstr every time you want to print an error message. Also, by encapsulating error message printing into a subroutine, you can change the format of your error messages uniformly throughout your script simply by making a change to the subroutine.

The dump_members2 script has a test following the row-fetching loop that dump_members did not have. Because dump_members2 doesn't automatically exit if an error occurs in fetchrow_array(), it's prudent to determine whether the loop terminated because the result set was read completely (normal termination) or because an error occurred. The loop terminates either way, of course, but if an error occurs, output from the script will be truncated. Without an error check, the person running the script wouldn't have any idea that anything was wrong! If you're checking for errors yourself, be sure to test the result of your fetch loops.

Handling Queries That Return No Result Set

Statements such as DELETE, INSERT, REPLACE, and UPDATE that do not return rows are relatively easy to process compared to statements such as SELECT, DESCRIBE, EXPLAIN, and SHOW, which do return rows. To process a non-SELECT statement, pass it to do() using the database handle. The do() method prepares and executes the query in one step. For example, to begin a new member entry for Marcia Brown with an expiration date of June 3, 2002, you can do this:

```
$rows = $dbh->do ("INSERT member (last_name,first_name,expiration)"
                . " VALUES('Brown','Marcia','2002-6-3')");
```

The do() method returns a count of the number of rows affected, or undef if an error occurs. An error may occur for various reasons. (For example, the query may be malformed or you may not have permission to access the table.) For a non-undef return, watch out for the case in which no rows are affected. When this happens, do() doesn't return the number 0; instead, it returns the string "0E0" (Perl's scientific notation form of zero). "0E0" evaluates to 0 in a numeric context but is considered true in conditional tests so that it can be distinguished easily from undef. If do() returned 0, it would be more difficult to distinguish between the occurrence of an error (undef) and the "no rows affected" case. You can check for an error using either of the following tests:

```
if (!defined ($rows)) { # error }
if (!$rows) { # error }
```

In numeric contexts, "0E0" evaluates as 0. The following code will correctly print the number of rows for any non-undef value of $rows:

```
if (!$rows)
{
    print "error\n";
}
else
{
    $rows += 0; # force conversion to number if "0E0"
    print "$rows rows affected\n";
}
```

You could also print $rows using a '%d' format with printf() to force an implicit conversion to a number:

```
if (!$rows)
{
    print "error\n";
}
else
{
    printf "%d rows affected\n", $rows;
}
```

The do() method is equivalent to prepare() followed by execute(). The preceding INSERT statement could be issued like this rather than by calling do():

```
$sth = $dbh->prepare ("INSERT member (last_name,first_name,expiration)"
                . " VALUES('Brown','Marcia','2002-6-3')");
$rows = $sth->execute ();
```

Handling Queries That Return a Result Set

This section provides more information on several options you have for performing the row-fetching loop for SELECT queries (or other SELECT-like queries that return rows, such as DESCRIBE, EXPLAIN, and SHOW). It also discusses how to get a count of the number of rows in a result, how to handle result sets for which no loop is necessary, and how to retrieve an entire result set all at once.

Writing Row-Fetching Loops

The dump_members script retrieved data using a standard sequence of DBI methods: prepare() to let the driver preprocess the query, execute() to begin executing the query, fetchrow_array() to fetch each row of the result set, and finish() to release resources associated with the query.

prepare(), execute(), and finish() are pretty standard parts of processing any query that returns rows. However, for fetching the rows, fetchrow_array() is actually only one choice from among several methods (see Table 7.3).

Table 7.3 **DBI Row-Fetching Methods**

Method Name	Return Value
fetchrow_array()	Array of row values
fetchrow_arrayref()	Reference to array of row values
fetch()	Same as fetchrow_arrayref()
fetchrow_hashref()	Reference to hash of row values, keyed by column name

The following examples show how to use each row-fetching method. The examples loop through the rows of a result set, and for each row, print the column values separated by commas. There are more efficient ways to write the printing code in some cases, but the examples are written the way they are to illustrate the syntax for accessing individual column values.

fetchrow_array() is used as follows:

```
while (@ary = $sth->fetchrow_array ())
{
    $delim = "";
    for ($i = 0; $i < @ary; $i++)
    {
        print $delim . $ary[$i];
        $delim = ",";
    }
    print "\n";
}
```

Each call to fetchrow_array() returns an array of row values, or an empty array when there are no more rows.

As an alternative to assigning the return value to an array variable, you can fetch column values into a set of scalar variables. You might do this if you want to work with variable names that are more meaningful than $ary[0], $ary[1], etc. Suppose you want to retrieve the name and email values into variables. Using fetchrow_array(), you could select and fetch rows like this:

```
$sth = $dbh->prepare ("SELECT last_name, first_name, suffix, email"
                        . " FROM member ORDER BY last_name");
$sth->execute ();
while (($last_name, $first_name, $suffix, $email)
                            = $sth->fetchrow_array ())
{
    # do something with variables
}
```

When you use a list of variables this way, you must make sure your query selects columns in the proper order, of course. DBI has no idea of the order in which columns are named by your SELECT statement, so it's up to you to assign variables correctly. You can also cause column values to be assigned to individual variables automatically when you fetch a row, using a technique known as parameter binding. This is discussed further in "Placeholders and Parameter Binding."

fetchrow_arrayref() is similar to fetchrow_array(), but instead of returning an array containing the column values for the current row, it simply returns a reference to the array, or undef when there are no more rows. It's used like this:

```
while ($ary_ref = $sth->fetchrow_arrayref ())
{
    $delim = "";
    for ($i = 0; $i < @{$ary_ref}; $i++)
    {
        print $delim . $ary_ref->[$i];
        $delim = ",";
    }
    print "\n";
}
```

You access array elements through the array reference, $ary_ref. This is something like deferencing a pointer, so you use $ary_ref->[$i] rather than $ary[$i]. To treat the reference as a full array, use the @{$ary_ref} construct.

fetchrow_arrayref() is unsuitable for fetching variables into a list. For example, the following loop does not work:

```
while (($last_name, $first_name, $suffix, $email)
                                    = @{$sth->fetchrow_arrayref ()})
{
    # do something with variables
}
```

As long as fetchrow_arrayref() actually fetches a row, the loop functions properly. But when there are no more rows, fetchrow_arrayref() returns undef, and @{undef} isn't legal. (It's like trying to de-reference a NULL pointer in a C program.)

The third row-fetching method, fetchrow_hashref(), is used like this:

```
while ($hashref = $sth->fetchrow_hashref ())
{
    $delim = "";
    foreach $key (keys (%{$hashref}))
    {
        print $delim . $hashref->{$key};
        $delim = ",";
    }
    print "\n";
}
```

Each call to `fetchrow_hashref()` returns a reference to a hash of row values keyed on column names, or `undef` when there are no more rows. In this case, column values don't come out in any particular order; members of Perl hashes are unordered. However, the hash elements are keyed on column names, so `$hashref` gives you a single variable through which you can access any column value by name. This allows you to pull out values (or any subset of them) in any order you want, and you don't have to know the order in which the columns were retrieved by the `SELECT` query. For example, if you wanted to access the name and email fields, you could do this:

```
while ($hashref = $sth->fetchrow_hashref ())
{
    $delim = "";
    foreach $key ("last_name", "first_name", "suffix", "email")
    {
        print $delim . $hashref->{$key};
        $delim = ",";
    }
    print "\n";
}
```

`fetchrow_hashref()` is especially useful when you want to pass a row of values to a function without requiring the function to know the order in which columns were named in the `SELECT` statement. In this case, you would call `fetchrow_hashref()` to retrieve rows and write a function that accesses values from the row hash using column names.

Keep in mind the following caveats when you use `fetchrow_hashref()`:

- If you need every bit of performance, `fetchrow_hashref()` is not the best choice because it's not as efficient as `fetchrow_array()` or `fetchrow_arrayref()`.

- The column names used as key values in the hash have the lettercase of columns as they are written in the `SELECT` statement. In MySQL, column names are not case sensitive, so the query will work the same way no matter what lettercase you use to write column names. But Perl hash key names are case sensitive, which may cause you problems. To avoid potential lettercase mismatch problems, you can tell `fetchrow_hashref()` to force column names into a particular lettercase by passing it a `NAME_lc` or `NAME_uc` attribute:

  ```
  $hash_ref = $sth->fetchrow_hashref ('NAME_lc'); # use lowercase names
  $hash_ref = $sth->fetchrow_hashref ('NAME_uc'); # use uppercase names
  ```

- The hash contains one element per unique column name. If you're performing a join that returns columns from multiple tables with overlapping names, you won't be able to access all the column values. For example, if you issue the following query, `fetchrow_hashref()` will return a hash having only one element:

  ```
  SELECT a.name, b.name FROM a, b WHERE a.name = b.name
  ```

Determining the Number of Rows Returned by a Query

How can you tell the number of rows returned by a SELECT or SELECT-like query?
One way is to count the rows as you fetch them, of course. In fact, this is the only
portable way to know how many rows a SELECT query returns. Using the MySQL
driver, you can call the rows() method using the statement handle after invoking
execute(), but this is not portable to other database engines. And even for MySQL,
rows() doesn't return the correct result until you've fetched all the rows if you've set
the mysql_use_result attribute. (See Appendix G for more information.) So you may
as well just count the rows as you fetch them.

Fetching Single-Row Results

It's not necessary to run a loop to get your results if the result set consists of a single
row. Suppose you want to write a script count_members that tells you the current
number of Historical League members. The code to perform the query looks like this:

```
# issue query
$sth = $dbh->prepare ("SELECT COUNT(*) FROM member");
$sth->execute ();

# read results of query, then clean up
$count = $sth->fetchrow_array ();
$sth->finish ();
$count = "can't tell" if !defined ($count);
print "$count\n";
```

The SELECT statement will return only one row, so there is no need for a loop; we call
fetchrow_array() just once. In addition, because we're selecting only one column, it's
not even necessary to assign the return value to an array. When fetchrow_array() is
called in a scalar context (where a single value rather than a list is expected), it returns
the first column of the row, or undef if no more rows are available.

Another type of query for which you expect at most a single record is one that
contains LIMIT 1 to restrict the number of rows returned. A common use for this is to
return the row that contains the maximum or minimum value for a particular column.
For example, the following query prints the name and birth date of the president who
was born most recently:

```
$query = "SELECT last_name, first_name, birth"
       . " FROM president ORDER BY birth DESC LIMIT 1";
$sth = $dbh->prepare ($query);
$sth->execute ();

# read results of query, then clean up
($last_name, $first_name, $birth) = $sth->fetchrow_array ();
$sth->finish ();
if (!defined ($last_name))
{
    print "Query returned no result\n";
}
```

```
else
{
    print "Most recently born president: $first_name $last_name ($birth)\n";
}
```

Other types of queries for which no fetch loop is necessary are those that use MAX()
or MIN() to select a single value. But in all these cases, an even easier way to get a
single-row result is to use the database handle method selectrow_array(), which
combines prepare(), execute() and the row fetching into a single call. It returns an
array (not a reference), or an empty array if an error occurred. The previous example
could be written like this using selectrow_array():

```
$query = "SELECT last_name, first_name, birth"
       . " FROM president ORDER BY birth DESC LIMIT 1";
($last_name, $first_name, $birth) = $dbh->selectrow_array ($query);
if (!defined ($last_name))
{
    print "Query returned no result\n";
}
else
{
    print "Most recently born president: $first_name $last_name ($birth)\n";
}
```

Working with Complete Result Sets

When you use a fetch loop, DBI doesn't provide any way to seek randomly into the
result set, or to process the rows in any order other than that in which they are
returned by the loop. Also, after you fetch a row, the previous row is lost unless you
take steps to maintain it in memory. This behavior isn't always suitable:

- You may want to process rows in non-sequential order. Consider a situation
  where you want to present a quiz based on the US presidents listed in the
  Historical League president table. If you want to ask questions in a different
  order each time the quiz is presented, you could select all the rows from the
  president table. Then you could pick rows in a random order to vary the order
  of the presidents about which you ask questions. To pick a row at random, you
  must have access to all the rows simultaneously.

- You may want to use only a subset of the rows returned, chosen on a random
  basis. For example, to present a multiple-choice question asking where a president was born, you could pick one row at random to choose the president (and
  the correct answer), then pick several other rows from which to draw the decoy
  choices.

- You may want to hang onto the entire result set even if you do process it in
  sequential order. This might be necessary if you need to make multiple passes
  through the rows. For example, in a statistical calculation, you may go through
  the result set once to assess some general numeric properties of your data, then
  go through the rows again performing a more specific analysis.

You can access your result set as a whole in a couple different ways. You can perform the usual fetch loop and save each row as you fetch it, or you can use a method that returns an entire result set all at once. Either way, you end up with a matrix containing one row per row in the result set, and as many columns as you selected. You can process elements of the matrix in any order you want, as many times as you want. The following discussion describes both approaches.

One way to use a fetch loop to capture the result set is to use `fetchrow_array()` and save an array of references to the rows. The following code does the same thing as the fetch-and-print loop in `dump_members`, except that it saves all the rows, then prints the matrix to illustrate how to determine the number of rows and columns in the matrix and how to access individual members of the matrix.

```perl
my (@matrix) = (); # array of array references

while (my @ary = $sth->fetchrow_array ())   # fetch each row
{
    push (@matrix, [ @ary ]); # save reference to just-fetched row
}
$sth->finish ();

# determine dimensions of matrix
my ($rows) = scalar (@matrix);
my ($cols) = ($rows == 0 ? 0 : scalar (@{$matrix[0]}));

for (my $i = 0; $i < $rows; $i++)              # print each row
{
my ($delim) = "";
    for (my $j = 0; $j < $cols; $j++)
    {
        print $delim . $matrix[$i][$j];
        $delim = ",";
    }
    print "\n";
}
```

When determining the dimensions of the matrix, the number of rows must be determined first because calculation of the number of columns is contingent on whether or not the matrix is empty. If `$rows` is 0, the matrix is empty and `$cols` becomes 0 as well. Otherwise, the number of columns can be calculated as the number of elements in a row array, using the syntax `@{$matrix[$i]}` to access row `$i` as a whole.

In the preceding example, we fetch each row, then save a reference to it. You might suppose that it would be more efficient to call `fetchrow_arrayref()` instead to retrieve row references directly:

```perl
my (@matrix) = (); # array of array references

while (my $ary_ref = $sth->fetchrow_arrayref ())
{
```

```
        # this will not work!
        push (@matrix, $ary_ref); # save reference to just-fetched row
}
$sth->finish ();
```

That doesn't work, because `fetchrow_arrayref()` reuses the array to which the reference points. The resulting matrix is an array of references, each of which points to the same row—the final row retrieved. Therefore, if you want to fetch a row at a time, use `fetchrow_array()` rather than `fetchrow_arrayref()`.

As an alternative to using a fetch loop, you can use one of the DBI methods that return the entire result set. For example, `fetchall_arrayref()` returns a reference to an array of references, each of which points to the contents of one row of the result set. That's a mouthful, but in effect, the return value is a reference to a matrix. To use `fetchall_arrayref()`, call `prepare()` and `execute()`, then retrieve the result like this:

```
my ($matrix_ref);  # reference to array of references

$matrix_ref = $sth->fetchall_arrayref ();   # fetch all rows

# determine dimensions of matrix
my ($rows) = (!defined ($matrix_ref) ? 0 : scalar (@{$matrix_ref}));
my ($cols) = ($rows == 0 ? 0 : scalar (@{$matrix_ref->[0]}));

for (my $i = 0; $i < $rows; $i++)            # print each row
{
my ($delim) = "";
    for (my $j = 0; $j < $cols; $j++)
    {
        print $delim . $matrix_ref->[$i][$j];
        $delim = ",";
    }
    print "\n";
}
```

`fetchall_arrayref()` returns a reference to an empty array if the result set is empty. The result is `undef` if an error occurs, so if you don't have `RaiseError` enabled, be sure to check the return value before you start using it.

The number of rows and columns are determined by whether or not the matrix is empty. If you want to access an entire row `$i` of the matrix as an array, use the syntax `@{$matrix_ref->[$i]}`.

It's certainly simpler to use `fetchall_arrayref()` to retrieve a result set than to write a row-fetching loop, although the syntax for accessing array elements becomes a little trickier. A method that's similar to `fetchall_arrayref()` but that does even more work is `selectall_arrayref()`. This method performs the entire `prepare()`, `execute()`, fetch loop, `finish()` sequence for you. To use `selectall_arrayref()`, pass your query directly to it using the database handle:

```
my ($matrix_ref);  # reference to array of references

$matrix_ref =
    $dbh->selectall_arrayref ("SELECT last_name, first_name, suffix, email,"
    . "street, city, state, zip, phone FROM member ORDER BY last_name");

# determine dimensions of matrix
my ($rows) = (!defined ($matrix_ref) ? 0 : scalar (@{$matrix_ref}));
my ($cols) = ($rows == 0 ? 0 : scalar (@{$matrix_ref->[0]}));

for (my $i = 0; $i < $rows; $i++)                  # print each row
{
my ($delim) = "";
    for (my $j = 0; $j < $cols; $j++)
    {
        print $delim . $matrix_ref->[$i][$j];
        $delim = ",";
    }
    print "\n";
}
```

Checking for NULL Values

When you retrieve data from a database, you may need to distinguish between column values that are NULL and those that are zero or the empty string. This is easy to do because DBI returns NULL column values as undef. However, you must be sure to use the right test. If you try the following code fragment, it prints "false!" all three times:

```
$col_val = undef; if (!$col_val) { print "false!\n"; }
$col_val = 0;     if (!$col_val) { print "false!\n"; }
$col_val = "";    if (!$col_val) { print "false!\n"; }
```

Furthermore, this fragment prints "false!" for both tests:

```
$col_val = undef; if ($col_val eq "") { print "false!\n"; }
$col_val = "";    if ($col_val eq "") { print "false!\n"; }
```

This fragment does the same:

```
$col_val = "";
if ($col_val eq "") { print "false!\n"; }
if ($col_val == 0)  { print "false!\n"; }
```

To distinguish between NULL column values and non-NULL values, use defined(). After you know a value doesn't represent NULL, you can distinguish between other types of values using appropriate tests. For example:

```
if (!defined ($col_val)) { print "NULL\n"; }
elsif ($col_val eq "")   { print "empty string\n"; }
elsif ($col_val == 0)    { print "zero\n"; }
else                     { print "other\n"; }
```

It's important to perform the tests in the proper order because both the second and third comparisons are true if $col_val is an empty string. If you reverse the order of those comparisons, you'll incorrectly identify empty strings as zero.

Quoting Issues

Thus far, we have constructed queries in the most basic way possible, using simple quoted strings. That causes a problem at the Perl lexical level when your quoted strings contain quoted values. You can also have problems at the SQL level when you want to insert or select values that contain quotes, backslashes, or binary data. If you specify a query as a Perl quoted string, you must escape any occurrences of the quoting character that occur within the query string itself:

```
$query = 'INSERT absence VALUES(14,\'1999-9-16\')';
$query = "INSERT absence VALUES(14,\"1999-9-16\")";
```

Both Perl and MySQL allow you to quote strings using either single or double quotes, so you can sometimes avoid escaping by mixing quote characters:

```
$query = 'INSERT absence VALUES(14,"1999-9-16")';
$query = "INSERT absence VALUES(14,'1999-9-16')";
```

However, the two types of quotes are not equivalent in Perl. Variable references are interpreted only within double quotes. Therefore, single quotes are not very useful when you want to construct queries by embedding variable references in the query string. For example, if the value of $var is 14, the following two strings are not equivalent:

```
"SELECT * FROM member WHERE id = $var"
'SELECT * FROM member WHERE id = $var'
```

The strings are interpreted as follows; clearly, the first string is more like something you'd want to pass to the MySQL server:

```
"SELECT * FROM member WHERE id = 14"
'SELECT * FROM member WHERE id = $var'
```

An alternative to quoting strings with double quotes is to use the qq{} construct, which tells Perl to treat everything between 'qq{' and '}' as a double-quoted string. (Think of double-q as meaning "double-quote.") For example, these two lines are equivalent:

```
$date = "1999-9-16";
$date = qq{1999-9-16};
```

You can construct queries without thinking so much about quoting issues when you use qq{} because you can use quotes (single *or* double) freely within the query string without having to escape them. In addition, variable references are interpreted. Both properties of qq{} are illustrated by the following INSERT statement:

```
$id = 14;
$date = "1999-9-16";
$query = qq{INSERT absence VALUES($id,"$date")};
```

You don't have to use '{' and '}' as the qq delimiters. Other forms, such as qq() and qq//, will work, too, as long as the closing delimiter doesn't occur within the string. I prefer qq{} because '}' is less likely than ')' or '/' to occur within the text of the query and be mistaken for the end of the query string. For example, ')' occurs within the INSERT statement just shown, so qq() would not be a useful construct for quoting the query string.

The qq{} construct crosses line boundaries, which is useful if you want to make the query string stand out from the surrounding Perl code:

```
$id = 14;
$date = "1999-9-16";
$query = qq{
    INSERT absence VALUES($id,"$date")
};
```

This is also useful if you simply want to format your query on multiple lines to make it more readable. For example, the SELECT statement in the dump_members script looks like this:

```
$sth = $dbh->prepare ("SELECT last_name, first_name, suffix, email,"
    . "street, city, state, zip, phone FROM member ORDER BY last_name");
```

With qq{}, it could be written like this instead:

```
$sth = $dbh->prepare (qq{
            SELECT
                last_name, first_name, suffix, email,
                street, city, state, zip, phone
            FROM member
            ORDER BY last_name
        });
```

It's true that double-quoted strings can cross line boundaries, too. But I much prefer qq{} for writing multiple-line strings. I find that when I see an unmatched quote on a line, my automatic response is to think, "Is this a syntax error?" Then I waste time looking for the matching quote.

The qq{} construct takes care of quoting issues at the Perl lexical level so that you can get quotes into a string easily without having Perl complain about them. However, you must also think about SQL-level syntax. Consider this attempt to insert a record into the member table:

```
$last = "O'Malley";
$first = "Brian";
$expiration = "2002-9-1";
$rows = $dbh->do (qq{
    INSERT member (last_name,first_name,expiration)
    VALUES('$last','$first','$expiration')
});
```

The string that do() sends to MySQL looks like this:

```
INSERT member (last_name,first_name,expiration)
VALUES('O'Malley','Brian','2002-9-1')
```

That is not legal SQL because a single quote occurs within a single-quoted string. We encountered a similar quoting problem in Chapter 6. There we dealt with the problem using mysql_escape_string(). DBI provides a similar mechanism—for each quoted

value you want to use literally in a statement, call the `quote()` method and use its
return value instead.

The preceding example is more properly written as follows:

```
$last = $dbh->quote ("O'Malley");
$first = $dbh->quote ("Brian");
$expiration = $dbh->quote ("2002-9-1");
$rows = $dbh->do (qq{
    INSERT member (last_name,first_name,expiration)
    VALUES($last,$first,$expiration)
});
```

Now the string that `do()` sends to MySQL looks like this, with the quote that occurs
within the quoted string properly escaped for the server:

```
INSERT member (last_name,first_name,expiration)
VALUES('O\'Malley','Brian','2002-9-1')
```

Note that when you refer to `$last` and `$first` in the query string, you do not add
any surrounding quotes; the `quote()` method supplies them for you. If you add quotes,
your query will have too many quotes, as shown by the following example:

```
$value = "paul";
$quoted_value = $dbh->quote ($value);

print "... WHERE name = $quoted_value\n";
print "... WHERE name = '$quoted_value'\n";
```

These statements produce the following output:

```
... WHERE name = 'paul'
... WHERE name = ''paul''
```

Placeholders and Parameter Binding

In the preceding sections, we've constructed queries by putting values to be inserted
or used as selection criteria directly in the query string. It's not necessary to do this.
DBI allows you to place special markers called placeholders into a query string, then
supply the values to be used in place of those markers when the query is executed.
The main reason to do this is for improved performance, especially when you're executing a query over and over in a loop.

As an illustration of how placeholders work, suppose you're beginning a new
semester at school and you want to clear out the `student` table for your gradebook
and then initialize it with the new students by using a list of student names contained
in a file. Without placeholders, you can delete the existing table contents and load the
new names like this:

```
$dbh->do (qq{ DELETE FROM student } );   # delete existing rows
while (<>)                               # add new rows
{
    chomp;
    $_ = $dbh->quote ($_);
    $dbh->do (qq{ INSERT student SET name = $_ });
}
```

That's inefficient, because the basic form of the INSERT query is the same each time, and do() calls prepare() and execute() each time through the loop. It's more efficient to call prepare() a single time to set up the INSERT statement before entering the loop and invoke only execute() within the loop. That avoids all invocations of prepare() but one. DBI allows us to do this as follows:

```
$dbh->do (qq{ DELETE FROM student } );  # delete existing rows
$sth = $dbh->prepare (qq{ INSERT student SET name = ? });
while (<>)                              # add new rows
{
    chomp;
    $sth->execute ($_);
}
$sth->finish();
```

Note the '?' in the INSERT query. That's the placeholder. When execute() is invoked, you pass the value to be substituted for the placeholder when the query is sent to the server. In general, if you find yourself calling do() inside a loop, it's better to invoke prepare() prior to the loop and execute() inside it.

Some things to note about placeholders:

- Do not enclose the placeholder character in quotes within the query string. If you do, it will not be recognized as a placeholder.

- Do not use the quote() method to specify placeholder values, or you will get extra quotes in the values you're inserting.

- You can have more than one placeholder in a query string, but be sure to pass as many values to execute() as there are placeholder markers.

- Each placeholder must specify a single value, not a list of values. For example, you cannot prepare and execute a statement like this:

```
$sth = $dbh->prepare (qq{{
            INSERT member last_name, first_name VALUES(?)
});
$sth->execute ("Adams,Bill,2003-09-19");
```

You must do it like this:

```
$sth = $dbh->prepare (qq{{
            INSERT member last_name, first_name VALUES(?,?,?)
});
$sth->execute ("Adams","Bill","2003-09-19");
```

- To specify NULL as a placeholder value, use undef.

- Do not try to use a placeholder for keywords. It won't work because placeholder values are processed automatically by quote(). The keyword will be placed into the query surrounded by quotes, and the query will fail with a syntax error.

For some database engines, you get another performance benefit from using place-holders in addition to improved efficiency in loops. Certain engines cache prepared queries as well as the plan they generate for executing the query efficiently. That way, if the same query is received by the server later, it can be reused without generating a new execution plan. Query caching is especially helpful for complex SELECT state-ments because it may take some time to generate a good execution plan. Placeholders give you a better chance of finding a query in the cache because they make queries more generic than queries constructed by embedding specific column values directly in the query string. For MySQL, placeholders don't improve performance in this way because queries aren't cached. However, you may still want to write your queries using placeholders; if you happen to port a DBI script to an engine that does maintain a query cache, your script will execute more efficiently than without placeholders.

Placeholders allow you to substitute values into a query string at query execution time. In other words, you can parameterize the "input" to the query. DBI also provides a corresponding output operation called parameter binding that allows you to parame-terize the "output" by retrieving column values into variables automatically when you fetch a row without having to assign values to the variables yourself.

Suppose you have a query to retrieve member names from the member table. You can tell DBI to assign the values of the selected columns to Perl variables. When you fetch a row, the variables are automatically updated with the corresponding column values. Here's an example that shows how to bind the columns to variables and then access them in the fetch loop:

```
$sth = $dbh->prepare (qq{
            SELECT last_name, first_name, suffix
            FROM member
            ORDER BY last_name, first_name
});
$sth->execute ();
$sth->bind_col (1, \$last_name);
$sth->bind_col (2, \$first_name);
$sth->bind_col (3, \$suffix);
print "$last_name, $first_name, $suffix\n" while $sth->fetch;
```

Each call to bind_col() should specify a column number and a reference to the vari-able you want to associate with the column. Column numbers begin with 1. bind_col() should be called after execute().

As an alternative to individual calls to bind_col(), you can pass all the variable ref-erences in a single call to bind_columns():

```
$sth = $dbh->prepare (qq{
            SELECT last_name, first_name, suffix
            FROM member
            ORDER BY last_name, first_name
});
$sth->execute ();
$sth->bind_columns (\$last_name, \$first_name, \$suffix);
print "$last_name, $first_name, $suffix\n" while $sth->fetch;
```

Specifying Connection Parameters

The most direct way to establish a server connection is to specify all the connection parameters when you invoke the connect() method:

```
$data_source = "DBI:mysql:db_name:host_name";
$dbh->connect ($data_source, user_name, password);
```

If you leave out connection parameters, DBI does the following:

- The DBI_DSN environment variable is used if the data source is undefined or is the empty string. The DBI_USER and DBI_PASS environment variables are used if the username and password are undefined (but not if they are the empty string). Under Windows, the USER variable is used if the username is undefined.

- If you leave out the hostname, it defaults to localhost.

- If you specify undef or an empty string for the username, it defaults to your UNIX login name. Under Windows, the username defaults to ODBC.

- If you specify undef or an empty string for the password, no password is sent.

You can specify certain options in the data source by appending them to the initial part of the string, each preceded by a semicolon. For example, you can use the mysql_read_default_file option to specify an option file pathname:

```
$data_source =
    "DBI:mysql:samp_db;mysql_read_default_file=/u/paul/.my.cnf";
```

When the script executes, it will read the file for connection parameters. Suppose /u/paul/.my.cnf contains the following contents:

```
[client]
host=pit-viper.snake.net
user=paul
password=secret
```

Then the connect() call will attempt to connect to the MySQL server on pit-viper.snake.net and will connect as user paul with password secret. If you want to allow your script to be used by anyone who has an option file set up properly, specify the data source like this:

```
$data_source =
    "DBI:mysql:samp_db;mysql_read_default_file=$ENV{HOME}/.my.cnf";
```

$ENV{HOME} contains the pathname to the home directory of the user running the script, so the hostname, username, and password that the script uses will be pulled out of each user's own option file. By writing a script in this way, you don't have to embed connection parameters literally in the script.

You can also use the mysql_read_default_group option, to specify an option file group. This automatically causes the user's .my.cnf file to be read, and allows you to specify an option group to be read in addition to the [client] group. For example, if you have options that are specific to your DBI scripts, you can list them in a [dbi] group and then use a data source value like this:

```
$data_source =
    "DBI:mysql:samp_db;mysql_read_default_group=dbi";
```

mysql_read_default_file and mysql_read_default_group require MySQL 3.22.10 or newer, and DBD::mysql 1.21.06 or newer. For more details on options for specifying the data source string, see Appendix G. For more information on the format of MySQL option files, see Appendix E, "MySQL Program Reference."

Using an option file doesn't prevent you from specifying connection parameters in the connect() call (for example, if you want the script to connect as a particular user). Any explicit hostname, username, and password values specified in the connect() call will override connection parameters found in the option file. For example, you might want your script to parse --host, --user, and --password options from the command line and use those values, if they are given, in preference to any found in the option file. That would be useful because it's the way the standard MySQL clients behave. Your DBI scripts would therefore be consistent with that behavior.

For the remaining command line scripts that we develop in this chapter, I'll use some standard connection setup and teardown code. I'll just show it once here so that we can concentrate on the main body of each script as we write it:

```
#! /usr/bin/perl

use DBI;
use strict;

# parse connection parameters from command line if given

use Getopt::Long;
$Getopt::Long::ignorecase = 0; # options are case sensitive

# default parameters - all missing
my ($host_name, $user_name, $password) = (undef, undef, undef);

# GetOptions doesn't seem to allow -uuser_name form, only -u user_name?
GetOptions(
    # =s means a string argument is required after the option
    "host|h=s"      => \$host_name
    ,"user|u=s"      => \$user_name
    # :s means a string argument is optional after the option
    ,"password|p:s"  => \$password

) or exit (1);

# solicit password if option specified without option value
if (defined ($password) && !$password)
{
```

continues

continued

```
        # turn off echoing but don't interfere with STDIN
        open (TTY, "/dev/tty") or die "Cannot open terminal\n";
        system ("stty -echo < /dev/tty");
        print STDERR "Enter password: ";
        chomp ($password = <TTY>);
        system ("stty echo < /dev/tty");
        close (TTY);
        print STDERR "\n";
    }

    # construct data source
    my ($dsn) = "DBI:mysql:samp_db";
    $dsn .= ":hostname=$host_name" if $host_name;
    $dsn .= ";mysql_read_default_file=$ENV{HOME}/.my.cnf";

    # connect to server
    my (%attr) = ( RaiseError => 1 );
    my ($dbh) = DBI->connect ($dsn, $user_name, $password, \%attr);
```

This code initializes DBI, looks for connection parameters on the command line, and then makes the connection to the MySQL server using parameters from the command line or found in the `~/.my.cnf` file of the user running the script. If you set up the `.my.cnf` file in your home directory, you won't have to enter any connection parameters when you run the scripts. (Remember to set the mode so that no one else can read the file. See Appendix E for instructions.)

The final part of our scripts will be similar from script to script, too; it simply terminates the connection and exits:

```
    $dbh->disconnect ();
    exit (0);
```

When we get to the Web programming section, "Using DBI in Web Applications," we'll modify the connection setup code a bit, but the basic idea will be similar.

Debugging

When you want to debug a malfunctioning DBI script, two techniques are commonly used, either alone or in tandem. First, you can sprinkle print statements throughout your script. This allows you to tailor your debugging output the way you want it, but you must add the statements manually. Second, you can use DBI's built-in tracing capabilities. This is more general but more systematic, and it occurs automatically after you turn it on. DBI tracing also shows you information about the operation of the driver that you cannot get otherwise.

Debugging Using Print Statements

A common question on the MySQL mailing list runs like this: "I have a query that works fine when I execute it in `mysql`, but it doesn't work from my DBI script. How come?" It's not unusual to find the DBI script issuing a different query than the questioner expects. If you print a query before executing it, you may be surprised to see what you're actually sending to the server. Suppose a query as you type it into mysql looks like this (without the terminating semicolon):

```
INSERT member (last_name,first_name,expiration)
VALUES("Brown","Marcia","2002-6-3")
```

Then you try the same thing in a DBI script:

```
$last = "Brown";
$first = "Marcia";
$expiration = "2002-6-3";
$query =
qq{
    INSERT member (last_name,first_name,expiration)
    VALUES($last,$first,$expiration)
};
$rows = $dbh->do ($query);
```

This doesn't work, even though it's the same query. Or is it? Try printing it:

```
print "$query\n";
```

Here is the result:

```
INSERT member (last_name,first_name,expiration)
VALUES(Brown,Marcia,2002-6-3)
```

From this output, you can see that you forgot the quotes around the column values in the VALUES() list. The proper way to specify the query is like this:

```
$last = $dbh->quote ("Brown");
$first = $dbh->quote ("Marcia");
$expiration = $dbh->quote ("2002-6-3");
$query =
qq{
    INSERT member (last_name,first_name,expiration)
    VALUES($last,$first,$expiration)
};
```

Alternatively, you could specify your query using placeholders and pass the values to be inserted directly to the do() method:

```
$last = "Brown";
$first = "Marcia";
$expiration = "2002-6-3";
$query =
qq{
    INSERT member (last_name,first_name,expiration)
    VALUES(?,?,?)
};
$rows = $dbh->do ($query, undef, $last, $first, $expiration);
```

Unfortunately, when you do this, you cannot see what the complete query looks like by using a print statement because the placeholder values aren't evaluated until you invoke do().When you use placeholders, tracing may be a more helpful debugging method.

Debugging Using Tracing

You can tell DBI to generate trace (debugging) information when you're trying to figure out why a script doesn't work properly. Trace levels range from 0 (off) to 9 (maximum information). Generally trace levels 1 and 2 are the most useful. A level 2 trace shows you the text of queries you're executing (including the result of placeholder substitutions), the result of calls to quote(), and so forth. This can be of immense help in tracking down a problem.

You can control tracing from within individual scripts using the trace() method, or you can set the DBI_TRACE environment variable to affect tracing for all DBI scripts you run.

To use the trace() call, pass a trace level argument and optionally a filename. If you specify no filename, all trace output goes to STDERR; otherwise, it goes to the named file. Some examples:

DBI->trace (1)	Level 1 trace to STDERR
DBI->trace (2, "trace.out")	Level 2 trace to "trace.out"
DBI->trace (0)	Turn trace output off

When invoked as DBI->trace(), all DBI operations are traced. For a more fine-grained approach, you can enable tracing at the individual handle level. This is useful when you have a good idea where a problem in your script lies and you don't want to wade through the trace output for everything that occurs up to that point. For example, if you're having problems with a particular SELECT query, you can trace the statement handle associated with the query:

```
$sth = $dbh->prepare (qq{ SELECT ... }); # create the statement handle
$sth->trace (1);                         # enable tracing on the statement
$sth->execute ();
```

If you specify a filename argument to any trace() call, whether for DBI as a whole or for an individual handle, *all* trace output goes to that file.

To turn on tracing globally for all DBI scripts you run, set the DBI_TRACE environment variable from your shell. The syntax for this depends on the shell you use:

% **setenv DBI_TRACE** value	For csh, tcsh
$ **DBI_TRACE**=value	For sh, ksh, bash
$ **export DBI_TRACE**	
C:\> **set DBI_TRACE**=value	For Windows

The format of value is the same for all shells: a number n to turn on tracing at level n to STDERR; a filename to turn on level 2 tracing to the named file, or n=file_name to turn on level *n* tracing to the named file. Here are some examples, using `csh` syntax:

```
% setenv DBI_TRACE 1                Level 1 trace to STDERR
% setenv DBI_TRACE 1=trace.out      Level 1 trace to "trace.out"
% setenv DBI_TRACE trace.out        Level 2 trace to "trace.out"
```

If you turn on tracing to a file from your shell, be sure to turn it off once you've resolved the problem. Debugging output is appended to the trace file without over-writing it, so the file can become quite large if you're not careful. It's a particularly bad idea to define `DBI_TRACE` in a shell startup file such as `.cshrc`, `.login`, or `.profile`! Under UNIX, you can turn off tracing using either of the following commands (`csh` syntax):

```
% setenv DBI_TRACE 0
% unsetenv DBI_TRACE
```

For `sh`, `ksh`, or `bash`, do this:

```
$ DBI_TRACE=0
$ export DBI_TRACE
```

On Windows, you can turn off tracing using either of these commands:

```
C:\> unset DBI_TRACE
C:\> set DBI_TRACE=0
```

Using Result Set Metadata

You can use DBI to gain access to result set metadata—that is, descriptive information about the rows selected by a query. Access the attributes of the statement handle asso-ciated with the query that generated the result set to get this information. Some of these attributes are provided as standard DBI attributes that are available across all data-base drivers (such as `NUM_OF_FIELDS`, the number of columns in the result set). Others, which are MySQL-specific, are provided by DBD::mysql, the MySQL driver for DBI. These attributes, such as `mysql_max_length`, which tell you the maximum width of the values in each column, are not applicable to other database engines. To the extent that you use any of the MySQL-specific attributes, you risk making your scripts non-portable to other databases. On the other hand, they can make it easier to get the information you want.

You must ask for metadata at the right time. Generally, result set attributes are not available for a `SELECT` statement until after you've invoked `prepare()` and `execute()`. In addition, attributes may become invalid after you invoke `finish()`.

Let's see how to use one of the MySQL metadata attributes, `mysql_max_length`, in conjunction with the DBI-level `NAME` attribute that holds the names of query columns. We can combine the information provided by these attributes to write a script `box_out` that produces output from `SELECT` queries in the same boxed style that you get when you run the `mysql` client program in interactive mode. The main body of box_out is as follows (you can replace the SELECT statement with any other; the output-writing routines are independent of the particular query):

```perl
my ($sth) = $dbh->prepare (qq{
    SELECT last_name, first_name, city, state
    FROM president ORDER BY last_name, first_name
});
$sth->execute (); # attributes should be available after this call

# actual maximum widths of column values in result set
my (@wid) = @{$sth->{mysql_max_length}};
# number of columns
my ($ncols) = scalar (@wid);

# adjust column widths if column headings are wider than data values
for (my $i = 0; $i < $ncols; $i++)
{
my ($name_wid) = length ($sth->{NAME}->[$i]);

    $wid[$i] = $name_wid if $wid[$i] < $name_wid;
}

# print output
print_dashes (\@wid, $ncols);              # row of dashes
print_row ($sth->{NAME}, \@wid, $ncols);   # column headings
print_dashes (\@wid, $ncols);              # row of dashes
while (my $ary_ref = $sth->fetch)
{
    print_row ($ary_ref, \@wid, $ncols);   # row data values
}
print_dashes (\@wid, $ncols);              # row of dashes
$sth->finish ();
```

After the query has been initiated with execute(), we can grab the metadata we need. $sth->{NAME} and $sth->{mysql_max_length} give us the column names and maximum width of each column's values. The value of each attribute is a reference to an array that contains one value for each column of the result set, in the order that columns are named in the query.

The remaining calculations are very much like those used for the client5 program developed in Chapter 6. For example, to avoid misaligned output, we adjust the column width values upward if the name of a column is wider than any of the data values in the column.

The output functions, print_dashes() and print_row(), are written as follows. They too are similar to the corresponding code in client5:

```perl
sub print_dashes
{
my ($wid_ary_ref) = shift;  # column widths
my ($cols) = shift;         # number of columns

    print "+";
    for (my $i = 0; $i < $cols; $i++)
    {
```

```
        print "-" x ($wid_ary_ref->[$i]+2) . "+";
    }
    print "\n";
}

# print row of data.  (doesn't right-align numeric columns)

sub print_row
{
my ($val_ary_ref) = shift;  # column values
my ($wid_ary_ref) = shift;  # column widths
my ($cols) = shift;         # number of columns

    print "|";
    for (my $i = 0; $i < $cols; $i++)
    {
        printf " %-*s |", $wid_ary_ref->[$i],
            defined ($val_ary_ref->[$i]) ? $val_ary_ref->[$i] : "NULL";
    }
    print "\n";
}
```

The output from box_out looks like this:

```
+------------+---------------+---------------------+-------+
| last_name  | first_name    | city                | state |
+------------+---------------+---------------------+-------+
| Adams      | John          | Braintree           | MA    |
| Adams      | John Quincy   | Braintree           | MA    |
| Arthur     | Chester A.    | Fairfield           | VT    |
| Buchanan   | James         | Mercersburg         | PA    |
| Bush       | George W.     | Milton              | MA    |
+------------+---------------+---------------------+-------+
```

Our next script uses column metadata to produce output in a different format. This script, show_member, allows you to take a quick look at Historical League member entries without entering any queries. Given a member's last name, it displays the selected entry like this:

```
% show_member artel
last_name:  Artel
first_name: Mike
suffix:
expiration: 2003-04-16
email:      mike_artel@venus.org
street:     4264 Lovering Rd.
city:       Miami
state:      FL
zip:        12777
phone:      075-961-0712
interests:  Civil Rights,Education,Revolutionary War
member_id:  63
```

You can also invoke show_members using a membership number, or using a pattern to match several last names. The following commands show the entry for member 23, and the entries for members with last names starting with "C":

```
% show_member 23
% show_member c%
```

The main body of the show_member script is shown below. It uses the NAME attribute to determine the labels to use for each row of output and the NUM_OF_FIELDS attribute to find out how many columns the result set contains:

```perl
my ($count) = 0;    # number of entries printed so far
my (@label) = ();   # column label array
my ($label_wid) = 0;

while (@ARGV)        # run query for each argument on command line
{
my ($arg) = shift (@ARGV);
my ($sth, $clause, $address);

    # default is last name search; do id search if argument is numeric
    $clause = "last_name LIKE " . $dbh->quote ($arg);
    $clause = "member_id = " . $dbh->quote ($arg) if $arg =~ /^\d/;

    # issue query
    $sth = $dbh->prepare (qq{
        SELECT * FROM member
        WHERE $clause
        ORDER BY last_name, first_name
    });
    $sth->execute ();

    # get column names to use for labels and
    # determine max column name width for formatting
    # (only do this the first time through the loop, though)
    if ($label_wid == 0)
    {
        @label = @{$sth->{NAME}};
        foreach my $label (@label)
        {
            $label_wid = length ($label) if $label_wid < length ($label);
        }
    }

    # read and print query results, then clean up
    while (my @ary = $sth->fetchrow_array ())
    {
        # print newline before 2nd and subsequent entries
        print "\n" if ++$count > 1;
        foreach (my $i = 0; $i < $sth->{NUM_OF_FIELDS}; $i++)
        {
            # print label, and value if there is one
```

```
            printf "%-*s", $label_wid+1, $label[$i] . ":";
            print " " . $ary[$i] if $ary[$i];
            print "\n";
        }
    }
    $sth->finish ();
}
```

The purpose of show_member is to show the entire contents of an entry, no matter what the fields are. By using SELECT * to retrieve all the columns and the NAME attribute to find out what they are, this script will work without modification even if columns are added or dropped from the member table.

If you just want to know what columns a table contains without retrieving any rows, you can issue this query:

```
SELECT * FROM tbl_name WHERE 1 = 0
```

After invoking prepare() and execute() in the usual way, you can get the column names from @{$sth->{NAME}}. Be aware, however, that although this little trick of using an "empty" query works for MySQL, it's not portable and doesn't work for all database engines.

For more information on the attributes provided by DBI and by DBD::mysql, see Appendix G. It's up to you to determine whether you want to strive for portability by avoiding MySQL-specific attributes, or take advantage of them at the cost of portability.

Putting DBI To Work

At this point you've seen a number of the concepts involved in DBI programming, so let's move on to some of the things we wanted to be able to do with our sample database. Our goals were outlined initially in Chapter 1, "Introduction to MySQL and SQL." Those that we'll tackle by writing DBI scripts in this chapter are listed here.

For the grade-keeping project, we want to be able to retrieve scores for any given quiz or test.

For the historical league, we want to do the following:

- Produce the member directory in different formats. We want a names-only list for use in the annual banquet program in a format we can use for generating the printed directory.
- Find League members that need to renew their memberships soon, then send them email to let them know about it.
- Edit member entries. (We'll need to update their expiration dates when they renew their memberships, after all.)
- Find members that share a common interest.
- Put the directory online.

For some of these tasks, we'll write scripts that run from the command line. For the others, we'll create scripts in the next section, "Using DBI in Web Applications," that you can use in conjunction with your Web server. At the end of the chapter, we'll still have a number of goals left to accomplish. We'll finish up those that remain in Chapter 8, "The PHP API."

Generating the Historical League Directory

One of our goals is to be able to produce information from the Historical League directory in different formats. The simplest format we'll generate is a list of member names for the annual banquet program. That can be a simple plain text listing. It will become part of the larger document used to create the program, so all we need is something that can be pasted into that document.

For the printable directory, a better representation than plain text is needed because we want something nicely formatted. A reasonable choice here is RTF (Rich Text Format), a format developed by Microsoft that is understood by many word processors. Word is one such program, of course, but many others such as WordPerfect and AppleWorks understand it as well. Different word processors support RTF to varying degrees, but we'll use a basic subset of the full RTF specification that should be understandable by any word processor that is RTF-aware to even a minimal degree.

The procedures for generating the banquet list and RTF directory formats are essentially the same: Issue a query to retrieve the entries, then run a loop that fetches and formats each entry. Given that basic similarity, it would be nice to avoid writing two separate scripts. To that end, let's write a single script, gen_dir, that can generate output from the directory in different formats. We can structure the script as follows:

1. Before writing out entry contents, perform any initialization that might be necessary for the output format. No special initialization is necessary for the banquet program member list, but we'll need to write out some initial control language for the RTF version.

2. Fetch and print each entry, formatted appropriately for the type of output we want.

3. After all the entries have been processed, perform any necessary cleanup and termination. Again, no special handling is needed for the banquet list, but some closing control language is required for the RTF version.

In the future, we might want to use this script to write output in other formats, so let's make it extensible by setting up a "switchbox"—a hash with an element for each output format. Each element specifies functions that generate output appropriately for a given format: an initialization function, an entry-writing function, and a cleanup function:

```
# switchbox containing formatting functions for each output format
my (%switchbox) =
```

```
(
    "banquet" =>                          # functions for banquet list
    {
        "init"      => undef,             # no initialization needed
        "entry"     => \&format_banquet_entry,
        "cleanup"   => undef              # no cleanup needed
    },
    "rtf" =>                              # functions for RTF format
    {
        "init"      => \&rtf_init,
        "entry"     => \&format_rtf_entry,
        "cleanup"   => \&rtf_cleanup
    }
);
```

Each element of the switchbox is keyed by a format name ("banquet" and "rtf" in this case). We'll write the script so that you just specify the format you want on the command line when you run it:

```
% gen_dir banquet
% gen_dir rtf
```

By setting up a switchbox this way, we can add the capability for a new format easily:

1. Write three formatting functions.

2. Add to the switchbox a new element that points to those functions.

3. To produce output in the new format, invoke gen_dir and specify the format name on the command line.

The code for selecting the proper switchbox entry according to the first argument on the command line is shown below. It's based on the fact that the output format names are the keys in the %switchbox hash. If no such key exists in the switchbox, the format is invalid. It's not necessary to hardwire format names into the code; if a new format is added to the switchbox, it's detected automatically. If no format name or an invalid name is specified on the command line, the script produces an error message and displays a list of the allowable names:

```
# make sure one argument was specified on the command line
@ARGV == 1
    or die "Usage: gen_dir format_type\nAllowable formats: "
            . join (" ", sort (keys (%switchbox))) . "\n";

# determine proper switchbox entry from argument on command line
# if no entry was found, the format type was invalid
my ($func_hashref) = $switchbox{$ARGV[0]};

defined ($func_hashref)
    or die "Unknown format: $ARGV[0]\nAllowable formats: "
            . join (" ", sort (keys (%switchbox))) . "\n";
```

If a valid format name is specified on the command line, the preceding code sets
$func_hashref. Its value will be a reference to the hash that points to the output writ-
ing functions for the selected format. Then we can run the entry-selection query. After
that, we invoke the initialization function, fetch and print the entries, and invoke the
cleanup function:

```
# issue query
my ($sth) = $dbh->prepare (qq{
    SELECT * FROM member ORDER BY last_name, first_name
});
$sth->execute ();

# invoke initialization function if there is one
&{$func_hashref->{init}} if defined ($func_hashref->{init});

# fetch and print entries if there is an entry formatting function
if (defined ($func_hashref->{entry}))
{
    while (my $entry_ref = $sth->fetchrow_hashref ("NAME_lc"))
    {
        # pass entry reference to formatting function
        &{$func_hashref->{entry}} ($entry_ref);
    }
}
$sth->finish ();

# invoke cleanup function if there is one
&{$func_hashref->{cleanup}} if defined ($func_hashref->{cleanup});
```

The entry-fetching loop uses fetchrow_hashref() for a reason. If the loop fetched an
array, the formatting functions would have to know the order of the columns. It's possible to figure that out by accessing the $sth->{NAME} attribute (which contains col-
umn names in the order in which they are returned), but why bother? By using a hash
reference, formatting functions can just name the column values they want using
$entry_ref->{col_name}. That's not especially efficient, but it's easy and can be used
for any format we want to generate because we know that any fields we need will be
in the hash.

All that remains is to write the functions for each output format (that is, for the
functions named by the switchbox entries).

Generating the Banquet Program Member List

For this output format, we simply want the member names. No initialization or
cleanup calls are necessary. We need only an entry formatting function:

```
sub format_banquet_entry
{
my ($entry_ref) = shift;
my ($name);
```

```
    $name = $entry_ref->{first_name} . " " . $entry_ref->{last_name};
    if ($entry_ref->{suffix})              # there is a name suffix
    {
        # no comma for suffixes of I, II, III, etc.
        $name .= "," unless $entry_ref->{suffix} =~ /^[IVX]+$/;
        $name .= " " . $entry_ref->{suffix} if $entry_ref->{suffix};
    }
    print "$name\n";
}
```

The argument to `format_banquet_entry()` is a reference to the hash of column values for a row. The function glues together the first and last names, plus any suffix that might be present. The trick here is that suffixes such as "Jr." or "Sr." should be preceded by a comma and a space, whereas suffixes such as "II" or "III" should be preceded only by a space:

```
Michael Alvis IV
Clarence Elgar, Jr.
Bill Matthews, Sr.
Mark York II
```

Because the letters 'I', 'V', and 'X' cover all generations, from the 1st to the 39th, we can determine whether or not to add a comma by using the following test:

```
$name .= "," unless $hash_ref->{suffix} =~ /^[IVX]+$/;
```

The code in `format_banquet_entry()` that puts the name together is something we'll need for the RTF version of the directory as well. However, instead of duplicating that code in `format_rtf_entry()`, let's stuff it into a function:

```
sub format_name
{
my ($entry_ref) = shift;
my ($name);

    $name = $entry_ref->{first_name} . " " . $entry_ref->{last_name};
    if ($entry_ref->{suffix})              # there is a name suffix
    {
        # no comma for suffixes of I, II, III, etc.
        $name .= "," unless $entry_ref->{suffix} =~ /^[IVX]+$/;
        $name .= " " . $entry_ref->{suffix} if $entry_ref->{suffix};
    }
    return ($name);
}
```

Putting the code that determines the name string into the `format_name()` function reduces `format_banquet_entry()` to almost nothing:

```
sub format_banquet_entry
{
    printf "%s\n", format_name ($_[0]);
}
```

Generating the Print-Format Directory

Generating the RTF version of the directory is a little more involved than generating the banquet program member list. For one thing, we need to print more information from each entry. For another, we need to put out some RTF control language with each entry to achieve the effects that we want. A minimal framework for an RTF document looks like this:

```
{\rtf0
{\fonttbl {\f0 Times;}}
\plain \f0 \fs24
    ...document content goes here...

}
```

The document begins and ends with curly braces '{' and '}'. RTF keywords begin with a backslash, and the first keyword of the document must be \rtf*n*, where *n* is the RTF specification version number the document corresponds to. 0 is fine for our purposes.

Within the document, we specify a font table to indicate the font to use for the entries. Font table information is listed in a group consisting of curly braces containing a leading \fonttbl keyword and some font information. The font table shown in the framework defines font number 0 to be in Times. (We only need one font, but you could use more if you wanted to be fancier.)

The next few directives set up the default formatting style: \plain selects plain format, \f0 selects font 0 (which we've defined as Times in the font table), and \fs24 sets the font size to 12 points (the number following \fs indicates the size in half points). It's not necessary to set up margins; most word processors will supply reasonable defaults.

To take a very simple approach, we can print each entry as a series of lines, with a label on each line. If the information corresponding to a particular output line is missing, the line is omitted. (For example, the "Email:" line is not printed for members that have no email address.) Some lines (such as the "Address:" line) are composed of the information in multiple columns (street, city, state, zip), so the script must be able to deal with various combinations of missing values. Here's a sample of the output format we'll use:

```
Name: Mike Artel
Address: 4264 Lovering Rd., Miami, FL 12777
Telephone: 075-961-0712
Email: mike_artel@venus.org
Interests: Civil Rights,Education,Revolutionary War
```

For the formatted entry just shown, the RTF representation looks like this:

```
\b Name: Mike Artel\b0\par
Address: 4264 Lovering Rd., Miami, FL 12777\par
Telephone: 075-961-0712\par
Email: mike_artel@venus.org\par
Interests: Civil Rights,Education,Revolutionary War\par
```

To make the "Name:" line bold, surround it by \b (with a space afterward) to turn boldface on and \b0 to turn boldface off. Each line has a paragraph marker (\par) at the end to tell the word processor to move to the next line—nothing too complicated.

The initialization function puts out the leading RTF control language (note the double backslashes to get single backslashes in the output):

```
sub rtf_init
{
    print "{\\rtf0\n";
    print "{\\fonttbl {\\f0 Times;}}\n";
    print "\\plain \\f0 \\fs24\n";
}
```

Similarly, the cleanup function puts out the terminating control language (not that there is much!):

```
sub rtf_cleanup
{
    print "}\n";
}
```

The real work is involved in formatting the entry, but even this is relatively simple. The primary complications are formatting the address string and determining which output lines should be printed:

```
sub format_rtf_entry
{
my ($entry_ref) = shift;
my ($address);

    printf "\\b Name: %s\\b0\\par\n", format_name ($entry_ref);
    $address = "";
    $address .= $entry_ref->{street} if $entry_ref->{street};
    $address .= ", " . $entry_ref->{city} if $entry_ref->{city};
    $address .= ", " . $entry_ref->{state} if $entry_ref->{state};
    $address .= " " . $entry_ref->{zip} if $entry_ref->{zip};
    print "Address: $address\\par\n" if $address;
    print "Telephone: $entry_ref->{phone}\\par\n" if $entry_ref->{phone};
    print "Email: $entry_ref->{email}\\par\n" if $entry_ref->{email};
    print "Interests: $entry_ref->{interests}\\par\n" if $entry_ref->{interests};
    print "\\par\n";
}
```

You're not locked into this particular formatting style, of course. You can change how you print any of the fields, so you can change the style of your printed directory almost at will, simply by changing format_rtf_entry(). With the directory in its original form (a word processing document), that's something not so easily done!

The gen_dir script is now complete. We can generate the directory in either output format by running commands such as these:

```
% gen_dir banquet > names.txt
% gen_dir rtf > directory.rtf
```

Under Windows, I can run `gen_dir`, and the files are ready for use from within a Windows-based word processor. Under UNIX, I might run those commands and then mail the output files to myself as attachments so that I can pick them up from my Macintosh and load them into a word processor. I happen to use the `mutt` mailer, which allows attachments to be specified from the command line using the `-a` option. I can send myself a message with both files attached to it as follows:

```
% mutt -a names.txt -a directory.rtf paul@snake.net
```

Other mailers may allow attachment creation, too. Alternatively, the files can be transferred by other means, such as FTP. In any case, after the files are where we want them, it's an easy step to read the name list and paste it into the annual program document or to read the RTF file into any word processor that understands RTF.

DBI made it easy to extract the information we wanted from MySQL, and Perl's text-processing capabilities made it easy to put that information into the format we wanted to see. MySQL doesn't provide any particularly fancy way of formatting output, but it doesn't matter because of the ease with which you can integrate MySQL's database handling abilities into a language such as Perl, which has excellent text manipulation capabilities.

Sending Membership Renewal Notices

When the Historical League directory is maintained as a word processing document, it's a time-consuming and error prone activity to determine which members need to be notified that their membership should be renewed. Now that we have the information in a database, let's see how to automate the renewal-notification process a bit. We want to identify members who need to renew via email so that we don't have to contact them by phone or surface mail.

What we need to do is determine which members are due for renewal within a certain number of days. The query for this involves a date calculation that's relatively simple:

```
SELECT ... FROM member
WHERE expiration < DATE_ADD(CURRENT_DATE, INTERVAL cutoff DAY)
```

cutoff signifies the number of days of leeway we want to grant. The query selects member entries that are due for renewal in fewer than that many days. As a special case, a cutoff value of 0 finds memberships with expiration dates in the past (that is, those memberships that have actually expired).

After we've identified the records that qualify for notification, what should we do with them? One option would be to send mail directly from the same script, but it might be useful first to be able to review the list without sending any messages. For this reason, we'll use a two-stage approach:

- **Stage 1:** Run a script `need_renewal` to identify members that need to renew. You can simply examine this list, or you can use it as input to the second stage to send the renewal notices.

- **Stage 2:** Run a script `renewal_notify`, which sends members a "please renew" notice by email. The script should warn you about members without email addresses so that you can contact them by other means.

For the first part of this task, the `need_renewal` script must identify which members need to renew. This can be done as follows:

```perl
# default cutoff is 30 days; reset if numeric argument given
my ($cutoff) = 30;
$cutoff = shift (@ARGV) if @ARGV && $ARGV[0] =~ /^\d+$/;

warn "Using cutoff of $cutoff days\n";

my ($sth) = $dbh->prepare (qq{
        SELECT
            member_id, email, last_name, first_name, expiration,
            TO_DAYS(expiration) - TO_DAYS(CURRENT_DATE) AS days
        FROM member
        WHERE expiration < DATE_ADD(CURRENT_DATE, INTERVAL ? DAY)
        ORDER BY expiration, last_name, first_name
});
$sth->execute ($cutoff);    # pass cutoff as placeholder value

while (my $hash_ref = $sth->fetchrow_hashref ())
{
    print join ("\t",
                $hash_ref->{member_id},
                $hash_ref->{email},
                $hash_ref->{last_name},
                $hash_ref->{first_name},
                $hash_ref->{expiration},
                $hash_ref->{days} . " days")
        . "\n";
}
$sth->finish ();
```

The output from the `need_renewal` script looks something like the following (you'll get different output because the results are determined against the current date, which will be different for you while reading this book than for me while writing it):

```
89  g.steve@pluto.com       Garner  Steve   1999-08-03  -32 days
18  york_mark@earth.com     York    Mark    1999-08-24  -11 days
82  john_edwards@venus.org  Edwards John    1999-09-12  8 days
```

Observe that some memberships need to be renewed in a negative number of days. That means they've already expired! (This happens when you maintain records manually; people slip through the cracks. Now that we have the information in a database, we're finding out that we missed a few people before.)

The second part of the renewal notification task involves a script renewal_notify that sends out the notices by email. To make renewal_notify a little easier to use, we can make it understand three kinds of command-line arguments: membership ID numbers, email addresses, and filenames. Numeric arguments signify membership ID values, and arguments with the '@' character signify email addresses. Anything else is interpreted as the name of a filename that should be read to find ID numbers or email addresses. This method enables you to specify members by their ID number or email address, and you can do so either directly on the command line or by listing them in a file. (In particular, you can use the output of need_renewal as input to renewal_notify.)

For each member who is to be sent a notice, the script looks up the relevant member table entry, extracts the email address, and sends a message to that address. If there is no email address in the entry, renewal_notify generates a message to warn you that you need to contact these members in some other way.

To send mail, renewal_notify opens a pipe to the sendmail program and shoves the mail message into the pipe.[1] The pathname to sendmail is set as a parameter near the beginning of the script. You may need to change this path because the location of sendmail varies from system to system:

```
# change path to match your system
my ($sendmail) = "/usr/lib/sendmail -t -oi";
```

The main argument-processing loop operates as follows. If no arguments were specified on the command line, we read the standard input for input. Otherwise, we process each argument by passing it to interpret_argument() for classification as an ID number, an email address, or a filename:

```
if (@ARGV == 0)      # no arguments, read STDIN for values
{
    read_file (\*STDIN);
}
else
{
    while (my $arg = shift (@ARGV))
    {
        # interpret argument, with filename recursion
        interpret_argument ($arg, 1);
    }
}
```

The function read_file() reads the contents of a file (assumed to be open already) and looks at the first field of each line. (If we feed the output of need_renewal to renewal_notify, each line has several fields, but we want to look only at the first one.)

---

[1] This will not work for Windows, which doesn't have sendmail. You'd need to find a mail-sending module and use that instead.

```
sub read_file
{
my ($fh) = shift;
my ($arg);

    while (defined ($arg = <$fh>))
    {
        # strip off everything past column 1, including newline
        $arg =~ s/\s.*//s;
        # interpret argument, without filename recursion
        interpret_argument ($arg, 0);
    }
}
```

The interpret_argument() function classifies each argument to determine whether it's an ID number, an email address, or a filename. For ID numbers and email addresses, it looks up the appropriate member entry and passes it to notify_member(). We have to be careful with members specified by email address. It's possible that two members have the same address (for example, a husband and wife), and we don't want to send a message to someone to whom it doesn't apply. To avoid this, we look up the member ID corresponding to an email address to make sure there is exactly one. If the address matches more than one ID number, it's ambiguous and we ignore it after printing a warning.

If an argument doesn't look like an ID number or email address, it's taken to be the name of a file to read for further input. We have to be careful here, too—we don't want to read a file if we're already reading a file in order to avoid the possibility of an infinite loop:

```
sub interpret_argument
{
my ($arg, $recurse) = @_;
my ($query, $ary_ref);

    if ($arg =~ /^\d+$/)         # numeric membership ID
    {
        notify_member ($arg);
    }
    elsif ($arg =~ /@/)          # email address
    {
        # get member_id associated with address
        # (there should be exactly one)
        $query = qq{ SELECT member_id FROM member WHERE email = ? };
        $ary_ref = $dbh->selectcol_arrayref ($query, undef, $arg);
        if (scalar (@{$ary_ref}) == 0)
        {
            warn "Email address $arg matches no entry: ignored\n";
        }
        elsif (scalar (@{$ary_ref}) > 1)
        {
            warn "Email address $arg matches multiple entries: ignored\n";
```

continues

continued

```
            }
            else
            {
                notify_member ($ary_ref->[0]);
            }
        }
        else                        # filename
        {
            if (!$recurse)
            {
                warn "filename $arg inside file: ignored\n";
            }
            else
            {
                open (IN, $arg) or die "Cannot open $arg: $!\n";
                read_file (\*IN);
                close (IN);
            }
        }
    }
}
```

The code for the notify_member() function that actually sends the renewal notice is as
follows. If it turns out that the member has no email address, there is nothing to be
done, but notify_member() prints a warning so that you know you need to contact
the member in some other way. You can invoke show_member with the membership ID
number shown in the message to see the full entry—to find out what the member's
phone number and address are, for example.

```
# notify member that membership will soon be in arrears

sub notify_member
{
my ($member_id) = shift;
my ($query, $sth, $entry_ref, @col_name);

    warn "Notifying $member_id...\n";
    $query = qq{ SELECT * FROM member WHERE member_id = ? };
    $sth = $dbh->prepare ($query);
    $sth->execute ($member_id);
    @col_name = @{$sth->{NAME}};
    $entry_ref = $sth->fetchrow_hashref ();
    $sth->finish ();
    if (!$entry_ref)            # no member found!
    {
        warn "NO ENTRY found for member $member_id!\n";
        return;
    }
    open (OUT, "| $sendmail") or die "Cannot open mailer\n";
    print OUT <<EOF;
To: $entry_ref->{email}
Subject: Your USHL membership is in need of renewal
```

```
Greetings.  Your membership in the US Historical League is
due to expire soon.  We hope that you'll take a few minutes to
contact the League office to renew your membership.  The
contents of your member entry are shown below.  Please note
particularly the expiration date.

Thank you.

EOF
    foreach my $col_name (@col_name)
    {
        printf OUT "%s: %s\n", $col_name, $entry_ref->{$col_name};
    }
    close (OUT);
}
```

You could get fancier with this—for example, by adding a column to the member table to record when the most recent renewal reminder was sent out. Doing so would help you to not send out notices too frequently. As it is, we'll just assume you won't run this program more than once a month or so.

The two scripts are done now, so you can use them like this:

```
% need_renewal > junk
% (take a look at junk to see if it looks reasonable)
% renewal_notify junk
```

To notify individual members, you can specify them by ID number or email address:

```
% need_renewal 18 g.steve@pluto.com
```

Historical League Member Entry Editing

After we start sending out renewal notices, it's safe to assume that some of the people we notify will renew their memberships. When that happens, we'll need a way to update their entries with new expiration dates. In the next chapter, we'll develop a way to edit member records from a Web browser, but here we'll develop a command-line script edit_member, which enables you to update entries using a simple approach of prompting for new values for each part of an entry. It works like this:

- If invoked with no argument on the command line, edit_member assumes you want to enter a new member, prompts for the initial information to be placed in the member's entry, and creates a new entry.

- If invoked with a membership ID number on the command line, edit_member looks up the existing contents of the entry, then prompts for updates to each column. If you enter a value for a column, it replaces the current value. If you press Enter, the column is not changed. (If you don't know a member's ID number, you can run show_member last_name to find out what it is.)

It's probably overkill to allow an entire entry to be edited this way if all you want to do is update a member's expiration date. On the other hand, a script like this also provides a simple general-purpose way to update any part of an entry without knowing any SQL. (One special case is that edit_member won't allow you to change the member_id field because that's automatically assigned when an entry is created and shouldn't change thereafter.)

The first thing edit_member needs to know is the names of the columns in the member table:

```
# get member table column names
my ($sth) = $dbh->prepare (qq{ SELECT * FROM member WHERE 1 = 0 });
$sth->execute ();
my (@col_name) = @{$sth->{NAME}};
$sth->finish ();
```

Then we can enter the main loop:

```
if (@ARGV == 0) # if no arguments, create new entry
{
        new_member (\@col_name);
}
else              # otherwise edit entries using arguments as member IDs
{
my (@id);

    # save @ARGV, then empty it so that reads from STDIN
    # don't use the arguments as filenames
    @id = @ARGV;
    @ARGV = ();
    # for each ID value, look up the entry, then edit it
    while (my $id = shift (@id))
    {
    my ($entry_ref);

        $sth = $dbh->prepare (qq{
                SELECT * FROM member WHERE member_id = ?
            });
        $sth->execute ($id);
        $entry_ref = $sth->fetchrow_hashref ();
        $sth->finish ();
        if (!$entry_ref)
        {
            warn "No member with member ID = $id\n";
            next;
        }
        edit_member (\@col_name, $entry_ref);
    }
}
```

The code for creating a new member entry is as follows. It solicits values for each member table column, then issues an INSERT statement to add a new record:

```
# create new member entry

sub new_member
{
my ($col_name_ref) = shift;
my ($entry_ref);
my ($col_val, $query, $delim);

    return unless prompt ("Create new entry? ") =~ /^y/i;
    # prompt for new values; user types in new value,
    # "null" to enter a NULL value, "exit" to exit
    # early.
    foreach my $col_name (@{$col_name_ref})
    {
        next if $col_name eq "member_id";   # skip key field
        $col_val = col_prompt ($col_name, "", 0);
        next if $col_val eq "";              # user pressed Enter
        return if $col_val =~ /^exit$/i;    # early exit
        $col_val = undef if $col_val =~ /^null$/i;
        $entry_ref->{$col_name} = $col_val;
    }
    # show values, ask for confirmation before inserting
    show_member ($col_name_ref, $entry_ref);
    return unless prompt ("\nInsert this entry? ") =~ /^y/i;

    # construct an INSERT query, then issue it.
    $query = "INSERT INTO member";
    $delim = " SET "; # put "SET" before first column, "," before others
    foreach my $col_name (@{$col_name_ref})
    {
        # only specify values for columns that were given one
        next if !defined ($entry_ref->{$col_name});
        # quote() quotes undef as the word NULL (without quotes),
        # which is what we want.
        $query .= sprintf ("%s %s=%s", $delim, $col_name,
                            $dbh->quote ($entry_ref->{$col_name}));
        $delim = ",";
    }
    warn "Warning: entry not inserted?\n"
        unless $dbh->do ($query) == 1;
}
```

The prompt routines used by new_member() look like this:

```
# ask a question, prompt for an answer

sub prompt
{
my ($str) = shift;

    print STDERR $str;
```

continues

continued

```
        chomp ($str = <STDIN>);
        return ($str);
}

# prompt for a column value; show current value in prompt if
# $show_current is true

sub col_prompt
{
my ($name, $val, $show_current) = @_;
my ($prompt, $str);

    $prompt = $name;
    $prompt .= " [$val]" if $show_current;
    $prompt .= ": ";
    print STDERR $prompt;
    chomp ($str = <STDIN>);
    return ($str ? $str : $val);
}
```

The reason that col_prompt() takes a $show_current parameter is that we also use this function for soliciting column values for existing member entries when the script is used to update an entry. $show_current will be 0 when we're creating a new entry because there are no current values to show. It will be non-zero when we're editing an existing entry. The prompt in the latter case will display the current value, which the user can accept simply by pressing Enter.

The code for editing an existing member is similar to that for creating a new member. However, we have an entry to work with, so the prompt routine displays the current entry values, and the edit_member() function issues an UPDATE statement rather than an INSERT:

```
# edit existing contents of an entry

sub edit_member
{
my ($col_name_ref, $entry_ref) = @_;
my ($col_val, $query, $delim);

    # show initial values, ask for okay to go ahead and edit
    show_member ($col_name_ref, $entry_ref);
    return unless prompt ("\nEdit this entry? ") =~ /^y/i;
    # prompt for new values; user types in new value to replace
    # existing value, "null" to enter a NULL value, "exit" to exit
    # early, or Enter to accept existing value.
    foreach my $col_name (@{$col_name_ref})
    {
        next if $col_name eq "member_id";    # skip key field
        $col_val = $entry_ref->{$col_name};
        $col_val = "NULL" unless defined ($col_val);
        $col_val = col_prompt ($col_name, $col_val, 1);
        return if $col_val =~ /^exit$/i;     # early exit
```

```
            $col_val = undef if $col_val =~ /^null$/i;
            $entry_ref->{$col_name} = $col_val;
    }
    # show new values, ask for confirmation before updating
    show_member ($col_name_ref, $entry_ref);
    return unless prompt ("\nUpdate this entry? ") =~ /^y/i;

    # construct an UPDATE query, then issue it.
    $query = "UPDATE member";
    $delim = " SET "; # put "SET" before first column, "," before others
    foreach my $col_name (@{$col_name_ref})
    {
        next if $col_name eq "member_id";   # skip key field
        # quote() quotes undef as the word NULL (without quotes),
        # which is what we want.
        $query .= sprintf ("%s %s=%s", $delim, $col_name,
                            $dbh->quote ($entry_ref->{$col_name}));
        $delim = ",";
    }
    $query .= " WHERE member_id = ?";
    warn "Warning: entry not updated?\n"
        unless $dbh->do ($query, undef, $entry_ref->{member_id}) == 1;
}
```

A problem with `edit_member` is that it doesn't do any input value validation. For most fields in the `member` table, there isn't much to validate—they're just string fields. But for the `expiration` column, input values really should be checked to make sure they look like dates. In a general-purpose data entry application, you'd probably want to extract information about a table to determine the types of all its columns. Then you could base validation constraints on those types. That's more involved than I want to go into here, so I'm just going to add a quick hack to the `col_prompt()` function to check the format of the input if the column name is `"expiration"`. A minimal date value check can be done like this:

```
sub col_prompt
{
my ($name, $val, $show_current) = @_;
my ($prompt, $str);

loop:
    $prompt = $name;
    $prompt .= " [$val]" if $show_current;
    $prompt .= ": ";
    print STDERR $prompt;
    chomp ($str = <STDIN>);
    # perform rudimentary check on the expiration date
    if ($str && $name eq "expiration")  # check expiration date format
    {
        $str =~ /^\d+[^\d]\d+[^\d]\d+$/
            or goto loop;
    }
    return ($str ? $str : $val);
}
```

The pattern tests for three sequences of digits separated by non-digit characters. This is only a partial check because it doesn't detect values such as "1999-14-92" as being illegal. To make the script better, you could give it more stringent date checks and other checks, such as requiring the first and last name fields to be given non-empty values.

Some other improvements might be to skip the update if no columns were changed and to notify the user if the record was already changed by someone else while the user was editing it. You could do this by saving the original values of the member entry columns and then writing the UPDATE statement to update only those columns that had changed. If there were none, the statement need not even be issued. Also, the WHERE clause can be written to include AND *col_name* = *col_val* for each original column value. This would cause the UPDATE to fail if someone else had changed the record, which provides feedback that two people are trying to change the entry at the same time.

Finding Historical League Members with Common Interests

One of the duties of the Historical League secretary is to process requests from members who'd like a list of other members who share a particular interest within the field of US history, such as in the Great Depression or the life of Abraham Lincoln. It's easy enough to find such members when the directory is maintained in a word processor document by using the word processor's "Find" function. However, producing a list consisting only of the qualifying member entries is more difficult because it involves a lot of copy and paste. With MySQL, the job becomes much easier because we can just run a query like this:

```
SELECT * FROM member WHERE interests LIKE "%lincoln%"
ORDER BY last_name, first_name
```

Unfortunately, the results don't look very nice if we run this query from the mysql client. Let's put together a little DBI script, interests, that produces better-looking output. The script first checks to make sure there is at least one argument named on the command line because there is nothing to search for otherwise. Then, for each argument, the script runs a search on the interests column of the member table:

```
@ARGV or die "Usage: interests keyword\n";
search_members (shift (@ARGV)) while @ARGV;
```

To search for the keyword string, we put '%' wildcard characters on each side so that the string can be found anywhere in the interests column. Then we print the matching entries:

```
sub search_members
{
my ($interest) = shift;
my ($sth, $count);
```

```
    print "Search results for keyword: $interest\n\n";
    $sth = $dbh->prepare (qq{
            SELECT * FROM member WHERE interests LIKE ?
            ORDER BY last_name, first_name
        });
    # look for string anywhere in interest field
    $sth->execute ("%" . $interest . "%");
    $count = 0;
    while (my $hash_ref = $sth->fetchrow_hashref ())
    {
        format_entry ($hash_ref);
        ++$count;
    }
    print "$count entries found\n\n";
}
```

The format_entry() function isn't shown here. It's essentially the same as the format_rtf_entry() function from the gen_dir script, with the RTF control words stripped out.

Putting the Historical League Directory Online

In the next section, "Using DBI in Web Applications," we'll start writing scripts that connect to the MySQL server to extract information and write that information in the form of Web pages that appear in a client's Web browser. Those scripts generate HTML dynamically according to what the client requested. Before we reach that point, let's begin thinking about HTML by writing some DBI code that generates a static HTML document that can be loaded into a Web server's document tree. A good candidate for this is a Historical League directory you create in HTML format because one of our goals was to put the directory online anyway.

An HTML document generally has a structure something like the following:

```
<HTML>                              ← beginning of document
<HEAD>                              ← end of document head
<TITLE>My Page Title</TITLE>        ← title of document
</HEAD>                             ← beginning of document head
<BODY>                              ← beginning of document body
<H1>My Level 1 Heading</H1>         ← a level 1 heading

... content of document body ...

</BODY>                             ← end of document body
</HTML>                             ← end of document
```

To generate the directory in this format, it's not necessary for you to write an entire script. Recall that when we wrote the gen_dir script, we used an extensible framework so that we'd be able to plug in code for producing the directory in additional formats. This means that to add code for generating HTML output, we need to write document initialization and cleanup functions, as well as a function to format individual entries. Then we need to create a switchbox element that points to these functions.

The document outline just shown breaks down pretty easily into prolog and epilog sections that can be handled by the initialization and cleanup functions, as well as a middle part that can be generated by the entry-formatting function. The HTML initialization function generates everything up through the level 1 heading, and the cleanup function generates the closing `</BODY>` and `</HTML>` tags:

```perl
sub html_init
{
    print "<HTML>\n";
    print "<HEAD>\n";
    print "<TITLE>US Historical League Member Directory</TITLE>\n";
    print "</HEAD>\n";
    print "<BODY>\n";
    print "<H1>US Historical League Member Directory</H1>\n";
}

sub html_cleanup
{
    print "</BODY>\n";
    print "</HTML>\n";
}
```

The real work, as usual, lies in formatting the entries. But even this isn't very difficult. We can copy the `format_rtf_entry()` function, make sure any special characters in the entry are encoded, and replace the RTF control words with HTML markup tags:

```perl
sub format_html_entry
{
my ($entry_ref) = shift;
my ($address);

    # encode characters that are special in HTML
    foreach my $key (keys (%{$entry_ref}))
    {
        $entry_ref->{$key} =~ s/&/&amp;/g;
        $entry_ref->{$key} =~ s/\"/&quot;/g;
        $entry_ref->{$key} =~ s/>/&gt;/g;
        $entry_ref->{$key} =~ s/</&lt;/g;
    }
    printf "<STRONG>Name: %s</STRONG><BR>\n", format_name ($entry_ref);
    $address = "";
    $address .= $entry_ref->{street} if $entry_ref->{street};
    $address .= ", " . $entry_ref->{city} if $entry_ref->{city};
    $address .= ", " . $entry_ref->{state} if $entry_ref->{state};
    $address .= " " . $entry_ref->{zip} if $entry_ref->{zip};
    print "Address: $address<BR>\n" if $address;
    print "Telephone: $entry_ref->{phone}<BR>\n" if $entry_ref->{phone};
    print "Email: $entry_ref->{email}<BR>\n" if $entry_ref->{email};
    print "Interests: $entry_ref->{interests}<BR>\n"
```

```
                              if $entry_ref->{interests};
        print "<BR>\n";
    }
```

Now we just add to the switchbox another element that points to the HTML–writing functions, and the modifications to gen_dir are complete:

```
# switchbox containing formatting functions for each output format
my (%switchbox) =
(
    "banquet" =>                        # functions for banquet list
    {
        "init"      => undef,           # no initialization needed
        "entry"     => \&format_banquet_entry,
        "cleanup"   => undef            # no cleanup needed
    },
    "rtf" =>                            # functions for RTF format
    {
        "init"      => \&rtf_init,
        "entry"     => \&format_rtf_entry,
        "cleanup"   => \&rtf_cleanup
    },
    "html" =>                           # functions for HTML format
    {
        "init"      => \&html_init,
        "entry"     => \&format_html_entry,
        "cleanup"   => \&html_cleanup
    }
);
```

To produce the directory in HTML format, run the following command and install the resulting output file in your Web server's document tree:

```
% gen_dir html > directory.html
```

When you update the directory, you can run the command again to update the online version. Another strategy is to set up a cron job that executes periodically. That way, the online directory will be updated automatically. For example, I might use a crontab entry like this one to run gen_dir every morning at 4 a.m.:

```
0 4 * * * /u/paul/samp_db/gen_dir > /usr/local/apache/htdocs/directory.html
```

The user that this cron job runs as must have permission both to execute scripts that are located in my samp_db directory and to write files into the Web server document tree.

Using DBI in Web Applications

The DBI scripts that we've written thus far have been designed for use from the shell in a command-line environment, but DBI is useful in other contexts as well, such as in the development of Web-based applications. When you write DBI scripts that can be invoked from your Web browser, you open up new and interesting possibilities for interacting with your databases.

For example, if you display data in tabular form, you can easily turn each column heading into a link that you can select to re-sort the data on that column. This allows you to view your data in a different way with a single click, without entering any queries. Or you can provide a form into which a user can enter criteria for a database search, then display a page containing the results of the search. Simple capabilities like this can dramatically alter the level of interactivity you provide for accessing the contents of your databases. In addition, Web browser display capabilities typically are better than what you get with a terminal window, so the output often looks nicer as well.

In this section, we'll create the following Web-based scripts:

- **A general browser for the tables in the `samp_db` database.** This isn't related to any specific task we want to accomplish with the database, but it illustrates several Web programming concepts and provides a convenient means of seeing what information the tables contain.

- **A score browser allowing us to see the scores for any given quiz or test.** It's handy as a quick means of reviewing grade event results, and it's useful when we need to establish the grading curve for a test so we can mark papers with letter grades.

- **A script to find Historical League members who share a common interest.** This is done by allowing the user to enter a search phrase, then searching the `interests` field of the `member` table for that phrase. We've already written a command-line script to do this, but a Web-based version provides an instructive point of reference, allowing comparison of two approaches to the same task.

We'll write these scripts using the CGI.pm Perl module, which is the easiest way to link DBI scripts to the Web. (For instructions on obtaining the CGI.pm module, see Appendix A.) CGI.pm is so called because it helps you write scripts that use the Common Gateway Protocol defining how a Web server communicates with other programs. CGI.pm handles the details involved in a number of common housekeeping tasks, such as collecting the values of parameters passed as input to your script by the Web server. CGI.pm also provides convenient methods for generating HTML output, which reduces the chance of writing out malformed HTML compared to writing raw HTML tags yourself.

You'll learn enough about CGI.pm in this chapter to write your own Web applications, but of course not all of its capabilities are covered. To learn more about this module, see *Official Guide to Programming with CGI.pm*, by Lincoln Stein (John Wiley, 1998), or check the online documentation at:

```
http://stein.cshl.org/WWW/software/CGI/
```

Setting up Apache for CGI Scripts

In addition to DBI and CGI.pm, there's one more component we need for writing Web-based scripts: a Web server. The instructions here are geared toward using scripts with the Apache server, but you can probably use a different server if you like by adapting the instructions a bit.

The various parts of an Apache installation commonly are located under /usr/ local/apache. For our purposes, the most important subdirectories of this directory are htdocs (for the HTML document tree), cgi-bin (for executable scripts and programs to be invoked by the Web server), and conf (for configuration files). These directories may be located somewhere else on your system. If so, make the appropriate adjustments to the following notes.

You should verify that the cgi-bin directory is not within the Apache document tree so that the scripts within it cannot be requested as plain text. This is a safety precaution. You don't want malicious clients to be able to examine your scripts for security holes by siphoning off the text of the scripts and studying them.

To install a CGI script for use with Apache, put it in the cgi-bin directory, then change the script's ownership to the user that Apache runs as and change its mode to be executable and readable only to that user. For example, if Apache runs as a user named www, use the following commands:

```
% chown www script_name
% chmod 500 script_name
```

You'll probably need to run these commands as www or as root. If you don't have permission to install scripts in the cgi-bin directory, you can ask your system administrator to do so on your behalf.

After the script has been installed, you can request it from your browser by sending the proper URL to the Web server. Typically the URL is something like this:

```
http://your.host.name/cgi-bin/script_name
```

Requesting the script from your Web browser causes it to be executed by the Web server. The script's output is sent back to you, and the result appears as a Web page in your browser.

If you want to use CGI scripts with mod_perl for better performance, do the following:

1. Make sure you have at least the following versions of the necessary software: Perl 5.004, CGI.pm 2.36, and mod_perl 1.07.

2. Make sure mod_perl is compiled into your Apache executable.

3. Set up a directory in which to store scripts. I use /usr/local/apache/cgi-perl. The cgi-perl directory should not be located within your Apache document tree for the same security reasons that cgi-bin shouldn't be there.

4. Tell Apache to associate scripts that are located in the cgi-perl directory with mod_perl:

```
Alias /cgi-perl/ /usr/local/apache/cgi-perl

<Location /cgi-perl>
    SetHandler perl-script
    PerlHandler Apache::Registry
    Options ExecCGI
</Location>
```

If you are using a current version of Apache that uses a single configuration file, put all these directives in httpd.conf. If your version of Apache uses the older three-file approach to configuration information, put the Alias directive in srm.conf and the Location lines in access.conf.

Do not enable mod_perl, PerlSendHeader, or PerlSetupEnv directives for the cgi-perl directory. These are handled automatically by CGI.pm, and enabling them may introduce processing conflicts.

The URL for a mod_perl script is similar to that of a standard CGI script. The only difference is that you specify cgi-perl instead of cgi-bin:

```
http://your.host.name/cgi-perl/script_name
```

For more information, visit the mod_perl area of the Apache Web site at the following location:

```
http://perl.apache.org/
```

A Brief Introduction to CGI.pm

To write a Perl script that uses the CGI.pm module, put a use line near the beginning of the script, then create a CGI object that gives you access to CGI.pm methods and variables:

```
use CGI;
my ($cgi) = new CGI;
```

Our CGI scripts use CGI.pm's capabilities by invoking methods using the $cgi variable. For example, to generate a level 1 heading, we'll use the h1() method like this:

```
print $cgi->h1 ("My Heading");
```

CGI.pm also supports a style of use that allows you to call its methods as functions, without the leading '$cgi->'. I don't use that syntax here because the '$cgi->' notation is more similar to the way DBI is used, and because it prevents CGI.pm function names from conflicting with the names of any functions you may define.

Checking for Input Parameters and Writing Output

One of the things CGI.pm does for you is to take care of all the ugly details involved in collecting input information provided by the Web server to your script. All you need to do to get that information is invoke the param() method. You can get the names of all available parameters like this:

```
my (@param) = $cgi->param ();
```

To retrieve the value of a particular parameter, just name the one in which you're interested:

```
if (!$cgi->param ("my_param"))
{
    print "my_param is not set\n";
}
else
{
    printf "my_param value: %s\n", $cgi->param ("my_param");
}
```

CGI.pm also provides methods for generating output to be sent to the client browser. Consider the following HTML document:

```
<HTML>
<HEAD>
<TITLE>My Page Title</TITLE>
</HEAD>
<BODY>
<H1>My Level-1 Heading</H1>
<P>Paragraph 1.
<P>Paragraph 2.
</BODY>
</HTML>
```

This code uses $cgi to produce the equivalent document:

```
print $cgi->header ();
print $cgi->start_html (-title => "My Page Title");
print $cgi->h1 ("My Page Heading");
print $cgi->p ();
print "Paragraph 1.\n";
print $cgi->p ();
print "Paragraph 2.\n";
print $cgi->end_html ();
```

Some of the advantages of using CGI.pm to generate output instead of writing raw HTML yourself are that you can think in logical units rather than in terms of individual markup tags, and your HTML is less likely to contain errors. (The reason I say "less likely" is that CGI.pm won't prevent you from doing bizarre things, such as including a list inside of a heading.) In addition, for non-tag text that you write, CGI.pm provides automatic escaping of characters such as '<' and '>' that are special in HTML.

Use of CGI.pm output-generating methods doesn't preclude you from writing out raw HTML yourself if you want. You can mix the two approaches, combining calls to CGI.pm methods with print statements that generate literal tags.

Escaping HTML and URL Text

If you write non-tag text via CGI.pm methods such as start_html() or h1(), special characters in the text are escaped for you automatically. For example, if you generate a title using the following statement, the '&' character in the title text will be converted to '&' for you by CGI.pm:

```
print $cgi->start_html (-title => "A, B & C");
```

If you write non-tag text without using a CGI.pm output-generating method, you should probably pass it through escapeHTML() first to make sure any special characters are escaped properly. This is also true when you construct URLs that may contain special characters, although in that case you should use the escape() method instead. It's important to use the appropriate encoding method because each method treats different sets of characters as special and encodes special characters using formats that differ from one another. Consider the following short Perl script:

```
#! /usr/bin/perl
use CGI;
$cgi = new CGI;

$s = "x<=y, right?";
print $cgi->escapeHTML ($s) . "\n"; # encode for use as HTML text
print $cgi->escape ($s) . "\n";     # encode for use in a URL
```

If you run this script, it produces the following output, from which you can see that encoding for HTML text is not the same as encoding for URLs:

```
x&lt;=y, right?
x%3C%3Dy%2C%20right%3F
```

Writing Multiple-Purpose Pages

One of the primary reasons to write Web-based scripts that generate HTML instead of writing static HTML documents is that a script can produce different kinds of pages depending on the way it's invoked. All of the CGI scripts we're going to write have that property. Each one operates as follows:

1. When you first request the script from your browser, it generates an initial page allowing you to select what kind of information you want.

2. When you make a selection, the script is re-invoked, but this time it retrieves and displays in a second page the specific information you requested.

The primary problem here is that you want the selection that you make from the first page to determine the contents of the second page, but Web pages normally are independent of one another unless you make some sort of special arrangements. The trick is to have the script generate pages that set a parameter to a value that tells the next invocation of the script what you want. When you first invoke the script, the parameter has no value; this tells the script to present its initial page. When you indicate what information you'd like to see, the page invokes the script again, but with the parameter set to a value that instructs the script what to do.

There are different ways of passing instructions from a page back to a script. One way is to provide a form that the user fills in. When the user submits the form, its contents are submitted to the Web server. The server passes the information along to the script, which can find out what was submitted by invoking the `param()` method. This is what we'll do for our third CGI script (the one that allows the user to enter a keyword for searching the Historical League directory).

Another way of specifying instructions to a script is to pass information as part of the URL that you send to the Web server when you request the script. This is what we'll do for our `samp_db` table browser and score browser scripts. The way this works is that the script generates a page containing hyperlinks. Selecting a link invokes the script again, but specifies a parameter value that instructs the script what to do. In effect, the script invokes itself in different ways to provide different kinds of results, depending on which link the user selects.

A script can allow itself to be invoked by sending to the browser a page containing a hyperlink to its own URL. For instance, a script `my_script` can write out a page containing this link:

```
<A HREF="/cgi-bin/my_script">Click Me!</A>
```

When the user clicks on the text `"Click Me!"`, the user's browser sends a request for `my_script` back to the Web server. Of course, all that will do is cause the script to send out the same page again because no other information is supplied. However, if you attach a parameter to the URL, that parameter is sent back to the Web server when the user selects the link. The server invokes the script, and the script can call `param()` to detect that the parameter was set and take action according to its value.

To attach a parameter to the end of the URL, add a '?' character followed by a name/value pair. To attach multiple parameters, separate them by '&' characters. For example:

```
/cgi-bin/my_script?name=value
/cgi-bin/my_script?name=value&name2=value2
```

To construct a self-referencing URL with attached parameters, a CGI script should begin by calling the `script_name()` method to obtain its own URL, then append parameters to it like this:

```
$url = $cgi->script_name ();    # get URL for script
$url .= "?name=value";          # add first parameter
$url .= "&name2=value2";        # add second parameter
```

After the URL is constructed, you can generate a hyperlink `<A>` tag containing it by using CGI.pm's `a()` method:

```
print $cgi->a ({-href => $url}, "Click Me!");
```

It's easier to see how this works by examining a short CGI script. When first invoked, the following script, `flip_flop`, presents a page called Page A that contains a single hyperlink. Selecting the link invokes the script again, but with the `page` parameter set to tell it to display Page B. Page B also contains a link to the script, but with no value for the `page` parameter. Therefore, selecting the link in Page B causes the original page

to be redisplayed. Subsequent invocations of the script flip the page back and forth
between Page A and Page B:

```
use CGI;

my ($cgi) = new CGI;
my ($url) = $cgi->script_name ();   # this script's own URL

print $cgi->header ();
if ($cgi->param ("page") ne "b")    # display page A
{
    print $cgi->start_html (-title => "Flip-Flop: Page A");
    print "This is Page A.<BR>To select Page B, ";
    $url .= "?page=b";       # attach parameter to select page B
    print $cgi->a ({-href => $url}, "click here");
}
else                                # display page B
{
    print $cgi->start_html (-title => "Flip-Flop: Page B");
    print "This is Page B.<BR>To select Page A, ";
    print $cgi->a ({-href => $url}, "click here");
}
print $cgi->end_html ();
```

If another client comes along and requests flip_flop, the initial page is presented
because different clients' browsers don't interfere with each other.

The value of $url actually was set in pretty cavalier fashion by the preceding exam-
ples. It's preferable to use the escape() method to encode your parameter names and
values when you append them to a URL in case they contain special characters. Here's
a better way to construct a URL with parameters attached to it:

```
$url = $cgi->script_name ();    # get URL for script
$url .= sprintf ("?%s=%s",       # add first parameter
            $cgi->escape ("name"), $cgi->escape ("value"));
$url .= sprintf ("&%s=%s",       # add second parameter
            $cgi->escape ("name2"), $cgi->escape ("value2"));
```

Connecting to the MySQL Server from Web Scripts

The command-line scripts we developed in the previous section, "Putting DBI To
Work," shared a common preamble for establishing a connection to the MySQL
server. Our CGI scripts share some code, too, but it's a little different:

```
use DBI;
use CGI;
use strict;

# default connection  parameters - all missing
my ($host_name, $user_name, $password) = (undef, undef, undef);
my ($db_name) = "samp_db";

# construct data source
```

```
my ($dsn) = "DBI:mysql:$db_name";
$dsn .= ":hostname=$host_name" if $host_name;
$dsn .= ";mysql_read_default_file=/usr/local/apache/conf/samp_db.cnf";

# connect to server
my (%attr) = ( RaiseError => 1 );
my ($dbh) = DBI->connect ($dsn, $user_name, $password, \%attr);
```

This preamble differs from the one we used for command-line scripts in the following respects:

- The first section now contains a use CGI statement.

- We no longer parse arguments from the command line.

- The code still looks for connection parameters in an option file, but doesn't use the .my.cnf file in the home directory of the user running the script (that is, the home directory of the Web server user). The Web server may run scripts for accessing other databases, and there's no reason to assume all those scripts will use the same connection parameters. Instead, we look for the option file stored in a different location (/usr/local/apache/conf/samp_db.cnf). You should change the option file pathname if you want to use a different file.

Scripts invoked through a Web server run as the Web server user, not as you. This raises some security issues because you're no longer in control after the Web server takes over. You should set the ownership of the option file to the user that the Web server runs as (perhaps www or nobody or something similar) and set the mode to 400 or 600 so that no other user can read it. Unfortunately, the file can still be read by anyone who can install a script for the Web server to execute. All they have to do is write a script that explicitly opens the option file and displays its contents in a Web page. Because their script runs as the Web server user, it will have full permission to read the file.

For this reason, you may find it prudent to create a MySQL user that has read–only (SELECT) privileges on the samp_db database, then list that user's name and password in the samp_db.cnf file, rather than your own name and password. That way you don't risk allowing scripts to connect to your database as a user that has permission to modify its tables. Chapter 11, "General MySQL Administration," discusses how to create a MySQL user account with restricted privileges.

Alternatively, you can arrange to execute scripts under Apache's suEXEC mechanism. This allows you to execute a script as a specific trusted user, and then write the script to get the connection parameters from an option file that is readable only to that user. You might do this for scripts that need write access to the database, for example.

Still another approach is to write a script to solicit a username and password from the client user, and use those values to establish a connection to the MySQL server. This is more suitable for scripts that you create for administrative purposes than for scripts that you provide for general use. In any case, you should be aware that some methods of name and password solicitation are subject to attack by anyone who can put a sniffer on the network between you and the server.

As you may gather from the preceding paragraphs, Web script security can be a tricky thing. It's definitely a topic about which you should read more for yourself, because it's a big subject to which I cannot really do justice here. A good place to start is with the security material in the Apache manual. You may also find the WWW security FAQ instructive; it's available at the following location:

```
http://www.w3.org/Security/Faq/
```

A samp_db Database Browser

For our first Web-based application, we'll develop a simple script—samp_browse—that allows you to see what tables exist in the samp_db database and to examine the contents of any of these tables interactively from your Web browser. samp_browse works like this:

- When you first request samp_browse from your browser, it connects to the MySQL server, retrieves a list of tables in the samp_db database, and sends your browser a page in which each table is presented as a link that you can select. When you select a table name from this page, your browser sends a request to the Web server asking samp_browse to display the contents of that table.

- If samp_browse receives a table name from the Web server when it's invoked, it retrieves the contents of the table and presents the information to your Web browser. The heading for each column of data is the name of the column in the table. Headings are presented as links; if you select one of them, your browser sends a request to the Web server to display the same table, but is sorted by the column you selected.

A note of warning here: The tables in the samp_db database are relatively small, so it's no big deal to send the entire contents of a table to your browser. If you edit samp_browse to display tables from a different database containing large tables, you should think about adding a LIMIT clause to the row retrieval statements.

In the main body of the samp_browse script, we create the CGI object and put out the initial part of the Web page. Then we check whether or not we're supposed to display some particular table based on the value of the tbl_name parameter:

```
my ($cgi) = new CGI;

# put out initial part of page
my ($title) = "$db_name Database Browser";
print $cgi->header ();
print $cgi->start_html (-title => $title);
print $cgi->h1 ($title);

# parameters to look for in URL
my ($tbl_name) = $cgi->param ("tbl_name");
```

```
my ($sort_column) = $cgi->param ("sort_column");

# if $tbl_name has no value, display a clickable list of tables.
# Otherwise, display contents of the given table.  $sort_column, if
# set, indicates which column to sort by.
if (!$tbl_name)
{
    display_table_list ()
}
else
{
    display_table ($tbl_name, $sort_column);
}

print $cgi->end_html ();
```

It's easy to find out what value a parameter has because CGI.pm does all the work of finding out what information the Web server passes to the script. We need only call param() with the name of the parameter in which we're interested. In the main body of samp_browse, that parameter is tbl_name. If it's not defined or is empty, this is the initial invocation of the script and we display the table list. Otherwise, we display the contents of the table named by the tbl_name parameter, sorted by the values in the column named by the sort_column parameter. After displaying the appropriate information, we call end_html() to put out the closing HTML tags.

The display_table_list() function generates the initial page. display_table_list() retrieves the table list and writes out a single-column HTML table containing the name of one database table in each cell:

```
sub display_table_list
{
my ($ary_ref, $url);

    print "Select a table by clicking on its name:<BR><BR>\n";

    # retrieve reference to single-column array of table names
    $ary_ref =
        $dbh->selectcol_arrayref (qq{ SHOW TABLES FROM $db_name });

    # display table with a border
    print "<TABLE BORDER>\n";
    print "<TR>\n";
    display_cell ("TH", "Table Name", 1);
    print "</TR>\n";
    foreach my $tbl_name (@{$ary_ref})
    {
        $url = $cgi->script_name ();
        $url .= sprintf ("?tbl_name=%s", $cgi->escape ($tbl_name));
        print "<TR>\n";
        display_cell ("TD", $cgi->a ({-href => $url}, $tbl_name), 0);
        print "</TR>\n";
```

continues

continued

```
        }
        print "</TABLE>\n";
    }
```

The page generated by `display_table_list()` contains links that look like this:

```
/cgi-bin/samp_browse?tbl_name=absence
/cgi-bin/samp_browse?tbl_name=event
/cgi-bin/samp_browse?tbl_name=member
...
```

If the `tbl_name` parameter has a value when `samp_browse` is invoked, the script passes
the value to `display_table()`, along with the name of the column to sort the results
by. If no column is named, we sort on the first column (we can refer to columns by
position, so this is easily accomplished using an `ORDER BY 1` clause):

```
sub display_table
{
my ($tbl_name, $sort_column) = @_;
my ($sth, $url);

    # if sort column not specified, use first column
    $sort_column = "1" unless $sort_column;

    # present a link that returns user to table list page
    print $cgi->a ({-href => $cgi->script_name ()}, "Show Table List");
    print "<BR><BR>\n";

    $sth = $dbh->prepare (qq{
                SELECT * FROM $tbl_name ORDER BY $sort_column
            });
    $sth->execute ();

    print "<B>Contents of $tbl_name table:</B><BR>\n";

    # display table with a border
    print "<TABLE BORDER>\n";
    # use column names for table headings; make each heading a link
    # that sorts output on the corresponding column
    print "<TR>\n";
    foreach my $col_name (@{$sth->{NAME}})
    {
        $url = $cgi->script_name ();
        $url .= sprintf ("?tbl_name=%s", $cgi->escape ($tbl_name));
        $url .= sprintf ("&sort_column=%s", $cgi->escape ($col_name));
        display_cell ("TH", $cgi->a ({-href => $url}, $col_name), 0);
    }
    print "</TR>\n";

    # display table rows
    while (my @ary = $sth->fetchrow_array ())
    {
```

```
        print "<TR>\n";
        foreach my $val (@ary)
        {
            display_cell ("TD", $val, 1);
        }
        print "</TR>\n";
    }

    $sth->finish ();
    print "</TABLE>\n";
}
```

A table display page associates column headings with links that redisplay the table; these links include a `sort_column` parameter that explicitly specifies the column to sort on. For example, for a page that displays the contents of the `event` table, the column heading links look like this:

```
/cgi-bin/samp_browse?tbl_name=event&sort_column=date
/cgi-bin/samp_browse?tbl_name=event&sort_column=type
/cgi-bin/samp_browse?tbl_name=event&sort_column=event_id
```

Both `display_table_list()` and `display_table()` use `display_cell()`, a utility function that displays a value as a cell in an HTML table. This function uses a little trick of turning empty values into a non-breaking space (' ') because in a table with borders, empty cells don't display the borders properly. Putting a non-breaking space in the cell fixes that problem. `display_cell()` also takes a third parameter controlling whether or not to encode the cell value. This is necessary because `display_cell()` is called to display some cell values that have already been encoded, such as column headings that include URL information.

```
# display a value in a table cell; put non-breaking
# space in "empty" cells so borders show up

sub display_cell
{
my ($tag, $value, $encode) = @_;

    $value = $cgi->escapeHTML ($value) if $encode;
    $value = " " unless $value;
    print "<$tag>$value</$tag>\n";
}
```

If you want to write a more general script, you could alter `samp_browse` to browse multiple databases. For example, you could have the script begin by displaying a list of databases on the server, rather than a list of tables within a particular database. Then you could pick a database to get a list of its tables and go from there.

Grade-Keeping Project Score Browser

Each time we enter the scores for a test, we need to generate an ordered list of scores so that we can determine the grading curve and assign letter grades. Note that all we will do with this list is print it so that we can determine where each letter grade cut-off lies. Then we'll mark the grades on the students' test papers before returning them. We're not going to record the letter grades in the database because grades at the end of the grading period are based on numeric scores, not letter grades. Note also that, strictly speaking, we should have a way of entering the scores before we create a way of retrieving them. I'm saving the script for entering scores until the next chapter. In the meantime, we do have several sets of scores in the database already from the early part of the grading period. We can use our script with those scores, even in the absence of a convenient score entry method.

Our score-browsing script, `score_browse`, has some similarities to `samp_browse`, but is intended for the more specific purpose of looking at scores for a given quiz or test. The initial page presents a list of the possible grade events from which to choose, and allows the user to select any of them to see the scores associated with the event. Scores for a given event are sorted by score with the highest scores first, so you can print out the result and use it to determine the grading curve.

The `score_browse` script needs to examine only one parameter, `event_id`, to see whether or not a particular event was specified. If not, `score_browse` displays the rows of the event table so that the user can select one. Otherwise, it displays the scores associated with the chosen event:

```
# parameter that tells us which event to display scores for
my ($event_id) = $cgi->param ("event_id");

# if $event_id has a value, display the event list.
# otherwise display the scores for the given event.
if (!$event_id)
{
    display_events ()
}
else
{
    display_scores ($event_id);
}
```

The `display_events()` function pulls out information from the `event` table and displays it in tabular form, using column names from the query for the table column headings. Within each row, the `event_id` value is displayed as a link that can be selected to trigger a query that retrieves the scores corresponding to the event. The URL for each event is simply the path to `score_browse` with a parameter attached, which specifies the event number:

```
/cgi-bin/score_browse?event_id=number
```

The `display_events()` function is written as follows:

```
sub display_events
{
my ($sth, $url);
```

```
    print "Select an event by clicking on its number:<BR><BR>\n";

    # get list of events
    $sth = $dbh->prepare (qq{
        SELECT event_id, date, type
        FROM event
        ORDER BY event_id
    });
    $sth->execute ();

    # display table with a border
    print "<TABLE BORDER>\n";
    # use column names for table column headings
    print "<TR>\n";
    foreach my $col_name (@{$sth->{NAME}})
    {
        display_cell ("TH", $col_name, 1);
    }
    print "</TR>\n";

    # associate each event id with a link that will show the
    # scores for the event; return rows using a hash to make
    # it easy to refer to the event_id column value by name.
    while (my $hash_ref = $sth->fetchrow_hashref ())
    {
        print "<TR>\n";
        $url = $cgi->script_name ();
        $url .= sprintf ("?event_id=%s",
                         $cgi->escape ($hash_ref->{event_id}));
        display_cell ("TD",
                      $cgi->a ({-href => $url}, $hash_ref->{event_id}), 0);
        display_cell ("TD", $hash_ref->{date}, 1);
        display_cell ("TD", $hash_ref->{type}, 1);
        print "</TR>\n";
    }
    $sth->finish ();
    print "</TABLE>\n";
}
```

When the user selects an event, the browser sends a request for score_browse that has an event ID value attached. score_browse finds the event_id parameter set and calls display_scores() to list all the scores for the specified event. The page also displays the text "Show Event List" as a link back to the initial page so that the user can return to the event list page easily. The URL for this link refers to the score_browse script but does not specify any value for the event_id parameter. display_scores() is shown in the following listing:

```
sub display_scores
{
my ($event_id) = shift;
```

continues

continued

```perl
    my ($sth);

        # a URL without any event_id parameter will
        # cause the event list to be displayed.
        print $cgi->a ({-href => $cgi->script_name ()}, "Show Event List");
        print "<BR><BR>\n";

        # select scores for the given event
        $sth = $dbh->prepare (qq{
            SELECT
                student.name, event.date, score.score, event.type
            FROM
                student, score, event
            WHERE
                student.student_id = score.student_id
                AND score.event_id = event.event_id
                AND event.event_id = ?
            ORDER BY
                event.date ASC, event.type ASC, score.score DESC
        });
        $sth->execute ($event_id);  # pass event ID as placeholder value

        print "<B>Scores for event $event_id</B><BR>\n";

        # display table with a border
        print "<TABLE BORDER>\n";
        # use column names for table column headings
        print "<TR>\n";
        foreach my $col_name (@{$sth->{NAME}})
        {
            display_cell ("TH", $col_name, 1);
        }
        print "</TR>\n";

        while (my @ary = $sth->fetchrow_array ())
        {
            print "<TR>\n";
            display_cell ("TD", shift (@ary), 1) while @ary;
            print "</TR>\n";
        }

        $sth->finish ();
        print "</TABLE>\n";
    }
```

The query that display_scores() runs is quite similar to one that we developed way back in Chapter 1 in the section "Retrieving Information From Multiple Tables" that describes how to write joins. In that chapter, we asked for scores for a given date because dates are more meaningful than event ID values. In contrast, when we use score_browse, we know the exact event ID. That's not because we think in terms of event IDs (we don't), but because the script presents us with a list of them from which to choose. You can see that this type of interface reduces the need to know particular details. We don't need to know an event ID; we need only to be able to recognize the event we want.

Historical League Common-Interest Searching

The samp_browse and score_browse scripts allow the user to make a selection by presenting a list of choices in an initial page, where each choice is a link that re-invokes the script with a particular parameter value. Another way to allow users to make a choice is to put a form in a page containing an editable field. This is more appropriate when the range of possible choices isn't constrained to some easily determined set of values. Our next script demonstrates this method of soliciting user input.

In the section "Putting DBI To Work," we constructed a command-line script for finding Historical League members who share a particular interest. However, that script isn't something that League members have access to; the League secretary must run the script and then mail the result to the member who requested the list. It'd be nice to make this search capability more widely available so that members could use it for themselves. Writing a Web script is one way to do that.

This script, interests, puts up a little form into which the user can enter a keyword, then searches the member table for qualifying members and displays the results. The search is done by adding the '%' wildcard character to both ends of the keyword so that it can be found anywhere in the interests column value.

The keyword form is displayed on every page so that the user can enter a new search immediately, even from those pages that display search results. In addition, the search string from the previous page is displayed in the keyword form so that if the user wants to run a similar search, the string can be edited. That way, it's not necessary to do a lot of retyping:

```
# parameter to look for
my ($interest) = $cgi->param ("interest");

# Display a keyword entry form.  In addition, if $interest is defined,
# search for and display a list of members who have that interest.
# Note that the current $interest value is displayed as the default
# value of the interest field in the form.

print $cgi->start_form (-method => "POST");
print $cgi->textfield (-name => "interest",
                          -value => $interest,
                          -size => 40);
print $cgi->submit (-name => "button", -value => "Search");
print $cgi->end_form ();

# run a search if a keyword was specified
search_members ($interest) if $interest;
```

The script communicates information to itself a little differently than `samp_browse` or `score_browse`. The `interest` parameter is not added to the end of a URL. Instead, the information in the form is encoded by the browser and sent as part of a POST request. However, `CGI.pm` makes it irrelevant how the information is sent; the parameter value is still obtained by calling `param()`.

The function for performing the search and displaying the results is shown in the following listing. The function that formats the entry, `format_html_entry()`, is not shown because it's the same as the one in the `gen_dir` script:

```
sub search_members
{
my ($interest) = shift;
my ($sth, $count);

    printf "Search results for keyword: %s<BR><BR>\n",
                                $cgi->escapeHTML ($interest);
    $sth = $dbh->prepare (qq{
                SELECT * FROM member WHERE interests LIKE ?
                ORDER BY last_name, first_name
            });
    # look for string anywhere in interest field
    $sth->execute ("%" . $interest . "%");
    $count = 0;
    while (my $hash_ref = $sth->fetchrow_hashref ())
    {
        format_html_entry ($hash_ref);
        ++$count;
    }
    print $cgi->p ("$count entries found");
}
```

8

The PHP API

PHP IS A SCRIPTING LANGUAGE THAT LETS you write Web pages containing embedded code that is executed whenever a page is accessed and that can generate dynamic content to be included as part of the output sent to a client's Web browser. This chapter describes how to use PHP to write Web-based applications that use MySQL. For a comparison of PHP with the C and Perl DBI APIs for MySQL programming, see Chapter 5, "Introduction to MySQL Programming."

The examples in this chapter draw on our sample database, samp_db, using the tables that we created for the grade-keeping project and for the Historical League in Chapter 1, "Introduction to MySQL and SQL." We'll cover PHP 3, although as I write PHP 4 is in beta testing and may be available by the time you read this. Compatibility with PHP 3 is one of the explicit design goals for PHP 4, so almost everything said here about PHP 3 should apply to PHP 4. A set of migration notes for PHP 4 describes changes from PHP 3. You should read those notes if you're using PHP 4.

This chapter was written under the assumption that you'll use PHP in conjunction with the Apache Web server. The MySQL C client library and header files must be installed as well; those files are needed when you build PHP, or PHP will not know how to access MySQL databases. If you need to obtain any of this software, see

Appendix A, "Obtaining and Installing Software." Instructions for obtaining the example scripts developed in this chapter are also given in that appendix. You can download the scripts to avoid typing them in yourself.

Under UNIX, PHP may be used with Apache either as a built-in module that is linked into the Apache executable binary, or as a standalone interpreter used as a traditional CGI program. Under Windows, PHP can run only as a standalone program at the moment, though there is work underway to develop an Apache PHP 4 module that will run under Windows NT.

For the most part, this chapter describes PHP functions only as they are needed for the discussion here. For a more comprehensive listing of all MySQL-related functions, see Appendix H, "PHP API Reference." You'll likely also want to consult the PHP manual, which describes the full range of functions that PHP provides, including functions for using databases other than MySQL (PHP is not limited to working with MySQL any more than DBI is). The manual is available from the PHP Web site at http://www.php.net/. This Web site also has the notes for migrating from PHP 3 to PHP 4.

PHP Script Characteristics

Filenames for PHP scripts are typically written with an extension that allows your Web server to recognize them and execute the PHP interpreter to process them. If you use an extension that isn't recognized, your PHP scripts will be served as plain text. The extension used in this chapter is .php. Other common extensions are .php3 and .phtml. For instructions on configuring Apache to recognize the extension you want to use, see Appendix A. If you are not in control of the Apache installation on your machine, check with the system administrator to find out the proper extension to use.

PHP Basics

The basic function of PHP is to interpret a script to produce a Web page that is sent to a client. The script typically contains a mix of HTML that is sent literally to the client and PHP code that is executed as a program. Whatever output the code produces is sent to the client, so the client never sees the code; it sees only the resulting output.

When PHP begins reading a file, it simply copies whatever it finds there to the output, with the assumption that the contents of the file represent literal HTML. When the PHP interpreter encounters a special opening tag, it switches from HTML mode to PHP code mode and starts interpreting the file as PHP code to be executed. The end of the code is indicated by another special tag, at which point the interpreter switches from code mode back to HTML mode. This allows you to mix static text (the HTML part) with dynamically generated results (output from the PHP code part) to produce a page that varies depending on the circumstances under which it is called.

For example, you might use a PHP script to process the result of a form into which a user has entered parameters for a database search. The search parameters may be different each time the form is filled out, so when the script performs searches, each resulting page will reflect a different search.

Let's see how this works by looking at an extremely simple PHP script:

```
<HTML>
<BODY>
hello, world
</BODY>
</HTML>
```

This script is not very interesting because it contains no PHP code! What good is that, you ask? That's a reasonable question. The answer is that it's sometimes useful to set up a script containing just the HTML framework for the page you want to produce and then to add the PHP code later. This is perfectly legal, and the PHP interpreter has no problem with it.

To include PHP code in a script, you distinguish it from the surrounding text with two special tags, '<?php' to begin the script and '?>' to end the script. When the PHP interpreter encounters the opening '<?php' tag, it switches from HTML mode to PHP code mode and interprets whatever it finds as PHP code until it sees the closing '?>' tag. The script between the tags is interpreted and replaced by any output it produces. The previous example could be rewritten to include a little PHP code like this:

```
<HTML>
<BODY>
<?php print ("hello, world\n"); ?>
</BODY>
</HTML>
```

In this case, the code part is minimal, consisting of a single line. When the code is interpreted, it produces the output hello, world, which becomes part of the output sent to the client's browser. Thus, the Web page produced by this script is identical to the one produced by the preceding example, in which the script consisted entirely of HTML.

You can use PHP code to generate any part of a Web page. We've already seen one extreme, in which the entire script consisted of literal HTML and contained no PHP code. The other extreme is for the entire script to be PHP code and contain no literal HTML:

```
<?php
print ("<HTML>\n");
print ("<BODY>\n");
print ("hello, world\n");
print ("</BODY>\n");
print ("</HTML>\n");
?>
```

This demonstrates that PHP gives you a lot of flexibility in how you produce output. PHP leaves it up to you to decide whatever combination of HTML and PHP code is appropriate. PHP is also flexible in that you don't need to put all your code in one place. You can switch between HTML and PHP code mode throughout the script however you please, as often as you want.

PHP Script Tags

PHP understands other script tags in addition to those used for examples in this chapter. You may see these in PHP code that other people write, or you may want to use them yourself. PHP recognizes four tag styles:

- **Default tag style.** This is the style that PHP is configured to use by default:

  ```
  <?php print ("hello, world\n"); ?>
  ```
- **Short-open-tag style.** This is like the default style except that the opening tag is shorter:

  ```
  <? print ("hello, world\n"); ?>
  ```
- **ASP-compatible style.** This style is common within Active Server Page environments:

  ```
  <% print ("hello, world\n"); %>
  ```
- **<SCRIPT> tag style.** This style is useful if you use an HTML editor that doesn't like any of the other tag styles. It's certainly more verbose, but you may find it necessary if an editor won't leave your PHP code alone when you use other tag styles:

  ```
  <SCRIPT LANGUAGE="php"> print ("hello, world\n"); </SCRIPT>
  ```
  The short-open-tag and ASP-compatible tag styles are not enabled by default. See Appendix H for instructions on enabling them.

Standalone PHP Scripts

It's possible to write standalone PHP scripts that you can invoke from the command line as you might do with a shell script or Perl script. Here's an example:

```
#! /usr/local/bin/php -q
<?php print ("hello, world\n"); ?>
```

The preceding script can be named hello.php, made executable with chmod +x, and invoked from the shell:

```
% hello.php
hello, world
```

We will not write any standalone scripts in this chapter. All examples are written with the expectation that they will be invoked by a Web server to generate a Web page.

The next script is a bit more substantial, but still relatively short. It shows how easily you can access a MySQL database from PHP and use the results of a query in a Web page. The following script was presented very briefly in Chapter 5; it forms a simple basis for a home page for the Historical League Web site. We'll make the script a bit more elaborate as we go on, but for now, all it does is display a short welcome message and a count of the current League membership:

```
<HTML>
<HEAD>
<TITLE>US Historical League</TITLE>
</HEAD>
<BODY>
<P>Welcome to the US Historical League Website.
<?php
$link = @mysql_pconnect ("pit-viper.snake.net", "paul", "secret")
    or exit ();
mysql_select_db ("samp_db")
    or exit ();
$result = mysql_query ("SELECT COUNT(*) FROM member")
    or exit ();
if ($row = mysql_fetch_array ($result))
    echo "<P>The League currently has " . $row[0] . " members";
mysql_free_result ($result);
?>
</BODY></HTML>
```

The welcome message is just static text, so it's easiest simply to write it as literal HTML. The membership count, on the other hand, is dynamic and changes from time to time, so it must be determined on the fly by querying the member table in the samp_db database.

The text of the code within the opening and closing script tags performs a simple task. First, it opens a connection to the MySQL server and makes the samp_db database the default database. Then it sends a query to the server to determine how many members the Historical League has at the moment (which we assess as the number of rows in the member table). The result of the query is displayed as part of a message containing the membership count and then disposed of.

If an error occurs at any point during this process, the script simply exits. No error output is produced because that's likely simply to be confusing to people visiting the Web site.[1]

Let's break down the script into pieces to see how it works. The first step is to connect to the server using mysql_pconnect():

```
$link = @mysql_pconnect ("pit-viper.snake.net", "paul", "secret")
    or exit ();
```

---

[1] If you generate your entire Web page by means of PHP code, exiting on an error without producing any output at all is likely to annoy people viewing your pages because some browsers will display a "this page contained no data" dialog box that must be dismissed.

`mysql_pconnect()` takes a hostname, username, and password as arguments. It returns a link identifier if the connection was established successfully and `FALSE` if an error occurs. If the connection attempt fails, our script calls `exit()`, which terminates the script immediately. No further output is produced.

What about that '@' character in front of the `mysql_pconnect()` call? That is the "Shut up, please" character. Some PHP functions write an error message when they fail, in addition to returning a status code. In the case of `mysql_pconnect()`, a failed connection attempt causes a message like this to appear in the Web page that is sent to the client's browser:

```
Warning: MySQL Connection Failed: Access denied for user:
'paul@pit-viper.snake.net' (Using password: YES)
```

That's ugly, and the person visiting our site may not know what to make of it or what to do about it. Putting '@' in front of the `mysql_pconnect()` call suppresses this error message so that we can choose how to deal with errors ourselves on the basis of the return value. For the script at hand, the best thing to do if an error occurs is to produce no output at all pertaining to the membership count. In this case, the page will contain only the welcome message.

You can use '@' with any PHP function, but in my experience, the initial `mysql_pconnect()` call is the one most likely to fail; hence, the examples in this chapter suppress messages only from that function.

Perhaps it makes you nervous that the name and password are embedded in the script for all to see. Well, it should. It's true that the name and password don't appear in the Web page that is sent to the client because the script's contents are replaced by its output. Nevertheless, if the Web server becomes misconfigured somehow and fails to recognize that your script needs to be processed by PHP, it will send your script as plain text, and your connection parameters will be exposed. We'll deal with this shortly, in the section "Using Functions and Include Files."

The link identifier returned by `mysql_pconnect()` can be passed to several other MySQL-related calls in the PHP API. However, for such calls, the identifier is always

---

`mysql_pconnect()` Versus `mysql_connect()`

A function that's similar to `mysql_pconnect()` is `mysql_connect()`. Both take hostname, username, and password arguments and return a link identifier or `FALSE` to indicate success or failure of the connection attempt. The difference between the two calls is that `mysql_pconnect()` establishes a persistent connection, whereas `mysql_connect()` establishes a non-persistent connection. A persistent connection differs from a non-persistent connection in that it is not closed when the script terminates. If another PHP script is executed later by the same Apache child process and calls `mysql_pconnect()` with the same arguments, the connection is reused. This is much more efficient than establishing each connection from scratch.

optional. For example, you can call `mysql_select_db()` using either of the following forms:

```
mysql_select_db ($db_name, $link);
mysql_select_db ($db_name);
```

If you omit the link argument from any MySQL-related PHP call that takes one, the call uses the most recently opened connection. Thus, if your script opens only a single connection, you never need to specify a link argument explicitly in any of your MySQL calls—that connection will be the default. This is quite different than MySQL programming with the C or DBI APIs, for which there is no such default.

I wrote the connection code in our simple home page script as follows using the `$link` variable to make it clearer what kind of value `mysql_pconnect()` returns:

```
$link = @mysql_pconnect ("pit-viper.snake.net", "paul", "secret")
    or exit ();
```

However, we don't actually use `$link` anywhere else in the script, so the code could have been written more simply like this:

```
@mysql_pconnect ("pit-viper.snake.net", "paul", "secret")
    or exit ();
```

Assuming the connection is established successfully, the next step is to select a database:

```
mysql_select_db ("samp_db")
    or exit ();
```

If `mysql_select_db()` fails, we exit silently. An error is unlikely to occur at this point if we've been able to connect to the server and the database exists, but it's still prudent to check for problems and take appropriate action. After selecting the database, we can send our query to the server, extract the result, display it, and free the result set:

```
$result = mysql_query ("SELECT COUNT(*) FROM member")
    or exit ();
if ($row = mysql_fetch_array ($result))
    echo "<P>The League currently has " . $row[0] . " members";
mysql_free_result ($result);
```

The `mysql_query()` function sends the query to the server to be executed. The query should not be terminated with a semicolon or with '\g'. `mysql_query()` returns FALSE if the query was illegal or couldn't be executed for some reason. Otherwise, it returns a result set identifier. This identifier is a value that we can use to obtain information about the result set. For our query, the result set consists of a single row with a single column value representing the membership count. To get this value, we pass the result set identifier to `mysql_fetch_array()` to fetch the row, assign the row to the variable `$row`, and access the first element (which also happens to be the only element) as `$row[0]`.

When we're done with the result set, we free it by passing it to `mysql_free_result()`. This call actually isn't necessary in our script because PHP automatically releases any active result sets when a script terminates.

`mysql_free_result()` is useful primarily in scripts that execute very large queries or a large number of queries; it prevents an excessive amount of memory from being used.

In order to use our script, we need to install it somewhere. I'll adopt the convention in this chapter that the US Historical League has its own directory called `ushl` at the top level of the Apache document tree, so the home page script can be installed as `ushl/index.php` in that tree. We'll be developing scripts for the grade-keeping project, too, so we'll give that a directory `gp`. If the Web site host is `pit-viper.snake.net`, pages in these two directories will have URLs that begin like this:

```
http://pit-viper.snake.net/ushl/
http://pit-viper.snake.net/gp/
```

For example, the home pages in each directory can be called `index.php` and accessed as follows:

```
http://pit-viper.snake.net/ushl/index.php
http://pit-viper.snake.net/gp/index.php
```

Using Functions and Include Files

PHP scripts differ from DBI scripts in that PHP scripts are located within your Web server document tree, whereas DBI scripts typically are located in a `cgi-bin` directory that's located outside of the document tree. This brings up a security issue: A server misconfiguration error can cause pages located within the document tree to leak out as plain text to clients. This means that usernames and passwords for establishing connections to the MySQL server are at a higher risk of being exposed to the outside world if they are used in a PHP script than in a DBI script.

Variables in PHP

In PHP you can make variables spring into existence simply by using them. Our home page script uses three variables, `$link`, `$result`, and `$row`, none of which are declared anywhere. (There are contexts in which you do declare variables, such as when you reference a global variable inside a function, but we'll get to that later.)

Variables are signified by an identifier preceded by a dollar sign ('$'). This is true no matter what kind of value it represents, although for arrays and objects you tack on some extra stuff to access individual elements of the value. If a variable $x represents a single value, such as a number or a string, you access it as just $x. If $x represents an array with numeric indices, you access its elements as $x[0], $x[1], etc. If $x represents an array with associative indices such as "yellow" or "large", you access its elements as $x["yellow"] or $x["large"].

PHP arrays can even have both numeric and associative elements. For example, $x[1] and $x["large"] both can be elements of the same array. If $x represents an object, it has properties that you access as $x->*property_name*. For example, $x->yellow and $x->large may be properties of $x. Numbers are not legal as property names, so $x->1 is not a valid construct in PHP.

Our initial Historical League home page script is subject to this problem because it contains the literal values of the MySQL username and password. Let's move these connection parameters out of the script using two of PHP's capabilities: functions and include files. We'll write a function `samp_db_connect()` to establish the connection, and put the function in an *include file*—a file that is not part of our main script but that can be referenced from it. Some advantages of this approach are:

- **It's easier to write connection establishment code.** We don't need to write out all the parameters, and we can have `samp_db_connect()` select the database for us after connecting so that one function does the work of two PHP functions. This tends to make scripts more understandable, too, because you can concentrate on the unique aspects of the script without being distracted by the connection setup code.

- **The include file can be accessed from our script but can be moved outside of the Apache document tree.** This makes its contents inaccessible to clients and thus connection parameters cannot be exposed to them, even if the Web server becomes misconfigured. Using an include file is a good strategy for hiding any kind of sensitive information that you don't want to be sent off-site by your Web server.

  This doesn't mean that the name and password are secure in all senses, though. Users that can log in on the Web server host may be able to read the include file directly if you don't take any precautions. See the section "Connecting to the MySQL Server from Web Scripts" in Chapter 7, "The Perl DBI API," and take note of the precautions that are described there for installing DBI configuration files so as to protect them from other users. The same precautions apply to the use of PHP include files.

PHP's Linguistic Influences

If you have experience with C programming, you've probably noticed that many of the syntactic constructs in our script are very similar to what you use for C programming. PHP syntax is in fact largely drawn from C, so the similarity is not coincidental. If you have some background in C, you'll be able to transfer much of it to PHP. In fact, if you're not sure how to write an expression or control structure in PHP, just try it the way you'd write it in C and it'll likely be correct.

Although PHP has its roots mainly in C, elements of Java and Perl are present, too. You can certainly see this in the comment syntax, where any of the following forms are allowed:

```
# Perl-style comment from '#' to end of line
// C++- or Java-style comment from '//' to end of line
/* C-style comment between slash-star to star-slash */
```

Other similarities with Perl include the '.' string concatenation operator (including '.=' as additive concatenation), and the way that variable references and escape sequences are interpreted within double quotes but not within single quotes.

- **The include file can be used by multiple scripts.** This promotes code reusability and makes code more maintainable. It also allows global changes to be made easily to every script that accesses the file. For example, if we move the samp_db database from pit-viper to boa, we don't need to change a bunch of individual scripts, we just change the hostname argument of the mysql_pcon-nect() call in the include file the contains the samp_db_connect() function.

To use include files, you need to have a place to put them, and you need to tell PHP to look for them. If your system already has such a location, you can use that. If not, use the following procedure to establish an include file location:

1. Create a directory in which to store PHP include files. This directory should not be located within the Web server document tree! I use a PHP include directory of /usr/local/apache/php, which is at the same level as my document tree (/usr/local/apache/htdocs), not within it.

2. Reference include files by full pathname or tell PHP what directories to look in when searching for them. The latter approach is more convenient because if we use the file's basename, PHP will find it for us.[2] To tell PHP where to look, modify the PHP initialization file (/usr/local/lib/php3.ini on my system), to change the value of include_path. If it has no value, set it to the full pathname of the new include directory:

   ```
   include_path = "/usr/local/apache/php"
   ```

   If include_path already has a value, add the new directory to that value:

   ```
   include_path = "current_value:/usr/local/apache/php"
   ```

3. Create the include file that you want to use and put it into the include directory. The file should have some distinctive name; for our purposes here, samp_db.inc will do. Its contents are shown in the following listing. For the scripts we develop here, when we connect to the MySQL server, we will always use the samp_db database, so the connection function samp_db_connect() may as well select that database for us. The function returns a link identifier if it successfully connects and selects the database, and it returns FALSE if an error occurs. It prints no message when an error occurs, which allows the caller to exit silently or print a message as circumstances warrant:

   ```
   <?php
   # samp_db.inc
   # samp_db sample database common functions
   ```

---

[2] PHP include files are somewhat analogous to C header files, including that PHP will look for them in several directories, just like the C preprocessor looks in multiple directories for C header files.

```
# Connect to the MySQL server using our top-secret name and password

function samp_db_connect ()
{
    $link = @mysql_pconnect ("pit-viper.snake.net", "paul", "secret");
    if ($link && mysql_select_db ("samp_db"))
        return ($link);
    return (FALSE);
}
?>
```

Observe that the contents of the `samp_db.inc` file are bracketed with '<?php' and '?>' tags. That's because PHP begins reading include files in HTML mode. Without the tags, PHP will send out the file as plain text rather than interpreting it as PHP code. If you intend to include literal HTML in the file, that's just fine. But if the file contains PHP code, you must enclose the code within script tags.

4. To reference the file from a script, use a line like this:

```
include ("samp_db.inc");
```

When PHP sees that line, it searches for the file and reads its contents. Anything in the file becomes accessible to the following parts of the script.

After setting up our include file `samp_db.inc`, we can modify the Historical League home page to reference the include file and connect to the MySQL server by calling the `samp_db_connect()` function:

```
<HTML>
<HEAD>
<TITLE>US Historical League</TITLE>
</HEAD>
<BODY>
<P>Welcome to the US Historical League Website.
<?php
include ("samp_db.inc");

samp_db_connect ()
    or exit ();
```

continues

---

include() **Versus** require()

PHP has a require() capability that is similar to include(). Where they differ is that for include(), the file is read and evaluated each time the include() statement is executed. For require(), the file is processed only once (in fact, the contents of the file replace the require() statement). This means that if you have code containing one of these directives and the code may be executed several times, it's more efficient to use require(). On the other hand, if you want to read a different file each time you execute your code or you have a loop that iterates through a set of files, you want include()because you can set a variable to the name of the file you want to include, and use the variable as the argument to include().

continued

```
$result = mysql_query ("SELECT COUNT(*) FROM member")
    or exit ();
if ($row = mysql_fetch_array ($result))
    echo "<P>The League currently has " . $row[0] . " members";
mysql_free_result ($result);
?>
</BODY></HTML>
```

You may be thinking that we haven't really saved all that much coding in the home page by using an include file. But just wait. The `samp_db.inc` file will be useful for other functions as well, and we can use it as a convenient repository for various other things. In fact, we can create two more functions to put in that file right now. Every script we write will generate a fairly stereotypical set of HTML tags at the beginning of a page and another set at the end. Rather than writing them out literally in each script, we can write functions `html_begin()` and `html_end()` to do that for us. The `html_begin()` function can take a couple of arguments that specify a page title and header. The code for the two functions looks like this:

```
# Put out initial HTML tags for page. $title and $header, if
# present, are assumed to have any special characters properly
# encoded.

function html_begin ($title, $header)
{
    print ("<HTML>\n");
    print ("<HEAD>\n");
    if ($title)
        print ("<TITLE>$title</TITLE>\n");
    print ("</HEAD>\n");
    print ("<BODY>\n");
    if ($header)
        print ("<H2>$header</H2>\n");
}


# put out final HTML tags for page.

function html_end ()
{
    print ("</BODY></HTML>\n");
}
```

Then we can change the Historical League home page to use the two new functions so that it looks like this:

```
<?php
include ("samp_db.inc");

$title = "US Historical League";
html_begin ($title, $title);
?>
```

```
<P>Welcome to the US Historical League Website.

<?php
samp_db_connect ()
    or exit ();
$result = mysql_query ("SELECT COUNT(*) FROM member")
    or exit ();
if ($row = mysql_fetch_array ($result))
    echo "<P>The League currently has " . $row[0] . " members";
mysql_free_result ($result);

html_end ();
?>
```

Notice that the code has been split into two pieces, with the literal HTML text of the welcome message appearing between the pieces.

The use of functions for generating the initial and final part of the page gives us an important capability. If we want to change the look of the header or footer of all pages that use these functions, we can just include some code in the functions. Every script that uses them will then be affected automatically. For instance, you might want to put a message "Copyright USHL" at the bottom of each Historical League page. A page-trailer function such as `html_end()` is an easy way to do that.

A Simple Query Page

The script that we've embedded in the Historical League home page runs a query that returns just a single row. Our next script shows how to process a multiple-line result set. It fetches and displays the contents of the member table. This is the PHP equivalent of the `dump_members` DBI script we developed in Chapter 7, so we'll call it `dump_members.php`. It's different than the DBI version in that it's intended for use in a Web environment rather than from the command line. For this reason, it needs to produce HTML output rather than simply writing tab-delimited text. To make rows and columns line up nicely, we'll write the member records as an HTML table. The script looks like this:

```
<?php
# dump_members.php - dump Historical League's membership list

include ("samp_db.inc");

$title = "US Historical League Member List";
html_begin ($title, $title);

samp_db_connect ()
    or die ("Cannot connect to server");

# issue query
$query = "SELECT last_name, first_name, suffix, email,"
```

continues

continued

```
                    . "street, city, state, zip, phone FROM member ORDER BY last_name";
        $result = mysql_query ($query)
              or die ("Cannot execute query");

        print ("<TABLE>\n");
        # read results of query, then clean up
        while ($row = mysql_fetch_row ($result))
        {
            print ("<TR>\n");
            for ($i = 0; $i < mysql_num_fields ($result); $i++)
            {
                # escape any special characters and print
                printf ("<TD>%s</TD>\n", htmlspecialchars ($row[$i]));
            }
            print ("</TR>\n");
        }
        mysql_free_result ($result);
        print ("</TABLE>\n");

        html_end ();
        ?>
```

This script uses the die() function to print a message and to exit if an error occurs.[3]
This is a different approach to error handling than we used in the Historical League
home page, where we exited silently. In dump_members.php, we're expecting to see a
particular result, so it's reasonable to print an error message indicating that a problem
occurred.

The script can be installed in the ushl directory and accessed as http://pit-
viper.snake.net/ushl/dump_members.php. We can then add a link to our new script
in the Historical League home page so that people know about it:

```
<?php
include ("samp_db.inc");

$title = "US Historical League";
html_begin ($title, $title);
?>

<P>Welcome to the US Historical League Website.

<?php
samp_db_connect ()
    or exit ();
$result = mysql_query ("SELECT COUNT(*) FROM member")
    or exit ();
if ($row = mysql_fetch_array ($result))
    echo "<P>The League currently has " . $row[0] . " members.";
```

---

[3] The die() function is similar to exit(), but it prints a message before exiting.

```
mysql_free_result ($result);
?>

<P>
You can view the directory of members
<A HREF="dump_members.php">here</A>.

<?php
html_end ();
?>
```

Processing Query Results

In this section, we'll examine in more detail how to execute MySQL queries and handle result sets. In PHP, all queries are issued by calling the `mysql_query()` function, which takes a query string and a link identifier as arguments. The link identifier is optional, so you can invoke `mysql_query()` using either of the following forms:

```
$result = mysql_query ($query, $link);   # use explicit connection
$result = mysql_query ($query);          # use default connection
```

For queries that don't return rows (non-`SELECT` queries such as `DELETE`, `INSERT`, `REPLACE`, and `UPDATE`), `mysql_query()` returns `TRUE` or `FALSE` to indicate the success or failure of the query. For a successful query, you can call `mysql_affected_rows()` to find out how many rows were changed (deleted, inserted, replaced, or updated, as the case may be).

For `SELECT` statements, `mysql_query()` returns a result set identifier or `FALSE` to indicate the success or failure of the query. For a successful query, you use the result set identifier to obtain further information about the result set. For instance, you can find out how many rows or columns the result set has or fetch the rows contained within the set.

When `mysql_query()` returns `FALSE` (that is, zero), it means a query failed—in other words, some error occurred and the query couldn't even be executed. A query may fail for any number of reasons:

- It may be malformed and contain a syntax error.
- The query may be syntactically correct but be semantically meaningless, such as when you try to select a column from a table containing no such column.
- You may not have sufficient privileges to perform the query.
- The MySQL server host may have become unreachable due to network problems.

In each of these cases (and there are others), `mysql_query()` returns `FALSE`. If you want to know the particular reason for the error, call `mysql_error()` or `mysql_errno()` to obtain the error message string or numeric error code. (See "Handling Errors.")

Two of the most common mistakes made with `mysql_query()` are to think that the return value is a row count or that it contains the data returned by your query. Neither is true.

Handling Queries That Return No Result Set

The following code uses DELETE to illustrate how to process a query that does not return any rows:

```
$result = mysql_query ("DELETE FROM member WHERE member_id = 149");
if (!$result)
    print ("query failed\n");
else
    printf ("number of rows deleted: %d\n", mysql_affected_rows ());
```

If there is a member with an ID of 149, MySQL deletes the record and `mysql_query()` returns TRUE. What happens if there is no such member? In that case, `mysql_query()` still returns TRUE! This surprises people who labor under the misconception that the return value from `mysql_query()` is a row count. It isn't. The return value is TRUE in both cases because the query is legal regardless of whether or not it actually deletes any rows. The number of rows affected by the query is an entirely different thing. To get that value after a successful query, call `mysql_affected_rows()`.

Handling Queries That Return a Result Set

The following example provides a general outline of SELECT query processing:

```
$result = mysql_query ("SELECT * FROM member");
if (!$result)
    print ("query failed\n");
else
{
    printf ("number of rows returned: %d\n", mysql_num_rows ($result));
    while ($row = mysql_fetch_row ($result))
    {
        for ($i = 0; $i < mysql_num_fields ($result); $i++)
        {
            if ($i > 0)
                print (",");
            print ($row[$i]);
```

Don't Assume That `mysql_query()` Will Succeed

On the PHP mailing list, it's common for new PHP users to ask why the following error message occurs when executing a script:

```
Warning: 0 is not a MySQL result index in file on line n
```

This message indicates that a result set identifier value of zero was passed to some function (such as a row-fetching function) that expects a valid result set. This means that an earlier call to `mysql_query()` returned zero—that is, FALSE. In other words, `mysql_query()` failed and the script writer didn't bother to check the return value before using it with other functions. When you use `mysql_query()`, always test the return value.

```
        }
        print ("\n");
    }
    mysql_free_result ($result);
}
```

If the query fails, the result is FALSE, and we simply print a message to that effect. (Other responses to an error may be more appropriate, depending on the circumstances.) If the query succeeds, mysql_query() returns a result set identifier. This return value is useful in a number of ways (but *not* as a row count!). The result set identifier can be used for any of the following purposes:

- Pass it to mysql_num_rows() to determine the number of rows in the result set.
- Pass it to mysql_num_fields() to determine the number of columns in the result set.
- Pass it to a row-fetching routine to fetch successive rows of the result set. The example uses mysql_fetch_row(), but there are other choices, which we'll see shortly.
- Pass it to mysql_free_result() to free the result set and allow PHP to dispose of any resources associated with it.

PHP provides several row-fetching functions for retrieving a result set after mysql_query() successfully executes a SELECT query (see Table 8.1). Each of these functions takes a result set identifier as the argument and returns FALSE when there are no more rows.

Table 8.1 **PHP Row-Fetching Functions**

Function Name	Return Value
mysql_fetch_row()	An array; elements are accessed by numeric indices
mysql_fetch_array()	An array; elements are accessed by numeric or associative indices
mysql_fetch_object()	An object; elements are accessed as properties

The most basic call is mysql_fetch_row(), which returns the next row of the result set as an array. Elements of the array are accessed by numeric indices in the range from 0 to mysql_num_fields()−1. The following example shows how to use mysql_fetch_row() in a simple loop that fetches and prints the values in each row:

```
    $query = "SELECT * FROM president";
    $result = mysql_query ($query)
        or die ("Query failed");
    while ($row = mysql_fetch_row ($result))
    {
        for ($i = 0; $i < mysql_num_fields ($result); $i++)
```

continues

continued

```
        {
            if ($i > 0)
                print ("\t");
            print ($row[$i]);
        }
        print ("\n");
    }
```

The variable $row is an array. You access elements as $row[$i], where $i is the numeric column index. If you're familiar with the PHP count() function, you may be tempted to use it to determine the number of elements in each row rather than using mysql_num_fields()—don't do it. count() counts only the number of elements in the array that are set, and PHP doesn't set elements that correspond to NULL column values. count() is an unreliable measure of the number of columns returned because that's not what it is intended for. This applies to the other two row-fetching functions as well.

The second row-fetching function listed in Table 8.1, mysql_fetch_array(), is similar to mysql_fetch_row(), but elements of the array that it returns are available both by numeric index and associative index. In other words, you can access elements by number or by name:

```
        $query = "SELECT last_name, first_name FROM president";
        $result = mysql_query ($query)
            or die ("Query failed");
        while ($row = mysql_fetch_array ($result))
        {
            printf ("%s %s\n", $row[0], $row[1]);
            printf ("%s %s\n", $row["first_name"], $row["last_name"]);
        }
```

The information returned by mysql_fetch_array() is a superset of the information returned by mysql_fetch_row(). Despite that, the performance differences between the two functions are negligible, and you can call mysql_fetch_array() with no particular performance penalty.

The third row-fetching function, mysql_fetch_object(), returns the next row of the result set as an object. This means you access elements of the row using $row->*col_name* syntax. For example, if you retrieve the last_name and first_name values from the president table, you access those columns as $row->last_name and $row->first_name:

Testing for NULL values in Query Results

To check whether or not a column value returned from a SELECT query is NULL, use the isset() function. For example, if your row is contained in the $row array, isset($row[$i]) is FALSE if $row[$i] corresponds to a NULL value and TRUE if it is non-NULL. A related function is empty(), but empty() returns the same result for NULL that it does for empty strings, so it's not useful as a NULL value test.

```
$query = "SELECT last_name, first_name FROM president";
$result = mysql_query ($query)
    or die ("Query failed");
while ($row = mysql_fetch_object ($result))
    printf ("%s %s\n", $row->first_name, $row->last_name);
```

What if your query contains calculated columns? For example, you might issue a query that returns values that are calculated as the result of an expression:

```
SELECT CONCAT(first_name, " ", last_name) FROM president
```

A query that is written like that is unsuitable for use with `mysql_fetch_object()`. The name of the selected column is the expression itself, which isn't a legal property name. However, you can supply a legal name by giving the column an alias. The following query aliases the column as `full_name`, which allows it to be accessed as `$row->full_name` if you fetch the results with `mysql_fetch_object()`:

```
SELECT CONCAT(first_name, " ", last_name) AS full_name FROM president
```

Handling Errors

PHP puts three means at your disposal for dealing with errors:

- **Use '@' to suppress error messages.** You can use '@' with any function that might display a message. We've been doing this when we call `mysql_pconnect()` to prevent error messages from that function from appearing in the page sent to the client.

- **Use the `error_reporting()` function.** This function turns error reporting on or off at any of the following levels:

Error Level	Types of Errors Reported
1	Normal Function Errors
2	Normal Warnings
4	Parser Errors
8	Notices

To control error reporting, call the `error_reporting()` function with an argument equal to the sum of the levels you want enabled. Turning off level 1 and level 2 warnings should be sufficient to suppress messages from MySQL functions:

```
error_reporting (4 + 8);
```

You probably don't want to turn off level 4 warnings about parse errors; if you do, you may have a difficult time debugging any changes you make to your scripts! Level 8 warnings often can be ignored, but sometimes indicate a problem with your script that you should pay attention to, so you may want to leave that level enabled as well. There are also error levels of 16 and 32, but those come from the PHP core engine and not from functions, so normally you need not be concerned about them.

- **Use `mysql_error()` and `mysql_errno()`.** These functions report error information that is returned by the MySQL server. They are similar to the corresponding C API calls. `mysql_error()` returns an error message in string form (an empty string if no error occurred). `mysql_errno()` returns an error number (0 if no error occurred). Both functions take a link identifier argument specifying a connection to the MySQL server, and both return error information for the most recently invoked MySQL function on that connection that returns a status. The link identifier is optional; if it's missing, the most recently opened connection is used. For example, you could report an error from `mysql_query()` this way:

```
if (!($result = mysql_query ( ... )))
{
    print ("errno: " . mysql_errno());
    print ("error: " . mysql_error());
}
```

The PHP versions of the `mysql_error()` and `mysql_errno()` functions differ from their C API counterparts in one important respect. In C, you can get error information even when an attempt to connect to the server fails. By contrast, the PHP calls do not return useful information for a connection until the connection has been established successfully. In other words, if a connection attempt fails, you cannot use `mysql_error()` or `mysql_errno()` to report the reason why. If you want to report a specific reason for connection failure rather than some generic message, you must take special measures. See Appendix H, "PHP API Reference," for instructions on how to do this.

The scripts in this chapter print fairly generic error messages such as "query failed" as they detect an error. However, while you're developing a script, you'll often find it useful to add a call to `mysql_error()` to help you discover the particular reason for an error.

Quoting Issues

When you're constructing query strings in PHP, it's necessary to be aware of quoting issues, just as it is in C and in Perl. The way that quoting problems are dealt with is similar, too, although the function names are different in the various languages. Suppose you're constructing a query to insert a new record into a table; you might put quotes around a value to be inserted into a string column:

```
$last = "O'Malley";
$first = "Brian";
$expiration = "2002-9-1";
```

```
$query = "INSERT member (last_name,first_name,expiration)"
        . " VALUES('$last','$first','$expiration')"
```

The problem here is that one of the quoted values itself contains a quote
(`"O'Malley"`), which results in a syntax error if you send the query to the MySQL
server. To deal with this in C, we would call `mysql_escape_string()`. In a Perl DBI
script, we would use `quote()`. PHP has a function `addslashes()` that accomplishes
much the same thing. For example, a call to `addslashes ("O'Malley")` returns the
value `"O\'Malley"`. The previous example should be written as follows to prevent
quoting problems:

```
$last = addslashes ("O'Malley");
$first = addslashes ("Brian");
$expiration = addslashes ("2002-9-1");
$query = "INSERT member (last_name,first_name,expiration)"
        . " VALUES('$last','$first','$expiration')"
```

The DBI `quote()` method adds surrounding quotes to the string. `addslashes()` does
not, so we still need to specify those explicitly in the query string around the values to
be inserted.

Quoting issues also occur when writing information to be presented in Web pages.
If you're writing a string that should appear as HTML or as part of a URL, it's best to
encode it if the string may contain characters that are special within HTML or URLs.
The PHP functions `htmlspecialchars()` and `urlencode()` can be used for this.
They're similar to the CGI.pm `escapeHTML()` and `escape()` methods.

Putting PHP to Work

In the remaining part of this chapter, we'll tackle the goals we set for ourselves in
Chapter 1 that we have yet to accomplish:

- For the grade-keeping project, we need to write a script that allows us to enter
  and edit test and quiz scores.
- For the Historical League, we want to develop an online quiz about US presidents, and make it interactive so that the questions can be generated on the fly
  for visitors to the Web site.
- We also want to allow Historical League members to edit their directory entries
  online to keep the information up to date and reduce the amount of entry editing we do ourselves.

Each of these scripts generates multiple Web pages and communicates from one invocation of the script to the next by means of information embedded in the pages it creates. If you're not familiar with the concept of inter-page communication, you might
want to read the section "Writing Multiple-Purpose Pages" in Chapter 7.

Entering Student Scores

In this section, we'll turn our attention to the grade-keeping project. The URL for this area on our Web site is `http://pit-viper.snake.net/gp/`, and we should probably write a short home page `index.php` for it. The following page will do for now. It contains a link to the `score_browser` script that we wrote in Chapter 7 because that script pertains to the grade-keeping project:

```php
<?php
include ("samp_db.inc");

$title = "Grade-Keeping Project";
html_begin ($title, $title);
?>

<P>
<A HREF="/cgi-bin/score_browse">View</A> scores for quizzes and tests

<?php
html_end ();
?>
```

Now let's consider how to design and implement the script `score_entry.php`, which will let us enter a new set of test or quiz scores or edit an existing set of scores. The latter capability is necessary for handling scores of students who take a test or quiz later than the rest of the class due to absence for illness or other reason (or, perish the thought, in case we enter a score incorrectly). The outline for the score entry script is as follows:

1. The initial page presents a list of known grade events and allows you to choose one or to specify that a new event should be created.

2. If you choose to create a new event, the script presents a page that allows you to specify the date and type of event. After the event record is created, the script redisplays the event list page to show the new event.

3. When you choose an event, the script presents a score-entry page showing the event information at the top (event ID, date, type), followed by a list with one entry per student. For new events, the entries will be blank. For existing events, the entries will show each student's existing score. When you select the Submit button, the scores are entered into the `score` table.

The script needs to perform several different actions, which means that we'll need to pass a status variable around from page to page so that the script can tell what it's supposed to do each time it's invoked. It's easy to do this in PHP because PHP processes variables passed as URL parameters and converts them to variables with the same names as the parameters. For example, we can encode a parameter `action` at the end of our script's URL like this:

```
http://pit-viper.snake.net/gp/score_entry.php?action=value
```

When `score_entry.php` is invoked that way, the `action` parameter is encoded as the `$action` variable, which can be accessed directly. This works for fields in forms, too. Suppose a form contains fields called `name` and `address`. When a client submits the form, the Web server invokes a script to process the form's contents. The script can find out what values were entered into the form by checking the values of the `$name` and `$address` variables. For forms that contain a lot of fields, it can be inconvenient to give them all unique names. PHP makes it easy to pass arrays in and out of forms. If you use field names such as `x[0]`, `x[1]`, and so forth, PHP will encode them as elements of the `$x` array. You can access the elements as `$x[0]`, `$x[1]`, etc.

We'll communicate information from one invocation of the `score_entry.php` script to the next by using a parameter called `action` in our pages, and check its value using the `$action` variable in the script. The framework of the script looks like this:

```php
<?php
# score_entry.php - Score Entry script for grade-keeping project

include ("samp_db.inc");

# define action constants
define (INITIAL_PAGE, 0);
define (SOLICIT_EVENT, 1);
define (ADD_EVENT, 2);
define (DISPLAY_SCORES, 3);
define (ENTER_SCORES, 4);

/* ... put functions here ... */

$title = "Grade-Keeping Project — Score Entry";
html_begin ($title, $title);

samp_db_connect()
    or die ("Cannot connect to database server");

if (empty ($action))
    $action = INITIAL_PAGE;

switch ($action)        # what are we supposed to do?
{
case INITIAL_PAGE:      # present initial page
    display_events ();
    break;
case SOLICIT_EVENT:     # ask for new event information
    solicit_event_info ();
    break;
case ADD_EVENT:         # add new event to database
    add_new_event ();
    display_events ();
    break;
case DISPLAY_SCORES:    # display scores for selected event
    display_scores ();
```

continues

continued

```
        break;
    case ENTER_SCORES:       # enter new or edited scores
        enter_scores ();
        display_events ();
        break;
    default:
        die ("Unknown action code ($action)");
    }

    html_end ();
    ?>
```

The $action variable can take on several values, which we test in the switch() statement. (To avoid having to use literal numbers in the script, we use PHP's define() construct to define constants.) The PHP switch() statement is like its C counterpart. In score_entry.php, it's used to determine what action to take and to call the functions that implement the action.

Let's examine the functions that handle these actions one at a time. The first one, display_events(), retrieves rows of the event table from MySQL and displays them. Each row of the table lists the event ID, date, and event type (test or quiz), with the event ID written as a link that you can select to edit the scores for that event:

```
function display_events ()
{
global $PHP_SELF;

    print ("Select an event by clicking on its number,\n");
    print ("or select New Event to create a new grade event:<BR><BR>\n");
    $query = "SELECT event_id, date, type"
            . " FROM event"
            . " ORDER BY event_id";
    $result = mysql_query ($query)
        or die ("Cannot execute query");
    print ("<TABLE BORDER>\n");
    print ("<TR>\n");
    display_cell ("TH", "Event ID", 1);
    display_cell ("TH", "Date", 1);
    display_cell ("TH", "Type", 1);
    print ("</TR>\n");

    # associate each event id with a link that will show the
    # scores for the event; use mysql_fetch_array() so we
    # can refer to columns by name.
    while ($row = mysql_fetch_array ($result))
    {
        print ("<TR>\n");
        $url = sprintf ("%s?action=%d&event_id=%d",
                        $PHP_SELF, DISPLAY_SCORES, $row["event_id"]);
```

```
        display_cell ("TD",
                      "<A HREF=\"$url\">" . $row["event_id"] . "</A>",
                      0);
        display_cell ("TD", $row["date"], 1);
        display_cell ("TD", $row["type"], 1);
        print ("</TR>\n");
    }
    # add one more link for "new event"
    print ("<TR ALIGN=CENTER>\n");
    $url = sprintf ("%s?action=%d", $PHP_SELF, SOLICIT_EVENT);
    display_cell ("TD COLSPAN=3",
                  "<A HREF=\"$url\">" . "New Event" . "</A>",
                  0);
    print ("</TR>\n");

    print ("</TABLE>\n");
}
```

The links in the table are constructed using $PHP_SELF. This variable contains the
URL for the script itself, which provides a convenient way for the script to re-invoke
itself. However, notice the `global` line near the beginning of the function:

```
global $PHP_SELF;
```

In PHP functions, global variables are not accessible unless you explicitly declare that
you want to use them. Without the `global` line, $PHP_SELF would be treated as a local
variable (and because we don't assign it a value, it would be empty). It's also necessary
inside a function to use `global` to refer to parameters passed to your script by means
of URL parameters or as form fields.

The `display_cell()` function that is used to generate the table is similar to the
DBI function of the same name that we wrote in Chapter 7. The PHP version looks
like this:

```
function display_cell ($tag, $value, $encode)
{
    if ($encode)
        $value = htmlspecialchars ($value);
    if ($value == "")
        $value = " ";
    print ("<$tag>$value</$tag>\n");
}
```

If you select the "New Event" link in the table that `display_events()` presents, the
script is re-invoked with an action of SOLICIT_EVENT. That triggers a call to
`solicit_event_info()`, which displays a form that allows you to enter information
for the new event:

```
function solicit_event_info ()
{
global $PHP_SELF;
```

continues

continued

```
    printf ("<FORM METHOD=\"post\" ACTION=\"%s?action=%d\">\n",
                                    $PHP_SELF, ADD_EVENT);
    print ("Enter information for new grade event:<BR><BR>\n");
    print ("Date: <INPUT TYPE=text NAME=\"date\"");
    print (" VALUE=\"\" SIZE=10> ");
    print ("Type: ");
    print ("<INPUT TYPE=\"radio\" NAME=\"type\" VALUE=\"T\" CHECKED>Test\n");
    print ("<INPUT TYPE=\"radio\" NAME=\"type\" VALUE=\"Q\">Quiz\n");
    print ("<BR><BR>\n");
    print ("<INPUT TYPE=\"submit\" NAME=\"button\" VALUE=\"Submit\">\n");
    print ("</FORM>\n");
}
```

The form generated by solicit_event_info() contains an edit field for entering the data, a pair of radio buttons for specifying whether the new event is a test or a quiz, and a Submit button. When you submit the form, score_entry.php is invoked with an action of ADD_EVENT. The add_new_event() function is called to enter a new row in the event table:

```
function add_new_event ()
{
global $date, $type;

    if (empty ($date))  # make sure a date was entered
        die ("No date specified");
    $query = sprintf ("INSERT INTO event (date,type) VALUES(\"%s\",\"%s\")",
                    addslashes ($date), addslashes ($type));
    if (!mysql_query ($query))
        die ("Could not add event");
}
```

In add_new_event(), we use global to access the values of the fields that are used in the new-event entry form (date and type, accessible as the $date and $type variables). After a minimal safety check to make sure the date isn't blank, we enter a new record into the event table. The main program displays the event list again after entering the event record so that you can select the new event and begin entering scores.

The display_scores() function takes care of looking up any existing scores for a given event and displaying a form that shows them, together with student names:

```
function display_scores ()
{
global $PHP_SELF, $event_id;

    # select scores for the given event
    $query = "
        SELECT
            student.student_id, student.name, event.date,
            score.score AS score, event.type
        FROM student, event
            LEFT JOIN score ON student.student_id = score.student_id
                    AND event.event_id = score.event_id
```

```
        WHERE event.event_id = $event_id
        ORDER BY student.name
    ";
    $result = mysql_query ($query)
        or die ("Cannot execute query");

    printf ("<FORM METHOD=\"post\" ACTION=\"%s?action=%d&event_id=%d\">\n",
                          $PHP_SELF, ENTER_SCORES, $event_id);

    # print scores in a table, and print the event date and type
    # preceding the table. (however, we cannot print the date and
    # type until we've fetched the first row of the result set)

    $needheading = 1;
    while ($row = mysql_fetch_array ($result))
    {
        if ($needheading)
        {
            printf ("Event ID: %s, Event date: %s, Event type: %s\n",
                          $event_id, $row["date"], $row["type"]);
            print ("<BR><BR>\n");
            print ("<TABLE BORDER>\n");
            print ("<TR>\n");
            display_cell ("TH", "Name", 1);
            display_cell ("TH", "Score", 1);
            print "</TR>\n";
            $needheading = 0;
        }
        print ("<TR>\n");
        display_cell ("TD", $row["name"], 1);
        $col_val =
            sprintf ("<INPUT TYPE=text NAME=\"score[%s]\"",
                                      $row["student_id"]);
        $col_val .=
            sprintf (" VALUE=\"%s\" SIZE=5><BR>\n",
                                      $row["score"]);
        display_cell ("TD", $col_val, 0);
        print ("</TR>\n");
    }

    print ("</TABLE>\n");
    print ("<BR>\n");
    print ("<INPUT TYPE=\"submit\" NAME=\"button\" VALUE=\"Submit\">\n");
    print "</FORM>\n";
}
```

The query that `display_scores()` uses to retrieve score information for the selected event is not just a simple join between tables because that won't select a row for any student who has no score for the event. In particular, for a new event, the join would select no records, and we'd have an empty entry form! We want to use a LEFT JOIN to force a row to be retrieved for each student, whether or not the student already has a score in the `score` table. The background for a query similar to the one that `display_scores()` uses to retrieve score records from MySQL was given in Chapter 3, "MySQL SQL Syntax and Use," in the section "Checking for Values Not Present in a Table." The query there selected only missing scores; here we select only scores for a particular event.

The scores are encoded in the form using fields with names like `score[n]`, where *n* is a `student_id` value. When the form is sent back to the Web server, PHP will convert these fields into elements of the `$score` array, and we can access elements of the array to recover the contents of the form.

When you finish entering or editing scores and submit the form, `score_entry.php` is invoked with the `ENTER_SCORES` action, and the `enter_scores()` function is called to process the form information:

```
function enter_scores ()
{
global $score, $event_id;

    $invalid = 0;
    $blank = 0;
    $nonblank = 0;
    while (list ($student_id, $newscore) = each ($score))
    {
        $newscore = trim ($newscore);
        if (empty ($newscore))  # no score, delete if present in table
        {
            ++$blank;
            $query = "DELETE FROM score"
                . " WHERE event_id = $event_id"
                . " AND student_id = $student_id";
        }
        else if (ereg ("^[0-9]+$", $newscore))  # must be integer
        {
            ++$nonblank;
            $query = "REPLACE INTO score (event_id,student_id,score)"
                . " VALUES($event_id,$student_id,$newscore)";
        }
        else
        {
            ++$invalid;
            continue;
        }
        if (!mysql_query ($query))
            die ("score entry failed, event_id $event_id, student_id
$student_id");
    }
    printf ("Scores entered: %d<BR>\n", $nonblank);
    printf ("Scores missing: %d<BR>\n", $blank);
```

```
    printf ("Invalid scores: %d<BR>\n", $invalid);
    print ("<BR>\n");
}
```

The student ID values and associated scores are obtained by iterating through the $score array with PHP's each function. Each score is processed as follows:

- If the score is blank, there is nothing to be entered, but we try to delete the score in case it existed before. (Perhaps we mistakenly entered a score earlier for a student who actually was absent.)

- If the score is not blank, we perform some rudimentary validation of the value. After stripping off leading and trailing whitespace using the trim() function, we accept the result if what remains is blank or an integer. However, form values are always encoded as strings, so we can't check whether or not a value is an integer by using is_long() or is_int(). Those functions would return FALSE, even if the value contained only digits. In this case, a pattern match works better. The following test is TRUE if every character from the beginning to the end of the string is a digit:

```
    ereg ("^[0-9]+$", $str)
```

If the score is okay, we add it to the score table. The query uses REPLACE rather than INSERT because we may be replacing an existing score rather than entering a new one. (REPLACE will work in either case.)

That takes care of the score_entry.php script. All score entry and editing can be done from your Web browser now. One obvious shortcoming is that the script provides no security; anyone who can connect to the Web server can edit scores. The script that we'll write later for Historical League member entry editing shows a simple authentication scheme that could be adapted for this script. You could also use the PHPLIB package to provide more sophisticated authentication.

US President Quiz

One of the goals for the Historical League Web site was to use it to present an online version of a quiz, similar to some of the quizzes that the League publishes in the children's section of its newsletter, "Chronicles of US Past." We created the president table, in fact, so that we could use it as a source of questions for a history-based quiz. To present this quiz, we'll write a script called pres_quiz.php.

The basic idea is to pick a president at random, ask a question about him, and then solicit an answer from the user and see whether or not the answer is correct. To keep it simple, we'll confine the topic to asking where a president was born. Another simplifying measure is to present the questions in multiple-choice format. That's easier for the user, who need only pick from among a set of choices, rather than typing in a response. It's also easier for us because we don't have to do any tricky string matching to check whatever the user might have typed in. We need only a simple comparison of the user's choice and the value that we're looking for.

A script that presents this quiz must perform two functions. First, for its initial invocation, it should generate and display a new question by looking up information from the `president` table. Second, if the script has been called because the user is submitting a response, the response needs to be checked and some feedback needs to be given to indicate whether or not it was correct. If so, the script should generate and display a new question. If the response was incorrect, the same question should be redisplayed.

To generate the questions, we'll use one of the features that appeared in MySQL 3.23, `ORDER BY RAND()`. Using this function, we can select rows randomly from the `president` table. For example, to pick a president name and birthplace randomly, this query does the job:

```
SELECT CONCAT(first_name, ' ', last_name) AS name,
    CONCAT(city, ', ', state) AS place
    FROM president ORDER BY RAND() LIMIT 1
```

The name will be the selected president, and the birthplace will be the correct answer to the question, "Where was this president born?" We'll also need to present some incorrect choices, which we can select using a similar query:

```
SELECT DISTINCT CONCAT(city, ', ', state) AS place
    FROM president ORDER BY RAND()
```

From the result of this query, we'll select the first four values that differ from the correct response. The function that issues these queries and retrieves the results looks like this:

```
function setup_quiz ()
{
    # issue query to pick a president and get birthplace
    $query = "SELECT CONCAT(first_name, ' ', last_name) AS name,"
        . " CONCAT(city, ', ', state) AS place"
        . " FROM president ORDER BY RAND() LIMIT 1";
    $result = mysql_query ($query)
        or die ("Cannot execute query");
    $row = mysql_fetch_array ($result)
        or die ("Cannot fetch result");
    $name = $row["name"];
    $place = $row["place"];

    # Construct the set of birthplace choices to present.
    # Set up the $choice array containing five birthplaces, one
    # of which is the correct response.
    $query = "SELECT DISTINCT CONCAT(city, ', ', state) AS place"
        . " FROM president ORDER BY RAND()";
    $result = mysql_query ($query)
        or die ("Cannot execute query");
    $choice[] = $place; # initialize array with correct choice
    while (count ($choice) < 5 && $row = mysql_fetch_array ($result))
```

```
    {
        if ($row["place"] == $place)
            continue;
        $choice[] = $row["place"];  # add another choice
    }
    # randomize choices, then display form
    shuffle ($choice);
    display_form ($name, $place, $choice);
}
```

To present the quiz question information, we use a form that displays the name of the president, a set of radio buttons that lists the possible choices, and a Submit button. This form needs to do two things: It must present the quiz information to the client, and it must transmit that information back to the Web server when the user submits a response so that we can check whether or not the response is correct.

To arrange for the form to take these actions, we include the quiz information in the form using several hidden fields. We'll call the fields name, place, and choice to represent the president's name and birthplace and the set of possible choices. The choices can be encoded as a single string easily by using implode() to concatenate the values together with a special character. (We need the special character so that we can break apart the string later with explode() if we have to redisplay the question.) The form-display function looks like this:

```
function display_form ($name, $place, $choice)
{
global $PHP_SELF;

    printf ("<FORM METHOD=\"post\" ACTION=\"%s\">\n", $PHP_SELF);
    hidden_field ("name", $name);
    hidden_field ("place", $place);
    hidden_field ("choice", implode ("#", $choice));
    printf ("Where was %s born?<BR><BR>\n", $name);
    for ($i = 0; $i < 5; $i++)
    {
        print ("<INPUT TYPE=\"radio\" NAME=\"response\"\n");
        printf ("VALUE=\"%s\">%s<BR>\n", $choice[$i], $choice [$i]);
    }
    print ("<BR><INPUT TYPE=\"Submit\" VALUE=\"Submit\">\n");
    print ("</FORM>\n");
}
```

The hidden_field() function writes HTML for a hidden field in the form:

```
function hidden_field ($name, $value)
{
    printf ("<INPUT TYPE=\"HIDDEN\" NAME=\"%s\" VALUE=\"%s\">\n",
                                            $name, $value);
}
```

When the user makes a choice and submits the form, the response is encoded as the value of the response field in the form contents that are sent back to the Web server. We can discover the values of the name, place, choice, and response fields by checking the $name, $place, $choice, and $response variables. That also gives us a way to figure out whether the script is being called for the first time or whether the user is submitting a response to a previously displayed form: None of those variables will be set if this is a first-time invocation. Thus, the main body of the script determines what it should do by checking one of these variables:

```
if (!$name)          # called for first time
    setup_quiz ();
else                 # user submitted response to form
    check_response ();
```

We still need to write the check_response() function that compares the user's response to the correct answer. We encoded the correct answer in the place field of the form, and the user's response will be in the response field, so all we need to do is compare $place to $response. Based on the result of the comparison, we provide some feedback and then either generate and display a new question or redisplay the same question:

```
function check_response ()
{
global $name, $place, $choice;
global $response;

    if ($place == $response) # correct response; generate new question
    {
        print ("That is Correct!<BR>\n");
        printf ("%s was born in %s.<BR>\n", $name, $place);
        print ("Try the next question:<BR><BR>\n");
        setup_quiz();
    }
    else                          # incorrect response; redisplay question
    {
        print ("That is not correct.  Please try again.<BR><BR>\n");
        $choice = explode ("#", $choice);
        display_form ($name, $place, $choice);
    }
}
```

We're done. Add a link for pres_quiz.php to the Historical League home page, and visitors can try out the quiz to test their knowledge.

Historical League Online Member Entry Editing

Our final script, edit_member.php, will allow the Historical League members to edit their own entries online. Then members can correct or update their membership information whenever they want without having to contact the league office to submit the changes. Providing this capability should help keep the member directory more up to date, and, not incidentally, reduce the workload of the League secretary.

One precaution we need to take is to prevent entries from being modified by anyone but the member the entry is for. This means we need some form of security. As a
demonstration of a simple form of authentication, we'll use MySQL to store passwords
for each member and require that a member supply the correct password to gain
access to the editing form that our script presents. The script works as follows:

- When initially invoked, `edit_script.php` presents a form containing fields for
  the member ID and a password.
- When the initial form is submitted, the script looks in the password table using
  the member ID as a key to find the associated password. If the password
  matches, the script looks up the member entry from the `member` table and displays it for editing.
- When the edited form is submitted, we update the entry using the contents of
  the form.

The framework for `edit_member.php` is as follows:

```php
<?php
# edit_member.php - Edit Historical League member entries via the Web

include ("samp_db.inc");

# define action constants
define (INITIAL_PAGE, 0);
define (DISPLAY_ENTRY, 1);
define (UPDATE_ENTRY, 2);

/* ... put functions here ... */

if (empty ($action))
    $action = INITIAL_PAGE;

$title = "US Historical League — Member Editing Form";
html_begin ($title, $title);

samp_db_connect ()
    or die ("Cannot connect to server");

switch ($action)
{
case INITIAL_PAGE:
    solicit_member_id ();
    break;
case DISPLAY_ENTRY:
    display_entry ();
    break;
case UPDATE_ENTRY:
    update_entry ();
    break;
```

continues

continued

```
default:
    die ("Unknown action code ($action)");
}

html_end ();
?>
```

The initial page presents a form to solicit the member ID and password:

```
function solicit_member_id ()
{
global $PHP_SELF;

    printf ("<FORM METHOD=\"post\" ACTION=\"%s?action=%d\">\n",
                            $PHP_SELF, DISPLAY_ENTRY);
    print ("Enter your membership ID number and password,\n");
    print ("then select Submit.\n<BR><BR>\n");
    print ("<TABLE>\n");
    print ("<TR>");
    print ("<TD>Member ID</TD><TD>");
    print ("<INPUT TYPE=text NAME=\"member_id\" SIZE=10><BR>\n");
    print ("</TD></TR>");
    print ("<TR>");
    print ("<TD>Password</TD><TD>");
    print ("<INPUT TYPE=password NAME=\"password\" SIZE=10><BR>\n");
    print ("</TD></TR>");
    print ("</TABLE>\n");
    print ("<INPUT TYPE=\"submit\" NAME=\"button\" VALUE=\"Submit\">\n");
    print "</FORM>\n";
}
```

We'll need some passwords, of course. An easy way to do this is to generate them randomly. The following statements set up a table `member_pass`, then create a password for each member by generating an MD5 checksum from a random number. It's more likely that you'd let members pick their own passwords, but you can invoke `mysql` and issue these statements as a quick and easy way to set something up:

```
CREATE TABLE member_pass
(
    member_id INT UNSIGNED NOT NULL PRIMARY KEY,
    password CHAR(8)
)
INSERT INTO member_pass (member_id, password)
    SELECT
        member_id,
        LEFT(MD5(RAND()), 8) AS password
    FROM member
```

We'll also add a special entry to this table for member 0, with a password that will serve as the administrative (superuser) password. We can use this password to get access to any entry we like:

```
INSERT INTO member_pass (member_id, password) VALUES(0, "secret");
```

After you create the password table, you might want to disable the `samp_browse` script that we wrote in Chapter 7, which allows anyone to browse the contents of any table in the `samp_db` database—including the `member_pass` table.

When a member enters an ID and password and submits the form, `edit_member.php` displays the entry for editing:

```
function display_entry ()
{
global $PHP_SELF;
global $member_id, $password;

    $member_id = trim ($member_id);
    if (empty ($member_id))
        die ("No member ID specified");
    if (!ereg ("^[0-9]+$", $member_id)) # must be integer
        die ("Invalid member ID specified (must be number)");
    if (empty ($password))
        die ("No password specified");
    if (check_pass ($member_id, $password)) # regular member
        $admin = 0;
    else if (check_pass (0, $password))      # administrator
        $admin = 1;
    else
        die ("Invalid password");

    $query = "SELECT last_name, first_name, suffix, email,"
        . "street, city, state, zip, phone, interests,"
        . "member_id, expiration"
        . " FROM member"
        . " WHERE member_id = $member_id"
        . " ORDER BY last_name";
    $result = mysql_query ($query)
        or die ("Cannot execute query");
    if (mysql_num_rows ($result) == 0)
        die ("No user with member_id = $member_id found");
    if (mysql_num_rows ($result) > 1)
        die ("More than one user with member_id = $member_id found");

    printf ("<FORM METHOD=\"post\" ACTION=\"%s?action=%d\">\n",
                            $PHP_SELF, UPDATE_ENTRY);
    hidden_field ("member_id", $member_id);
    hidden_field ("password", $password);
    print ("<TABLE>\n");
    # read results of query and format for editing
    $row = mysql_fetch_array ($result);
    display_column ("Member ID", $row, "member_id", 0);
    # allow user with admin password to edit expiration
    display_column ("Expiration", $row, "expiration", $admin);
    display_column ("Last name", $row, "last_name", 1);
    display_column ("First name", $row, "first_name", 1);
    display_column ("Suffix", $row, "suffix", 1);
```

continues

continued

```
        display_column ("Email", $row, "email", 1);
        display_column ("Street", $row, "street", 1);
        display_column ("City", $row, "city", 1);
        display_column ("State", $row, "state", 1);
        display_column ("Zip", $row, "zip", 1);
        display_column ("Phone", $row, "phone", 1);
        display_column ("Interests", $row, "interests", 1);
        print ("</TABLE>\n");
        print ("<INPUT TYPE=\"submit\" NAME=\"button\" VALUE=\"Submit\">\n");
        print "</FORM>\n";

    }
```

The first thing that `display_entry()` needs to do is verify the password. If the password entered in the form matches the password stored in the `member_pass` table for the given member ID, or if it matches the administrative password (that is, the password for member 0), `edit_member.php` displays the entry for editing. The password-checking function `check_pass()` runs a simple query to yank a record from the `member_pass` table:

```
function check_pass ($id, $pass)
{
    $query = "SELECT password FROM member_pass WHERE member_id = $id";
    if (!($result = mysql_query ($query)))
        die ("Error reading password table");
    if (!($row = mysql_fetch_array ($result)))
        return (FALSE);
    return ($row["password"] == $pass); # TRUE if password matches
}
```

The editing form displays the member ID value as read-only text because it shouldn't be changed. For normal members, the expiration date is also displayed as read-only text because we don't want members changing it. However, if the administrative password were given, the expiration date would be made editable, allowing the League secretary to update the date for members renewing their memberships.

Columns from the `member` table entry are displayed by the `display_column()` function. It adds columns to the editing form as editable text or as read-only text according to the value of its third argument:

```
# Display a column of a member entry.  $label is the visible label
# displayed to the user.  $row is the array containing the entry.
# $col_name is the name of a column in the entry.  $value is the
# column value.  $editable is non-zero if the user is allowed to
# change the value.  The value is displayed as non-editable text
# otherwise.  Field names are constructed as row[col_name] so that
# when the form is submitted, values can be accessed using an array
# rather than a bunch of individual variables.

function display_column ($label, $row, $col_name, $editable)
{
    print ("<TR>\n");
```

```
    printf ("<TD>%s</TD>\n", htmlspecialchars ($label));
    $value = htmlspecialchars ($row[$col_name]);
    if ($editable)  # display as edit field
    {
        $str = sprintf ("<INPUT TYPE=text NAME=\"row[%s]\"", $col_name);
        $str .= sprintf (" VALUE=\"%s\" SIZE=\"80\">\n", $value);
    }
    else            # display as read-only text
        $str = $value;
    printf ("<TD>%s</TD>\n", $str);
    print ("</TR>\n");
}
```

The display_entry() function embeds the member_id and password values as hidden fields in the form so that they will carry over to the next invocation of edit_script.php when the member submits the edited entry. This allows the password for the ID to be verified automatically without asking the member to enter it again. (Notice that our simple authentication method involves passing the password back and forth in clear text. In general, this isn't a great idea, but the Historical League is not a high-security operation, and this method suffices for our purposes. You'd probably want something stronger if you were performing financial transactions, for example.)

The function that updates the entry looks like this:

```
function update_entry ()
{
global $row, $member_id, $password;

    $member_id = trim ($member_id);
    if (empty ($member_id))
        die ("No member ID specified");
    if (!ereg ("^[0-9]+$", $member_id)) # must be integer
        die ("Invalid member ID specified (must be number)");
    if (!check_pass ($member_id, $password) && !check_pass (0, $password))
        die ("Invalid password");

    # We'll need a result set to use for assessing nullability of
    # member table columns.  This query gives us one without
    # selecting any rows.
    $result = mysql_query ("SELECT * FROM member WHERE 1 = 0");
    if (!$result)
        die ("Cannot query member table");

    # iterate through each field in the form, using the values to
    # construct the UPDATE statement.

    $query = "UPDATE member ";
    $delim = "SET "; # put "SET" before first column, "," before others
    while (list ($col_name, $val) = each ($row))
    {
        $query .= "$delim $col_name =";
        $delim = ",";
```

continues

continued

```
                    # if a value is empty, update the value with NULL if the
                    # column is nullable.  This prevents trying to put an
                    # empty string in the expiration when it should be NULL,
                    # for example.
                    $val = trim ($val);
                    if (empty ($val))
                    {
                        if (nullable ($result, $col_name))
                            $query .= "NULL";    # enter NULL
                        else
                            $query .= "\"\"";    # enter empty string
                    }
                    else
                        $query .= "\"" . addslashes ($val) . "\"";
                }
                $query .= " WHERE member_id = $member_id";
                if (mysql_query ($query) && mysql_affected_rows () > 0)
                    print ("Entry updated successfully.\n");
                else
                    print ("Entry not updated.\n");
            }
```

First we re-verify the password to make sure someone isn't attempting to hoax us by
sending a faked form, then the entry is updated. The update requires some care
because if a field in the form is blank, it may need to be entered as NULL rather than as
an empty string. The expiration column is an example of this. A NULL membership
expiration date has the special meaning of "lifetime membership." If we insert an
empty string into this column, the value will be converted to "0000-00-00", and the
member will no longer have a lifetime membership.

To handle this problem, we look up the metadata for the column and check
whether it's declared as NULL or NOT NULL. This information is returned by the
mysql_fetch_field() function; unfortunately, that function looks up columns by
numeric index. It's more convenient to refer to columns in the member table by name,
so we'll write a little function nullable(), which takes a column name and finds the
appropriate metadata object:

```
    # Determine whether or not the column with the given name in
    # the result set is nullable.

    function nullable ($result, $col_name)
    {
        for ($i = 0; $i < mysql_num_fields ($result); $i++)
        {
            if (!($fld = mysql_fetch_field ($result, $i)))
                continue;
            if ($fld->name == $col_name)
                return (!$fld->not_null);
        }
        return (0);
    }
```

The `mysql_fetch_field()` function requires a result set identifier for the table whose columns we're checking. We get that by executing a trivial SELECT query that returns no rows. The query returns an empty result set, but it's a sufficient means of retrieving the metadata that we need for assessing the nullability of the `member` table columns:

```
SELECT * FROM member WHERE 1 = 0
```

That's it. Install the script, let the members know their passwords, and they can update their own membership information.

MySQL Administration

9

Introduction to MySQL Administration

AS DATABASE SYSTEMS GO, MySQL IS RELATIVELY simple to use, and the effort required to bring up a MySQL installation and use it is low as well. MySQL's simplicity probably accounts for much of its popularity, especially among people who aren't, and don't want to be, programmers. It helps to be a trained computer professional, of course, but that's certainly not a requirement for running a successful MySQL installation.

Nevertheless, a MySQL installation won't run itself, regardless of your level of expertise. Someone must watch over it to make sure it operates smoothly and efficiently, and someone must know what to do when problems occur. If the job falls on you to make sure MySQL is happy at your site, keep reading.

In Part II of this book, we'll examine the various aspects of MySQL administration. This chapter provides an overview of what you should know about the responsibilities that are involved in administrating a MySQL installation. It provides a brief description of these responsibilities, and the following chapters provide instructions for carrying them out.

If you are a new or inexperienced MySQL administrator, don't let the long list of responsibilities presented in this chapter scare you. Each task listed in the following sections is important, but you need not learn them all at once. If you like, you can use the chapters in this part of the book as a reference, looking up topics as you discover that you need to know about them.

If you have experience administrating other database systems, you will find that running a MySQL installation is similar in some ways and that your experience is a valuable resource. But MySQL administration has its own unique requirements; this part of the book will help you become familiar with them.

Overview of Administrative Duties

The MySQL database system consists of several components. You should be familiar with what these components are and the purpose of each. This allows you to understand both the nature of the system you're administrating and the tools available to help you do your job. If you take the time to understand what you're overseeing, your work will be much easier. To that end, you should acquaint yourself with the following aspects of MySQL:

- **The MySQL server.** The server `mysqld` performs all manipulation of databases and tables. `safe_mysqld` is a related program used to start up the server, monitor it, and restart it in case it goes down.

- **The MySQL clients and utilities.** Several MySQL programs are available to help you communicate with the server and to perform administrative tasks. The most important of these are:

  - `mysql`, an interactive program that allows you to issue SQL statements to the server and to view the results.

  - `mysqladmin`, an administrative program that lets you perform tasks such as shutting down the server and creating or dropping databases. You can also use `mysqladmin` to check the server's status if it appears not to be functioning properly.

  - `isamchk` and `myisamchk`, utilities that help you perform table analysis and optimization, as well as crash recovery if tables become damaged.

  - `mysqldump`, a tool for backing up your databases or copying databases to another server.

- **The server's language, SQL.** Some administrative duties can be performed using only the `mysqladmin` command-line utility, but you're better off if you can also talk to the server in its own language. As a simple example, you may need to find out why a user's privileges aren't working the way you expected them to work. There is no substitute for being able to go in and communicate with the server directly. You can do this by using the `mysql` client program to issue SQL queries that let you examine the grant tables. And if your version of MySQL predates the introduction of the `GRANT` statement, you'll need to use `mysql` to set up each user's privileges in the first place.

  If you don't know any SQL, be sure to acquire at least a basic understanding of it. A lack of SQL fluency will only hinder you, whereas the time you take to learn will be repaid many times over. A real mastery of SQL takes some time, but the basic skills can be attained quickly. If you need some instruction in SQL or the use of the `mysql` command-line client, see Chapter 1, "Introduction to MySQL and SQL."

- **The MySQL data directory.** The data directory is where the server stores its databases and status files. It's important to understand the structure and contents of the data directory so that you know how the server uses the file system to represent databases and tables, as well as where files such as the logs are located and what's in them. You should also know your options for managing allocation of disk space across file systems should you find that the file system on which the data directory is located is becoming too full.

General Administration

General administration deals primarily with the operation of `mysqld`, the MySQL server, and in providing your users with access to the server. In carrying out this responsibility, the following duties are the most important:

- **Server startup and shutdown.** You should be able to start and stop the server manually from the command line and know how to arrange for automatic startup and shutdown when your system starts up and shuts down. It's also important to know what to do to get the server going again if it crashes or will not start properly.

- **User account maintenance.** You should understand the difference between MySQL users and UNIX or Windows users. You should know how to set up MySQL user accounts by specifying which users can connect to the server and where they can connect from. New users should also be advised on the proper connection parameters that they will need to use to connect to the server successfully. It's not their job to figure out how you've set up their accounts!

- **Log file maintenance.** You should understand what types of log files you can maintain, as well as when and how to perform log file maintenance. Log rotation and expiration are essential to prevent the logs from filling up your file system.

- **Database backup and copying.** Database backups are of crucial importance in the event of a severe system crash. You want to be able to restore your databases to the state they were in at the time of the crash with as little data loss as possible. Note that backing up your databases is not the same thing as performing general system backups, as is done, for example, by using the UNIX `dump` program. The files corresponding to your database tables may be in flux due to server activity when system backups take place, so restoring those files will not give you internally consistent tables. The `mysqldump` program generates backup files that are more useful for database restoration, and it allows you to create backups without taking down the server.

If you decide to run a database on a faster host, or you want to replicate it, you'll need to copy its contents to a different machine. You should understand the procedure for doing this, should the need arise. Database files may be system dependent, so you can't necessarily just copy the files.

- **Server tuning.** Your users want the server to perform at its best. The quick-and-dirty method for improving how well your server runs is to buy more memory or to get faster disks. But those brute-force techniques are no substitute for understanding how the server works. You should know what parameters are available for tuning the server's operation and how they apply to your situation. At some sites, queries tend to be mostly retrievals. At others, inserts and updates dominate. The choice of which parameters to change will be influenced by the query mix that you observe at your own site.

- **Multiple servers.** It's useful to run multiple servers under some circumstances. You can test a new MySQL release while leaving your current production installation in place, or provide better privacy for different groups of users. (The latter scenario is particularly relevant to ISPs.) For such situations, you should know how to set up multiple simultaneous installations.

- **MySQL updates.** New MySQL releases appear frequently. You should know how to keep up to date with these releases to take advantage of bug fixes and new features. Understand the circumstances under which it's more reasonable to hold off on upgrading, and know how to choose between the stable and development releases.

Security

When you run a MySQL installation, it's important to make sure that the data your users are storing is kept secure. The MySQL administrator is responsible for controlling access to the data directory and the server, and should understand the following issues:

- **File system security.** A UNIX machine may host several user accounts that have no MySQL-related administrative duties. It's important to ensure that these accounts have no access to the data directory. This prevents them from compromising data on a file system level by copying database tables or removing them, or by being able to read log files that may contain sensitive information. You should know how to set up a UNIX user account for the MySQL server, how to set up the data directory so that it is owned by that user, and how to start up the server to run with that user's privileges.

- **Server security.** You must understand how the MySQL security system works so that when you set up user accounts, you grant the proper privileges. Users connecting to the server over the network should have permission to do only what they are supposed to be able to do. You don't want to inadvertently grant superuser access to anonymous users due to faulty understanding of the security system!

Database Repair and Maintenance

Every MySQL administrator hopes to avoid having to deal with corrupted or destroyed database tables. But just hoping won't keep problems from occurring. There are steps you can take to minimize your risks and learn what to do if bad things do happen:

- **Crash recovery.** Should disaster strike in spite of your best efforts, you should know how to repair or restore your tables. Crash recovery should be necessary only rarely, but when it is, it's an unpleasant, high-stress business (especially with the phone ringing and people knocking on the door while you're scrambling to fix things). Nevertheless, you must know how to do it because your users will be quite unhappy otherwise! Be familiar with the table-checking and repair capabilities of isamchk and myisamchk. Know how to recover as well as possible from your backup files and how to use the update logs to recover changes that were made after your most recent backup.

- **Preventive Maintenance.** A regular program of preventive maintenance should be put in place to minimize the likelihood of database corruption or damage. You should also be making backups, of course, but preventive maintenance reduces the chance that you'll need to use them.

The preceding outline summarizes the responsibilities you undertake by becoming a MySQL administrator. The next few chapters discuss them in more detail and provide procedures to follow so that you can carry out these responsibilities effectively. We'll discuss the MySQL data directory first; that's the resource you're maintaining and you should understand its layout and contents. From there we move on to general administrative duties, a discussion of MySQL's security system, and maintenance and troubleshooting

10

The MySQL Data Directory

CONCEPTUALLY, MOST RELATIONAL DATABASE systems are similar: They are each made up of a set of databases, and each database includes a set of tables. But every system has its own way of organizing the data it manages, and MySQL is no exception.

By default, all data managed by the MySQL server mysqld is stored under a location called the MySQL data directory. All databases are stored here, as well as the status files that provide information about the server's operation. You should be familiar with the layout and use of the data directory if you perform any administrative duties for a MySQL installation.

This chapter covers the following topics:

- **How to determine the location of the data directory.** You need to know this so that you can administer its contents effectively.

- **How the server organizes and provides access to the databases and tables it manages.** This is important for setting up preventive maintenance schedules, and for performing crash recovery should table corruption ever occur.

- **Where to find the status files generated by the server and what they contain.** Their contents provide useful information about how the server is running, which is useful if you encounter problems.

- **How to change the default placement or organization of the data directory or individual databases.** This can be important for managing the allocation of disk resources on your system—for example, by balancing disk activity across drives or by relocating data to file systems with more free space. You can also use this knowledge in planning placement of new databases.

You can benefit from reading this chapter even if you don't perform any MySQL administration; it never hurts to have a better idea of how the server operates.

Location of the Data Directory

A default data directory location is compiled into the server. Typical defaults are /usr/local/var if you install MySQL from a source distribution, /usr/local/mysql/data if you install from a binary distribution, and /var/lib/mysql if you install from an RPM file.

The data directory location may be specified explicitly when you start up the server by using a --datadir=/path/to/dir option. This is useful if you want to place the data directory somewhere other than its default location.

As a MySQL administrator, you should know where your data directory is. If you run multiple servers, you should know where all the data directories are. But if you don't know the location (perhaps you are taking over for a previous administrator who left poor notes), there are several ways to find out:

- **Use mysqladmin variables to get the data directory pathname directly from your server.** On UNIX, the output looks like this:

```
% mysqladmin variables
+------------------------------+------------------------------+
| Variable_name                | Value                        |
+------------------------------+------------------------------+
| back_log                     | 5                            |
| connect_timeout              | 5                            |
| basedir                      | /var/local/                  |
| datadir                      | /usr/local/var/              |
...
```

This output indicates a data directory location of /usr/local/var on the server host.

On Windows, the output might look like this instead:

```
C:\> mysqladmin variables
+------------------------------+------------------------------+
| Variable_name                | Value                        |
+------------------------------+------------------------------+
| back_log                     | 5                            |
| connect_timeout              | 5                            |
| basedir                      | c:\mysql\                    |
| datadir                      | c:\mysql\data\               |
...
```

If you have multiple servers running, they will be listening on different TCP/IP port numbers or sockets. You can get data directory information from each of them in turn by supplying appropriate `--port` or `--socket` options to connect to the port or socket on which each server is listening:

```
% mysqladmin --port=port_num variables
% mysqladmin --socket=/path/to/socket variables
```

The mysqladmin command can be run on any host from which you can connect to the server. Use a `--host=host_name` option if you need to connect to a server on a remote host:

```
% mysqladmin --host=host_name variables
```

On Windows, you can contact a Windows NT server that is listening on a named pipe by using `--pipe` to force a named pipe connection and `--socket=pipe_name` to specify the pipe name:

```
C:\> mysqladmin --pipe --socket=pipe_name variables
```

- **You can use ps to see the command line of any currently executing mysqld process.** Try one of the following commands (depending on which version of ps your system supports) and look for `--datadir` in the commands that are shown in the output:

`% ps axww | grep mysqld`	BSD-style ps
`% ps -ef | grep mysqld`	System V-style ps

  The `ps` command can be especially useful if your system runs multiple servers because you can discover multiple data directory locations at once. The drawbacks are that ps must be run on the server host and that no useful information is produced unless the `--datadir` option was specified explicitly on the mysqld command line.

- **If MySQL was installed from a source distribution, you can examine its configuration information to determine the data directory location.** For example, the location is available in the top-level Makefile. But be careful: The location is the value of the localstatedir variable in the Makefile, not datadir, as you might expect. Also, if the distribution is located on an NFS-mounted file system and is used to build MySQL for several hosts, the configuration information reflects the host on which the distribution was most recently built. That may not show you the data directory for the host in which you're interested.

- **Failing any of the previous methods, you can use find to search for database files.** The following command searches for .frm (description) files, which are part of any MySQL installation:

```
% find / -name "*.frm" -print
```

In the examples that follow throughout this chapter, I denote the location of the MySQL data directory as DATADIR. You should interpret that as the location of the data directory on your own machine.

Structure of the Data Directory

The MySQL data directory contains all of the databases and tables managed by the server. These are organized into a tree structure that is implemented in straightforward fashion by taking advantage of the hierarchical structure of the UNIX or Windows file systems:

- Each database corresponds to a directory under the data directory.
- Tables within a database correspond to files in the database directory.

The data directory also contains several status files that are generated by the server, such as the log files. These files provide important information about the server's operation and are valuable for administrators, especially when something goes wrong and you're trying to determine the cause of the problem. If some particular query kills the server, for example, you can identify the offending query by examining the log files.

How the MySQL Server Provides Access to Data

Everything under the data directory is managed by a single entity, the MySQL server mysqld. Client programs never manipulate data directly. Instead, the server provides the sole point of contact though which databases are accessed, acting as the intermediary between client programs and the data they wish to use. (See Figure 10.1.)

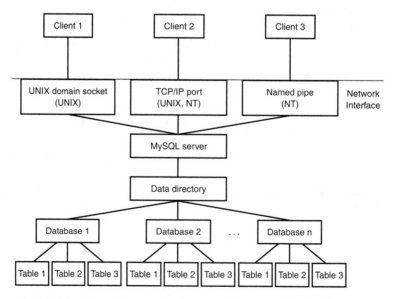

Figure 10.1   How the MySQL server controls access to the data directory.

When the server starts up, it opens the log files if any were requested, then presents a network interface to the data directory by listening for network connections. To access data, client programs establish a connection to the server, then communicate requests as SQL queries to perform the desired operations (for example, creating a table, selecting records, updating records). The server performs each operation and sends back the result to the client. The server is multi-threaded and can service multiple simultaneous client connections. However, because update operations are performed one at a time, the practical effect is to serialize requests so that two clients can never change the same record at exactly the same time.

Under normal conditions, having the server act as the sole arbiter of database access provides assurance against the kinds of corruption that can result from multiple processes accessing the database tables at the same time. Nevertheless, administrators should be aware that there are times when the server does not have exclusive control of the data directory:

- **When you run multiple servers on a single data directory.** Normally you run a single server to manage all databases on a host, but it's possible to run multiple servers. If this is done to provide access to multiple independent data directories, there is no problem of interaction. But it's possible to start multiple servers and point them at the same data directory. In general, this is not a good idea. If you try it, you'd better make sure your system provides good file locking or the servers will not cooperate properly. You also risk having your log files become a source of confusion (rather than a source of helpful information) if you have multiple servers writing to them at the same time.

- **When you run `isamchk` and `myisamchk`.** The isamchk and myisamchk utilities are used for table maintenance, troubleshooting, and repair. As you might guess, because these utilities can change table contents, allowing them to operate on tables at the same time the server is doing so can cause table damage. It's important to understand how to limit this type of interaction so that you don't damage your tables. See Chapter 13, "Database Maintenance and Repair," for instructions on the proper use of these programs.

Database Representation

Each database managed by the MySQL server has its own database directory. This exists as a subdirectory of the data directory, with the same name as the database it represents. For example, a database my_db corresponds to the database directory *DATADIR*/my_db.

This representation allows several database-level statements to be almost trivial in their implementation. CREATE DATABASE *db_name* creates an empty directory *db_name* in the data directory, with an ownership and mode that allow access only to the MySQL server user (the UNIX user the server runs as). This is equivalent to creating the database manually by executing the following commands as the server user on the server host:

```
% mkdir DATADIR/db_name        Create database directory
% chmod 700 DATADIR/db_name    Make it accessible only to the MySQL server user
```

The minimal approach of representing a new database by an empty directory contrasts with some other database systems that create a number of control or system files even for an "empty" database.

The DROP DATABASE statement is implemented easily as well. DROP DATABASE db_name removes the db_name directory in the data directory, along with any table files contained within it. This is almost the same as the following command:

```
% rm -rf DATADIR/db_name
```

(The difference is that the server removes only files with extensions known to be used for tables. If you've created other files in the database directory, the server leaves them intact, and the directory itself is not removed.)

SHOW DATABASES is essentially nothing more than a list of the names of the directories located within the data directory. Some database systems keep a master table that lists all the databases maintained, but there is no such construct in MySQL. Given the simplicity of the data directory structure, the list of databases is implicit in the contents of the data directory and such a table would be unnecessary overhead.

Database Table Representation

Each table within a database exists as three files in the database directory: a form (description) file, a data file, and an index file. The basename of each file is the table name, and the filename extension indicates the file type. The extensions are shown in Table 10.1. The data and index file extensions indicate whether the table uses the older ISAM indexing or the newer MyISAM indexing.

Table 10.1   **MySQL File Types**

File Type	Filename Extension	File Contents
Form file	.frm	Describes the structure of the table (its columns, column types, indexes, and so forth).
Data file	.ISD (ISAM) or .MYD (MyISAM)	Contains the table's data—that is, its rows.
Index file	.ISM (ISAM) or .MYI (MyISAM)	Contains the index trees for any indexes on the data file. The index file exists whether or not the table has any indexes.

When you issue a CREATE TABLE *tbl_name* statement defining a table's structure, the server creates a *tbl_name*.frm file containing the internal encoding of that structure. It also creates empty data and index files, initialized to contain information indicating no records and no indexes. (If the CREATE TABLE statement includes index specifications, the index file reflects those indexes.) The ownership and mode of the files representing the table are set to allow access only to the MySQL server user.

When you issue an ALTER TABLE statement, the server re-encodes *tbl_name*.frm and modifies the contents of the data and index files to reflect the structural change indicated by the statement. This is true for CREATE INDEX and DROP INDEX as well because they are treated by the server as equivalent ALTER TABLE statements. DROP TABLE is implemented by removing the three files representing the table.

You cannot create or alter a table manually, although you can remove a table by removing the three files in the database directory to which the table corresponds. For example, if my_db is the current database, DROP TABLE my_tbl is roughly equivalent to the following command:

```
% rm -f DATADIR/my_db/my_tbl.*
```

The output from SHOW TABLES my_db is just a listing of the basenames of the .frm files in the my_db database directory. Some database systems maintain a registry that lists all tables contained in a database. MySQL does not because it is unnecessary; the "registry" is implicit in the structure of the data directory.

Operating System Constraints on Database and Table Naming

MySQL has general rules for naming databases and tables:

- Names may be constructed from alphanumeric characters in the current character set, as well as the underscore and dollar ('_' and '$').
- Names may be up to 64 characters long.

However, because names of databases and tables correspond to names of directories and files, the operating system on which a server runs may impose additional constraints.

First, you are limited in database and table names to the characters that are legal in filenames. For example, '$' is allowed in a name by MySQL's rules, but if your OS doesn't allow it, you can't use it in directory or table names, either. In practice, this is not a concern for either UNIX or Windows. The greatest difficulty you might have is referring to names directly from the shell when performing database administration. For example, if you give a database a name such as $my_db that includes a dollar sign, any reference to that name from a shell command line may be interpreted by the shell as a variable reference:

```
% ls $my_db
my_db: Undefined variable.
```

If this happens, you must escape the '$' character or use quoting to suppress its special meaning:

```
% ls \$my_db
% ls '$my_db'
```

If you use quotes, use single quotes. Double quotes do not suppress variable interpretation.

Second, although MySQL allows database and table names to be up to 64 characters long, the length of names is also bound by the length allowed by your operating system. Normally, this is not a problem, although under UNIX you may run into System V-ish systems that enforce an older 14-character limit. In that case, your effective limit on database names is 14 characters. The limit for table names is 10 characters because names of files representing tables end with a period and a three-character extension.

Third, case sensitivity of the underlying file system affects how you name and refer to databases and tables. If the file system is case sensitive (as in UNIX), the two names my_tbl and MY_TBL refer to different tables. If the file system is not case sensitive (as in Windows), my_tbl and MY_TBL refer to the same table. You should keep that in mind if you use a UNIX server to develop a database, and if there is a possibility you might move the database to a Windows server sometime.

Implications of Data Directory Structure for System Performance

The structure of the data directory is easy to understand because it uses the hierarchical structure of the file system in such a natural way. At the same time, this structure has certain performance implications, particularly regarding operations that open the files that represent database tables.

One consequence of the data directory structure is that because tables are represented by multiple files, each open table can require multiple file descriptors, not one. The server caches descriptors intelligently, but a busy server can easily use up lots of them servicing many simultaneous client connections or executing complex queries that reference several tables. File descriptors are a scarce resource on many systems, particularly systems that set the default per-process limit fairly low. Chapter 11, "General MySQL Administration," provides information on assessing the number of descriptors you'll need, and on reconfiguring your server or operating system if necessary.

Another effect of representing each table by its own files is that table-opening time increases with the number of tables. Operations that open tables map onto the file-opening operations provided by the operating system, and as such are bound by the efficiency of the system's directory-lookup routines. Normally this isn't an issue, but it is something to consider if you'll need large numbers of tables in a database.

For example, if you want to have 10,000 tables, your database directory will contain 30,000 files. With that many files, you may notice a slowdown due to the time taken by file-opening operations. (Linux ext2 and Solaris file systems are subject to this problem.) If this is cause for concern, you might be wise to reconsider the structure of your tables in relation to the needs of your applications and reorganize your tables accordingly. Ask whether or not you really require so many tables; sometimes applications multiply tables needlessly. An application that creates a separate table per user results in many tables, all of which have identical structures. If you wanted to combine the tables into a single table, you might be able to do so by adding another column identifying the user to which each row applies. If this significantly reduces the number of tables, the application's performance improves.

As always in database design, you must consider whether or not this particular strategy is worthwhile for a given application. Reasons not to combine tables in the manner just described are as follows:

- **Increased disk space requirements.** Combining tables reduces the number of tables required (decreasing table-opening times), but adds another column (increasing disk space requirements). This is a typical time versus space tradeoff and you'd need to decide which factor is most important. If speed is paramount, you'd probably be willing to sacrifice a little extra disk space. If space is tight, it might be more acceptable to use multiple tables and live with a slight delay.

- **Security considerations.** These may constrain your ability or desire to combine tables. One reason to use a separate table per user is to allow access to each table only to that user by means of table-level privileges. If you combined tables, all users' data would be in the same table.

  MySQL has no provision for restricting access to particular rows to a given user; thus, you might not be able to merge tables without compromising access control. On the other hand, if all access to the data is controlled by your application (users never connect directly to the database), you can merge the tables and use application logic to enforce row-level access to the combined result.

MySQL has its own internal limit on table sizes, but because it represents tables as files, MySQL is also bound by the maximum file size allowed by your operating system. The effective maximum table size is therefore the smaller of MySQL's internal limit and the system file size limit.

In general, the trend is for constraints on sizes to be relaxed over time. For example, IBM AIX 4.1 has a 2GB file size limit, but the limit in AIX 4.2 is approximately 64GB. The internal table size limit in MySQL increases with newer releases, too. Prior to the 3.23 series, the internal limit is 4GB. As of 3.23, the limit is approximately 9 million terabytes. Table 10.2 illustrates how the MySQL internal table size limit and the AIX file size limit interact to determine the effective maximum table size. Similar interactions may apply for other operating systems as well.

Table 10.2 **Interaction of MySQL and Operating System Size Limits**

MySQL Version	AIX Version	Maximum Table Size	Constraining Factor
MySQL 3.22.22	AIX 4.1	2GB	AIX 2GB maximum file size
MySQL 3.22.22	AIX 4.2	4GB	MySQL 4GB maximum table size
MySQL 3.23.0	AIX 4.1	2GB	AIX 2GB maximum file size
MySQL 3.23.0	AIX 4.2	64GB	AIX 64GB maximum file size

MySQL Status Files

In addition to database directories, the MySQL data directory contains a number of status files. These files are summarized in Table 10.3, then described in more detail. The default name for most of the files is generated from the server host name, denoted as HOSTNAME in the table.

The server writes its process ID (PID) into the PID file when it starts up and removes the file when it shuts down. The PID file is the means by which the server allows itself to be found by other processes. For example, if you run the mysql.server script at system shutdown time to shut down the MySQL server, that script examines the PID file to determine which process it needs to send a termination signal to.

The error log is created by safe_mysqld as a redirection of the server's standard error output; it contains any messages the server writes to stderr. This means the error log exists only if you start the server by invoking safe_mysqld. (That is the preferred method for starting the server anyway because safe_mysqld restarts the server if it exits due to an error.)

The general log and update log are optional; you can turn on just the logging types you need, using the --log and --log-update server options.

Table 10.3 **MySQL Status Files**

File Type	Default Name	File Contents
Process ID	HOSTNAME.pid	The server process ID
Error log	HOSTNAME.err	Startup and shutdown events and error conditions
General log	HOSTNAME.log	Connect/disconnect events and query information
Update log	HOSTNAME.nnn	Text of all queries that modify table contents or structure

The general log provides general information about server operation: who is connecting from where and what queries they are issuing. The update log provides query information, too, but only for queries that modify database contents. The contents of the update log are written as SQL statements that can be executed by providing them as input to the mysql client. Update logs are useful if you have a crash and must revert to backup files because you can repeat the updates performed since the time of the crash by feeding update logs to the server. This allows you to bring your databases up to the state they were in when the crash occurred.

Here is a sample of the kind of information that appears in the general log as the result of a short client session that creates a table in the test database, inserts a row into the table, and then drops the table:

```
990509  7:34:09      492 Connect      paul@localhost on test
                      492 Query        show databases
                      492 Query        show tables
                      492 Field List tbl_1
                      492 Field List tbl_2
                      ...
990509  7:34:22      492 Query        CREATE TABLE my_tbl (val INT)
990509  7:34:34      492 Query        INSERT INTO my_tbl VALUES(1)
990509  7:34:38      492 Query        DROP TABLE my_tbl
990509  7:34:40      492 Quit
```

The general log contains columns for date and time, server thread ID, event type, and event-specific information.

The same session appears in the update log like this:

```
use test;
CREATE TABLE my_tbl (val INT);
INSERT INTO my_tbl VALUES(1);
DROP TABLE my_tbl;
```

For the update log, an extended form of logging is available using the --log-long-format option. Extended logging provides information about who issued each query and when. This uses more disk space, of course, but may be useful if you want to know who is doing what without trying to correlate update log contents with the connection events in the general log.

For the session just shown, extended update logging produces this information:

```
# Time: 990509  7:43:42
# User@Host: paul [paul] @ localhost []
use test;
CREATE TABLE my_tbl (val INT);
# User@Host: paul [paul] @ localhost []
INSERT INTO my_tbl VALUES(1);
# Time: 990509  7:43:43
# User@Host: paul [paul] @ localhost []
DROP TABLE my_tbl;
```

It's a good idea to make sure your log files are secure and not readable by arbitrary users. The general and update logs both may contain sensitive information such as passwords because they contain the text of queries. Here's the type of log entry you don't want just anyone to be able to read because it displays the password for the root user:

```
990509  7:47:24      4 Query       UPDATE user SET Password=PASSWORD("secret")
                                    WHERE user="root"
```

For information on checking and setting your data directory permissions, see Chapter 12, "Security." The short instructions for securing the data directory consist of the following command:

```
% chmod 700 DATADIR
```

Run this command as the UNIX user who owns the data directory. Make sure the server runs as that user, too, or the command not only will keep other people out of the data directory (which you want), but it will prevent the server from accessing your databases (which you don't want!).

Status files appear at the top level of the data directory, just like database directories, so you may wonder whether names of those files can conflict with or be mistaken for database names (for example, when the server is executing a SHOW DATABASES statement). The answer is no. Status and log information is stored in files, and databases are directories, so executable programs can distinguish them with a simple stat() call. (That's how the server tells them apart.) If you're looking through the data directory yourself, you can distinguish status files from database directories by using ls -l and examining the first character of the mode information to see whether it's a '-' or a 'd':

```
% ls -l DATADIR
total 31
drwxrwx---  1 mysqladm     mysqlgrp      1024 May  8 13:22 bigdb
drwxrwx---  2 mysqladm     mysqlgrp      1024 Dec 15 22:34 mysql
-rw-rw----  1 mysqladm     mysqlgrp        69 May  9 20:11 pit-viper.001
-rw-rw-r--  1 mysqladm     mysqlgrp     24168 May  9 20:11 pit-viper.err
-rw-rw----  1 mysqladm     mysqlgrp      4376 May  9 20:11 pit-viper.log
-rw-r--r--  1 mysqladm     mysqlgrp         5 May  9 20:11 pit-viper.pid
drwxrwx---  7 mysqladm     mysqlgrp       512 Sep 10  1998 sql-bench
drwxrwx---  2 mysqladm     mysqlgrp       512 May  9 07:44 test
```

You can also tell simply by looking at names: All status file names contain a period, whereas no database directory name does (period is not a legal character in a database name).

For information on log file maintenance and rotation techniques, see Chapter 11.

Relocating Data Directory Contents

The preceding section discusses the data directory structure in its default configuration. All databases and status files are contained within it. However, you have some latitude in determining the placement of the data directory's contents. This section discusses why you might want to move parts of the data directory (or even the directory itself), what can be moved, and how you go about making these changes.

MySQL allows you to relocate the data directory or elements within it. There are several reasons why you might want to do this:

- You can put the data directory on a file system with a greater capacity than the file system on which it's located by default.
- If your data directory is on a busy disk, you can put it on a less active drive to balance disk activity across physical devices. You can put databases and log files on separate drives or distribute databases across drives for similar reasons.
- You might want to run multiple servers, each with its own data directory. This is one way to work around problems with per-process file descriptor limits, especially if you cannot reconfigure the kernel for your system to allow higher limits.
- Some systems keep server PID files in a directory such as /var/run. You might want to put the MySQL PID file there, too, for consistency of system operation.

Relocation Methods

There are two ways to relocate elements of the data directory:

- You can specify an option at server startup time, either on the command line or in the [mysqld] group of an option file.
- You can move the thing to be relocated, then make a symlink (symbolic link) in the original location that points to the new location.

Neither method works universally for everything that you can relocate. Table 10.4 summarizes what can be relocated and which relocation methods can be used. If you use an option file, it is possible to specify options in the global option file /etc/my.cnf (C:\my.cnf on Windows). The current Windows version also looks in the system directory (C:\windows or C:\NT).

Table 10.4 **Relocation Method Summary**

Entity To Relocate	Applicable Relocation Methods
Entire data directory	Startup option or symlink
Individual database directories	Symlink
Individual database tables	Symlink
PID file	Startup option
General log file	Startup option
Update log file	Startup option

You can also use the option file `my.cnf` in the default data directory (the directory compiled into the server). I don't recommend using this file. If you want to relocate the data directory itself, you have to leave the default data directory intact so that you can place an option file in it that specifies where the server should find the "real" data directory! That is confusing. If you want to use an option file to specify server options, it's best to use `/etc/my.cnf`.

Assessing the Effect of Relocation

Before attempting to relocate anything, it's a good idea to verify that the operation will have the desired effect. I tend to favor the `du`, `df`, and `ls -l` commands for obtaining disk space information, but all of these depend on correctly understanding the layout of your file system.

The following example illustrates a subtle trap to watch out for when assessing a data directory relocation. Suppose your data directory is `/usr/local/var` and you want to move it to `/var/mysql` because `df` indicates the `/var` file system has more free space (as shown by the following example):

```
% df /usr /var
Filesystem  1K-blocks     Used    Avail Capacity  Mounted on
/dev/wd0s3e    396895   292126    73018    80%    /usr
/dev/wd0s3f   1189359  1111924   162287    15%    /var
```

How much space will relocating the data directory free up on the `/usr` file system? To find out, use `du -s` to see how much space that directory uses:

```
% cd /usr/local/var
% du -s
133426   .
```

That's about 130MB, which should make quite a difference on `/usr`. But will it really? Try `df` in the data directory:

```
% df /usr/local/var
Filesystem  1K-blocks     Used    Avail Capacity  Mounted on
/dev/wd0s3f   1189359  1111924   162287    15%    /var
```

That's odd. If we're requesting the free space for the file system containing `/usr/local/var`, why does `df` report the space on `var`? Here `ls -l` provides the answer:

```
% ls -l /usr/local
...
lrwxrwxr-x  1 root  wheel  10 Dec 11 23:46 var -> /var/mysql
...
```

This output shows that `/usr/local/var` is a symlink to `/var/mysql`. In other words, the data directory *already* has been relocated to the `/var` file system and replaced with a symlink that points there. So much for freeing up a lot of space on `/usr` by moving the data directory to `/var`!

Moral: A few minutes spent assessing the effect of relocation is a worthwhile investment. It doesn't take long, and it can keep you from wasting a lot of time moving things around, only to find that you've failed to achieve your objective.

Relocating the Data Directory

To relocate the data directory, bring down the server and move the data directory to its new location. Then you should either remove the original data directory and replace it with a symlink that points to the new location or restart the server with an option that explicitly indicates the new location. Table 10.5 illustrates command line and option file syntax for specifying the location.

Relocating Databases

Databases can be moved only by the symlink method. To relocate a database, bring down the server and move the database directory. Remove the original database directory, replace it with a symlink that points to the new location, and restart the server.

The following example shows how you might move a database `bigdb` to a different location:

```
% mysqladmin -u root -p shutdown
Enter password: ********
% cd DATADIR
% tar cf - bigdb | (cd /var/db; tar xf -)
% mv bigdb bigdb.orig
% ln -s /var/db/bigdb .
% safe_mysqld &
```

Table 10.5 **Data Directory Relocation Syntax**

Option Source	Syntax
Command line	--datadir=/path/to/dir
Option file	[mysqld] datadir=/path/to/dir

Relocation Precautions

You should bring down the server before performing any relocation operation, then restart it afterward. For some types of relocations, such as moving a database directory, it is possible (although not recommended) to keep the server running. If you do that, you must make sure the server is not accessing the database you're moving. You should also be sure to issue a FLUSH TABLES statement before moving the database to make sure the server closes all open table files. Failure to observe these precautions can result in damaged tables.

You should execute these commands as the data directory owner. The original database directory is renamed to `bigdb.orig` for safekeeping. After you've verified that the server works properly with the relocated database, you can remove the original one:

```
% rm -rf bigdb.orig
```

Relocating Database Tables

It's not a good idea to relocate individual tables. You can do it by moving a table's files to a different location and creating symlinks in the database directory that point to those files. However, if you ever issue an `ALTER TABLE` or `OPTIMIZE TABLE` statement, your changes will be undone.

Each statement operates by creating a temporary table in the database directory that implements your alteration or optimization, then deleting the original table and renaming the temporary table to the original name. The result is that your symlinks are removed and the new table ends up right back in the database directory, where your original table was before you moved it. Furthermore, the old table files that you moved out of the database directory are still in the location where you moved them—and you might not even realize they are there, continuing to take up space. Also, the symlinks have been destroyed, so when you realize later what has happened, you may not have any good way of tracking down the files if you've forgotten where you moved them.

Because it's difficult to guarantee that no one with access to the table will ever alter or optimize it (and thus undo any attempted relocation), it's best to leave tables in the database directory.

Relocating Status Files

You can relocate the PID file, the general log, and the update log using startup options. The error log is created by `safe_mysqld` and cannot be relocated (unless you edit `safe_mysqld`).

To write a status file in a different location, bring down the server, then restart it with the appropriate option specifying the new status file location. Table 10.6 shows the command line and option file syntax for each file.

> **Removing a Relocated Database**
>
> You can remove a database with the `DROP DATABASE` statement, but older versions of MySQL have trouble removing a database that has been relocated. The tables in the database are removed correctly, but an error occurs when the server attempts to remove the database directory because the directory is a symlink and not a real directory. The MySQL administrator must manually remove the database directory and the symlink that points to it. This problem is fixed as of the MySQL 3.23 series.

Table 10.6 **Status File Relocation Syntax**

Option Source	Syntax
Command line	`--pid-file=pidfile`
	`--log=logfile`
	`--log-update=updatefile`
Option file	`[mysqld]`
	`pid-file=pidfile`
	`log=logfile`
	`log-update=updatefile`

If you specify the name of a status file as an absolute pathname, the file is created using that pathname. Otherwise, the file is created under the data directory. For example, if you specify `--pid-file=/var/run/mysqld.pid`, the PID file is `/var/run/mysqld.pid`. If you specify `--pid-file=mysqld.pid`, the PID file is `DATADIR/mysqld.pid`.

If you specify an update log name that has no extension, MySQL generates sequential names each time it opens the update log. These names are created with an extension of `.nnn`, where `.nnn` is the first number not already used by an existing update log file (for example, `update.001`, `update.002`, and so forth). You can override sequential name generation by specifying a name containing an explicit extension. Then the server will use only the name you specify.

11

General MySQL Administration

THIS CHAPTER DISCUSSES THE DUTIES a MySQL administrator needs to perform to keep MySQL running smoothly. These responsibilities include making sure the server is up and running as much as possible, setting up user accounts so that clients can access the server, maintaining log files, and performing database backups. The administrator also may want to run multiple servers or modify the server's operating parameters for better performance. Finally, because MySQL is under active development, the administrator must be able to determine when to upgrade MySQL by installing new releases. Other significant administrative concerns are covered in Chapter 12, "Security," and Chapter 13, "Database Maintenance and Repair."

Several programs are covered in these chapters that are useful for MySQL administrators:

- `mysqladmin` performs miscellaneous administrative operations.
- `safe_mysqld` and `mysql.server` are scripts for starting up the MySQL server, `mysqld`.
- `mysqldump` is used for database backup and copying operations.
- `myisamchk` and `isamchk` are used for table integrity checking and repair operations.

Additional information about most of these programs is provided in Appendix E, "MySQL Program Reference."

Securing a New MySQL Installation

You may be reading this chapter because you've just installed MySQL according to the instructions in Appendix A, "Obtaining and Installing Software." If so, you need to set up the password for the MySQL root user—for a new MySQL installation, the server is running with privileges that are insecure. I assume that you have initialized your data directory and the mysql database that contains the grant tables. Under UNIX, this is done by running the mysql_install_db script. Under Windows, the data directory and mysql database are initialized by running the Setup program in the server distribution. I assume also that the server is running.

When you install MySQL for the first time on a machine, the privileges in the grant tables of the mysql database are initialized as follows:

- You can connect as root from the local host *without a password*. The root user has all privileges (including administrative privileges) and can do anything. (By the way, the fact that the MySQL superuser and the UNIX superuser both have the name root is coincidental. They have nothing to do with each other.)

- Anonymous access is granted to users that connect from the local host for the database named test or any databases with names that begin with 'test_'. Anonymous users can do anything with such databases, but have no administrative privileges.

Connections to the server from the local host are allowed whether the connecting user specifies a hostname of localhost or the actual hostname. For example, if the server is on pit-viper.snake.net, a client on that host can connect to the server without a password to use the test database with either of these commands:

```
% mysql -h localhost test
% mysql -h pit-viper.snake.net test
```

The fact that you can even connect to the MySQL server as the root user with no password means the initial installation is insecure. Therefore, one of your first acts as a MySQL administrator should be to set the password for the root user. Then, depending on the method you use to set the password, you may also need to tell the server to reload the grant tables so that it notices the change. (When the server starts up, it loads the tables into memory and may not recognize that you've changed them. If not, you must tell it explicitly to re-read them.)

For MySQL 3.22 and up, you can set the password using the mysqladmin program as follows, substituting whatever password you choose for "*my password*" in the command:

```
% mysqladmin -u root password "your password"
```

For any version of MySQL, you can use the `mysql` program and update the user grant table in the `mysql` database directly:

```
% mysql -u root mysql
mysql> UPDATE user SET Password=PASSWORD("your password")
    -> WHERE User="root";
```

Use `mysql` and an `UPDATE` statement if you have an older version of MySQL; this includes the Windows shareware version.

After you set the password, find out if you need to tell the server to reload the grant tables by running the following command:

```
% mysqladmin -u root status
```

If the server still lets you connect as `root` without a password, tell it to re-read the grant tables like this:[1]

```
% mysqladmin -u root reload
```

After you have set the `root` password (and reloaded the grant tables if necessary), you'll need to specify your new password whenever you connect to the server as `root`.

Arranging for MySQL Server Startup and Shutdown

One general goal that you have as a MySQL administrator is to make sure the server is running as much as possible so that clients have access to it. Sometimes, however, it's best to bring down the server. (For example, if you're relocating a database, you don't want the server updating tables in that database.) The tension between the need to keep the server running and the need to bring it down occasionally is something this book can't resolve for you. But we can at least discuss how to get the server started and stopped so that you have the ability to do either one as you see fit.

The instructions in this chapter apply only to UNIX systems. If you're running under Windows, you can skip them, because Appendix A, "Obtaining and Installing Software," contains all the startup and shutdown commands you need.

Invoking Commands Shown in This Chapter

In most cases, programs such as `mysqladmin`, `mysqldump`, and so forth are shown in this chapter without any `-h`, `-u`, or `-p` options for the purpose of brevity. I assume that you'll invoke programs with any options that are necessary for making a connection to the server

---

[1] Versions of MySQL from 3.22.11 and up also allow you to reload the tables using the `mysqladmin flush-privileges` command and the `FLUSH PRIVILEGES` SQL statement.

Running the MySQL Server Using an Unprivileged User Account

Before discussing how to start the server, let's consider which account it should be run under when it does start. The server can be started manually or automatically. If you start it manually, the server runs as the UNIX user you happen to be logged in as. That is, if I log in as paul and start the server, it runs as paul. If instead I switch user to root using the su command and then start the server, it runs as root.

However, most of the time you probably won't want to start the server manually. It's more likely that you'll arrange for the server to run automatically at system boot time as part of the standard startup procedure. Under UNIX, this startup procedure is performed by the system as the UNIX root user, and any processes started during the procedure run with root privileges.

You should keep in mind two goals for your MySQL server startup procedures:

- **You want the server to run as some non-root user.** In general, you want to limit the power of any process unless it really needs root access, and mysqld does not.

- **You want the server to run as the same user all the time.** It's inconsistent for the server to run as one user sometimes and another user other times. That leads to files and directories being created under the data with different ownerships and can even result in the server not being able to access databases or tables, depending on which user it runs as. Consistently running the server as the same user enables you to avoid this problem.

To run the server as a normal, unprivileged user, follow this procedure:

1. Choose an account to use for running the server. mysqld can run as any user, but it's cleaner conceptually to create a separate account for MySQL activity. You can designate a group specifically for MySQL as well. I'll call these user and group names mysqladm and mysqlgrp. If you use different names, substitute them anywhere you see mysqladm and mysqlgrp throughout this book.

   If you have installed MySQL under your own account and have no special administrative privileges on your system, you'll probably be running the server under your own user ID. In this case, substitute your own login name and group name for mysqladm and mysqlgrp.

   If you installed MySQL under RedHat Linux using an RPM file, the installation will have created an account under the name mysql automatically. Substitute that name for mysqladm.

2. Create the server account if necessary using your system's usual account-creation procedure. You'll need to do this as root.

3. Bring down the server if it's running.

4. Modify the ownership of the data directory and any subdirectories and files so that the `mysqladm` user owns them. For example, if the data directory is `/usr/local/var`, you can set up ownership for the `mysqladm` user as follows (you'll need to run these commands as `root`):

    ```
    # cd /usr/local/var
    ```
    Move into the data directory

    ```
    # chown -R mysqladm.mysqlgrp
    ```
    Set ownership of all directories and files

5. Modify the permissions on the data directory and any subdirectories and files so that only the `mysqladm` user can access them. Setting the mode to keep other people out is a good security precaution. If the data directory is `/usr/local/var`, you can set up everything to be owned by the `mysqladm` user as follows (you'll need to run these commands as `root`):

    ```
    # cd /usr/local/var
    ```
    Move into the data directory

    ```
    # chmod -R go-rwx
    ```
    Make everything accessible only to `mysqladm`

When you set the ownership and mode of the data directory and its contents, watch out for symbolic links. You'll need to follow them and change the ownership and mode of the files or directories they point to. This can be troublesome if the directory in which the linked files are located doesn't belong to you, so you may need to be `root`.

After you've completed the preceding procedure, you should make sure always to start the server either while logged in as `mysqladm`, or as `root`. In the latter case, be sure to specify an option of `--user=mysqladm` so that the server can switch its user ID to `mysqladm` (which also applies during the system startup procedure).

The `--user` option was added to `mysql` in MySQL 3.22. If you have a version older than that, you can use the `su` command to tell the system to run the server under a particular account when you start the server while running as `root`. You'll need to read the manual page for `su` because the syntax for running a command as a given user varies.

Methods for Starting the Server

After you've decided what account you'll use to run the server, you can choose how to arrange to start the server. You can run it manually from the command line or automatically during the system startup procedure. There are three primary methods for starting the server:

- **Invoke `mysqld` directly.** This is probably the least common method. I won't discuss it further, except to say that `mysqld --help` is a useful command for finding out what options you can use with the other startup methods.

- **Invoke the `safe_mysqld` script.** `safe_mysqld` attempts to determine the location of the server program and the data directory, and then invokes the server with options reflecting those values. `safe_mysqld` redirects the standard error output from the server into an error file in the data directory so that there is a record of it. After starting the server, `safe_mysqld` also monitors it and restarts it if it dies. `safe_mysqld` is commonly used on BSD-style versions of UNIX.

  The error log will be owned by `root` if you ever start up `safe_mysqld` as `root` or during system startup. This may cause a "permission denied" error later if you try to invoke `safe_mysqld` as an unprivileged user. Remove the error log and try again.

- **Invoke the `mysql.server` script.** This script starts up the server by running `safe_mysqld`. `mysql.server` is intended for use on systems that use the System V startup/shutdown system. This system includes several directories that contain scripts to be invoked when the machine enters or exits a given run level. It can be invoked with an argument of `start` or `stop` to indicate whether you want the server to start or stop.

The `safe_mysqld` script is installed in the `bin` directory under the MySQL installation directory or can be found in the `scripts` directory of the MySQL source distribution. The `mysql.server` script is installed under the `share/mysql` directory under the MySQL installation directory or can be found in the `support-files` directory of the MySQL source distribution. You'll need to copy it to the proper startup directory if you want to use it.

For BSD-style systems, it's common to have a few files in the `/etc` directory that initiate services at boot time. These files often have names that begin with 'rc', and it's likely that there is a file named `rc.local` (or something similar) intended specifically for starting locally installed services. On such a system, you might add lines like the following to `rc.local` to start up the server (change the path to `safe_mysqld` if it's different on your system):

```
if [ -x /usr/local/bin/safe_mysqld ]; then
    /usr/local/bin/safe_mysqld &
fi
```

For System V–style systems, you can install `mysql.server` by placing it in the appropriate startup directory under `/etc`. This may have been done for you already if you run Linux and installed MySQL from an RPM file. Otherwise, install the script in the main startup script directory, and place links to it in the appropriate run level directory. You can also make the script executable only by `root`.

The layout for startup file directories varies from system to system, so you'll need to check around to see how your system organizes them. For example, under LinuxPPC, the directories are `/etc/rc.d/init.d` and `/etc/rc.d/rc3.d`. I could install the script like this:

```
# cp mysql.server /etc/rc.d/init.d
# cd /etc/rc.d/init.d
# chmod 500 mysql.server
# cd /etc/rc.d/rc3.d
# ln -s ../init.d/mysql.server S99mysql
```

Under Solaris, the main script directory is /etc/init.d, and the run level directory is /etc/rc2.d, so the commands would look like this instead:

```
# cp mysql.server /etc/init.d
# cd /etc/init.d
# chmod 500 mysql.server
# cd /etc/rc2.d
# ln -s ../init.d/mysql.server S99mysql
```

At system startup time, the S99mysql script will be invoked automatically with an argument of start.

If you have a chkconfig command (which is common under Linux, for example), you can use it to help you install the mysql.server script instead of manually running the commands like those just shown.

Specifying Startup Options

If you want to specify additional startup options when the server starts up, you can do so in two ways. You can modify the startup script you use (safe_mysqld or mysql.server) and specify the options directly on the line that invokes the server. Or you can specify options in an option file. I recommend that you specify server options in a global option file if possible. The usual location for this is /etc/my.cnf under UNIX and C:\my.cnf under Windows. (See Appendix E for details on using option files.)

Some kinds of information cannot be specified as server options. For these you'll probably need to modify safe_mysqld. For example, if your server doesn't pick up the local time zone properly and returns time values in GMT, you can set the TZ environment variable to give it a hint. If you start the server using safe_mysqld or mysql.server, you can add a time zone setting to safe_mysqld. Find the line that starts the server and add commands such as the following before that line:

```
TZ=US/Central
export TZ
```

This sets TZ to the US Central time zone. You'll need to use the time zone appropriate for your location. The syntax shown is for Solaris; your system may use something different. For example, another common syntax for setting the TZ variable is:

```
TZ=CST6CDT
export TZ
```

If you do modify your startup script, be aware that the next time you install MySQL (for example, to upgrade to a newer version), your changes will be lost unless you copy the startup script somewhere else first. After installing the new version, compare your script to the newly installed one to see what modifications you need to re-establish.

Checking Your Tables at Startup Time

In addition to arranging for your server to start up when the system boots, you may want to install a script that runs `myisamchk` and `isamchk` to check your tables before the server starts. You may be restarting after a crash, and it's possible that tables were damaged. Checking them before the server starts is a good way to discover problems. Chapter 13 has details on writing and installing such a script.

Shutting Down the Server

To shut down the server manually, use `mysqladmin`:

```
% mysqladmin shutdown
```

To shut down the server automatically, you shouldn't need to do anything special. BSD systems normally shut down services by sending processes a `TERM` signal. They either respond to it appropriately or are killed unceremoniously. `mysqld` responds by terminating when it receives this signal. For System V-style systems that start the server with `mysql.server`, the shutdown process will invoke that script with an argument of `stop` to tell the server to shut down—assuming that you've installed `mysql.server`, of course.

Regaining Control of the Server If You Can't Connect

Under certain circumstances you may need to restart the server manually due to an inability to connect to it. Of course, this is somewhat paradoxical, because typically you shut down the server manually by connecting to it and telling it to terminate. How then can this situation arise?

First, the MySQL `root` password might have gotten set to a value that you don't know. This can happen when you change the password—for example, if you accidentally type an invisible control character when you enter the new password value. You might also simply have forgotten the password.

Second, connections to `localhost` are usually made through a UNIX domain socket file, which is typically `/tmp/mysql.sock`. If the socket file gets removed, local clients won't be able to connect. This might happen if your system runs a `cron` job that removes temporary files in `/tmp` now and then.

If you can't connect because you've lost the socket file, you can get it back simply by restarting the server because the server recreates it at startup time. The trick here is that you can't use the socket to establish a connection because it's gone. You must establish a TCP/IP connection instead. For example, if the server host is `pit-viper.snake.net`, you can connect like this:

```
% mysqladmin -p -u root -h pit-viper.snake.net shutdown
```

If the socket file is being removed by a `cron` job, the problem will recur until you change the `cron` job or use a different socket file. You can specify a different socket using the global option file. For example, if the data directory is `/usr/local/var`, you can move the socket file there by adding these lines to `/etc/my.cnf`:

```
[mysqld]
socket=/usr/local/var/mysql.sock

[client]
socket=/usr/local/var/mysql.sock
```

The pathname is specified both for the server and for client programs so that they all use the same socket file. If you set the pathname only for the server, client programs will still expect to find the socket at the old location. Restart the server after making the change so that it creates the socket in the new location.

If you can't connect because you can't remember the `root` password or have changed it to a value that's different than what you thought, you need to regain control of the server so that you can set the password again:

- **Bring down the server.** If you can log in as `root` on the server host, you can terminate the server using the `kill` command. You can find out the server's process ID by using the `ps` command, or by looking in the server's PID file (which is usually located in the data directory).

  It's best to try killing the server with a normal `kill` first that just sends a `TERM` signal to the server to see if it will respond by shutting down normally. That way, tables and logs will be flushed properly. If the server is jammed and unresponsive to a normal termination signal, you can use `kill -9` to forcibly terminate it. That is a last resort because there may be unflushed modifications, and you risk leaving tables in an inconsistent state.

  If you terminated the server with `kill -9`, be sure to check your tables with `myisamchk` and `isamchk` before restarting the server (see Chapter 13).

- **Restart the server with the `--skip-grant-tables` option.** This tells the server not to use the grant tables to verify connections. That allows you to connect as `root` with no password. After you've connected, change the `root` password as shown in "Securing a New MySQL Installation."

- **Tell the server to start using the grant tables again with `mysqladmin flush-privileges`.** If your version of `mysqladmin` does not recognize `flush-privileges`, try `reload` instead.

Managing User Accounts

The MySQL administrator should know how to set up MySQL user accounts by specifying which users can connect to the server, where they can connect from, and what they can do while connected. MySQL 3.22.11 introduced two statements that make this task much easier: The GRANT statement creates MySQL users and specifies their privileges, and the REVOKE statement removes privileges. These two statements act as a front end to the grant tables in the mysql database and provide an alternative to manipulating the contents of those tables directly. The GRANT and REVOKE statements affect four tables:

Grant Table	Contents
user	Users who can connect to the server and any global privileges they have
db	Database-level privileges
tables_priv	Table-level privileges
columns_priv	Column-level privileges

There is a fifth grant table, (host), but it is not affected by GRANT or REVOKE.

When you issue a GRANT statement for a user, an entry is created for that user in the user table. If the statement specifies any global privileges (administrative privileges or privileges that apply to all databases), those are recorded in the user table, too. If you specify database, table, or column privileges, they are recorded in the db, tables_priv, and columns_priv tables.

It's easier to use GRANT and REVOKE than to modify the grant tables directly. However, it's advisable to supplement the material in this chapter by reading Chapter 12, which discusses the grant tables in more detail. These tables are extremely important, and as an administrator you should understand how they work beyond the level of the GRANT and REVOKE statements.

In the rest of this section, we'll describe how to set up MySQL user accounts and grant privileges. We'll also cover how to revoke privileges and remove users from the grant tables entirely, and we'll consider a privilege puzzle that afflicts many new MySQL administrators.

You may also want to consider using the mysqlaccess and mysql_setpermission scripts, which are part of the MySQL distribution. These are Perl scripts that provide an alternative to the GRANT statement for setting up user accounts. mysql_setpermission requires that you have DBI support installed.

Creating New Users and Granting Privileges

The syntax for the GRANT statement looks like this:

```
GRANT privileges (columns)
    ON what
    TO user IDENTIFIED BY "password"
    WITH GRANT OPTION
```

To use the statement, you need to fill in the following parts:

- *privileges*

    The privileges to assign to the user. The privilege specifiers that can be used with the GRANT statement are listed in the following table:

Privilege Specifier	Operation Allowed by Privilege
ALTER	Alter tables and indexes
CREATE	Create databases and tables
DELETE	Delete existing records from tables
DROP	Drop (remove) databases and tables
INDEX	Create or drop indexes
INSERT	Insert new records into tables
REFERENCES	Unused
SELECT	Retrieve existing records from tables.
UPDATE	Modify existing table records
FILE	Read and write files on the server
PROCESS	View information about the threads executing within the server or kill threads
RELOAD	Reload the grant tables or flush the logs, the host cache, or the table cache
SHUTDOWN	Shut down the server
ALL	Anything; ALL PRIVILEGES is a synonym
USAGE	A special "no privileges" privilege

The privilege specifiers in the first group shown in the preceding table apply to databases, tables, and columns. The specifiers in the second group are administrative privileges. Normally, these are granted relatively sparingly because they allow users to affect the operation of the server. (The SHUTDOWN privilege is not one you hand out on an everyday basis, for example.) The specifiers in the third group are special. ALL means "all privileges." USAGE means "no privileges"—that is, "create the user, but don't grant any privileges."

- *columns*

  The columns that the privileges apply to. This is optional, and you use it only to set up column-specific privileges. If more than one column is named, they should be separated by commas.

- *what*

  The level at which the privileges apply. Privileges can be global (apply to all databases and all tables), database-specific (apply to all tables in a database), or table-specific. Privileges can be made column specific by specifying a *columns* clause.

- *user*

  The user who the privileges are for. This consists of a username and a hostname; in MySQL, you specify not only who can connect but from where. This allows you to have two users with the same name that connect from different locations. MySQL lets you distinguish between them and assign privileges to each independently of the other.

  A username in MySQL is just the name that you specify when you connect to the server. The name has no necessary connection to your UNIX login name or Windows name. By default, client programs will use your login name as your MySQL username if you don't specify a name explicitly, but that's just a convention. There is also nothing special about the name root as the MySQL superuser that can do anything. It's just a convention. You could just as well change this name to nobody in the grant tables and then connect as nobody to perform operations requiring superuser privileges.

- *password*

  The password to assign to the user. This is optional. If you specify no IDENTIFIED BY clause for a new user, that user is assigned no password (which is insecure). For an existing user, any password you specify replaces the old one. If you don't specify a new password, the user's old password remains unchanged. When you do use IDENTIFIED BY, the password string should be the literal text of the password; GRANT will encode the password for you. Don't use the PASSWORD() function as you do with the SET PASSWORD statement.

The WITH GRANT OPTION clause is optional. If you include it, the user may give any privileges granted by the GRANT statement to other users. You can use this clause to delegate privilege-granting capabilities to other users.

Usernames, passwords, and database and table names are case sensitive in grant table entries. Hostnames and column names are not.

You can generally figure out the kind of GRANT statement you need by asking some simple questions:

- Who can connect, and from where?
- What level of privileges should the user have, and what should they apply to?
- Should the user be allowed to administer privileges?

Let's ask these questions and look at some examples of the way you can use the GRANT statement to set up MySQL user accounts.

Who Can Connect, and From Where?

You can allow a user to connect from as specific or broad a set of hosts as you like. At the one extreme, you can limit access to a single host if you know users will be connecting only from that host:

```
GRANT ALL ON samp_db.* TO boris@localhost IDENTIFIED BY "ruby"
GRANT ALL ON samp_db.* TO fred@ares.mars.net IDENTIFIED BY "quartz"
```

(The notation samp_db.* means "all tables in the samp_db database.") At the other extreme, you may have a user max who travels a lot and needs to be able to connect from hosts all over the world. In this case, you can allow him to connect no matter where he connects from:

```
GRANT ALL ON samp_db.* TO max@% IDENTIFIED BY "diamond"
```

The '%' character functions as a wildcard with the same meaning as in a LIKE pattern match. In the preceding statement, it means "any host." If you give no hostname part at all, it's the same as specifying '%'. Thus, max and max@% are equivalent. This is the easiest way to set up a user, but the least secure.

To take a middle ground, you can allow a user to connect from a limited set of hosts. For example, to allow mary to connect from any host in the snake.net domain, use a hostname specifier of %.snake.net:

```
GRANT ALL ON samp_db.* TO mary@%.snake.net IDENTIFIED BY "topaz"
```

The host part of the user identifier can be given using an IP address rather than a hostname if you like. You can specify a literal IP address or an address that contains pattern characters. Also, as of MySQL 3.23, you can specify IP numbers with a netmask indicating the number of bits to use for the network number:

```
GRANT ALL ON samp_db.* TO joe@192.168.128.3 IDENTIFIED BY "water"
GRANT ALL ON samp_db.* TO ardis@192.168.128.% IDENTIFIED BY "snow"
GRANT ALL ON samp_db.* TO rex@192.168.128.0/17 IDENTIFIED BY "ice"
```

The first of these statements indicates a specific host from which the user can connect. The second specifies an IP pattern for the 192.168.128 Class C subnet. In the third statement, 192.168.128.0/17 specifies a 17-bit network number and matches any host with 192.168.128 in the first 17 bits of its IP address.

If MySQL complains about the user value that you specify, you may need to use quotes (but quote the username and hostname parts separately):

```
GRANT ALL ON samp_db.president TO "my friend"@"boa.snake.net"
```

What Level of Privileges Should the User Have, and What Should They Apply To?

You can grant different levels of privileges. Global privileges are the most powerful because they apply to any database. To make `ethel` a superuser who can do anything, including being able to grant privileges to other users, issue this statement:

```
GRANT ALL ON *.* TO ethel@localhost IDENTIFIED BY "coffee"
    WITH GRANT OPTION
```

The `*.*` specifier in the `ON` clause means "all databases, all tables." As a safety precaution, we've specified that `ethel` can connect only from the local host. Limiting the hosts from which a superuser can connect is usually wise because it limits the hosts from which password-cracking attempts can be mounted.

Some privileges (`FILE`, `PROCESS`, `RELOAD`, and `SHUTDOWN`) are administrative and can only be granted using the `ON *.*` global-privilege specifier. You can, if you wish, grant these privileges without also granting database-level privileges. For example, the following statement sets up a `flush` user that can do nothing but issue `FLUSH` statements. This can be useful in administrative scripts in which you need to perform operations such as flushing the logs during log file rotation:

```
GRANT RELOAD ON *.* TO flush@localhost IDENTIFIED BY "flushpass"
```

Generally, you want to grant administrative privileges only sparingly because users that have them can affect the operation of your server.

Database-level privileges apply to all tables in a particular database. These are granted by using an `ON db_name.*` clause:

```
GRANT ALL ON samp_db.* TO bill@racer.snake.net IDENTIFIED BY "rock"
GRANT SELECT ON menagerie.* TO ro_user@% IDENTIFIED BY "dirt"
```

The first of these statements grants `bill` full privileges for any table in the `samp_db` database. The second creates a restricted-access user `ro_user` ("read-only user") that can access any table in the `menagerie` database, but only for reading. That is, the user can issue only `SELECT` statements.

How to Specify Your Local Hostname in Grant Table Entries

It's common to have problems connecting from the server host if you use the server's hostname rather than `localhost`. This can occur due to a mismatch between the way the name is specified in the grant tables and the way your name resolver routines report the name to programs. If the resolver reports an unqualified name, such as `pit-viper`, but the grant tables contain entries with the fully qualified name—such as `pit-viper.snake.net` (or vice versa)—this mismatch will occur.

To determine if this is happening on your system, try connecting to the local server using a `-h` option that specifies the name of your host. Then look in the server's general log file. How does it report the hostname? Is it in unqualified or fully qualified form? Whichever form it's in, that tells you how you'll need to specify the hostname part of user specifiers when you issue `GRANT` statements.

You can list a number of individual privileges to be granted at the same time. For example, if you want a user to be able to read and modify the contents of existing tables, but not to create new tables or drop tables, grant those privileges as follows:

```
GRANT SELECT,INSERT,DELETE,UPDATE ON samp_db.* TO jennie@%
    IDENTIFIED BY "boron"
```

For more fine-grained access control, you can grant privileges on the individual tables, or even on individual columns in tables. Column-specific privileges are useful when there are parts of a table you want to hide from a user, or when you want a user to be able to modify only particular columns. Suppose someone volunteers to help you out at the Historical League office with the duties that you perform as the League secretary. That's good news, but you decide to begin by granting your new assistant read-only access to the member table that contains membership information, plus a column-specific UPDATE privilege on the expiration column of that table. That way, your assistant can begin with the modest task of updating expiration dates as people renew their memberships. The statements to set up this MySQL user are as follows:

```
GRANT SELECT ON samp_db.member
    TO assistant@localhost IDENTIFIED BY "officehelp"
GRANT UPDATE (expiration) ON samp_db.member
    TO assistant@localhost
```

The first statement grants read access to the entire member table and sets up a password. The second statement adds the UPDATE privilege, but only for the expiration column. It's not necessary to specify the password again because that was done by the first statement.

If you want to grant column-specific privileges for more than one column, specify a list of columns separated by commas. For example, to add UPDATE privileges for the address fields of the member table for the assistant user, use the following statement. The new privileges will be added to any that already exist for the user:

```
GRANT UPDATE (street,city,state,zip) ON samp_db.member
    TO assistant@localhost
```

Normally, you don't want to grant privileges that are any broader than what a user really needs. However, one reason to grant fairly permissive privileges on a database occurs when you want your users to be able to create scratch tables to hold intermediate results, but you don't want them to do so in a database containing data that they shouldn't be modifying. You can accomplish this by setting up a separate database (I'll call it tmp) and granting users all privileges in this database. For example, if you want any user from hosts in the mars.net domain to be able to use the tmp database, you can issue this GRANT statement:

```
GRANT ALL ON tmp.* TO ""@%.mars.net
```

After you've done that, users can create and refer to tables in the tmp database using names of the form tmp.tbl_name. (The "" in the user specifier creates an anonymous user entry; any user matches the blank username.)

Should the User Be Allowed to Administer Privileges?

You can allow the owner of a database to control access to the database by granting the owner all privileges on the database, and specifying the WITH GRANT OPTION when you do. For example, if you want alicia to be able to connect from any host in the big-corp.com domain and administer privileges for all tables in the sales database, you could use this GRANT statement:

```
GRANT ALL ON sales.*
    TO alicia@%.big-corp.com IDENTIFIED BY "applejuice"
    WITH GRANT OPTION
```

In effect, the WITH GRANT OPTION clause allows you to delegate access-granting rights to another user. Be aware that two users with the GRANT privilege can grant each other their own privileges. If you've given one user only the SELECT privilege but another user has GRANT plus other privileges in addition to SELECT, the second user can make the first one "stronger."

Revoking Privileges and Removing Users

To take away a user's privileges, use the REVOKE statement. The syntax for REVOKE is very much like that for the GRANT statement, except that TO is replaced by FROM and there are no IDENTIFIED BY or WITH GRANT OPTION clauses:

```
REVOKE privileges (columns) ON what FROM user
```

The *user* part must match the *user* part of the original GRANT statement for the user whose privileges you want to revoke. The *privileges* part need not match; you can grant privileges with a GRANT statement, then revoke only some of them with REVOKE.

The REVOKE statement removes only privileges, not users. An entry for the user remains in the user table even if you revoke all of the user's privileges. This means the user can still connect to the server. To remove a user entirely, you must explicitly delete the user record from the user table with a DELETE statement:

```
% mysql -u root mysql
mysql> DELETE FROM user
    -> WHERE User = "user_name" and Host = "host_name";
mysql> FLUSH PRIVILEGES;
```

The DELETE statement removes the user's entry, and the FLUSH statement tells the server to reload the grant tables. (The tables are reloaded automatically when you use GRANT or REVOKE, but not when you modify the grant tables directly.)

The next section describes a situation that illustrates why you might want to delete user table entries.

A Privilege Puzzle, Part I

Here's a scenario that comes up repeatedly on the MySQL mailing list: A new MySQL administrator adds an entry for a user, but uses a hostname part that is specified using a pattern. For example:

```
GRANT ALL ON samp_db.* TO fred@%.snake.net IDENTIFIED BY "cocoa"
```

The intent here is to allow the user `fred` to connect from any host in the `snake.net` domain and have all privileges for the `samp_db` database. In fact, `fred` will be able to connect from those hosts, *except* from the server host itself! When `fred` tries to connect from the server host, the attempt fails with an "access denied" message, even though he specifies the correct password.

This situation happens if your grant tables contain the default entries installed by the `mysql_install_db` initialization script. The reason it occurs is that when the server validates `fred`'s connection attempt, one of the anonymous-user entries takes precedence over `fred`'s entry. The anonymous-user entry requires the user to connect with no password, and a password mismatch results. Additional background on this problem is given in the section "A Privilege Puzzle, Part II" of Chapter 12, "Security." For now, suffice it to say that the way to fix the problem is to delete the anonymous-user entries from the `user` table. We can't use `REVOKE` for this because it only revokes privileges. To get rid of the entries entirely, do this:

```
% mysql -u root mysql
mysql> DELETE FROM user where User="";
mysql> FLUSH PRIVILEGES;
```

Now when `fred` attempts to connect from the local host, he'll succeed.

Maintaining Log Files

When the MySQL server starts up, it examines its command-line options to see whether or not it should perform logging and opens the appropriate log files if it should. There are two primary types of logs you can tell the server to generate:

- **The general log file.** This reports client connections, queries, and various other miscellaneous events. It is useful for tracking server activity: who is connecting, from where, and what they are doing.

- **The update log.** This reports queries that modify the database. The term "update" in this context refers not just to UPDATE statements, but to any statement that modifies a database. For this reason, it contains a record of queries such as DELETE, INSERT, REPLACE, CREATE TABLE, DROP TABLE, GRANT, and REVOKE. Update log contents are written as SQL statements in a form that can be used as input to mysql. This is useful in conjunction with backups if you have to restore tables after a crash. You can restore a database from your backup files, then rerun any queries that modified the database subsequent to the backup by using the update logs as input to mysql. That way you can bring the tables to the state they were in at the time of the crash.

To enable logging, use the --log option to turn on the general log and the --log-update option to turn on the update log. You can specify these options on the command line for mysqld, safe_mysqld, or mysql.server, or in the [mysqld] group in an option file. When you enable logging, the log files are written to the server's data directory by default.

I recommend that you enable both types of logging when you first start using MySQL. After you have gained some experience with it, you may want to get by with only the update log to reduce your disk space requirements.

After you've enabled logging, you need to make sure you don't fill up your disks with huge amounts of log information, particularly if you have a busy server that is processing lots of queries. You can use log file rotation and expiration to keep the last few logs available online while preventing log files from growing without bound.

Log file rotation works as follows. Suppose the log file is named log. At the first rotation, log is renamed to log.0 and the server begins writing a new log file. At the second rotation, log.0 is renamed to log.1, log is renamed to log.0, and the server begins writing another new log file. In this way, each file rotates through the names log.0, log.1, and so forth. When the file reaches a certain point in the rotation, you expire it.

Update Logs and LOAD DATA Statements

Currently, when the server executes a LOAD DATA statement, it writes only the statement itself to the update log, not the contents of the rows that are loaded. This means a recovery operation that uses the update logs will be incomplete unless the data file remains accessible. To ensure this, you shouldn't delete the data file until the database has been backed up.

System Backups

Your update logs won't be any good for database recovery if a disk crash causes you to lose them. Make sure you're performing regular file system backups. It's also a good idea to write update logs to a different disk than the one where your databases are stored. See Chapter 10, "The MySQL Data Directory," for instructions on relocating log files.

For example, if you rotate the logs daily and you want to keep a week's work of logs, you would keep `log.0` through `log.6`. At the next rotation, you would expire `log.6` by letting `log.5` overwrite it to become the new `log.6`. In this way, you would retain a number of logs but also prevent them from overrunning your disk.

The frequency of log rotation and the number of old logs you keep will depend on how busy your server is (active servers generate more log information) and how much disk space you're willing to devote to old logs. When you rotate the general logs, you can tell the server to close the current log file and open a new one using the `mysqladmin flush-logs` command.

A script to perform general log rotation might look like this (modify it to reflect your log basename and data directory location, and perhaps the number of old logs you wish to keep):

```
#! /bin/sh

base=basename
datadir=DATADIR

cd $datadir
mv $base.5 $base.6
mv $base.4 $base.5
mv $base.3 $base.4
mv $base.2 $base.3
mv $base.1 $base.2
mv $base.0 $base.1
mv $base $base.0
mysqladmin flush-logs
```

It's best to run this script from the `mysqladm` account to make sure that the log files are owned by that user. If you keep your connection parameters in your `.my.cnf` option file, you don't need to specify any parameters on the `mysqladmin` command in the script. If you don't, you might want to set up a limited-privilege user that can't do anything but issue flush commands. Then you can put that user's password in the script with minimal risk. If you want to do this, the user should have only the `RELOAD` privilege. For example, to call the user `flush` and assign a password of `flushpass`, use the following `GRANT` statement:

```
GRANT RELOAD ON *.* TO flush@localhost IDENTIFIED BY "flushpass"
```

When you need to perform a flush operation in a script, you can do so like this:

```
mysqladmin -u flush -pflushpass flush-logs
```

Under Linux, you may prefer to use `logrotate` to install the `mysql-log-rotate` script that comes with the MySQL distribution, rather than writing your own script. Look in the `support-files` directory of your MySQL distribution if `mysql-log-rotate` wasn't installed automatically by an RPM file.

Log file rotation is a bit different for update logs than for the general logs because of the way the server handles update log filenames. If you tell the server to use an update log filename with no extension, such as `update`, it automatically creates update log filenames using the sequence `update.001`, `update.002`, and so forth. A new update log file is created when the server starts up and when the logs are flushed. If you turn on update logging without specifying a filename, the server generates a sequence of update log files using your hostname as the basename.

When you expire a sequence of files that are generated this way, you'll probably want to expire them based on age (assessed as time of last modification) rather than name. The reason for this is that you don't know when `flush-logs` commands might be issued, so you can't count on a fixed number of update logs being created in any give time period. For example, if you back up tables with `mysqldump` and use the `--flush-logs` option, a new file in the update log name sequence is created with each backup.

For update logs with sequenced filenames that are automatically generated by the server, an expiration script based on age might look like this:

```
#! /bin/sh

find DATADIR -name "update.[0-9]*" -type f -mtime +6 | xargs rm -f
mysqladmin flush-logs
```

The `find` command locates and removes update log files last modified more than a week ago. It's important to use the `-name` argument to test for a numeric filename extension to avoid removing a table named `update` by mistake.

You can tell the server to use a fixed update log filename if you want. This is useful if you want to rotate update logs the same way as the general logs. To use a fixed update log name, specify a name that includes an extension. For example, you can start the server with a `--log-update=update.log` option to use the name `update.log`. The server will still close and open the log each time a `flush-logs` command is received, but it will not generate a new file each time. In this case, the log rotation script used for update logs differs from that used for the general logs only in the basename of the files you're rotating.

You'll probably want to perform log rotation and expiration automatically. You can do so using `cron`. Assume the scripts for rotating the general and update logs are called `rotate-logs` and `rotate-update-logs`, and that they're installed in `/usr/users/mysql/bin`. Log in as `mysqladm`, then edit the `mysqladm` user's `crontab` file using this command:

```
% crontab -e
```

This command will allow you to edit a copy of your current `crontab` file (which may be empty if you haven't done this before). Add lines to the file that look like this:

```
0 4 * * * /usr/users/mysqladm/bin/rotate-logs
0 4 * * * /usr/users/mysqladm/bin/rotate-update-logs
```

This entry tells cron to run the script at 4 a.m. every morning. You can vary the time or scheduling as desired; check the crontab manual page for instructions.

Backing Up and Copying Databases

It's important to back up your databases in case tables are lost or damaged. If a system crash occurs, you want to be able to restore your tables to the state they were in at the time of the crash with as little data loss as possible. Likewise, a user who issues an unwise DROP DATABASE or DROP TABLE will likely show up at your door requesting that you perform data recovery. Sometimes it's the MySQL administrator who causes the damage. Administrators have been known to damage table files by trying to edit them directly using an editor such as vi or emacs. This is certain to do bad things to a table!

The two main methods for backing up databases are to use the mysqldump program or to directly copy database files (for example, with cp, tar, or cpio). Each method has its own advantages and disadvantages:

- mysqldump operates in cooperation with the MySQL server. Direct-copy methods are external to the server, and you must take steps to ensure that no clients are modifying the tables while you copy them. This is the same problem that occurs if you try to use file system backups to back up databases: If a database table is being updated during the file system backup, the table files that go into the backup are in an inconsistent state and are worthless for restoring the table later. The difference between file system backups and direct-copy files is that for the latter you have control over the backup schedule, so you can take steps to make sure the server leaves the tables alone.

- mysqldump is slower than direct-copy techniques.

- mysqldump generates text files that are portable to other machines, even those with a different hardware architecture. Direct-copy files are not portable to other machines unless the tables you're copying use the MyISAM storage format. ISAM tables can be copied only between machines of like hardware architecture. For example, copying files from Solaris on SPARC to Solaris on SPARC will work, but copying files from Solaris on SPARC to Solaris on Intel or vice-versa will not work. The MyISAM table storage format introduced in MySQL 3.23 solves this problem because the format is machine independent. Therefore, directly copied files can be moved to a machine with a different hardware architecture if two conditions are satisfied: The other machine must also be running MySQL 3.23 or later, and the files must represent MyISAM tables, not ISAM tables.

Whichever backup method you choose, there are certain principles to which you should adhere to assure the best results if you ever need to restore database contents:

- Perform backups regularly. Set a schedule and stick to it.

- Tell the server to perform update logging (see the earlier section, "Maintaining Log Files"). Update logs help you when you need to restore a database after a crash. After you use your backup files to restore a database to the state it was in at the time of the backup, you can reapply the changes that were made subsequent to the backup by running the queries in the update logs. This restores the tables in the database to their state at the time the crash occurred.

  In the language of file system backups, database backup files represent full dumps, and update logs represent incremental dumps.

- Use a consistent and understandable backup file-naming scheme. Names like `backup1`, `backup2`, and so forth are not particularly meaningful. When it comes time to perform your restore, you'll waste time figuring out what's in the files. You may find it useful to construct backup filenames using database names and dates. For example:

  ```
  % mysqldump samp_db > /usr/archives/mysql/samp_db.1999-10-02
  % mysqldump menagerie > /usr/archives/mysql/menagerie.1999-10-02
  ```

  You might want to compress backup files after you generate them. Backups tend to be large, after all! You'll also need to expire your backup files to keep them from filling your disk, just like you expire your log files. See the section "Maintaining Log Files" for information on log file expiration. You can use the same techniques to expire your backup files.

- Back up your backup files using file system backups. If you have a complete crash that wipes out not only your data directory but also the disk drive containing your database backups, you'll be in real trouble. Back up your update logs, too.

- Put your backup files on a different file system than the one you use for your databases. This reduces the likelihood of filling up the file system containing the data directory as a result of generating backups.

The techniques that are used for creating backups are also useful for copying databases to another server. Most commonly, a database is transferred to a server running on another host, but you can also transfer data to another server running on the same host. You might do this if you're running a server for a new release of MySQL and want to test it with some real data from your production server. Or you might have gotten a new machine and want to move all your databases onto it.

Using `mysqldump` to Back Up and Copy Databases

When you use the `mysqldump` program to generate database backup files, by default the contents of the file consist of `CREATE TABLE` statements that create the tables being dumped and `INSERT` statements containing the data for the rows in the tables. In other words, `mysqldump` creates output that can be used later as input to `mysql` to re-create the database.

You can dump an entire database into a single text file like this:

```
% mysqldump samp_db > /usr/archives/mysql/samp_db.1999-10-02
```

The beginning of the output file looks like this:

```
# MySQL dump 6.0
#
# Host: localhost    Database: samp_db
#--------------------------------------------------------
# Server version       3.23.2-alpha-log
#
# Table structure for table 'absence'
#
CREATE TABLE absence (
  student_id int(10) unsigned DEFAULT '0' NOT NULL,
  date date DEFAULT '0000-00-00' NOT NULL,
  PRIMARY KEY (student_id,date)
);
#
# Dumping data for table 'absence'
#
INSERT INTO absence VALUES (3,'1999-09-03');
INSERT INTO absence VALUES (5,'1999-09-03');
INSERT INTO absence VALUES (10,'1999-09-06');
...
```

The rest of the file consists of more INSERT and CREATE TABLE statements.

If you want to compress the backup as you generate it, use a command like this instead:

```
% mysqldump samp_db | gzip > /usr/archives/mysql/samp_db.1999-10-02.gz
```

If you have a huge database, the output file also will be huge and may be difficult to manage. If you like, you can dump the contents of individual tables by naming them after the database name on the mysqldump command line. This partitions the dump into smaller, more manageable files. The following example shows how to dump some of the samp_db tables into separate files:

```
% mysqldump samp_db student score event absence > gradebook.sql
% mysqldump samp_db member president > hist-league.sql
```

If you're generating backup files that are intended to be used to periodically refresh the contents of another database, you may want to use the --add-drop-table option. This tells mysqldump to write DROP TABLE IF EXISTS statements into the backup file. Then, when you take the backup file and load it into the second database, you won't get an error if the tables already exist. If you're running a second test server, you can use this technique to periodically reload it with a copy of the data from the databases on your production server.

If you are dumping a database so that you can transfer the database to another server, you don't even need to create backup files. Make sure that the database exists on the other host, then dump the database using a pipe so that `mysql` reads the output of `mysqldump` directly. For example, if you want to copy the `samp_db` database from `pit-viper.snake.net` to `boa.snake.net`, that's easily done like this:

```
% mysqladmin -h boa.snake.net create samp_db
% mysqldump samp_db | mysql -h boa.snake.net samp_db
```

Later, if you want to refresh that database on `boa.snake.net` again, skip the `mysqladmin` command, but add the `--add-drop-table` to the `mysqldump` to avoid getting errors about tables already existing:

```
% mysqldump --add-drop-table samp_db | mysql -h boa.snake.net samp_db
```

Other useful `mysqldump` options include the following:

- The combination of `--flush-logs` and `--lock-tables` is helpful for checkpointing your database. `--lock-tables` locks all the tables that you're dumping, and `--flush-logs` closes and reopens the update log file. If you're generating sequenced update logs, the new update log will contain only queries that modify databases from the point of the backup. This checkpoints your update log to the time of the backup. (Locking all the tables is not so good for client access during the backups if you have clients that need to perform updates, however.)

  If you use `--flush-logs` to checkpoint the update logs to the time of the backup, it's probably best to dump the entire database. If you dump individual files, it's harder to synchronize update log checkpoints against your backup files. During restore operations, you usually extract update log contents on a per-database basis. There is no option for extracting updates for individual tables, so you'll have to extract them yourself.

- By default, `mysqldump` reads the entire contents of a table into memory before writing it out. This isn't really necessary, and in fact is almost a recipe for failure if you have really large tables. You can use the `--quick` option to tell `mysqldump` to write each row as soon as it has been retrieved. To further optimize the dump process, use `--opt` instead of `--quick`. The `--opt` option turns on other options that speed up dumping the data and reading it back in.

  Performing backups using `--opt` is probably the most common method because of the benefits for backup speed. Be warned, however, that the `--opt` option does have a price; what `--opt` optimizes is your backup procedure, not access by other clients to the database. The `--opt` option prevents anyone from updating any of the tables that you're dumping by locking all the tables at once. You can easily see for yourself the effect of this on general database access. Just try running a backup at the time of day when your database is normally most heavily used. It won't take long for your phone to start ringing with people calling to find out what's going on. (I'd appreciate it if you would refrain from asking yourself how it is that I happen to know this.)

- An option with something of the opposite effect of `--opt` is `--delayed`. This option causes `mysqldump` to write `INSERT DELAYED` statements rather than `INSERT` statements. If you are loading a data file into another database and you want to minimize the impact of this operation on other queries that may be taking place in that database, `--delayed` is helpful for achieving that end.

- The `--compress` option is helpful when you're copying a database to another machine because it reduces the number of bytes travelling over the network. Here is an example; notice that the `--compress` option is given for the program that communicates with the server on the remote host, not the one that communicates with the local host:

```
% mysqldump --opt samp_db | mysql --compress -h boa.snake.net samp_db
```

`mysqldump` has many other options. Consult Appendix E for more information.

Using Direct-Copy Database Backup and Copying Methods

Another way to back up a database or tables that doesn't involve `mysqldump` is to copy table files directly. Typically this is done using utilities such as `cp`, `tar`, or `cpio`. The examples in this section use `cp`.

When you use a direct-copy backup method, you must make sure the tables aren't being used. If the server is changing a table while you're copying it, the copies will be worthless.

The best way to ensure the integrity of your copies is to bring down the server, copy the files, and restart the server. If you don't want to bring down the server, you should refer to Chapter 13. Take a look at the techniques described there for locking the server while performing table checking. If the server is running, the same constraints apply to copying files, and you should use the same locking protocol to keep the server quiet.

Assuming that the server is either down or that you've locked the tables you want to copy, the following example shows how to back up the entire `samp_db` database to a backup directory (`DATADIR` represents the server's data directory):

```
% cd DATADIR
% cp -r samp_db /usr/archive/mysql
```

Individual tables can be backed up like this:

```
% cd DATADIR/samp_db
% cp member.* /usr/archive/mysql/samp_db
% cp score.* /usr/archive/mysql/samp_db
...
```

When you're done backing up, you can restart the server (if you brought it down) or release the locks you have on the tables (if you left the server running).

To use direct-copy files to copy a database from one machine to another, just copy the files to the appropriate database directory on the other server host. Make sure the files are for MyISAM tables or that both machines have the same hardware architecture, though. Your tables may appear to have very strange contents on the second host otherwise. You should also make sure the server on the second host doesn't attempt to access the tables while you're installing them.

Replicating Databases

The term "replication" can mean something as simple as copying a database to another server, or it can involve live updating of a secondary database as changes are made to the contents of a master database. If you simply want to copy a database to another server, you can use commands for this that were already shown earlier. Support for replication based on live updating has begun to appear in MySQL as of the 3.23 version. This capability is still in its infancy, so I won't say more about it other than you should keep an eye on current versions as they are released to see what new developments are taking place if you're interested.

Using Backups for Data Recovery

Database damage occurs for a number of reasons and varies in extent. If you're lucky, you may simply have minor damage to a table or two (for example, if your machine goes down briefly due to a power outage). If you're not so lucky, you may have to replace your entire data directory (for example, if a disk died and took your data directory with it). Recovery is also needed under other circumstances, such as when users mistakenly drop databases or tables or delete a table's contents. Whatever the reason for these unfortunate events, you'll need to perform some sort of recovery.

If tables are damaged but not lost, try to repair them using `myisamchk` or `isamchk`. You may not need to use backup files at all if the damage is such that the repair utilities can fix it. The procedure for table repair is described in Chapter 13. If tables are lost or irreparable, you'll need to restore them.

Recovery procedures involve two sources of information: your backup files and your update logs. The backup files restore tables to the state they were in at the time the backup was performed. However, tables typically will have been modified between the time of the dump and the time at which problems occurred. The update logs contain the queries used to make those changes. You can repeat the queries by using the update logs as input to `mysql`. (This is why you should enable update logging. If you haven't yet done so, you should do so right now and generate a new backup before reading further.)

The recovery procedure varies depending on how much information you must restore. In fact, it may be easier to restore an entire database than a single table because it's easier to apply the update logs for a database than for a table.

Recovering an Entire Database

First of all, if the database you want to recover is the `mysql` database that contains the grant tables, you'll need to run the server using the `--skip-grant-tables` option. Otherwise, it will complain about not being able to find the grant tables. After you've restored the tables, execute `mysqladmin flush-privileges` to tell the server to load the grant tables and start using them.

- Copy the contents of the database directory somewhere else. You may want them later—for example, to perform post-mortem examination of the corpses of crashed tables.

- Reload the database using your most recent backup files. If you're using files generated by `mysqldump`, use them as input to `mysql`. If you're using files that were directly copied from the database (for example, with `tar` or `cp`), copy them directly back into the database directory. In this case, however, you should bring down the server before copying the files and restart it afterward.

- Use the update logs to repeat the queries that modified database tables subsequent to the time at which the backup was made. For any applicable update log, use it as input to `mysql`. Specify the `--one-database` option so that `mysql` executes queries only for the database you're interested in recovering. If you know you need to apply all the update log files, you can use this command in the directory containing the logs:

```
% ls -t -r -1 update.[0-9]* | xargs cat | mysql --one-database db_name
```

The `ls` command produces a single-column list of update log files, sorted according to the order in which they were generated by the server. (Be aware that if you modify any of the files, you will change the sort order, which will result in the update logs being applied in the wrong order.)

It's more likely that you'll have to apply just some update logs. For example, if the logs made since the time of your backup are named `update.392`, `update.393`, and so forth, you can rerun the commands in them like this:

```
% mysql --one-database db_name < update.392
% mysql --one-database db_name < update.393
...
```

If you're performing recovery and using update logs to restore information that was lost due to an ill-advised `DROP DATABASE`, `DROP TABLE`, or `DELETE` statement, be sure to remove that statement from the update log in which it appears before applying the log!

Recovering Individual Tables

Recovering individual tables is more difficult. If you have a backup file generated by `mysqldump` and it doesn't contain the data just for the table in which you're interested, you'll need to extract the relevant lines and use them as input to `mysql`. That's the easy part. The hard part is pulling out the pieces of the update log that apply to just that table. You may find the `mysql_find_rows` utility helpful for this; it can extract multiple-line queries from update logs.

Another possibility is to restore the entire database using another server, then copy the files for the table you want to the original database. This may actually be easier! Make sure the server for the original database is down when you copy the files back into the database directory.

Tuning the Server

The MySQL server has several parameters (variables) that affect how it operates. If the default parameter values are not appropriate, you can change them to values that are better for the environment in which your server runs. For example, if you have plenty of memory, you can tell the server to use larger buffers for disk and index operations. This will hold more information in memory and decrease the number of disk accesses that need to be made. If your system is more modest, you can tell the server to use smaller buffers to prevent it from hogging system resources to the detriment of other processes.

The current values of the server's variables can be examined by executing the `mysqladmin variables` command. Variables can be set with the `--set-variable var_name=value` option on the command line (`-O var_name=value` is equivalent.) If you want to set several variables, use multiple `--set-variable` options. You can also set variables in the `[mysqld]` group in an option file using this syntax:

```
set-variable=var_name=value
```

A complete list of server variables is given in Appendix E under the entry for the `mysqld` program. Those that are most likely to be useful for performance tuning are shown in the following list. You can also find additional discussion of this topic in the chapter "Getting Maximum Performance from MySQL" in the MySQL Reference Manual.

- `back_log`

  The number of incoming client connection requests that can be queued while processing requests from the current clients. If you have a very busy site, you may want to increase the value of this variable.

- `delayed_queue_size`

  This variable controls the number of rows from `INSERT DELAYED` statements that can be queued. If the queue is full, further `INSERT DELAYED` statements block until there is room in the queue, which prevents the clients that issue those statements from continuing. If you have many clients that perform this kind of `INSERT` and you find that they are blocking, increasing this variable will allow more of them to continue more quickly. (`INSERT DELAYED` is discussed in the section "Scheduling and Locking Issues" of Chapter 4, "Query Optimization.")

- `flush_time`

  If your system has problems and tends to lock up or reboot often, setting this variable to a non-zero value causes the server to flush the table cache every `flush_time` seconds. Writing out table changes in this way degrades performance but can reduce the chance of table corruption or data loss.

  Under Windows, you can start the server with the `--flush` option on the command line to force table changes to be flushed after every update.

- `key_buffer_size`

  The size of the buffer used to hold index blocks. Creating and modifying indexes is faster if you increase the value of this variable. Larger values make it more likely that MySQL will find key values in memory, which reduces the number of disk accesses needed for index processing.

  This variable is called `key_buffer` in versions of MySQL prior to 3.23. MySQL 3.23 and up recognizes both names.

- `max_allowed_packet`

  The maximum size to which the buffer used for client communications can grow. If you have clients that send large `BLOB` or `TEXT` values, this server variable may need to be increased.

  Clients currently use a default buffer size of 24MB. If you have older clients that use a smaller buffer, you may need to make the client buffer larger. For example, `mysql` can be invoked like this to specify a 24MB packet limit:

  ```
  mysql --set-variable max_allowed_packet=24M
  ```

- `max_connections`

  The maximum number of simultaneous client connections the server will allow. If your server is busy, you may need to increase this value. For example, if your MySQL server is used by your Web server to process queries generated by DBI or PHP scripts, and you have a lot of Web traffic, visitors to your site may find requests being refused if this variable is set too low.

- `table_cache`

  The size of the table cache. Increasing this value allows `mysqld` to keep more tables open simultaneously and reduces the number of file opens and closes that must be done.

If you increase the values of `max_connections` or `table_cache`, the server will require a larger number of file descriptors. That may cause problems with operating system limits on the per-process number of file descriptors, in which case you'll need to increase the limit or work around it. Procedures vary for increasing the limit on the number of file descriptors. You may be able to do this at runtime using the `ulimit` command in the script that you use to start up the server, or you may need to reconfigure your system. Some systems can be configured simply by editing a system description file and rebooting. For others, you must edit a kernel description file and rebuild the kernel. Consult the documentation for your system to see how to proceed.

One way to work around per-process file descriptor limits is to split your data directory into multiple data directories and run multiple servers. This effectively multiplies the number of file descriptors available by the number of servers you run. On the other hand, other complications can cause you problems. To name two, you cannot access databases in different data directories from a single server, and you might need to replicate privileges in the grant tables across different servers for users that need access to more than one server.

Two variables that administrators sometimes increase in hopes of improving performance are `record_buffer` and `sort_buffer`. These buffers are used during join and sort operations, but the values are per connection. That is, each client gets its own buffers. If you make the values of these variables quite large, performance may actually suffer due to exorbitant system resource consumption. If you want to modify these variables, execute `mysqladmin variables` to see what values they currently have, then adjust up the values incrementally. This will allow you to assess the effect of the change with less likelihood of serious performance degradation.

Running Multiple Servers

Most people run a single MySQL server on a given machine, but there are circumstances under which it can be useful to run multiple servers:

- You may want to test a new version of the server while leaving your production server running. In this case, you'll be running different server binaries.
- Operating systems typically impose per-process limitations on the number of open file descriptors. If your system makes it difficult to raise the limit, running multiple servers is one way to work around that limitation. (For example, raising the limit may require recompiling the kernel, and you may not be able to do that if you're not in charge of administering the machine.) In this case, you may be running multiple instances of the same server binary.
- Internet service providers often provide customers with their own MySQL installation, which necessarily involves separate servers. In this case, you may be running multiple instances of the same binary or different binaries if different customers want different versions of MySQL.

Naturally, running several servers is more complicated than running just one. If you're installing multiple versions, you can't just install them all in the same place. When the servers run, certain parameters must be or are likely to be unique to each server. Some of these include where the server is installed, the pathname to its data directory, its TCP/IP port and UNIX domain socket pathname, and the UNIX account used to run the server (if you don't run all servers under the same account). If you decide to run multiple servers, be sure to keep good notes on the parameters you're using so that you don't lose track of what's going on.

Configuring and Installing Multiple Servers

If you're going to run different versions of the server rather than multiple instances of the same server, you should install them in different locations. If you install binary (not RPM) distributions, they'll be installed under a directory name that includes the version number. If you install from source, the easiest way to keep different distributions separate is to use the `--with-prefix` option when you run `configure` during the MySQL installation process for each version. That will cause everything to be installed under a single directory, and you can tie that directory to the distribution version number. For example, you can configure a MySQL distribution as follows, where *version* is the MySQL version number:

```
% ./configure --with-prefix=/usr/local/mysql-version
```

The `--with-prefix` option will also determine a unique data directory for the server. You may want to add options to configure other server-specific values, such as the TCP/IP port number and socket pathname (`--with-tcp-port`, and `--with-unix-socket`).

If you're going to run multiple instances of the same server binary, any option that must be set on a server-specific basis will need to be specified at run time.

Multiple Server Startup Procedures

Starting up multiple servers is more complicated than using a single server, because `safe_mysqld` and `mysql.server` both work best in a single-server setting. I recommend that you study `safe_mysqld` carefully and use it as a basis for your startup procedures, but that you use modified copies that you can tailor more precisely to your own requirements.

One problem you must deal with is how to specify options in option files. With multiple servers, you can't use `/etc/my.cnf` for settings that vary on a per-server basis. You can only use that file for settings that you want to be the same for all servers. If each server has a different compiled-in data directory location, you can specify server-specific parameters in the `my.cnf` file in each server's data directory. In other words, use `/etc/my.cnf` for settings you want all servers to use and *DATADIR*`/my.cnf` for server-specific settings, where *DATADIR* varies per server.

Another way to specify server options is to use `--defaults-file=`*path_name* as the first option on the command line to tell the server to read options from the file named by *path_name*. This way, you can put a server's options in a file unique to that server, then tell it to read that file at startup time. Note that if you specify this option, none of the usual option files, such as `/etc/my.cnf`, will be used.

Updating MySQL

When MySQL was first released publicly, it was at version 3.11.1. It's now in the version 3.22 series for stable releases and the 3.23 series for development releases. The stable release series is always one minor number behind the development series. After 3.23 becomes stable, work will begin on using 3.24 as the development series. The MySQL developers apparently work without sleep, so updates appear fairly often (several times a year). Updates are issued for both the stable and development series. The pace of ongoing development raises the question for the MySQL administrator as to whether or not you should upgrade your existing MySQL installation when new releases appear. This section provides some guidelines to help you make this decision.

The first thing you should do when a new release appears is to find out how it differs from previous releases. Check the "Change Notes" appendix in the MySQL Reference Manual to familiarize yourself with what's different. Then ask yourself these questions:

- Are you experiencing problems with your current version that the new version fixes?
- Does the new version have additional features that you want or need?
- Is performance improved for certain types of operations that you use?

If the answer to all of these questions is no, then you don't have any compelling reason to upgrade. If the answer to any of them is yes, you may want to go ahead. At this point, it's often useful to wait a few days and watch the MySQL mailing list to see what other people report about the release. Was the upgrade helpful? Were bugs or other problems found?

Some other factors to consider that may help you make your decision are as follows:

- Releases in the stable series are most often for bug fixes, not new features. There is generally less risk for upgrades within the stable series than within the development series. (Of course, if you're running a development series server, you may not be that concerned about risk anyway!)
- It's possible that if you upgrade MySQL, you'll need to upgrade other programs that are built with the MySQL C client library linked in. For example, after a MySQL upgrade, you may also need to rebuild PHP, Apache, and the Perl DBD::mysql module to link the new client library into those programs. (An obvious symptom that you need to do this is when all your MySQL-related DBI and PHP scripts start dumping core after you upgrade MySQL.) It's not generally a big deal to rebuild these programs, but if you prefer to avoid it, you may be better off not upgrading MySQL. If you use statically linked rather than dynamically linked programs, the likelihood of this problem is much reduced. However, then your system memory requirements increase.

If you're still not sure whether or not to upgrade, you can always test the new server independently of your current server. You can do this either by running it in parallel with your production server, or by installing it on a different machine. It's easier to maintain independence between servers if you use a different machine. If you don't have the luxury of a separate machine to use for testing, you can run the new server on your production machine. If you do this, be *sure* to run the new server with different values for parameters such as the installation location, the data directory, and the network port and socket on which the server listens for connections. See the section "Running Multiple Servers" earlier in this chapter.

In either case, you'll probably want to test the server using a copy of the data in your existing databases. See the section "Backing Up and Copying Databases" for instructions on copying databases.

If you do decide to upgrade, see if there are any remarks in the "Change Notes" appendix in the MySQL Reference Manual about any special steps you must take when upgrading. Usually there aren't any, but check anyway.

Don't Be Afraid to Try Development Releases

You may prefer not to use development releases with your production databases, but I'd encourage you to at least try a separate test server, perhaps with a copy of your production data. The more people that try new releases, the better it helps to find bugs. With some database products, finding bugs is a dreaded thing. With MySQL, bug reports are a significant factor in helping development move forward because the developers actually fix problems that the user community reports.

12

Security

$\mathbf{T}$HE FOCUS OF THIS CHAPTER IS ON what you can do as a MySQL administrator to maintain the security and integrity of your MySQL installation. We have already touched on a few security-related topics in Chapter 11, "General MySQL Administration," such as the importance of setting up the initial MySQL root password and how to set up user accounts. Those topics were dealt with as part of the process of getting your installation up and running. In this chapter, we'll look more closely at security-related issues:

- Why security is important and what kind of attacks you should guard against
- What risks you face from users on the server host (internal security) and what you can do about it
- What risks you face from clients connecting to the server over the network (external security) and what you can do about it

The MySQL administrator is responsible for keeping the contents of databases secure so that records can be accessed only by those who have the proper authorization. This involves both internal and external security.

Internal security concerns the issues involved at the file system level—that is, protecting the MySQL data directory from attack by people who have accounts on the machine on which the server runs. It won't do you much good to make sure the grant tables controlling client access over the network are set up properly if the file permissions on the data directory contents are so permissive that someone can simply replace the files corresponding to those tables!

External security concerns the issues involved with clients connecting from outside—that is, protecting the MySQL server from attack through connections coming in over the network to the server asking for access to database contents. You want to set up the MySQL grant tables so they don't allow access to the databases managed by the server unless a valid name and password is supplied.

This chapter provides a guide to the issues you should be aware of and gives instructions showing how to prevent unauthorized access at both the internal and external levels.

Internal Security: Securing Data Directory Access

The MySQL server provides a flexible privilege system implemented through the grant tables in the `mysql` database. You can set up the contents of these tables to allow or deny database access to clients any way you want. This provides you with security against unauthorized network access to your data. However, it won't do you any good to set up good security for network access to your databases if other users on the server host have direct access to the contents of the data directory. Unless you know you are the only person who ever logs in on the machine where the MySQL server is running, you need to be concerned about the possibility of other people on that machine gaining access to the data directory.

Here's what you want to protect:

- **Database files.** Clearly you want to maintain the privacy of the databases maintained by the server. Database owners usually, and rightly, consider database contents private. Even if they don't, it's up to them to make the contents of a database public, not to have those contents be exposed by poor security of the database directory.

- **Log files.** The general and update logs must be kept secure because they contain the text of queries. This is a general concern in that anyone with log file access can monitor the transactions occurring on databases.

A more specific security concern relating to log files is that queries such as GRANT and SET PASSWORD are logged. The general and update log files contain the text of sensitive queries, including passwords. (MySQL uses password encryption, but this applies to connection establishment after passwords already have been set up. The process of setting up a password involves a query such as GRANT, INSERT, or SET PASSWORD, and such queries are logged in plain text form.) If an attacker has read access to the logs, it's only necessary to run grep on the log for words such as GRANT or PASSWORD to discover sensitive information.

Obviously you don't want other users on the server host to have write access to data directory files, because then they can stomp all over your status files or database tables. But read access is just as dangerous. If a table's files can be read, it is trivial to steal the files and to get MySQL itself to show you the contents of the table in plain text. How? Like this:

1. Install your own rogue MySQL server on the server host, but with a port, socket, and data directory that are different than those used by the official server.

2. Run mysql_install_db to initialize your data directory. This gives you access to your server as the MySQL root user, so you have full control over the server's access mechanism. It also sets up a test database.

3. Copy the files corresponding to the table or tables that you want to steal into the test directory under your server's data directory.

4. Start your rogue server. Presto! You can access the tables at will. SHOW TABLES FROM test shows that you have a copy of the stolen tables, and SELECT * shows the entire contents of any of them.

5. If you want to be really nasty, open up the permissions on the anonymous user accounts for your server so that anyone can connect to the server from anywhere to access your test database. You have now effectively published the stolen tables to the world.

Think about that for a moment, then reverse the perspective. Do you want someone to do that to you? Of course not.

You can determine whether or not your data directory contains insecure files or directories by executing ls -l in the data directory. Look for files or directories that have the "group" or "other" permissions turned on. Here's a partial listing of a data directory that is insecure, as are some of the database directories within it:

```
% ls -l
total 10148
drwxrwxr-x  11 mysqladm wheel        1024 May  8 12:20 .
drwxr-xr-x  22 root     wheel         512 May  8 13:31 ..
drwx------   2 mysqladm mysqlgrp      512 Apr 16 15:57 menagerie
drwxrwxr-x   2 mysqladm wheel         512 Jan 25 20:43 mysql
drwxrwxr-x   7 mysqladm wheel         512 Aug 31  1998 sql-bench
drwxrwxr-x   2 mysqladm wheel        1536 May  6 06:11 test
drwx------   2 mysqladm mysqlgrp     1024 May  8 18:43 tmp
...
```

As you can see, some database directories have proper permissions, and others do not. The situation in this example resulted over time. The less-restrictive permissions were created by older servers that were less stringent than more recent servers about setting permissions. (Notice that the more restrictive directories, menagerie and tmp, all have more recent dates.) Current versions of MySQL make sure these files are readable only to the user the server runs as.

Let's fix up these permissions so that only the server user can access them. Your principal means of protection comes from the tools provided by the UNIX file system itself to set the ownership and mode of files and directories. Here's what to do:

1. Move into the data directory:

   ```
   % cd DATADIR
   ```

2. Set the ownership of all the files under the data directory to be owned by the account used to run the server. (You must perform this step as root.) In this book, I use mysqladm and mysqlgrp for the user and group names of this account. You can change ownerships using either of the following commands:

   ```
   # chown -R mysqladm.mysqlgrp .
   # find . -follow -type d -print | xargs chown mysqladm.mysqlgrp
   ```

3. Change the mode of your data directory and database directories so that they are readable only to mysqladm. This prevents other users from accessing the contents of your data directory. You can do this with either of the following commands, which can be run either as root or as mysqladm (the latter is preferable, to minimize the number of commands that are run as root):

   ```
   % chmod -R go-rwx .
   % find . -follow -type d -print | xargs chmod go-rwx
   ```

4. The ownership and mode of data directory contents are set for the mysqladm user. Now you should make sure that you always run the server as mysqladm because that is the only user who now has access to the data directory. The procedure for running the server as a non-root is described in Chapter 11.

After following the preceding instructions, you should end up with data directory permissions like this:

```
% ls -l
total 10148
drwxrwx---  11 mysqladm mysqlgrp   1024 May  8 12:20 .
drwxr-xr-x  22 root     wheel       512 May  8 13:31 ..
drwx------   2 mysqladm mysqlgrp    512 Apr 16 15:57 menagerie
drwx------   2 mysqladm mysqlgrp    512 Jan 25 20:43 mysql
drwx------   7 mysqladm mysqlgrp    512 Aug 31  1998 sql-bench
drwx------   2 mysqladm mysqlgrp   1536 May  6 06:11 test
drwx------   2 mysqladm mysqlgrp   1024 May  8 18:43 tmp
...
```

External Security: Securing Network Access

The MySQL security system is flexible. It allows you to set up user access privileges in many different ways. Normally, you do this by using the GRANT and REVOKE statements, which modify for you the grant tables that control client access. However, you may have an older version of MySQL that does not support these statements (they were not functional prior to MySQL 3.22.11), or you may find that user privileges don't seem to be working the way you want. For situations like this, it's helpful to understand the structure of the MySQL grant tables and how the server uses them to determine access permissions. Such an understanding allows you to add, remove, or modify user privileges by modifying the grant tables directly. It also allows you to diagnose privilege problems when you examine the tables.

I assume that you've read "Managing User Accounts" in Chapter 11 and that you understand how the GRANT and REVOKE statements work. GRANT and REVOKE provide a convenient way for you to set up MySQL user accounts and associate privileges with them, but they are just a front end. All the real action takes place in the MySQL grant tables.

Structure and Contents of the MySQL Grant Tables

Access to MySQL databases by clients that connect to the server over the network is controlled by the contents of the grant tables. These tables are located in the mysql database and are initialized during the process of installing MySQL on a machine for the first time (as described in Appendix A, "Obtaining and Installing Software," for example). The five grant tables, user, db, host, tables_priv, and columns_priv, are shown in Tables 12.1 and 12.2.

Table 12.1   user, db, **and** host **Grant Table Structure**

	Scope of Access Columns	
user	**db**	**host**
Host	Host	Host
User	Db	Db
Password	User	

	Database/Table Privilege Columns	
Alter_priv	Alter_priv	Alter_priv
Create_priv	Create_priv	Create_priv
Delete_priv	Delete_priv	Delete_priv
Drop_priv	Drop_priv	Drop_priv
Index_priv	Index_priv	Index_priv
Insert_priv	Insert_priv	Insert_priv
References_priv	References_priv	References_priv
Select_priv	Select_priv	Select_priv
Update_priv	Update_priv	Update_priv

continues

Table 12.1 **Continued**

ADMINISTRATIVE PRIVILEGE COLUMNS		
user	**db**	**host**
File_priv	Grant_priv	Grant_priv
Grant_priv		
Process_priv		
Reload_priv		
Shutdown_priv		

Table 12.2 `tables_priv` **and** `columns_priv` **Grant Table Structure**

SCOPE OF ACCESS COLUMNS	
tables_priv	**columns_priv**
Host	Host
Db	Db
User	User
Table_name	Table_name
Column_name	

PRIVILEGE COLUMN	
Table_priv	Column_priv

The contents of the grant tables are used as follows:

- user

    The user table lists users that may connect to the server and their passwords, and it specifies which global (superuser) privileges they have, if any. Any privileges that are enabled in the user table entry are global privileges and apply to all databases. If you enable the DELETE privilege here, the user listed in the entry can delete records from any table, for example. Think carefully before you do this.

    Generally, it's best to leave all the privileges turned off in user table entries and specify privileges using the other tables, which are more restrictive. The exceptions are for superusers such as root, but these are usually rare.

- db

    The db table lists databases and which users have privileges for accessing them. A privilege specified here applies to all tables in a database.

- host

    The host table is used in combination with the db table to control database access privileges to particular hosts at a finer level than is possible with the db table alone. This table is unaffected by the GRANT and REVOKE statements, so you may find that you never use it at all.

- tables_priv

  The tables_priv table specifies table-level privileges. A privilege specified here applies to all columns in a table.

- columns_priv

  The columns_priv table specifies column-level privileges. A privilege specified here applies to a particular column in a table.

In the section "Setting Up Users Without GRANT," we'll discuss how the GRANT statement acts to modify these tables and how you can achieve the same results by modifying the grant tables directly.

The tables_priv and columns_priv tables were introduced in MySQL 3.22.11 (at the same time as the GRANT statement). If you have an older version of MySQL, your mysql database will have only the user, db, and host tables. If you have upgraded to 3.22.11 or later from an older version, but do not have the tables_priv and columns_priv tables, run the mysql_fix_privileges_tables script to create them.

There is no rows_priv table because MySQL doesn't provide record-level privileges. For example, you cannot restrict a user to only those rows in a table that contain a particular value in some column. If you need this capability, you must provide it using application programming. If you want to perform advisory record-level locking, you can do that using the GET_LOCK() function described in Appendix C, "Operator and Function Reference."

The grant tables contain two kinds of columns: scope columns that determine when an entry applies, and privilege columns that determine which privileges an entry grants. (Some of the grant tables contain other miscellaneous columns, but they don't concern us here.)

Grant Table Scope Columns

The grant table scope columns specify when table entries apply. Each grant table entry contains User and Host columns to indicate that the entry applies when the given user connects from the given host. (The host table is an exception; it's used in a special way that we won't get into just yet.) The other tables contain additional scope columns. For example, the db table contains a Db column to indicate which database the entry applies to. Similarly, the tables_priv and columns_priv tables contain scope fields that narrow the scope to a particular table in a database or column in a table.

Grant Table Privilege Columns

The grant tables also contain privilege columns. These indicate which privileges are held by the user who is specified in the scope columns. The privileges supported by MySQL are shown in the following list. The list uses the privilege names that are used for the GRANT statement. For the most part, the names of the privilege columns in the

user, db, and host tables bear an obvious resemblance to the privilege names discussed in connection with the GRANT statement in Chapter 11. For example, the
Select_priv column corresponds to the SELECT privilege.

Database and Table Privileges

The following privileges apply to operations on databases and tables:

- ALTER

  Allows you to use the ALTER TABLE statement. This actually is simply a first-level
  privilege; you must have additional privileges, depending on what you want to
  do with the table.

- CREATE

  Allows you to create databases and tables. This does not allow you to create
  indexes.

- DELETE

  Allows you to remove existing records from tables.

- DROP

  Allows you to drop databases and tables. This does not allow you to drop
  indexes.

- INDEX

  Allows you to create or drop indexes from tables.

- INSERT

  Allows you to insert new records in tables.

- REFERENCES

  This is currently unused.

- SELECT

  Allows you to retrieve data from tables using SELECT statements. This privilege is
  unnecessary for SELECT statements that do not involve tables, such as SELECT
  NOW() or SELECT 4/2.

- UPDATE

  Allows you to modify existing records in tables.

Administrative Privileges

The following privileges apply to administrative operations that control the operation
of the server or a user's ability to grant privileges:

- FILE

  Allows you to tell the server to read or write files on the server host. This privilege should not be granted without just cause; it is dangerous, as discussed in

"Grant Table Risks to Avoid." The server does take certain precautions to keep the use of this privilege within certain bounds. You can read only files that are world-readable, and thus likely not to be considered protected in any way. A file that you are writing must not already exist. This prevents you from coercing the server into overwriting important files, such as /etc/passwd, or database files in a database belonging to someone else. For example, if this constraint were not enforced, you could completely replace the contents of the grant tables in the mysql database.

If you grant the FILE privilege, be sure not to run the server as the UNIX root user, because root can create new files anywhere in the file system. If you run the server as an unprivileged user, the server can create files only in directories accessible to that user.

- GRANT

Allows you to give to other users the privileges you have yourself, including the GRANT privilege.

- PROCESS

Allows you to view information about the threads (processes) currently executing within the server by using the SHOW PROCESSLIST statement or the mysqladmin processlist command. This privilege also allows you to kill threads with the KILL statement or the mysqladmin kill command.

You can always see or kill your own threads. The PROCESS privilege gives you the ability to do these things with any thread.

- RELOAD

Allows you to perform a variety of server administration operations. You can issue the FLUSH SQL statement. You can also perform the mysqladmin commands reload, refresh, flush-hosts, flush-logs, flush-privileges, and flush-tables.

This is not normally a dangerous privilege to grant, even though it is administrative in nature.

- SHUTDOWN

Allows you to shut down the server with mysqladmin shutdown.

In the user, db, and host tables, each privilege is specified as a separate column. These columns are all declared with a type of ENUM("N","Y"), so the default value for every privilege is "N" (off). Privileges in the tables_priv and columns_priv tables are represented by a SET, which allows privileges to be specified in any combination using a single column. These two tables are newer than the other three, which is why they use the more efficient representation. (It's possible that the user, db, and host tables may be reorganized in the future to represent privileges by SET columns as well.)

The `Table_priv` column in the `tables_priv` table is defined like this:

```
SET('Select','Insert','Update','Delete','Create','Drop',
    'Grant','References','Index','Alter')
```

The `Column_priv` column in the `columns_priv` table is defined like this:

```
SET('Select','Insert','Update','References')
```

There are fewer column privileges than table privileges because fewer operations make sense at the column level. For example, you can create a table, but you can't create an isolated column.

The `user` table contains columns for some privileges that are not present in any of the other grant tables: `File_priv`, `Process_priv`, `Reload_priv`, and `Shutdown_priv`. These privileges apply to operations you tell the server to perform that aren't associated with any particular database or table. It doesn't make sense to allow a user to shut down the server based on what the current database is, for example.

How the Server Controls Client Access

There are two stages of client access control when you use MySQL. The first stage occurs when you attempt to connect to the server. The server looks at the `user` table to see if it can find an entry that matches your name, the host you're connecting from, and the password you supplied. If there is no match, you can't connect. If there is a match, the connection is established and you proceed to the second stage. In this stage, for each query you issue, the server checks the grant tables to see whether or not you have sufficient privileges to perform the query. The second stage continues until your session with the server ends.

This section describes in more detail the rules that the MySQL server uses to match grant table entries to incoming client connection requests and to queries. This includes the types of values that are legal in the grant table scope columns, the way privilege information in the grant tables is combined, and the order in which table entries are checked.

Scope Column Contents

Some of the scope columns require literal values, but most of them allow wildcard or other special values.

- Host

  A `Host` column value may be a hostname or an IP number. The value `localhost` means the local host, but it matches only if you actually connect using a host value of `localhost`, not if you connect using the hostname. Suppose the name of the local host is `pit-viper.snake.net` and there are two entries for you in the `user` table, one with a `Host` value or `localhost` and the other with a value of `pit-viper.snake.net`. The entry with `localhost` will match only if you connect

to `localhost`. The other will match only if you connect to `pit-viper.snake.`
`net`. If you want users to be able to connect either way, you need two entries in
the `user` table.

You may also specify `Host` values using wildcards. The SQL pattern characters '`%`'
and '`_`' may be used and have the same meaning as when you use the `LIKE` operator in a query. (`REGEX` patterns are not allowed.) The SQL pattern characters
work for both names and IP numbers. For example, `%.wisc.edu` matches any
host in the `wisc.edu` domain, and `%.edu` matches any host at any educational
institution. Similarly, `192.168.%` matches any host in the 192.168 class B subnet,
whereas `192.168.3.%` matches any host in the 192.168.3 class C subnet.

The value `%` matches any host at all, and may be used to allow a user to connect
from anywhere. A blank `Host` value is the same as `%`. (Exception: In the `db` table,
a blank `Host` value means "check the `host` table for further information." This
process is described in "Query Access Verification."

As of MySQL 3.23, you can also specify IP numbers with a netmask indicating
the number of bits to use for the network number. For example,
`192.168.128.0/17` specifies a 17-bit network number and matches any host with
`192.168.128` in the first 17 bits of its IP address.

- `User`

  Usernames must be either literal values or blank (empty). A blank value matches
  any user. `%` as a `User` value does *not* mean blank; instead, it matches a user with a
  literal name of '`%`', which is probably not what you want.

  When an incoming connection is verified against the `user` table and the entry
  that matches contains a blank `User` value, the client is considered to be an
  anonymous user.

- `Password`

  Password values are either blank (empty) or non-blank, and wildcards are not
  allowed. A blank password doesn't mean that any password matches. It means
  that the user must specify no password.

  Passwords are stored as encrypted values, not literal text. If you store a literal
  password in the `Password` column, the user will not be able to connect! The
  `GRANT` statement and the `mysqladmin password` command encrypt the password
  for you automatically, but if you use statements such as `INSERT`, `REPLACE`,
  `UPDATE`, or `SET PASSWORD`, be sure to specify the password using
  `PASSWORD("new_password")` rather than simply using `"new_password"`.

- `Db`

  In the `columns_priv` and `tables_priv` tables, `Db` values must be literal database
  names; patterns and blanks are not allowed. In the `db` and `host` tables, `Db` values
  may be specified literally or by using the SQL pattern characters '`%`' or '`_`' to
  specify a wildcard. A value of `%` or blank matches any database.

- Table_name, Column_name

Values in these columns must be literal table or column names; patterns and blanks are not allowed.

Some scope columns are treated by the server as case sensitive; others are not. The rules are summarized in Table 12.3. Note in particular that Table_name values are always treated as case sensitive, even though treatment of table names in queries depends on the case sensitivity of the file system on which the server runs (case sensitive under UNIX, but not under Windows).

Table 12.3 **Case Sensitivity in Grant Table Scope Columns**

Column	Case Sensitive
Host	No
User	Yes
Password	Yes
Db	Yes
Table_name	Yes
Column_name	No

Query Access Verification

Each time you issue a query, the server checks whether or not you have sufficient privileges to execute it. It does this by checking, in order, the user, db, tables_priv, and columns_priv tables, until it either determines you have proper access or it has searched all the tables in vain. More specifically:

1. The server checks the user table entry that matched when you connected initially to see what global privileges you have. If you have any and they are sufficient for the query, the server executes it.

2. If your global privileges are insufficient, the server looks for an entry for you in the db table adds the privileges in that entry to your global privileges. If the result is sufficient for the query, the server executes it.

How Passwords are Stored in the user Table

Passwords are listed in the user table as encrypted strings, so you can't tell what a user's password is even if you have read access to this table. It seems to be a common assumption that the PASSWORD() function performs the same kind of encryption as is used for UNIX passwords, but it doesn't.

The two kinds of encryption are similar in that both are one-way and not reversible, but MySQL doesn't use the same encryption algorithm that UNIX does. This means that even if you use your UNIX password as your MySQL password, you shouldn't expect the encrypted password strings to match. If you want UNIX encryption for an application, use the CRYPT() function rather than PASSWORD().

3. If the combination of your global and database-level privileges is insufficient, the server keeps looking, first in the `tables_priv` table and then in the `columns_priv` table.

4. If you don't have permission after all the tables have been checked, the server rejects your attempt to execute the query.

In boolean terms, the privileges in the grant tables are used by the server like this:

```
user OR db OR tables_priv OR columns_priv
```

I see that you're wondering why the preceding description refers to only four grant tables when there are five grant tables. Okay, you caught me. The way the server really checks access permissions is like this:

```
user OR (db AND host) OR tables_priv OR columns_priv
```

I showed the simpler expression first because the `host` table is not affected by the `GRANT` or `REVOKE` statements. If you always use `GRANT` and `REVOKE` to manage user privileges, you'll never need to think about the `host` table. But here's how it works, if you want to know:

- When the server checks for database-level privileges, it looks at the `db` table entry for the client. If the `Host` column value is blank, it means "Check the `host` table to find out which hosts can access the database."

- The server looks in the `host` table for entries with the same `Db` column value as the entry from the `db` table. If no `host` table entry matches the client host, no database-level privileges are granted. If any of those entries do have a `Host` column value that matches the host from which the client is connecting, the `db` table entry and the `host` table entry are combined to produce the client's database-level privileges.

  However, the privileges are combined using a logical `AND`, which means that the client doesn't have a given privilege unless it's present in both entries. In this way, you can grant a basic set of privileges in the `db` table entry, then selectively disable them for particular hosts using `host` table entries. For example, you might allow access to a database from all hosts in your domain, but turn off database privileges for hosts that are located in less secure areas.

The preceding description no doubt makes access checking sound like a rather complicated process, especially when you consider that the server checks privileges for every single query that clients issue. However, the process is quite fast because the server doesn't actually look up information from the grant tables for every query. Instead, it reads the contents of the tables into memory when it starts up, then verifies queries using the in-memory copies. This gives a performance boost to access-checking operations, but has a rather important side effect: If you change the contents of the grant tables directly, the server won't notice the privilege change.

For example, if you add a new MySQL user by using an `INSERT` statement to add a new record to the `user` table, the user named in the entry won't be able to connect to the server. This is something that often confuses new administrators (and sometimes more-experienced ones!), but the solution is quite simple: Tell the server to reload the contents of the grant tables after you change them. You can do this by issuing a `FLUSH PRIVILEGES` statement or by executing `mysqladmin flush-privileges` (or `mysqladmin reload` if you have an old version that doesn't support `flush-privileges`).

Scope Column Matching Order

The MySQL server sorts entries in the grant tables in a particular way, then tries to match incoming connections by looking through the entries in order. The first match found determines the entry that is used. It's important to understand the sorting order that MySQL uses, especially for the `user` table. This seems to trip up a lot of people in their attempts to understand MySQL security.

When the server reads the contents of the `user` table, it sorts entries according to the values in the `Host` and `User` column. The `Host` value is the dominant value (entries with the same `Host` value are sorted together, then ordered according to the `User` value). However, sorting is *not* lexicographic, or rather, it's only partially so. The principle to keep in mind is that literal values are preferred over patterns. This means that if you're connecting from `boa.snake.net` and there are entries with `Host` values of `boa.snake.net` and `%.snake.net`, the first entry will be preferred. Similarly, `%.snake.net` is preferred over `%.net`, which is in turn preferred over `%`. IP number matching works that way, too. For a client connecting from a host with an IP number of `192.168.3.14`, entries with `Host` values of `192.168.3.14`, `192.168.3.%`, `192.168.%`, `192.%`, and `%` will match, in that order.

Grant Table Risks to Avoid

This section describes some precautions to observe when you grant privileges, and the attendant risks of unwise choices. In general, you want to grant superuser privileges sparingly. That is, don't enable privileges in `user` table entries. Use the other grant tables instead, to restrict user privileges to particular databases, tables, or columns. Privileges in the `user` table allow the user to affect the operation of your server or to access any table in any database.

Don't grant privileges for the `mysql` database. A user with privileges on the database containing the grant tables may be able to modify the tables to acquire privileges on any other database as well. Granting privileges that allow a user to modify the `mysql` database tables also effectively gives that user a global `GRANT` privilege. If the user can modify the tables directly, it's pretty much equivalent to being able to issue any `GRANT` statement you can think of.

The `FILE` privilege is particularly dangerous; don't grant it lightly. Here's an example of something a user with the `FILE` privilege can do:

```
CREATE TABLE etc_passwd (pwd_entry TEXT);
LOAD DATA INFILE "/etc/passwd" INTO TABLE etc_passwd;
SELECT * FROM etc_passwd;
```

After issuing these statements, the user has the contents of your password file. In fact, the contents of *any* publicly readable file on the server can be accessed over the network by any user with the FILE privilege.

The FILE privilege also can be exploited to compromise databases on systems that aren't set up with sufficiently restrictive file permissions. This is a reason why you should set the data directory contents to be readable only by the server. If files corresponding to database tables are world readable, not only can any user with an account on the server host read them, but any client user with the FILE privilege can connect over the network and read them, too! The following procedure demonstrates how:

- Create a table with a LONGBLOB column:

  ```
  USE test
  CREATE TABLE tmp (b LONGBLOB)
  ```

- Use the table to read in the contents of each file corresponding to the table you want to steal, then write out the table contents to a file in your own database:

  ```
  LOAD DATA INFILE "./other_db/x.frm" INTO TABLE tmp
      FIELDS ESCAPED BY "" LINES TERMINATED BY ""
  SELECT * FROM tmp INTO OUTFILE "y.frm"
      FIELDS ESCAPED BY "" LINES TERMINATED BY ""
  DELETE FROM tmp
  LOAD DATA INFILE "./other_db/x.ISD" INTO TABLE tmp
      FIELDS ESCAPED BY "" LINES TERMINATED BY ""
  SELECT * FROM tmp INTO OUTFILE "y.ISD"
      FIELDS ESCAPED BY "" LINES TERMINATED BY ""
  DELETE FROM tmp
  LOAD DATA INFILE "./other_db/x.ISM" INTO TABLE tmp
      FIELDS ESCAPED BY "" LINES TERMINATED BY ""
  SELECT * FROM tmp INTO OUTFILE "y.ISM"
      FIELDS ESCAPED BY "" LINES TERMINATED BY ""
  ```

- You now have a new table y containing the contents of other_db.x, and you have full access to it.

To avoid having someone attack you in the same way, set the permissions on your data directory contents according to the instructions in "Internal Security: Securing Data Directory Access." You can also use the --skip-show-database option when you start the server to limit users from using SHOW DATABASES and from using SHOW TABLES for databases they have no access to. This helps prevent users from finding out about databases and tables they shouldn't be accessing.

The ALTER privilege can be used in ways you may not intend. Suppose you want user1 to be able to access table1 but not table2. A user with the ALTER privilege may be able to subvert your intent by using ALTER TABLE to rename table2 to table1.

Be careful with the GRANT privilege. Two users with different privileges that both have the GRANT privilege can make each other's access rights more powerful.

Setting Up Users Without GRANT

If you have a version of MySQL prior to 3.22.11, you can't use the GRANT (or REVOKE) statements to set up users and access privileges, but you can modify the contents of the grant tables directly. Much of this is easier if you understand how the GRANT statement acts to modify the grant tables. Then you can just do the same thing yourself by issuing INSERT statements manually. (The INSERT statement may be ugly and difficult to enter correctly, but that's a different issue. This ugliness is in fact one reason why GRANT is so much easier to use.)

When you issue a GRANT statement, you specify a username and hostname, and possibly a password. A user table entry is created for the user, and these values are recorded in the User, Host, and Password columns of the entry. If you specify global privileges in the GRANT statement, those privileges are recorded in the privileges columns of the entry. One thing to be careful about is that the GRANT statement encrypts the password for you, but INSERT does not; you'll need to use the PASSWORD() function to encrypt passwords in your INSERT statements.

If you specified database-level privileges, the username and hostname are recorded in the User and Host columns of a db table entry. The database you granted privileges for is recorded in the Db column, and the privileges you granted are recorded in the privileges columns.

For table-level and column-level privileges, the effects are similar. Entries are created in the tables_priv and columns_priv tables to record the username, hostname, and database, as well as the table or table and column as necessary. The privileges granted are recorded in the privilege columns.

If you keep the preceding description in mind, you should be able to do what GRANT does even without the GRANT statement. Remember that when you modify the grant tables directly, you'll need to tell the server to reload the grant tables or it won't notice your changes. You can force a reload by executing a mysqladmin flush-privileges or mysqladmin reload command. If you forget to do this, you'll be wondering why the server isn't doing what you want.

The following GRANT statement creates a superuser with all privileges, including the ability to grant privileges to other users:

```
GRANT ALL ON *.* TO ethel@localhost IDENTIFIED BY "coffee"
    WITH GRANT OPTION
```

The statement will create an entry for ethel@localhost in the user table, and turn on all the privileges there because that's where superuser (global) privileges are stored. To do the same thing with INSERT, the statement is:

```
INSERT INTO user VALUES("localhost","ethel",PASSWORD("coffee"),
    "Y","Y","Y","Y","Y","Y","Y","Y","Y","Y","Y","Y","Y","Y")
```

That's one ugly INSERT statement! You may even find that it doesn't work, depending on your version of MySQL. The structure of the grant tables has changed on occasion and you may not have 14 privilege columns in your user table. Use SHOW COLUMNS to find out just what privilege columns each of your grant tables contains, and adjust your INSERT statements accordingly.

The following GRANT statement also creates a user with superuser status, but for only a single privilege:

```
GRANT RELOAD ON *.* TO flush@localhost IDENTIFIED BY "flushpass"
```

You may remember this statement from when we created the flush user in Chapter 11. The INSERT statement for this example is a bit simpler than for the preceding one; it's easier to list the column names and specify only the one privilege column. All the others will be set to the default of "N":

```
INSERT INTO user (Host,User,Password,Reload_priv)
    VALUES("localhost","flush",PASSWORD("flushpass"),"Y")
```

Database-level privileges are granted with an ON *db_name*.* clause rather than ON *.*:

```
GRANT ALL ON samp_db.* TO boris@localhost IDENTIFIED BY "ruby"
```

These privileges are not global, so they won't be stored in the user table. We still need to create an entry in the user table (so that the user can connect), but we also need to create a db table entry to record the database-level privileges:

```
INSERT INTO user (Host,User,Password)
    VALUES("localhost","boris",PASSWORD("ruby"))
INSERT INTO db VALUES("localhost","samp_db","boris",
    "Y","Y","Y","Y","Y","Y","N","Y","Y","Y")
```

The "N" column is for the GRANT privilege; for a database-level GRANT statement that has WITH GRANT OPTION at the end, you'd set that column to "Y" instead.

To set table-level or column-level privileges, you use INSERT statements for the tables_priv or columns_priv tables. Of course, if you don't have the GRANT statement, you won't have those tables, either, because they all appeared in MySQL at the same time. If you do have the tables and want to manipulate them manually for some reason, be aware that you don't enable privileges using individual columns. You set either the tables_priv.Table_priv or columns_priv.Column_priv column to a SET value consisting of the privileges you want to enable. For example, to enable SELECT and INSERT privileges for a table, you'd set the Table_priv column to a value of "Select,Insert" in the relevant tables_priv entry.

If you want to modify privileges for a user whose MySQL account already exists, use UPDATE rather than INSERT. This is true whether you are adding or revoking privileges. To remove a user entirely, use DELETE to remove entries from each grant table in which the user has them.

If you prefer to avoid issuing queries to modify the grant tables directly, you may want to take a look at the mysqlaccess and mysql_setpermissions scripts that come with the MySQL distribution.

A Privilege Puzzle, Part II

In Chapter 11, in the section "A Privilege Puzzle, Part I," we looked at a privilege-granting situation in which the privileges did not have the intended effect. To recount that discussion briefly, a problem that often occurs with new MySQL installations is that the administrator wants to add an entry for a user that allows them to connect from several hosts. The obvious way to do this is to use a hostname specifier containing the '%' wildcard character, so the administrator creates a user using a statement something like this:

```
GRANT ALL ON samp_db.* TO fred@%.snake.net IDENTIFIED BY "cocoa"
```

fred happens to have an account on the server host, so he tries to connect from there:

```
% mysql -u fred -pcocoa samp_db
ERROR 1045: Access denied for user: 'fred@localhost'
(Using password: YES)
```

Why is this? To understand what's going on, you have to consider both how mysql_install_db sets up the initial grant tables and how the server uses user table entries to match client connections. When you initialize your databases by running mysql_install_db, it creates user table entries with Host and User values like this:

```
+---------------------+------+
| Host                | User |
+---------------------+------+
| localhost           | root |
| pit-viper.snake.net | root |
| localhost           |      |
| pit-viper.snake.net |      |
+---------------------+------+
```

The first two entries allow root to connect to the local host by specifying either localhost or the hostname. The second two allow anonymous connections from the local host. When the entry for fred is added, the table contains these entries:

```
+---------------------+------+
| Host                | User |
+---------------------+------+
| localhost           | root |
| pit-viper.snake.net | root |
| localhost           |      |
| pit-viper.snake.net |      |
| %.snake.net         | fred |
+---------------------+------+
```

When the server starts up, it reads the entries and sorts them (by host first, then by user within host), with more specific values first and less specific values last:

```
+----------------------+------+
| Host                 | User |
+----------------------+------+
| localhost            | root |
| localhost            |      |
| pit-viper.snake.net  | root |
| pit-viper.snake.net  |      |
| %.snake.net          | fred |
+----------------------+------+
```

The two entries with `localhost` sort together, and the entry for `root` is put first because that's more specific than the blank value. The entries with `pit-viper.snake.net` sort together in a similar way. All of these entries have literal `Host` values without any wildcard characters, so they all sort ahead of the entry for `fred`, which does use a wildcard character. In particular, the anonymous user entries take precedence over `fred`'s entry in the sorting order.

The result is that when `fred` attempts to connect from the local host, one of the entries with a blank username matches before the entry containing `%.snake.net` in the `Host` column. The password in that entry is blank, because the default anonymous users have no password. Because `fred` specified a password when he connected, there was a mismatch and the connection failed.

The thing to keep in mind here is that, although it's very convenient to use wildcards to specify the hosts from which users can connect, you may have problems for connections from the local host as long as you leave the anonymous user entries in the `user` table.

In general, I'd recommend you delete entries for the anonymous user. It'll make your life easier:

```
mysql> DELETE FROM user WHERE User = "";
```

If you want to be more thorough, delete any anonymous user entries in the other grant tables as well. Those that have `User` columns are `db`, `tables_priv`, and `columns_priv`.

The puzzle presented in this section addresses a specific situation, but contains a more general lesson. If privileges for a user don't work the way you expect, look in the grant tables to see if there's some entry containing `Host` values that are more specific than the entry for the user in question and that will match connection attempts by that user. If so, that may explain the problem. You may need to make the user's entry more specific (or add another entry to cover the more specific case).

13

Database Maintenance and Repair

IDEALLY, MySQL RUNS SMOOTHLY FROM the time that you first install it. But problems sometimes do occur for a variety of reasons, ranging from power outages to hardware failure to improper shutdown of the MySQL server (such as when you terminate it with kill -9 or the machine crashes). Circumstances such as these, many of which are beyond your control, can result in damage to database tables, typically caused by incomplete writes in the middle of a change to a table.

This chapter focuses on detecting and solving problems with your tables, regardless of how those problems arise. For table checking and repair, the MySQL administrator's best friends are the myisamchk and isamchk utilities. These two programs have several capabilities. We've already discussed how to use them to perform index key distribution analysis and index deactivation and reactivation in Chapter 4, "Query Optimization." You can also use them for checking tables and repairing those that have problems. This enables you to correct damage before it becomes worse, possibly making tables unusable.

For a full listing of the options supported by myisamchk and isamchk, see Appendix E, "MySQL Program Reference." For additional background, see the chapter "Maintaining a MySQL Installation" in the MySQL Reference Manual.

Checking and Repairing Database Tables

The general procedure for table damage detection and correction is as follows:

1. Check the table for errors.

    If the table checks okay, you're done. Otherwise, you must repair it.

2. Make copies of the table files before beginning repair, just in case something goes wrong.

3. Try to repair the table.

4. If the repair operation fails, restore the table from your database backups and update logs.

The final step of the preceding procedure assumes that you've been performing database backups and have update logging enabled. If that's not true, you're living dangerously. Go read Chapter 11, "General MySQL Administration," to find out how to use `mysqldump` and how to turn on update logging. You don't ever want to be in the position of having irretrievably lost a table because you were lax about backing up.

Before you use `myisamchk` or `isamchk` to check or repair tables, some preliminary requirements should be satisfied:

-   Institute regular database backup procedures and enable update logging, in case worse comes to worse and a table is damaged beyond repair. Perhaps I've mentioned this before?

-   Read all the way through this section before trying out any of it. In particular, you should *not* use these instructions before you have read "Avoiding Interactions with the MySQL Server." That section discusses the problems that arise if the server is using a table at the same time you're trying to perform checking or repair procedures on it. It also describes how to prevent those problems from occurring by keeping the server at bay while you're working.

-   When performing table checking or repair, you should be logged in under the account that is used to run `mysqld` because you need read and write access to the table files.

`myisamchk` and `isamchk` Invocation Syntax

MySQL's `myisamchk` and `isamchk` utilities are very similar and are used in the same way most of the time. The primary difference between them is the type of table they are used with. For MyISAM tables, use `myisamchk`, and for ISAM tables, use `isamchk`. You can tell which storage format a table uses by the filename extension on the table's index file. The extension `".MYI"` indicates a MyISAM table, whereas `".ISM"` indicates an ISAM table.

To use either utility, tell it what tables you want to check or repair, along with the options that indicate what type of operation to perform:

```
% myisamchk options tbl_name ...
% isamchk options tbl_name ...
```

A `tbl_name` argument may be either a table name or the name of the table's index file. If you specify multiple tables, you can easily use a filename pattern to pick up all the relevant files in a directory:

```
% myisamchk options *.MYI
% isamchk options *.ISM
```

You won't destroy a table by telling the wrong program to check it, but the program won't do anything except issue a warning message. For example, the first of the following statements will check all the MyISAM tables in the current directory, while the second will simply print warnings:

```
% myisamchk *.MYI      Correct
% myisamchk *.ISM      Incorrect—wrong type of file
```

Neither myisamchk nor isamchk make any assumptions about where the tables are located, so you should either run the programs in the directory containing the table files, or specify the pathname to the tables. This enables you to copy table files to another directory and work with the copies.

Checking Tables

Both myisamchk and isamchk provide table-checking methods that vary in how thoroughly they examine a table. The normal method is usually sufficient. If the normal check reports no errors but you still suspect damage (perhaps because queries do not seem to be working properly), you may want to perform a more thorough check. To perform a normal table check with either utility, invoke it with no options:

```
% myisamchk tbl_name
% isamchk tbl_name
```

To perform an extended check, use the `--extend-check` option. This can be very slow, but it is extremely thorough; for each record in the table's data file, the associated key for every index in the index file is checked to make sure it really points to the correct record. myisamchk also has an intermediate option, `--medium-check`, which is less thorough than extended checking, but faster.

If no errors are reported for a check with `--extend-check`, you can be sure your table is okay. If you still have problems with the table, the cause must lie elsewhere. Re-examine any queries that seem to yield problematic results to verify that they are written correctly. If you believe the problem may be with the MySQL server, consider filing a bug report or upgrading to a newer version.

If myisamchk or isamchk report that a table has errors, you should repair it using the instructions in the next section.

Repairing Tables

Table repair is an ugly business, made more so by the fact that the details tend to be very incident-specific. Nevertheless, there are general guidelines and procedures you can follow to significantly increase your chances of being able to fix the tables. Generally, you begin with the fastest repair method to see if that will correct the damage. If you find that this is not sufficient, you can escalate to more thorough (but slower) repair methods, until either the damage has been repaired or you cannot escalate further. (In practice, most problems are fixable without going to more extensive and slower repair modes.) If the table cannot be repaired, then restore the table from your backups. Instructions for recovery using backup files and update logs are given in Chapter 11.

Performing a Standard Table Repair

To repair a table, take the following steps:

1. Try to fix the table using the --recover option, but use the --quick option as well to attempt recovery based only on the contents of the index file. This will repair the table without touching the data file:

   ```
   % myisamchk --recover --quick tbl_name
   % isamchk --recover --quick tbl_name
   ```

2. If problems remain, try the command from the previous step, but omit the --quick option to allow myisamchk or isamchk to go ahead and modify the data file, too:

   ```
   % myisamchk --recover tbl_name
   % isamchk --recover tbl_name
   ```

3. If that doesn't work, try the --safe-recover repair mode. This is slower than regular recovery mode, but is capable of fixing a few problems that --recover mode will not:

   ```
   % myisamchk --safe-recover tbl_name
   % isamchk --safe-recover tbl_name
   ```

If myisamchk or isamchk stop at any of these steps with an error message of the form "Can't create new temp file: file_name", you should repeat the command and add the --force option to force removal of the temporary file. This may have been left around from a previous failed repair attempt.

> **Copy Your Tables Before Repairing Them**
>
> One general precaution you should follow before performing table repair is to make copies of the table files in case something goes awry. That is unlikely, but if it happens, you can make a new copy of the table from the copied files and try a different recovery method.

What To Do When Standard Table Repair Fails

If the standard repair procedure fails to repair the table, your index file may be missing or damaged beyond repair. It's also possible, though unlikely, that the table description file is missing. In either of these cases, you'll need to replace the affected files, then try the standard repair procedure again.

To regenerate the index file, use the following procedure:

1. Move into the database directory that contains the crashed table.

2. Move the table's data file to a safe place.

3. Invoke mysql and re-create a new empty table by executing the following statement, which uses the table description file `tbl_name.frm` to regenerate new data and index files from scratch:

   ```
   mysql> DELETE FROM tbl_name;
   ```

4. Exit mysql and move the original data file back into the database directory, replacing the new empty data file you just created.

5. Attempt a standard table repair again.

To recover the table description file, restore it from your backup files, then attempt a standard repair again. If for some reason you have no backup, but you know the CREATE TABLE statement that must be issued to create the table, you still may be able to repair it:

1. Move into the database directory that contains the crashed table.

2. Move the table's data file to a safe place. Move the index file, too, if you want to try to use it.

3. Invoke mysql and issue the CREATE TABLE statement that creates the table.

4. Exit mysql and move the original data file back into the database directory, replacing the new data file you just created. If you moved the index file in step 2, move it back into the database directory, too.

5. Attempt a standard table repair again.

Avoiding Interactions with the MySQL Server

When you're running a table check/repair utility, you don't want the MySQL server and the utility to access a table simultaneously. It's obviously a bad thing if both programs are writing to the table, but having one of them read while the other program is writing isn't good, either. The program doing the reading may become confused if the table is being changed by the other program at the same time.

You can guarantee that there will be no interaction between the server and myisamchk or isamchk if you bring down the server. But administrators are understandably reluctant to take the server completely offline because that makes undamaged databases and tables unavailable, too. The procedures described in this section will help you avoid interaction between the server and myisamchk or isamchk.

The server has two kinds of locking. It uses internal locking to keep requests from clients from interfering with each other—for example, to keep one client's SELECT query from being interrupted by another client's UPDATE query. The server also uses external locking (file system level locking) to keep other programs from modifying table files while it's using them. Normally, the server uses external locking for cooperation with myisamchk or isamchk during table checking operations. However, external locking is disabled on some systems because it doesn't work reliably. The procedure you should choose for running myisamchk and isamchk depends on whether or not the server uses external locking. If it does not, you must use an internal locking protocol.

External locking is disabled if the server is run with the --skip-locking option. This option is the default on some systems, such as Linux. You can determine whether or not the server is able to use external locking by running the mysqladmin variables command. Check the value of the skip_locking variable and proceed as follows:

- If skip_locking is off, external locking is enabled. You can go ahead and run either utility to check tables. The server and the utility will cooperate for table access. However, you should flush the table cache with mysqladmin flush-tables before running either utility. To repair tables, you should use the table repair locking protocol.

- If skip_locking is on, external locking is disabled, and the server won't know when myisamchk or isamchk are checking or repairing a table. It's best to bring the server down. If you insist on leaving the server up, you need to make sure no clients access the table while you're using it. Be sure to use an appropriate locking protocol to tell the server to leave the table alone and to block clients from accessing it.

The locking protocols described here use the server's internal locking mechanism to prevent it from accessing a table while you work on it with myisamchk or isamchk. The general idea is that you invoke mysql and issue a LOCK TABLE statement for the table you want to check or repair. Then, with mysql idle (that is, running but not doing anything with the table except keeping it locked), you run myisamchk or isamchk. After myisamchk or isamchk have finished, you can switch back to your mysql session and release the lock to tell the server it's okay to use the table again.

The locking protocols for checking and repairing are somewhat different. For checking, you only need to acquire a read lock. In this case, you're reading the table, but not modifying it, so it's okay to allow other clients to read it as well. The read lock suffices to prevent other clients from modifying the table. For repair, you must acquire a write lock to prevent any clients from modifying the table while you're working on it.

The locking protocols use LOCK TABLE and UNLOCK TABLE statements to acquire and release locks. The protocols also use FLUSH TABLES to tell the server to flush any pending changes to disk and to reopen the table after it's been modified by a table repair utility. You *must* perform all the LOCK, FLUSH, and UNLOCK statements from within a single mysql session. If you lock a table and then quit mysql, the lock will be released, and it will not be safe to run myisamchk or isamchk!

It's easiest to perform the locking procedures if you keep two windows open, one for running mysql and the other for running myisamchk or isamchk. This allows you to switch between programs easily. If you're not working in a windowing environment, you'll need to suspend and resume mysql using your shell's job control facilities while you run myisamchk or isamchk. The following instructions show commands for both myisamchk or isamchk; use the one that's appropriate for the table or tables you're working with.

Locking a Table for Checking Operations

This procedure is for checking a table only, not for repairing it. In window 1, invoke mysql and issue the following statements:

```
% mysql db_name
mysql> LOCK TABLE tbl_name READ;
mysql> FLUSH TABLES;
```

The lock prevents other clients from writing to the table and modifying it while you're checking it. The FLUSH statement causes the server to close the table files, which flushes out any unwritten changes that may still be cached.

With mysql sitting idle, switch to window 2 and check the table:

```
% myisamchk tbl_name
% isamchk tbl_name
```

When myisamchk or isamchk finishes, switch back to the mysql session in window 1 and release the table lock:

```
mysql> UNLOCK TABLE;
```

If myisamchk or isamchk indicated that a problem was found with the table, you'll need to perform table repair.

Locking a Table for Repair Operations

The locking procedure for repairing a table is similar to procedure for checking it, with two differences. First, you must obtain a write lock rather than a read lock. You'll be modifying the table, so you can't let clients access it at all. Second, you must issue a FLUSH TABLES statement after performing the repair because myisamchk and isamchk build a new index file, and the server won't notice that unless you flush the table cache again. To perform this procedure, invoke mysql in window 1 and issue the following statements:

```
% mysql db_name
mysql> LOCK TABLE tbl_name WRITE;
mysql> FLUSH TABLES;
```

With `mysql` idle, switch to window 2, make copies if the table files if you haven't already, then run `myisamchk` or `isamchk`:

```
% cp tbl_name.* /some/other/directory
% myisamchk --recover tbl_name
% isamchk --recover tbl_name
```

The `--recover` option is for illustration only. The particular options you choose will depend on the type of repair you're performing. After `myisamchk` or `isamchk` has finished, switch back to the `mysql` session in window 1, flush the table cache again and release the table lock:

```
mysql> FLUSH TABLES;
mysql> UNLOCK TABLE;
```

Getting `myisamchk` and `isamchk` To Run Faster

`myisamchk` and `isamchk` can take a long time to run, especially if you're working with a big table or using one of the more-extensive checking or repair methods. You may be able to speed up these programs by telling them to use more memory when they

Reducing Server Downtime

Another way to keep the server from accessing the table that you're working with is to work with copies of the table files outside of the data directory. This doesn't eliminate the interaction problem because you still have to keep the server from accessing (and possibly changing!) the table while you're making the copies. However, this route can be a means of minimizing server downtime, and may be attractive to you if you're otherwise reluctant to take your server offline. Bring down the server briefly while you copy the table files you need into another directory, then bring the server back up.

Future Plans for `myisamchk`

The table checking and repair functions of `myisamchk` are scheduled to be merged into the server at some point during the MySQL 3.23 version series. When that happens, checking and repairing tables will become a lot easier because issues of server interaction with `myisamchk` won't arise.

Also, you'll be able to tell the server to check tables at startup time, so it won't be necessary to set up any special commands to be executed at boot time before starting up the server. None of this will work for ISAM tables, though, so when the server gets table checking and repair capabilities, I'd encourage you to consider converting your ISAM tables to MyISAM tables. Check the MySQL Reference Manual for new releases to see what developments may be taking place in this area. You can convert a table by using an ALTER TABLE statement:

```
ALTER TABLE tbl_name TYPE = MYISAM
```

run. Both utilities have several operating parameters that can be set. The most important of these variables control the buffer sizes used by the programs:

Variable	Meaning
key_buffer_size	Size of buffer used to hold index blocks
read_buffer_size	Size of buffer used for read operations
sort_buffer_size	Size of buffer used for sorting
write_buffer_size	Size of buffer used for write operations

To find out what values either program uses for these variables by default, run it with the --help option. To specify a different value, use --set-variable *variable=value* or -O *variable=value* on the command line. You can abbreviate the variable names as key, read, sort, and write. For example, to tell myisamchk to use a 16MB sort buffer and 1MB read and write buffers, invoke it like this:

```
% myisamchk -O sort=16M -O read=1M -O write=1M ...
```

sort_buffer_size is used only with the --recover option (not with --safe_recover), and in that case, key_buffer is not used.

Scheduling Preventive Maintenance

You should consider setting up a schedule of preventive maintenance to help detect problems automatically so that you can take steps to correct them:

1. Perform regular database backups and enable update logging. I've mentioned this before, right?

2. Arrange for periodic table checking on a regular basis. By checking your tables, you'll reduce the chance of having to use your backups. This is most easily accomplished by using a cron job, typically invoked from the crontab file of the account used to run the server. For example, if you run the server as the mysqladm user, then you can set up periodic check from the crontab file for mysqladm. If you don't know how to use cron, check the relevant UNIX manual pages using these commands:

   ```
   % man cron
   % man crontab
   ```

3. Check database tables during the system boot procedure before the server starts up. The machine may be rebooting because it crashed earlier. If so, database tables may be damaged and should be checked.

To run an automatic table check, you can write a script that changes directory into the server's data directory and runs myisamchk and isamchk on all your database tables. We'll use both programs in the scripts shown in the following discussion. If you have only MyISAM tables or only ISAM tables, you need only one of the programs, and can leave the irrelevant one out of the scripts.

myisamchk and isamchk both produce some output in table-checking mode to let you know which tables they're checking, even when there are no problems. For crontab entries, you'll normally want to suppress output unless there are errors in the tables. (cron jobs typically generate a mail message if a job produces any output at all, and there's little reason to receive mail for table-checking jobs that find no problems.) If you invoke either utility with the --silent option, it generates output only when problems are found. In addition, myisamchk supports a --fast option that lets it skip any table that hasn't been modified since it was last checked.

A simple script to check all tables under the server's data directory looks like this (DATADIR should be changed to a value appropriate for your system):

```
#! /bin/sh
cd DATADIR
myisamchk --silent --fast */*.MYI
isamchk --silent */*.ISM
```

A potential problem with this script is that if you have many tables, the wildcard patterns '*/*.MYI' or '*/*.ISM' may blow up the shell with a "too many arguments" error. An alternative script can be written like this (again, change DATADIR to a value appropriate for your system):

```
#! /bin/sh
datadir=DATADIR
find $datadir -name "*.MYI" -print | xargs myisamchk --silent --fast
find $datadir -name "*.ISM" -print | xargs isamchk --silent
```

Whichever form of the script you choose to use, I'll assume that you call it check_mysql_tables. Make sure to change the mode to make it executable. Then you should invoke it manually to verify that it works properly:

```
% chmod +x check_mysql_tables
% check_mysql_tables
```

Ideally, there will be no output. If your system doesn't support external locking, it's possible that the server will change a table while you're checking it. In this case, the script may report problems for tables that are actually okay. This is somewhat unfortunate, but it's better than the opposite problem: having the script report no damage when there is some damage. If your system supports external locking, this problem won't occur.

The following sections show how to set up the script to be executed automatically by cron and at system startup time. In the examples in these sections, I assume the script is installed in /usr/users/mysqladm/bin. You'll need to adjust the path appropriately for your system.

If you run multiple servers on your system, you'll need to modify the procedure to check the tables for each server's data directory. You can do this using different copies of check_mysql_tables or by modifying it to accept a command-line argument that specifies the data directory you want checked.

Checking Tables Periodically with `cron`

Suppose you want to invoke the `check_mysql_tables` script from the `crontab` file for the `mysqladm` user. Log in as that user, then edit your `crontab` file using this command:

```
% crontab -e
```

This command will drop you into an editor with a copy of your current `crontab` file (which may be empty if you haven't done this before). Add a line to the file that looks like this:

```
0 3 * * 0 /usr/users/mysqladm/bin/check_mysql_tables
```

This entry tells `cron` to run the entry at 3 a.m. every Sunday. You can vary the time or scheduling as desired. Check the `crontab` manual page for the format of the entries.

Checking Tables at System Startup Time

If you're using a BSD-style system and you've added the server startup command to `/etc/rc.local` or the equivalent, you can simply invoke `check_mysql_tables` from that same file before starting up the server.

If you're using the System V-style startup method that invokes `mysql.server` from one of the `/etc/rc.d` directories, the procedure is a little more complex. The startup scripts in these directories should understand `start` and `stop` arguments so that they can take appropriate action for system startup and shutdown. To perform table checking, we can write such a script that invokes `check_mysql_tables` when the argument is `start` and does nothing when the argument is `stop`. Let's call the script `mysql.check`; it looks like this:

```
#! /bin/sh

# See how we were called.
case "$1" in
  start)
    echo -n "Checking MySQL tables: "
    if [ -x /usr/users/mysqladm/bin/check_mysql_tables ]; then
        /usr/users/mysqladm/bin/check_mysql_tables
    fi
    ;;
  stop)
    # don't do anything
    ;;
  *)
    echo "Usage: $0 {start|stop}"
    exit 1
esac

exit 0
```

Now you can install `mysql.check` using a procedure similar to the one described in Chapter 11 for installing `mysql.server`. Be sure to give `mysql.check` a lower prefix number in the run level directory so that it runs before `mysql.server`. For example, if you link to `mysql.server` as `S99mysql.server` from the run level directory, you could link to `mysql.check` as `S98mysql.check`.

IV

Appendixes

A

Obtaining and Installing Software

THIS APPENDIX DESCRIBES HOW TO OBTAIN and install the software you'll need to run MySQL and the related third-party software described in this book, such as Perl DBI and CGI.pm support, PHP, and Apache. It also indicates how to obtain the files associated with the samp_db sample database used throughout the book.

The purpose of this chapter is to bring together installation instructions for all the packages in one place, not to replace the instructions that come with each package. In fact, I encourage you to read those instructions. This appendix provides general instructions that should suffice for most situations, but each software distribution also contains instructions that help you troubleshoot problems when a standard installation procedure fails. For example, the MySQL manual contains an extensive chapter dealing with installation procedures and includes solutions to many system-specific problems.

Choosing What to Install

You must install MySQL if you haven't already, but you need install only those third-party tools you plan to use:

- If you want to write Perl scripts that access MySQL databases, you must install MySQL client programming support and the DBI modules. If you plan to write DBI scripts that provide Web access to your databases, you'll probably want to install the CGI.pm module, and you'll need a Web server. The Apache server is used in this book, but others may work, too.

- If you want to write PHP scripts, you must install MySQL client programming support and PHP. Normally, PHP is used for Web scripting, which means you also need a Web server. The Apache server is used in this book because Apache has module support for PHP. That means you can install PHP as a built-in part of your Apache binary. If you cannot modify your copy of Apache (for example, if you are on an ISP host and the ISP controls Apache), or if you run a different Web server, you can build PHP as a standalone program and run PHP scripts as standard CGI scripts. Installing PHP as an Apache module provides better performance than running it as a standalone program.

Precompiled binaries are available for many of the installation packages. Various RPM files are available for Linux. If you prefer to compile software from source, or if a binary distribution isn't available for your platform, you'll need a C compiler (C++ for MySQL). The MySQL developers recommend that you use gcc 2.95.1 or newer to build MySQL. Versions of egcs from 1.03 and up are also known to work.

Other tools you'll need include gunzip and tar (if you install from compress tar files) or rpm (if you install from RPM files).

Obtaining the Software

The primary distribution points for each of the packages you'll need are shown in the following table. Some packages can be obtained from multiple locations:

Package	Location
MySQL	http://www.mysql.com/ ftp://ftp.mysql.com/pub/mysql/
DBI	http://www.symbolstone.org/ technology/perl/DBI/ http://www.mysql.com/Contrib/
PHP	http://www.php.net/ ftp://ftp.php.net/
Apache	http://www.apache.org/ ftp://ftp.apache.org/
CGI.pm	http://stein.cshl.org/WWW/software/CGI/

If you use FTP to transfer files, be sure to transfer them in binary mode to avoid file corruption.

There are many mirror sites for MySQL. www.mysql.com is located in Scandinavia, so if you pick a mirror site that's closer to you, you'll probably get better download times. Mirror sites are listed at the following address:

http://www.mysql.com/mirrors.html

For Perl software, you can always use `http://cpan.perl.org/` to locate mirrors for the modules you want.

Choosing Which Version to Install

The version of a package you install depends on your needs:

- If you need maximum stability, you probably should be conservative and use the most recent stable (non-beta) version of a package. That gives you the benefit of the newest features and the greatest number of bug fixes without exposing you to experimental code in beta versions.

- If you're interested in being on the cutting edge, or if you're a developer, you might want to use the latest beta. Of course, if you absolutely require a feature that's available only in a beta version, you have no choice but to use that version.

- For MySQL, pre-built binary and RPM distributions often are built using optimization flags that are better than what the configuration script in the source distribution might figure out by itself. The MySQL developers also build distributions using some commercial optimizing compilers to make MySQL even faster. Consequently, programs in these types of distributions may run faster than those you'd compile yourself. If you want the highest performance, you may want to try a pre-built distribution.

The Web sites for each package indicate which versions are the latest stable releases and which are beta releases. They also provide per-version feature change lists to help you decide which release is best for you.

If you are working with binary or RPM distributions, unpacking a distribution is equivalent to installing it because the files are unpacked into the directories where you want them to end up. You may need to be `root` to unpack a distribution if it installs files in protected directories.

For source distributions, you can unpack them into an area that you use for compiling and then install the software into the installation locations. You may need to be `root` to perform the install step but not for any configuration or compilation steps.

Subscribing to Mailing Lists for Help

When you install a package, it's a good idea to subscribe to the general discussion list for that package so that you can ask questions and receive helpful answers. If you install beta-quality releases, you definitely should be prepared to join and read the mailing list associated with the software to stay abreast of bug reports and fixes. If you don't join a general discussion list, you should at least subscribe to the announcement list so that you receive notices of new releases. Instructions for subscribing to mailing lists and using them are provided in the Introduction. The Web sites for each package also provide subscription information.

If you are installing from source, several packages are configured with the `config-ure` utility, which makes it easy to set up and build software on a variety of systems. If a build fails, you may need to rerun `configure` with different options than those you originally specified. Should this be necessary, you need to prevent `configure` from picking up information that it saved from the previous time you ran it. You can clean out stored configuration like this:

```
% make distclean
```

Alternatively, you can clean it out like this:

```
% rm config.cache
% make clean
```

In either case, you should then run `configure` again.

Installing MySQL on UNIX

Distributions are available for several versions of MySQL. The current stable releases have version numbers in the 3.22 series. The current development releases are in the 3.23 series. Generally, you should use the highest-numbered version in the series you want to use that is available in the distribution format you want to work with.

MySQL distributions come in binary, RPM, and source format. Binary and RPM distributions are easier to install, but you must accept the installation layout and configuration defaults that are built into the distribution. Source distributions are more difficult to install because you must compile the software, but you also get more control over configuration parameters. For example, you can compile the distribution for client support only without building the server, and you can change the location where you want to install the software.

The distributions contain one or more of the following components:

- The `mysqld` server
- Client programs (`mysql`, `mysqladmin`, and so forth), and client programming support (libraries and header files)
- Documentation
- The benchmark database
- Language support

Source and binary distributions contain all of these items. Each RPM file contains only some of them, so you may need to install multiple RPMs to get everything you need.

If you plan to connect to a server that's already running on another machine, you don't need to install a server. But you should always install client software:

- If you don't run a server, you'll need the clients so that you can connect to a server on another machine.

- If you do run a server, you'll want to be able to connect to it from the server host, not be forced to log in on another machine that has the client software just to test your server.

Overview of MySQL Installation

Installing MySQL on UNIX involves the following steps:

1. Create a UNIX account for the user and group that the server will run as (if you are installing the server).
2. Obtain and unpack any distributions you want to install. If you are using a source distribution, compile it and install it.
3. Run the `mysql_install_db` script to initialize the data directory and grant tables (first-time installation only).
4. Start the server.
5. Read Chapter 11, "General MySQL Administration," to become familiar with general administrative procedures. In particular, you should read the sections on server startup and shutdown and on running the server as an unprivileged user.

Creating an Account for the MySQL User

You can skip this section if you're running MySQL client software only and are not going to run a MySQL server.

The MySQL server can be run as any UNIX user on your system, but for security and administrative reasons, it's best that you not run the server as `root`. I recommend that you create a separate account to use for MySQL administration and that you run the server as that user. That way, you can log in as that user and have full privileges in the data directory for performing maintenance and troubleshooting. Procedures for creating user accounts vary from system to system. Consult your local documentation for specific details.

This book uses `mysqladm` and `mysqlgrp` for the UNIX user and group names of this account. If you plan to install MySQL only for your own use, you can run it as yourself, in which case you'll use your own login and group names wherever you see `mysqladm` and `mysqlgrp` in this book. If you are installing from RPM files, a user named `mysql` is created automatically as part of the RPM installation procedure. In that case, you will want to substitute `mysql` for `mysqladm`.

Advantages of using a separate, unprivileged account rather than `root` for running MySQL are:

- If you do not run MySQL as `root`, no one can exploit the server as a security hole to gain `root` access.

- It's safer to perform MySQL administrative tasks as an unprivileged user than as root.

- The server will create files owned by mysqladm rather than by root. The fewer root-owned files on your system, the better.

- It's cleaner conceptually to separate MySQL activity into its own account, and it's easier to see what things on your system are MySQL related. For example, in the directory where cron files are kept, you'll have a separate file for the MySQL user, mysqladm. Otherwise, the MySQL cron jobs would be in root's file, along with everything else done as root on a periodic basis.

Obtaining and Installing the MySQL Distribution

In the following instructions, I use *version* to stand for the version number of the MySQL distribution you're working with and *platform* to stand for the name of the platform on which you're installing it. These are used in distribution filenames so that distributions can be identified easily and distinguished one from another. A version number is something like 3.22.26 or 3.23.4-alpha. A platform name is something like sgi-irix6.3-mips or dec-osf4.0b-alpha.

Installing a Binary Distribution

Binary distribution files have names such as mysql-*version*-*platform*.tar.gz. Obtain the distribution file for the version and platform you want and put it in the directory under which you want to install MySQL—for example, /usr/local.

Unpack the distribution using one of the following commands (use the second command if your version of tar doesn't understand the z option for uncompressing the distribution):

```
% tar zxf mysql-version-platform.tar.gz
% gunzip < mysql-version-platform.tar.gz | tar xf -
```

Unpacking the distribution creates a directory, mysql-*version*-*platform*, containing the contents of the distribution. To make it easier to refer to this directory, create a symbolic link:

```
% ln -s mysql-version-platform mysql
```

Now you can refer to the installation directory as /usr/local/mysql if you installed MySQL under /usr/local.

If you are going to use only the client support provided by the distribution and are not running a server, you're done installing MySQL. If you are installing MySQL for the first time, however, go to the section "Initializing the Data Directory and Grant Tables." If you are updating an existing installation, go to the section "Starting the Server."

Installing an RPM Distribution

RPM files are available for installing MySQL on Linux systems. These have filenames like the following:

- MySQL-`version-platform`.rpm

  The server software.

- MySQL-client.`version-platform`.rpm

  The client programs.

- MySQL-devel.`version-platform`.rpm

  Development support (client libraries and header files) for writing client programs. You'll need this if you want to use or write Perl DBI scripts for accessing MySQL databases.

- MySQL-bench.`version-platform`.rpm

  Benchmarks and tests. These require Perl and the `Msql-Mysql-modules` module. You can get an RPM for `Msql-Mysql-modules` at `www.mysql.com`.

- MySQL-`version`.src.rpm

  The source for the server, clients, benchmarks, and tests.

You don't need to be in any particular directory when you install from an RPM because RPM files include information indicating where the files they contain should be installed. For any RPM file `rpm_file`, you can find out where its contents will be installed with the following command:

```
% rpm -qpl rpm_file
```

To install an RPM file, use this command:

```
% rpm -i rpm_file
```

Various parts of MySQL are divided into different RPM files, so you may need to install more than one RPM. To install client support, use this command:

```
% rpm -i MySQL-client-version-platform.rpm
```

For server support, use this command:

```
% rpm -i MySQL-version-platform.rpm
```

If you plan to write your own programs using the client programming support, make sure to install the development RPM file:

```
% rpm -i MySQL-devel-version-platform.rpm
```

If you plan to use only the client support provided by the distribution and are not running a server, you're done installing MySQL. If you are installing MySQL for the first time, however, go to the section "Initializing the Data Directory and Grant Tables." If you are updating an existing installation, go to the section "Starting the Server."

If you want to install from the source RPM file, the following command should be
sufficient:

```
% rpm --recompile MySQL-version.src.rpm
```

Installing a Source Distribution

Source distributions have names such as `mysql-version.tar.gz`, where `version` is the
MySQL version number. Pick the directory under which you want to unpack the distribution and move into it. Obtain the distribution file and unpack it using one of the
following commands (use the second command if your version of `tar` doesn't understand the `z` option for uncompressing the distribution):

```
% tar zxf mysql-version.tar.gz
% gunzip < mysql-version.tar.gz | tar xf -
```

Unpacking the distribution creates a directory `mysql-version` containing the contents
of the distribution. Move into this directory:

```
% cd mysql-version
```

Now you need to configure and compile the distribution before you can install it.
If these steps fail, check the chapter "Installing MySQL" in the MySQL Reference
Manual, particularly any system-specific notes it may contain about your type of
machine.

Use the `configure` command to configure the distribution:

```
% ./configure
```

You may want to specify options for `configure`. To obtain a list of available options,
run this command:

```
% ./configure --help
```

The following list shows some configuration options many people find helpful:

- `--without-server`

  Configure for building client support only (client programs or client libraries).
  You might do this if you're planning to access a server that's already running on
  another machine.

- `--prefix=path_name`

  By default, the installation root directory is `/usr/local`. The data directory,
  clients, the server, client libraries, and header files are installed in the `var`, `bin`,
  `libexec`, `lib`, and `include` directories under this directory. If you want to change
  the installation root, use the `--prefix` option.

- `--localstatedir=path_name`

  This option changes the location of the data directory. You can use this if you
  don't want to keep your databases under `/usr/local/var`.

- `--with-low-memory`

  The `sql/sql_yacc.cc` source file requires a lot of memory to compile, which sometimes causes the build to blow up. Symptoms of this problem include error messages about "fatal signal 11" or exhaustion of virtual memory. The `--with-low-memory` option causes the compiler to be invoked with options that result in lower memory use.

After you run `configure`, compile the distribution and then install it:

```
% make
% make install
```

You may need to be `root` to run the install command if you haven't used the `--prefix` option to specify an installation directory in which you have write permission.

If you are going to use only the client support provided by the distribution and are not running a server, you're done installing MySQL. If you are installing MySQL for the first time, however, go to the next section. If you are updating an existing installation, go to the section "Starting the Server."

Initializing the Data Directory and Grant Tables

Before you can use your MySQL installation, you need to initialize the `mysql` database that contains the grant tables controlling network access to your server. This step is needed only for a new installation and only if you will run a server. Those performing client-only installations can skip it. For a binary distribution, run the commands from the installation directory (the parent of the `bin` directory created by the distribution). For a source distribution, run the commands from the top-level directory of the distribution.

DATADIR is the pathname to your data directory. Normally, you run the following commands as `root`. If you're logged in as `mysqladm` or you're installed MySQL under your own account because you intend to run it for yourself, you can run the commands without being `root` and can skip the `chown` and `chmod` commands.

Set up the default grant tables by running the `mysql_install_db` script:[1]

```
# scripts/mysql_install_db
```

If `mysql_install_db` fails, consult the chapter "Installing MySQL" in the MySQL Reference Manual to see if it says anything about the problem you're encountering, and then try again. Note that if `mysql_install_db` doesn't run to completion successfully, any grant tables it creates are likely incomplete. You should remove them because `mysql_install_db` may not try to re-create any tables that it finds already existing. You can remove the entire `mysql` database like this:

```
# rm -rf DATADIR/mysql
```

---

[1] You need not do this if you are installing from RPM files because `mysql_install_db` will be run for you automatically.

After running `mysql_install_db`, shut down the server if you are installing a version of MySQL older than 3.22.10 (with newer versions, `mysql_install_db` does this automatically):

```
# bin/mysqladmin --user=root shutdown
```

With the server down, change the user and group ownership and mode of all files under the data directory:

```
# chown -R mysqladm.mysqlgrp DATADIR
# chmod -R go-rwx DATADIR
```

The `chown` command changes the ownership to the MySQL user, and the `chmod` changes the mode to keep everybody out of the data directory except `mysqladm`.

Starting the Server

This step is needed only if you will run a server. Those performing client-only installations can skip it. Run the commands in this section from the same directory indicated in the previous section. Normally, you run the commands as `root`. If you're logged in as `mysqladm` or you're installed MySQL under your own account, you can run the commands without being `root` and should omit the `--user` option.

Use the following command to start the server:

```
# bin/safe_mysqld --user=mysqladm &
```

The `--user` option tells the server to run as `mysqladm`. If you want to enable logging, use this command instead:

```
# bin/safe_mysqld --user=mysqladm --log &
```

The default installation allows the MySQL `root` user to connect without a password. It's a good idea to establish a password. You should also arrange for the server to start up and shut down when your system starts up and shuts down. In addition, it's recommended that you enable update logging because that can be useful for data recovery procedures. For instructions on performing any of these actions, see Chapter 11.

Installing Perl DBI Support

Install the DBI software if you want to write Perl scripts that access MySQL databases. DBI requires that you've installed MySQL client programming support because it uses the MySQL C client library. You can also install the CGI.pm module if you want to write Web-based DBI scripts. The DBI software requires a reasonably recent version of Perl (5.004 or later). If you don't have Perl installed, visit `http://www.perl.com/`, download a Perl distribution, and install it before you install DBI support.

DBI support requires three modules, which you can install from source or from RPM files:

- **Data-Dumper.** A module for processing Perl data structures conveniently.
- **DBI.** The main DBI driver.
- **Msql-Mysql-modules.** The MySQL-specific driver used by DBI when you connect to a MySQL server.

If you install from source, install the modules in the order shown in the preceding list. Otherwise, the test step of the following installation instructions won't work.

Installation for all three modules is similar. When you install from source, you unpack a distribution file using one of the following commands (use the second command if your version of `tar` doesn't understand the `z` option for uncompressing the distribution):

```
% tar zxf dist_file.tar.gz
% gunzip < dist_file.tar.gz | tar xf -
```

Then move into the distribution directory created by the `tar` command and run these commands (you may need to be `root` to run the installation step):

```
% perl Makefile.PL
% make
% make test
% make install
```

If you run the preceding commands for the Msql-Mysql-modules distribution, the `perl` command will ask you some questions when you generate the `Makefile`:

- **Which drivers do you want to install?** There are choices for various combinations of MySQL and mSQL. Unless you also run mSQL, select MySQL to keep things simple.

- **Do you want to install the MysqlPerl emulation?** MysqlPerl is the old Perl interface for MySQL. It is obsolete. Answer no to this unless you have old MysqlPerl scripts and want to enable emulation support for them in the DBI module.

- **Where is your MySQL installed?** This should be the grandparent of the directory containing your MySQL header files, probably `/usr/local` or `/usr/local/mysql` unless you installed MySQL in a non-standard location.

- **Which database should I use for testing the MySQL drivers?** The default is `test`, which should be okay, unless you've turned off anonymous access to it. In that case, you'll need to give a database name to which you have access and then specify a valid MySQL username and password for the next couple of questions.

- **On which host is the database running?** `localhost` should be sufficient if you're running a local server. If not, name a host that is running a server to which you have access. The MySQL server must be running on this host when you run the `make test` command or the tests will fail.

- **User name for connecting to the database?**

  Password for connecting to the database?

  The name and password to use for connecting to the MySQL server for testing. The default is undef for both questions. This causes the driver to connect as the anonymous user. Specify non-blank values if you need to connect non-anonymously.

If you have problems installing the Perl modules, consult the README file for the relevant distribution as well as the mail archives for the DBI mailing list because the answers for most installation problems can be found there.

If you want to use CGI.pm, it may already be present in your Perl installation. Try running the command perldoc CGI. If it displays CGI documentation, CGI is installed. Otherwise, obtain the distribution and unpack and install it using the same instructions as for the other Perl modules.

If you want to install the mod_perl Apache module for use with Web-based DBI scripts, visit the mod_perl area of the Apache Web site at the following location for more information:

    http://perl.apache.org/

Installing PHP and Apache

The following instructions should get you going. If you encounter problems, check the "VERBOSE INSTALL" section of the INSTALL file included with the PHP distribution. (It's not a bad idea to read that file anyway. It contains lots of useful information.)

These instructions assume you have an Apache source distribution available and that you'll run PHP as an Apache module. They also assume that you have Apache 1.3.9 and PHP 3.0.12 and that you are in a directory under which the apache_1.3.9 and php-3.0.12 directories containing the source distributions are located. If you have different versions or locations, substitute your actual version numbers and pathnames when you use the following instructions.

To configure and build PHP, begin by running the following commands (the procedure looks a little strange because you begin with the Apache distribution, but that's correct):

    % cd apache_1.3.9
    % ./configure

The configure command for Apache is necessary because some of the header files that PHP needs are generated at configuration time. If you don't run configure in the Apache distribution, the PHP configuration process won't be able to find the files. After configuring Apache, move into the PHP distribution directory, configure PHP, build it, and install it. You can also install a copy of the PHP initialization file:

```
% cd ../php-3.0.12
% ./configure --with-mysql --with-apache=../apache_1.3.9 --enable-track-vars
% make
% make install
% cp php3.ini-dist /usr/local/lib/php3.ini
```

The `configure` command for PHP tells it that you want MySQL support and indicates where the Apache source tree is located. The `--enable-track-vars` option turns on automatic conversion of form input into variables that you can access easily from within your PHP pages. The `make` commands compile and install PHP. You might need to be `root` to install the initialization file `php3.ini`.

When you build PHP as a module, "installing" it simply copies the module into the Apache source tree so that it can be linked into the Apache binary. After that is done, you can compile and install Apache:

```
% cd ../apache_1.3.9
% ./configure --activate-module=src/modules/php3/libphp3.a
% make
% make install
```

These steps reconfigure Apache so that it knows about the PHP module file and then build and install it. You should edit your Apache configuration file `httpd.conf` so that Apache recognizes PHP scripts. PHP recognition is based on the filename extension that you use for PHP scripts. For example, if you want Apache to recognize both `.php` and `.php3`, include the following lines in the configuration file:

```
AddType application/x-httpd-php3 .php
AddType application/x-httpd-php3 .php3
```

The suffixes to use depend on how you plan to name your PHP scripts. `.php` and `.php3` are probably the most common. Another common extension is `.phtml`. You can simply enable them all if you want. This may be best anyway if you're going to be installing pages that you obtain from other people that use one or another of these extensions.

You can also tell Apache to recognize `index.php` or `index.php3` as the default file for a directory when no filename is specified at the end of a URL. You'll probably find a line in the configuration file that looks like this:

```
DirectoryIndex index.html
```

Change it to this:

```
DirectoryIndex index.html index.php index.php3
```

After editing the Apache configuration file, bring down the `httpd` server if one was already running, and then start the new `httpd` that you just installed. On many systems, the following commands (executed as `root`) accomplish this:

```
# /usr/local/apache/bin/apachectl stop
# /usr/local/apache/bin/apachectl start
```

You should also set up Apache to start up and shut down at system startup and shut-down time. See the Apache documentation for instructions. Normally, this involves running `apachectl start` at boot time and `apachectl stop` at shutdown time.

Installing MySQL on Windows

You can run MySQL under Windows 95, Windows 98, or Windows NT. To do so, you must have TCP/IP support installed, and your Winsock software must be at least version 2.

You can install two kinds of MySQL software under Windows:

- Standalone programs, such as those you install for UNIX (the `mysqld` server and client programs such as `mysql` and `mysqladmin`).
- MyODBC, the MySQL driver for ODBC that allows other programs (such as Access) to communicate with MySQL servers.

The Windows distributions are all available from the MySQL Web site as zip files. To unpack such a file, just double-click it. If that does not work, use a program such as Winzip or pkunzip to unpack files. The primary distributions include the following:

- `mysqlwin-version.zip`

  The full distribution (server and clients).

- `winclients-version.zip`

  Client-only software (`mysql`, `mysqladmin`, `mysqldump`, and so forth). You can use this if you don't want to run the server under Windows.

- `myodbc-version-win95.zip`
  `myodbc-version-nt.zip`

  MyODBC support for Windows 95 (or Windows 98), and for Windows NT.

- `mysqlclient-version-cygwin-b20.tar.gz`

  MySQL clients compiled with the Cygnus toolkit. This includes `mysqlc`, a version of the `mysql` client that has command-line history editing capability. If you install this, you'll need to copy the library file `cygwinb19.dll` from `C:\mysql\lib` to your Windows system directory.

Installing a Client-Only or Client/Server Distribution

If you have the `winclients-version.zip` distribution containing client software only, unpack it to produce a `mysql` folder. Move this folder to `C:\`.

If you have the `mysqlwin-version.zip` distribution containing the server and the clients, unpack it first. In the resulting folder, run the `Setup` program to install MySQL in `C:\mysql`.

Choose from the following servers:

Server	Description
mysqld	Standard server
mysqld-opt	Server optimized for Pentium processors
mysqld-nt	Server that can be installed as a service under Windows NT

You can run any of the servers under NT, but the last one may only be run under NT.

To run mysqld or mysqld-opt, start the server as follows:

```
C:\> C:\mysql\bin\mysqld
C:\> C:\mysql\bin\mysqld-opt
```

To shut down the server, use the mysqladmin utility:

```
C:\> C:\mysql\bin\mysqladmin -u root shutdown
```

Under Windows NT, you can run the mysqld-nt server as a service:

```
C:\> C:\mysql\bin\mysqld-nt --install
```

If you start mysqld-nt this way, you can specify other options by putting them in the option file C:\my.cnf. They cannot be specified on the command line. When mysqld-nt is running as a service, you can start or stop it using the following commands:

```
C:\> net start mysql
C:\> net stop mysql
```

You can also use the Services Control Manager utility found in the Control Panel folder to start or stop the server, or you can use the mysqladmin utility to stop the server from the command line:

```
C:\> C:\mysql\bin\mysqladmin -u root shutdown
```

To run mysqld-nt as a standalone program, invoke it like this:

```
C:\> C:\mysql\bin\mysqld-nt --standalone
```

In this case, you can specify other options on the command line after the --standalone option if you want. To shut down the server, use mysqladmin.

If you have problems getting the server to run, check the Windows notes in the chapter "Installing MySQL" in the MySQL Reference Manual.

The default installation allows the MySQL root user to connect without a password. For instructions on establishing a password, see Chapter 11.

Installing MyODBC

Unpack the appropriate distribution (there is one for Windows 95 or 98, and another for Windows NT). In the resulting folder, run the Setup program to install the

MySQL ODBC driver. An ODBC control panel is also installed that you can use to configure the driver.

If you encounter an error, such as "Problems while copying MFC30.DLL," while installing MyODBC, then MFC30.DLL is being used by some application. In this case, try restarting Windows in safe mode and run the Setup program again.

When you run the ODBC control panel, you'll see a window that allows you to set up a data source name (DSN). Click the User DSN tab and then click the Add button to bring up a window that lists the available data source drivers. Select the MySQL driver from the list and click the Finish button. You'll see a window that allows you to enter connection parameters for the data source. Fill in parameters that are appropriate for the connection that you want to establish and then click the OK button. For example, to set up a data source for the samp_db database using the server and user account that I use throughout most of this book, I'd fill in the fields as follows:

Field Name	Field Value
Windows DSN name:	`samp_db`
MySQL host (name or IP):	`pit-viper.snake.net`
MySQL database name:	`samp_db`
User:	`paul`
Password:	`secret`

Now you should be able to use ODBC aware programs to access MySQL databases.

Installing Perl DBI Support

The easiest thing to do is to get the ActiveState Perl distribution from the ActiveState Web site (`http://www.activestate.com/`) and install it. Then fetch and install the additional Perl modules that you need. The ppm (Perl Package Manager) program is used for this. To find out what modules are already installed, use this command:

```
C:\> C:\perl\bin\ppm info
```

Then install the modules you need using the appropriate commands from the following list. It's likely that CGI.pm will already be installed, but you'll probably need to install the DBI-related packages.

```
C:\> C:\perl\bin\ppm install Data-Dumper
C:\> C:\perl\bin\ppm install DBI
C:\> C:\perl\bin\ppm install DBD-mysql
C:\> C:\perl\bin\ppm install CGI
```

Installing PHP and Apache

Under Windows, PHP is a separate executable, and MySQL support is a DLL file. For complete instructions on installing PHP on Windows, the best thing to do is to visit the following Web page:

```
http://www.umesd.k12.or.us/php/win32install.html
```

Obtaining and Installing the samp_db Sample Database Distribution

The files used to set up and access the samp_db sample database are available at the following address (note that it is case sensitive and must be typed exactly as shown):

```
http://mysql.he.net/Downloads/Contrib/Examples/
```

Retrieve the distribution file samp_db.tar.gz, move into the directory under which you want to install it, and unpack it using one of these commands:

```
% tar zxf samp_db.tar.gz
% gunzip < samp_db.tar.gz | tar xf -
```

When you unpack the distribution, it will create a directory named samp_db containing several items:

- Files for creating and loading the samp_db database. These are used in Chapter 1, "Introduction to MySQL and SQL."
- The C programs from Chapter 6, "The MySQL C API."
- The Perl DBI scripts and the samp_db.cnf option file from Chapter 7, "The Perl DBI API."
- The PHP scripts and the samp_db.inc include file from Chapter 8, "The PHP API."

The samp_db directory contains a README file that you should consult for instructions on using the distribution files.

B

Column Type Reference

THIS APPENDIX DESCRIBES EACH COLUMN type provided by MySQL. More information on the use of each type is available in Chapter 2, "Working with Data in MySQL." Unless otherwise indicated, the types listed have been present in MySQL at least as far back as MySQL 3.21.0.

Type name specifications are written using the following conventions:

- **Square brackets ([ ]).** Optional information.
- *M.* The maximum display width; unless otherwise specified, *M* should be an integer from 1 to 255.
- *D.* The number of digits following the decimal point for types that have a fractional part; *D* should be an integer from 0 to 30. *D* should also be no greater than *M*−2. Otherwise, the value of *M* is adjusted to be *D*+2.

In ODBC terminology, *M* and *D* correspond to "precision" and "scale."

For each type description, one or more of the following kinds of information are provided:

- **Meaning.** A short description of the type.
- **Allowable attributes.** Optional attribute keywords that may be associated with the column type in CREATE TABLE or ALTER TABLE statements. Attributes are listed in alphabetical order, but this does not necessarily correspond to the order

imposed by the syntax of CREATE TABLE or ALTER TABLE. See Appendix D, "SQL Syntax Reference," for the syntax of those statements. The attributes listed in each column type description are in addition to the global attributes listed below.

- **Allowable length.** The maximum allowable length of column values for string types.

- **Range.** For numeric or date and time types, the range of values the type can represent. For integer numeric types, two ranges are given because integer columns can be signed or unsigned, and the ranges are different for each case.

- **Zero value.** For date and time types, the "zero" value that is stored if an illegal value is inserted into the column.

- **Default value.** The default value if no explicit DEFAULT attribute is given in the type specification.

- **Storage required.** The number of bytes required to store values of the type. For some types, this value is fixed. The amount varies for other types depending on the length of the value stored in the column.

- **Comparisons.** Whether or not comparisons are case sensitive for string types. This applies to sorting and indexing too because those operations are based on comparisons.

- **Synonyms.** Any synonyms for the type name.

- **Notes.** Any miscellaneous observations about the type.

- **Global attributes.** Some attributes apply to all or almost all column types; they are listed here rather than in each type description. NULL or NOT NULL may be specified for every type. DEFAULT *default_value* may be specified for all types except BLOB and TEXT types.

Numeric Types

MySQL provides numeric types for integer and floating point values. Types may be chosen according to the range of values you need to represent.

For integer types, a column must be a PRIMARY KEY or a UNIQUE index if the AUTO_INCREMENT attribute is specified. Inserting NULL into an AUTO_INCREMENT column inserts a value that is one greater than the column's current maximum value. Negative values are not allowed for integer types if the UNSIGNED attribute is specified.

Values for numeric types are padded with leading zeroes to the column's display width if the ZEROFILL attribute is specified.

TINYINT[(*M*)]

Meaning. A very small integer

Allowable attributes. AUTO_INCREMENT, UNSIGNED, ZEROFILL

Range. −128 to 127 (-2^7 to 2^7-1), or 0 to 255 (0 to 2^8-1) if UNSIGNED

Default value. NULL if column can be NULL, 0 if NOT NULL

Storage required. 1 byte

SMALLINT[(*M*)]

Meaning. A small integer

Allowable attributes. AUTO_INCREMENT, UNSIGNED, ZEROFILL

Range. −32768 to 32767 (-2^{15} to $2^{15}-1$), or 0 to 65535 (0 to $2^{16}-1$) if UNSIGNED

Default value. NULL if column can be NULL, 0 if NOT NULL

Storage required. 2 bytes

MEDIUMINT[(*M*)]

Meaning. A medium-sized integer

Allowable attributes. AUTO_INCREMENT, UNSIGNED, ZEROFILL

Range. −8388608 to 8388607 (-2^{23} to $2^{23}-1$), or 0 to 16777215 (0 to $2^{24}-1$) if UNSIGNED

Default value. NULL if column can be NULL, 0 if NOT NULL

Storage required. 3 bytes

INT[(*M*)]

Meaning. A normal-sized integer

Allowable attributes. AUTO_INCREMENT, UNSIGNED, ZEROFILL

Range. −2147483648 to 2147483647 (-2^{31} to $2^{31}-1$), or 0 to 4294967295 (0 to $2^{32}-1$) if UNSIGNED

Default value. NULL if column can be NULL, 0 if NOT NULL

Storage required. 4 bytes

Synonyms. INTEGER[(*M*)]

BIGINT[(*M*)]

Meaning. A large integer

Allowable attributes. AUTO_INCREMENT, UNSIGNED, ZEROFILL

Range. −9223372036854775808 to 9223372036854775807 (-2^{63} to $2^{63}-1$), or 0 to 18446744073709551615 (0 to $2^{64}-1$) if UNSIGNED

Default value. NULL if column can be NULL, 0 if NOT NULL

Storage required. 8 bytes

FLOAT[(*M*,*D*)]

Meaning. A small floating-point number; single-precision (less precise than DOUBLE)

Allowable attributes. ZEROFILL

Range. Minimum non-zero values are ±1.175494351E−38; maximum non-zero values are ±3.402823466E+38

Default value. NULL if column can be NULL, 0 if NOT NULL

Storage required. 4 bytes

Synonyms. Prior to MySQL 3.23, FLOAT(4) is a synonym for FLOAT with the default *M* and *D* values.

Note. As of MySQL 3.23, FLOAT(4) is a true floating-point type (values are stored to the full precision allowed by your hardware, not rounded to the default number of decimal places).

DOUBLE[(*M*,*D*)]

Meaning. A large floating-point number; double-precision (more precise than FLOAT)

Allowable attributes. ZEROFILL

Range. Minimum non-zero values are ±2.2250738585072014E−308, maximum non-zero values are ±1.7976931348623157E+308

Default value. NULL if column can be NULL, 0 if NOT NULL

Storage required. 8 bytes

Synonyms. DOUBLE PRECISION[(*M*,*D*)] and REAL[(*M*,*D*)] are synonyms for DOUBLE[(*M*,*D*)]. Prior to MySQL 3.23, FLOAT(8) is a synonym for DOUBLE with the default *M* and *D* values.

Note. As of MySQL 3.23, FLOAT(8) is a true floating-point type. (Values are stored to the full precision allowed by your hardware, not rounded to the default number of decimal places.)

DECIMAL(*M*,*D*)

Meaning. A floating-point number, stored as a string (1 byte per digit, decimal point, or '·' sign).

Allowable attributes. ZEROFILL

Range. Maximum range is the same as for DOUBLE; effective range for a given DECIMAL type is determined by *M* and *D*. If *D* is 0, column values have no decimal point or a fractional part.

Default value. NULL if column can be NULL, 0 if NOT NULL

Storage required. *M* bytes for versions of MySQL earlier than 3.23, *M*+2 bytes for MySQL 3.23 and up

Synonyms. NUMERIC(*M*,*D*)

Note. As of MySQL 3.23, the value of *M* does not include the bytes needed for the sign character or decimal point, in conformance with ANSI SQL.

String Types

The MySQL string types are commonly used to store text, but are general and may hold arbitrary data. Types are available to hold values of varying maximum lengths and can be chosen according to whether or not you want values to be treated in case sensitive fashion.

CHAR(*M*)

Meaning. A fixed-length character string 0 to *M* bytes long. *M* should be an integer from 1 to 255 prior to MySQL 3.23, and from 0 to 255 as of MySQL 3.23. Strings shorter than *M* characters are right-padded with spaces when stored. Strings longer than *M* characters are chopped to length *M* when stored. Trailing spaces are removed when values are retrieved.

Allowable attributes. BINARY

Allowable length. 0 to *M* bytes

Default value. NULL if column can be NULL, "" if NOT NULL

Storage required. *M* bytes

Comparisons. Not case sensitive (case sensitive if BINARY)

VARCHAR(*M*)

Meaning. A variable-length character string 0 to *M* bytes long. *M* should be an integer from 1 to 255, or from 0 to 255 as of MySQL 3.23. Trailing spaces are removed from values when stored. Strings longer than *M* characters are chopped to length *M* when stored.

Allowable attributes. BINARY

Allowable length. 0 to *M* bytes

Default value. NULL if column can be NULL, "" if NOT NULL

Storage required. Length of value, plus 1 byte to record the length

Comparisons. Not case sensitive (case sensitive if BINARY)

TINYBLOB

Meaning. A small BLOB value

Allowable attributes. None other than the global attributes

Allowable length. 0 to 255 (0 to 2^8-1) bytes

Default value. NULL if column can be NULL, "" if NOT NULL

Storage required. Length of value, plus 1 byte to record the length

Comparisons. Case sensitive

BLOB

Meaning. A normal-sized BLOB value

Allowable attributes. None other than the global attributes

Allowable length. 0 to 65535 (0 to $2^{16}-1$) bytes

Default value. NULL if column can be NULL, "" if NOT NULL

Storage required. Length of value, plus 2 bytes to record the length

Comparisons. Case sensitive

MEDIUMBLOB

Meaning. A medium-sized BLOB value

Allowable attributes. None other than the global attributes

Allowable length. 0 to 16777215 (0 to $2^{24}-1$) bytes

Default value. NULL if column can be NULL, "" if NOT NULL

Storage required. Length of value, plus 3 bytes to record the length

Comparisons. Case sensitive

LONGBLOB

Meaning. A large BLOB value

Allowable attributes. None other than the global attributes

Allowable length. 0 to 4294967295 (0 to $2^{32}-1$) bytes

Default value. NULL if column can be NULL, "" if NOT NULL

Storage required. Length of value, plus 4 bytes to record the length

Comparisons. Case sensitive

TINYTEXT

Meaning. A small TEXT value

Allowable attributes. None other than the global attributes

Allowable length. 0 to 255 (0 to 2^8-1) bytes

Default value. NULL if column can be NULL, "" if NOT NULL

Storage required. Length of value, plus 1 byte to record the length

Comparisons. Not case sensitive

TEXT

Meaning. A normal-sized TEXT value

Allowable attributes. None other than the global attributes

Allowable length. 0 to 65535 (0 to $2^{16}-1$) bytes

Default value. NULL if column can be NULL, "" if NOT NULL

Storage required. Length of value, plus 2 bytes to record the length

Comparisons. Not case sensitive

MEDIUMTEXT

Meaning. A medium-sized TEXT value

Allowable attributes. None other than the global attributes

Allowable length. 0 to 16777215 (0 to $2^{24}-1$) bytes

Default value. NULL if column can be NULL, "" if NOT NULL

Storage required. Length of value, plus 3 bytes to record the length

Comparisons. Not case sensitive

LONGTEXT

Meaning. A large TEXT value

Allowable attributes. None other than the global attributes

Allowable length. 0 to 4294967295 (0 to $2^{32}-1$) bytes

Default value. NULL if column can be NULL, " " if NOT NULL

Storage required. Length of value, plus 4 bytes to record the length

Comparisons. Not case sensitive

ENUM("value1","value2",...)

Meaning. An enumeration; column values may be assigned exactly one member of the value list

Allowable attributes. None other than the global attributes

Default value. NULL if column can be NULL, first enumeration value if NOT NULL

Storage required. 1 byte for enumerations with 1 to 255 members, 2 bytes for enumerations with 256 to 65535 members

Comparisons. Not case sensitive (case sensitive prior to MySQL 3.22.1)

SET("value1","value2",...)

Meaning. A set; column values may be assigned zero or more members of the value list

Allowable attributes. None other than the global attributes

Default value. NULL if column can be NULL, " " (empty set) if NOT NULL

Storage required. 1 byte (for sets with 1 to 8 members), 2 bytes (9 to 16 members), 3 bytes (17 to 24 members), 4 bytes (25 to 32 members), or 8 bytes (33 to 64 members)

Comparisons. Not case sensitive (case sensitive prior to MySQL 3.22.1)

Date and Time Types

MySQL provides types to represent temporal data in various forms. Date and time types are available, either together or in combination. There is a special timestamp type that is updated automatically when a record changes and a type for storing years if you don't need a complete date.

DATE

Meaning. A date, in `"YYYY-MM-DD"` format

Allowable attributes. None other than the global attributes

Range. `"1000-01-01"` to `"9999-12-31"`

Zero value. `"0000-00-00"`

Default value. NULL if column can be NULL, `"0000-00-00"` if NOT NULL

Storage required. 3 bytes (4 bytes prior to MySQL 3.22)

TIME

Meaning. A time, in `"hh:mm:ss"` format (`"-hh:mm:ss"` for negative values); represents elapsed time but may be treated as time of day

Allowable attributes. None other than the global attributes

Range. `"-838:59:59"` to `"838:59:59"`

Zero value. `"00:00:00"`

Default value. NULL if column can be NULL, `"00:00:00"` if NOT NULL

Storage required. 3 bytes

Note. Although `"00:00:00"` is used as the zero value when illegal values are inserted into a TIME column, that is also a legal value that lies within the normal value range.

DATETIME

Meaning. A date and time (both parts are required), in `"YYYY-MM-DD hh:mm:ss"` format

Allowable attributes. None other than the global attributes

Range. `"1000-01-01 00:00:00"` to `"9999-12-31 23:59:59"`

Zero value. `"0000-00-00 00:00:00"`

Default value. NULL if column can be NULL, `"0000-00-00 00:00:00"` if NOT NULL

Storage required. 8 bytes

TIMESTAMP[(*M*)]

Meaning. A timestamp (date and time), in *YYYYMMDDhhmmss* format

Allowable attributes. None other than the global attributes

Range. 19700101000000 to sometime in the year 2037

Zero value. 00000000000000

Default value. The current date and time. Note that DESCRIBE and SHOW COLUMNS report the default value as NULL.

Storage required. 4 bytes

Note. Inserting a NULL into the first TIMESTAMP column of a table inserts the current date and time. Changing the value of any other column in the row causes the first TIMESTAMP column to be updated to the modification date and time. Values are stored and used in calculations internally to full 14-character precision, regardless of the display width. If NOT NULL is specified as an attribute, it is ignored.

YEAR

Meaning. A year, in *YYYY* format

Allowable attributes. None other than the global attributes

Range. 1900 to 2155

Zero value. 0000

Default value. NULL if column can be NULL, 0000 if NOT NULL

Storage required. 1 byte

Note. YEAR was introduced in MySQL 3.22.

C

Operator and Function Reference

THIS APPENDIX LISTS ALL THE MySQL functions that you can use in SQL statements. It also lists the operators used to construct expressions. Evaluating an expression often involves type conversion of the values in that expression. See Chapter 2, "Working with Data in MySQL," for details on the circumstances under which type conversion occurs and the rules that MySQL uses to convert values from one type to another.

Unless otherwise indicated, the operators and functions listed have been present in MySQL at least as far back as MySQL 3.21.0. If an operator or function appears to behave differently than described here, check the change notes in the MySQL Reference Manual. It's very possible that old versions of MySQL have bugs that have since been fixed.

Operator and function examples are written in the following format:

expression   → *result*

The *expression* demonstrates how to use an operator or function, and the *result* shows the result from evaluating the expression. For example:

LOWER("ABC")   → "abc"

This means that the function call LOWER("ABC") produces the string result "abc".

You can try out the examples shown in this appendix for yourself using the `mysql` program. To try the preceding example, invoke `mysql`, type in the example expression with `SELECT` in front of it and a semicolon after it, and press Enter:

```
mysql> SELECT LOWER("ABC");
+--------------+
| LOWER("ABC") |
+--------------+
| abc          |
+--------------+
```

MySQL does not require a `SELECT` statement to have a `FROM` clause, which makes it easy to experiment with operators and functions by entering arbitrary expressions in this way. (Some database systems don't let you issue a `SELECT` without a `FROM`—an unfortunate restriction.)

Examples include complete `SELECT` statements for functions that cannot be demonstrated otherwise. The section "Summary Functions" is written that way because those functions make no sense except in reference to a particular table.

Function names, as well as operators that are words, such as `BETWEEN`, may be specified in any lettercase.

Certain types of function arguments occur repeatedly and are represented by names with a fixed meaning:

- *expr* represents an expression; depending on the context, this may be a numeric, string, or date or time expression, and may incorporate constants, references to table columns, or other expressions.
- *str* represents a string; it can be a literal string, a reference to a string-valued table column, or an expression that produces a string.
- *n* represents an integer (as do letters near to *n* in the alphabet).
- *x* represents a floating-point number (as do letters near to *x* in the alphabet).

Other argument names are used less often and are defined where used. Optional parts of operator or function call sequences are indicated by square brackets ([ ]).

Operators

Operators are used to combine terms in expressions to perform arithmetic, compare values, perform bitwise or logical operations, and match patterns.

Operator Precedence

Operators have varying levels of precedence. The levels are shown in the following list, from highest to lowest. Operators on the same line have the same precedence. Operators at a given precedence level are evaluated left to right. Operators at a higher precedence level are evaluated before operators at a lower precedence level.

```
BINARY
NOT  !
- (unary minus)
*  /  %
+  -
<<  >>
&
|
<  <=  =  <=>  !=  <>  >=  >  IN  IS  LIKE  REGEXP  RLIKE
BETWEEN
AND  &&
OR  ||
```

The unary operators (unary minus, NOT, and BINARY) bind more tightly than the binary operators. That is, they group with the immediately following term in an expression, not with the rest of the expression as a whole.

```
-2+3                                    → 1
-(2+3)                                  → -5
```

Grouping Operators

Parentheses—(and)—may be used to group parts of an expression to override the default operator precedence that determines the order in which terms of an expression are evaluated (see "Operator Precedence"). Parentheses may also be used simply for visual clarity, to make an expression more readable.

```
1 + 2 * 3 / 4                           → 2.50
(((1 + 2) * 3) / 4)                     → 2.25
```

Arithmetic Operators

These operators perform standard arithmetic. The arithmetic operators work on numbers, not strings (although strings that look like numbers are converted automatically to the corresponding numeric value). Arithmetic involving NULL values produces a NULL result.

- +

  Evaluates to the sum of the arguments.

  ```
  2 + 2                                 → 4
  3.2 + 4.7                             → 7.9
  "43bc" + "21d"                        → 64
  "abc" + "def"                         → 0
  ```

  The final example in this listing shows that '+' does not serve as the string concatenation operator the way it does in some languages. Instead, the strings are converted to numbers before the arithmetic operation takes place. Strings that don't look like numbers are converted to 0. Use the CONCAT() function to concatenate strings.

- -

  Evaluates to the difference of the operands when used between two terms of
  an expression. Evaluates to the negative of the operand when used in front of a
  single term (that is, it flips the sign of the term).

`10 - 7`	→ 3
`-(10 - 7)`	→ -3

- *

  Evaluates to the product of the operands.

`2 * 3`	→ 6
`2.3 * -4.5`	→ -10.3

- /

  Evaluates to the quotient of the operands. Division by zero produces a `NULL`
  result.

`3 / 1`	→ 3.00
`1 / 3`	→ 0.33
`1 / 0`	→ NULL

- %

  The modulo operator; evaluates to the remainder of m divided by n. m % n is the
  same as `MOD(m,n)`. As with division, the modulo operator with a divisor of zero
  returns `NULL`.

`12 % 4`	→ 0
`12 % 5`	→ 2
`12 % 0`	→ NULL

For '+', '-', and '*', arithmetic is performed with `BIGINT` values (64-bit integers) if both
arguments are integers. This means expressions involving large values might exceed the
range of 64-bit integer calculations, with unpredictable results:

`999999999999999999 * 999999999999999999`	→ -7527149226598858751
`99999999999 * 99999999999 * 99999999999`	→ -1504485813132150785
`18014398509481984 * 18014398509481984`	→ 0

For '/', and '%', `BIGINT` values are used only when the division is performed in a context where the result is converted to an integer.

Comparison Operators

Comparison operators return 1 if the comparison is true and 0 if the comparison is
false. You can compare numbers or strings. Operands are converted as necessary
according to the following rules:

- With the exception of the '<=>' operator, comparisons involving `NULL` values
  evaluate as `NULL`. ('<=>' is like '=', except that `NULL <=> NULL` is true.)
- If both operands are strings, they are compared lexicographically as strings.
  String comparisons are performed using the character set in force on the server.

- If both operands are integers, they are compared numerically as integers.
- Hexadecimal constants that are not compared to a number are compared as binary strings.
- If either operand is a TIMESTAMP or DATETIME value and the other is a constant, the operands are compared as TIMESTAMP values. This is done to make comparisons work better for ODBC applications.
- If none of the preceding rules apply, the operands are compared numerically as floating-point values. Note that this includes the case of comparing a string and a number. The string is converted to a number, which results in a value of 0 if the string doesn't look like a number. For example, "14.3" converts to 14.3, but "L4.3" converts to 0.

The following comparisons illustrate these rules:

```
2 < 12                                          → 1
"2" < "12"                                      → 0
"2" < 12                                        → 1
```

The first comparison involves two integers, which are compared numerically. The second comparison involves two strings, which are compared lexicographically. The third comparison involves a string and a number, so they are compared as floating-point values.

String comparisons are not case sensitive unless the comparison involves a binary string. Thus, a case-sensitive comparison is performed if you use the BINARY keyword or are comparing values from CHAR BINARY, VARCHAR BINARY, or BLOB columns.

- =

    Evaluates to 1 if the operands are equal, 0 otherwise.

    ```
    1 = 1                                       → 1
    1 = 2                                       → 0
    "abc" = "abc"                               → 1
    "abc" = "def"                               → 0
    "abc" = "ABC"                               → 1
    BINARY "abc" = "ABC"                        → 0
    BINARY "abc" = "abc"                        → 1
    "abc" = 0                                   → 1
    ```

    "abc" is equal to both "abc" and "ABC" because string comparisons are not case sensitive by default. String comparisons can be made case sensitive by using the BINARY operator. "abc" is equal to 0 because it's converted to a number in accordance to the comparison rules. Because "abc" doesn't look like a number, it's converted to 0.

- `<=>`

  NULL–safe equality operator; it's similar to '=', except that it evaluates to 1 when the operands are equal, even when they are NULL.

  ```
  1 <=> 1                                           → 1
  1 <=> 2                                           → 0
  NULL <=> NULL                                     → 1
  NULL = NULL                                       → NULL
  ```

  The final two examples show how '=' and '<=>' handle NULL comparisons differently.

  '<=>' was introduced in MySQL 3.23.0.

- `!= or <>`

  Evaluates to 1 if the operands are unequal, 0 otherwise.

  ```
  3.4 != 3.4                                        → 0
  "abc" <> "ABC"                                    → 0
  BINARY "abc" <> "ABC"                             → 1
  "abc" != "def"                                    → 1
  ```

- `<`

  Evaluates to 1 if the left operand is less than the right operand, 0 otherwise.

  ```
  3 < 10                                            → 1
  105.4 < 10e+1                                     → 0
  "abc" < "ABC"                                     → 0
  "abc" < "def"                                     → 1
  ```

- `<=`

  Evaluates to 1 if the left operand is less than or equal to the right operand, 0 otherwise.

  ```
  "abc" <= "a"                                      → 0
  "a" <= "abc"                                      → 1
  13.5 <= 14                                        → 1
  (3 * 4) - (6 * 2) <= 0                            → 1
  ```

- `>=`

  Evaluates to 1 if the left operand is greater than or equal to the right operand, 0 otherwise.

  ```
  "abc" >= "a"                                      → 1
  "a" >= "abc"                                      → 0
  13.5 >= 14                                        → 0
  (3 * 4) - (6 * 2) >= 0                            → 1
  ```

- \>

    Evaluates to 1 if the left operand is greater than the right operand, 0 otherwise.

    ```
    PI() > 3                                      → 1
    "abc" > "a"                                   → 1
    SIN(0) > COS(0)                               → 0
    ```

- *expr* BETWEEN *min* AND *max*

    Evaluates to 1 if *min* is less than or equal to *expr* and *max* is greater than or equal to *expr*. If the operands *expr*, *min*, and *max* are all of the same type, these expressions are equivalent:

    ```
    expr BETWEEN min AND max
    (min <= expr AND expr <= max)
    ```

    If the operands are not of the same type, type conversion occurs and those two expressions may not be equivalent. BETWEEN is evaluated using comparisons determined according to the type of *expr*:

    - If *expr* is a string, the operands are compared lexicographically as strings. The comparisons are case sensitive or not, according to whether or not *expr* is a binary string.

    - If *expr* is an integer, the operands are compared numerically as integers.

    - If neither of the preceding rules is true, the operands are compared numerically as floating-point numbers.

    ```
    "def" BETWEEN "abc" and "ghi"                 → 1
    "def" BETWEEN "abc" and "def"                 → 1
    13.3 BETWEEN 10 and 20                        → 1
    13.3 BETWEEN 10 and 13                        → 0
    2 BETWEEN 2 and 2                             → 1
    "B" BETWEEN "A" and "a"                       → 0
    BINARY "B" BETWEEN "A" and "a"                → 1
    ```

    BETWEEN was introduced in MySQL 3.21.2.

- *expr* IN (*value1,value2,...*)
    expr NOT IN (*value1,value2,...*)

    IN evaluates to 1 if *expr* is one of the values in the list, 0 otherwise. For NOT IN, the opposite is true. The following expressions are equivalent:

    ```
    expr NOT IN (value1,value2,...)
    NOT (expr IN (value1,value2,...))
    ```

    If all values in the list are constants, MySQL sorts them and evaluates the IN test using a binary search, which is very fast.

    ```
    3 IN (1,2,3,4,5)                              → 1
    "d" IN ("a","b","c","d","e")                  → 1
    "f" IN ("a","b","c","d","e")                  → 0
    3 NOT IN (1,2,3,4,5)                          → 0
    ```

```
"d" NOT IN ("a","b","c","d","e")                    → 0
"f" NOT IN ("a","b","c","d","e")                    → 1
```

IN was introduced in MySQL 3.21.0.

- *expr* IS NULL

  expr IS NOT NULL

  IS NULL evaluates to 1 if the value of *expr* is NULL, 0 otherwise. IS NOT NULL is the opposite. The following expressions are equivalent:

  ```
  expr IS NOT NULL
  NOT (expr IS NULL)
  ```

  IS NULL and IS NOT NULL should be used to determine whether or not the value of *expr* is NULL. You cannot use the regular comparison operators '=' and '!=' for this purpose.

  ```
  NULL IS NULL                    → 1
  0 IS NULL                       → 0
  NULL IS NOT NULL                → 0
  0 IS NOT NULL                   → 1
  NOT (0 IS NULL)                 → 1
  NOT (NULL IS NULL)              → 0
  NOT NULL IS NULL                → 1
  ```

  The last example returns the result that it does because NOT binds more tightly than IS (see "Operator Precedence").

Bit Operators

Bit operations are performed using BIGINT values (64-bit integers), which limits the maximum range of the operations. Bit operations involving NULL values produce a NULL result.

- |

  Evaluates to the bitwise OR (union) of the operands.

  ```
  1 | 1                           → 1
  1 | 2                           → 3
  1 | 2 | 4 | 8                   → 15
  1 | 2 | 4 | 8 | 15              → 15
  ```

- &

  Evaluates to the bitwise AND (intersection) of the operands.

  ```
  1 & 1                           → 1
  1 & 2                           → 0
  7 & 5                           → 5
  ```

- `<<`

  Shifts the leftmost operand left the number of bit positions indicated by the right operand. Shifting by a negative amount results in a value of zero.

1 << 2	→ 4
2 << 2	→ 8
1 << 62	→ 4611686018427387904
1 << 63	→ -9223372036854775808
1 << 64	→ 0

  The last two examples demonstrate the limits of 64-bit calculations.

  '<<' was introduced in MySQL 3.22.2.

- `>>`

  Shifts the leftmost operand right the number of bit positions indicated by the right operand. Shifting by a negative amount results in a value of zero.

16 >> 3	→ 2
16 >> 4	→ 1
16 >> 5	→ 0

  '>>' was introduced in MySQL 3.22.2.

Logical Operators

Logical operators (also known as boolean operators, after the mathematician George Boole, who formalized their use) test the truth or falsity of expressions. All logical operations return 1 for true and 0 for false. Logical operators interpret non-zero operands as true and operands of 0 as false. NULL values are handled as indicated in the operator descriptions.

Logical operators expect operands to be numbers, so string operands are converted to numbers before the operator is evaluated.

- `NOT or !`

  Logical negation; evaluates to 1 if the following operand is false and 0 if the operand is true, except that NOT NULL is NULL.

NOT 0	→ 1
NOT 1	→ 0
NOT NULL	→ NULL
NOT 3	→ 0
NOT NOT 1	→ 1
NOT "1"	→ 0
NOT "0"	→ 1
NOT ""	→ 1
NOT "abc"	→ 1

- OR or ||

    Logical OR; evaluates to 1 if either operand is true (not zero or NULL), zero otherwise.

    ```
    0 OR 0                                    → 0
    0 OR 3                                    → 1
    4 OR 2                                    → 1
    1 OR NULL                                 → 1
    ```

- AND or &&

    Logical AND; evaluates to 1 if both operands are true (not zero or NULL), zero otherwise.

    ```
    0 AND 0                                   → 0
    0 AND 3                                   → 0
    4 AND 2                                   → 1
    1 AND NULL                                → 0
    ```

In MySQL, '!', '||', and '&&' indicate logical operations, as they do in C. Note in particular that '||' does not perform string concatenation as it does in some versions of SQL. Use the CONCAT() function instead to concatenate strings.

Cast Operators

BINARY causes the following operand to be treated as a binary string so that comparisons involving the string are case sensitive. If the following operand is a number, it is converted to string form:

```
"abc" = "ABC"                             → 1
"abc" = BINARY "ABC"                       → 0
BINARY "abc" = "ABC"                        → 0
"2" < 12                                   → 1
"2" < BINARY 12                            → 0
```

BINARY causes a number-to-string conversion; the comparison is then performed lexicographically because both operands are strings.

BINARY was introduced in MySQL 3.23.0.

Pattern-Matching Operators

MySQL provides SQL pattern matching using LIKE and extended regular expression pattern matching using REGEXP. SQL pattern matches are not case sensitive unless the string to be matched or the pattern string are binary strings. Extended regular expression pattern matches are always case sensitive.

SQL pattern matching succeeds only if the pattern matches the entire string to be matched. Extended regular expression pattern matching succeeds if the pattern is found anywhere in the string.

- `str LIKE pat [ESCAPE 'c']`
  `str NOT LIKE pat [ESCAPE 'c']`

  LIKE performs a simple SQL pattern match and evaluates to 1 if the pattern string pat matches the entire string expression str. If it does not match, it evaluates to 0. For NOT LIKE, the opposite is true. These two expressions are equivalent:

  ```
  str NOT LIKE pat [ESCAPE 'c']
  NOT (str LIKE pat [ESCAPE 'c'])
  ```

  The result is NULL if either string is NULL.

  Two characters have special meaning in SQL patterns and serve as wildcards, as indicated here:

Character	Meaning
%	Match any sequence of characters other than NULL (including an empty string)
_	Match any single character

  Patterns may contain either or both wildcard characters:

  ```
  "catnip" LIKE "cat%"        → 1
  "dogwood" LIKE "%wood"      → 1
  "bird" LIKE "____"          → 1
  "bird" LIKE "___"           → 0
  "dogwood" LIKE "%wo__"      → 1
  ```

  Case sensitivity of SQL pattern matching using LIKE is determined by the strings being compared. Normally, comparisons are not case sensitive. If either string is a binary string, the comparison is case sensitive:

  ```
  "abc" LIKE "ABC"            → 1
  BINARY "abc" LIKE "ABC"     → 0
  "abc" LIKE BINARY "ABC"     → 0
  ```

  Because '%' matches any sequence of characters, it even matches no characters:

  ```
  "" LIKE "%"                 → 1
  "cat" LIKE "cat%"           → 1
  ```

  In MySQL, you can use LIKE with numeric expressions:

  ```
  50 + 50 LIKE "1%"           → 1
  200 LIKE "2__"              → 1
  ```

  To match a wildcard character literally, turn off its special meaning in the pattern string by preceding it with the escape character, '\':

  ```
  "100% pure" LIKE "100%"       → 1
  "100% pure" LIKE "100\%"      → 0
  "100% pure" LIKE "100\% pure" → 1
  ```

If you want to use an escape character other than '\', specify it using an ESCAPE clause:

```
"100% pure" LIKE "100^%" ESCAPE '^'                → 0
"100% pure" LIKE "100^% pure" ESCAPE '^'           → 1
```

- *str* REGEXP *pat*

  str NOT REGEXP *pat*

  REGEXP performs an extended regular expression pattern match. Extended regular expressions are similar to the patterns used by the UNIX utilities grep and sed. The pattern sequences you can use are shown in Table C.1.

  REGEXP evaluates to 1 if the pattern string pat matches the string expression *str*, 0 otherwise. NOT REGEXP is the opposite. These two expressions are equivalent:

```
str NOT REGEXP pat
NOT (str REGEXP pat)
```

  The result is NULL if either string is NULL.

  The pattern need not match the entire string, it just needs to be found somewhere in the string.

  The [...] and [^...] constructs specify character classes. Within a class, a range of characters may be indicated using a dash between the two endpoint characters of the range. For example, [a-z] matches any lowercase letter, and [0-9] matches any digit. For you to be able to indicate a literal ']' within a class, it must be the first character of the class. In order for you to indicate a literal '-', it must be the first or last character of the class. And for you to indicate a literal '^', it must not be the first character after the '['.

Table C.1   **Extended Regular Expression Sequences**

Sequence	Meaning
^	Match the beginning of the string
$	Match the end of the string
.	Match any single character, including newline
[...]	Match any character appearing between the brackets
[^...]	Match any character not appearing between the brackets
e*	Match zero or more instances of pattern element *e*
e+	Match one or more instances of pattern element *e*
e?	Match zero or one instances of pattern element *e*
e1¦e2	Match pattern element *e1* or *e2*
e{m}	Match *m* instances of pattern element *e*
e{m,}	Match *m* or more instances of pattern element *e*
e{,n}	Match zero to *n* instances of pattern element *e*
e{m,n}	Match *m* to *n* instances of pattern element *e*
(...)	Group pattern elements into a single element
other	Non-special characters match themselves

Several other more complicated special constructions having to do with collating sequences and equivalence classes may be used within a character class. See the MySQL Reference Manual for more information.

An extended regular expression match succeeds if the pattern is found anywhere in the string being matched, but you can use '^' and '$' to force the pattern to match only at the beginning or end of the string.

```
"abcde" REGEXP "b"                    → 1
"abcde" REGEXP "^b"                   → 0
"abcde" REGEXP "b$"                   → 0
"abcde" REGEXP "^a"                   → 1
"abcde" REGEXP "e$"                   → 1
"abcde" REGEXP "^a.*e$"               → 1
```

Extended regular expression pattern matches are case sensitive:

```
"abc" REGEXP "ABC"                    → 0
"ABC" REGEXP "ABC"                    → 1
```

- *str* RLIKE *pat*
  str NOT RLIKE *pat*

  RLIKE and NOT RLIKE are synonyms for REGEXP and NOT REGEXP.

MySQL uses syntax similar to C for escape sequences within strings. For example, '\n', '\t', and '\\' are interpreted as newline, tab, and backslash. To specify such characters in a pattern, double the backslashes ('\\n', '\\t', and '\\\\'). One backslash is stripped off when the query is parsed, and the remaining escape sequence is interpreted when the pattern match is performed.

Functions

Functions are called to perform a calculation and return a value. Functions must be invoked with no space between the function name and the parenthesis following it:

```
NOW()               Correct
NOW ()              Incorrect
```

If you pass multiple arguments to a function, arguments must be separated by commas. Spaces are allowed around function arguments:

```
CONCAT("abc","def")        This is okay
CONCAT( "abc" , "def" )    This is okay, too
```

Comparison Functions

- GREATEST(*expr1,expr2,...*)

  Returns the largest argument, where "largest" is defined according to the following rules:

- If the function is called in an integer context or all the arguments are integers, the arguments are compared as integers.
- If the function is called in a floating-point context or all the arguments are floating-point values, the arguments are compared as floating-point values.
- If the preceding two rules are not true, the arguments are compared as strings. The comparisons are not case sensitive unless some argument is a binary string.

```
GREATEST(2,3,1)                        → 3
GREATEST(38.5,94.2,-1)                 → 94.2
GREATEST("a","ab","abc")               → "abc"
GREATEST(1,3,5)                        → 5
GREATEST("A","b","C")                  → "C"
GREATEST(BINARY "A","b","C")           → "b"
```

GREATEST() was introduced in MySQL 3.22.5. In earlier versions, you can use MAX() instead.

- IF(*expr1,expr2,expr3*)

If *expr1* is true (not 0 or NULL), returns *expr2*; otherwise, it returns *expr3*. IF() returns a number or string according to the context in which it is used.

```
IF(1,"true","false")                   → "true"
IF(0,"true","false")                   → "false"
IF(NULL,"true","false")                → "false"
IF(1.3,"non-zero","zero")              → "non-zero"
IF(0.3,"non-zero","zero")              → "zero"
IF(0.3 != 0,"non-zero","zero")         → "non-zero"
```

expr is evaluated as an integer value, and the last three examples indicate how this behavior may catch you unaware if you're not careful. 1.3 converts to the integer value 1, which is true. But 0.3 converts to the integer value 0, which is false. The last example in the listing shows the proper way to use a floating-point number: Test it using a comparison because the comparison returns 1 or 0, depending on the result of the test.

- IFNULL(*expr1,expr2*)

Returns *expr2* if the value of the expression *expr1* is NULL; otherwise, it returns *expr1*. IFNULL() returns a number or string according to the context in which it is used.

```
IFNULL(NULL,"null")                    → "null"
IFNULL("not null","null")              → "not null"
```

- INTERVAL(*n*,*n1*,*n2*,...)

  Returns 0 if *n* < *n1*, 1 if *n* < *n2*, and so on, or −1 if *n* is NULL. The values *n1*, *n2*, ... must be in strictly increasing order (*n1* < *n2* < ...) because a fast binary search is used. INTERVAL() will behave unpredictably otherwise.

INTERVAL(1.1,0,1,2)	→ 2
INTERVAL(7,1,3,5,7,9)	→ 4

- ISNULL(*expr*)

  Returns 1 if the value of the expression *expr* is NULL; otherwise, it returns 0.

ISNULL(NULL)	→ 1
ISNULL(0)	→ 0
ISNULL(1)	→ 0

- LEAST(*expr1*,*expr2*,...)

  Returns the smallest argument, where "smallest" is defined using the same comparison rules as for the GREATEST() function.

LEAST(2,3,1)	→ 1
LEAST(38.5,94.2,-1)	→ -1.0
LEAST("a","ab","abc")	→ "a"

  LEAST() was introduced in MySQL 3.22.5. In earlier versions, you can use MIN() instead.

- STRCMP(*str1*,*str2*)

  This function returns 1,0, or -1 if the first argument is lexicograhically greater than, equal to, or less than the second argument. If either argument is NULL, the function returns NULL.

STRCMP("a","a")	→ 0
STRCMP("a","A")	→ 1
STRCMP("A","a")	→ -1

Numeric Functions

Numeric functions return NULL if an error occurs. For example, if you pass arguments to the function that are out of range or otherwise invalid, the function will return NULL.

- ABS(*x*)

  Returns the absolute value of *x*.

ABS(13.5)	→ 13.5
ABS(-13.5)	→ 13.5

- ACOS(*x*)

  Returns the arccosine of *x*, or NULL if *x* is not in the range from −1 to 1.

ACOS(1)	→ 0.000000
ACOS(0)	→ 1.570796
ACOS(-1)	→ 3.141593

ACOS() was introduced in MySQL 3.21.8.

- ASIN(*x*)

Returns the arcsine of *x*, or NULL if *x* is not in the range from −1 to 1.

ASIN(1)	→ 1.570796
ASIN(0)	→ 0.000000
ASIN(-1)	→ -1.570796

ASIN() was introduced in MySQL 3.21.8.

- ATAN(*x*)

Returns the arctangent of *x*.

ATAN(1)	→ 0.785398
ATAN(0)	→ 0.000000
ATAN(-1)	→ -0.785398

ATAN() was introduced in MySQL 3.21.8.

- ATAN2(*x*,*y*)

This is like ATAN2(*x*,*y*), but it uses the signs of the arguments to determine the quadrant of the return value.

ATAN2(1,1)	→ 0.785398
ATAN2(1,-1)	→ 2.356194
ATAN2(-1,1)	→ -0.785398
ATAN2(-1,-1)	→ -2.356194

- CEILING(*x*)

Returns the smallest integer not less than *x*.

CEILING(3.8)	→ 4
CEILING(-3.8)	→ -3

- COS(*x*)

Returns the cosine of *x*. *x* is measured in radians.

COS(0)	→ 1.000000
COS(PI())	→ -1.000000
COS(PI()/2)	→ 0.000000

COS() was introduced in MySQL 3.21.8.

- COT(*x*)

Returns the cotangent of *x*. *x* is measured in radians.

COT(PI()/2)	→ 0.00000000
COT(PI()/4)	→ 1.00000000

COT() was introduced in MySQL 3.21.16.

- DEGREES(*x*)

Returns the value of *x*, converted from radians to degrees.

DEGREES(PI())	→ 180
DEGREES(PI()*2)	→ 360

```
DEGREES(PI()/2)                                          → 90
DEGREES(-PI())                                           → -180
```

DEGREES() was introduced in MySQL 3.21.16.

- EXP(*x*)

Returns *e^x*, where *e* is the base of natural logarithms.

```
EXP(1)                                                   → 2.718282
EXP(2)                                                   → 7.389056
EXP(-1)                                                  → 0.367879
1/EXP(1)                                                 → 0.36787944
```

- FLOOR(*x*)

Returns the largest integer not greater than *x* .

```
FLOOR(3.8)                                               → 3
FLOOR(-3.8)                                              → -4
```

- LOG(*x*)

Returns the natural (base *e*) logarithm of *x*.

```
LOG(0)                                                   → NULL
LOG(1)                                                   → 0.000000
LOG(2)                                                   → 0.693147
LOG(EXP(1))                                              → 1.000000
```

You can use LOG() to compute the logarithm of *x* for an arbitrary base *b*; use LOG(*x*)/LOG(*b*).

```
LOG(100)/LOG(10)                                         → 2.00000000
LOG10(100)                                               → 2.000000
```

- LOG10(*x*)

Returns the logarithm of *x* to the base 10.

```
LOG10(0)                                                 → NULL
LOG10(10)                                                → 1.000000
LOG10(100)                                               → 2.000000
```

- MOD(*m*,*n*) MOD(*m*,*n*)

This is the same as *m* % *n*. See "Arithmetic Operators."

- PI()

Returns the value of π.

```
PI()                                                     → 3.141593
```

PI() was introduced in MySQL 3.21.8.

- POW(*x*,*y*)

  Returns x^y—that is, *x* raised to the power *y*.

POW(2,3)	→ 8.000000
POW(2,-3)	→ 0.125000
POW(4,.5)	→ 2.000000
POW(16,.25)	→ 2.000000

- POWER(*x*,*y*)

  This function is a synonym for POW(). It was introduced in MySQL 3.21.16.

- RADIANS(*x*)

  Returns the value of *x*, converted from degrees to radians.

RADIANS(0)	→ 0
RADIANS(360)	→ 6.28319
RADIANS(-360)	→ -6.28319

  RADIANS() was introduced in MySQL 3.21.16.

- RAND()
  RAND(*n*)

  RAND() returns a random floating-point value in the range from 0.0 to 1.0. RAND(*n*) does the same thing, using *n* as the seed value for the randomizer. All calls with the same value of *n* return the same result; you can use this property when you need a repeatable sequence of numbers.

RAND(10)	→ 0.181091
RAND(10)	→ 0.181091
RAND()	→ 0.117195
RAND()	→ 0.358596
RAND(10)	→ 0.181091

  In the examples, notice how sequential calls to RAND() behave when you supply an argument compared to when you do not.

- ROUND(*x*)
  ROUND(*x*,*d*)
  ROUND(*x*)

  Returns the value of *x*, rounded to an integer. ROUND(*x*,*d*) returns the value of *x*, rounded to a number with *d* decimal places. If *d* is 0, the result has no decimal point or fractional part.

ROUND(15.3)	→ 15
ROUND(15.5)	→ 16
ROUND(-33.27834,2)	→ -33.28
ROUND(1,4)	→ 1.0000

- SIGN(*x*)

  Returns −1, 0, or 1, depending on whether the value of *x* is negative, zero, or positive.

SIGN(15.803)	→ 1
SIGN(0)	→ 0
SIGN(-99)	→ -1

- SIN(*x*)

  Returns the sine of *x*. *x* is measured in radians.

SIN(0)	→ 0.000000
SIN(PI())	→ 0.000000
SIN(PI()/2)	→ 1.000000

  SIN() was introduced in MySQL 3.21.8

- SQRT(*x*)

  Returns the non-negative square root of *x*.

SQRT(625)	→ 25.000000
SQRT(2.25)	→ 1.500000
SQRT(-1)	→ NULL

- TAN(*x*)

  Returns the tangent of *x*. *x* is measured in radians.

TAN(0)	→ 0.000000
TAN(PI()/4)	→ 1.000000

  TAN() was introduced in MySQL 3.21.8.

- TRUNCATE(*x*,*d*)

  Returns the value *x*, with the fractional part truncated to *d* decimal places. If *d* is 0, the result has no decimal point or fractional part. If *d* is greater than the number of decimal places in *x*, the fractional part is padded with trailing zeros to the desired width.

TRUNCATE(1.23,1)	→ 1.2
TRUNCATE(1.23,0)	→ 1
TRUNCATE(1.23,4)	→ 1.2300

  TRUNCATE() was introduced in MySQL 3.21.16.

String Functions

Most of the functions in this section return a string result. Some of them, such as LENGTH(), take strings as arguments and return a number. For functions that operate on strings based on string positions, the position of the first (leftmost) character is 1 (not 0).

- ASCII(*str*)

  Returns the ASCII code of the leftmost character of the string *str*. It returns 0 if *str* is empty or NULL if *str* is NULL.

  ```
  ASCII("abc")                                → 97
  ASCII("")                                   → 0
  ASCII(NULL)                                 → NULL
  ```

  ASCII() was introduced in MySQL 3.21.2.

- BIN(*n*)

  Returns the value of *n* in binary form as a string. The following two expressions are equivalent:

  ```
  BIN(n)
  CONV(n,10,2)
  ```

  See the description of CONV() for more information.

  BIN() was introduced in MySQL 3.22.4.

- CHAR(*n1*,*n2*,...)

  Interprets the arguments as ASCII codes and returns a string consisting of the concatenation of the corresponding character values. NULL arguments are ignored.

  ```
  CHAR(65)                                    → "A"
  CHAR(97)                                    → "a"
  CHAR(89,105,107,101,115,33)                 → "Yikes!"
  ```

  CHAR() was introduced in MySQL 3.21.0.

- CHARACTER_LENGTH(*str*)

  This function is a synonym for LENGTH().

- CHAR_LENGTH(*str*)

  This function is a synonym for LENGTH().

- COALESCE(*expr1*,*expr2*,...)

  Returns the first non-NULL element in the list.

  ```
  COALESCE(NULL,1/0,2,"a",45+97)              → "2"
  ```

  COALESCE() was introduced in MySQL 3.23.3.

- CONCAT(*str1*,*str2*,...)

  Returns a string consisting of the concatenation of all of its arguments. Returns NULL if any argument is NULL. CONCAT() may be called with several arguments.

  ```
  CONCAT("abc","def")                         → "abcdef"
  CONCAT("abc")                               → "abc"
  CONCAT("abc",NULL)                          → NULL
  CONCAT("Hello",", ","goodbye")              → "Hello, goodbye"
  ```

- CONV(*n*,*from_base*,*to_base*)

  Given a number *n* represented in base *from_base*, returns a string representation of *n* in base *to_base*. The result is NULL if any argument is NULL. *from_base* and *to_base* should be integers in the range from 2 to 36. *n* is treated as a BIGINT value (64-bit integer) but may be specified as a string because numbers in bases higher than 10 may contain non-decimal digits. (This is also the reason that CONV() returns a string; the result may contain characters from 'A' to 'Z' for bases 11 to 36.) The result is 0 if *n* is not a legal number in base *from_base*. (For example, if *from_base* is 16 and *n* is "abcdefg", the result is 0 because 'g' is not a legal hexadecimal digit.)

  Non-decimal characters in *n* may be specified in either uppercase or lowercase. Non-decimal characters in the result will be uppercase.

  n is treated as an unsigned number by default. If you specify *to_base* as a negative number, *n* is treated as a signed number.

  Convert 14 specified as a hexadecimal number to binary:

  ```
  CONV("e",16,2)                              → "1110"
  ```

  Convert 255 specified in binary to octal:

  ```
  CONV(11111111,2,8)                          → "377"
  CONV("11111111",2,8)                        → "377"
  ```

  CONV() was introduced in MySQL 3.22.4.

- ELT(*n*,*str1*,*str2*,...)

  Returns the *n*-th string from the list of strings *str1*, *str2*, ... Returns NULL if there is no *n*-th string or if that string or *n* are NULL. The index of the first string is 1. ELT() is complementary to FIELD().

  ```
  ELT(3,"a","b","c","d","e")                  → "c"
  ELT(0,"a","b","c","d","e")                  → NULL
  ELT(6,"a","b","c","d","e")                  → NULL
  ELT(FIELD("b","a","b","c"),"a","b","c")     → "b"
  ```

- EXPORT_SET(*n*,*on*,*off*,[*separator*,[*bit_count*]])

  Returns a string consisting of the strings *on* and *off*, separated by the string *separator*. *on* is used for each bit that is set in *n*, and *off* is used for each bit that is clear. *bit_count* indicates the maximum number of bits in *n* to examine. The default *separator* string is a comma, and the default *bit_count* value is 64.

  ```
  EXPORT_SET(7,"+","-","",5)                  → "+++.."
  EXPORT_SET(0xa,"1","0","",6)                → "010100"
  EXPORT_SET(97,"Y","N",",",8)                → "Y,N,N,N,N,Y,Y,N"
  ```

  EXPORT_SET() was introduced in MySQL 3.23.2.

- FIELD(*str*,*str1*,*str2*,...)

  Finds *str* in the list of strings *str1*, *str2*, ... and returns the index of the matching string. Returns 0 if there is no match or if *str* is NULL. The index of the first string is 1. FIELD() is complementary to ELT().

FIELD("b","a","b","c")	→ 2
FIELD("d","a","b","c")	→ 0
FIELD(NULL,"a","b","c")	→ 0
FIELD(ELT(2,"a","b","c"),"a","b","c")	→ 2

- FIND_IN_SET(*str*,*str_list*)

  str_list is a string consisting of substrings separated by commas (that is, it is like a SET value). FIND_IN_SET() returns the index of *str* within *str_list*. Returns 0 if *str* is not present in *str_list*, or NULL if either argument is NULL. The index of the first substring is 1.

FIND_IN_SET("cow","moose,cow,pig")	→ 2
FIND_IN_SET("dog","moose,cow,pig")	→ 0

  FIND_IN_SET() was introduced in MySQL 3.21.22.

- FORMAT(X,D)

  Formats the number *x* to a string with *d* decimals to a format like "nn,nnn.nnn". If *d* is 0, the result has no decimal point or fractional part.

FORMAT(1234.56789,3)	→ "1,234.568"
FORMAT(999999.99,2)	→ "999,000.00"
FORMAT(999999.99,0)	→ "1,000,000"

  Note the rounding behavior exhibited in the last example in the listing.

- HEX(*n*)

  Returns the value of *n* in hexadecimal form, as a string. The following two expressions are equivalent:

  ```
  HEX(n)
  CONV(n,10,16)
  ```

  See the description of CONV() for more information.

  HEX() was introduced in MySQL 3.22.4.

- INSERT(*str*,*pos*,*len*,*new_str*)

  Returns the string *str* with the substring beginning at position *pos* and *len* characters long replaced by the string *new_str*. Returns the original string if *pos* is out of range, or NULL if any argument is NULL.

INSERT("nighttime",6,4,"fall")	→ "nightfall"
INSERT("sunshine",1,3,"rain or ")	→ "rain or shine"
INSERT("sunshine",0,3,"rain or ")	→ "sunshine"

- INSTR(*str,substr*)

  INSTR() is like the two-argument form of LOCATE(), but with the arguments reversed. The following two expressions are equivalent:

  ```
  INSTR(str,substr)
  LOCATE(substr,str)
  ```

- LCASE(*str*)

  Returns the string *str* with all the characters converted to lowercase, or NULL if *str* is NULL.

LCASE("New York, NY")	→ "new york, ny"
LCASE(NULL)	→ NULL

- LEFT(*str,len*)

  Returns the leftmost *len* characters from the string *str*, or the entire string if there aren't that many characters. Returns NULL if *str* is NULL. Returns the empty string if *len* is NULL or less than 1.

LEFT("my left foot", 2)	→ "my"
LEFT(NULL,10)	→ NULL
LEFT("abc",NULL)	→ ""
LEFT("abc",0)	→ ""

- LENGTH(*str*)

  Returns the length of the string *str*.

LENGTH("abc")	→ 3
LENGTH("")	→ 0
LENGTH(NULL)	→ NULL

- LOCATE(*substr,str*)
  LOCATE(*substr,str,pos*)

  The two-argument form of LOCATE() returns the position of the first occurrence of the string *substr* within the string *str*, or 0 if *substr* does not occur within *str*. Returns NULL if any argument is NULL. If the position argument *pos* is given, LOCATE() starts looking for *substr* at that position. The test is case sensitive.

LOCATE("b","abc")	→ 2
LOCATE("b","ABC")	→ 0

- LOWER(*str*) This function is a synonym for LCASE().

- LPAD(*str,len,pad_str*)

  Returns a string consisting of the value of the string *str*, left-padded with the string *pad_str* to a length of *len* characters. Returns *str* if *str* is already *len* characters long.

LPAD("abc",12,"def")	→ "defdefdefabc"
LPAD("abc",10,".")	→ ".......abc"
LPAD("abc",2,".")	→ "abc"

  LPAD() was introduced in MySQL 3.22.2.

- LTRIM(*str*)

Returns the string *str* with leading spaces removed, or NULL if *str* is NULL.

```
LTRIM(" abc ")                                    → "abc "
```

- MAKE_SET(*n*,*bit0_str*,*bit1_str*,...)

Constructs a SET value (a string consisting of substrings separated by commas) based on the value of the integer *n* and the strings *bit0_str*, *bit1_str*.... For each bit that is set in the value of *n*, the corresponding string is included in the result. (If bit 0 is set, the result includes *bit0_str*, and so on.) If *n* is 0, the result is the empty string. If *n* is NULL, the result is NULL. If any string in the list is NULL, it is ignored when constructing the result string.

```
MAKE_SET(8,"a","b","c","d","e")                   → "d"
MAKE_SET(7,"a","b","c","d","e")                   → "a,b,c"
MAKE_SET(2+16,"a","b","c","d","e")                → "b,e"
MAKE_SET(2¦16,"a","b","c","d","e")                → "b,e"
MAKE_SET(-1,"a","b","c","d","e")                  → "a,b,c,d,e"
```

The last example selects every string because −1 has all bits turned on.

MAKE_SET() was introduced in MySQL 3.22.2.

- MID(*str*,*pos*,*len*)

Returns a substring of the string *str* beginning at position *pos* and *len* characters long. Returns NULL if any argument is NULL.

```
MID("what a dull example",8,4)                    → "dull"
```

- OCT(*n*)

Returns the value of *n* in octal form, as a string. The following two expressions are equivalent:

```
OCT(n)
CONV(n,10,8)
```

See the description of CONV() for more information.

OCT() was introduced in MySQL 3.22.4.

- OCTET_LENGTH(*str*)

This function is a synonym for LENGTH().

- POSITION(*substr* IN *str*) POSITION()

This is like the two-argument form of LOCATE(). The following expressions are equivalent:

```
POSITION(substr IN str)
LOCATE(substr,str)
```

- REPEAT(*str,n*)

  Returns a string consisting of the string *str* repeated *n* times. Returns the empty string if *n* is non-positive, or NULL if either argument is NULL.

  ```
  REPEAT("x",10)                      → "xxxxxxxxxx"
  REPEAT("abc",3)                     → "abcabcabc"
  ```

  REPEAT() was introduced in MySQL 3.21.10.

- REPLACE(*str,from_str,to_str*)

  Returns a string consisting of the string *str* with all occurrences of the string *from_str* replaced by the string *to_str*. Returns NULL if any argument is NULL. If *to_str* is empty, the effect is to delete occurrences of *from_str*. If *from_str* is empty, REPLACE() returns *str* unchanged.

  ```
  REPLACE("abracadabra","a","oh")     → "ohbrohcohdohbroh"
  REPLACE("abracadabra","a","")       → "brcdbr"
  REPLACE("abracadabra","","x")       → "abracadabra"
  ```

- REVERSE(*str*)

  Returns a string consisting of the string *str* with the characters reversed. Returns NULL if *str* is NULL.

  ```
  REVERSE("abracadabra")              → "arbadacarba"
  REVERSE("Madam, I'm Adam")          → "madA m'I ,madaM"
  ```

  REVERSE() was introduced in MySQL 3.21.19.

- RIGHT(*str,len*)

  Returns the rightmost *len* characters from the string *str*, or the entire string if there aren't that many characters. Returns NULL if *str* is NULL. Returns the empty string if *len* is NULL or less than 1.

  ```
  RIGHT("rightmost",4)                → "most"
  ```

- RPAD(*str,len,pad_str*)

  Returns a string consisting of the value of the string *str*, right-padded with the string *pad_str* to a length of *len* characters. Returns *str* if *str* is already *len* characters long.

  ```
  RPAD("abc",12,"def")                → "abcdefdefdef"
  RPAD("abc",10,".")                  → "abc......."
  RPAD("abc",2,".")                   → "abc"
  ```

  RPAD() was introduced in MySQL 3.22.2.

- RTRIM(*str*)

  Returns the string *str* with trailing spaces removed, or NULL if *str* is NULL.

  ```
  RTRIM("  abc  ")                    → "  abc"
  ```

- SOUNDEX(*str*)

Returns a soundex string calculated from the string *str*. Non-alphanumeric characters in *str* are ignored. International non-alphabetic characters outside the range from 'A' to 'Z' are treated as vowels.

```
SOUNDEX("Cow")                          → "C000"
SOUNDEX("Cowl")                         → "C400"
SOUNDEX("Howl")                         → "H400"
SOUNDEX("Hello")                        → "H400"
```

- SPACE(*n*)

Returns a string consisting of *n* spaces, the empty set if *n* is non-positive, or NULL if *n* is NULL.

```
SPACE(6)                                → "      "
SPACE(0)                                → ""
SPACE(NULL)                             → NULL
```

SPACE() was introduced in MySQL 3.21.16.

- SUBSTRING(*str*,*pos*)
  SUBSTRING(*str*,*pos*,*len*)
  SUBSTRING(*str* FROM*pos*)
  SUBSTRING(*str* FROM *pos* FOR *len*)

Returns a substring from the string *str*, beginning at position *pos*. If a *len* argument is given, returns a substring that many characters long; otherwise, it returns the entire rightmost part of *str*, beginning at position *pos*.

```
SUBSTRING("abcdef",3)                   → "cdef"
SUBSTRING("abcdef",3,2)                 → "cd"
```

The following expressions are equivalent:

```
SUBSTRING(str,pos,len)
SUBSTRING(str FROM pos FOR len)
MID(str,pos,len)
```

- SUBSTRING_INDEX(*str*,*delim*,*n*)

Returns a substring from the string *str*. If *n* is positive, SUBSTRING_INDEX() finds the *n*-th occurrence of the delimiter string *delim*, then returns everything to the left of that delimiter. If *n* is negative, SUBSTRING_INDEX() finds the *n*-th occurrence of *delim*, counting back from the right end of *str*, then returns everything to the right of that delimiter. If *delim* is not found in *str*, the entire string is returned. Returns NULL if any argument is NULL.

```
SUBSTRING_INDEX("jar-jar","j",-2)       → "ar-jar"
SUBSTRING_INDEX(USER(),"@",1)           → "paul"
```

SUBSTRING_INDEX() was introduced in MySQL 3.21.15.

- TRIM([[LEADING | TRAILING | BOTH] [*trim_str*] FROM] *str*)

  Returns the string *str* with leading and/or trailing instances of the string *trim_str* trimmed off. If LEADING is specified, TRIM() strips leading occurrences of *trim_str*. If TRAILING is specified, TRIM() strips trailing occurrences of *trim_str*. If BOTH is specified, TRIM() strips leading and trailing occurrences of *trim_str*. The default is BOTH if none of the following is specified: LEADING, TRAILING, or BOTH. TRIM() strips spaces if *trim_str* is not specified.

TRIM("^" FROM "^^^XYZ^^")	→ "XYZ"
TRIM(LEADING "^" FROM "^^^XYZ^^")	→ "XYZ^^"
TRIM(TRAILING "^" FROM "^^^XYZ^^")	→ "^^^XYZ"
TRIM(BOTH "^" FROM "^^^XYZ^^")	→ "XYZ"
TRIM(BOTH FROM " ABC ")	→ "ABC"
TRIM(" ABC ")	→ "ABC"

  TRIM() was introduced in MySQL 3.21.12.

- UCASE(*str*)

  Returns the string *str* with all the characters converted to uppercase, or NULL if *str* is NULL.

UCASE("New York, NY")	→ "NEW YORK, NY"
UCASE(NULL)	→ NULL

- UPPER(*str*)

  This function is a synonym for UCASE().

Date and Time Functions

The date and time functions take various types of arguments. In general, a function that expects a DATE argument will also accept a DATETIME or TIMESTAMP argument and will ignore the time part of the value.

- ADDDATE(*date*,INTERVAL *expr interval*)

  This function is a synonym for DATE_ADD().

- CURDATE()

  Returns the current date as a string in "*YYYY-MM-DD*" format, or as a number in *YYYYMMDD* format, according to the context in which it is used.

CURDATE()	→ "1999-08-10"
CURDATE() + 0	→ 19990810

Legal Date and Time Values

If you don't supply legal date or time values to date and time functions, you can't expect a reasonable result. Verify your arguments first.

- CURRENT_DATE

  This function is a synonym for CURDATE(); note the lack of parentheses.

- CURRENT_TIME

  This function is a synonym for CURTIME(); note the lack of parentheses.

- CURRENT_TIMESTAMP

  This function is a synonym for NOW(); note the lack of parentheses.

- CURTIME()

  Returns the current time of day as a string in "hh:mm:ss" format, or as a number in hhmmss format, according to the context in which it is used.

  ```
  CURTIME()                                       → "16:41:01"
  CURTIME() + 0                                   → 164101
  ```

  CURTIME() was introduced in MySQL 3.21.12.

- DATE_ADD(date,INTERVAL expr interval)

  Takes a date or date and time value date, adds a time interval to it, and returns the result. expr specifies the time value to be added to date (or subtracted, if expr begins with '-'), and interval specifies how to interpret the interval. The result is a DATE value if date is a DATE value and no time-related values are involved in calculating the result. If that is not true, the result is a DATETIME value. The result is NULL if date is not a legal date.

  ```
  DATE_ADD("1999-12-01",INTERVAL 1 YEAR)              → "2000-12-01"
  DATE_ADD("1999-12-01",INTERVAL 60 DAY)             → "2000-01-30"
  DATE_ADD("1999-12-01",INTERVAL -3 MONTH)           → "1999-09-01"
  DATE_ADD("1999-12-01 08:30:00",INTERVAL 12 HOUR)   → "1999-12-01 20:30:00"
  ```

  Table C.2 shows the allowable interval values, their meanings, and the format in which values for each interval type should be specified. The keyword INTERVAL and the interval specifiers may be given in any lettercase.

  The expression expr that is added to the date may be specified as a number or as a string, unless it contains non-digit characters, in which case it must be a string. The delimiter characters are arbitrary and may be any-punctuation character:

  ```
  DATE_ADD("1999-12-01",INTERVAL "2:3" YEAR_MONTH)   → "2002-03-01"
  DATE_ADD("1999-12-01",INTERVAL "2-3" YEAR_MONTH)   → "2002-03-01"
  ```

  The parts of the value of expr are matched from right to left against the parts to be expected based on the interval specifier. For example, the expected format for HOUR_SECOND is "hh:mm:ss". An expr value of "15:21" is interpreted as "00:15:21", not as "15:21:00".

  ```
  DATE_ADD("1999-12-01 12:00:00",INTERVAL "15:21" HOUR_SECOND)
                                                     → "1999-12-01 12:15:21"
  ```

Table C.2 `DATE_ADD()` **Interval Types**

Type	Meaning	Value Format
SECOND	Seconds	*ss*
MINUTE	Minutes	*mm*
HOUR	Hours	*hh*
DAY	Days	*DD*
MONTH	Months	*MM*
YEAR	Years	*YY*
MINUTE_SECOND	Minutes and seconds	*"mm:ss"*
HOUR_MINUTE	Hours and minutes	*"hh:mm"*
HOUR_SECOND	Hours, minutes, and seconds	*"hh:mm:ss"*
DAY_HOUR	Days and hours	*"DD hh"*
DAY_MINUTE	Days, hours, and minutes	*"DD hh:mm"*
DAY_SECOND	Days, hours, minutes, and seconds	*"DD hh:mm:ss"*
YEAR_MONTH	Years and months	*"YY-MM"*

If *interval* is YEAR, MONTH, or YEAR_MONTH and the day part of the result is larger than the number of days in the result month, the day is set to the maximum number of days in that month.

```
DATE_ADD("1999-12-31",INTERVAL 2 MONTH)          → "2000-02-29"
```

DATE_ADD() was introduced in MySQL 3.22.4.

- `DATE_FORMAT(date,format)`

Formats a date or date and time value *date* according to the formatting string *format* and returns the resulting string. DATE_FORMAT() can be used to reformat DATE or DATETIME values from the form MySQL uses to provide any format you want.

```
DATE_FORMAT("1999-12-01","%M %e, %Y")            → "December 1, 1999"
DATE_FORMAT("1999-12-01","The %D of %M")         → "The 1st of December"
```

Table C.3 shows the available specifiers that may be used in the formatting string.

As of MySQL 3.23.0, the '%' character preceding the format code is required. In earlier versions, the '%' is allowed but is optional. Characters present in the formatting string that are not listed in the table are copied to the result string literally.

If you refer to time specifiers for a DATE value, the time part of the value is treated as "00:00:00".

```
DATE_FORMAT("1999-12-01","%i")                   → "00"
```

DATE_FORMAT() was introduced in MySQL 3.21.14.

Table C.3 DATE_FORMAT() **Formatting Specifiers**

Specifier	Meaning
%S, %s	Second in two-digit numeric form (00, 01, ..., 59)
%i	Minute in two-digit numeric form (00, 01, ..., 59)
%H	Hour in two-digit numeric form, 24-hour time (00, 01, ..., 23)
%h, %I	Hour in two-digit numeric form, 12-hour time (01, 02, ..., 12)
%k	Hour in numeric form, 24-hour time (0, 1, ..., 23)
%l	Hour in numeric form, 12-hour time (1, 2, ..., 12)
%T	Time in 24-hour form (*hh:mm:ss*)
%r	Time in 12-hour form (*hh:mm:ss* AM or *hh:mm:ss* PM)
%p	AM or PM
%W	Weekday name (Sunday, Monday, ..., Saturday)
%a	Weekday name in abbreviated form (Sun, Mon, ..., Sat)
%d	Day of the month in two-digit numeric form (00, 01, ..., 31)
%e	Day of the month in numeric form (1, 2, ..., 31)
%D	Day of the month with English suffix (1st, 2nd, 3rd, ...)
%w	Day of the week in numeric form (0=Sunday, 1=Monday, ..., 6=Saturday)
%j	Day of the year in three-digit numeric form (001, 002, ..., 366)
%U	Week (0, 1, ..., 52), where Sunday is the first day of the week
%u	Week (0, 1, ..., 52), where Monday is the first day of the week
%M	Month name (January, February, ..., December)
%b	Month name in abbreviated form (Jan, Feb, ..., Dec)
%m	Month in two-digit numeric form (01, 02, ..., 12)
%c	Month in numeric form (1, 2, ..., 12)
%Y	Year in 4-digit numeric form
%y	Year in 2-digit numeric form
%%	A literal '%'

- DATE_SUB(*date*,INTERVAL *expr interval*)

  Performs date arithmetic in the same manner as DATE_ADD(), except that *expr* is subtracted from the date value *date*. See DATE_ADD() for more information.

  ```
  DATE_SUB("1999-12-01",INTERVAL 1 MONTH)           → "1999-11-01"
  DATE_SUB("1999-12-01",INTERVAL "13-2" YEAR_MONTH) → "1986-10-01"
  DATE_SUB("1999-12-01 04:53:12",INTERVAL "13-2" MINUTE_SECOND)
                                                    → "1999-12-01 04:40:10"
  DATE_SUB("1999-12-01 04:53:12",INTERVAL "13-2" HOUR_MINUTE)
                                                    → "1999-11-30 15:51:12"
  ```

  DATE_SUB() was introduced in MySQL 3.22.4.

- DAYNAME(*date*)

  Returns a string containing the weekday name for the date value *date*.

DAYNAME("1999-12-01")	→ "Wednesday"
DAYNAME("1900-12-01")	→ "Saturday"

  DAYNAME() was introduced in MySQL 3.21.23.

- DAYOFMONTH(*date*)

  Returns the numeric value of the day of the month for the date value *date*, in the range from 1 to 31.

DAYOFMONTH("1999-12-01")	→ 1
DAYOFMONTH("1999-12-25")	→ 25

  DAYOFMONTH() was introduced in MySQL 3.21.22.

- DAYOFWEEK(*date*)

  Returns the numeric value of the weekday for the date value *date*. Weekday values are in the range from 1 for Sunday to 7 for Saturday, per the ODBC standard. See also the WEEKDAY() function.

DAYOFWEEK("1999-12-05")	→ 1
DAYNAME("1999-12-05")	→ "Sunday"
DAYOFWEEK("1999-12-11")	→ 7
DAYNAME("1999-12-11")	→ "Saturday"

  DAYOFWEEK() was introduced in MySQL 3.21.15.

- DAYOFYEAR(*date*)

  Returns the numeric value of the day of the year for the date value *date*, in the range from 1 to 366.

DAYOFYEAR("1999-12-01")	→ 335
DAYOFYEAR("2000-12-31")	→ 366

  DAYOFYEAR() was introduced in MySQL 3.21.22.

- EXTRACT(*interval* FROM *datetime*)

  Returns the part of the date and time value *datetime* indicated by *interval*, which may be any of the interval specifiers that are allowed for DATE_ADD().

EXTRACT(YEAR FROM "1999-12-01 13:42:19")	→ 1999
EXTRACT(MONTH FROM "1999-12-01 13:42:19")	→ 12
EXTRACT(DAY FROM "1999-12-01 13:42:19")	→ 1
EXTRACT(HOUR_MINUTE FROM "1999-12-01 13:42:19")	→ 1342
EXTRACT(SECOND FROM "1999-12-01 13:42:19")	→ 19

  EXTRACT() can also be used with DATE values; extracting a time in this case returns NULL.

  EXTRACT() was introduced in MySQL 3.23.0.

- FROM_DAYS(*n*)

  Given a numeric value representing the number of days since the year 0 (typically obtained by calling TO_DAYS()), returns the corresponding date.

  ```
  TO_DAYS("1999-12-01")                      → 730454
  FROM_DAYS(730454 + 3)                      → "1999-12-04"
  ```

  FROM_DAYS() is intended only for dates covered by the Gregorian calendar (1582 on).

- FROM_UNIXTIME(*unix_timestamp*)

  FROM_UNIXTIME(*unix_timestamp,format*)

  Given a UNIX timestamp value *unix_timestamp* such as is returned by UNIX_TIMESTAMP(), returns a date and time value in "*YYYY-MM-DD hh:mm:ss*" format, or as a number in *YYYYMMDDhhmmss* format, according to the context in which it is used. If the *format* argument is given, the return value is formatted as a string just as it would be by the DATE_FORMAT() function.

  ```
  FROM_UNIXTIME(934340541)                   → "1999-08-10 22:02:21"
  FROM_UNIXTIME(944028000)                   → "1999-12-01 00:00:00"
  FROM_UNIXTIME(944028000,"%Y")              → "1999"
  ```

  FROM_UNIXTIME() was introduced in MySQL 3.21.5. The two-argument form was introduced in MySQL 3.21.8.

- HOUR(*time*)

  Returns the numeric value of the hour for the time value *time*, in the range from 0 to 23.

  ```
  HOUR("12:31:58")                           → 12
  ```

  HOUR() was introduced in MySQL 3.21.22.

- MINUTE(*time*)

  Returns the numeric value of the minute for the time value *time*, in the range from 0 to 59.

  ```
  MINUTE("12:31:58")                         → 31
  ```

  MINUTE() was introduced in MySQL 3.21.22.

- MONTH(*date*)

  Returns the numeric value of the month of the year for the date value *date*, in the range from 1 to 12.

  ```
  MONTH("1999-12-01")                        → 12
  ```

  MONTH() was introduced in MySQL 3.21.22.

- MONTHNAME(*date*)

  Returns a string containing the month name for the date value *date*.

  ```
  MONTHNAME("1999-12-01")                    → "December"
  ```

  MONTHNAME() was introduced in MySQL 3.21.23.

- NOW()

  Returns the current date and time as a string in `"YYYY-MM-DD hh:mm:ss"` format, or as a number in `YYYYMMDDhhmmss` format, according to the context in which it is used.

NOW()	→ "1999-08-10 18:51:43"
NOW() + 0	→ 19990810185143

- PERIOD_ADD(*period*,*n*)

  Adds *n* months to the period value *period* and returns the result. The return value format is *YYYYMM*. The *period* argument format may be *YYYYMM* or *YYMM*. Neither is a date value.

PERIOD_ADD(199902,12)	→ 200002
PERIOD_ADD(9902,-3)	→ 199811

- PERIOD_DIFF(*period1*,*period2*)

  Takes the difference of the period-valued arguments and returns the number of months between them. The arguments may be in the format *YYYYMM* or *YYMM*. Neither is a date value.

PERIOD_DIFF(200002,199902)	→ 12
PERIOD_DIFF(199811,9902)	→ -3

- QUARTER(*date*)

  Returns the numeric value of the quarter of the year for the date value *date*, in the range from 1 to 4.

QUARTER("1999-12-01")	→ 4
QUARTER("2000-01-01")	→ 1

  QUARTER() was introduced in MySQL 3.21.22.

- SECOND(*time*)

  Returns the numeric value of the second for the time value *time*, in the range from 0 to 59.

SECOND("12:31:58")	→ 58
SECOND(123158)	→ 58

  SECOND() was introduced in MySQL 3.21.22.

- SEC_TO_TIME(*seconds*)

  Given a number of seconds *seconds*, returns the corresponding time value as a string in `"hh:mm:ss"` format, or as a number in `hhmmss` format, according to the context in which it is used.

SEC_TO_TIME(29834)	→ "08:17:14"
SEC_TO_TIME(29834) + 0	→ 81714

  SEC_TO_TIME() was introduced in MySQL 3.21.5.

- SUBDATE(*date*,INTERVAL *expr interval*)

This function is a synonym for DATE_SUB().

- SYSDATE().

This function is a synonym for NOW().

- TIME_FORMAT(*time*,*format*)

Formats the time value *time* according to the formatting string *format* and returns the resulting string. The formatting string is like that used by DATE_FORMAT(), but the only specifiers that may be used are those that are time-related. Other specifiers result in a NULL value or 0.

```
TIME_FORMAT("12:31:58","%H %i")          → "12 31"
TIME_FORMAT(123158,"%H %i")              → "12 31"
```

TIME_FORMAT() was introduced in MySQL 3.21.3.

- TIME_TO_SEC(*time*)

Given a value *time* representing elapsed time, returns a number representing the corresponding number of seconds.

```
TIME_TO_SEC("08:17:14")                  → 29834
```

TIME_TO_SEC() was introduced in MySQL 3.21.16.

- TO_DAYS(*date*)

Returns a numeric value representing the date value *date* converted to the number of days since the year 0. The value may be passed to FROM DAYS() to convert it back to a date.

```
TO_DAYS("1999-12-01")                    → 730454
FROM_DAYS(730454 - 365)                  → "1998-12-01"
```

TO_DAYS() is intended only for dates covered by the Gregorian calendar (1582 on).

- UNIX_TIMESTAMP()
  UNIX_TIMESTAMP(*date*)

When called with no arguments, returns the number of seconds since the UNIX epoch ("1970-01-01 00:00:00" GMT). When called with a date-valued argument *date*, returns the number of seconds between the epoch and that date. *date* may be specified several ways: as a DATE or DATETIME string, a TIMESTAMP value, or a number in the format *YYYYMMDD* or *YYMMDD* in local time.

```
UNIX_TIMESTAMP()                         → 934341073
UNIX_TIMESTAMP("1999-12-01")             → 944028000
UNIX_TIMESTAMP(991201)                   → 944028000
```

- WEEK(*date*)
  WEEK(*date*,*first*)

  When called with a single argument, returns a number representing the week of the year for the date value *date*, in the range from 0 to 52. The week is assumed to start on Sunday. When called with two arguments, returns the same kind of value, but the *first* argument indicates the day on which the week starts. If *first* is 0, the week starts on Sunday. If *first* is 1, the week starts on Monday.

WEEK("1999-12-05")	→ 49
WEEK("1999-12-05",0)	→ 49
WEEK("1999-12-05",1)	→ 48

  WEEK() was introduced in MySQL 3.21.22. The two-argument form was introduced in MySQL 3.22.1.

- WEEKDAY(*date*)

  Returns the numeric value of the weekday for the date value *date*. Weekday values are in the range from 0 for Monday to 6 for Sunday; see also the DAYOFWEEK() function.

WEEKDAY("1999-12-05")	→ 6
DAYNAME("1999-12-05")	→ "Sunday"
WEEKDAY("1999-12-13")	→ 0
DAYNAME("1999-12-13")	→ "Monday"

- YEAR(*date*)

  Returns the numeric value of the year for the date value *date*, in the range from 1000 to 9999.

YEAR("1999-12-01")	→ 1999

  YEAR() was introduced in MySQL 3.21.22.

Summary Functions

Summary functions are also known as *aggregate functions*. They calculate a single value based on a group of values. However, the resulting value is based only on non-NULL values from the selected rows (with the exception that COUNT(*) counts all rows). Summary functions can be used to summarize entire columns, or to summarize values when grouped by distinct values in some other column or combination of columns. See "Generating Summaries" in Chapter 1, "Introduction to MySQL and SQL."

For the examples in this section, assume you have a table my_table with an integer column my_col that contains six rows with the values 1, 3, 5, 7, 9, and NULL.

- AVG(*expr*)

  Returns the average value of *expr* for all non-NULL values in the selected rows.

SELECT AVG(my_col) FROM my_table	→ 5.0000
SELECT AVG(my_col)*2 FROM my_table	→ 10.0000
SELECT AVG(my_col*2) FROM my_table	→ 10.0000

- BIT_AND(*expr*)

  Returns the bitwise AND value of *expr* for all non-NULL values in the selected rows.

  ```
  SELECT BIT_AND(my_col) FROM my_table            → 1
  ```

  BIT_AND() was introduced in MySQL 3.21.11.

- BIT_OR(*expr*)

  Returns the bitwise OR value of *expr* for all non-NULL values in the selected rows.

  ```
  SELECT BIT_OR(my_col) FROM my_table             → 15
  ```

  BIT_OR() was introduced in MySQL 3.21.11.

- COUNT(*expr*)

  With any argument other than '*', returns a count of the number of non-NULL values in the result set. With an argument of '*', returns a count of all rows in the result set, whether or not the rows contain NULL values.

  ```
  SELECT COUNT(my_col) FROM my_table              → 5
  SELECT COUNT(*) FROM my_table                   → 6
  ```

  COUNT(*) with no WHERE clause is optimized to return the number of records in the table named in the FROM clause very quickly. When more than one table is named, COUNT(*) returns the product of the number of rows in the individual tables:

  ```
  SELECT COUNT(*) FROM my_table AS m1, my_table AS m2
                                                  → 36
  ```

- MAX(*expr*)

  Returns the maximum value of *expr* for all non-NULL values in the selected rows. MAX() may also be used with strings, in which case it returns the lexicographically greatest value.

  ```
  SELECT MAX(my_col) FROM my_table                → 9
  ```

- MIN(*expr*)

  Returns the minimum value of *expr* for all non-NULL values in the selected rows. MIN() may also be used with strings, in which case it returns the lexicographically least value.

  ```
  SELECT MIN(my_col) FROM my_table                → 1
  ```

- STD(*expr*)

  Returns the standard deviation of *expr* for all non-NULL values in the selected rows.

  ```
  SELECT STD(my_col) FROM my_table                → 2.8284
  ```

- STDDEV(*expr*)

This function is a synonym for STD().

- SUM(*expr*)

Returns the sum of *expr* for all non-NULL values in the selected rows.

```
SELECT SUM(my_col) FROM my_table                    → 25
```

Miscellaneous Functions

The functions in this section do not fall into any of the other categories.

- BENCHMARK(*count*,*expr*)

Evaluates the expression *expr* repetitively *count* times. BENCHMARK() is something of an unusual function in that it is intended for use within the mysql client program. Its return value is always 0, and thus of no use. The value of interest is the elapsed time that mysql prints after displaying the result of the query:

```
mysql> SELECT BENCHMARK(100000,PASSWORD("secret"));
+--------------------------------------+
| BENCHMARK(100000,PASSWORD("secret")) |
+--------------------------------------+
|                                    0 |
+--------------------------------------+
1 row in set (1.63 sec)
```

The time is only an approximate indicator of how quickly the server evaluates the expression since it represents wall-clock time on the client, not CPU time on the server. The time can be influenced by factors such as the load on the server, whether the server is in a runnable state or swapped out when the query arrives, and so forth. You may want to execute it several times to see what a representative value is.

BENCHMARK() was introduced in MySQL 3.22.15.

- BIT_COUNT(*n*)

Returns the number of bits that are set in the argument, which is treated as a BIGINT value (a 64-bit integer).

```
BIT_COUNT(0)                              → 0
BIT_COUNT(1)                              → 1
BIT_COUNT(2)                              → 1
BIT_COUNT(7)                              → 3
BIT_COUNT(-1)                             → 64
```

- DATABASE()

Returns a string containing the current database name, or the empty string if there is no current database.

```
DATABASE()                                → "samp_db"
```

- DECODE(*str*,*password*)

Given an encrypted string *str* obtained as a result of a call to ENCODE(), decrypts it using the password string *password* and returns the resulting string.

```
DECODE(ENCODE("secret","scramble"),"scramble")    → "secret"
```

- ENCODE(*str*,*password*)

Encrypts the string *str* using the password string *password* and returns the result as a binary string. The string may be decoded with DECODE(). Because the encrypted result is a binary string, you should use a column that is one of the BLOB column types if you want to store it.

- ENCRYPT(*str*)

ENCRYPT(*str*,*salt*)

Encrypts the string *str* and returns the resulting string. This is a non-reversible encryption. The *salt* argument, if given, should be a string with two characters. By specifying a *salt* value, the encrypted result for *str* will be the same each time. With no *salt* argument, identical calls to ENCRYPT() yield different results over time.

```
ENCRYPT("secret","AB")                          → "ABS5SGh1EL6bk"
ENCRYPT("secret","AB")                          → "ABS5SGh1EL6bk"
ENCRYPT("secret")                               → "z1oPSN18WRwFA"
ENCRYPT("secret")                               → "12FJgqDtVOg7Q"
```

ENCRYPT() uses the UNIX crypt() system call, and depends on it two ways. First, if crypt() is unavailable on your system, ENCRYPT() always returns NULL. Second, ENCRYPT() is subject to the way crypt() operates for systems on which it is present. In particular, crypt() looks only at the first eight characters of the string to be encrypted on some systems.

ENCRYPT() was introduced in MySQL 3.21.12. As of MySQL 3.22.16, *salt* can be longer than two characters.

- GET_LOCK(*str*,*timeout*)

GET_LOCK() is used in conjunction with RELEASE_LOCK() to perform advisory (cooperative) locking. You can use the two functions to write applications that cooperate based on the status of an agreed-upon lock name.

GET_LOCK() is called with a lock name indicated by the string *str* and a timeout value of *timeout* seconds. It returns 1 if the lock was obtained successfully within the timeout period, 0 if the lock attempt failed due to timing out, or NULL if an error occurred. The *timeout* value determines how long to wait while attempting to obtain the lock, not the duration of the lock. After it is obtained, the lock remains in force until released.

The following call acquires a lock named "Nellie", waiting up to 10 seconds for it:

```
GET_LOCK("Nellie", 10)
```

The lock applies only to the string itself. It does not lock a database, a table, or any rows or columns within a table. In other words, the lock does not prevent any other client from doing anything to database tables, which is why `GET_LOCK()` locking is advisory only—it simply allows other cooperating clients to determine whether or not the lock is in force.

A client that has a lock on a name blocks attempts by other clients to lock the name (or attempts by other threads within a multi-threaded client that maintains multiple connections to the server). Suppose client 1 locks the string `"Nellie"`. If client 2 attempts to lock the same string, it will block until client 1 releases the lock or until the timeout period expires. In the former case, client 2 will acquire the lock successfully; in the latter case, it will fail.

Because two clients cannot lock a given string at the same time, applications that agree on a name can use the lock status of that name as an indicator of when it is safe to perform operations related to the name. For example, you can construct a lock name based on a unique key value for a row in a table to allow cooperative locking of that row.

A lock is released explicitly by calling `RELEASE_LOCK()` with the lock name:

```
RELEASE_LOCK("Nellie")
```

`RELEASE_LOCK()` returns 1 if the lock was released successfully, 0 if the lock was held by another connection (you can only release your own locks), or `NULL` if no such lock exists.

Any lock held by a client connection is also automatically released when the connection terminates, or if the client issues another `GET_LOCK()` call (a client connection can lock only one string at a time). In the latter case, the lock being held is released before the new lock is obtained, even if the lock name is the same.

`GETLOCK(str,0)` may be used as a simple poll to determine without waiting whether or not a lock on `str` is in force. (This will of course lock the string if it is not currently locked, so remember to call `RELEASE_LOCK()` as appropriate.)

`GET_LOCK()` was introduced in MySQL 3.21.7.

- `LAST_INSERT_ID()`
  `LAST_INSERT_ID(expr)`

  With no argument, returns the `AUTO_INCREMENT` value that was most recently generated during the current server session, or 0 if no such value has been generated. With an argument, `LAST_INSERT_ID()` is intended to be used in an `UPDATE` statement. The result is treated the same way as an automatically generated value, which is useful for generating sequences.

  More details may be found in Chapter 2, "Working with Data in MySQL." For both forms of `LAST_INSERT_ID()`, the value is maintained by the server on a per-connection basis and will not be changed by other clients, even by those that cause new automatically generated values to be created.

The form of `LAST_INSERT_ID()` that takes an argument was introduced in MySQL 3.22.9.

- `LOAD_FILE(file_name)`

Reads the file `file_name` and returns the contents as a string. The file must be located on the server, must be specified as an absolute (full) pathname, and must be world-readable to ensure that you're not trying to read a protected file. Because the file must be on the server, you must have the `FILE` privilege. If any of these conditions fail, `LOAD_FILE()` returns `NULL`.

`LOAD_FILE()` was introduced in MySQL 3.23.0.

- `MD5(str)`

Calculates a checksum from the string `str` based on the RSA Data Security, Inc. MD5 Message-Digest algorithm. The return value is a string consisting of 32 hexadecimal digits.

```
MD5("secret")                     → "5ebe2294ecd0e0f08eab7690d2a6ee69"
```

`MD5()` was introduced in MySQL 3.23.2.

- `PASSWORD(str)`

Given a string `str`, calculates and returns an encrypted password string of the form used in the MySQL grant tables. This is a non-reversible encryption.

```
PASSWORD("secret")                        → "428567f408994404"
```

Note that `PASSWORD()` does *not* use the same algorithm as the one used on UNIX to encrypt user account passwords. For that type of encryption, use `ENCRYPT()`.

- `RELEASE_LOCK(str)`

`RELEASE_LOCK()` is used in conjunction with `GET_LOCK()`. See the description of `GET_LOCK()` for details.

`RELEASE_LOCK()` was introduced in MySQL 3.21.7.

- `SESSION_USER()`

This function is a synonym for `USER()`.

- `SYSTEM_USER()`

This function is a synonym for `USER()`.

- `USER()`

Returns a string representing the current client user name. As of MySQL 3.22.1, the string is of the form `"user@host"`, where `user` is the user name and `host` is the name of the host from which the client connected to the server.

```
USER()                                     → "paul@localhost"
SUBSTRING_INDEX(USER(),"@",1)              → "paul"
SUBSTRING_INDEX(USER(),"@",-1)             → "localhost"
```

- VERSION()

Returns a string describing the server version, for example, `"3.22.25-log"`. The suffixes you may see following the server version number are `-log` (logging is on), `-debug` (the server is running debug mode), or `-demo` (the server is running in demo mode).

```
VERSION()                                      → "3.23.1-alpha-log"
```

VERSION() was introduced in MySQL 3.21.13.

D

SQL Syntax Reference

THIS APPENDIX DESCRIBES EACH OF THE SQL statements provided by MySQL. The syntax for writing comments in SQL code is also described. Comments are used to write descriptive text that is ignored by the server and to hide MySQL-specific keywords (these keywords will be executed by MySQL but ignored by other database servers). See the section "Comment Syntax."

MySQL development is ongoing, so enhancements to its SQL implementation are made on a regular basis. You will find it useful to consult the online MySQL Reference Manual occasionally to see what new capabilities are being added. The manual is available at http://www.mysql.com/.

The syntax descriptions use the following conventions:

- Optional information is enclosed in square brackets ([ ]). If a list is enclosed in square brackets, one alternative may be chosen.

- If a list is enclosed in curly brackets ({ }), one alternative must be chosen.

- Vertical bars (|) separate alternative items in a list.

- Ellipsis notation (...) indicates that the term preceding the ellipsis may be repeated.

Unless otherwise indicated, the statements listed here have been present in MySQL at least as far back as MySQL 3.22.0.

SQL Statements

This section describes the syntax and meaning of each of MySQL's SQL statements. A statement will fail if you do not have the necessary privileges to perform it. For example, USE *db_name* fails if you have no permission to access the database *db_name*.

ALTER TABLE

```
ALTER [IGNORE] TABLE tbl_name action_list
```

ALTER TABLE allows you to rename tables or modify their structure. To use it, specify the table name *tbl_name*, then give the specifications for one or more actions to be performed on the table. The IGNORE keyword comes into play if duplicate values result in unique keys in the new table. Without IGNORE, the effect of the ALTER TABLE statement is cancelled. With IGNORE, the rows that duplicate values for unique keys are deleted.

The *action_list* specifies one or more actions separated by commas. Each action is performed in turn. An action may be any of the following:

- ADD [COLUMN] *col_declaration* [FIRST | AFTER *col_name*)]

  Adds a column to the table. *col_declaration* is the column declaration; it is in the same format as that used for the CREATE TABLE statement. The column becomes the first column in the table if the FIRST keyword is given or is placed after the named column if AFTER *col_name* is given. If the column placement is not specified, the column becomes the last column of the table.

  ```
  ALTER TABLE member
      ADD member_id INT UNSIGNED NOT NULL AUTO_INCREMENT PRIMARY KEY
  ALTER TABLE member
      ADD member_id INT UNSIGNED NOT NULL AUTO_INCREMENT PRIMARY KEY
      FIRST
  ALTER TABLE member
      ADD member_id INT UNSIGNED NOT NULL AUTO_INCREMENT PRIMARY KEY
      AFTER suffix
  ```

- ADD INDEX [*index_name*] (*index_columns*)

  Adds an index to the table. The index is based on the columns named in *index_columns*, each of which must be a column in *tbl_name*. If multiple columns are named, they should be separated by commas. For CHAR and VARCHAR columns, you can index a prefix of the column, using *col_name*(*n*) syntax to index the first *n* characters of column values. For BLOB and TEXT columns, you *must* specify a prefix value; you cannot index the entire column. If the index name *index_name* is not specified, a name is chosen automatically based on the name of the first indexed column.

- ADD PRIMARY KEY (*index_columns*)

  Adds a primary key on the given columns. The key is given the name PRIMARY. *index_columns* is specified as it is for the ADD INDEX clause. An error occurs if a primary key already exists.

  ```
  ALTER TABLE president ADD PRIMARY KEY (last_name, first_name)
  ```

- ADD UNIQUE [*index_name*] (*index_columns*)

  Adds a unique-valued index to *tbl_name*. *index_name* and *index_columns* are specified as they are for the ADD INDEX clause.

  ```
  ALTER TABLE absence ADD UNIQUE id_date (student_id, date)
  ```

- ALTER [COLUMN] *col_name* {SET DEFAULT *value* | DROP DEFAULT}

  Modifies the given column's default value, either to the specified value, or by dropping the current default value. In the latter case, a new default value is assigned, as described in the entry for the CREATE TABLE statement.

  ```
  ALTER TABLE event ALTER type SET DEFAULT "Q"
  ALTER TABLE event ALTER type DROP DEFAULT
  ```

- CHANGE [COLUMN] *col_name col_declaration*

  Changes a column's name and definition. *col_name* is the column's current name, and *col_declaration* is the declaration to which the column should be changed. *col_declaration* is in the same format as that used for the CREATE TABLE statement. Note that the declaration includes the new column name; if you want to leave the name unchanged, you will specify the same name twice.

  ```
  ALTER TABLE student CHANGE name name VARCHAR(40)
  ALTER TABLE student CHANGE name student_name CHAR(30) NOT NULL
  ```

- DROP [COLUMN] *col_name*

  Removes the given column from the table. If the column is part of any indexes, it is removed from those indexes. If all columns from an index are removed, the index is removed as well.

  ```
  ALTER TABLE president DROP suffix
  ```

- DROP INDEX *index_name*

  Removes the given index from the table.

  ```
  ALTER TABLE member DROP INDEX name
  ```

- DROP PRIMARY KEY

  Removes the primary key from the table. If a table has no unique index that was created as a PRIMARY KEY but has one or more UNIQUE indexes, the first one of those is dropped.

  ```
  ALTER TABLE president DROP PRIMARY KEY
  ```

- MODIFY [COLUMN] *col_declaration*

  Changes the declaration of a column. The column declaration *col_declaration* is given, using the same format as for column descriptions in the entry for the CREATE TABLE statement. The declaration begins with a column name, which is how the column to be modified is indicated. MODIFY was introduced in MySQL 3.22.16.

  ```
  ALTER TABLE student MODIFY name VARCHAR(40) DEFAULT "" NOT NULL
  ```

- RENAME [AS] *new_tbl_name*

  Renames the table *tbl_name* to *new_tbl_name*.

  ```
  ALTER TABLE president RENAME prez
  ```

- *table_options*

  Specifies table options of the sort that may be given in the *table_options* part of a CREATE TABLE statement.

  ```
  ALTER TABLE score TYPE = MYISAM CHECKSUM = 1
  ```

CREATE DATABASE

```
CREATE DATABASE db_name
```

Creates a database with the given name. The statement fails if the database already exists or if you don't have the proper privilege to create it.

CREATE FUNCTION

```
CREATE [AGGREGATE] FUNCTION function_name
    RETURNS {STRING | REAL | INTEGER}
    SONAME shared_library_name
```

Specifies a user-defined function (UDF) to be loaded into the func table in the mysql database. *function_name* is the name by which you want to refer to the function in SQL statements. The keyword following RETURNS indicates the return type of the function. *shared_library_name* is the pathname of the file that contains the executable code or the function.

The AGGREGATE keyword indicates that the function is a group function like SUM() or MAX(). AGGREGATE was introduced in MySQL 3.23.5.

CREATE FUNCTION requires that the server be built as a dynamically linked binary (not as a static binary), because the UDF mechanism requires dynamic linking. For instructions on writing user-defined functions, refer to the MySQL Reference Manual.

CREATE INDEX

```
CREATE [UNIQUE] INDEX index_name ON tbl_name (index_columns)
```

Adds an index named *index_name* to the table *tbl_name*. This statement is handled as an ALTER TABLE ADD INDEX or ALTER TABLE ADD UNIQUE statement, according to the absence or presence of the UNIQUE keyword. See the entry for ALTER TABLE for details. CREATE INDEX was introduced in MySQL 3.22.

CREATE TABLE

```
CREATE [TEMPORARY] TABLE [IF NOT EXISTS] tbl_name
    (create_definition,...)
    [table_options]
    [[IGNORE | REPLACE] select_statement]

create_definition:
    {   col_declaration
      | PRIMARY KEY (index_columns)
      | KEY [index_name] (index_columns)
      | INDEX [index_name] (index_columns)
      | UNIQUE [INDEX] [index_name] (index_columns)
      | [CONSTRAINT symbol] FOREIGN KEY index_name (index_columns)
      | [reference_definition]
      | CHECK (expr) }

col_declaration:
    col_name col_type
        [NOT NULL | NULL] [DEFAULT default_value]
        [AUTO_INCREMENT] [PRIMARY KEY] [reference_definition]

reference_definition:
    REFERENCES tbl_name [(index_columns)]
        [MATCH FULL | MATCH PARTIAL]
        [ON DELETE reference_option]
        [ON UPDATE reference_option]

reference_option:
    {RESTRICT | CASCADE | SET NULL | NO ACTION | SET DEFAULT}
```

The CREATE TABLE statement creates a new table named *tbl_name*. If the TEMPORARY keyword is given, the table exists only until the current client connection ends (either normally or abnormally), or until a DROP TABLE statement is issued. A temporary table is visible only to the client that created it.

Normally, attempting to create a table with a name that already exists will result in an error. No error occurs under two conditions. First, if the IF NOT EXISTS clause is specified, the table is not created but no error occurs. Second, if TEMPORARY is specified and the original table is not a temporary table, the new temporary table is created, but the original table named *tbl_name* becomes hidden to the client while the temporary table exists. The original table remains visible to other clients. The original table becomes visible again either at the next client session or if an explicit DROP TABLE is issued for the temporary table.

The *create_definition* list names the columns and indexes that you want to create. The list is optional if you create the table by means of a trailing SELECT statement. The *table_options* clause allows you to specify various properties for the table. If a trailing *select_statement* is specified (in the form of an arbitrary SELECT statement), the table is created using the result set returned by the SELECT statement. These clauses are described more fully in the following sections.

The TEMPORARY keyword, the IF NOT EXISTS clause, the *table_options* clause, and the ability to create a table from the result of a SELECT statement were introduced in MySQL 3.23.

A *create_definition* may be a column declaration, an index definition, a FOREIGN KEY clause, a *reference_definition*, or a CHECK clause. The latter three are parsed for compatibility with other database systems, but otherwise ignored.

A column declaration *col_declaration* begins with a column name *col_name* and a type *col_type* and may be followed by several optional keywords. The column type may be any of the types listed in Appendix B, "Column Type Reference." See that appendix for type-specific attributes that apply to the columns you want to declare. The optional keywords that may follow the column type are as follows:

- NULL or NOT NULL

  Specifies that the column may or may not contain NULL values. If neither is specified, NULL is the default.

- DEFAULT *default_value*

  Specifies the default value for the column. This cannot be used for BLOB or TEXT types. If no default is specified, a default value is assigned. For columns that may take NULL values, the default is NULL. For columns that may not be NULL, the default is assigned as follows:

  - For numeric columns, the default is 0, except for AUTO_INCREMENT columns. For AUTO_INCREMENT, the default is the next number in the column sequence.

  - For date and time types other than TIMESTAMP, the default is the "zero" value for the type (for example, "0000-00-00" for DATE). For TIMESTAMP, the default is the current date and time.

  - For string types other than ENUM, the default is the empty string. For ENUM, the default is the first enumeration element.

- AUTO_INCREMENT

  This keyword applies only to integer column types. An AUTO_INCREMENT column is special in that when you insert NULL into it, the value actually inserted is one greater than the current maximum value in the column. AUTO_INCREMENT values

start at 1 by default; the first value may be specified explicitly with the
AUTO_INCREMENT table option. The column must also be specified as a UNIQUE
index or PRIMARY KEY and should be NOT NULL. There may be at most one
AUTO_INCREMENT column per table.

- PRIMARY KEY

  Specifies that the column is a PRIMARY KEY.

- UNIQUE

  Specifies that the column is a UNIQUE index. This attribute may be specified as of
  MySQL 3.23.

The PRIMARY KEY, UNIQUE, INDEX, and KEY clauses specify indexes. PRIMARY KEY and
UNIQUE specify indexes that must contain unique values. INDEX and KEY are synonyms;
they specify indexes that may contain duplicate values. The index is based on the
columns named in *index_columns*, each of which must be a column in *tbl_name*. If
there are multiple columns, they should be separated by commas. For CHAR and
VARCHAR columns, you can index a prefix of the column, using *col_name(n)* syntax to
index the first *n* characters of column values. For BLOB and TEXT columns, you *must*
specify a prefix value; you cannot index the entire column. If the index name
index_name is not specified, a name is chosen automatically based on the name of the
first indexed column.

Prior to MySQL 3.23, indexed columns must be declared NOT NULL. As of MySQL
3.23, only columns in PRIMARY KEY indexes must be declared NOT NULL.

The *table_options* clause is available as of MySQL 3.23. If present, it may contain
one or more of the options in the following list. If multiple options are present, they
should not be separated by commas. Each specifier applies to all table types unless otherwise noted.

- AUTO_INCREMENT = *n*

  The first AUTO_INCREMENT value to be generated for the table (MyISAM tables
  only).

- AVG_ROW_LENGTH = *n*

  The approximate average row length of your table. This option is used by
  MySQL to determine the maximum data file size and is needed only for tables
  with BLOB or TEXT columns where the table might become larger than 4GB.

- CHECKSUM = {0 | 1}

  If this is set to 1, MySQL maintains a checksum for each table row. There is a
  slight penalty for updates to the table, but this improves the table checking
  process (MyISAM tables only).

- COMMENT = "*string*"

  A comment for the table. The maximum length is 60 characters.

- `DELAY_KEY_WRITE = {0 | 1}`

  If this is set to 1, the index cache is flushed only occasionally for the table, rather than after each insert operation (MyISAM tables only).

- `MAX_ROWS = n`

  The maximum number of rows you plan to store in the table.

- `MIN_ROWS = n`

  The minimum number of rows you plan to store in the table.

- `PACK_KEYS = {0 | 1}`

  If this is set to 1, index blocks are packed to a higher percentage than usual. The usual effect is an update penalty and an improvement in retrieval performance. If this is set to 0, index blocks are not packed specially. In this case, only indexes with `CHAR` or `VARCHAR` key values 8 characters or longer are packed (MyISAM and ISAM tables only).

- `PASSWORD = "string"`

  Specifies a password for encrypting the table's description file. Normally, this has no effect; the option is enabled only for certain support contract customers.

- `TYPE = {ISAM | MYISAM | HEAP}`

  Specifies the table storage format. The characteristics of these storage formats are described in the section "Table Storage-Type Specifiers" in Chapter 3, "MySQL SQL Syntax and Use." The default format for MySQL as of version 3.23 is MyISAM. Prior to MySQL 3.23, `CREATE TABLE` always creates tables in ISAM format.

If a *select_statement* clause is specified (as a `SELECT` query), the table is created using the contents of the result set returned by the query. Rows that duplicate values on a unique index are either ignored or they replace existing rows according to whether `IGNORE` or `REPLACE` is specified. If neither is specified, an error occurs, and any remaining records are ignored.

Create a table with three columns. The `id` column is a `PRIMARY KEY`, and the two name columns are indexed together:

```
CREATE TABLE customer
(
    id SMALLINT UNSIGNED NOT NULL AUTO_INCREMENT,
    last_name CHAR(30) NOT NULL,
    first_name CHAR(20) NOT NULL,
    PRIMARY KEY (id),
    INDEX (last_name, first_name)
)
```

Create a temporary table and make it a HEAP (in-memory) table for greater speed:

```
CREATE TEMPORARY TABLE tmp_table
    (id MEDIUMINT NOT NULL UNIQUE, name CHAR(40))
    TYPE = HEAP
```

Create a table as a copy of another table:

```
CREATE TABLE prez_copy SELECT * FROM president
```

Create a table using only part of another table:

```
CREATE TABLE prez_alive SELECT last_name, first_name, birth
    FROM president WHERE death IS NULL
```

If creation declarations are specified for a table created and populated by means of a trailing SELECT statement, the declarations are applied after the table contents have been inserted into the table. For example, you can declare that a selected column should be made into a PRIMARY KEY:

```
CREATE TABLE new_tbl (PRIMARY KEY (a)) SELECT a, b, c FROM old_tbl
```

DELETE

```
DELETE [LOW_PRIORITY] FROM tbl_name
    [WHERE where_expr] [LIMIT n]
```

Deletes rows from the table *tbl_name*. The rows deleted are those that match the conditions specified in the expression *where_expr*:

```
DELETE FROM score WHERE event_id = 14
DELETE FROM member WHERE expiration < CURRENT_DATE
```

If the WHERE clause is omitted, *all records are deleted from the table.*

DELETE returns the number of records deleted, except when you delete all records by specifying no WHERE clause. MySQL optimizes this special case by re-creating the data and index files from scratch rather than deleting records on a row-by-row basis. This is extremely fast, but no row count is available, and a value of zero is returned. To obtain a true count, specify a WHERE clause that matches all records. For example:

```
DELETE FROM tbl_name WHERE 1 > 0
```

There is a significant performance penalty, however.

Specifying LOW_PRIORITY causes the statement to be deferred until no clients are reading from the table. LOW_PRIORITY was introduced in MySQL 3.22.5.

If the LIMIT clause is given, the value *n* specifies the maximum number of rows that will be deleted. LIMIT was introduced in MySQL 3.22.7.

DESCRIBE

```
{DESCRIBE | DESC} tbl_name {col_name | pattern}
```

This statement provides the same information as SHOW COLUMNS. See the SHOW entry for more information.

DROP DATABASE

```
DROP DATABASE [IF EXISTS] db_name
```

Drops (removes) the given database. After you drop a database, it's gone, so be careful. The statement fails if the database does not exist (unless you specify IF EXISTS) or if you don't have the proper privilege. The IF EXISTS clause may be specified to suppress the error message that normally results if the database does not exist. IF EXISTS was introduced in MySQL 3.22.2.

A database is represented by a directory under the data directory. If you have put non-table files in that directory, those files are not deleted by the DROP DATABASE statement. In that case, the database directory itself is not removed, either.

DROP FUNCTION

```
DROP FUNCTION function_name
```

Removes a user-defined function that was previously loaded with CREATE FUNCTION.

DROP INDEX

```
DROP INDEX index_name ON tbl_name
```

Drops the index index_name from the table tbl_name. This statement is handled as an ALTER TABLE DROP INDEX statement. See the entry for ALTER TABLE for details. DROP INDEX was introduced in MySQL 3.22.

DROP TABLE

```
DROP TABLE [IF EXISTS] tbl_name [, tbl_name] ...
```

Drops the named table or tables from the database they belong to. If the IF EXISTS clause is given, dropping a non-existent table is not an error. IF EXISTS was introduced in MySQL 3.22.2.

EXPLAIN

```
EXPLAIN tbl_name
EXPLAIN select_statement
```

The first form of this statement is equivalent to SHOW COLUMNS FROM tbl_name. See the description of the SHOW statement for more information.

The second form of the EXPLAIN statement provides information about how MySQL would execute the SELECT statement following the EXPLAIN keyword.

```
EXPLAIN SELECT score.* FROM score, event
    WHERE score.event_id = event.event_id AND event.event_id = 14
```

Output from EXPLAIN consists of one or more rows containing the following columns:

- table

  The table to which the output row refers.

- type

  The type of join that MySQL will perform. The possible types are, from best to worst: system, const, eq_ref, ref, range, index, and ALL. The better types are more restrictive, meaning that MySQL has to look at fewer rows from the table when performing the retrieval.

- possible_keys

  The indexes that MySQL considers candidates for finding rows in the table named in the row column. A value of NULL means that no indexes were found.

- key

  The index that MySQL actually will use for finding rows in the table. A value of NULL indicates that no index will be used.

- key_len

  How much of the index will be used. This may be less than the full index row length if MySQL will use a leftmost prefix of the index.

- ref

  The values to which MySQL will compare index values. The word const or '???' means the comparison is against a constant; a column name indicates a column-to-column comparison.

- rows

  An estimate of the number of rows from the table that MySQL must examine to perform the query. The product of the values in this column is an estimate of the total number of row combinations that must be examined from all tables.

- Extra

  Only index indicates that MySQL can retrieve information for the table using only information in the index without examining the data file. where used indicates the use of the information in the WHERE clause of the SELECT statement.

FLUSH

```
FLUSH flush_option [, flush_option] ...
```

Flushes various internal caches used by the server. *flush_option* may be any of the items in the following list:

- HOSTS

  Flushes the host cache.

- LOGS

  Flushes the log files by closing and reopening them.

- PRIVILEGES

  Reloads the grant tables.

- STATUS

  Reinitializes the status variables.

- TABLES

  Closes any open tables in the table cache.

The FLUSH statement was introduced in MySQL 3.22.9. The STATUS flush option was introduced in MySQL 3.22.11.

GRANT

```
GRANT priv_type [(column_list)] [, priv_type [(column_list)] ] ...
    ON {*.* | * | db_name.* | db_name.tbl_name | tbl_name}
    TO user [, user ] ...
    [WITH GRANT OPTION]
```

The GRANT statement grants access privileges to one or more MySQL users. The *priv_type* value specifies the privileges to be granted. It consists of one or more comma-separated privilege types chosen from the following list:

Privilege Specifier	Operation Allowed by Privilege
ALTER	Alter tables and indexes
CREATE	Create databases and tables
DELETE	Delete existing records from tables
DROP	Drop (remove) databases and tables
INDEX	Create or drop indexes
INSERT	Insert new records into tables
REFERENCES	Unused
SELECT	Retrieve existing records from tables
UPDATE	Modify existing table records

FILE	Read and write files on the server
PROCESS	View information about the threads executing within the server or kill threads
RELOAD	Reload the grant tables or flush the logs, the host cache, or the table cache
SHUTDOWN	Shut down the server
ALL	Anything; ALL PRIVILEGES is a synonym
USAGE	A special "no privileges" privilege

You can always view or kill your own threads. The PROCESS privilege allows you to view or kill any threads.

The ON clause specifies how widely the privileges should be granted, as shown in the following table:

Privilege Specifier	Level at Which Privileges Apply
.	Global privileges: all databases, all tables
*	Global privileges if no default database has been selected, database-level privileges for the current database otherwise
db_name.*	Database-level privileges; all tables in the named database
db_name.tbl_name	Table-level privileges; all columns in the named table
tbl_name	Table-level privileges; all columns in the named table in the default database

When a table is named in the ON clause, privileges may be made column-specific by naming one or more column-separated columns in the column_list clause.

The TO clause specifies one or more users to whom the privileges should be granted. Each user consists of a specifier in the user_name@host_name with an optional IDENTIFIED BY clause. The user_name may be a name or an empty string (""); the latter specifies an anonymous user. host_name may be given as localhost, a hostname, an IP address, or as a pattern matching a domain name or network number. The pattern characters are '%' and '_', with the same meaning as for the LIKE operator. A user_name specified alone with no hostname is equivalent to user_name@%. As of MySQL 3.23, host_name can be an IP number/netmask pair in n.n.n.n/m notation, where n.n.n.n indicates the IP address and m indicates the number of bits to use for the network number.

The IDENTIFIED BY clause, if given, assigns a password to the user. The password should be specified in plain text, without using the PASSWORD function, in contrast to the way passwords are specified for the SET PASSWORD statement. If the user already exists and IDENTIFIED BY is specified, the new password replaces the old one. The existing password remains unchanged otherwise.

The GRANT statement was introduced in MySQL 3.22.11.

The following statements demonstrate some ways in which the GRANT statement can be used. See Chapter 11, "General MySQL Administration," for other examples.

Create a user paul who can access all tables in the samp_db database from any host. The following two statements are equivalent because a missing hostname part in the *user* identifier is equivalent to "%":

```
GRANT ALL ON samp_db.* TO paul IDENTIFIED BY "secret"
GRANT ALL ON samp_db.* TO paul@% IDENTIFIED BY "secret"
```

Create a user with read-only privileges for the tables in the menagerie database. The user can connect from any host in the xyz.com domain:

```
GRANT SELECT ON menagerie.* TO lookonly@%.xyz.com
    IDENTIFIED BY "ragweed"
```

Create a user with full privileges, but only for the member table in the samp_db database. The user can connect from a single host:

```
GRANT ALL ON samp_db.member TO member_mgr@boa.snake.net
    IDENTIFIED BY "doughnut"
```

Create a superuser who can do anything, including granting privileges to other users, but who must connect from the local host:

```
GRANT ALL ON *.* TO superduper@localhost IDENTIFIED BY "homer"
    WITH GRANT OPTION
```

Create an anonymous user of the menagerie database who can connect from the local host with no password:

```
GRANT ALL ON menagerie.* TO ""@localhost
```

INSERT

```
INSERT [LOW_PRIORITY | DELAYED] [IGNORE] [INTO]
    tbl_name [(column_list)] VALUES (expr [, expr] ...) [, (...)] ...
INSERT [LOW_PRIORITY | DELAYED] [IGNORE] [INTO]
    tbl_name [(column_list)] SELECT ...
INSERT [LOW_PRIORITY | DELAYED] [IGNORE] [INTO]
    tbl_name SET col_name=expr [, col_name=expr] ...
```

Inserts rows into an existing table *tbl_name* and returns the number of rows inserted. The INTO keyword is required prior to MySQL 3.22.5.

LOW_PRIORITY causes the statement to be deferred until no clients are reading from the table. LOW_PRIORITY was introduced in MySQL 3.22.5.

DELAYED causes the rows to be placed into a queue for later insertion, and the statement returns immediately so that the client may continue on without waiting. However, in this case, LAST_INSERT_ID() will not return the AUTO_INCREMENT value for any AUTO_INCREMENT column in the table. DELAYED inserts were introduced in MySQL 3.22.15.

If IGNORE is specified, rows that duplicate values for unique keys in existing rows are discarded. If duplicate values occur without IGNORE, an error occurs and no more rows are inserted. IGNORE was introduced in MySQL 3.22.10.

The first form of INSERT requires a VALUES() list that specifies all values to be inserted. If no *column_list* is given, the VALUES() list must specify one value for each column in the table. If a *column_list* is given consisting of one or more comma-separated column names, one value per column must be specified in the VALUES() list. Columns not named in the column list are set to their default values. As of MySQL 3.22.5, multiple value lists may be specified, allowing multiple rows to be inserted using a single INSERT statement. As of MySQL 3.23.3, the VALUES() list may be empty, which inserts a row for which each column is set to its default value.

The second form of INSERT retrieves records according to the SELECT statement and inserts them into *tbl_name*. The SELECT statement must select as many columns as are in *tbl_name*, or as many columns as are named in *column_list* if a column list is specified. When a column list is specified, any columns not named in the list are set to their default values.

The third form of INSERT, available as of MySQL 3.22.10, inserts columns named in the SET clause to the values given by the corresponding expressions. Columns not named are set to their default values.

```
INSERT INTO absence (student_id, date) VALUES(14,"1999-11-03"),(34,NOW())
INSERT INTO absence SET student_id = 14, date = "1999-11-03"
INSERT INTO absence SET student_id = 34, date = NOW()
INSERT INTO score (student_id, score, event_id)
    SELECT student_id, 100 AS score, 15 AS event_id FROM student
```

KILL

```
KILL thread_id
```

Kills the server thread with the given *thread_id*. You must have the PROCESS privilege to kill the thread, unless it is one of your own.

The mysqladmin kill command performs the same operation, but allows multiple thread ID values to be specified on the command line. The KILL statement allows only a single ID.

This statement was introduced in MySQL 3.22.9.

LOAD DATA

```
LOAD DATA [LOW_PRIORITY] [LOCAL] INFILE 'file_name'
    [IGNORE | REPLACE]
    INTO TABLE tbl_name
    import_options
    [IGNORE n LINES]
    [(column_list)]
```

LOAD DATA reads records from the file *file_name* and loads them in bulk into the table *tbl_name*. This is faster than INSERT.

LOW_PRIORITY causes the statement to be deferred until no clients are reading from the table. LOW_PRIORITY was introduced in MySQL 3.23.

Normally, the file is read directly by the server on the server host. In this case, you must have the FILE privilege and the file must either be located in the database directory of the default database or world readable. If LOCAL is specified, the client reads the file on the client host and sends its contents over the network to the server. In this case, the FILE privilege is not required. LOCAL became functional in MySQL 3.22.15.

When LOCAL is not given, the server locates the file as follows:

- If *file_name* is an absolute pathname, the server looks for the file starting from the root directory.

- If *file_name* is a relative pathname, interpretation depends on whether or not the name contains a single component. If so, the server looks for the file in the database directory of the default database. If the filename contains multiple components, the server looks for the file beginning in the server's data directory.

If LOCAL is given, the filename is interpreted as follows:

- If *file_name* is an absolute pathname, the client looks for the file starting from the root directory.

- If *file_name* is a relative pathname, the client looks for the file beginning with your current directory.

Rows that duplicate values on a unique index are either ignored or replace existing rows according to whether IGNORE or REPLACE is specified. If neither is specified, an error occurs, and any remaining records are ignored.

The *import_options* clause indicates the format of the data. The options available in this clause also apply to the *export_options* clause for the SELECT ... INTO OUTFILE statement. The syntax for *import_options* is:

```
[FIELDS
    [TERMINATED BY 'string']
    [[OPTIONALLY] ENCLOSED BY 'char']
    [ESCAPED BY 'char' ]]
[LINES TERMINATED BY 'string']
```

The *string* and *char* values may include the following escape sequences to indicate special characters:

Sequence	Meaning
\0	ASCII 0
\b	Backspace
\n	Newline
\r	Carriage return
\s	Space
\t	Tab
\'	Single quote
\"	Double quote
\\	Backslash

As of MySQL 3.22.10, you may also use hexadecimal constants to indicate arbitrary characters. For example, `LINES TERMINATED BY 0x02` indicates that lines are terminated by Ctrl-B (ASCII 2) characters.

If `FIELDS` is given, at least one of the `TERMINATED BY`, `ENCLOSED BY`, or `ESCAPED BY` clauses must be given, and those that are given must be specified in the order shown. If both `FIELDS` and `LINES` are given, `FIELDS` must precede `LINES`. The parts of the `FIELDS` clause are used as follows:

- `TERMINATED BY` specifies the character or characters that delimit values within a line.

- `ENCLOSED BY` specifies a quote character that is stripped from the ends of field values if it is present. This occurs whether or not `OPTIONALLY` is present. For output (`SELECT ... INTO OUTFILE`), the `ENCLOSED BY` character is used to enclose field values in output lines. If `OPTIONALLY` is given, values are quoted only for `CHAR` and `VARCHAR` columns.

  To include an instance of the `ENCLOSED BY` character within an input field value, it should either be doubled or preceded by the `ESCAPED BY` character. Otherwise, it will be interpreted as signifying the end of the field. For output, instances of the `ENCLOSED BY` character within field values are preceded by the `ESCAPED BY` character.

- The `ESCAPED BY` character is used to specify escaping of special characters. In the following examples, assume that the escape character is backslash ('\'). For input, '\N' (backslash-N) is interpreted as `NULL`, and '\0' (backslash-ASCII '0') is interpreted as a zero-valued byte. For other characters, the escape character is stripped off, and the following character is used literally. For example, '\"' is interpreted as a double quote, even if field values are enclosed within double quotes.

  For output, the escape character is used to encode `NULL` and zero-valued bytes as '\N' and '\0'. In addition, instances of the `ESCAPED BY` and `ENCLOSED BY` characters are preceded by the escape character, as are the first characters of the field and line termination strings. If the `ESCAPED BY` character is empty (`ESCAPED BY ''`), no escaping is done. To specify an escape character of '\', double it (`ESCAPED BY '\\'`).

The `LINES TERMINATED BY` value specifies a character or characters that signify the ends of lines.

If neither `FIELDS` nor `LINES` is given, the defaults are as if you had specified them like this:

```
FIELDS
    TERMINATED BY '\t'
    ENCLOSED BY ''
    ESCAPED BY '\\'
LINES TERMINATED BY '\n'
```

In other words, fields within a line are tab-delimited without being quoted, backslash is treated as the escape character, and lines are terminated by newline characters.

If the TERMINATED BY and ENCLOSED BY values for the FIELDS clause are both empty, a fixed-width row format is used with no delimiters between fields. Column values are read (or written, for output) using the display widths of the columns. For example, VARCHAR(15) and MEDIUMINT(5) columns are read as 15-character and 5-character fields for input. For output, the columns are written using 15 characters and 5 characters. NULL values are written as strings of spaces.

If the IGNORE *n* LINES clause is given, the first *n* lines of the input are discarded. For example, if your data file has a row of column headers that you don't want to put into the database table, you can use IGNORE 1 LINES:

```
LOAD DATA LOCAL INFILE "my_tbl.txt" INTO TABLE my_tbl IGNORE 1 LINES
```

If no *column_list* is specified, input lines are assumed to contain one value per column in the table. If a list consisting of one or more comma-separated column names is given, input lines should contain a value for each named column. Columns not named in the list are set to their default values. If an input line is short of the expected number of values, columns for which values are missing are set to their default values.

If you have a tab-delimited text file that you created on Windows, you can use the default column separator, but the lines are probably terminated by carriage return/newline pairs. To load the file, specify a different line terminator ('\r' indicates a carriage return, and '\n' indicates a newline):

```
LOAD DATA LOCAL INFILE "my_tbl.txt" INTO TABLE my_tbl
    LINES TERMINATED BY "\r\n"
```

Unfortunately, for files created on Windows, you may end up with a malformed record in the database if the program that created the data file uses the odd MS-DOS convention of putting the Ctrl-Z character at the end of the file to indicate end-of-file. Either write the file using a program that doesn't do this, or delete the record after loading the file.

Comma-separated value (CSV) files have commas between fields, and fields may be quoted with double quotes. Assuming lines have newlines at the end, the LOAD DATA statement to load such a file looks like this:

```
LOAD DATA LOCAL INFILE "my_tbl.txt" INTO TABLE my_tbl
    FIELDS TERMINATED BY "," ENCLOSED BY "\""
```

The following statement shows how to read a file for which fields are separated by Ctrl-A (ASCII 1) characters, and lines are terminated by Ctrl-B (ASCII 2) characters:

```
LOAD DATA LOCAL INFILE "my_tbl.txt" INTO TABLE my_tbl
    FIELDS TERMINATED BY 0x01 LINES TERMINATED BY 0x02
```

LOCK TABLES

> LOCK TABLES *lock_list*

Obtains a lock on the tables named in `lock_list`, waiting if necessary until all locks are acquired. LOCK TABLE is a synonym for LOCK TABLES.

`lock_list` consists of one or more comma-separated items, each of which follows this syntax:

> *tbl_name* [AS *alias_name*] {READ | [LOW_PRIORITY] WRITE}

READ indicates a read lock. This blocks other clients that want to write to the table, but allows other clients to read the table. WRITE indicates a write lock. This blocks all other clients, whether they want to read from or write to the table. A LOW_PRIORITY WRITE lock request allows other readers to read the table if the request is waiting for another client that is already reading the table. The lock is not acquired until there are no more readers.

LOCK TABLES allows an alias to be specified so that you can lock a table that you are going to refer to using that alias in a subsequent query. If you use a table multiple times in a query, you must obtain a lock for each instance of the table, locking aliases as necessary.

LOCK TABLES releases any existing locks that you currently hold. Thus, to lock multiple tables, you must lock them all using a single LOCK TABLES statement. Any locks that are held by a client when it terminates are released automatically.

LOW_PRIORITY locks were introduced in MySQL 3.22.5.

```
LOCK TABLES student READ, score WRITE, event READ
LOCK TABLE member READ
```

OPTIMIZE TABLE

> OPTIMIZE TABLE *tbl_name*

Reclaims wasted space in a table. DELETE, REPLACE, and UPDATE statements may result in areas of unused space in a table, particularly for tables that have variable-length rows. The OPTIMIZE TABLE statement eliminates wasted space, resulting in a smaller table. This statement was introduced in MySQL 3.22.7. Additional table-maintenance options are scheduled to be added during the MySQL 3.23 version series, so be sure to check the online MySQL Reference Manual for the latest additions.

REPLACE

```
REPLACE [LOW_PRIORITY | DELAYED] [INTO]
    tbl_name [(column_list)] VALUES (expr [, expr] ...) [, (...)] ...
REPLACE [LOW_PRIORITY | DELAYED] [INTO]
    tbl_name [(column_list)] SELECT ...
REPLACE [LOW_PRIORITY | DELAYED] [INTO]
    tbl_name SET col_name=expr [, col_name=expr] ...
```

The REPLACE statement is like INSERT, with the exception that if a row to be inserted has a value for a UNIQUE index that duplicates the value in a row already present in the table, the old value is deleted before the new one is inserted. For this reason, there is no IGNORE clause option in the syntax of REPLACE.

See the INSERT entry for more information.

REVOKE

```
REVOKE priv_type [(column_list)] [, priv_type [(column_list)] ...]
    ON {*.* | * | db_name.* | db_name.tbl_name | tbl_name}
    FROM user [, user ] ...
```

This statement revokes privileges from the named user or users. The *priv_type*, *column_list*, and *user* clauses are specified the same way as the GRANT statement. The same kind of specifiers are allowed in the ON clause as well.

REVOKE does not remove the user from the user grant table. This means that the user can still connect to the MySQL server. To remove the user entirely, you must manually delete the user's entries from the grant tables.

The REVOKE statement was introduced in MySQL 3.22.11.

Revoke all privileges for superduper@localhost:

```
REVOKE ALL ON *.* FROM superduper@localhost
```

Revoke privileges that allow the member_mgr user to modify the member table in the samp_db database:

```
REVOKE INSERT,DELETE,UPDATE ON samp_db.member FROM member_mgr@boa.snake.net
```

Revoke all privileges for a single table in the menagerie database from the anonymous user on the local host:

```
REVOKE ALL ON menagerie.pet FROM ""@localhost
```

SELECT

```
SELECT
    [select_options]
    select_list
    [INTO OUTFILE 'file_name' export_options]
    [FROM tbl_list
    [WHERE where_expr]
    [GROUP BY column_list]
    [HAVING where_expr]
    [ORDER BY {unsigned_integer | col_name | formula} [ASC | DESC] , ...]
    [LIMIT [offset,] rows]
    [PROCEDURE procedure_name] ]
```

Retrieves rows from the specified tables. Actually, everything is optional except the SELECT keyword and the *select_list* clause, which allows for statements that simply evaluate expressions:

```
SELECT "one plus one =", 1+1
```

The *select_options* clause, if present, may contain the following options:

- ALL
  DISTINCT
  DISTINCTROW

  These keywords control whether or not duplicate rows are returned. ALL causes all rows to be returned. This is the default. DISTINCT and DISTINCT-ROW specify that duplicate rows should be eliminated from the result set.

- HIGH_PRIORITY

  Specifying HIGH_PRIORITY gives the statement a higher priority if it normally would have to wait. If other statements, such as INSERT or UPDATE, are waiting to write to tables named in the SELECT because some other client is reading the tables, HIGH_PRIORITY causes a SELECT statement to be given priority over those write statements. This should be done only for SELECT statements that you know will execute quickly and that must be done immediately because it slows down execution of the write statements. HIGH_PRIORITY was introduced in MySQL 3.22.9.

- SQL_BIG_RESULT
  SQL_SMALL_RESULT

  These keywords specify that the result set will be large or small, which gives the optimizer information that it can use to process the query more effectively. SQL_SMALL_RESULT was introduced in MySQL 3.22.12. SQL_BIG_RESULT was introduced in MySQL 3.23.

- STRAIGHT_JOIN

  Forces tables to be joined in the order named in the FROM clause. It may be used if you believe that the optimizer is not making the best choice.

The *select_list* clause names the output columns to be returned. Multiple columns should be separated by commas. Columns may be references to table columns or expressions. Any column may be assigned a column alias using AS *alias_name* syntax. The alias then becomes the column name in the output and may also be referred to in GROUP BY, ORDER BY, and HAVING clauses. However, you cannot refer to the alias in a WHERE clause.

The special notation * means "all columns from the tables named in the FROM clause," and *tbl_name*.* means "all columns from the named table."

The result of a SELECT statement may be written into a file *file_name* using an INTO '*file_name*' OUTFILE clause. You must have the FILE privilege, and the file must not already exist. The filename is interpreted using the same rules that apply when reading non-LOCAL files with LOAD DATA. The syntax of the *export_options* clause is the same as for the *import_options* clause of the LOAD DATA statement. See the LOAD DATA entry for more information.

The `FROM` clause names one or more tables from which rows should be selected. MySQL supports the following `JOIN` types for use in `SELECT` statements:

```
tbl_list:
    tbl_name
    tbl_list, tbl_name
    tbl_list [CROSS] JOIN tbl_name
    tbl_list INNER JOIN tbl_name
    tbl_list STRAIGHT_JOIN tbl_name
    tbl_list LEFT [OUTER] JOIN tbl_name ON conditional_expr
    tbl_list LEFT [OUTER] JOIN tbl_name USING (column_list)
    tbl_list NATURAL LEFT [OUTER] JOIN tbl_name
    { oj tbl_list LEFT OUTER JOIN tbl_name ON conditional_expr }
```

The join types select rows from the named tables as indicated in the following descriptions, though the rows actually returned to the client may be limited by `WHERE`, `HAVING`, or `LIMIT` clauses.

For a single table named by itself, `SELECT` retrieves rows from that table.

If multiple tables are named and separated by commas, `SELECT` returns all possible combinations of rows from the tables. Using `JOIN`, `CROSS JOIN`, or `INNER JOIN` is equivalent to using commas. `STRAIGHT_JOIN` is similar, but forces the optimizer to join the tables in the order that the tables are named. It may be used if you believe that the optimizer is not making the best choice.

`LEFT JOIN` retrieves rows from the joined tables, but forces a row to be generated for every row in the left table, even if there is no matching row in the right table. When there is no match, columns from the right table are returned as `NULL` values. Matching rows are determined according to the condition specified in the `ON` `conditional_expr` clause or the `USING (column_list)` clause. `conditional_expr` is an expression of the form that may be used in the `WHERE` clause. `column_list` consists of one or more comma-separated column names, each of which must be a column that occurs in both of the joined tables. `LEFT OUTER JOIN` is equivalent to `LEFT JOIN`, as is the syntax that begins with `oj` (which is included for ODBC compatibility).

`NATURAL LEFT JOIN` is equivalent to `LEFT JOIN USING (column_list)`, where `column_list` names every column that is common to both tables.

Tables may be assigned aliases in the `FROM` clause using either `tbl_name alias_name` or `tbl_name AS alias_name` syntax. References to an aliased column elsewhere in the `SELECT` statement must be made using the alias.

The `WHERE` clause specifies an expression that is applied to rows selected from the tables named in the `FROM` clause. Rows that do not satisfy the criteria given by the expression are rejected. The result set may be further limited by `HAVING` and `LIMIT` clauses.

The `GROUP BY column_list` clause groups rows of the result set according to the columns named in the list. This clause is used when you specify summary functions such as `COUNT()` or `MAX()` in the `select_list` clause. Columns may be referred to by column names or aliases, or by position within `select_list`. Column positions are numbered beginning with 1.

The HAVING clause specifies a secondary expression that is used to limit rows after they have satisfied the conditions named by the WHERE clause. Rows that do not satisfy the HAVING condition are rejected. HAVING is useful for expressions involving summary functions that cannot be tested in the WHERE clause. However, if a condition is legal in either the WHERE clause or the HAVING clause, it is preferable to place it in the WHERE clause where it will be subject to analysis by the optimizer.

ORDER BY indicates how to sort the result set. Like GROUP BY, columns may be referred to by column names or aliases, or by position within the column selection list. Output columns are sorted in ascending order by default. To specify a sort order for a column explicitly, follow the column indicator by ASC (ascending) or DESC (descending). As of MySQL 3.23.2, you may also specify an expression as a sort column. For example, ORDER BY RAND() returns rows in random order.

The LIMIT clause may be used to select a section of rows from the result set. LIMIT *n* returns the first *n* rows. LIMIT *m, n* returns *n* rows, beginning with row *m*. For LIMIT, rows are numbered beginning with 0, not 1.

PROCEDURE names a procedure to which the data in the result set will be sent before a result set is returned to the client. As of MySQL 3.23, you can use PROCEDURE ANALYSE() to obtain information about the characteristics of the data in the columns named in the column selection list.

The following statements demonstrate some ways in which the SELECT statement can be used. See Chapter 1, "Introduction to MySQL and SQL," for many other examples.

Select the entire contents of a table:

```
SELECT * FROM president
```

Select entire contents, but sort by name:

```
SELECT * FROM president ORDER BY last_name, first_name
```

Select records for presidents born on or after "1900-01-01":

```
SELECT * FROM president WHERE birth >= "1900-01-01"
```

Do the same, but sort in birth order:

```
SELECT * FROM president WHERE birth >= "1900-01-01" ORDER BY birth
```

Determine which states are represented by rows in the member table:

```
SELECT DISTINCT state FROM member;
```

Select rows from member table and write columns as comma-separated values into a file:

```
SELECT * INTO OUTFILE "/tmp/member.txt"
    FIELDS TERMINATED BY "," FROM member
```

Select the top five scores for a particular grade event:

```
SELECT * FROM score WHERE event_id = 9 ORDER BY score DESC LIMIT 5
```

SET

```
SET [OPTION] option_setting, ...
```

The SET statement is used to specify a variety of options. It is best to leave out the word OPTION because it will be removed in a future version of MySQL.

option_setting values may be any item in the following list:

- CHARACTER SET {charset_name | DEFAULT}

  Specifies the character set used by the client. Strings sent to and from the client are mapped using this character set. The only character set available currently is cp1251_koi8. The character set name DEFAULT restores the default character set.

  ```
  SET CHARACTER SET cp1251_koi8
  SET CHARACTER SET DEFAULT
  ```

- INSERT_ID = n

  Specifies the value to be used by the next INSERT statement when inserting an AUTO_INCREMENT column. This is used for update log processing.

  ```
  SET INSERT_ID = 1973
  ```

- LAST_INSERT_ID = n

  Specifies the value to be returned by LAST_INSERT_ID(). This is used for update log processing.

  ```
  SET LAST_INSERT_ID = 48731
  ```

- PASSWORD [FOR user] = PASSWORD("password")

  With no FOR clause, sets the password for the current user to "password". With a FOR clause, sets the password for the given user. You must have privileges for modifying the mysql database to be able to set another user's password. user is specified in user_name@host_name form, using the same types of values for user_name and host_name that are acceptable for the GRANT statement.

  ```
  SET PASSWORD = PASSWORD("secret")
  SET PASSWORD FOR paul = PASSWORD("secret")
  SET PASSWORD FOR paul@localhost = PASSWORD("secret")
  SET PASSWORD FOR bill@%.bigcorp.com = PASSWORD("old-sneep")
  ```

- SQL_AUTO_IS_NULL = {0 | 1}

  If this is set to 1, the last row that was inserted containing an AUTO_INCREMENT value can be selected using a WHERE clause of the form WHERE auto_inc_col IS NULL. This is used by some ODBC programs such as Access. The default is 1. This option was introduced in MySQL 3.23.5.

  ```
  SET SQL_AUTO_IS_NULL = 0
  ```

- SQL_BIG_SELECTS = {0 | 1}

  SELECT statements that will return more than `max_join_size` rows are allowed if this is set to 1. Otherwise, the query will be aborted. The default is 1.

  ```
  SET SQL_BIG_SELECTS = 0
  ```

- SQL_BIG_TABLES = {0 | 1}

  All temporary tables are stored on disk rather than in memory if this is set to 1. Performance is slower, but SELECT statements that require large temporary tables will not generate "table full" errors. The default is 0 (hold temporary tables in memory). This option normally is not needed for MySQL 3.23 and up.

  ```
  SET SQL_BIG_TABLES = 1
  ```

- SQL_LOG_OFF = {0 | 1}

  If this option is set to 1, the current client's queries are not logged in the general log file. If set to 0, logging for the client is enabled. The client must have the PROCESS privilege for this statement to have any effect. Logging to the update log is unaffected.

  ```
  SET SQL_LOG_OFF = 1
  ```

- SQL_LOG_UPDATE = {0 | 1}

  This is like SQL_LOG_OFF (including the requirement for the PROCESS privilege) except that it affects logging to the update log and not to the general log. SQL_LOG_UPDATE was introduced in MySQL 3.22.5.

  ```
  SET SQL_LOG_UPDATE = 1
  ```

- SQL_LOW_PRIORITY_UPDATES = {0 | 1}

  If this option is set to 1, statements that modify table contents (DELETE, INSERT, REPLACE, UPDATE) wait until no SELECT is active or pending for the table. SELECT statements that arrive while another is active begin executing immediately rather than waiting for low-priority modification statements.
  SQL_LOW_PRIORITY_UPDATES was introduced in MySQL 3.22.5.

  ```
  SET SQL_LOW_PRIORITY_UPDATES = 0
  ```

- SQL_SELECT_LIMIT = {n | DEFAULT}

  Specifies the maximum number of records to return from a SELECT statement. The presence of an explicit LIMIT clause in a statement takes precedence over this option. The default value is "no limit." A value of DEFAULT restores the default if you have changed it.

  ```
  SET SQL_SELECT_LIMIT = 100000
  SET SQL_SELECT_LIMIT = DEFAULT
  ```

- SQL_WARNINGS = {0 | 1}

  If set to 1, MySQL reports warning counts even for single-row inserts. Normally, warning counts are reported only for INSERT statements that insert multiple rows. The default is 0. SQL_WARNINGS was introduced in MySQL 3.22.11.

  ```
  SET SQL_WARNINGS = 1
  ```

- TIMESTAMP = {timestamp_value | DEFAULT}

  Specifies a TIMESTAMP value. This is used for update log processing.

  ```
  SET TIMESTAMP = DEFAULT
  ```

SHOW

```
SHOW COLUMNS FROM tbl_name [FROM db_name] [LIKE pattern]
SHOW DATABASES [LIKE pattern]
SHOW GRANTS FOR user_name
SHOW INDEX FROM tbl_name [FROM db_name]
SHOW PROCESSLIST
SHOW STATUS
SHOW TABLE STATUS [FROM db_name] [LIKE pattern]
SHOW TABLES [FROM db_name] [LIKE pattern]
SHOW VARIABLES [LIKE pattern]
```

The various forms of the SHOW statement provide information about databases, tables, columns, and indexes, or information about server operation. Several of the forms take an optional FROM db_name clause, allowing you to specify the database for which information should be shown. If the clause is not present, the default database is used. Some forms allow an optional LIKE pattern clause to limit output to values that match the pattern. The pattern should be a string or a SQL pattern containing '%' or '_' characters.

SHOW COLUMNS

The SHOW COLUMNS statement lists the columns for the given table. SHOW FIELDS is a synonym for SHOW COLUMNS.

```
SHOW COLUMNS FROM president
SHOW FIELDS FROM president
SHOW COLUMNS FROM president FROM samp_db
SHOW COLUMNS FROM tables_priv FROM mysql LIKE "%priv"
```

The output from SHOW COLUMNS contains the following columns:

- Field

  The table column name.

- Type

  The column type.

- Null

    Whether the column may contain NULL values. This is either YES or blank (no).

- Key

    Whether or not the column is indexed.

- Default

    The column's default value.

- Extra

    Extra information about the column.

- Privileges

    The privileges that you hold for the column. This information is shown only as of MySQL 3.23.

SHOW DATABASES

The SHOW DATABASES statement lists the databases available on the server host.

```
SHOW DATABASES
SHOW DATABASES LIKE "test%"
```

SHOW GRANTS

The SHOW GRANTS statement displays grant information about the specified user, which should be given in *user_name@host_name* form, using the same types of values for *user_name* and *host_name* that are acceptable for the GRANT statement. SHOW GRANTS was introduced in MySQL 3.23.4.

```
SHOW GRANTS FOR root@localhost
SHOW GRANTS FOR ""@pit-viper.snake.net
```

SHOW INDEX

The SHOW INDEX statement displays information about a table's indexes. SHOW KEYS is a synonym for SHOW INDEX.

```
SHOW INDEX FROM score
SHOW KEYS FROM score
SHOW INDEX FROM samp_db.score
SHOW INDEX FROM score FROM samp_db
```

The output from SHOW INDEX contains the following columns:

- Table

    The name of the table containing the index.

- Non_unique

    This value is 1 if the index can contain duplicate values and 0 if it cannot.

- Key_name

  The index name.

- Seq_in_index

  The number of the column within the index. Columns are numbered beginning with 1.

- Column_name

  The column name.

- Collation

  The column sorting order within the index. The values may be A (ascending), D (descending), or NULL (not sorted). Descending keys are not yet available, but will be implemented in the future.

- Cardinality

  The number of unique values in the index. This value is updated by running myisamchk or isamchk with the --analyze option.

- Sub_part

  The prefix length, if only a prefix of the column is indexed. This is NULL if the entire column is indexed.

- Packed

  How the key is packed, or NULL if it is not packed. This column is shown only for MySQL 3.23 and up.

- Comment

  Reserved for internal comments about the index. This column is shown only for MySQL 3.23 and up.

SHOW PROCESSLIST

SHOW PROCESSLIST displays information about the threads executing within the server. The output contains the following columns:

- Id

  The thread ID number for the client.

- User

  The client name associated with the thread.

- Host

  The host from which the client is connected.

- db

  The default database for the thread.

- Command

  The command being executed by the thread.

- Time

  The amount of time used by the command currently executing in the thread, in seconds.

- State

  Information about what MySQL is doing while processing a SQL statement. The value may be useful for reporting a problem with MySQL or when asking a question on the MySQL mailing list about why a thread stays in some state for a long time.

- Info

  The query being executed.

SHOW STATUS

The SHOW STATUS statement displays the server status variables and their values:

- Aborted_clients

  The number of client connections aborted due to clients not closing the connection properly.

- Aborted_connects

  The number of failed attempts to connect to the server.

- Connections

  The number of attempts to connect to the server (both successful and unsuccessful). If this number is quite high, you may want to look into using persistent connections in your clients if possible.

- Created_tmp_tables

  The number of temporary tables created while processing queries.

- Delayed_errors

  The number of errors occurring while processing INSERT DELAYED rows.

- Delayed_insert_threads

  The current number of INSERT DELAYED handlers.

- Delayed_writes

  The number of INSERT DELAYED rows that have been written.

- Flush_commands

  The number of FLUSH commands that have been executed.

- Handler_delete

  The number of requests to delete a row from a table.

- Handler_read_first

  The number of requests to read the first row from a table.

- Handler_read_key

  The number of requests to read a row based on an index value.

- Handler_read_next

  The number of requests to read the next row in index order.

- Handler_read_rnd

  The number of requests to read a row based on row position. If this number is much higher than all other reported numbers, you are either performing many queries that require full table scans or you are not using indexes properly.

- Handler_update

  The number of requests to update a row in a table.

- Handler_write

  The number of requests to insert a row in a table.

- Key_blocks_used

  The number of blocks in use in the index cache.

- Key_read_requests

  The number of requests to read a block from the index cache.

- Key_reads

  The number of physical reads of index blocks from disk.

- Key_write_requests

  The number of requests to write a block to the index cache.

- Key_writes

  The number of physical writes of index blocks to disk.

- Max_used_connections

  The maximum number of connections that have been open simultaneously.

- Not_flushed_delayed_rows

  The number of rows waiting to be written for INSERT DELAYED queries.

- Not_flushed_key_blocks

  The number of blocks in the key cache that have been modified but not yet flushed to disk.

- Open_files

  The number of open files.

- Open_streams

  The number of open streams. A stream is a file opened with `fopen()`; this applies only to log files.

- Open_tables

  The number of open tables.

- Opened_tables

  The total number of tables that have been opened. If this number is high, it may be a good idea to increase your table cache size.

- Questions

  The number of queries that have been received by the server (this includes both successful and unsuccessful queries).

- Slow_queries

  The number of queries that look longer than `long_query_time` seconds to execute.

- Threads_connected

  The number of currently open connections.

- Threads_running

  The number of threads that are not sleeping.

- Uptime

  The number of seconds since the server started running.

SHOW TABLE STATUS

The SHOW TABLE STATUS statement displays descriptive information about the tables in a database. SHOW TABLE STATUS was introduced in MySQL 3.23.

```
SHOW TABLE STATUS
SHOW TABLE STATUS FROM samp_db
SHOW TABLE STATUS FROM mysql LIKE "%priv"
```

The output from SHOW TABLE STATUS contains the following columns:

- Name

  The table name.

- Type

  The table type; this may be NISAM (ISAM), MyISAM, or HEAP.

- Row_format

  The row storage format; this can be `Fixed` (fixed-length rows), `Dynamic` (variable-length rows), or `Compressed`.

- Rows

  The number of rows in the table.

- Avg_row_length

  The average number of bytes used by table rows.

- Data_length

  The actual size in bytes of the table data file.

- Max_data_length

  The maximum size in bytes that the table data file can grow to.

- Index_length

  The actual size in bytes of the index file.

- Data_free

  The number of unused bytes in the data file. If this number is very high, it may be a good idea to issue an OPTIMIZE TABLE statement for the table.

- Auto_increment

  The next value that will be generated for an AUTO_INCREMENT column.

- Create_time

  The time when the table was created.

- Update_time

  The time when the table was most recently modified.

- Check_time

  The time at which the table was last checked or repaired by myisamchk; the value is NULL if the table has never been checked or repaired.

- Create_options

  Extra options that were specified in the *table_options* clause of the CREATE TABLE statement that created the table.

- Comment

  The text of any comment specified when the table was created.

SHOW TABLES

The SHOW TABLES statement displays a list of tables in a database.

```
SHOW TABLES
SHOW TABLES FROM samp_db
SHOW TABLES FROM mysql LIKE "%priv"
```

SHOW VARIABLES

The SHOW VARIABLES statement displays a list of server variables and their values. These variables are described in the entry for mysqld in Appendix E, "MySQL Program Reference."

```
SHOW VARIABLES
SHOW VARIABLES LIKE "%thread%"
```

UNLOCK TABLES

```
UNLOCK TABLES
```

This statement releases any table locks being held by the current client. UNLOCK TABLE is a synonym for UNLOCK TABLES.

UPDATE

```
UPDATE [LOW_PRIORITY] tbl_name
    SET col_name=expr [, col_name=expr ] ...
    [WHERE where_expr] [LIMIT n]
```

Modifies the contents of existing rows in the table tbl_name. The rows to be modified are those selected by the expression specified in the WHERE clause. For those rows that are selected, each column named in the SET clause is set to value of the corresponding expression.

```
UPDATE member SET expiration = NULL, phone = "197-602-4832"
    WHERE member_id = 14
```

If no WHERE clause is given, *all rows in the table are updated.*

UPDATE returns the number of rows that were updates. However, a row is not considered updated unless some column value actually changes. Setting a column to the value it already contains is not considered to affect the row. If your application really needs to know how many rows matched the WHERE clause regardless of whether or not the UPDATE actually changed any values, you should specify the CLIENT_FOUND_ROWS flag when you establish a connection to the server. See the entry for the mysql_real_connect() function in Appendix F, "C API Reference."

LOW_PRIORITY causes the statement to be deferred until no clients are reading from the table. LOW_PRIORITY was introduced in MySQL 3.22.5.

If the LIMIT clause is given, the value *n* specifies the maximum number of rows that will be updated. LIMIT was introduced in MySQL 3.23.3.

USE

```
USE db_name
```

Selects *db_name* to make it the current database (the default database for table references that include no explicit database name). The USE statement fails if the database doesn't exist or if you have no privileges for accessing it.

Comment Syntax

This section describes how to write comments in your SQL code. It also points out a shortcoming of the mysql client program with respect to comment interpretation. Comments are often used in query files that are executed using mysql in batch mode, so you should be particularly aware of this limitation when you're writing such files.

The MySQL server understands three types of comments:

- Anything from '#' to the end of the line is treated as a comment. This syntax is the same as is used in most shells and Perl.

- Anything between '/*' and '*/' is treated as a comment. This form of comment may span multiple lines. This syntax is the same as is used in the C language.

- As of MySQL 3.23.3, you can begin a comment with '-- ' (two dashes and a space); everything from the dashes to the end of the line is treated as a comment. This comment style is used by some other databases, except that the space is not required. MySQL requires the space as a disambiguation character so that expressions such as *value1-value2*, where *value2* is negative, will not be treated as comments.

Comments are ignored by the server when executing queries, with the exception that C-style comments that begin with '/*!' are given special treatment. The text of the comment should contain SQL keywords, and the keywords will be treated by the MySQL server as part of the statement in which the comment appears. For example, the following lines are considered equivalent by the server:

```
INSERT LOW_PRIORITY INTO my_tbl SET ...
INSERT /*! LOW_PRIORITY */ INTO my_tbl SET ...
```

This form of comment is intended to be used for MySQL-specific extensions and keywords. MySQL will recognize the keywords, and other SQL servers will ignore them. This makes it easier to write queries that take advantage of MySQL-specific features but that still work with other database systems. The '/*!' comment style was introduced in MySQL 3.22.7.

As of MySQL 3.22.26, you may follow the '/*!' sequence with a version number to tell MySQL to ignore the comment unless the server version number is at least as recent as that version. The comment in the following UPDATE statement is ignored unless the server is version 3.23.3 or later:

```
UPDATE my_table SET my_col = 100 WHERE my_col < 100 /*!32303 LIMIT 100 */
```

The mysql client is more limited than the MySQL server in its ability to understand comments. mysql gets confused if certain constructs appear in C-style comments

because it uses a less sophisticated parser than the server. For example, a quote character appearing inside of a C-style comment will fool it into thinking it's parsing a
string, and it continues looking for the end of the string until a matching quote is
seen. The following statements demonstrate this behavior:

```
mysql> SELECT /* I have no quote */ 1;
+---+
| 1 |
+---+
| 1 |
+---+
mysql> SELECT /* I've got a quote */ 1;
    '>
```

mysql parses the first statement without problems, sends it to the server for execution,
and prints another 'mysql>' prompt. The second statement contains a comment with an
unmatched quote. As a result, mysql goes into string-parsing mode. It's still in that
mode after you enter the line, as indicated by the ''>' prompt. To escape from this, type
a matching quote followed by a '\c' command to cancel the query. See Appendix E for
more information on the meaning of mysql's prompts.

E

MySQL Program Reference

THIS APPENDIX DESCRIBES THE MySQL programs named in the following list. Later in the appendix, each program is described in more detail, including a short description of its purpose, its invocation syntax, the options it supports, and a description of any internal variables it has.

- `isamchk` and `myisamchk`

  Utilities for checking and repairing tables, performing key distribution analysis, and de-activating and re-activating indexes.

- `myisampack` and `pack_isam`

  Utilities to produce compressed read-only tables.

- `mysql`

  Interactive program with line-editing capabilities for sending queries to the MySQL server; may also be used in batch mode to execute queries stored in a file.

- `mysql.server`

  Script for starting up and shutting down the MySQL server.

- mysqlaccess

  Script for testing access privileges.

- mysqladmin

  Utility for performing administrative operations.

- mysqlbug

  Script for generating bug reports.

- mysqld

  The MySQL server; this program must be running so that clients have access to the databases administered by the server.

- mysqldump

  Utility for dumping the contents of database tables.

- mysqlimport

  Utility for bulk loading of data into tables.

- mysqlshow

  Utility that provides information about databases or tables.

- safe_mysqld

  Script for starting up and monitoring the MySQL server.

In the syntax descriptions, optional information is indicated by square brackets ([ ]).

Specifying Program Options

Most MySQL programs understand several options that affect how the program operates. Options may be specified on the command line or in option files. In addition, some options may be specified by setting environment variables. Options specified on the command line take precedence over options specified any other way, and options in option files take precedence over environment variable values.

Getting Online Help from MySQL Programs

Each MySQL program except mysqlbug, mysql.server, and safe_mysqld understands the --help option. This option provides a quick way to get online help about a program from the program itself. For example, if you're not sure how to use mysqlimport, invoke it like this for instructions:

```
% mysqlimport --help
```

The -? option is the same as help, although your shell may interpret the '?' character as a filename wildcard character:

```
% mysqlimport -?
mysqlimport: No match.
```

If that happens to you, try this instead:

```
% mysqlimport -\?
```

Most options have both a short (single-letter) form and a long (full-word) form. The `-?` and `--help` options just shown are an example of this. If a short-form option is followed by a value, in most cases the option and the value may be separated by whitespace. For example, when you specify a username, `-upaul` is equivalent to `-u paul`. The `-p` (password) option is an exception; any password value must follow the `-p` with no intervening space.

Each program description lists all options a program currently understands. If a program doesn't seem to recognize an option listed in its description, you may have an older version of the program that precedes the addition of the option. (But double-check the syntax just to make sure you simply haven't specified the option incorrectly.)

Standard MySQL Program Options

Several options have a standard meaning across multiple MySQL programs. Rather than listing these in the description of each program that understands them, they are shown here once, and the "Standard Options Supported" section in each program description indicates which of these options a program understands. (That section lists only long-format names, but programs understand the corresponding short-format options as well, unless otherwise specified.)

The standard options are:

- `-C, --compress`

  Enables compression for the protocol used for communication between the client and the server if the server supports it. This option is used only by client programs. It was introduced in MySQL 3.22.3.

- `-# debug_options, --debug=debug_options`

  Turns on debugging output. This option has no effect unless MySQL was built with debugging support enabled. The `debug_options` string consists of colon-separated options. A typical value is `d:t:o,file_name`, which enables debugging, turns on function call entry and exit tracing, and sends output to the file `file_name`.

  If you expect to do much debugging, you should examine the file `dbug/dbug.c` in the MySQL source distribution for a description of all the options you can use.

- `--defaults-file=path_name`

  Specifies the pathname to an option file. Normally, programs search for option files in several locations, but if `--defaults-file` is specified, only the named file is read. If you use this option, it must be the first one on the command line. This option was introduced in MySQL 3.22.23.

- -?, --

  Tells the program to print a help message and exit.

- -h *host_name*, --host=*host_name*

  Specifies the host to connect to (that is, the host where the server is running). This option is used only by client programs.

- --no-defaults

  Suppresses the use of any option files. If you use this option, it must be the first one on the command line.

- -p[*password*], --password[=*password*]

  Specifies the password to use when connecting to the server. If *password* is not specified after the option name, the program will ask you to enter one. If *password* is given, it must immediately follow the option name with no space in between. This option is used only by client programs.

- -W, --pipe

  Uses a named pipe to connect to the server. This option is used only for client programs running under Windows.

- -P *port_num*, --port=*port_num*

  For client programs, this is the port number to use when connecting to the server. This is used for TCP/IP connections (connections where the host is not localhost). For mysqld, this option specifies the port on which to listen for TCP/IP connections.

- --print-defaults

  Prints the option values that will be used if you invoke the program with no options on the command line. This shows the values that will be picked up from option files (and environment variables). --print-defaults is useful for verifying proper setup of an option file. It's also useful if MySQL programs seem to be using options that you never specified. You can use --print-defaults to determine if options are being picked up from some option file. If you use this option, it must be the first one on the command line.

- -O *var=value*, --set-variable *var=value*

  Several programs have variables (operating parameters) that you can set. The --set-variable option allows you to set these variables. *var* is the variable name, and *value* is the value to assign to the variable. Values are in bytes for variables that represent buffer sizes or lengths. Values may be specified as an exact number, or as a number with the suffix 'K' or 'M' to indicate kilobytes or megabytes. Suffixes are not case sensitive; 'k' and 'm' are equivalent to 'K' and 'M'.

  Each program's variables are listed in the program's description in this appendix, and are also displayed when you invoke the program with the --help option.

- -s, --silent

  Specifies silent mode. This doesn't necessarily mean the program is completely silent, simply that it produces less output than usual. Several programs allow this option to be specified multiple times to cause the program to become increasingly silent (this works in option files, too).

- -S *path_name*, --socket=*path_name*

  For client programs, this is the full pathname of the socket file to use when connecting to the server. A socket file is used for connections to localhost.

- -u *user_name*, --user=*user_name*

  For client programs, this is the MySQL username to use when connecting to the server. The default if this option is not specified is your login name under UNIX and ODBC under Windows. For mysqld, this option indicates the name of the UNIX account to be used for running the server. (The server must be started as root for this option to be effective.)

- -v, --verbose

  Specify verbose mode; the program produces more output than usual. Several programs allow this option to be specified multiple times to cause the program to be increasingly verbose. (This works in option files, too.)

- -V, --version

  Tells the program to print its version information string and exit.

Option Files

Option files were introduced in MySQL 3.22. They allow you to store MySQL program options so that you don't have to type them on the command line each time you invoke a program. Option files are read by isamchk, myisamchk, myisampack, mysql, mysqladmin, mysqld, mysqldump, mysqlimport, mysql.server, and pack_isam. You can find an example option file, my-example.cnf, in the share/mysql directory under the MySQL installation directory, or in the support-files directory of a source distribution.

Any option specified in an option file may be overridden by specifying a different value for the option explicitly on the command line.

MySQL programs consult several files looking for options; however, it is not an error for an option file to be missing. Under UNIX, the following files are checked for options, in the order given:

Filename	Contents
/etc/my.cnf	Global options
DATADIR/my.cnf	Server-specific options
~/.my.cnf	User-specific options

592 Appendix E MySQL Program Reference

Under Windows, these files are read:

Filename	Contents
SYSTEMDIR\my.ini	Global options
C:\my.cnf	Global options
DATADIR\my.cnf	Server-specific options

DATADIR represents the pathname to the data directory on your machine. (This is the pathname compiled into the server; it cannot be changed with the --datadir option.) Under Windows, *DATADIR* is C:\mysql\data. *SYSTEMDIR* represents the pathname to the Windows system directory (usually something like C:\Windows or C:\WinNT). Although the Windows option file names are specified using '\' as the pathname component separator, pathnames specified within the files should be written using '/' as the pathname separator. If you want to use '\' as the separator, use '\\' because '\' is treated as an escape character.

Global option files are used by all programs that are option file-aware. A file in a server's data directory is used only by the corresponding server. User-specific files are used by programs run by that user.

Options are specified in groups. Here's an example:

```
[client]
user=paul
password=secret

[mysql]
no-auto-rehash

[mysqlshow]
status
```

Group names are given inside square brackets and usually correspond to a program name. In the preceding example, [mysql] indicates the option group for the mysql client and [mysqlshow] indicates the option group for mysqlshow. The special group name [client] allows you to specify options that apply to all client programs. The standard MySQL client programs look at both the [client] group and the group with the same name as the client name. For example, mysql looks at the [client] and [mysql] groups, and mysqlshow looks at the [client] and [mysqlshow] groups.

Any options following a group name are associated with that group. An option file may contain any number of groups, and groups listed later take precedence over groups listed earlier. If a given option is found multiple times in the groups a program looks at, the value listed last is used.

Each option should be specified on a separate line. The first word on the line is the option name, which must be specified in long-name format without the leading dashes. (For example, to specify compression on the command line, you can use either

-C or --compress, but in an option file, you can only use compress.) Any long-format option supported by a program may be listed in an option file. If the option requires a value, list the name and value separated by an '=' character.

Consider the following command line:

```
mysql --compress --user=paul --set-variable max_allowed_packet=24M
```

To specify the same information in an option file using the [mysql] group, you'd do so as follows:

```
[mysql]
compress
user=paul
set-variable=max_allowed_packet=24M
```

Observe that in an option file, set-variable is followed by a '=' character in addition to the '=' character between the variable name and its value.

Option file lines that are empty or that begin with '#' or ';' are treated as comments and ignored.

Certain escape sequences may be used in option values to indicate special characters:

Sequence	Meaning
\b	Backspace
\n	Newline
\r	Carriage return
\s	Space
\t	Tab
\\	Backslash

Be careful not to put options in the [client] group that really are understood only by a single client. For example, if you put the mysql-specific skip-line-numbers option in the [client] group, you will suddenly find that other client programs, such as mysqlimport, no longer work. (You'll get an error message, followed by the help message.) Move skip-line-numbers to the [mysql] group instead and you will be all right.

The options understood by all MySQL programs that read the [client] group are compress, debug, help, host, password, pipe, port, select, user, and version. (It doesn't make much sense to put help or version in an option file, of course.)

Keep User-Specific Option Files Private

Make sure that each user-specific option file is owned by the proper user and that the mode is set to 600 or 400 so that other users cannot read it. You don't want MySQL username and password information exposed to anyone other than the user the file applies to.

Environment Variables

MySQL programs look at the values of the several environment variables to obtain option settings. Environment variables have low precedence; options specified using environment variables may be overridden by options specified in an option file or on the command line.

MySQL programs check the following environment variables:

- MYSQL_DEBUG

  The options to use when debugging. This variable has no effect unless MySQL was built with debugging support enabled. Setting MYSQL_DEBUG is like using the --debug option.

- MYSQL_PWD

  The password to use when establishing connections to the MySQL server. Setting MYSQL_PWD is like using the --password option.

- MYSQL_TCP_PORT

  For clients, this is the port number to use when establishing a TCP/IP connection to the server. For mysqld, this is the port on which to listen for TCP/IP connections. Setting MYSQL_TCP_PORT is like using the --port option.

- MYSQL_UNIX_PORT

  For clients, this is the pathname of the socket file to use when establishing UNIX domain socket connections to the server running on localhost. For mysqld, this is the socket on which to listen for local connections. Setting MYSQL_UNIX_PORT is like using the --socket option.

- TMPDIR

  The pathname of the directory in which to create temporary files. Setting this variable is like using the --tmpdir option.

- USER

  This is the MySQL username to use when connecting to the server. This variable is used only by client programs running under Windows; setting it is like using the --user option.

The mysql client checks the value of the following environment variables:

- MYSQL_HISTFILE

  The name of the file to use for storing command-line history. The default value if this variable is not set is $HOME/.mysql_history, where $HOME is the location of your home directory.

- MYSQL_HOST

  The host to connect to when establishing a connection to the server. Setting this variable is like using the --host option.

isamchk **and** myisamchk

These utilities allow you to check and repair damaged tables, display table information, perform index key value distribution analysis, and disable or enable indexes. Chapter 4, "Query Optimization," provides more information on key analysis and index disabling. Chapter 13, "Database Maintenance and Repair," provides more information on table checking and repair.

myisamchk is used for tables that use the newer MyISAM storage format. These tables have data and index filenames with .MYD and .MYI suffixes. Use isamchk for tables that use the older ISAM storage format. These have data and index filenames with .ISD and .ISM suffixes. If you tell either utility to operate on a table of the wrong type, it will print a warning message and ignore the table.

Do not perform table checking or repair while the MySQL server is accessing the table! Chapter 13 discusses how to prevent the server from using a table while myisamchk or isamchk are working on it.

Usage

```
isamchk [options] tbl_name[.ISM] ...
myisamchk [options] tbl_name[.MYI] ...
```

With no options, these utilities check the named tables for errors. Otherwise, the tables are processed according to the meaning of the specified options. A *tbl_name* argument can be either the name of a table or the name of the index file (.ISM or .MYI) for the table. Using index file names is convenient because you can use filename wildcards to operate on all tables for a given storage type in a single command. For example, you can check all the tables in a directory like this:

```
% isamchk *.ISD
% myisamchk *.MYI
```

These utilities make no assumptions about where table files are located. You must specify the pathname to the files you want to use if they are not in the current directory. Because table files are not assumed to be located under the server's data directory, you can copy table files into another directory and operate on the copies rather than the originals.

Some of the options refer to index numbers. Indexes are numbered beginning with 1. You can issue a SHOW INDEX query or use the mysqlshow --keys command to find out the index numbering for a particular table. The Key_name column lists indexes in the same order that myisamchk and isamchk see them.

> MYSQL_PWD **is a Security Risk**
>
> Using the MYSQL_PWD variable to store a password constitutes a security risk because other users on your system can easily discover its value. For example, the ps utility will show the environment variable settings for other users.

Standard Options Supported by `isamchk` and `myisamchk`

```
--debug          --set-variable   --verbose
--help           --silent         --version
```

The `--silent` option means that only error messages are printed. The `--verbose` option prints more information when given with the `--description` or `--extend-check` options for either program, or when given with the `--check` option for `myisamchk`. The `--silent` and `--verbose` options may be specified multiple times for increased effect.

Options Common to `isamchk` and `myisamchk`

`isamchk` and `myisamchk` have many options in common:

- `-a`, `--analyze`

  Performs key distribution analysis. This can help the server perform index-based lookups and joins more quickly. You can obtain information about key distribution after the analysis by running `isamchk` or `myisamchk` again with the `--description` and `--verbose` options.

- `-b` *n*, `--block-search=n`

  Prints out the start of the table row that contains a block starting at block *n*. This is for debugging only.

- `-d`, `--description`

  Prints descriptive information about the table.

- `-e`, `--extend-check`

  Performs an extended table check. It should rarely be necessary to use this option because `myisamchk` and `isamchk` should find any errors with one of the less extensive checking modes.

- `-f`, `--force`

  Forces a table to be checked or repaired even if a temporary file for the table already exists. Normally, `myisamchk` and `isamchk` simply exit after printing an error message if they find a file *tbl_name*.`TMD` because that may indicate another instance of the program is already running. However, the file may also exist if you killed a previous invocation of the program while it was running, in which case the file may be removed safely. If you know that to be the case, use `--force` to tell either utility to run even if the temporary file exists. (Alternatively, you can remove the temporary file manually.)

  If you use `--force` when checking tables, the program automatically restarts with `--recover` for any table found to have problems.

- `-i, --information`

  Prints statistical information about table contents.

- `-k n, --keys-used=n`

  Used with `--recover`. Tells MySQL to update only the first *n* indexes. In other words, this de-activates indexes numbered higher than *n*. This option can be used to improve the performance of `INSERT`, `DELETE`, and `UPDATE` operations. Specifying an index number of 0 turns off all indexes. Specifying an index number equal to the highest-numbered index turns all indexing back on.

- `-l, --no-symlinks`

  If a table argument is a symbolic link, normally the table the symlink points to is repaired. When this option is specified, symlinks are not followed. Instead the symlink is *replaced* with the new (repaired) version of the file.

- `-q, --quick`

  This option is used in conjunction with `--recover` for faster repair than when `--recover` is used alone. The data file is not touched when both options are given. To force the program to modify the data file even if duplicate key values are found, specify the `--quick` option twice. If you use this option twice, be sure you have a backup of the data file first.

- `-r, --recover`

  Performs a normal recovery operation. This can fix most problems except duplicate values that are found in an index that should be unique.

- `-o, --safe-recover`

  Uses a recovery method that is slower than the `--recover` method, but that can fix a few problems that `--recover` cannot.

- `-S, --sort-index`

  Sorts the index blocks to speed up sequential block reads.

- `-R n, --sort-records=n`

  Sorts data records according to the order in which records are listed in index *n*. Subsequent retrievals based on the given index should be faster. The first time you perform this operation on a table, it may be very slow because your records will be unordered.

- `-u, --unpack`

  Unpacks a packed file. `myisamchk` can unpack MyISAM files packed with `myisampack`; `isamchk` can unpack ISAM files packed with `pack_isam`. This option can be used to convert a compressed read-only table to modifiable form.

- -w, --wait

  If a table is locked, waits until it is available. Without --wait, the program will wait 10 seconds for a lock and then print an error message if no lock can be obtained.

Options Specific to myisamchk

Although there are no options specific to isamchk, there are several specific to myisamchk.

- -c, --check

  Checks tables for errors. This is the default action if no options are specified.

- -D n, --data-file-length=n

  Specifies the maximum length to which the data file should be allowed to grow when rebuilding a data file that has become full. (This occurs when a file reaches the size limit imposed by MySQL or by the file size constraints of your operating system. It also occurs when the number of rows reaches the limit imposed by internal table data structures.) The value is specified in bytes. This option is effective only when used with --recover or --safe-recover.

- -F, --fast

  Does not check tables that have not been modified since they were last checked.

- -m, --medium-check

  Checks a table using a method that is faster than extended-check, but slightly less thorough. (The myisamchk help message says that this method finds "only" 99.99% of all errors.) This checking mode should be sufficient for most circumstances. Medium check mode works by calculating CRC values for the keys in the index and compares them with the CRC values calculated from the indexed columns in the data file.

- -T, --read-only

  Does not mark the table as having been checked.

- -A [n], --set-auto-increment[=n]

  Forces AUTO_INCREMENT values to start at n (or at a higher value if the table already contains records with AUTO_INCREMENT values as large as n). If no value is specified, this option sets the next AUTO_INCREMENT to one greater than the current maximum value.

- -t path_name, --tmpdir=path_name

  Specifies the pathname of the directory to use for temporary files. The default is the value of the TMPDIR environment variable or /tmp if that variable is not set.

Variables for `isamchk` and `myisamchk`

The following `isamchk` and `myisamchk` variables can be set with the `--set-variable` option:

- `key_buffer_size`

  The size of the buffer used for index blocks.

- `read_buffer_size`

  The read buffer size.

- `write_buffer_size`

  The write buffer size.

- `sort_buffer_size`

  The size of the buffer used for key value sorting operations. (This is used for `--recover`, but not for `--safe-recover`.)

- `sort_key_blocks`

  This variable is related to the depth of the B-tree structure used for the index. You should not need to change it.

- `decode_bits`

  The number of bits to use when decoding compressed tables. Larger values may result in faster operation but will require more memory. Generally, the default value is sufficient.

`myisampack` and `pack_isam`

The `myisampack` and `pack_isam` utilities produce compressed, read-only tables. They achieve typical storage requirement reductions of 40 to 70 percent while maintaining fast record access. `myisampack` packs MyISAM tables and works with all column types. `pack_isam` packs ISAM tables and works only with tables that contain no BLOB or TEXT columns.

`myisampack` and `pack_isam` are not included with MySQL by default but are available to customers that order 10 or more licenses or that have a support agreement at the extended support level or higher. This may change so that the programs are available under the same terms as the rest of the MySQL distribution. (See the MySQL Reference Manual for current support and licensing information.)

No special version of MySQL is needed to read tables that have been packed with these utilities. This makes them especially applicable for applications for which you wish to distribute a table containing archival or encyclopedic information that is read-only and need not be updated. If you want to convert a packed file back to unpacked and modifiable form, you can do so by using `myisamchk --unpack` (for MyISAM tables) or `isamchk --unpack` (for ISAM tables).

`myisampack` and `isam_pack` pack data files, but do not touch index files. To update the indexes, run `myisamchk -rq` after running `myisampack` or `isamchk -rq` after running `pack_isam`.

Usage

```
myisampack [options] tbl_name ...
pack_isam [options] tbl_name ...
```

A `tbl_name` argument can be either the name of a table or the name of the index file for the table (a `.MYI` file for MyISAM tables and an `.ISM` file for ISAM tables). Specify the pathname to the directory in which the table is located if you are not in that directory.

Standard Options Supported by `myisampack` and `pack_isam`

`--debug`	`--silent`	`--version`
`--help`	`--verbose`	

Options Common to `myisampack` and `pack_isam`

- `-b, --backup`

  Tells `myisampack` or `pack_isam` to make a backup of each `tbl_name` argument as `tbl_name.OLD` before packing it.

- `-f, --force`

  Forces a table to be packed even if the resulting packed file is larger than the original or if a temporary file for the table already exists. Normally, `myisampack` or `pack_isam` simply exit after printing an error message if they find a file `tbl_name.TMD` because that may indicate that another instance of the program is already running. However, the file may also exist if you killed a previous invocation of the program while it was running, in which case the file may be removed safely. If you know that to be the case, use `--force` to tell either utility to pack the table even if the temporary file exists.

- `-j join_tbl, --join=join_tbl`

  Joins (merges) all the tables named on the command line into a single packed table—`join_tbl`. All the tables to be merged must have the same structure. (Column names, types, and indexes must be identical.)

- `-t, --test`

  Runs in test mode. A packing test is run, and information is printed about the results you would obtain if you actually packed the table.

- -T *path_name*, --tmpdir=*path_name*

  Specifies the pathname of the directory to use for temporary files.

- -w, --wait

  Waits and retries if a table is in use. You don't want to pack a table if it might be updated while you're packing it.

Options Specific to `pack_isam`

Although there are no options specific to `myisampack`, there is one specific to `pack_isam`, -p *n*, --packlength=*n*. This option tells `pack_isam` to use a record length storage size of *n* bytes, where n is an integer from 1 to 3. `pack_isam` automatically attempts to determine the number of bytes needed to record the length of each record in the packed table. In some cases, it may determine that a smaller length could have been used. If so, `pack_isam` issues a message to that effect. You can run `pack_isam` again and explicitly specify the smaller length with a --packlength option to achieve some additional space savings.

mysql

The `mysql` client is an interactive program that allows you to connect to the server, issue queries, and view the results. `mysql` may also be used in batch mode to execute queries that are stored in a file if you redirect the input of the command to read from that file. For example:

```
% mysql -u paul -p -h pit-viper.snake.net samp_db < my_query_file
```

In interactive mode, when `mysql` starts up, it displays a prompt 'mysql>' to indicate that it's waiting for input. To issue a query, type it in (using multiple lines if necessary) and then indicate the end of the query by typing ';' (semicolon) or '\g'. `mysql` sends the query to the server, displays the results, and then prints another prompt to indicate that it's ready for another query.

`mysql` varies the prompt to indicate what it's waiting for as you enter input lines:

mysql>	Waiting for the first line of a new query
->	Waiting for the next line of the current query
'>	Waiting for completion of a single-quoted string in current query
">	Waiting for completion of a double-quoted string in current query

The ''>' and '">' prompts indicate that you've begun a single-quoted or double-quoted string on a previous line and have not yet entered the terminating quote. Usually, this happens when you've forgotten to terminate a string. If that's the case, to escape from string-collection mode, enter the appropriate matching quote that is indicated by the prompt, followed by '\c' to cancel the current query.

When `mysql` is used in interactive mode, it saves queries in a history file. This file is `$HOME/.mysql_history` by default or may be specified explicitly by setting the `MYSQL_HISTORY` environment variable. Queries may be recalled from the command history and re-issued, either with or without further editing. The following list shows some of these editing commands (the arrow keys may not work under Windows):

Key Sequence	Meaning
Up arrow, Ctrl-P	Recall previous line
Down arrow, Ctrl-N	Recall next line
Left arrow, Ctrl-B	Move cursor left (backward)
Right arrow, Ctrl-F	Move cursor right (forward)
Escape Ctrl-B	Move backward one word
Escape Ctrl-F	Move forward one word
Ctrl-A	Move cursor to beginning of line
Ctrl-E	Move cursor to end of line
Ctrl-D	Delete character under cursor
Delete	Delete character to left of cursor
Escape D	Delete word
Escape Backspace	Delete word to left of cursor
Ctrl-K	Erase everything from cursor to end of line
Ctrl-_	Undo last change; may be repeated

Some options suppress use of the history file. Generally, these are options that indicate non-interactive use of `mysql`, such as `--batch`, `--html`, and `--quick`.

Usage

```
mysql [options] [db_name]
```

If you specify a *db_name* argument, that database becomes the current (default) database for your session. If you specify no *db_name* argument, `mysql` starts with no current database and you'll need to either qualify all table references with a database name or issue a USE *db_name* statement to specify a default database.

Standard Options Supported by `mysql`

`--compress`	`--password`	`--silent`	`--version`
`--debug`	`--pipe`	`--socket`	
`--help`	`--port`	`--user`	
`--host`	`--set-variable`	`--verbose`	

`--silent` and `--verbose` may be specified multiple times for increased effect.

Options Specific to `mysql`

- `-B, --batch`

  Specifies that `mysql` should run in batch mode. Query results are displayed in tab-delimited format (each row on a separate line with tabs between column values). This is especially convenient for generating output that you want to import into another program, such as a spreadsheet. Query results include an initial row of column headings by default. To suppress these headings, use the `--skip-column-names` option.

- `-T, --debug-info`

  Prints debugging information when the program terminates.

- `-e query, --execute=query`

  Executes the query and quits. You should enclose the query in quotes to prevent the shell from interpreting it as multiple command-line arguments. Multiple queries may be specified by separating them with a semicolons in the *query* string.

- `-f, --force`

  Normally when `mysql` reads queries from a file, it exits if an error occurs. This option causes `mysql` to keep processing queries, regardless of errors.

- `-H, --html`

  Produces HTML output. This option became functional in MySQL 3.22.26.

- `-i, --ignore-space`

  Instructs the server to ignore spaces between function names and the '(' character that introduces the argument list. Normally, function names must be followed immediately by the parenthesis with no intervening spaces.

- `-A, --no-auto-rehash`

  When `mysql` starts up, it hashes database, table, and column names to construct a data structure that allows for fast completion of names. (You can type the initial part of a name when entering a query and then press Tab; `mysql` will complete the name unless it's ambiguous.) This option suppresses hash calculation, which allows `mysql` to start up more quickly, particularly if you have many tables. If you want to use name completion after starting `mysql`, you can use the `rehash` command at the 'mysql>' prompt.

- `-o, --one-database`

  This option is used when updating databases from the contents of an update log file. It tells `mysql` to update only the default database (the database named on the command line). Updates to other databases are ignored. If no database is named on the command line, no updates are performed.

- -q, --quick

  Normally mysql retrieves the entire result of a query from the server before displaying it. This option causes each row to be displayed as it is retrieved, which uses much less memory and may allow some large queries to be performed successfully that would fail otherwise. However, this option should not be specified for interactive use; if the user pauses the output or suspends mysql, the server continues to wait, which can interfere with other clients.

- -r, --raw

  Writes column values without escaping any special characters. This option is used in conjunction with the --batch option.

- -N, --skip-column-names

  Suppresses display of column names as column headers in query results. You can also achieve this effect by specifying the --silent option twice.

- -L, --skip-line-numbers

  Does not write line numbers when errors occur.

- -t, --table

  Produces output in tabular format, with values in each row delimited by bars and lined up vertically.

- -n, --unbuffered

  Flushes the buffer used for communication with the server after each query.

- -E, --vertical

  Prints query results vertically—that is, with each row of a result set displayed as a set of lines, one line per column. Each line consists of a column name and value. The display for each row is preceded by a line indicating the row number within the result set. Vertical display format may be useful when a query produces very long lines.

  If this option is not specified, you can turn on vertical display format for individual queries by terminating them with '\G' rather than with ';' or '\g'.

  This option was introduced in MySQL 3.22.5.

- -w, --wait

  If a connection to the server cannot be established, wait and retry.

Variables for mysql

The following mysql variables can be set with the --set-variable option:

- max_allowed_packet

  The maximum size of the buffer used for communication between the server and the client.

- net_buffer_length

  The initial size of the buffer used for communication between the server and the client. This buffer may be expanded up to max_allowed_packet bytes long.

mysql **Commands**

mysql understands several commands itself in addition to allowing you to send SQL statements to the MySQL server. Each command must be given on a single line; no semicolon is necessary at the end of the line. Most of the commands have a long form, consisting of a word, and a short form, consisting of a backslash followed by a single letter. Commands in long form are not case sensitive. Commands in short form must be specified using the lettercase shown in the following list:

- clear, \c

  Clears (cancels) the current query. The current query is the query that you are in the process of typing in; this command does not cancel a query that has already been sent to the server and for which mysql is displaying output.

- connect [*db_name* [*host_name*]], \r [*db_name* [*host_name*]]

  Connects to the given database on the given host. If the database name or hostname is missing, the most recently used values from the current mysql session are used.

- edit, \e

  Edits the current query. The editor to use is determined by the value of the EDITOR and VISUAL environment variables—or vi if neither of them is set.

- ego, \G

  Sends the current query to the server and displays the result vertically. This command was introduced in MySQL 3.22.11.

- exit

  Same as quit.

- go, \g, ;

  Sends the current query to the server and displays the result.

- help, \h, ?

  Displays a help message describing the available mysql commands.

- print, \p

  Prints the current query (the text of the query itself, not the results obtained by executing the query).

- quit, \q

  Quits mysql.

- rehash, \#

  Recalculates the information needed for database, table, and column name completion. See the description for the --no-auto-rehash option.

- status, \s

  Retrieves and displays status information from the server. This is useful if you want to check the server version and current database.

- use *db_name*, \u *db_name*

  Selects the given database to make it the current database.

mysql.server

mysql.server is a script that starts and stops the mysqld server by invoking safe_mysqld.

Usage

```
mysql.server start
mysqlserver stop
```

Normally, mysql.server is used on a System V style system and is installed in one of the runtime directories under the /etc directory. The system starts the server by invoking the script with an argument of start at system boot time. The system shuts down the server by invoking the script with an argument of stop at system shutdown time. The script also can be invoked by hand with the appropriate argument to start up or shut down the server.

mysqlaccess

This script allows you to connect to a server, retrieve access privilege information, and test the result of specifying user privileges. It does this using copies of the user, db, and host tables from the mysql database. (mysqlaccess cannot be used to experiment with table or column privileges, however.) You can also commit changes you make to the temporary tables back into the actual tables in the mysql database.

To use mysqlaccess, you must have sufficient privileges to access the grant tables yourself.

Usage

```
mysqlaccess [host_name [user_name [db_name]]] options
```

Standard Options Supported by `mysqlaccess`

--host   --password   --user   --version

Options Specific to `mysqlaccess`

- -b, --brief

  Displays results in single-line format.

- --commit

  Copies the temporary grant tables back to the `mysql` database. Be sure to execute a `mysqladmin flush-privileges` command afterward so that the server notices the changes.

- --copy

  Loads the grant tables into the temporary tables.

- -d *db_name*, --db=*db_name*

  Specifies the database name.

- --debug=*n*

  Specifies the debugging level. *n* should be an integer from 0 to 3.

- --howto

  Displays some examples demonstrating how to use `mysqlaccess`.

- --old_server

  Specifies that the server is older than MySQL 3.21. This causes `mysqlaccess` to make certain adjustments to the queries that it sends to the server.

- --plan

  Displays a list of enhancements planned for future releases of `mysqlaccess`.

- --preview

  Displays the privilege differences between the actual and temporary grant tables.

- --relnotes

  Prints the `mysqlaccess` release notes.

- -H *host_name*, --rhost=*host_name*

  Specifies the remote server host to connect to.

- --rollback

  Undoes the changes made to the temporary grant tables.

- -P *password*, --spassword=*password*

  Specifies the password for the MySQL superuser (a user with sufficient privileges to modify the grant tables).

- -U *user_name*, --superuser=*user_name*

  Specifies the username for the MySQL superuser.

- -t, --table

  Displays results in tabular format.

mysqladmin

The mysqladmin utility communicates with the MySQL server to perform a variety of administrative operations. You can use mysqladmin to obtain information from or control the operation of the server, set passwords, and create or drop databases.

Usage

```
mysqladmin [options] command ...
```

Standard Options Supported by mysqladmin

--compress	--host	--port	--user
--debug	--password	--silent	--version
--help	--pipe	--socket	

--silent causes mysqladmin to exit silently if it cannot connect to the server.

Options Specific to mysqladmin

- -f, --force

  This option has two effects. First, it causes mysqladmin not to ask for confirmation of the drop *db_name* command. Second, when multiple commands are specified on the command line, mysqladmin attempts to execute each command even if errors occur. Normally, mysqladmin will exit after the first error.

- --relative

  Shows the difference between the current and previous values when used with --sleep. Currently, this option works only with the extended-status command.

- -i *n*, --sleep=*n*

  Executes the commands named on the command line repeatedly with a delay of *n* seconds between each repetition.

- `-t` *n*, `--timeout=`*n*

  Waits *n* seconds before timing out when attempting to connect to the server. This option was introduced in MySQL 3.22.1.

- `-w` [*n*], `--wait`[`=`*n*]

  Specifies the number of times to wait and retry if a connection to the server cannot be established. The default value of *n* is 1 if no value is specified.

mysqladmin **Commands**

Following any options on the command line, you may specify one or more of the following commands. The command name may be shortened to a prefix, as long as the prefix is unique. For example, `processlist` may be shortened to `process` or `proc`, but not to `p`.

Several of these commands have an equivalent SQL statement. These are noted in the descriptions. For more information about the meaning of the SQL statements, see Appendix D, "SQL Syntax Reference."

- `create` *db_name*

  Creates a new database with the given name.

  This command is like the `CREATE DATABASE` *db_name* SQL statement.

- `drop` *db_name*

  Deletes the database with the given name, and any tables that may be in the database. Be careful with this command; you can't get the database back. `mysqladmin` asks for confirmation of this command unless the `--force` option was given.

  This command is like the `DROP DATABASE` *db_name* SQL statement.

- `extended-status`

  Displays the names and values of the server's status variables.

  This command is like the `SHOW STATUS` SQL statement.

  The `extended-status` command was introduced in MySQL 3.22.10.

- `flush-hosts`

  Flushes the host cache.

  This command is like the `FLUSH HOSTS` SQL statement.

- `flush-logs`

  Flushes (closes and reopens) the log files.

  This command is like the `FLUSH LOGS` SQL statement.

- `flush-privileges`

  Reloads the grant tables.

  This command is like the FLUSH PRIVILEGES SQL statement.

- `flush-status`

  Clears the status variables. (This resets several counters to zero.)

  This command is like the FLUSH STATUS SQL statement.

- `flush-tables`

  Flushes the table cache.

  This command is like the FLUSH TABLES SQL statement.

- `kill id,id,...`

  Kills the server threads specified by the given identifier numbers. If you specify multiple numbers, the ID list should contain no spaces so that it will not be confused for another command following the `kill` command. To find out what threads are currently running, use `mysqladmin processlist`.

  This command is like issuing a KILL SQL statement for each thread ID.

- `password new_password`

  Changes the password for the MySQL user that you connect to the server as when you run the `mysqladmin` command. The new password is `new_password`. You must be able to connect to the server as the MySQL user whose password is being changed, which serves as verification that you know the user's old password.

  This command is like the SET PASSWORD SQL statement.

  The `password` command was introduced in MySQL 3.22.

- `ping`

  Checks whether or not the MySQL server is running.

- `processlist`

  Displays a list of the currently executing server threads.

  This command is like the SHOW PROCESSLIST SQL statement.

- `refresh`

  Flushes the table cache and closes and reopens the log files.

- `reload`

  Reloads the grant tables.

  This command is like the FLUSH PRIVILEGES SQL statement.

- shutdown

  Tells the server to shut down.

- status

  Displays a short status message from the server.

- variables

  Displays the names and values of the server's variables.

  This command is like the SHOW VARIABLES SQL statement.

- version

  Retrieves and displays the server version information string.

mysqlbug

Chapter 2 of the MySQL Reference Manual contains a detailed procedure for filing a bug report. Following that procedure helps ensure that your report will be helpful and will contain sufficient information to resolve the problem you're reporting. A key part of this procedure is to use the mysqlbug script. It's used to create and send a bug report to the MySQL mailing list when you discover a problem with MySQL. mysqlbug gathers information about your system and MySQL configuration and then drops you into an editor containing the contents of the mail message to be sent. Edit the message to add as much information as you can about the problem you are reporting, and then write out the message to save your changes and exit the editor. mysqlbug will ask you whether or not to send the report and then mails it if you confirm.

Please use mysqlbug to report bugs, but don't use it lightly. In many cases, a "bug" isn't a bug at all or is a report of something that has already been documented in the Reference Manual. For example, it's been reported as a bug several times that the statement DELETE FROM *tbl_name* reports a rows-affected value of zero. That's true, but it's the intended behavior. It's also documented in the manual as such, as is the query to use instead if you want the true count. The MySQL mailing list archives are another useful source of information. Links to these can be found at http://www.mysql.com/doc.html.

Usage

```
mysqlbug [address]
```

The bug report is sent to the MySQL mailing list by default. If you specify an email address on the command line, the report is sent to that address instead. You can specify your own address to try out mysqlbug without sending the report to the mailing list; that's not a bad idea when you're first using the script and are perhaps not quite sure how it works.

mysqld

`mysqld` is the MySQL server. It provides database access to client programs, so it must be running or clients cannot use databases administered by the server. When `mysqld` starts up, it opens network ports to listen on and then waits for client connections. `mysqld` is multi-threaded and processes each client connection using a separate thread to provide concurrency among clients. Queries that write to the database are executed atomically; when the server begins executing such a query, it will execute no other query for the table involved until the current query has finished. For this reason, no two clients can ever modify the same row in a table at the same time.

Usage

```
mysqld [options]
```

Standard Options Supported by `mysqld`

--debug	--port	--user
--help	--socket	--version

Note that although `--socket` is supported, `-S` is not because the server uses the `-Sg` option with a meaning unrelated to the socket file.

If the `--user` option is given, it specifies the user name of the account to use for running the server. In this case, when the server starts up, it looks up the user and group ID values of the account from the password file and then changes its user and group IDs to match. In this way, the server runs with the privileges associated with that user, not `root` privileges. (The server must be started as `root` for the `--user` option to be effective; it will not be able to change its user ID otherwise.) This option was introduced in MySQL 3.22.

Options Specific to `mysqld`

- `-b path_name`, `--basedir=path_name`

  Specifies the pathname to the MySQL installation directory. Many other pathnames are resolved beginning at this directory if they are given as relative pathnames.

- `--big-tables`

  Allows large result sets to be processed by saving all temporary results to disk rather than by holding them in memory. This avoids most "table full" messages that occur as a result of having insufficient memory to hold large result sets. This option is no longer needed as of MySQL 3.23.

- `--bind-address=ip_addr`

  Binds to the given IP address. Normally, `mysqld` binds to the default IP address for the host on which the server is running. This option can be used to select an alternative address to bind to if the host has multiple addresses.

- `--bootstrap`

  This option is used by installation scripts when you first install MySQL.

- `--chroot=path_name`

  Runs the MySQL server anchored to a special root directory. The option specifies the pathname to that directory. See the `chroot()` UNIX manual page for more information on running in a `chroot()`-ed environment. This option was introduced in MySQL 3.22.2.

- `-h path_name, --datadir=path_name`

  Specifies the pathname to the MySQL data directory.

- `--default-table-type=type`

  Specifies the default table storage type. The `type` value should be `isam`, `myisam`, or `heap`. (The value is not case sensitive.) The default if this option is not specified is to use MyISAM tables. This option was introduced in MySQL 3.23.

- `--enable-locking`

  Enables external locking (file system locking) for systems such as Linux, where the default is `--skip-locking`. This option was introduced in MySQL 3.22.4.

- `-T [n], --exit-info[=n]`

  Prints debugging information when the program terminates. This option was introduced in MySQL 3.22.

- `--init-file=file_name`

  Specifies a file of SQL statements to be executed at startup time.

- `-L, --language=lang_name`

  Displays error messages to clients in the specified language. Normally, `lang_name` will be a value such as `english` or `german`.

- `-l [path_name], --log[=path_name]`

  Turns on logging to the general log file. The general log contains information about client connections and queries. If `path_name` is not given, the log file name is `host_name.log`, where `host_name` is the name of the server host. If `path_name` is given as a relative path, it is interpreted starting at the data directory.

- `--log-isam[=file_name]`

  Enables index file logging. This is used only for debugging ISAM/MyISAM operations.

- `--log-long-format`

  Writes additional information to the update log. This option was introduced in MySQL 3.22.7.

- `--log-update[=path_name]`

  Turns on logging to the update log file. The update log contains the text of any query that modifies database tables. If *path_name* is not given, the update log file name is *host_name.nnn*, where *host_name* is the name of the server host and *nnn* is a sequence number one greater than that of the previous update log.

  If *path_name* is given and the final component contains no extension, the server adds a numeric extension of the form *nnn* with a value as previously described. If the final component of the pathname includes an extension, that name is used without modification as the update log filename. If *path_name* is given as a relative path, it is interpreted starting at the data directory.

- `--low-priority-updates`

  Gives write operations lower priority than retrievals. This option was introduced in MySQL 3.23. (It was called `--low-priority-inserts` from MySQL 3.22.5 until MySQL 3.23.)

- `-n, --new`

  Uses new, possibly unsafe routines. These are features in MySQL that are not yet declared stable. This option should be used only if you are feeling adventurous.

- `-o, --old-protocol`

  Uses the protocol that was used for client/server communications prior to MySQL 3.21. This option may be needed if the server communicates with very old client programs.

- `--one-thread`

  Runs using a single thread; used for debugging under Linux, which normally uses three threads at a minimum. This option was introduced in MySQL 3.22.2.

- `--pid-file=path_name`

  When `mysqld` starts up, it writes its process ID (PID) into a file. This option specifies the pathname of the PID file. The file may be used by other processes to determine the server's process number, typically for purposes of sending a signal. For example, `mysql.server` reads the file when it sends a signal to the server to shut down.

- `--safe-mode`

  This option is like `--skip-new`, but disables even more things. You can try it if MySQL appears to be unstable or if complex queries seem to yield incorrect results. If using this option improves server operation, please note that fact when you use `mysqlbug` to report the problems you encounter.

- -Sg, --skip-grant-tables

  Does not use the grant tables to verify client connections. This gives any client full access to do anything. You can tell the server to begin using the grant tables by issuing a mysqladmin flush-privileges command.

- --skip-host-cache

  Disables use of the hostname cache.

- --skip-locking

  Suppresses use of system locking (file system locking). If you use this option, you must shut down the server before using isamchk or myisamchk to repair tables or you risk damaging them.

- --skip-name-resolve

  Does not try to resolve hostnames. If this option is specified, the grant tables must specify hosts by IP number or as localhost.

- --skip-networking

  Does not allow TCP/IP connections. Clients must connect from the local host using localhost.

- --skip-new

  Does not use new, possibly unsafe routines. See --new.

- --skip-show-database

  Does not allow unprivileged users to issue SHOW DATABASES queries or to use SHOW TABLES on databases for which they have no access. This option was introduced in MySQL 3.23.

- --skip-thread-priority

  Normally, queries that modify tables run at a higher priority than those that retrieve data. If that is undesirable, this option causes the server not to give different types of queries different priorities.

- -t path_name, --tmpdir=path_name

  Specifies the pathname of the directory to use for temporary files. This option was introduced in MySQL 3.22.4.

Windows-specific options are as follows:

- --console

  Displays a console window for error messages. This option was introduced in MySQL 3.22.4.

- --flush

  Flushes all tables to disk after each update. This reduces the risk of table corruption in the event of a crash but seriously degrades performance. This option was introduced in MySQL 3.22.9.

- `--install`

  Installs `mysqld-nt` as a service (Windows NT only).

- `--remove`

  Removes `mysqld-nt` as a service (Windows NT only).

- `--standalone`

  Starts `mysqld-nt` as a standalone program rather than as a service (Windows NT only).

Variables for `mysqld`

To see what values `mysqld` will use by default, use this command:

```
% mysqld --help
```

To see what values the currently executing `mysqld` is using, use this command:

```
% mysqladmin variables
```

You can also check the current variable values by issuing a `SHOW VARIABLES` query. The `mysqld` variables that can be set with the `--set-variable` option are shown in the following list:

- `back_log`

  The number of pending connection requests that can be queued while current connections are being processed.

- `connect_timeout`

  The number of seconds that `mysqld` will wait for packets during the initial connection handshake.

- `delayed_insert_timeout`

  When the handler for `INSERT DELAYED` operations finishes inserting queued rows, it waits this many seconds to see if any new `INSERT DELAYED` rows arrive. If so, it handles them; otherwise, it terminates.

- `delayed_insert_limit`

  The number of rows from `INSERT DELAYED` statements that will be inserted into a table before checking whether any new `SELECT` statements for the table have arrived. If any have, the insert operation is suspended to allow retrievals to execute.

- `delayed_queue_size`

  The number of rows that may be queued for `INSERT DELAYED` statements. If the queue is full, further `INSERT DELAYED` statements block until there is room in the queue.

- flush_time

  If this variable has a non-zero value, tables are closed to flush pending changes to disk every flush_time seconds. The default value for Windows is 30 minutes; use the --flush option to change this.

- join_buffer_size

  The size of the full-join buffer (that is, the buffer for joins that are performed without use of indexes).

  This was called join_buffer prior to MySQL 3.23.

- key_buffer_size

  The size of the buffer used for index blocks. This buffer is shared among connection-handler threads.

  This was called key_buffer prior to MySQL 3.23.

- long_query_time

  The number of seconds that defines a "slow" query. Any query taking longer than this causes the Slow_queries counter to be incremented.

- max_allowed_packet

  The maximum size of the buffer used for communication between the server and the client. The buffer is initially allocated to be net_buffer_length bytes long but may grow up to max_allowed_packet bytes as necessary.

- max_connections

  The maximum number of simultaneous client connections allowed.

- max_connect_errors

  The number of failed connections from a host that are allowed before the host is blocked from further connection attempts. This is done on the basis that someone may be attempting to break in from that host. The FLUSH HOSTS statement or mysqladmin flush-hosts command may be used to clear the host cache to re-enable blocked hosts.

- max_delayed_insert_threads

  The maximum number of handlers that will be initiated to handle INSERT DELAYED statements. Any such statements that are received while the maximum number of handlers is already in use will be treated as non-DELAYED statements.

- max_join_size

  The MySQL optimizer estimates how many rows a join will return. If the estimate exceeds max_join_size rows, an error is returned. This can be used if users tend to write indiscriminate SELECT queries that return an inordinate number of rows.

- max_sort_length

  BLOB or TEXT values are sorted using the first max_sort_length bytes of each value.

- net_buffer_length

  The initial size of the buffer used for communication between the server and the client. This buffer may be expanded up to max_allowed_packet bytes long.

- record_buffer

  The size of the buffer used by threads that perform sequential table scans.

- sort_buffer

  The size of the buffer used by threads for performing sort operations (GROUP BY or ORDER BY). This value is per thread. Normally, if you may have many threads that do sorting at the same time, it is unwise to make this value very large (more than 1MB).

- table_cache

  The maximum number of tables that can be open. This cache is shared between threads.

- tmp_table_size

  The maximum number of bytes allowed for temporary tables. If a table exceeds this size, mysqld returns an error to the client.

- thread_stack

  The stack size for each thread.

- wait_timeout

  The number of seconds a connection can remain idle before the server closes it

mysqldump

The mysqldump program writes the contents of database tables into text files. These files may be used for a variety of purposes, such as database backups, moving databases to another server, or setting up a test database based on the contents of an existing database.

By default, output for each dumped table consists of a CREATE TABLE statement that re-creates the table, followed by a set of INSERT statements that reload the contents of the table. If the --tab option is given, table contents are written to a data file in raw format, and the table creation SQL statement is written to a separate file.

Usage

```
mysqldump [options] db_name [tbl_name] ...
```

If no tables are named following the database name db_name, all tables in the database are dumped. Otherwise, only the named tables are dumped.

The most common way to use `mysqldump` is as follows:

```
% mysqldump --opt db_name > backup_file
```

Standard Options Supported by `mysqldump`

--compress	--host	--port	--user
--debug	--password	--set-variable	--verbose
--help	--pipe	--socket	--version

Options Specific to `mysqldump`

The following options control how `mysqldump` operates. The next section, "Data Format Options," describes options that may be used in conjunction with the `--tab` option to indicate the format of data files.

- `--add-drop-table`

  Adds a `DROP TABLE IF EXISTS` statement before each `CREATE TABLE` statement.

- `--add-locks`

  Adds `LOCK TABLE` and `UNLOCK TABLE` around the set of `INSERT` statements that load the data for each table.

- `--allow-keywords`

  Allows for the creation of column names that are keywords.

- `-c, --complete-insert`

  Uses `INSERT` statements that name each column to be inserted.

- `--delayed-insert`

  Writes `INSERT DELAYED` statements.

- `-e, --extended-insert`

  Writes multiple-row `INSERT` statements.

- `-F, --flush-logs`

  Flushes the server log files before starting the dump.

- `-f, --force`

  Continues even if errors occur.

- `--full`

  Adds additional information to the `CREATE TABLE` statements that `mysqldump` generates, such as the table type, beginning `AUTO_INCREMENT` value, and so forth. This is the information that you can specify in the `table_options` part of the `CREATE TABLE` syntax. (see Appendix D.)

- -l, --lock-tables

  Obtains lock for all tables being dumped before dumping them.

- -t, --no-create-info

  Does not write CREATE TABLE statements.

- -d, --no-data

  Does not write table data.

- --opt

  Optimizes table dumping speed and writes a dump file that is optimal for reloading speed. This option turns on --add-drop-table, --add-locks, --all, --extended-insert, --quick, and --lock-tables.

- -q, --quick

  By default, mysqldump reads the entire contents of a table into memory and then writes it out. This option causes each row to be written to the output as soon as it has been read from the server.

  If you use this option, you should not suspend mysqldump; that causes the server to wait, which can interfere with other clients.

- -T dump_dir, --tab=dump_dir

  This option causes mysqldump to write two files per table, using dump_dir as the location for the files. The directory must already exist. For each table tbl_name, a file dump_dir/table_name.txt is written containing the data from the table, and a file dump_dir/table_name.sql is written containing the CREATE TABLE statement for the table. You must have the FILE privilege to use this option.

  To avoid confusion, it is best to run mysqldump on the server host when you use this option. Otherwise, some of the files are written on the server and some are written on the client. dump_dir is used on the server host for the *.sql files and on the client host for the *.txt files. The *.sql files will be owned by the account used to run the server, and the *.txt files will be owned by you.

  By default, the data file contains newline-terminated lines consisting of tab-separated column values. This format may be changed using the options described under "Data Format Options."

- -w where_clause, --where=where_clause

  Only dumps records selected by the WHERE clause given by where_clause. You should enclose the clause in quotes to prevent the shell from interpreting it as multiple command-line arguments. This option was introduced in MySQL 3.22.7.

Data Format Options

If you specify the --tab or -T option to generate a separate data file for each table, several additional options apply. You may need to enclose the option value in appropriate quoting characters. These options are analogous to the data format options for the LOAD DATA statement. See the entry for LOAD DATA in Appendix D.

- --fields-enclosed-by=*char*

  Specifies that column values should be enclosed within the given character, usually a quote character. The default is not to enclose column values within anything.

- --fields-escaped-by=*char*

  Specifies the escape character for escaping special characters. The default is no escape character.

- --fields-optionally-enclosed-by=*char*

  Specifies that column values should be enclosed within the given character, usually a quote character. The character is used for non-numeric columns. The default is not to enclose column values within anything.

- --fields-terminated-by=*char*

  Specifies the column value separation character to use for data files. By default, values are separated by tabs.

- --lines-terminated-by=*str*

  Specifies the string (it may be multiple characters) to write at the end of output lines. The default is to write newlines.

Variables for mysqldump

The following mysqldump variables can be set with the --set-variable option:

- max_allowed_packet

  The maximum size of the buffer used for communication between the server and the client.

- net_buffer_length

  The initial size of the buffer used for communication between the server and the client. This buffer may be expanded up to max_allowed_packet bytes long.

mysqlimport

The `mysqlimport` utility is a bulk loader for reading the contents of text files into existing tables. It functions as a command-line interface to the LOAD DATA SQL statement, and is an efficient way to enter rows into tables.

Usage

```
mysqlimport [options] db_name file_name ...
```

The *db_name* argument specifies the database that contains the tables into which you want to load data. The tables to load are determined from the filename arguments. For each filename, any extension from the first period in the name is stripped off and the remaining basename is used as the name of the table into which the file should be loaded. For example, `mysqlimport` will load the contents of `president.txt` into the `president` table.

Standard Options Supported by `mysqlimport`

--compress	--host	--port	--user
--debug	--password	--silent	--verbose
--help	--pipe	--socket	--version

Options Specific to `mysqlimport`

The following options control how `mysqlimport` processes input files. The next section, "Data Format Options," describes options that may be used to indicate the format of the data in the input files.

- -d, --delete

  Empties each table before loading any data into it.

- -f, --force

  Continues loading rows even if errors occur.

- -i, --ignore

  When an input row contains a value for a unique key that already exists in the table, keeps the existing row and discards the input row.

- -L, --local

  By default, `mysqlimport` lets the server read the data file, which means that the file must be located on the server host and that you must have the FILE privilege. Specifying the --local option tells `mysqlimport` to read the data file itself and send it to the server. This is slower but works when you're running `mysqlimport` on a different machine than the server host, as well as on the server host—even if you don't have the FILE privilege.

The `--local` option was introduced in MySQL 3.22.15.

- `-l, --lock-tables`

Locks each table before loading data into it.

- `-r, --replace`

When an input row contains a value for a unique key that already exists in the table, replaces the existing row with the input row.

Data Format Options

By default, `mysqlimport` assumes that data files contain newline-terminated lines consisting of tab-separated values. The expected format may be altered using the following options. You may need to enclose the option value in appropriate quoting characters. These options are analogous to the data format options for the `LOAD DATA` statement. See the entry for `LOAD DATA` in Appendix D.

- `--fields-enclosed-by=char`

Specifies that column values are enclosed within the given character, usually a quote character. By default, values are assumed to not be enclosed by any character.

- `--fields-escaped-by=char`

Specifies the escape character used to escape special characters. The default is no escape character.

- `--fields-optionally-enclosed-by=char`

Specifies that column values may be enclosed within the given character, usually a quote character.

- `--fields-terminated-by=char`

Specifies the character that separates column values. By default, values are assumed to be separated by tabs.

- `--lines-terminated-by=str`

Specifies the string (it may be multiple characters) that terminates input lines. By default, lines are assumed to be terminated by newline characters.

mysqlshow

`mysqlshow` lists databases, tables within a database, or information about columns or indexes within a table. It acts as a command-line interface to the `SHOW` SQL statement.

Usage

```
mysqlshow [options] [db_name [tbl_name [col_name]]]
```

If no database name is specified, `mysqlshow` lists all databases on the server host. If a database name but no table name is specified, all tables in the database are listed. If database and table names are specified, but no column name is specified, it lists the columns in the table. If all the names are specified, `mysqlshow` shows information about the given column.

If the final argument contains a shell wildcard ('*' or '?'), output is limited to values that match the wildcard. '*' and '?' are treated as the '%' and '_' SQL wildcard characters for the LIKE operator.

Standard Options Supported by `mysqlshow`

--compress	--host	--port	--version
--debug	--password	--socket	
--help	--pipe	--user	

Options Specific to `mysqlshow`

- `-i, --status`

  Displays the same kind of table information displayed by the SHOW TABLE STATUS statement.

  The `--status` option was introduced in MySQL 3.23.

- `-k, --keys`

  Shows information about table indexes in addition to information about table columns. This option is meaningful only if you specify a table name.

safe_mysqld

`safe_mysqld` is a script that starts up the `mysqld` server and monitors it. If the server dies, `safe_mysqld` restarts it.

Usage

`safe_mysqld` understands the same options as `mysqld`.

C API Reference

THIS APPENDIX DESCRIBES THE C LANGUAGE application programming interface for the MySQL client library. The API consists of a set of functions for communicating with MySQL servers and accessing databases, and a set of data types used by those functions.

This appendix serves as a reference, so it includes only brief code fragments illustrating use of the client library. For complete client programs and notes on writing them, see Chapter 6, "The MySQL C API."

Compiling and Linking

At the source level, the client library is defined in the `mysql.h` header file, which your own source files can include:

```
#include <mysql.h>
```

To tell the compiler where to find this file, you may need to specify a `-I/path/to/include/dir` option. For example, if your MySQL header files are installed in `/usr/include/mysql` or `/usr/local/mysql/include`, you can compile source files by using commands that look something like this:

```
% gcc -I/usr/include/mysql -c myprog.c
% gcc -I/usr/local/mysql/include -c myprog.c
```

If you need to use other MySQL header files, they are located in the same directory as `mysql.h`. For example, `mysql_com.h` contains constants and macros for interpreting query result metadata. (`mysql_com.h` is included by `mysql.h`, so although you might want to look at it to see what's in it, you have access to it simply by including `mysql.h`.) The header files `errmsg.h` and `mysqld_error.h` contain constants for error codes.

At the object level, the client library is provided as the `mysqlclient` library. To link this library into your program, specify `-lmysqlclient` on the link command. You'll probably also need to tell the linker where to find the library using a `-L/path/to/lib/dir` option. For example:

```
% gcc -o myprog myprog.o -L/usr/lib/mysql -lmysqlclient
% gcc -o myprog myprog.o -L/usr/local/mysql/lib -lmysqlclient
```

C API Data Types

Data types for the MySQL client library are designed to represent the entities you deal with in the course of a session with the server. There are types for the connection itself, for results from a query, for a row within a result, and for metadata (descriptive information about the columns making up a result).

Note that the terms "column" and "field" are synonymous in the following discussion.

Scalar Data Types

MySQL's scalar data types represent values such as very large integers, boolean values, and field offsets.

- `my_ulonglong`

  A long integer type, used for return values of functions such as `mysql_affected_rows()`, `mysql_num_rows()`, and `mysql_insert_id()`, that return row counts or other potentially large numbers.

  To print a `my_ulonglong` value, cast it to `unsigned long` and use a format of '`%lu`'. The value will not print correctly on some systems if you don't do this.

- `my_bool`

  A boolean type, used for the return value of `mysql_change_user()` and `mysql_eof()`.

- `MYSQL_FIELD_OFFSET`

  This data type is used by the `mysql_field_tell()` and `mysql_field_seek()` functions to represent offsets within the set of `MYSQL_FIELD` structures for the current result set.

Non-Scalar Data Types

MySQL's non-scalar types represent structures or arrays. Every MYSQL and MYSQL_RES structure should be considered as a "black box." That is, you should refer only to the structure itself, not to elements within the structure. The MYSQL_ROW and MYSQL_FIELD types have no such restriction. You access them openly to obtain data and metadata returned as a result of a query.

- MYSQL

  The primary client library type is the MYSQL structure, which is used for connection handlers. A handler contains information about the state of a connection with a server. You initialize a MYSQL structure and then pass it to a connection routine to open a server session. After you've established the connection, you can use the handler to issue queries, generate result sets, get error information, and so forth.

- MYSQL_RES

  Queries such as SELECT or SHOW that return data to the client do so by means of a result set, represented as a MYSQL_RES structure. This structure contains information about the rows returned by the query.

  After you have a result set, you can call API functions to get result set data (the data values in each row of the set) or metadata (information about the result, such as how many columns there are, their types and lengths, and so forth).

- MYSQL_ROW

  The MYSQL_ROW type contains the values for one row of data, represented as an array of counted byte strings. All values are returned in string form (even numbers), except that if a value in a row is NULL, it is represented in the MYSQL_ROW structure by a C NULL pointer.

  The number of values in a row is given by mysql_num_fields(). The i-th column value in a row is given by row[i], where i ranges from 0 to mysql_num_fields(res_set)-1. (res_set is a pointer to a MYSQL_RES result set.)

  Note that the MYSQL_ROW type is already a pointer, so you declare a row variable like this:

  ```
  MYSQL_ROW row;        /* correct */
  ```

  You don't declare it like this:

  ```
  MYSQL_ROW *row;        /* incorrect */
  ```

  Values in a MYSQL_ROW type have terminating nulls, so non-binary values may be treated as null-terminated strings. However, data values that may contain binary data might contain null bytes internally and should be treated as counted strings. To get the lengths of the values in the row, call mysql_fetch_lengths() like this:

  ```
  unsigned long *length;
  length = mysql_fetch_lengths (res_set);
  ```

  The length returned by mysql_fetch_lengths() for NULL values is 0.

- MYSQL_FIELD

  The client library uses MYSQL_FIELD structures to represent metadata about the columns in the result set—one structure per column. The number of MYSQL_FIELD structures is given by mysql_num_fields(). You can access successive field structures by calling mysql_fetch_field() or move back and forth among structures with mysql_field_tell() and mysql_field_seek().

  The MYSQL_FIELD structure is useful for presenting or interpreting the contents of data rows. It looks like this:

  ```
  typedef struct st_mysql_field {
      char *name;
      char *table;
      char *def;
      enum enum_field_types type;
      unsigned int length;
      unsigned int max_length;
      unsigned int flags;
      unsigned int decimals;
  } MYSQL_FIELD;
  ```

  MYSQL_FIELD structure members have the following meanings:

  - name

    The column name, as a null-terminated string. If the column's values are calculated as the result of an expression, name is that expression in string form. If a column or expression is given a column alias, name is the alias name. For example, the following query results in name values of "my_col", "4*(my_col+1)", and "mc":

    ```
    SELECT my_col, 4*(my_col+1), my_col AS mc ...
    ```

  - table

    The name of the table that the column comes from, as a null-terminated string. If the column's values are calculated as the result of an expression, table is an empty string. For example, if you issue a query like the following, the table name for the first column (my_col) is my_tbl, whereas the table name for the second column (my_col+0) is the empty string:

    ```
    SELECT my_col, my_col+0 FROM my_tbl ...
    ```

  - def

    The default value for the column, as a null-terminated string. This member of the MYSQL_FIELD structure is set only if you call mysql_list_fields(), and is NULL otherwise. (Column default values can also be obtained by issuing a DESCRIBE *tbl_name* or SHOW FIELDS FROM *tbl_name* query and examining the result set.)

- type

  The column type. The type for a column calculated as the result of
  an expression is determined from the types of the elements in the
  expression. For example, if my_col is a VARCHAR(20) column, type is
  FIELD_TYPE_VAR_STRING, whereas type for LENGTH(my_col) is
  FIELD_TYPE_LONGLONG.

  The possible type values are listed in mysql_com.h and shown in Table F.1.

Table F.1   MYSQL_FIELD type **Member Values**

type **Value**	**Column Type**
FIELD_TYPE_BLOB	BLOB or TEXT
FIELD_TYPE_DATE	DATE
FIELD_TYPE_DATETIME	DATETIME
FIELD_TYPE_DECIMAL	DECIMAL or NUMERIC
FIELD_TYPE_DOUBLE	DOUBLE or REAL
FIELD_TYPE_ENUM	ENUM
FIELD_TYPE_FLOAT	FLOAT
FIELD_TYPE_INT24	MEDIUMINT
FIELD_TYPE_LONG	INT
FIELD_TYPE_LONGLONG	BIGINT
FIELD_TYPE_NULL	NULL
FIELD_TYPE_SET	SET
FIELD_TYPE_SHORT	SMALLINT
FIELD_TYPE_STRING	CHAR
FIELD_TYPE_TIME	TIME
FIELD_TYPE_TIMESTAMP	TIMESTAMP
FIELD_TYPE_TINY	TINYINT
FIELD_TYPE_VAR_STRING	VARCHAR
FIELD_TYPE_YEAR	YEAR

  You might see references to FIELD_TYPE_CHAR in older source files; that was a
  one-byte type that is now called FIELD_TYPE_TINY.

- length

  The length of the column, as specified in the CREATE TABLE statement used to
  create the table. The length for a column calculated as the result of an expression
  is determined from the elements in the expression.

- max_length

  The length of the longest column value actually present in the result set. For
  example, if a column in a result set contains the values "Bill," "Jack," and
  "Belvidere," max_length for the column is 9.

Because the `max_length` value can be determined only after all the rows have been seen, it is meaningful only for result sets created with `mysql_store_result()`. `max_length` is 0 for result sets created with `mysql_use_result()`.

- `flags`

  The `flags` member specifies attributes for the columns. Attributes are represented by individual bits within the `flags` value. The bits may be tested via the bitmask constants shown in Table F.2. For example, to determine whether or not a column's values are `UNSIGNED`, test the `flags` value like this:

  ```
  if (field->flags & UNSIGNED_FLAG)
      printf ("%s values are UNSIGNED\n", field->name);
  ```

Table F.2   `MYSQL_FIELD` flags **Member Values**

flags Value	Meaning
AUTO_INCREMENT_FLAG	Column has the AUTO_INCREMENT attribute
BINARY_FLAG	Column has the BINARY attribute
MULTIPLE_KEY_FLAG	Column is a part of a NON-UNIQUE index
NOT_NULL_FLAG	Column cannot contain NULL values
PRI_KEY_FLAG	Column is a part of a PRIMARY KEY
UNIQUE_KEY_FLAG	Column is a part of a UNIQUE index
UNSIGNED_FLAG	Column has the UNSIGNED attribute
ZEROFILL_FLAG	Column has the ZEROFILL attribute

A few `flags` constants indicate column types rather than column attributes; they are now deprecated because you should use `field->type` to determine the column type. Table F.3 lists these deprecated constants.

Table F.3   **Deprecated** `MYSQL_FIELD` flags **Member Values**

flags Value	Meaning
BLOB_FLAG	Column contains BLOB values
ENUM_FLAG	Column contains ENUM values
SET_FLAG	Column contains SET values
TIMESTAMP_FLAG	Column contains TIMESTAMP values

- `decimals`

  The number of decimals for numeric columns; `decimals` is zero for non-numeric columns. For example, a `DECIMAL(8,3)` column has a `decimals` value of 3, whereas a `BLOB` column has a value of 0.

Accessor Macros

mysql.h contains a few macros that allow you to test MYSQL_FIELD members more conveniently. IS_NUM() tests the type member; the others listed here test the flags member.

IS_NUM() is true (non-zero) if values in the column have a numeric type:

```
if (IS_NUM (field->type))
    printf ("Field %s is numeric\n", field->name);
```

IS_PRI_KEY() is true if the column is part of a primary key:

```
if (IS_PRI_KEY (field->flags))
    printf ("Field %s is part of primary key\n", field->name);
```

IS_NOT_NULL() is true if the column cannot contain NULL values:

```
if (IS_NOT_NULL (field->flags))
    printf ("Field %s values cannot be NULL\n", field->name);
```

IS_BLOB() is true if the column is a BLOB or TEXT. However, this macro tests the deprecated flags member BLOB_FLAG bit, so IS_BLOB() is deprecated as well.

C API Functions

The client library functions may be classified into the following categories:

- Connection management routines to establish and terminate connections to the server
- Status and error-reporting routines to get error codes and messages
- Query construction and execution routines to construct queries and send them to the server
- Result set processing routines to handle results from queries that return data
- Information routines that provide information about the client, server, protocol version, and the current connection
- Administration routines for controlling server operation
- Debugging routines to generate debugging information
- Deprecated routines that now are considered obsolete

Client library functions within each of these categories are described in detail in the following sections, listed alphabetically within category. Certain parameters appear recurrently in the function descriptions and have a standard meaning:

- conn is a pointer to the MYSQL connection handler for a server connection.
- res_set is a pointer to a MYSQL_RES result set structure.
- field is a pointer to a MYSQL_FIELD column information structure.
- row is a MYSQL_ROW data row from a result set.

For brevity, where these parameters are not mentioned in the descriptions of functions in which they occur, you may assume the meanings just given.

Unless otherwise indicated, you may assume any given function is present in the client library at least as far back as MySQL 3.21.0.

Connection Management Routines

These functions allow you to establish and terminate connections to a server, to set options affecting the way connection establishment occurs, and to re-establish connections that have timed out.

- `my_bool`

  `mysql_change_user` `(MYSQL *conn, char *user_name, char *password, char *db_name);`

  Changes the user and the default database on the connection specified by `conn`. The database becomes the default for table references that do not include a database specifier. If `db_name` is `NULL`, no default database is selected.

  `mysql_change_user()` returns true if the user is allowed to connect to the server and, if a database was specified, has permission to access the database. Otherwise, the function fails and the current user and database remain unchanged.

  `mysql_change_user()` was introduced in MySQL 3.23.3.

- `void`

  `mysql_close` `(MYSQL *conn);`

  Closes the connection specified by `conn`. Call this routine when you are done with a server session. If the connection handler was allocated automatically by `mysql_init()`, `mysql_close()` de-allocates it.

  Do not call `mysql_close()` if the attempt to open a connection failed.

- `MYSQL *`

  `mysql_init` `(MYSQL *conn);`

  Initializes a connection handler and returns a pointer to it. If `conn` points to an existing `MYSQL` structure, `mysql_init()` initializes that handler and returns its address:

  ```
  MYSQL conn_struct, *conn;
  conn = mysql_init (&conn_struct);
  ```

  If `conn` is `NULL`, `mysql_init()` allocates a new handler, initializes it, and returns its address:

  ```
  MYSQL *conn;
  conn = mysql_init (NULL);
  ```

  If `mysql_init()` fails, it returns `NULL`. This may happen if `mysql_init()` cannot allocate a new handler.

If `mysql_init()` allocates the handler, `mysql_close()` de-allocates it automatically when you close the connection.

`mysql_init()` was introduced in MySQL 3.22.1.

- `int`

  `mysql_options` (MYSQL *conn, enum mysql_option option, char *arg);

  This function allows you to tailor connection behavior more precisely than is possible with `mysql_real_connect()` alone. Call it after `mysql_init()` and before `mysql_real_connect()`. You may call `mysql_options()` multiple times if you want to set several options.

  The `option` argument specifies which connection option you want to set. Additional information needed to set the option, if any, is specified by the `arg` argument. (Note that `arg` is a pointer.) `arg` is `NULL` if no additional information is needed.

  The following options are available:

  - `MYSQL_INIT_COMMAND`

    Specifies a query to execute after connecting to the server. `arg` is a null-terminated string containing the query. The query is executed after reconnecting as well (for example, if you call `mysql_ping()`). Any result set returned by the query is discarded.

  - `MYSQL_OPT_COMPRESS`

    Specifies that the connection should use the compressed client/server protocol if the server supports it. `arg` is `NULL`.

    It is also possible to specify compression when you call `mysql_real_connect()`.

  - `MYSQL_OPT_CONNECT_TIMEOUT`

    Specifies the connection timeout, in seconds. `arg` is a pointer to an `unsigned int` containing the timeout value.

  - `MYSQL_OPT_NAMED_PIPE`

    Specifies that the connection to the server should use a named pipe. `arg` is `NULL`. This option is for Windows 95/98/NT clients only and only for connections to Windows NT servers.

  - `MYSQL_READ_DEFAULT_FILE`

    Specifies an option file to read for connection parameters. Options are read from the `[client]` group in the file.

  - `MYSQL_READ_DEFAULT_GROUP`

    Specifies a group to read from the option file that you name with `MYSQL_READ_DEFAULT_FILE`. The named group is read in addition to the `[client]` group. If no option file is named, the client library looks for the standard option files and reads them.

If you call `mysql_options()` multiple times to set a given option, `mysql_real_connect()` uses the most recently specified value for that option.

`mysql_options()` returns zero for success and non-zero if the `option` value is unknown.

The following options may be used in an option file (in either the `[client]` group or a group that you specify with the `MYSQL_READ_DEFAULT_GROUP` option):

```
compress
database=db_name
debug
host=host_name
init-command=query
password=your_password
pipe
port=port_num
return-found-rows
socket=socket_name
timeout=seconds
user=user_name
```

The `mysql_options()` calls in the following example set connection options so that `mysql_real_connect()` connects with a named pipe using the compressed protocol and a timeout of 10 seconds. It reads `C:\my.cnf.special` for information from the `[client]` and `[mygroup]` groups. When the connection is established, a `SET SQL_BIG_TABLES` statement is executed.

```
MYSQL *conn;
unsigned int timeout;

if ((conn = mysql_init (NULL)) == NULL)
    ... deal with error ...
timeout = 10;
mysql_options (conn, MYSQL_OPT_CONNECT_TIMEOUT, (char *) &timeout);
mysql_options (conn, MYSQL_OPT_COMPRESS, NULL);
mysql_options (conn, MYSQL_OPT_NAMED_PIPE, NULL);
mysql_options (conn, MYSQL_READ_DEFAULT_FILE, "C:\my.cnf.special");
mysql_options (conn, MYSQL_READ_DEFAULT_GROUP, "mygroup");
mysql_options (conn, MYSQL_INIT_COMMAND, "SET SQL_BIG_TABLES=1");
if (mysql_real_connect (conn, ...) == NULL)
    ... deal with error ...
```

`mysql_options()` was introduced in MySQL 3.22.1.

`MYSQL_INIT_COMMAND`, `MYSQL_READ_DEFAULT_FILE`, and `MYSQL_READ_DEFAULT_GROUP` were introduced in MySQL 3.22.10.

- `int`
  mysql_ping (MYSQL *conn);

  Checks whether the connection indicated by `conn` is still up. If not, `mysql_ping()` reconnects using the same parameters that were used initially to make the connection. Thus, you should not call `mysql_ping()` without first successfully having called `mysql_real_connect()`.

  `mysql_ping()` was introduced in MySQL 3.22.1.

- `MYSQL *`
  mysql_real_connect (MYSQL *conn, char *host_name,
                      char *user_name, char
                      *password, char *db_name,
                      unsigned int port_num, char
                      *socket_name,
                      unsigned int flags);

  Connects to a server and returns a pointer to the connection handler. `conn` should be a pointer to an existing connection handler that was initialized by `mysql_init()`. The address of the handler is the return value for a successful connection. `NULL` is returned if an error occurs.

  If the connection attempt fails, you can pass the `conn` handler value to `mysql_errno()` and `mysql_error()` to obtain error information. However, you should not pass the `conn` value to any other client library routines that assume the handler reflects a successful connection.

  `host_name` is the server to connect to. Table F.4 shows how the client attempts to connect for various `host_name` values for UNIX and Windows clients. (If you connect using a UNIX socket or named pipe, the `socket_name` parameter specifies the socket or pipe name.)

Table F.4 **Client Connection Types By Server Hostname Type**

Hostname Value	UNIX Connection Type	Windows Connection Type
hostname	TCP/IP connection to the named host	TCP/IP connection to the named host
IP number	TCP/IP connection to the named host	TCP/IP connection to the named host
localhost	UNIX socket connection to the local host	TCP/IP connection to the local host
.	Does not apply	Named pipe connection to the local host

continues

Table F.4 **Continued**

Hostname Value	UNIX Connection Type	Windows Connection Type
NULL	UNIX socket connection to the local host	TCP/IP connection to the local host, except that on Windows NT, a named pipe connection is attempted first before falling back to TCP/IP

user_name is your MySQL username. If this is NULL, the client library sends a default name. Under UNIX, the default is your login name. Under Windows, the default is your name as specified in the USER environment variable if that variable is set and "ODBC" otherwise.

password is your password. If this is NULL, you will only be able to connect if the user grant table contains an entry matching your username and the host from which you are connecting and that entry has a blank password.

db_name is the database to use. If this is NULL, no initial database is selected.

port_num is the port number to use for TCP/IP connections. If this is 0, the default port number is used.

socket_name is the socket name to use for connections to the local host. If this is NULL, the default socket name is used.

The port number and socket name are used according to the value of host_name. If you are connecting to the local host, mysql_real_connect() attempts a connection using a UNIX domain socket (under UNIX) or a named pipe (under Windows). Otherwise, it connects using TCP/IP.

flags can be 0 to specify no options or one or more of the values shown in Table F.5. The options affect the operation of the server.

Table F.5 flags **Values for** mysql_real_connect()

Flag Value	Effect on Server Operation
CLIENT_FOUND_ROWS	For UPDATE queries, return the number of rows matched rather than the number of rows changed.
CLIENT_NO_SCHEMA	Don't allow db_name.tbl_name.col_name syntax.
CLIENT_COMPRESS	Use compressed communications protocol, if the server supports it.
CLIENT_ODBC	Treat the client as an ODBC client.

If you specify CLIENT_NO_SCHEMA, the server allows only references of the forms tbl_name.col_name, tbl_name, or col_name in queries.

The flag values are bit values, so you can combine them using '|' or '+', for example, CLIENT_COMPRESS|CLIENT_ODBC or CLIENT_COMPRESS+CLIENT_ODBC.

mysql_real_connect() was introduced in MySQL 3.21.10. The db_name parameter was added in 3.22.0. The use of mysql_init() to initialize MYSQL arguments began in 3.22.1.

Status and Error-Reporting Routines

The functions in this section allow you to determine and report the causes of errors.

- unsigned int
  mysql_errno (MYSQL *conn);

  Returns an error code for the most recently invoked client library routine that returned a status. The error code is 0 if no error occurred and non-zero otherwise. The possible error codes are listed in the MySQL header files errmsg.h and mysqld_error.h.

  ```
  if (mysql_errno (conn) == 0)
      printf ("Everything is okay\n");
  else
      printf ("Something is wrong!\n");
  ```

  mysql_errno() was introduced in MySQL 3.21.7.

- char *
  mysql_error (MYSQL *conn);

  Returns a null-terminated string containing an error message for the most recently invoked client library routine that returned a status. The return value is the empty string if no error occurred (this is the zero-length string "", not a NULL pointer). Although normally you call mysql_error() after you already know an error occurred, the return value itself can be used to detect the occurrence of an error:

  ```
  if (mysql_error (conn)[0] == '\0') /* empty string? */
      printf ("Everything is okay\n");
  else
      printf ("Something is wrong!\n");
  ```

  mysql_error() was introduced in MySQL 3.21.7 (possibly a little later).

Query Construction and Execution Routines

The functions in this section allow you to send queries to the server. mysql_escape_string() helps you construct queries by escaping characters that need special treatment.

- unsigned int
  mysql_escape_string (char *to_str, char *from_str, unsigned int from_len);

Encodes a string that may contain special characters so that it can be used in an SQL statement. Table F.6 lists the characters that are considered special and their encodings.

Table F.6 `mysql_escape_string()` **Character Encodings**

Special Character	Encoding
NUL (ASCII 0)	\0 (backslash-'0', not backslash-null)
Backslash	\\ (backslash-backslash)
Single quote	\' (backslash-single quote)
Double quote	\" (backslash-double quote)
Newline	\n (backslash-'n')
Carriage return	\r (backslash-'r')
Ctrl-Z	\Z (backslash-'Z')

The buffer to be encoded is specified as a counted string. `from_str` points to that buffer, and `from_len` indicates the number of bytes in it. `mysql_escape_string()` writes the result into the buffer pointed to by `to_str` and adds a null byte. `to_str` must point to an existing buffer that is at least `(from_len*2)+1` bytes long. (In the worst case scenario, every character in `from_str` might need to be encoded as a two-character sequence, and you also need room for the terminating null.)

`mysql_escape_string()` returns the length of the encoded string, not counting the terminating null byte.

The resulting encoded string contains no internal nulls but is null-terminated, so you can use it with functions such as `strlen()` or `strcat()`.

When you write literal strings in your program, take care not to confuse the lexical escape conventions of the C programming language with the encoding done by `mysql_escape_string()`. Consider the following example, and the output produced by it:

```
to_len = mysql_escape_string (to_str, "\0\\\'\"\n\r\032", 7);
printf ("to_len = %d, to_str = %s\n", to_len, to_str);
```

The output is:

```
to_len = 14, to_str = \0\\\'\"\n\r\Z
```

The printed value of `to_str` looks very much like the string specified as the second argument of the `mysql_escape_string()` call, but is in fact quite different.

- int
  mysql_query (MYSQL *conn, char *query_string);

  Given a query specified as a null-terminated string, `mysql_query()` sends the query to the server to be executed. The string should not contain binary data; in particular, it should not contain null bytes, which `mysql_query()` interprets as the end of the query. If your query does contain binary data, use `mysql_real_query()` instead.

The query must consist of a single SQL statement, and should not end with a semicolon (';') or '\g'. (';' and '\g' are conventions of the `mysql` client program, not of the client library.)

`mysql_query()` returns zero for success and non-zero for failure. A successful query is one that the server accepts as legal and executes without error. Success does not imply anything about the number of rows affected or returned.

- int
  `mysql_real_query` (MYSQL *conn, char *query_string, unsigned int length);

  Given a query specified as a counted string, `mysql_real_query()` sends the query to the server to be executed. The string may contain binary data (including null bytes). The query text is given by `query_string`, and the length is indicated by `length`.

  The query must consist of a single SQL statement, and should not end with a semicolon (';') or '\g'. (';' and '\g' are conventions of the `mysql` client program, not of the client library.)

  `mysql_real_query()` returns zero for success and non-zero for failure. A successful query is one that the server accepts as legal and executes without error. Success does not imply anything about the number of rows affected or returned.

- int
  `mysql_select_db` (MYSQL *conn, char *db_name);

  Selects the database named by `db_name` as the current database, which becomes the default for table references that contain no explicit database specifier. You must have permission to access the database; otherwise, `mysql_select_db()` fails.

  `mysql_select_db()` returns zero for success, non-zero for failure.

Result Set Processing Routines

When a query produces a result set, the functions in this section allow you to retrieve the set and access its contents. The `mysql_store_result()` and `mysql_use_result()` functions create the result set and one or the other must be called before using any other functions in this section. Table F.7 compares the two functions.

Table F.7 **Comparison of** `mysql_store_result()` **and** `mysql_use_result()`

`mysql_store_result()`	`mysql_use_result()`
All rows in the result set are fetched by `mysql_store_result()` itself.	`mysql_use_result()` initializes the result set, but defers row retrieval to `mysql_fetch_row()`.
Uses more memory; all rows are stored in client.	Uses less memory; one row is stored at a time.
Slower due to overhead involved in allocating memory for entire result set.	Faster because memory need be allocated only for the current row.
NULL return from `mysql_fetch_row()` indicates end of result set; never indicates an error.	NULL return from `mysql_fetch_row()` indicates end of result set or an error because communications failure can disrupt retrieval of current record.
`mysql_num_rows()` can be called anytime after `mysql_store_result()` has been called.	`mysql_num_rows()` returns correct row count only after all rows have been fetched.
`mysql_affected_rows()` is a synonym for `mysql_num_rows()`.	`mysql_affected_rows()` cannot be used.
Random access to result set rows is possible with `mysql_data_seek()`, `mysql_row_seek()`, and `mysql_row_tell()`.	No random access into result set; rows must be processed in order as returned by server; `mysql_data_seek()`, `mysql_row_seek()`, and `mysql_row_tell()` should not be used.
You need not call `mysql_fetch_row()` at all because all rows have already been retrieved to client.	You *must* call `mysql_fetch_row()` to fetch all rows, or "leftover" rows will leak into the result of the next query, causing an "out of sync" error.
Tables are read-locked for no longer than necessary to fetch data rows.	Tables can stay read-locked if client pauses in mid-retrieval, locking out other clients attempting to modify them.

`mysql_store_result()`	`mysql_use_result()`
The `max_length` member of result set `MYSQL_FIELD` structures is set to the longest value actually in the result set for the columns in the set.	`max_length` is not set to any meaningful value because it cannot be known until all rows are retrieved.

- `my_ulonglong`
  `mysql_affected_rows` `(MYSQL *conn);`

  Returns the number of rows changed by the most recent DELETE, INSERT, REPLACE, or UPDATE query. For such queries, `mysql_affected_rows()` may be called immediately after a successful call to `mysql_query()`. You can also call this function after issuing a statement that returns rows. In this case, the function acts the same way as `mysql_num_rows()` and is subject to the same constraints on which the value is meaningful, as well as the additional constraint that `mysql_affected_rows()` is never meaningful when you use `mysql_use_result()`.

  `mysql_affected_rows()` returns zero if no query has been issued or if the query was one that returns rows but no rows were selected. A return value greater than zero indicates the number of rows changed (for DELETE, INSERT, REPLACE, UPDATE) or returned (for queries that return rows). A return value of -1 indicates either an error, or that you (erroneously) called `mysql_affected_rows()` after issuing a query that returns rows but before actually retrieving the result set. Because `mysql_affected_rows()` returns an unsigned value, you should perform the comparison by casting its result to a signed value:

  ```
  if ((long) mysql_affected_rows (conn) == -1)
      fprintf (stderr, "Error!\n");
  ```

  If you have specified that the client should return the number of rows matched for UPDATE queries, `mysql_affected_rows()` returns that value rather than the number of rows actually modified. (MySQL does not update a row if the columns to be modified are the same as the new values.) This behavior can be selected either by specifying `return-found-rows` in an option file or by passing `CLIENT_FOUND_ROWS` in the `flags` parameter to `mysql_real_connect()`.

  See the note about printing values of type `my_ulonglong` in the section "Scalar Data Types."

- void
  mysql_data_seek (MYSQL_RES *res_set, unsigned int offset);

  Seeks to a particular row of the result set. The value of offset may range from 0 to mysql_num_rows(res_set)-1. The results are unpredictable if offset is out of range.

  mysql_data_seek() requires that the entire result set has been retrieved, so you can use it only if the result set was created by mysql_store_result(), not by mysql_use_result().

- MYSQL_FIELD *
  mysql_fetch_field (MYSQL_RES *res_set);

  Returns a structure containing information (metadata) about a column in the result set. After you successfully execute a query that returns rows, the first call to mysql_fetch_field() returns information about the first column. Subsequent calls return information about successive columns following the first, and NULL when no more columns are left.

  You can also call mysql_field_tell() to determine the current column position, or mysql_field_seek() to select a particular column to be returned by the next call to mysql_fetch_field().

  The following example seeks the first MYSQL_FIELD, then fetches successive column information structures:

  ```
  MYSQL_FIELD    *field;
  unsigned int   i;

  mysql_field_seek (res_set, 0);
  for (i = 0; i < mysql_num_fields (res_set); i++)
  {
      field = mysql_fetch_field (res_set);
      printf ("column %u: name = %s max_length = %lu\n",
              i, field->name, field->max_length);
  }
  ```

- MYSQL_FIELD *
  mysql_fetch_fields (MYSQL_RES res_set);

  Returns an array of all column information structures for the result set. You access them as follows:

  ```
  MYSQL_FIELD    *field;
  unsigned int   i;

  field = mysql_fetch_fields (res_set);
  for (i = 0; i < mysql_num_fields (res_set); i++)
  {
      printf ("column %u: name = %s max_length = %lu\n",
              i, field[i].name, field[i].max_length);
  }
  ```

Compare this to the example shown for `mysql_fetch_field()`. Note that although both functions return values of the same type, those values are accessed using slightly different syntax for each function.

- `MYSQL_FIELD *`

  `mysql_fetch_field_direct` `(MYSQL_RES *res_set, unsigned int field_num);`

  Given a column index, returns the information structure for that column. The value of `field_num` may range from `0` to `mysql_num_fields()-1`. The results are unpredictable if `field_num` is out of range.

  The following example accesses `MYSQL_FIELD` structures directly:

  ```
  MYSQL_FIELD    *field;
  unsigned int   i;

  for (i = 0; i < mysql_num_fields (res_set); i++)
  {
      field = mysql_fetch_field_direct (res_set, i);
      printf ("column %u: name = %s max_length = %lu\n",
              i, field->name, field->max_length);
  }
  ```

  `mysql_fetch_field_direct()` does not work properly prior to MySQL 3.23.

- `unsigned long *`

  `mysql_fetch_lengths` `(MYSQL_RES *res_set);`

  Returns a pointer to an array of `unsigned long` values representing the lengths of the columns in the current row of the result set. You must call `mysql_fetch_lengths()` each time you call `mysql_fetch_row()` or your lengths will be out of sync with your data values.

  The length for `NULL` values is zero, but a zero length does not by itself indicate a `NULL` data value. Because an empty string also has a length of zero, you must check whether or not the data value is a `NULL` pointer to distinguish between the two cases.

  The following example displays lengths and values for the current row, printing "`NULL`" if the value is `NULL`:

  ```
  unsigned long *length;

  length = mysql_fetch_lengths (res_set);
  for (i = 0; i < mysql_num_fields (res_set); i++)
  {
      printf ("length is %lu, value is %s\n",
              length[i], (row[i] != NULL ? row[i] : "NULL"));
  }
  ```

  `mysql_fetch_lengths()` appeared in MySQL 3.20.5. Prior to MySQL 3.22.7, the return type of `mysql_fetch_lengths()` was `unsigned int`.

- MYSQL_ROW
  mysql_fetch_row (MYSQL_RES *res_set);

  Returns a pointer to the next row of the result set, represented as an array of strings (except that NULL column values are represented as NULL pointers). The i-th value in the row is the i-th member of the value array.

  Values for all data types, even numeric types, are returned as strings. If you want to perform a numeric calculation with a value, you must convert it yourself—for example, with atoi() or atof().

  mysql_fetch_row() returns NULL when there are no more rows in the data set. (If you use mysql_use_result() to initiate a row-by-row result set retrieval, mysql_fetch_row() also returns NULL if a communications error occurs.)

  Data values are null-terminated, but you should not treat values that can contain binary data as null-terminated strings. Treat them as counted strings instead. (To determine column value lengths, call mysql_fetch_lengths().)

  The following code shows how to loop through a row of data values and determine whether or not each value is NULL:

  ```
  MYSQL_ROW      row;
  unsigned int   i;

  while ((row = mysql_fetch_row (res_set)) != NULL)
  {
      for (i = 0; i < mysql_num_fields (res_set); i++)
      {
          printf ("column %u: value is %s\n",
                  i, (row[i] == NULL ? "NULL" : "not NULL"));
      }
  }
  ```

  To determine the types of the column values, use the column metadata stored in the MYSQL_FIELD column information structures, obtained by calling mysql_fetch_field(), mysql_fetch_fields(), or mysql_fetch_field_direct().

- unsigned int
  mysql_field_count (MYSQL *conn);

  Returns the number of columns for the most recent query on the given connection. This function is usually used when mysql_store_result() or mysql_use_result() return NULL. mysql_field_count() tells you whether or not a result set should have been returned. A return value of 0 indicates no result set and no error. A non-zero value indicates that columns were expected and that, because none were returned, an error occurred.

The following example illustrates how to use `mysql_field_count()` for error-detection purposes:

```
res_set = mysql_store_result (conn);
if (res_set == NULL)    /* no result set was returned */
{
    /*
     * does the lack of a result set mean that an error
     * occurred or that no result set should be expected?
     */
    if (mysql_field_count (conn) > 0)
    {
        /*
         * a result set was expected, but mysql_store_result()
         * did not return one; this means an error occurred
         */
        printf ("Problem processing result set\n");
    }
    else
    {
        /*
         * a result set was not expected; query returned no data
         * (it was not a SELECT, SHOW, DESCRIBE, or EXPLAIN),
         * so just report number of rows affected by query
         */
        printf ("%lu rows affected\n",
                    (unsigned long) mysql_affected_rows (conn));
    }
}
else    /* a result set was returned */
{
    /* ... process rows here ... */
    mysql_free_result (res_set);
}
```

`mysql_field_count()` was introduced in MySQL 3.22.24. Prior to that version, `mysql_num_fields()` was used for the same purpose. To write code that will work with any version of MySQL, include the following fragment in any file that uses `mysql_field_count()`:

```
#if !defined(MYSQL_VERSION_ID) || MYSQL_VERSION_ID<32224
#define mysql_field_count mysql_num_fields
#endif
```

This maps `mysql_field_count()` to `mysql_num_fields()` when the source is compiled under older versions of MySQL.

- MYSQL_FIELD_OFFSET
mysql_field_seek (MYSQL_RES *res_set, MYSQL_FIELD_OFFSET offset);

Seeks to the column information structure specified by offset. The next call to mysql_fetch_field() will return the information structure for the given column. offset is *not* a column index; it is a MYSQL_FIELD_OFFSET value obtained from an earlier call to mysql_field_tell() or to mysql_field_seek().

To reset to the first column, pass an offset value of 0.

- MYSQL_FIELD_OFFSET
mysql_field_tell (MYSQL_RES *res_set);

Returns the current column information structure offset. This value may be passed to mysql_field_seek().

- void
mysql_free_result (MYSQL_RES *res_set);

De-allocates the memory used by the result set. You must call mysql_free_result() for each result set you work with. Typically, result sets are generated by calling mysql_store_result() or mysql_use_result(). However, some client library functions generate result sets implicitly, and you are responsible for freeing those sets, too. These functions are mysql_list_dbs(), mysql_list_fields(), mysql_list_processes(), and mysql_list_tables().

- char *
mysql_info (MYSQL *conn);

Returns a string containing information about the effect of the most recently executed query of the following types. The string format is given immediately following each query:

```
ALTER TABLE ...
    Records: 0 Duplicates: 0 Warnings: 0
INSERT INTO ... SELECT ...
    Records: 0 Duplicates: 0 Warnings: 0
INSERT INTO ... VALUES (...),(...),...
    Records: 0 Duplicates: 0 Warnings: 0
LOAD DATA ...
    Records: 0 Deleted: 0 Skipped: 0 Warnings: 0
UPDATE ...
    Rows matched: 0 Changed: 0 Warnings: 0
```

The numbers will vary according to the particular query you've executed, of course.

For statements not shown in the preceding list, mysql_info() returns NULL. mysql_info() returns non-NULL for INSERT INTO ... VALUES only if the statement contains more than one value list.

The string returned by `mysql_info()` is in the language used by the server, so you can't necessarily count on being able to parse it by looking for certain words.

- `my_ulonglong`

  `mysql_insert_id` `(MYSQL conn);`

  Returns the `AUTO_INCREMENT` value generated by the most recently executed query on the given connection. Returns zero if no query has been executed or if the previous query did not generate an `AUTO_INCREMENT` value. This means you should call `mysql_insert_id()` immediately after a query that you expect to generate a new value. If any other query intervenes between that query and the point at which you want to use the value, the value of `mysql_insert_id()` will be reset by the intervening query.

  A zero return value is distinct from any valid `AUTO_INCREMENT` value because such values start at 1. (Exception: If you create an `AUTO_INCREMENT` column and then insert a literal negative number, the sequence will begin with that number and may eventually reach 0 as a valid member of the sequence. It's assumed in this case that you know what you're doing, particularly because `mysql_insert_id()` returns an unsigned number and you'll need to play tricks with the return value.)

  Note that the behavior of `mysql_insert_id()` differs from that of the SQL function `LAST_INSERT_ID()`. `mysql_insert_id()` is maintained in the client and is set for each query. The value of `LAST_INSERT_ID()` is maintained in the server and persists from query to query.

  The values returned by `mysql_insert_id()` are connection specific and are not affected by `AUTO_INCREMENT` activity on other connections.

  See the note about printing values of type `my_ulonglong` in the section "Scalar Data Types."

- `unsigned int`

  `mysql_num_fields` `(MYSQL_RES *res_set);`

  Returns the number of columns in the result set. `mysql_num_rows()` is often used to iterate through the columns of the current row of the set, as illustrated by the following example:

  ```
  MYSQL_ROW       row;
  unsigned int    i;

  while ((row = mysql_fetch_row (res_set)) != NULL)
  {
      for (i = 0; i < mysql_num_fields (res_set); i++)
      {
          /* do something with row[i] here ... */
      }
  }
  ```

Prior to MySQL 3.22.24, `mysql_num_fields()` was also used to perform the function now performed by `mysql_field_count()`—that is, to test whether or not a NULL return from `mysql_store_result()` or `mysql_use_result()` indicates an error. This is why in older source code you will sometimes see `mysql_num_fields()` being called with a pointer to a connection handler rather than with a pointer to a result set. `mysql_num_fields()` used to be callable both ways. Use of `mysql_num_fields()` with a connection handler is now deprecated. You should write programs using `mysql_field_count()` instead; the description for that function shows how to use it even for older versions of MySQL.

- my_ulonglong
  mysql_num_rows (MYSQL_RES *res_set);

Returns the number of rows in the result set. If you generate the result set with `mysql_store_result()`, you can call `mysql_num_rows()` anytime thereafter:

```
if ((res_set = mysql_store_result (conn)) == NULL)
{
    /* mysql_num_rows() can be called now */
}
```

If you generate the result set with `mysql_use_result()`, `mysql_num_rows()` doesn't return the correct value until you have fetched all the rows:

```
if ((res_set = mysql_use_result (conn)) == NULL)
{
    /* mysql num rows() cannot be called yet */
    while ((row = mysql_fetch_row (res_set)) != NULL)
    {
        /* mysql_num_rows() still cannot be called */
    }
    /* mysql_num_rows() can be called now */
```

See the note about printing values of type `my_ulonglong` in the section "Scalar Data Types."

- MYSQL_ROW_OFFSET
  mysql_row_seek (MYSQL_RES *res_set, MYSQL_ROW_OFFSET offset);

Seeks to a particular row of the result set. `mysql_row_seek()` is similar to `mysql_data_seek()`, but the `offset` value is not a row number. `offset` must be a value obtained from a call to `mysql_row_tell()` or `mysql_row_seek()`.

`mysql_row_seek()` returns the previous row offset.

`mysql_row_seek()` requires that the entire result set has been retrieved, so you can use it only if the result set was created by `mysql_store_result()`, not by `mysql_use_result()`.

- MYSQL_ROW_OFFSET
  mysql_row_tell (MYSQL_RES *res_set);

Returns an offset representing the current row position in the result set. This is not a row number; the value may be passed only to `mysql_row_seek()`, not to `mysql_data_seek()`.

`mysql_row_tell()` requires that the entire result set has been retrieved, so you can use it only if the result set was created by `mysql_store_result()`, not by `mysql_use_result()`.

- `MYSQL_RES *`
  `mysql_store_result` (MYSQL *conn);

  Following a successful query, returns the result set and stores it in the client. Returns NULL if the query returns no data or an error occurred. When `mysql_store_result()` returns NULL, call `mysql_field_count()` or one of the error-reporting functions to determine whether a result set was not expected or whether an error occurred.

  When you are done with the result set, pass it to `mysql_free_result()` to de-allocate it.

  See the comparison of `mysql_store_result()` and `mysql_use_result()` in Table F.7.

- `MYSQL_RES *`
  `mysql_use_result` (MYSQL *conn);

  Following a successful query, initiates a result set retrieval but does not retrieve any data rows itself. You must call `mysql_fetch_row()` to fetch the rows one by one. Returns NULL if the query returns no data or an error occurred. When `mysql_use_result()` returns NULL, call `mysql_field_count()` or one of the error-reporting functions to determine whether a result set was not expected or whether an error occurred.

  When you are done with the result set, pass it to `mysql_free_result()` to de-allocate it.

  See the comparison of `mysql_store_result()` and `mysql_use_result()` in Table F.7.

  `mysql_store_result()` and `mysql_use_result()` both are used to retrieve result sets, but they affect the way you can use other result set–handling functions.

Information Routines

These functions provide information about the client, server, protocol version, and the current connection.

- char *
  mysql_get_client_info (void);

  Returns a null-terminated string describing the client library version—for example, "3.22.25".

- char *
  mysql_get_host_info (MYSQL *conn);

  Returns a null-terminated string describing the current connection—for example, "Localhost via UNIX socket" or "your.host.com via TCP/IP".

- unsigned int
  mysql_get_proto_info (MYSQL *conn);

  Returns a number indicating the client/server protocol version used for the current connection.

- char *
  mysql_get_server_info (MYSQL *conn);

  Returns a null-terminated string describing the server version—for example, "3.22.25-log". The suffixes you may see following the server version number are -log (logging is on), -debug (the server is running debug mode), or -demo (the server is running in demo mode).

- char *
  mysql_stat (MYSQL *conn);

  Returns a null-terminated string containing server status information or NULL if an error occurred. The format of the string is subject to change. Currently it looks something like this:

  ```
  Uptime: 864034  Threads: 1  Questions: 32736  Slow queries: 50  Opens: 1428
  Flush tables: 1  Open tables: 61
  ```

  These values may be interpreted as follows:

  - Uptime is the number of seconds the server has been up.
  - Threads is the number of threads currently running in the server.
  - Questions is the number of queries the server has executed.
  - Slow queries is the number of queries that take longer than the server's long_query_time parameter.
  - Opens is the number of tables the server has opened.
  - Flush tables is the number of times that FLUSH, REFRESH, and RELOAD commands have been executed.
  - Open tables is the number of tables the server currently has open.

  The information returned by mysql_stat() is the same as that reported by the mysqladmin status command. (Where do you think mysqladmin gets the information?)

- unsigned long
mysql_thread_id (MYSQL *conn);

Returns the thread number that the server associates with the current connection. You can use this number as an identifier for mysql_kill().

It's not a good idea to execute mysql_thread_id() until just before you need the value. If you get the value and store it, intending to use it later, the value may be incorrect. This can happen if your connection goes down and then is re-established (for example, with mysql_ping()) because the server will assign a new thread identifier.

Administrative Routines

The functions in this section allow you to control aspects of server operation.

- int
mysql_kill (MYSQL *conn, unsigned long thread_id);

Kill the server thread identified by thread_id.

If you have the PROCESS privilege, you can kill any thread. Otherwise, you can kill only your own threads.

mysql_kill() returns zero for success and non-zero for failure.

- int
mysql_refresh (MYSQL *conn, unsigned int options);

This function is similar in effect to the SQL FLUSH statement, except that you can tell the server to flush several kinds of things at once. The options value should be one or more of the values shown in Table F.8.

Table F.8 mysql_refresh() **Options**

Option Value	Action Taken by the Server
REFRESH_GRANT	Reload grant table contents
REFRESH_LOG	Begin new general and update logs (whichever ones are currently open)
REFRESH_TABLES	Close all open tables
REFRESH_HOSTS	Flush the host cache
REFRESH_STATUS	Reset status variables to zero

The options in Table F.8 are bit values, so you can combine them using '|' or '+'—for example, REFRESH_LOG|REFRESH_TABLES or REFRESH_LOG+REFRESH_TABLES.

For more information on flush operations, see the description of the FLUSH statement in Appendix D, "SQL Syntax Reference."

mysql_refresh() returns zero for success and non-zero for failure.

- int
  mysql_shutdown (MYSQL *conn);

  Instructs the server to shut down. You must have the SHUTDOWN privilege to do this.

  mysql_shutdown() returns zero for success, non-zero for failure.

Debugging Routines

These functions allow you to generate debugging information on either the client or server end of the connection. This requires MySQL to be compiled to support debugging. (Use the --with-debug option when you configure the MySQL distribution.)

- void
  mysql_debug (char *debug_string);

  Performs a DBUG_PUSH operation using the string debug_string. The format of the string is described in the MySQL Reference Manual.

  To use mysql_debug(), the client library must be compiled with debugging support.

- int
  mysql_dump_debug_info (MYSQL *conn);

  Instructs the server to write debugging information to the log. You must have the PROCESS privilege to do this.

  mysql_dump_debug_info() returns zero for success, non-zero for failure.

Deprecated Routines

The MySQL client library includes a number of functions that now are deprecated because there are preferred ways to do the same thing. Most of these functions can be replaced by passing an equivalent query to mysql_query(). For example, mysql_create_db("*db_name*") can be replaced with this call:

```
mysql_query (conn, "CREATE DATABASE db_name")
```

A few functions, such as mysql_connect() and mysql_eof(), are deprecated because they have been replaced by functions that do more or that provide more information.

Over time, more functions have become deprecated as MySQL understands more SQL statements. For example, when the SQL FLUSH PRIVILEGES statement was added, mysql_reload() became deprecated. The following descriptions indicate the version of MySQL at which each function became deprecated and the preferred way to perform each function now. If your client library is older than the MySQL version listed, you must still use the deprecated function, of course.

If you want to plan for the future, you should avoid all functions listed in this section. Some or all of them will disappear in MySQL 4.0.

- MYSQL *

  mysql_connect (MYSQL *conn, char *host_name,
            char *user_name, char *password);

  This is the predecessor of mysql_real_connect(). It is, in fact, now implemented as a call to mysql_real_connect().

  This function is deprecated as of MySQL 3.22.0.

- int

  mysql_create_db (MYSQL *conn, char *db_name);

  Creates a database with the name given by db_name. This can be done now by issuing a CREATE DATABASE command with mysql_query().

  mysql_create_db() returns zero for success and non-zero for failure.

  This function is deprecated as of MySQL 3.21.15.

- int

  mysql_drop_db (MYSQL *conn, char *db_name);

  Drops the database named by db_name. This can be done now by issuing a DROP DATABASE command with mysql_query().

  mysql_drop_db() returns zero for success and non-zero for failure.

  This function is deprecated as of MySQL 3.21.15.

- my_bool

  mysql_eof (MYSQL_RES *res_set);

  Returns non-zero if the end of a result set has been reached and zero if an error occurred. mysql_eof() is used when you use the combination of mysql_use_result() to initiate a result set retrieval and mysql_fetch_row() to fetch the data rows one at a time. With mysql_use_result(), a NULL return from mysql_fetch_row() may mean either that the end of the set has been reached or that an error occurred. mysql_eof() distinguishes between the two outcomes.

  mysql_errno() and mysql_error() may be used now to achieve the same effect, though actually they return more information. (They indicate the reason for any error that may have occurred, rather than simply whether or not it did occur.)

  This function is deprecated as of MySQL 3.21.17.

- MYSQL_RES *

  mysql_list_dbs (MYSQL *conn, char *wild);

  Returns a result set listing database names on the server or NULL if an error occurred. The list contains all databases matching the SQL regular expression indicated by wild (which may contain the wildcard characters '%' and '_') or all databases if wild is NULL. You are responsible for calling mysql_free() to free the result set.

  The list produced by mysql_list_dbs() may be obtained by executing a SHOW DATABASES command with mysql_query() and then processing the result set.

  This function is deprecated as of MySQL 3.22.0.

- MYSQL_RES *

  mysql_list_fields (MYSQL *conn, char *tbl_name, char *wild);

  Returns a result set listing column names in the given table or NULL if an error occurred. The list contains all column names matching the SQL regular expression indicated by wild (which may contain the wildcard characters '%' and '_') or all columns if wild is NULL. You are responsible for calling mysql_free() to free the result set.

  The list produced by mysql_list_fields() may be obtained by executing a SHOW COLUMNS command with mysql_query() and then processing the result set.

  This function is deprecated as of MySQL 3.22.0.

- MYSQL_RES *

  mysql_list_processes (MYSQL *conn);

  Returns a result set containing a list of the processes running in the server or NULL if an error occurred. If you have the PROCESS privilege, the list contains all server processes. If you do not, the list contains only your own processes. You are responsible for calling mysql_free() to free the result set.

  The list produced by mysql_list_fields() may be obtained by executing a SHOW PROCESSLIST query with mysql_query() and then processing the result set.

  This function is deprecated as of MySQL 3.22.0.

- MYSQL_RES *

  mysql_list_tables (MYSQL *conn, char *wild);

  Returns a result set listing tables in the current database or NULL if an error occurred. The list contains all table names matching the SQL regular expression indicated by wild (which may contain the wildcard characters '%' and '_') or all tables if wild is NULL. You are responsible for calling mysql_free() to free the result set.

  The list produced by mysql_list_tables() may be obtained by executing a SHOW TABLES command with mysql_query() and then processing the result set.

  This function is deprecated as of MySQL 3.22.0.

- int

  mysql_reload (MYSQL *conn);

  Instructs the server to reload the grant tables. This can be done now by issuing a FLUSH PRIVILEGES query with mysql_query(). You must have the RELOAD privilege to use mysql_reload().

  mysql_reload() returns zero for success and non-zero for failure.

  This function is deprecated as of MySQL 3.21.9.

G

Perl DBI API Reference

THIS APPENDIX DESCRIBES THE PERL DBI application-programming interface. The API consists of a set of methods and attributes for communicating with database servers and accessing databases from Perl scripts. The appendix also describes MySQL-specific extensions to DBI provided by DBD::mysql, the MySQL database driver.

Some DBI methods and attributes are not discussed here, either because they do not apply to MySQL or because they are new, experimental methods that may change as they are developed or may even be dropped. Some MySQL-specific DBD methods are not discussed due to being obsolete. If you want more information about new or obsolete methods, see the DBI documentation or the MySQL DBD documentation, which you can get by running the following commands:

```
% perldoc DBI
% perldoc DBI::FAQ
% perldoc DBD::mysql
```

This appendix serves as a reference, so it includes only brief code fragments illustrating use of the Perl DBI API. For complete client scripts and notes on writing them, see Chapter 7, "The Perl DBI API."

Writing Scripts

Every Perl script that uses the DBI module must include the following line:

```
use DBI;
```

It's not necessary to include a use line for a particular DBD-level module because DBI will take care of activating the proper module when you connect to the server.

Normally, a DBI script will open a connection using the connect() method, issue queries, and then close the connection with disconnect(). The methods used to issue queries vary. Non-SELECT queries typically are performed with the do() method. SELECT queries typically are performed by passing the query to prepare(), then calling execute(), and finally retrieving query results a row at a time in a loop that repeatedly invokes a row-fetching method, such as fetchrow_array() or fetchrow_hashref().

DBI Methods

The method descriptions here are written in a somewhat different format than is used for the C functions in Appendix F, "C API Reference," and for the PHP functions in Appendix H, "PHP API Reference." Functions in those appendixes are written in prototype form, with return value types and parameter types listed explicitly. Perl generally doesn't use prototypes in the same way, so the descriptions here indicate return value types and parameter types by variables, for which the leading character of the variable indicates the type of value: '$' for a scalar, '@' for an array, and '%' for a hash (associative array). In addition, for any parameter listed with a leading '\', a reference to the variable should be passed, not the variable itself. A variable name ending of '_ref' signifies that the variable value is a reference.

Several variables are used with specific meanings throughout this appendix. They are shown in Table G.1.

Table G.1   **Conventional Perl DBI Variable Names**

Name	Meaning
$drh	A handle to a driver object
$dbh	A handle to a database object
$sth	A handle to a statement (query) object
$fh	A handle to an open file
$h	A "generic" handle; the meaning depends on context
$rc	The return code from operations that return true or false
$rv	The return value from operations that return an integer
$rows	The return value from operations that return a row count
@ary	An array (list) representing a row of values returned by a query

Many methods accept a hash argument %attr containing attributes that affect the way the method works. This hash should be passed by reference. You can do this in two ways. One way is to set up the contents of the hash value %attr before invoking the method and then pass it to the method.

```
my (%attr) = (AttrName1 => value1, AttrName2 => value2);
$ret_val = $h->method (..., \%attr);
```

The other is to supply an anonymous hash directly in the method invocation:

```
$ret_val = $h->method (..., {AttrName1 => value1, AttrName2 => value2});
```

Optional information is indicated by square brackets ([ ]). The way in which a method or function is used is indicated by the calling sequence. 'DBI->' indicates a DBI class method, 'DBI::' indicates a DBI function, and '$DBI::' indicates a DBI variable. For methods that are called using handles, the handle name indicates the scope of the method. '$dbh->' indicates a database handle method, '$sth->' indicates a statement handle method, and '$h->' indicates a method that may be called with different kinds of handles. Here's an example calling sequence:

```
@row_ary = $dbh->selectrow_array ($statement, [\%attr [, @bind_values]]);
```

This indicates that the selectrow_array() method is called as a database handle method, because it's invoked using '$dbh->'. The parameters are $statement (a scalar value), %attr (a hash that should be passed as a reference, as indicated by the leading '\'), and @bind_values (an array). The second and third parameters are optional. The return value is an array.

The method descriptions indicate what the return value is in case of an error, but an error can be returned only if the RaiseError attribute is disabled. The script will terminate automatically if RaiseError is enabled.

In the descriptions that follow, the term "SELECT query" should be taken to mean a SELECT query or any other query that returns rows, such as DESCRIBE, EXPLAIN, or SHOW.

DBI Class Methods

The %attr parameter for methods in this section may be used to specify method-processing attributes. For MySQL, the most important of these are PrintError and RaiseError. For example, to turn on automatic script termination when a DBI error occurs, enable RaiseError:

```
$dbh = DBI->connect ($data_source, $user_name, $password, {RaiseError => 1});
```

PrintError and RaiseError are discussed in the section "General Handle Attributes."

- @ary = DBI->**available_drivers** ([$quiet]);

  Returns a list of available DBI drivers. A warning is issued if multiple drivers with the same name are found. You can suppress the warning by passing a value of 1 for the $quiet parameter.

- $dbh = DBI->**connect** ($data_source, $user_name, $password [, \%attr]);

  connect() establishes a connection to a database server and returns a database handle. The handle is undef if the connection attempt fails. To terminate a successfully established connection, invoke the disconnect() method using the database handle returned by connect().

  For connect(), any attributes specified in the %attr parameter affect DBI processing globally.

  The data source can be given in several forms. The first part is always "DBI:mysql", where "DBI" may be given in any lettercase and the driver name, "mysql", must be lowercase. Everything after the driver name part of the data source is interpreted by the driver, so the syntax described in the following discussion does not necessarily apply to any driver other than DBD::mysql.

  Following the driver name, you may also specify a database name and hostname in the initial part of the data source string:

  ```
  $data_source = "DBI:mysql:db_name";
  $data_source = "DBI:mysql:db_name:host_name";
  ```

  The database may be specified as *db_name* or as database=*db_name*. The hostname may be specified as *host_name* or as host=*host_name*.

  Following the initial part of the data source string, you may specify several options in *attribute=value* format. Each option must be preceded by a semicolon. The MySQL driver understands the following options:

  - host=*host_name*

    The host to connect to. A port number may also be specified by using *host_name:port_num* format.

  - port=*port_num*

    The port number to connect to.

  - mysql_compression=1

    This option enables compressed communication between the client and the MySQL server.

    mysql_compression requires MySQL 3.22.3 or later, and DBD::mysql 1.19.20 or later.

  - mysql_read_default_file=*file_name*

    By default, DBI scripts do not read any MySQL option files for connection parameters. This option allows you to specify an option file to read. The filename should be a full pathname. (Otherwise, it will be interpreted relative to the directory in which you execute the script, and you will get inconsistent results.)

    To read the .my.cnf file in the home directory of whatever user happens to be running the script, specify the filename as $ENV{HOME}/.my.cnf. This is useful when you expect a script to be used by several people and you want them to connect as themselves rather than as a user that you hardwire into the script.

mysql_read_default_file requires MySQL 3.22.10 or later, and DBD::mysql 1.21.06 or later.

- mysql_read_default_group=*group_name*

   If you read an option file for connection parameters, the [client] group is read by default. The mysql_read_default_group option allows you to specify a group to read in addition to the [client] group. For example, mysql_read_default_group=dbi specifies that the [dbi] group should be read as well as the [client] group. The precedence of parameters found in multiple groups is described in Appendix E, "MySQL Program Reference."

   mysql_read_default_group requires MySQL 3.22.10 or later, and DBD::mysql 1.21.06 or later.

- mysql_socket=*socket_name*

   This option specifies the pathname of the UNIX domain socket to use for connections to localhost if the default socket path is unsuitable.

   mysql_socket requires MySQL 3.21.15 or later. DBI consults several environment variables for connection parameters:

   - If the data source is undefined or empty, the value of the DBI_DSN variable is used.

   - If the driver name is missing from the data source, the value of the DBI_DRIVER variable is used.

   - If the *user_name* or *password* parameters of the connect() call are undefined, the values of the DBI_USER and DBI_PASS variables are used. This does *not* occur if the parameters are empty strings.

   Use of DBI_PASS is a security risk, so you shouldn't use it in any situation where security is important. (Environment variable values are visible to other users by means of commands like ps.)

If some connection parameters remain unknown after all information sources have been consulted, DBI uses default values. If the hostname is unspecified, it defaults to localhost. If the username is unspecified, it defaults to your login name under UNIX and to ODBC under Windows. If the password is unspecified, there is no default. Instead, no password is sent.

- $drh = DBI->**install_driver** ($driver_name);

Activates a DBD-level driver and returns a driver handle for it. For MySQL, the driver name is "mysql" (it must be lowercase). Normally, it is not necessary to use this method because DBI activates the proper driver automatically when you invoke the connect() method. However, install_driver() may be of use if you're using the `func()` method to perform administrative operations. (See "MySQL-Specific Administrative Methods.")

Database Handle Methods

The methods in this section are invoked through a database handle and may be used after you have obtained such a handle by calling the `connect()` method.

The `%attr` parameter for methods in this section may be used to specify method-processing attributes. For MySQL, the most important of these are `PrintError` and `RaiseError`. For example, you can enable `RaiseError` to cause automatic script termination if a DBI error occurs during processing of a particular query like this:

```
$rows = $dbh->do ($statement, {RaiseError => 1});
```

`PrintError` and `RaiseError` are discussed in the section "General Handle Attributes."

- `$rc = $dbh->disconnect ();`

  Terminates the connection associated with the handle. If a connection is still active when the script exits, a warning is printed and the connection is terminated automatically.

- `$rows = $dbh->do ($statement [, \%attr [, @bind_values]]);`

  Prepares and executes the query indicated by `$statement`. The return value is the number of rows affected— -1 if the number of rows is unknown, and `undef` if an error occurs. If the number of rows affected is zero, the return value is the string `"0E0"`, which evaluates as zero but is considered true.

  `do()` is used primarily for statements that do not retrieve rows, such as `DELETE`, `INSERT`, `REPLACE`, or `UPDATE`. If you try to use it for a `SELECT` statement, you won't get back a statement handle and you won't be able to fetch any rows.

  `@bind_values` is used when the statement contains placeholders (indicated by the '?' character within the query string). `@bind_values` is a list of the values to be bound to the placeholders. There must be as many values as there are placeholders. If you specify values to be bound but no attributes, pass `undef` as the value of the `\%attr` parameter.

- `$rc = $dbh->ping ();`

  Checks whether the connection to the server is still active, and returns true or false accordingly.

- `$sth = $dbh->prepare ($statement [, \%attr]);`

  Prepares the query indicated by `$statement` for later execution and returns a statement handle. The return handle may be used with `execute()` to execute the query.

- $str = $dbh->**quote** ($value [, $data_type]);

Processes a string to perform quoting and escaping of characters that are special in SQL statements so that the string will not cause a syntax error when you execute the statement. For example, the string "I'm happy" is returned as "'I\'m happy'" (without the double quotes). If $value is undef, it is returned as the string "NULL" (unquoted).

The $data_type parameter is usually unnecessary because MySQL converts values specified as strings in queries to other types automatically. $data_type may be specified as a hint that a value is of a particular type—for example, DBI::SQL_INTEGER to indicate the $value represents an integer.

Do not use quote() with values that you are going to insert into a query using placeholders; DBI quotes such values automatically.

- $ary_ref = $dbh->**selectall_arrayref** ($statement [, \%attr [, @bind_values]]);

Executes the query specified by $statement and returns the result by combining prepare(), execute(), and fetchall_arrayref(). Returns undef if an error occurs.

If the $statement parameter is a previously prepared statement, the prepare() step is omitted.

The @bind_values parameter has the same meaning as for the do() method.

- $ary_ref = $dbh->**selectcol_arrayref** ($statement, [\%attr [, @bind_values]]);

Executes the query specified by $statement and returns the first column of the result by combining prepare() and execute(). The result is returned as a reference to an array containing the first column from each row. undef is returned if an error occurs.

If the $statement parameter is a previously prepared statement, the prepare() step is omitted.

The @bind_values parameter has the same meaning as for the do() method.

- @row_ary = $dbh->**selectrow_array** ($statement [, \%attr [, @bind_values]]);

Executes the query specified by $statement and returns the first row of the result by combining prepare(), execute(), and fetchrow_array().

If the $statement parameter is a previously prepared statement, the prepare() step is omitted.

When called in a list context, selectrow_array() returns an array representing row values, or an empty array if an error occurs. In a scalar context, selectrow_array() returns the value of the first element of the array (the first column of the row). It returns undef if an error occurs.

The @bind_values parameter has the same meaning as for the do() method.

Statement Handle Methods

The methods in this section are invoked through a statement handle, which you obtain by calling prepare().

- $rc = $sth->**bind_col** ($col_num, \$var_to_bind);

Binds a given column for a SELECT query to a Perl variable, which should be passed as a reference. $col_num should be in the range from 1 to the number of columns selected by the query. Each time a row is fetched, the variable is updated automatically with the column value.

bind_col() should be called after prepare() and before execute().

bind_col() returns false if the column number is not in the range from 1 to the number of columns selected by the query.

- $rc = $sth->**bind_columns** (\$var_to_bind1, \$var_to_bind2, ...);

Binds a list of variables to columns returned by a prepared SELECT statement. See the description of the bind_col() method.

bind_columns() returns false if the number of references doesn't match the number of columns selected by the query.

- $rv = $sth->**bind_param** ($n, $value [, \%attr]);
$rv = $sth->**bind_param** ($n, $value [, $bind_type]);

Binds a value to a placeholder ('?') in a statement. It should be called after prepare() and before execute().

$n specifies the number of the placeholder to which the value $value should be bound and should be in the range from 1 to the number of placeholders. To bind the NULL value, pass undef.

The \%attr or $bind_type parameter may be supplied as a hint about the type of the value to be bound. For example, to specify that the value represents an integer, you could invoke bind_param() in either of the following ways:

```
$rv = $sth->bind_param ($n, $value , { TYPE => DBI::SQL_INTEGER });
$rv = $sth->bind_param ($n, $value , DBI::SQL_INTEGER);
```

The default is to treat the variable as a VARCHAR. This is normally sufficient because MySQL converts string values in queries to other data types as necessary.

- `$rows = $sth->dump_results ([$maxlen [, $line_sep [, $field_sep [, $fh]]]]);`

  Fetches all rows from the statement handle `$sth`, formats them by calling the utility function `DBI::neat_list()`, and prints them to the given file handle. Returns the number of rows fetched.

  The defaults for the `$maxlen`, `$line_sep`, `$field_sep`, and `$fh` parameters are 35, `"\n"`, `", "` and `STDOUT`.

- `$rv = $sth->execute ([@bind_values]);`

  Executes a prepared statement. Returns true if the statement executed successfully, or `undef` if an error occurs.

  The `@bind_values` parameter has the same meaning as for the `do()` method.

- `$ary_ref = $sth->fetch ();`

  `fetch()` is an alias for `fetchrow_arrayref()`.

- `$tbl_ary_ref = $sth->fetchall_arrayref ([$slice_array_ref]);`
  `$tbl_ary_ref = $sth->fetchall_arrayref ([$slice_hash_ref]);`

  Fetches all rows from the statement handle `$sth` and returns a reference to an array that contains one reference for each row fetched. The meaning of each reference in the array depends on the argument you pass. With no argument or an array slice reference argument, each element of `$tbl_ary_ref` is a reference to an array containing the values for one row of the result. With a hash slice reference argument, each element of `$tbl_ary_ref` is a reference to a hash containing the values for one row of the result.

- `@ary = $sth->fetchrow_array ();`

  When called in a list context, `fetchrow_array()` returns an array containing column values for the next row of the result set, or an empty array if there are no more rows or if an error occurs. In a scalar context, `fetchrow_array()` returns the value of the first element of the array (that is, the first column of the row), or `undef` if there are no more rows or if an error occurs.

  You can distinguish between normal exhaustion of the result set and an error by checking `$sth->err()`. A value of zero indicates you've reached the end of the result set without error.

- `$ary_ref = $sth->fetchrow_arrayref ();`

  Returns a reference to an array containing column values for the next row of the result set. It returns `undef` if there are no more rows or an error occurs.

  You can distinguish between normal exhaustion of the result set and an error by checking `$sth->err()`. A value of zero indicates you've reached the end of the result set without error.

- $hash_ref = $sth->**fetchrow_hashref** ([$name]);

Returns a reference to a hash containing column values for the next row of the result set. It returns undef if there are no more rows or an error occurs. Hash index values are the column names, and elements of the hash are the column values.

The $name argument may be specified to indicate the statement handle attribute to use for hash key values. It defaults to "NAME". This may cause a problem in that column names are not case insensitive in queries, but hash keys are case sensitive. To force hash keys to be lowercase or uppercase, you can specify a $name value of "NAME_lc" or "NAME_uc" instead.

You can distinguish between normal exhaustion of the result set and an error by checking $sth->err(). A value of zero indicates you've reached the end of the result set without error.

- $rc = $sth->**finish** ();

Frees any resources associated with the statement handle. Normally, you do not need to invoke this method explicitly, but if you are fetching only part of a result set, calling finish() lets DBI know that you are done fetching data.

Calling finish() may invalidate statement attributes; it's best to access them immediately after invoking execute().

- $rv = $sth->**rows** ();

Returns the number of rows affected by the statement associated with $sth, or −1 if an error occurred. This method is used primarily for statements that do not return rows. For SELECT statements, you should not rely on the rows() method; count the rows as you fetch them instead.

General Handle Methods

The methods in this section are not specific to particular types of handles. They may be invoked using driver, database, or statement handles.

- $h->**err** ();

Returns the numeric error code for the most recently invoked driver operation. 0 indicates no error.

- $h->**errstr** ();

Returns the string error message for the most recently invoked driver operation. The empty string indicates no error.

- DBI->**trace** ($trace_level [, $trace_filename]);
  $h->**trace** ($trace_level [, $trace_filename]);

Sets a trace level. Tracing provides information about DBI operation. The trace level can be in the range from 0 (off) to 9 (maximum information). Tracing can be enabled for all DBI operations within a script by invoking trace as a DBI class method, or for an individual handle:

```
DBI->trace (2);         Turn on script tracing
$sth->trace (2);        Turn on handle tracing
```

Tracing can also be enabled on a global level for all DBI scripts you run by setting the DBI_TRACE environment variable.

Trace output goes to STDERR by default. The $filename parameter may be supplied to direct output to a different file. Output is appended to any existing contents of the file.

Each trace call causes output from *all* traced handles to go to the same file. If a file is named, all trace output goes there. If no file is named, all trace output goes to STDERR.

- DBI->**trace_msg** ($str [, $min_level])
  $h->**trace_msg** ($str [, $min_level])

  Writes a message to the trace output if the handle is being traced or if tracing has been enabled at the DBI level. trace_msg() may be called as DBI->trace_msg() to write a message if DBI-level tracing is enabled.

  The $min_level parameter may be supplied to specify that the message should be written only if the trace level is at least at that level.

MySQL-Specific Administrative Methods

This section describes the func() method that DBI provides as a means of accessing driver-specific operations directly.

```
$rc = $drh->func('createdb',
                  $db_name, $host_name, $user_name, $password, 'admin');
$rc = $drh->func('dropdb',
                  $db_name, $host_name, $user_name, $password, 'admin');
$rc = $drh->func('shutdown',
                  $host_name, $user_name, $password, 'admin');
$rc = $drh->func('reload',
                  $host_name, $user_name, $password, 'admin');

$rc = $dbh->func('createdb', $db_name, 'admin');
$rc = $dbh->func('dropdb', $db_name, 'admin');
$rc = $dbh->func('shutdown', 'admin');
$rc = $dbh->func('reload', 'admin');
```

The func() method is accessed either through a driver handle or through a database handle. A driver handle is not associated with an open connection, so if you access func() that way, you must supply arguments for the hostname, user name, and password to allow the method to establish a connection. If you access func() with a database handle, those arguments are unnecessary. A driver handle may be obtained, if necessary, as follows:

```
$drh = DBI->install_driver("mysql");     # ("mysql" must be lowercase)
```

- createdb

  Creates the database named by $db_name. You must have the CREATE privilege for the database to do this.

- dropdb

  Drops (removes) the database named by $db_name. You must have the DROP privilege for the database to do this.

  Be careful; if you drop a database, it's gone. You can't get it back.

- shutdown

  Shuts down the server. You must have the SHUTDOWN privilege to do this.

- reload

  Tells the server to reload the grant tables. This is necessary if you modify the contents of the grant tables directly using DELETE, INSERT, or UPDATE rather than using GRANT or REVOKE. You must have the RELOAD privilege to use reload.

DBI Utility Functions

These functions are invoked as DBI::*func_name*(), rather than as DBI->*func_name*().

- @bool = DBI::**looks_like_number** (@array);

  Takes a list of values and returns an array with one member for each element of the list. Each member indicates whether the corresponding argument looks like a number: true if it does, false if it doesn't, and undef if the argument is undefined or empty.

- $str = DBI::**neat** ($value [, $maxlen]);

  Returns a string containing a nicely formatted representation of the $value argument. Strings are quoted; numbers are not. (But note that quoted numbers are considered to be strings.) Undefined values are reported as undef, and unprintable characters are reported as '.'.

  The $maxlen argument controls the maximum length of the result. If the result is longer than $maxlen, it is shortened to $maxlen−4 characters and an ellipsis ('…') is added. If $maxlen is 0, undef, or missing, it defaults to $DBI::neat_maxlen (400).

  Don't use neat() for query construction; if you need to perform quoting or escaping, use quote() instead.

- $str = DBI::**neat_list** (\@listref [, $maxlen [, $field_sep]]);

  Calls neat() for each element of the list pointed to by the first argument, joins them with the separator string $field_sep, and returns the result as a single string.

  The $maxlen argument is applied to individual arguments, not to the string resulting from the calls to neat().

  If $field_sep is missing, the default is ", ".

DBI Attributes

DBI provides attribute information at several levels. Most attributes are associated with database handles or statement handles, but not with both. Some attributes, such as PrintError and RaiseError, may be associated with either database handles or statement handles. In general, each handle has its own attributes, but some attributes that hold error information, such as err and errstr, are dynamic in that they associate with the most recently used handle.

General Handle Attributes

These attributes may be applied to individual handles or specified in the %attr parameter to methods that take such a parameter to affect the operation of the method. If used with the connect() method, DBI processing is affected globally throughout the script.

- $h->{'**ChopBlanks**'};

  Determines whether row-fetching methods will chop trailing blanks from CHAR column values. ChopBlanks is disabled by default for most database drivers, but for MySQL it doesn't matter anyway because the server always chops blanks from CHAR values.

- $h->{'**PrintError**'};

  If enabled, the occurrence of a DBI-related error causes a warning message to be printed. PrintError is enabled by default.

- $h->{'**RaiseError**'};

  If enabled, the occurrence of a DBI-related error causes automatic script termination. RaiseError is disabled by default.

Dynamic Attributes

These attributes are associated with the most recently used handle, represented by $h in the following descriptions:

- **$DBI::err**

  This is the same as calling $h->err().

- **$$DBI::errstr**

  This is the same as calling $h->errstr().

- **$DBI::rows**

  This is the same as calling $h->rows().

MySQL-Specific Database Handle Attributes

These attributes are specific to the DBI MySQL driver, DBD::mysql.

- $str = $dbh->{'**info**'};

  This attribute contains the same information that is returned by the C API function mysql_info(). See the description of that function in Appendix F.

- $rv = $dbh->{'**mysql_insertid**'};

  The AUTO_INCREMENT value that was most recently generated on the connection associated with $dbh.

- $rv = $dbh->{'**thread_id**'};

  The thread number of the connection associated with $dbh.

Statement Handle Attributes

Generally these attributes apply to a SELECT (or SELECT–like) query and are not valid until the query has been passed to prepare() to obtain a statement handle and execute() has been called for that handle. In addition, finish() may invalidate some statement attributes.

Many of these attributes have values that are a reference to an array of values, one value per column of the query. The number of elements in the array is given by the $sth->{'NUM_OF_FIELDS'} attribute. For a statement attribute *stmt_attr* that is a reference to an array, you can refer to the entire array as @{$sth->{*stmt_attr*}}, or loop through the elements in the array like this:

```
for (my $i = 0; $i < $sth->{NUM_OF_FIELDS}; $i++)
{
    $value = $sth->{stmt_attr}->[$i];
}
```

- $sth->{'**NAME**'};

  A reference to an array of strings indicating the name for each column. The lettercase of the names is as specified in the SELECT statement.

- `$sth->{'NAME_lc'};`

  A reference to an array of strings indicating the name for each column. The names are returned as lowercase strings.

- `$sth->{'NAME_uc'};`

  A reference to an array of strings indicating the name for each column. The names are returned as uppercase strings.

- `$sth->{'NULLABLE'};`

  A reference to an array of values indicating whether or not each column can be NULL. Values for each element can be 0 (no), 1 (yes), or 2 (unknown). At least, that's what the DBI documentation says. It appears the value is actually the empty string if the column cannot be NULL.

- `$sth->{'NUM_OF_FIELDS'};`

  The number of columns that a prepared statement will return, or zero for a non-SELECT statement.

- `$sth->{'NUM_OF_PARAMS'};`

  The number of placeholders in a prepared statement.

- `$sth->{'PRECISION'};`

  A reference to an array of values indicating the precision of each column. DBI uses "precision" in the ODBC sense, which for MySQL means the maximum width of the column. For numeric columns, this is the display width. For string columns, it's the maximum length of the column.

- `$sth->{'SCALE'};`

  A reference to an array of values indicating the scale of each column. DBI uses "scale" in the ODBC sense, which for MySQL means the number of decimal places for floating-point columns. For other columns, the scale is 0.

- `$sth->{'Statement'};`

  The text of the statement associated with $sth. The text is that seen by prepare() before any placeholder substitution takes place.

- `$sth->{'TYPE'};`

  A reference to an array of values indicating the numeric type of each column.

MySQL-Specific Statement Handle Attributes

Most of these statement handle attributes should be considered read-only and should be accessed after invoking execute(). Exceptions are mysql_store_result and mysql_use_result. DBD::mysql provides the capability for controlling the result set processing style used by your script. The statement handle attributes `mysql_store_result` and `mysql_use_result` select the result set processing behavior of the C API functions `mysql_store_result()` and `mysql_use_result()`. See Appendix F for a discussion of these two functions and how they differ.

By default, DBI uses `mysql_store_result()`, but you can enable the `mysql_use_result` attribute, which tells DBI to use `mysql_use_result()` instead. Do this after `prepare()` but before `execute()`:

```
$sth = $dbh->prepare (...);
$sth->{mysql_use_result} = 1;
$sth->execute();
```

Several of the MySQL-specific attributes that were available in older versions of DBD::mysql are now deprecated and have been replaced by newer preferred forms, as indicated in Table G.2. If your version of DBD::mysql is old and does not support the newer attributes, try the deprecated forms instead (or else upgrade to a newer version).

Note that `insertid` is a statement handle attribute, whereas its preferred form, `mysql_insertid`, is a database handle attribute.

Table G.2 **Deprecated MySQL-Specific Attributes**

Deprecated Attribute	**Preferred Attribute**
insertid	mysql_insertid
is_blob	mysql_is_blob
is_key	mysql_is_key
is_not_null	mysql_is_not_null
is_num	mysql_is_num
is_pri_key	mysql_is_pri_key
length	PRECISION
max_length	mysql_max_length
table	mysql_table

- `$sth->{'mysql_is_blob'};`

  A reference to an array of values indicating whether or not each column is a BLOB type.

- `$sth->{'mysql_is_key'};`

  A reference to an array of values indicating whether or not each column is part of a non-unique key.

- `$sth->{'mysql_is_not_null'};`

  A reference to an array of values indicating whether or not each column may be NULL. A false value indicates that the column may contain NULL values. This attribute contains information that is the "inverse" of the information in the information in the NULLABLE attribute.

- `$sth->{'mysql_is_num'};`

  A reference to an array of values indicating whether or not each column is a numeric type.

- `$sth->{'mysql_is_pri_key'};`

  A reference to an array of values indicating whether or not each column is part of a PRIMARY KEY.

- `$sth->{'mysql_max_length'};`

  A reference to an array of values indicating the actual maximum length of the column values in the result set.

- `$sth->{'mysql_store_result'};`

  If `mysql_store_result` is enabled (set to 1), result sets are retrieved from the MySQL server using the `mysql_store_result()` C API function rather than by using `mysql_use_result()`. See Appendix F for a discussion of these two functions and how they differ.

  If you set the `mysql_store_result` attribute, do so after invoking `prepare()` and before invoking `execute()`.

- `$sth->{'mysql_table'};`

  A reference to an array of values indicating the name of the table from which each column comes. The table name for a calculated column is the empty string.

- `$sth->{'mysql_type'};`

  A reference to an array of values indicating the number of the MySQL type for each column in the result set.

- `$sth->{'mysql_type_name'};`

  A reference to an array of values indicating the name of the MySQL type for each column in the result set.

- `$sth->{'mysql_use_result'};`

  If `mysql_use_result` is enabled (set to 1), result sets are retrieved from the MySQL server using the `mysql_use_result()` C API function rather than by using `mysql_store_result()`. See Appendix F for a discussion of these two functions and how they differ.

  Note that use of this attribute causes some attributes such as `mysql_max_length` to become invalid. It also invalidates the use of the `rows()` method, although it's better to count rows when you fetch them anyway.

  If you set the `mysql_use_result` attribute, do so after invoking `prepare()` and before invoking `execute()`.

DBI Environment Variables

DBI consults several environment variables, listed in Table G.3. All of them except `DBI_TRACE` are used by the `connect()` method. `DBI_TRACE` is used by the `trace()` method.

Table G.3 **DBI Environment Variables**

Name	Meaning
DBI_DRIVER	DBD-level driver name ("`mysql`" for MySQL)
DBI_DSN	Data source name
DBI_PASS	Password
DBI_TRACE	Trace level and/or trace output file
DBI_USER	Username

H

PHP API Reference

THIS APPENDIX DESCRIBES THE PHP application-programming interface for MySQL. The API consists of a set of functions for communicating with MySQL servers and accessing databases.

This appendix serves as a reference, so it includes only brief code fragments illustrating use of the PHP API. For complete client scripts and notes on writing them, see Chapter 8, "The PHP API." The functions described here are those that pertain directly to MySQL. The PHP manual (currently almost 800 pages) contains more than 600 pages of reference material, so obviously this appendix can do no more than summarize a small part of PHP's capabilities. To obtain the complete PHP manual, visit the PHP Web site at the following location:

```
http://www.php.net/
```

Writing PHP Scripts

PHP scripts are plain text files that may contain a mixture of HTML and PHP code. The script is interpreted to produce a Web page as output that is sent to the client. The HTML is copied to the output without interpretation. PHP code is interpreted and replaced by whatever output the code produces (possibly none).

PHP begins interpreting a file in HTML mode. You can switch into and out of PHP code mode using special tags that signify the beginning and end of PHP code. You can switch between modes any number of times within a file. PHP understands four types of tags, although some of them must be explicitly enabled if you want to use them. One way to do this is by turning them on in the PHP initialization file, `php3.ini`. The location of this file is system dependent; it's often found in `/usr/local/lib`.

PHP understands the following tag styles:

- The default style uses '`<?php`' and '`?>`' tags:

  ```
  <?php echo ("Some PHP code here"); ?>
  ```

- Short-open-tag style uses '`<?`' and '`?>`' tags:

  ```
  <? echo ("Some PHP code here"); ?>
  ```

  This tag style can be enabled with a directive in the PHP initialization file:

  ```
  short_open_tag = On;
  ```

- Active Server Page-compatible style uses '`<%`' and '`%>`' tags:

  ```
  <% echo ("Some PHP code here"); %>
  ```

  ASP-style tags can be enabled with a directive in the PHP initialization file:

  ```
  asp_tags = On;
  ```

  Support for ASP tags was introduced in PHP 3.0.4.

- If you use an HTML editor that doesn't understand the other tags, you can use `<SCRIPT>` and `</SCRIPT>` tags:

  ```
  <SCRIPT LANGUAGE="php"> echo ("Some PHP code here"); </SCRIPT>
  ```

Functions

The following descriptions discuss each of PHP's MySQL-related functions. Optional parameters are indicated by square brackets (`[ ]`).

Many functions take an optional `link_id` (link identifier) parameter that indicates a connection to a MySQL server. If the link identifier is missing from a function call, the most recently opened connection is used. Some functions will try to establish a connection if no connection is specified and there isn't one open.

A `result_id` parameter indicates a result set identifier, typically returned by `mysql_db_query()` or `mysql_query()`.

Some functions produce an error message if an error occurs, in addition to returning a status value. In Web contexts, this message appears in the output sent to the client browser, which may not be what you want. A function name may be preceded by '`@`' to suppress the (possibly cryptic) error message the function would normally produce. For example, to suppress the error message from a `mysql_pconnect()` call so that you can report failure in a more suitable manner, you might do something like this:

```
<?php
    $link = @mysql_pconnect ("pit-viper.snake.net", "paul", "secret")
        or die ("Could not connect");
    print ("Connected successfully");
?>
```

Another way to suppress error messages is to use the `error_reporting()` function:

```
<?php
    error_reporting (0); # suppress all error messages
    $link = mysql_pconnect ("pit-viper.snake.net", "paul", "secret")
        or die ("Could not connect");
    print ("Connected successfully");
?>
```

Many of the example scripts in this appendix print "Connected successfully" after establishing a connection to the MySQL server. The reason they do this is to make sure the script prints some output, in case you try the script for yourself. A PHP script that produces no output triggers a "page contains no data" warning in some browsers.

In the descriptions that follow, the term "SELECT query" should be taken to mean a SELECT query or any other query that returns rows, such as DESCRIBE, EXPLAIN, or SHOW.

Connection Management Routines

The routines in this section allow you to open and close connections to the MySQL server.

- int
  mysql_close ([int link_id]);

  Closes the connection to the MySQL server identified by `link_id`. If no connection is specified, `mysql_close()` closes the most recently opened connection.

  `mysql_close()` returns true for success or false for an error. For persistent connections opened with `mysql_pconnect()`, `mysql_close()` ignores the close request but returns true. If you are going to close a connection, you should open it using `mysql_connect()` rather than `mysql_pconnect()`.

  ```
  <?php
      $link = mysql_connect ("pit-viper.snake.net", "paul", "secret")
          or die ("Could not connect");
      print ("Connected successfully");
      mysql_close ($link);
  ?>
  ```

- int
  mysql_connect ([string host_name] [, string user_name [, string password]]);

  Opens a connection to the MySQL server on host `host_name` for user `user_name` with the given password. Returns the link identifier (a positive number) associated with the new connection; returns false if an error occurred.

As of PHP 3.0B4, the hostname parameter may be specified with an optional port number, in "*host_name:port_num*" form. As of PHP 3.0.10, if the hostname is `localhost`, the hostname parameter may be specified with an optional pathname to specify the UNIX domain socket path, in "`localhost:`*socket_name*" form. The socket should be specified as a full pathname.

If the hostname parameter is missing, the default is `localhost`. If the username parameter is missing or empty, the default is the username that PHP is running as. (This is the name of the user the Web server is running as if PHP is running as an Apache module, or the name of the user PHP is running as if PHP is running as a standalone program.) If the password parameter is missing or empty, the empty password is sent.

While the connection is open, if `mysql_connect()` is called with the same connection parameters (hostname, username, password), no new connection is generated; `mysql_connect()` returns the existing link identifier instead.

The connection may be closed by calling `mysql_close()`. If the connection is open when the script terminates, the connection is closed automatically.

```php
<?php
    $link = mysql_connect ("pit-viper.snake.net", "paul", "secret")
        or die ("Could not connect");
    print ("Connected successfully");
    mysql_close ($link);
?>
```

- int

mysql_pconnect ([string host_name] [, string user_name [, string password]]);

`mysql_pconnect()` is like `mysql_connect()` except that it opens a persistent connection. That is, the connection stays open when the script terminates. If another call is made to `mysql_pconnect()` with the same connection parameters (hostname, username, password) while the connection is open, the connection will be reused. This avoids the overhead of tearing down and reopening connections and is more efficient than non-persistent connections.

Persistent connections only make sense when PHP is executing as a module within a Web server that continues to run after the PHP script terminates. In a script executed by a standalone version of PHP, the connection is closed when the script terminates because the PHP process terminates as well.

Calling `mysql_close()` on a persistent connection is nonsensical; in this case, `mysql_close()` returns true but leaves the connection open.

```php
<?php
    $link = mysql_pconnect ("pit-viper.snake.net", "paul", "secret")
        or die ("Could not connect");
    print ("Connected successfully");
?>
```

Status- and Error-Reporting Routines

The `mysql_errno()` and `mysql_error()` functions return error number and message information for MySQL-related PHP functions. However, no error information is available from either function without a valid link identifier. This means that they are not useful for reporting the result of failed `mysql_connect()` or `mysql_pconnect()` calls because no valid link identifier is available until a connection has been established successfully. If you want to get the MySQL error message for failed connection attempts, enable the `track_errors` variable with a directive in the PHP initialization file:

```
track_errors = On;
```

Then restart your Web server if you're running PHP as an Apache module. After you've done that, you can obtain the error string for failed connection attempts by referring to the `$php_errormsg` variable:

```php
<?php
    $link = @mysql_connect("badhost","baduser", "badpass")
        or die ("Could not connect: " . $php_errormsg);
    print ("Connected successfully");
?>
```

- int

  mysql_errno ([int link_id]);

  For the given connection, returns the error number for the MySQL-related function that most recently returned a status. A value of zero means no error occurred.

  ```php
  <?php
      $link = mysql_pconnect ("pit-viper.snake.net", "paul", "secret")
          or die ("Could not connect");
      print ("Connected successfully");
      $query = "SELECT * FROM president";
      $result = mysql_query ($query)
          or die ("query failed, error code = " . mysql_errno ());
  ?>
  ```

- string

  mysql_error ([int link_id]);

  For the given connection, returns a string containing the error message for MySQL-related function that most recently returned a status. An empty string means no error occurred.

  ```php
  <?php
      $link = mysql_pconnect ("pit-viper.snake.net", "paul", "secret")
          or die ("Could not connect");
      print ("Connected successfully");
      $query = "SELECT * FROM president";
      $result = mysql_query ($query)
          or die ("query failed, error message = " . mysql_error ());
  ?>
  ```

Query Construction and Execution Routines

The routines in this section are used to issue queries to the MySQL server.

- int
  mysql_db_query (string db_name, string query [, int link_id]);

  mysql_db_query() is like mysql_query() except that it takes an additional database name argument and makes it the default database before executing the query. (Compare the following example to the example for mysql_query().)

  ```php
  <?php
      $link = mysql_pconnect ("pit-viper.snake.net", "paul", "secret")
          or die ("Could not connect");
      print ("Connected successfully");
      $query = "SELECT * FROM president";
      $result = mysql_db_query ("samp_db", $query)
          or die ("Query failed");
  ?>
  ```

- int
  mysql_list_dbs ([int link_id]);

  Returns a result identifier for a result set consisting of the names of the databases the server knows about on the given connection, one database name per row of the result set. Returns false if an error occurs. A default database does not need to be selected. The result set may be processed by any of the usual row-fetching functions or by mysql_tablename().

  ```php
  <?php
      $link = mysql_pconnect ("pit-viper.snake.net", "paul", "secret")
          or die ("Could not connect");
      $result = mysql_list_dbs ()
          or die ("Query failed");
      print ("Databases (using mysql_fetch_row()):<BR>\n");
      while ($row = mysql_fetch_row ($result))
          printf ("%s<BR>\n", $row[0]);
      $result = mysql_list_dbs ()
          or die ("Query failed");
      print ("Databases (using mysql_tablename()):<BR>\n");
      for ($i = 0; $i < mysql_num_rows ($result); $i++)
          printf ("%s<BR>\n", mysql_tablename ($result, $i));
  ?>
  ```

- int
  mysql_list_fields (string db_name, string tbl_name [, int link_id]);

  Returns a result identifier for a result set containing information about the columns in a table; returns false if an error occurs. A default database does not need to be selected. The db_name and tbl_name parameters identify the database and table in which you're interested. The result identifier can be used with the functions `mysql_field_flags()`, `mysql_field_len()`, `mysql_field_name()`, and `mysql_field_type()`.

```php
<?php
    $link = mysql_pconnect ("pit-viper.snake.net", "paul", "secret")
        or die ("Could not connect");
    $result = mysql_list_fields ("samp_db", "member")
        or die ("Query failed");
    print ("member table column information:<BR>\n");
    for ($i = 0; $i < mysql_num_fields ($result); $i++)
    {
        printf ("column %d:", $i);
        printf (" name %s,\n", mysql_field_name ($result, $i));
        printf (" len %d,\n", mysql_field_len ($result, $i));
        printf (" type %s,\n", mysql_field_type ($result, $i));
        printf (" flags %s\n", mysql_field_flags ($result, $i));
        print "<BR>\n";
    }
?>
```

- int
  mysql_list_tables (string db_name [, int link_id]);

  Returns a result identifier for a result set consisting of the names of the tables in the given database name, one table name per row of the result set. Returns false if an error occurs. A default database does not need to be selected. The result set may be processed by any of the usual row-fetching functions or by `mysql_tablename()`.

```php
<?php
    $link = mysql_pconnect ("pit-viper.snake.net", "paul", "secret")
        or die ("Could not connect");
    $result = mysql_list_tables ("samp_db")
        or die ("Query failed");
    print ("samp_db tables (using mysql_fetch_row()):<BR>\n");
    while ($row = mysql_fetch_row ($result))
        printf ("%s<BR>\n", $row[0]);
    $result = mysql_list_tables ("samp_db")
        or die ("Query failed");
    print ("samp_db tables (using mysql_tablename()):<BR>\n");
    for ($i = 0; $i < mysql_num_rows ($result); $i++)
        printf ("%s<BR>\n", mysql_tablename ($result, $i));
?>
```

- int
  mysql_query (string query [, int link_id]);

  Sends the query string to the MySQL server on the given connection. For DELETE, INSERT, REPLACE, and UPDATE statements, `mysql_query()` returns true for success, and false if an error occurs. For a successful query, you can call mysql_affected_rows() to find out how many rows were modified.

For SELECT statements, mysql_query() returns a positive result set identifier for success, and false if an error occurs. For a successful query, the result identifier can be used with the various result set processing functions that take a result_id argument. The identifier may be passed to mysql_free_result() to free any resources associated with the result set.

A "successful" query is one that executes without error, but success implies nothing about whether or not the query returns any rows. The following query is perfectly legal but returns no rows:

```
SELECT * FROM president WHERE 1 = 0
```

A query may fail for any of several reasons. For example, it may be syntactically malformed, semantically invalid, or illegal because you don't have permission to access the tables named in the query.

If no link identifier is specified, the most recently opened connection is used. If there is no current connection, mysql_query() attempts to open a connection as if mysql_connect() were called with no arguments. mysql_query() fails if the connection attempt fails.

```php
<?php
    $link = mysql_pconnect ("pit-viper.snake.net", "paul", "secret")
        or die ("Could not connect");
    print ("Connected successfully");
    mysql_select_db ("samp_db")
        or die ("Could not select database");
    $query = "SELECT * FROM president";
    $result = mysql_query ($query)
        or die ("Query failed");
?>
```

Result Set Processing Routines

The routines in this section are used to retrieve the results of queries. They also provide access to information about the result, such as how many rows were affected, or the metadata for result set columns.

- int
  mysql_affected_rows ([int link_id]);

  Returns the number of rows affected (modified) by the most recent DELETE, INSERT, REPLACE, or UPDATE statement on the given connection. mysql_affected_rows() returns 0 if no rows were changed and −1 if an error occurred.

After a `SELECT` query, `mysql_affected_rows()` returns the number of rows selected. However, normally you use `mysql_num_rows()` with `SELECT` statements.

```php
<?php
    $link = mysql_pconnect ("pit-viper.snake.net", "paul", "secret")
        or die ("Could not connect");
    mysql_select_db ("samp_db")
        or die ("Could not select database");
    $query = "INSERT INTO member (last_name,first_name,expiration)"
        . " VALUES('Brown','Marcia','2002-6-3')";
    $result = mysql_query ($query)
        or die ("Query failed");
    printf ("%d row%s inserted\n",
            mysql_affected_rows (),
            mysql_affected_rows () == 1 ? "" : "s");
?>
```

- int

mysql_data_seek (int result_id, int row_num);.

Each result set returned by a `SELECT` query has a row cursor to indicate which row should be returned by the next call to the row-fetching functions (`mysql_fetch_array()`, `mysql_fetch_object()`, or `mysql_fetch_row()`. `mysql_data_seek()` sets the cursor for the given result set to the given row. The row number should be in the range from 0 to `mysql_num_rows()`−1. `mysql_data_seek()` returns true if the row number is legal and false otherwise.

```php
<?php
    $link = mysql_pconnect ("pit-viper.snake.net", "paul", "secret")
        or die ("Could not connect");
    mysql_select_db ("samp_db")
        or die ("Could not select database");
    $query = "SELECT last_name, first_name FROM president";
    $result = mysql_query ($query)
        or die ("Query failed");
    # fetch rows in reverse order
    for ($i = mysql_num_rows ($result) - 1; $i >=0; $i—)
    {
        if (!mysql_data_seek ($result, $i))
        {
            printf ("Cannot seek to row %d\n", $i);
            continue;
        }
        if(!($row = mysql_fetch_object ($result)))
            continue;
        printf ("%s %s<BR>\n", $row->last_name, $row->first_name);
    }
    mysql_free_result ($result);
?>
```

- array

mysql_fetch_array (int result_id [, int result_type]);

Returns the next row of the given result set as an array. Returns false if there are no more rows. The array contains values stored both by numeric column indices and associatively keyed by column names. In other words, each column value may be accessed using either its numeric column index or its name. Associative indices are case sensitive and must be given in the same case that was used to name columns in the query. Suppose you issue the following query:

```
SELECT last_name, first_name FROM president
```

If you fetch rows from the result set into an array named $row, array elements may be accessed as follows:

```
$row[0]                  Holds last_name value
$row[1]                  Holds first_name value
$row["last_name"]        Holds last_name value
$row["first_name"]       Holds first_name value
```

Keys are not qualified by the table names of the corresponding columns, so if you select columns with the same name from different tables, a name clash results. Precedence is given to the column named last in the list of columns selected by the query. To access the hidden column, use its numeric index, or write the query to provide an alias for the column.

The result_type parameter may be MYSQL_ASSOC (return values by name indices only), MYSQL_NUM (return values by numeric indices only), or MYSQL_BOTH (return values by both types of indices). The default if result_type is missing is MYSQL_BOTH.

```php
<?php
    $link = mysql_pconnect ("pit-viper.snake.net", "paul", "secret")
        or die ("Could not connect");
    mysql_select_db ("samp_db")
        or die ("Could not select database");
    $query = "SELECT last_name, first_name FROM president";
    $result = mysql_query ($query)
        or die ("Query failed");
    while ($row = mysql_fetch_array ($result))
    {
        # print each name twice, once using numeric indices,
        # once using associative (name) indices
        printf ("%s %s<BR>\n", $row[0], $row[1]);
        printf ("%s %s<BR>\n", $row["last_name"], $row["first_name"]);
    }
    mysql_free_result ($result);
?>
```

- object

mysql_fetch_field (int result_id [, int col_num]);

Returns metadata information about the given column in the result set; returns false if there is no such column. If col_num is omitted, successive calls to mysql_fetch_field() return information about successive columns of the result set. The return value is false if no more columns remain. If col_num is specified, it should be in the range from 0 to mysql_num_fields()−1. In this case, mysql_fetch_field() returns information about the given column; returns false if col_num is out of range.

The information is returned as an object that has the properties shown in Table H.1.

```php
<?php
    $link = mysql_pconnect ("pit-viper.snake.net", "paul", "secret")
        or die ("Could not connect");
    mysql_select_db ("samp_db")
        or die ("Could not select database");
    $query = "SELECT * FROM president";
    $result = mysql_query ($query)
        or die ("Query failed");
    # get column metadata
    for ($i = 0; $i < mysql_num_fields ($result); $i++)
    {
        printf ("Information for column %d:<BR>\n", $i);
        $meta = mysql_fetch_field ($result);
        if (!$meta)
        {
            print ("No information available<BR>\n");
            continue;
        }
        print ("<PRE>\n");
        printf ("blob:          %s\n", $meta->blob);
        printf ("max_length:    %s\n", $meta->max_length);
        printf ("multiple_key: %s\n", $meta->multiple_key);
        printf ("name:          %s\n", $meta->name);
        printf ("not_null:      %s\n", $meta->not_null);
        printf ("numeric:       %s\n", $meta->numeric);
        printf ("primary_key:  %s\n", $meta->primary_key);
        printf ("table:         %s\n", $meta->table);
        printf ("type:          %s\n", $meta->type);
        printf ("unique_key:    %s\n", $meta->unique_key);
        printf ("unsigned:      %s\n", $meta->unsigned);
        printf ("zerofill:      %s\n", $meta->zerofill);
        print ("</PRE>\n");
    }
?>
```

Table H.1 `mysql_fetch_field()` **Properties**

Property	Meaning
blob	1 if the column is a BLOB type, 0 otherwise
max_length	The length of the largest column value in the result set
multiple_key	1 if the column is a part of a non-unique index, 0 otherwise
name	The column name
not_null	1 if the column cannot contain NULL values, 0 otherwise
numeric	1 if the column has a numeric type, 0 otherwise
primary_key	1 if the column is a part of a PRIMARY KEY, 0 otherwise
table	The name of the table containing the column (empty for calculated columns)
type	The name of the type of the column
unique_key	1 if the column is a part of a UNIQUE index, 0 otherwise
unsigned	1 if the column has the UNSIGNED attribute, 0 otherwise
zerofill	1 if the column has the ZEROFILL attribute, 0 otherwise

- array
  mysql_fetch_lengths (int result_id);

  Returns an array containing the lengths of the column values in the row most recently fetched by any of the functions `mysql_fetch_array()`, `mysql_fetch_object()`, or `mysql_fetch_row()`. Returns false if no row has yet been fetched or if an error occurred.

```php
<?php
    $link = mysql_pconnect ("pit-viper.snake.net", "paul", "secret")
        or die ("Could not connect");
    mysql_select_db ("samp_db")
        or die ("Could not select database");
    $query = "SELECT * FROM president";
    $result = mysql_query ($query)
        or die ("Query failed");
    $row_num = 0;
    while (mysql_fetch_row ($result))
    {
        ++$row_num;
        # get lengths of column values
        printf ("Lengths of values in row %d:<BR>\n", $row_num);
        $len = mysql_fetch_lengths ($result);
        if (!$len)
        {
            print ("No information available<BR>\n");
            break;
        }
        print ("<PRE>\n");
```

```
            for ($i = 0; $i < mysql_num_fields ($result); $i++)
                printf ("column %d: %s\n", $i, $len[$i]);
            print ("</PRE>\n");
        }
    ?>
```

- object

  mysql_fetch_object (int result_id [, int result_type]);

  Returns the next row of the given result set as an object; returns false if there are no more rows. Column values may be accessed as properties of the object. The property names are the names of the columns selected in the query from which the result set was generated.

  The result_type parameter may be MYSQL_ASSOC (return values by name indices only), MYSQL_NUM (return values by numeric indices only), or MYSQL_BOTH (return values by both types of indices). The default if result_type is missing is MYSQL_BOTH. (It's not clear to me what the utility of specifying MYSQL_NUM is, given that numbers are not legal property names.)

  ```
  <?php
      $link = mysql_pconnect ("pit-viper.snake.net", "paul", "secret")
          or die ("Could not connect");
      mysql_select_db ("samp_db")
          or die ("Could not select database");
      $query = "SELECT last_name, first_name FROM president";
      $result = mysql_query ($query)
          or die ("Query failed");
      while ($row = mysql_fetch_object ($result))
          printf ("%s %s<BR>\n", $row->last_name, $row->first_name);
      mysql_free_result ($result);
  ?>
  ```

- array

  mysql_fetch_row (int result_id);

  Returns the next row of the given result set as an array; returns false if there are no more rows.

  Column values may be accessed as array elements, using column indices in the range from 0 to mysql_num_fields()−1.

  ```
  <?php
      $link = mysql_pconnect ("pit-viper.snake.net", "paul", "secret")
          or die ("Could not connect");
      mysql_select_db ("samp_db")
          or die ("Could not select database");
      $query = "SELECT last_name, first_name FROM president";
      $result = mysql_query ($query)
          or die ("Query failed");
      while ($row = mysql_fetch_row ($result))
  ```

continues

continued

```
        printf ("%s %s<BR>\n", $row[0], $row[1]);
    mysql_free_result ($result);
?>
```

- string
  mysql_field_name (int result_id, int col_num);.

Returns the name of the given column of the result set.

col_num should be in the range from 0 to mysql_num_fields()–1.

```
<?php
    $link = mysql_pconnect ("pit-viper.snake.net", "paul", "secret")
        or die ("Could not connect");
    mysql_select_db ("samp_db")
        or die ("Could not select database");
    $query = "SELECT * FROM president";
    $result = mysql_query ($query)
        or die ("Query failed");
    # get column names
    for ($i = 0; $i < mysql_num_fields ($result); $i++)
    {
        printf ("Name of column %d: ", $i);
        $name = mysql_field_name ($result, $i);
        if (!$name)
            print ("No name available<BR>\n");
        else
            print ("$name<BR>\n");
    }
?>
```

- int
  mysql_field_seek (int result_id, int col_num);

Sets the index for subsequent calls to mysql_fetch_field().The next call to mysql_fetch_field() that is issued without an explicit column number will return information for column col_num. Returns true if the seek succeeds and false otherwise.

col_num should be in the range from 0 to mysql_num_fields()–1.

```
<?php
    $link = mysql_pconnect ("pit-viper.snake.net", "paul", "secret")
        or die ("Could not connect");
    mysql_select_db ("samp_db")
        or die ("Could not select database");
    $query = "SELECT * FROM president";
    $result = mysql_query ($query)
        or die ("Query failed");
    # get column metadata
    for ($i = 0; $i < mysql_num_fields ($result); $i++)
    {
```

```
        printf ("Information for column %d:<BR>\n", $i);
        if (!mysql_field_seek ($result, $i))
        {
            print ("Cannot seek to column<BR>\n");
            continue;
        }
        $meta = mysql_fetch_field ($result, $i);
        if (!$meta)
        {
            print ("No information available<BR>\n");
            continue;
        }
        print ("<PRE>\n");
        printf ("blob:         %s\n", $meta->blob);
        printf ("max_length:   %s\n", $meta->max_length);
        printf ("multiple_key: %s\n", $meta->multiple_key);
        printf ("name:         %s\n", $meta->name);
        printf ("not_null:     %s\n", $meta->not_null);
        printf ("numeric:      %s\n", $meta->numeric);
        printf ("primary_key:  %s\n", $meta->primary_key);
        printf ("table:        %s\n", $meta->table);
        printf ("type:         %s\n", $meta->type);
        printf ("unique_key:   %s\n", $meta->unique_key);
        printf ("unsigned:     %s\n", $meta->unsigned);
        printf ("zerofill:     %s\n", $meta->zerofill);
        print ("</PRE>\n");
    }
?>
```

- string
  mysql_field_table (int result_id, int col_num);

Returns the name of the table that contains the given column of the result set.
For calculated columns, the name is empty.

col_num should be in the range from 0 to mysql_num_fields()−1.

```
<?php
    $link = mysql_pconnect ("pit-viper.snake.net", "paul", "secret")
        or die ("Could not connect");
    mysql_select_db ("samp_db");
    $query = "SELECT * FROM president";
    $result = mysql_query ($query)
        or die ("Query failed");
    for ($i = 0; $i < mysql_num_fields ($result); $i++)
    {
        printf ("column %d:", $i);
        printf (" name %s,\n", mysql_field_name ($result, $i));
        printf (" table %s\n", mysql_field_table ($result, $i));
```

continues

continued

```
            print "<BR>\n";
        }
    ?>
```

- string

    mysql_field_type (int result_id, int col_num);

    Returns the name of the type for the given column of the result set. Type names are listed in Appendix B, "Column Type Reference."

    col_num should be in the range from 0 to mysql_num_fields()−1.

```php
<?php
    $link = mysql_pconnect ("pit-viper.snake.net", "paul", "secret")
        or die ("Could not connect");
    mysql_select_db ("samp_db");
    $query = "SELECT * FROM president";
    $result = mysql_query ($query)
        or die ("Query failed");
    for ($i = 0; $i < mysql_num_fields ($result); $i++)
    {
        printf ("column %d:", $i);
        printf (" name %s,\n", mysql_field_name ($result, $i));
        printf (" type %s\n", mysql_field_type ($result, $i));
        print "<BR>\n";
    }
?>
```

- string

    mysql_field_flags (int result_id, int col_num);

    Returns metadata information about the given column in the result set as a string; returns false if an error occurred. The string consists of space-separated words indicating which of a column's flag values are true. For flags that are false, the corresponding word is not present in the string. Table H.2 lists the words that may be present in the string.

    col_num should be in the range from 0 to mysql_num_fields()−1.

```php
<?php
    $link = mysql_pconnect ("pit-viper.snake.net", "paul", "secret")
        or die ("Could not connect");
    mysql_select_db ("samp_db");
    $query = "SELECT * FROM member";
    $result = mysql_query ($query)
        or die ("Query failed");
    for ($i = 0; $i < mysql_num_fields ($result); $i++)
    {
        printf ("column %d:", $i);
        printf (" name %s,\n", mysql_field_name ($result, $i));
        printf (" flags %s\n", mysql_field_flags ($result, $i));
```

```
            print "<BR>\n";
        }
    ?>
```

Table H.2 `mysql_field_flags()` **Values**

Property	Meaning
auto_increment	Column has the AUTO_INCREMENT attribute
binary	Column has the BINARY attribute
blob	Column is a BLOB type
enum	Column is an ENUM
multiple_key	Column is a part of a non-unique index
not_null	Column cannot contain NULL values
primary_key	Column is a part of a PRIMARY KEY
timestamp	Column is a TIMESTAMP
unique_key	Column is a part of a UNIQUE index
unsigned	Column has the UNSIGNED attribute
zerofill	Column has the ZEROFILL attribute

- int
  mysql_field_len (int result_id, int col_num);

  Returns the maximum possible length of values in the given column of the result set.

  col_num should be in the range from 0 to `mysql_num_fields()`–1.

  ```php
  <?php
      $link = mysql_pconnect ("pit-viper.snake.net", "paul", "secret")
          or die ("Could not connect");
      mysql_select_db ("samp_db");
      $query = "SELECT * FROM member";
      $result = mysql_query ($query)
          or die ("Query failed");
      for ($i = 0; $i < mysql_num_fields ($result); $i++)
      {
          printf ("column %d:", $i);
          printf (" name %s,\n", mysql_field_name ($result, $i));
          printf (" len %d\n", mysql_field_len ($result, $i));
          print "<BR>\n";
      }
  ?>
  ```

- int
  mysql_free_result (int result_id);

  Frees any resources associated with the given result set. Result sets are freed automatically when a script terminates, but you may wish to call this function explicitly in a script that generates many result sets. For example, this script will use a considerable amount of memory:

```php
<?php
    $link = mysql_connect ("localhost", "paul", "secret");
    mysql_select_db ("samp_db");
    for ($i = 0; $i < 10000; $i++)
    {
        $result = mysql_query ("SELECT * from president");
    }
?>
```

Adding a `mysql_free_result()` call after the `mysql_query()` call will reduce the amount of result set memory used to almost nothing:

```php
<?php
    $link = mysql_connect ("localhost", "paul", "secret");
    mysql_select_db ("samp_db");
    for ($i = 0; $i < 10000; $i++)
    {
        $result = mysql_query ("SELECT * from president");
        mysql_free_result ($result);
    }
?>
```

- int
  mysql_insert_id ([int link_id]);

Returns the `AUTO_INCREMENT` value generated by the most recently executed query on the given connection. Returns zero if no such value has been generated during the life of the connection. Generally, you should call `mysql_insert_id()` immediately after a query that you expect to generate a new value; if any other query intervenes between that query and the point at which you want to use the value, the value of `mysql_insert_id()` may be reset to zero by the intervening query.

Note that the behavior of `mysql_insert_id()` differs from that of the SQL function `LAST_INSERT_ID()`. `mysql_insert_id()` is maintained in the client and is set for each query. The value of `LAST_INSERT_ID()` is maintained in the server and persists from query to query.

The values returned by `mysql_insert_id()` are connection-specific and are not affected by `AUTO_INCREMENT` activity on other connections.

```php
<?php
    $link = mysql_pconnect ("pit-viper.snake.net", "paul", "secret")
        or die ("Could not connect");
    mysql_select_db ("samp_db")
        or die ("Could not select database");
    $query = "INSERT INTO member (last_name,first_name,expiration)"
        . " VALUES('Brown','Marcia','2002-6-3')";
```

```
        $result = mysql_query ($query)
            or die ("Query failed");
        printf ("membership number for new member: %d\n", mysql_insert_id());
    ?>
```

- int
  mysql_num_fields (int result_id);

  Returns the number of columns in the given result set.

```
    <?php
        $link = mysql_pconnect ("pit-viper.snake.net", "paul", "secret")
            or die ("Could not connect");
        mysql_select_db ("samp_db")
            or die ("Could not select database");
        $query = "SELECT * FROM president";
        $result = mysql_query ($query)
            or die ("Query failed");
        printf ("Number of columns: %d\n", mysql_num_fields ($result));
    ?>
```

- int
  mysql_num_rows (int result_id);

  Returns the number of rows in the given result set.

```
    <?php
        $link = mysql_pconnect ("pit-viper.snake.net", "paul", "secret")
            or die ("Could not connect");
        mysql_select_db ("samp_db")
            or die ("Could not select database");
        $query = "SELECT * FROM president";
        $result = mysql_query ($query)
            or die ("Query failed");
        printf ("Number of rows: %d\n", mysql_num_rows ($result));
    ?>
```

- int
  mysql_result (int result_id, int row, mixed field);

  Returns a value from the given row of a result set. The column is identified by the `field` parameter, which may be either a numeric column index or the column name specified in the query.

  This function is slow; it's preferable to use `mysql_fetch_array()`, `mysql_fetch_object()`, or `mysql_fetch_row()` instead.

```
    <?php
        $link = mysql_pconnect ("pit-viper.snake.net", "paul", "secret")
            or die ("Could not connect");
        mysql_select_db ("samp_db")
            or die ("Could not select database");
        $query = "SELECT last_name, first_name FROM president";
```

continues

continued

```php
        $result = mysql_query ($query)
            or die ("Query failed");
        for ($i = 0; $i < mysql_num_rows ($result); $i++)
        {
            for ($j = 0; $j < mysql_num_fields ($result); $j++)
            {
                if ($j > 0)
                    print (" ");
                print (mysql_result ($result, $i, $j));
            }
            print "<BR>\n";
        }
        mysql_free_result ($result);
    ?>
```

- string

mysql_tablename (int result_id, int row_num);

Given a result identifier returned by mysql_list_dbs() or mysql_list_tables() and a row index row_num, returns the name stored in the given row of the result set.

The row index should be in the range from 0 to mysql_num_rows()−1.

```php
    <?php
        $link - mysql_poonncot ("pit-viper.snake.net", "paul", "secret")
            or die ("Could not connect");
        $result = mysql_list_tables ("samp_db")
            or die ("Query failed");
        print ("samp_db tables:<BR>\n");
        for ($i = 0; $i < mysql_num_rows ($result); $i++)
            printf ("%s<BR>\n", mysql_tablename ($result, $i));
    ?>
```

Database Routines

The routines in this section allow you to create and destroy databases. They also allow you to select a default database for the current server session.

- int

mysql_create_db (string db_name [, int link_id]);

Tells the MySQL server identified by link_id to create the database with the given name. Returns true if the database was created successfully; returns false if an error occurred. You must have the CREATE privilege on the database to create it.

It is preferable to use mysql_query() to issue a CREATE DATABASE statement than to use mysql_create_db().

```
<?php
    $link = mysql_pconnect ("pit-viper.snake.net", "paul", "secret")
        or die ("Could not connect");
    if (mysql_create_db ("my_db"))
        print ("Database created successfully\n");
    else
        printf ("Error creating database: %s\n", mysql_error ());
?>
```

- int

  mysql_drop_db (string db_name [, int link_id]);

  Tells the MySQL server identified by link_id to drop (remove) the database with the given name. Returns true if the database was removed successfully; returns false if an error occurred. You must have the DROP privilege on the database to remove it.

  Be careful with this function; if you drop a database, it's gone. You can't get it back.

  It is preferable to use mysql_query() to issue a DROP DATABASE statement than to use mysql_drop_db().

```
<?php
    $link = mysql_pconnect ("pit-viper.snake.net", "paul", "secret")
        or die ("Could not connect");
    if (mysql_drop_db ("my_db"))
        print ("Database dropped successfully\n");
    else
        printf ("Error dropping database: %s\n", mysql_error ());
?>
```

- int

  mysql_select_db (string db_name [, int link_id]);

  Selects the given database to make it the default database for the given connection. Returns true for success; returns false if an error occurs.

  If no connection is specified, the current connection is used. If there is no current connection, mysql_select_db() attempts to open a connection as if mysql_connect() were called with no arguments. mysql_select_db() fails if the connection attempt fails.

```
<?php
    $link = mysql_pconnect ("pit-viper.snake.net", "paul", "secret")
        or die ("Could not connect");
    print ("Connected successfully");
    mysql_select_db ("samp_db")
        or die ("Could not select database");
?>
```

I

Useful Third-Party Tools

THIS APPENDIX GIVES YOU A BRIEF, illustrative overview of the types of third-party tools available to help you use MySQL more easily and effectively. A more comprehensive, frequently updated list of software is available at the MySQL Web site. My goal here is simply to make you aware of some of the types of tools available and to encourage you to take a look at some of them for yourself. See `http://www.mysql.com/Contrib/` for more information. You'll find many different packages that can help you. These come in several categories:

- **Language APIs and programming tools.** MySQL is well-represented by programming interfaces. In addition to the Perl and PHP interfaces that were discussed in Chapters 7, "The Perl DBI API," and 8, "The PHP API," interfaces for several other languages are available. These include C++, Delphi, Eiffel, Guile, Java, Matlab, Pike, Python, Ruby, Smalltalk, and Tcl. There are also wrapper libraries, such as a C library that presents a Visual Basic-style interface to the host program.

  Other tools are available that help you use the APIs. You can take output produced by `mysqldump` that describes table structures and convert it into a C header file. This is useful for writing C programs that use the MySQL C API to access the table. If you use Tcl/Tk, an interface screen generator is available.

- **Packages that extend MySQL's capabilities.** These include tools to provide full text searching and tools that help you replicate MySQL databases.

- **Data conversion tools.** These include programs that make it easier to convert data used in other programs for use with MySQL, and vice versa. For example, you can convert between .dbf files and MySQL tables, or between Access tables and MySQL tables.

- **ODBC support.** The ODBC (Open Database Connectivity) standard developed by Microsoft allows ODBC-compliant programs to access MySQL databases if a MySQL driver is available. For example, you can install MyODBC on Windows and then use ODBC programs under Windows to access MySQL. One common application involving MyODBC is to connect to a MySQL server from Microsoft Access. To do this, you must have MyODBC set up under Windows, and you should have created a data source name (DSN) for connecting to MySQL. (If you haven't set up MyODBC or created a DSN, see Appendix A, "Obtaining and Installing Software.") After ODBC has been set up, use the following procedure to connect to the MySQL server from within Access:

    1. Start the Access program.
    2. Create a new empty database.
    3. From the File menu, select "External Data," then "Link Tables."
    4. In the window that appears, click on the "Files of type" popup menu and select "ODBC Databases."
    5. Select the DSN that you specified in the ODBC Control Panel for connecting to MySQL.
    6. Start linking.
    7. Select the tables you wish to see.
    8. To open a table, double-click its name.

- **Interfaces to other programs.** Several tools have been written to help you incorporate MySQL as the back end for other programs. There are patches for Apache and WU-ftpd to make these programs perform logging into MySQL tables. You can use MySQL to perform mail user authentication for qmail and the Cyrus IMAP server. pam authentication can be done using MySQL as well.

- **Administrative tools.** Programs to make it easier to manage your MySQL installation come in several different forms. Some are command-line programs, and several others are GUI tools. Some graphical clients are based on the X Windows System, another runs under Windows, and still others, written in Perl and PHP, are Web-based.

J

Internet Service Providers

MANY PEOPLE HAVE FULL–TIME ACCESS TO the Internet and to MySQL over a fast connection. This is especially common in university environments and in businesses large enough to have their own computing services departments. But for many others this is not true, and access to online services comes through an Internet Service Provider (ISP). In addition to basic Internet connectivity for services such as email and Web browsing, many ISPs offer other services, such as access to MySQL and a Web server.

This chapter provides a guide to choosing an ISP appropriately for your requirements. You may need both a way to connect to the Internet and a host on which MySQL is provided. Alternatively, you may already have MySQL running on your machine and need a provider you can connect to that will enable incoming connections from the Internet to reach your machine.

One way to find candidate providers is to visit the Web sites for the packages you require to see if they have a page about ISPs that host the service. For example, the PHP Web site has a search page intended for finding ISPs that have PHP service. One of the search criteria allows you to look for providers that have MySQL. There is also a site that lists MySQL providers. You can visit these sites at the following addresses:

```
http://hosts.php.net/search.php3
http://www.wix.com/mysql-hosting/
```

ISPs are not all the same, so it's important to do a comparative analysis before picking one. Choose carefully; a bad ISP can take all the pleasure out of using MySQL, whereas a good one can help you immeasurably. It's more work to shop around, but if you don't, you may make a bad choice and then you'll have to invest the time later anyway.

Most of the criteria presented in this chapter must be assessed on a relative basis. You may not be able to find an ISP that satisfies your requirements completely, but you should be able to find one that satisfies those requirements better than other ISPs.

As you shop, try to maintain your perspective. Internet Service Providers are not all bad guys, looking to bleed you for as much money as possible while offering as little real value as possible. But they're not all good guys either. It's important to do your homework so that you can find one of the ISPs that do know their stuff and that can help you accomplish your goals. As you proceed in your investigation, be wary of an ISP that evades specific questions about their business practices or technical capabilities. Also watch out for ISPs that give general answers when you press for details.

A note to service providers: MySQL represents a service that you can offer to your customers, with a much lower financial outlay than almost any other relational database system. And, of course, you can use MySQL for your own purposes internally (for example, to assist you in keeping track of customer records). If you are considering installing MySQL, read the chapter in reverse. That is, where it says "Ask the ISP such-and-such?" ask yourself whether or not you could answer the question. If not, why not? Where the chapter says, "Does the ISP provide this or that?" ask yourself whether or not you provide it. If not, what would you require to do so?

Getting Ready to Shop for an ISP

Your first step in finding a service provider is to assess your needs. Before you can choose a provider that meets your requirements, you must know what your requirements are for services and bandwidth. Perhaps that is stating the obvious; unfortunately, it's not unusual for people to look for an ISP with nothing more than the vague idea that they want to "get connected." That's a difficult goal to accomplish satisfactorily; it leaves many questions unanswered because they aren't even asked. Connected for what purpose? To pursue which activities? What cost is considered reasonable?

Once you know what you want, you can approach ISPs with a common set of questions and you'll be better able to compare them. If you don't figure out what you want in advance, you'll be learning what questions to ask with each successive ISP, you'll get incomplete information, and it will be more difficult to compare them.

As one part of your evaluation, you might consider making a few preliminary calls to see if you can find an ISP or two that offers an assessment service to help you determine what you need. If the service actually is geared toward helping you specify your requirements (as opposed to being simply another sales technique for pushing services you don't want or need), you may have found a provider with at least one strength: customer service.

Keep in mind as you shop that some organizations that provide services such as MySQL access and Web site hosting do not provide dialup service. You may actually be best served by choosing one provider for basic dialup connectivity, allowing you to access the Internet, and another for database and Web activities. (Or you already may have an ISP for dialup access that you are satisfied with, in which case you need to find a provider only for database and Web services.) The following "Bandwidth" and "Services" sections describe the types of concerns that are most appropriately addressed by each type of ISP.

Bandwidth

Providers offer various options, from dedicated lines (faster) to dialup modem connections (slower). In general, the tradeoff is between cost and speed: Fast access costs more. If you're going to shuttle a lot of data between your computer and the ISP's host, a modem connection may be too slow. In certain cases, however, you may be able to get by with a slower connection between the ISP and yourself. For example, if most of the activity you sustain on the ISP host is due to your customers accessing your database from upstream (through a Web site, for example), then most of your database traffic will be outbound from the ISP.

Services

The most obvious requirement for any candidate ISP is that it provides MySQL, but the following services might be necessary or desirable as well:

- **An email account.** This is essential for communicating with the ISP's technical support staff, and you can use it to join one or more of the MySQL mailing lists.

- **Telnet access to a shell account.** This gives you the ability to run standard UNIX utilities and to use MySQL command-line clients such as `mysql`, `mysqldump`, and `mysqlimport`. You may also be able to install your own software.

- **Additional MySQL-related services.** These might include Web site hosting, PHP, and CGI capabilities.

- **FTP.** This is useful for transferring files between your computer and the ISP's machine. For example, you'll likely have some data files you want to load into your database to populate it initially, or you may generate output from the database that you want to manipulate on your own machine. You may also want to allow people to download your files.

- **Domain name registration.** This gives you email and Web site addresses under your own domain name rather than under the domain of your ISP. This is a desirable service if you want to establish a Web or FTP presence under a name that can be readily identified with your organization or business.

Assessing an ISP—General Considerations

This section enumerates a number of general criteria you can use to evaluate candidate ISPs. The next section deals with issues that pertain specifically to MySQL. As you approach a new ISP, ask yourself the questions that follow:

✓ How easy is it to get information?

✓ What are the costs?

✓ What kind of client access software does the ISP provide?

✓ What kind of initial assistance do you receive from the ISP?

✓ Does the provider have good connectivity and bandwidth?

✓ What are the ISP's customer connectivity options?

✓ What kind of technical support does the ISP provide?

✓ Are there quotas? And if so, what are they?

✓ What kind of hardware do they provide?

✓ How do they handle privacy and security issues?

✓ What kind of reputation do they have, and how long have they been around?

✓ What are their plans for growth?

Let's discuss each of these questions in more depth.

✓ **How easy is it to get information?** When you call to inquire about the services an ISP provides, does the ISP answer? If you have difficulty getting through, maybe it's an operation run by someone out of a garage during the evening. If you reach an answering machine, does the ISP return your call?

Do customer service representatives have the answers to your questions? If not, do they find someone within their organization who does? Or do they try to convince you the issues you're raising are unimportant ("Oh, sure, we can handle that—don't worry.")? If you can't get answers to questions before they have your money, how will they treat you after they do?

Does the ISP staff communicate with you in terms you understand? If the only language anyone speaks is marketing drivel, you may be in contact with an outfit that's long on selling themselves and short on hard technical knowledge. On the other hand, if they overpower you with jargon, you might be dealing with a bunch of geeks that have their technical know-how down pat but who can't communicate well with "normal people."

Visit the provider's Web site if you have access to a browser. Is the site clear, informative, and easy to understand? If they can't put together a good home page, what else will they do poorly?

✓ **What are the costs?** This can vary considerably because it depends on so many factors. Is there an initial signup/setup fee in addition to the usual monthly fee? Is the monthly fee fixed or sliding? What does the fee include? Do you get unlimited connect time, or is there some hourly limit? If you exceed the limit, what happens? Do they simply refuse connections (which is inconvenient, but you incur no extra fee)? Or is there a surcharge on top of your normal monthly rate? If there is a charge, does it include disk space?

For dialup connections, the ISP presumably has a local number you can use within your calling area. Do they have an 800 number you can use when you're outside that area? Is there an extra charge for using it? If you live in a rural area, your options probably are more limited, and it's especially important to make sure that ISP access doesn't involve a toll call.

ISPs often include a modest amount of disk space in the basic fee (a few megabytes), with an option to purchase a larger allocation as needed. Get specific information about disk charges if you expect your database to be large or if you plan on hosting a Web site (particularly if it will be graphics heavy).

If you establish a Web or FTP presence on the ISP's host, how does the ISP charge for download volume when people access your Web pages or download files? Some ISPs impose a quota and shut you off until the next time period begins if you exceed the limit. Others may include a sliding fee based on download volume in your bill. Still others may reclassify you as a commercial customer (probably at a higher rate). Find out what your options are.

Is technical support free or is there a charge? If it's free, is that only for a limited time, such as your first 30 days? If there is a charge, do you pay a flat rate or a per-incident rate? Can you pay an extra fee to get premium support?

If you are presented with a fee prepayment plan, evaluate it with an eye to the history and reputation of the company. Prepayment options are sometimes used by startups as a means of raising operating capital, but such ISPs are also the most likely to fold, and if they do, your prepaid fees are likely to be unrecoverable.

Do you have to sign a long-term (a year or more) contract? If you're uncertain about an ISP's capabilities, you want to be able to back out after a month or two. It might be easy to get signed up; how easy is it to get out if you decide you don't like them? Can you get back the unused portion of your contract?

Perhaps you can get a free or low-cost trial account that will allow you to assess the ISP's technical competence and support services. Keep in mind that such an account typically will include limitations on your activities. For example, disk space constraints will limit the size of any trial database you may create.

✓ **What kind of client access software does the ISP provide?** Do they support your platform? Some ISPs may specify that they support only certain systems, such as Windows, which doesn't help you if you're running UNIX or Mac OS.[1]

Does the ISP provide an email client and Web browser if you need them? Do you have to use the ones they provide or can you use others if you prefer?

✓ **What kind of initial assistance do you receive from the ISP?** Do they offer help in getting you connected and getting your account working? Is there a fee for this service (which is likely if you have complex requirements)?

✓ **Does the provider have good connectivity and bandwidth?** How close is the provider to the Internet backbone? Are they directly connected, or do they go through another provider to get there? Do they have redundant connections in case of connection outage?

How big is the "pipe" between the ISP and the backbone? The type of connection determines its *bandwidth*—that is, the maximum amount of traffic the ISP can handle between the backbone and its own installation. T-3 and T-1 lines are high-bandwidth trunks that provide fast connections, but if the provider's own outbound connections are made via modems, that is a bottleneck and transmission rates will suffer.

Ask how much traffic they're actually moving over their connection—how much of their capacity is used? If you're sharing a connection to the backbone with many other active users, the bandwidth that is available to you decreases. This won't just slow you down—a saturated link slows down people connecting from upstream to your database or to your Web site if you have one.

✓ **What are the ISP's customer connectivity options?** You may have a 56Kbps modem, but the ISP must support it or you'll be limited to lower connection rates. Do they offer other higher-speed options, such as ISDN or DSL? If you expect to be moving large amounts of traffic between your site and the ISP, you might even want to set up a dedicated line. Will the ISP help you with that?

Don't Have Unreasonable Expectations of an ISP

You won't get unlimited access, unlimited disk space, and unlimited tech support for $20 a month. Are you willing to pay for good service and support? You want something for your money, but ISPs expect to be reasonably compensated for the services they provide, too.

---

[1] If you're connecting through PPP (point-to-point protocol) or SLIP (serial line IP), you probably can connect from virtually any platform.

If you'll be connecting by modem, you don't want to get a busy signal when you try to reach the service provider. You can ask candidate providers what their customer/modem ratio is, but that depends on customer activity. Residential customers who connect briefly to check email don't tie up the modem pool as much as commercial customers who camp out on a connection all day to conduct business. It's better to ask how often you'll get a busy signal, particularly at the time of day you typically expect to be connecting.

You can test this for yourself before signing up: Dial the ISP's number on a regular phone and listen for a modem screeching on the other end. Perform this test several times on different days. How often do you get a busy signal or no answer? Assess modem availability against your activities. If you're a business, you want to be sure you can connect whenever you want. For personal purposes, you may not mind the occasional busy signal.

✓ **What kind of technical support does the ISP provide?** Is it available at all times, or only during normal business hours? You may plan to connect only during the day, but if you don't, will someone be there to answer your questions? Do they provide both phone and email access to technical support staff? You want phone support because you can't send email if you can't log on. But you want email, too, so that you can mail technical information or program output to the support staff to avoid trying to describe it over the phone. Do they promise a response within a certain amount of time? (The problem may not necessarily be resolved within that time, but requests at least should be acknowledged promptly so that you know they're working on them.)

Is there online help? Is it clear and to the point, or confusing and vague? Can you navigate it easily to find the information you need? Is it searchable?

You can assess technical support availability for yourself the same way you test the dialup access numbers—call them. You might feel foolish doing this before you have an account with the ISP, but it can be instructive to find out whether or not you get put in a phone queue, and for how long. Also ask how many technical support personnel are there. Better yet, ask what the customer-to-technician ratio is.

✓ **Are there quotas? And if so, what are they?** Are there quotas for disk space or processing time? Are there time constraints on scripts executed by the Web server? It's not unreasonable for the ISP to put some limits on customer activities to prevent monopolization of resources shared by other customers, but you want to know what those limits are.

✓ **What kind of hardware do they provide?** It's possible to run basic Internet services on an old 386-class PC, but it won't be suitable for large numbers of users, to say nothing of trying to run more computationally intensive services such as MySQL. MySQL doesn't hog system resources the same way large database systems do, but you still want an ISP that runs hardware with some muscle. What kinds of load can the system handle comfortably?

Where is the server located? In someone's garage or basement? A provider located in a commercial district is likely to have an easier time getting the phone company to run additional trunk lines as capacity demands increase.

How does the ISP deal with equipment failure? Is there a recovery plan in place? Or are you just knocked offline until the equipment is repaired or replaced? What is their actual uptime percentage over the past several months? What accounts for the downtime incidents? Do they perform file system backups, and if so, how often? Or does the ISP consider that your responsibility?

Are there expected downtimes (for scheduled maintenance or backups, for example)? Does the ISP inform customers when those will be? If you run a Web server, you probably prefer that it be available 24 hours a day.

✓ **How do they handle privacy and security issues?** Do they have a policy regarding privacy of your files? What measures do they take to prevent your account from being compromised?

✓ **What kind of reputation do they have, and how long have they been around?** What is their reputation? What other customers do they have, and how well are those customers satisfied? Word of mouth can be useful; ask around to see if your acquaintances are familiar with candidate ISPs. You can ask the ISP for references, and it might be informative to ask for opinions on the MySQL mailing list as well. An ISP will probably refer you to people who are satisfied with their service. On the mailing list, you'll hear both sides. Subscribers there tend to be quite willing to relate whether or not their experience with an ISP is good or bad.

How long has the provider been in business? The ISP industry has a phenomenal number of failed or short-lived startups because it's easy to get started, and difficult to do well. A provider with some longevity is more likely to be around in the not-so-near future and be able to help you for the long term.

✓ **What are their plans for growth?** How big are they? You probably don't want to use a tiny new startup, but the biggest services aren't necessarily better. Smaller companies can be more in touch with the needs of their customers.

How fast are they growing? How many customers do they have now? A month ago? A year ago? You might want to go with a company that's prospering, but growth puts pressure on resources for bandwidth, customer access, and technical support. What is their policy for dealing with increased load?

Assessing an ISP—MySQL-Specific Considerations

The preceding section gives you a way to assess an ISP's general capabilities. This section discusses criteria for evaluating an ISP's MySQL services. When you see "MySQL," interpret that as including any other related services you require, such as Apache, PHP, and DBI.

✓ What MySQL-related services does the ISP provide?

✓ What version of MySQL is installed?

✓ What is ISP policy on updating MySQL?

✓ Are there known problems with MySQL on the ISP's operating system?

✓ Can you install your own software?

✓ Is the ISP concerned about privacy and security of your database?

✓ Do they help you get started?

✓ What kind of MySQL-specific technical support is provided?

✓ How many of their customers use MySQL?

Let's discuss each of these questions in more depth.

✓ **What MySQL-related services does the ISP provide?** The provider should have MySQL installed already, as well as any other related packages you need. The exception might be that you've already got an ISP with which you're otherwise satisfied, but that doesn't have MySQL. In this case, you might want to simply ask whether or not they'd be willing to install it for you. You'll probably need to make some sort of business case for doing so, and you may have to agree that any such installation is done with the understanding that MySQL is not a supported service in the same way as email or Web hosting.

Visit the ISP's Web site. Do they provide information in any detail about their MySQL services? Does it sound like they have any technical understanding, or is the site strong on the marketing language? Is the site easy to navigate? Do they provide an area with answers to common questions customers have about using their services so that you can look up information for yourself?

✓ **What version of MySQL is installed?** Is it a recent version, or is it some really old release that hasn't been touched since its installation? Check the change notes appendix in the MySQL Reference Manual to see what's been added after the version the ISP runs. Do you require those features?

✓ **What is ISP policy on updating MySQL?** The ISP has to balance the need for stability and known behavior with existing MySQL applications against customers' desire to take advantage of new features in recent releases. This isn't necessarily an easy issue to resolve, so don't treat an ISP's concerns about it as trivial. But you will want to know that there is at least some possibility for upgrades, perhaps on a separate host devoted to test purposes. If you offer to serve as a guinea pig for newer releases, you may be able to reach a cooperative solution because you'll be providing your ISP with a valuable testing service.

✓ **Are there known problems with MySQL on the ISP's operating system?** Check the installation chapter in the MySQL Reference manual to see if there are limitations that may affect you. Often there are workarounds to circumvent these problems.

✓ **Can you install your own software?** This allows you to enhance your own MySQL capabilities with third-party software or programs you've written yourself.

✓ **Is the ISP concerned about privacy and security of your database?** In addition to the ISP's general measures to protect customer data, does the ISP take any steps to protect MySQL data in particular? Do you get your own MySQL server? This is better from the customer's point of view because you can control who gets to see the contents of your database. But it's more work on the ISP's part.

✓ **Do they help you get started?** Don't expect the provider to teach you SQL and show you how to write your queries, but you need to be able to connect to the MySQL server. Do they tell you what you need to know to make a connection? Do you get a sample script you can run to verify that you can access your database?

✓ **What kind of MySQL-specific technical support is provided?** Now and then people post messages to the MySQL mailing list about problems with their ISP and getting MySQL to run properly. I've noticed that it's fairly common for an ISP to point its finger at the customer as the source of the problem. As in many disputes, there may be fault on both sides in a number of cases, but from the descriptions of the situations, it seems clear that many times the ISP has little idea how to deal with MySQL and is just guessing how to solve the problem. For this reason, it's important to determine ahead of time that a candidate ISP has administrative or technical staff with a decent grasp of MySQL. Question them about their level of technical expertise. Ask them if they have a MySQL support contract. If so, it's an indication that they take MySQL seriously and stand ready to assist you with problems that may arise.

For example, is the ISP experienced with each package you require so that they can provide real assistance? Or do they say, "Just ask the mailing list"? The ISP should be familiar with the material in Part III, "MySQL Administration," of this book.

Beware the Absentee Administrator

Watch out for ISPs that simply install MySQL so that they can add it to their list of services to attract customers. You don't want the kind of administrator that tries to get away with knowing as little as possible in performing administrative duties.

You'll need to assess the technical support provided against the control that the ISP gives you over your resources. If you want complete control over your MySQL server, and the ISP gives it to you, it's reasonable for the ISP to expect you to be capable of administering the server. In this case, you'll want the ISP to allow you to provide a script that will start your server at system boot time so that you need not do it manually each time the machine is restarted.

✓ **How many of their customers use MySQL?** If MySQL is used actively by many customers, there's a better chance that the ISP will provide good support for it than if just one or two customers use it.

Index

Symbols

C

D

G

N

temporary tables, 555
  CREATE TABLE statements, 148
TERMINATED BY clause
  (LOAD DATA statement), 567
terminating
  MySQL server, 421
  sessions, 20
  statements, 21
terminology
  architectural, 15-16
  query language, 15
  structural, RDBMS (relational database
    management systems), 12-13
--test program option, 600
testing type conversion, 136
text
  columns, strings, 98-100
  formatting, RTF (Rich Text Format), 10
  strings, 81
    double quoting, 82
    storage requirements, 98
TEXT data type, 84, 101, 505
third-party tools, 695
  administrative tools, 696
  data conversion tools, 696
  installing, 481-482
  language APIs, 695
  ODBC support, 696
  program interfaces, 696
threads
  KILL statement, 565
  SHOW PROCESSLIST statement,
    578-579
thread_id attribute (Perl DBI), 668
three-way joins, 63
TIME data type, 84, 108-109, 507
time values, 82
time zone, configuring, 419
time/date
  data types, 84, 107-109, 506
    ambiguous year values, 113-114
    attributes, 111
    DATE, 507
    DATETIME, 507
    formatting, 111-113

TIME, 507
TIMESTAMP, 109-111, 508
YEAR, 111, 508
functions, 535-543
values, rules of interpretation, 135-136
TIMESTAMP data type, 84, 109-111,
  508, 576
--timeout program option, 609
TIME_FORMAT( ) function, 542
TIME_TO_SEC( ) function, 542
TINYBLOB data type, 84, 504. See also
  BLOB data type
TINYINT data type, 83, 87, 501
  storage requirements, 88
TINYTEXT data type, 84, 505. See also
  TEXT data type
TMPDIR environment variable, 594
--tmpdir program option, 598, 601, 615
TO clause (GRANT statement), 563
tools. See third-party tools
TO_DAYS( ) date and time function,
  53, 542
trace( ) method (Perl DBI), 304, 664-665
trace_msg( ) method (Perl DBI), 665
tracing (debugging Perl scripts), 304-305
transactions, 171-174
triggers, 175
TRIM( ) string function, 535
trivial joins, 160
troubleshooting
  administration duties, 393
  C API
    failed result set, 272
    NULL column values, 272-273
    uninitialized buffer pointers, 273
    uninitialized connection handler pointers,
      271-272
  fully qualified names (name
    resolution), 426
  standard table repair, 471
TRUNCATE( ) numeric function, 527
truncated values (column size), 89

Related Titles from New Riders

UNIX/Linux Titles

Solaris 8 Essential Reference
By John P. Mulligan
2nd Edition
425 pages, $34.99
ISBN: 0-7357-1007-4

Looking for the fastest, easiest way to find the Solaris command you need? Need a few pointers on shell scripting? How about advanced administration tips and sound, practical expertise on security issues? Are you looking for trustworthy information about available third-party software packages that will enhance your operating system? Author John Mulligan—creator of the popular Unofficial Guide to Solaris Web site (solarisguide.com)—delivers all that and more in one attractive, easy-to-use reference book. With clear and concise instructions on how to perform important administration and management tasks and key information on powerful commands and advanced topics, *Solaris 8 Essential Reference* is the reference you need when you know what you want to do and you just need to know how.

Linux System Administration
By M Carling and James T. Dennis
1st Edition
450 pages, $29.99
ISBN: 1-56205-934-3

As an administrator, you probably feel that most of your time and energy is spent in endless firefighting. If your network has become a fragile quilt of temporary patches and workarounds, then this book is for you. For example, have you had trouble sending or receiving your email lately? Are you looking for a way to keep your network running smoothly with enhanced performance? Are your users always hankering for more storage, more services, and more speed? *Linux System Administration* advises you on the many intricacies of maintaining a secure, stable system. In this definitive work, the author addresses all the issues related to system administration, from adding users and managing file permissions to Internet services and Web hosting to recovery planning and security. This book fulfills the need for expert advice that will ensure a trouble-free Linux environment.

Developing Linux Applications
By Eric Harlow
1st Edition
400 pages, $34.99
ISBN: 0-7357-0021-4

We all know that Linux is one of the most powerful and solid operating systems in existence. And as the success of Linux grows, there is an increasing interest in developing applications with graphical user interfaces that really take advantage of the power of Linux. In this book, software developer Eric Harlow gives you an indispensable development handbook focusing on the GTK+ toolkit. More than an overview on the elements of application or GUI design, this is a hands-on book that delves deeply into the technology. With in-depth material on the various GUI programming tools and loads of examples, this book's unique focus will give you the information you need to design and launch professional-quality applications.

Linux Firewalls

By Robert Ziegler
1st Edition
400 pages, $39.99
ISBN: 0-7357-0900-9

New Riders is proud to offer the first book aimed specifically at Linux security issues. While there are a host of general UNIX security books, we think it is time to address the practical needs of the Linux network. Author Robert Ziegler takes a balanced approach to system security, discussing topics like planning a secure environment, firewalls, and utilizing security scripts. With comprehensive information on specific system compromises, and advice on how to prevent and repair them, this is one book that every Linux administrator should have on their shelf.

GIMP Essential Reference

by Alex Harford
1st Edition
400 pages, $24.95
ISBN: 0-7357-0911-4

GIMP Essential Reference is designed to fulfill a need for the computer expert. It is made to bring someone experienced in computers up to speed with the GNU Image Manipulation Program. It provides essential information on using this program effectively. This book is targeted at you if you want to efficiently use the GIMP. *GIMP Essential Reference* will show you how to quickly become familiar with the advanced user interface using a table-heavy format that will allow users to find what they're looking for quickly. *GIMP Essential Reference* is for users working with GIMP who know what they want to accomplish, but don't know exactly how to do it.

KDE Application Development

by Uwe Thiem
1st Edition
216 pages, $39.99
ISBN: 1-57870-201-1

KDE Application Development offers a head start into KDE and Qt. The book will cover the essential widgets available in KDE and Qt, and it offers a strong start without the "first try" annoyances that sometimes make strong developers and programmers give up. This book explains KDE and Qt by writing a real application from the very beginning stages, where it can't do anything but display itself and offer a button to quit. Then it will finally bring the user to a full-featured application. The process of developing such an application takes the potential KDE developer through all stages of excitement.

Grokking the GIMP

by Carey Bunks
1ct Edition,
352 pages, $45.00
ISBN: 0-7357-0924-6

This titles is a technical and inspirational reference covering the intricacies of the GIMP's feature set. Even if you have little background in image manipulation, you can succeed at using the GIMP to achieve your goals, using this book as a guide. Keeping in mind that all tools are not created equal, author Carey Bunks provides an in-depth look at the GIMP's most useful tools. The content focuses on the intermediate to advanced topics of interest to most users, like photo touchup and enhancement, compositing, and animations. Invaluable is the conceptual approach of the author, in which he avoids the cookbook approach to learning image manipulation and helps you become self-sufficient.

Inside Linux

by Michael Tobler
1st Edition,
800 pages, $39.99
ISBN: 0-7357-0940-8

With in-depth complete coverage on the installation process, editing and typesetting, graphical user interfaces, programming, system administration, and managing Internet sites, *Inside Linux* is the only book "smart" users new to Linux will need. If you have an understanding of computer technology and are looking for just the right reference to fit your sophisticated needs, this book guides you to a high level of proficiency with all the flavors of Linux, and helps you with crucial system administration chores. *Inside Linux* is different than other books available because it's a unique blend of a how-to and a reference guide.

Python Essential Reference

By David Beazley
1st Edition
300 pages, $34.95
ISBN: 0-7357-0901-7

This book describes the Python programming language and its library of standard modules. Python is an informal language that has become a highly valuable software development tool for many computing professionals. This language reference covers Python's lexical conventions, built-in datatypes, control flow, functions, statements, classes, and execution model. This book also covers the contents of the Python library as bundled in the standard Python distribution.

Development Titles

GTK+/Gnome Application Development

By Havoc Pennington
1st Edition
400 pages, $34.99
ISBN: 0-7357-0078-8

GTK+/Gnome Application Development provides the experienced programmer the knowledge to develop X Window applications with the powerful GTK+ toolkit. The author provides the reader with a checklist of features every application should have, advanced GUI techniques, and the ability to create custom widgets. The title also contains reference information for more experienced users already familiar with usage, but requires knowledge of function prototypes and detailed descriptions. These tools let the reader write powerful applications in record time.

Web Application Development with PHP 4.0

By Till Gerken, et al.
1 Edition
400 pages, $39.99
ISBN: 0-7357-0997-1

Web Application Development with PHP 4.0 explains PHP's advanced syntax including classes, recursive functions and variables. The authors present software development methodologies and coding conventions which are a must-know for industry quality products and make developing faster and more productive. Included is coverage on Web applications and insight into user and session management, e-commerce systems, XML applications and WDDX.

Linux Essential Reference

By Ed Petron
1st Edition
350 pages, $24.95
ISBN: 0-7357-0852-5

This title is all about getting things done by providing structured organization to the plethora of available Linux information. Providing clear and concise instructions on how to perform important administration and management tasks, as well as how to use some of the more powerful commands and more advanced topics, the scope of the Linux Essential Reference includes the best way to implement the most frequently used commands, deal with shell scripting, administer your own system, and utilize effective security.

Lotus Notes and Domino Titles

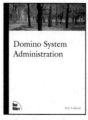

Domino System Administration

By Rob Kirkland
1st Edition
880 pages, $49.99
ISBN: 1-56205-948-3

Your boss has just announced that you will be upgrading to the newest version of Lotus Notes and Domino when it ships. As a Premium Lotus Business Partner, Lotus has offered a substantial price break to keep your company away from Microsoft's Exchange Server. How are you supposed to get this new system installed, configured, and rolled out to all of your end users? You understand how Lotus Notes works—you've been administering it for years. What you need is a concise, practical explanation about the new features, and how to make some of the advanced stuff really work. You need answers and solutions from someone like you, who has worked with the product for years, and understands what it is you need to know. *Domino System Administration* is the answer—the first book on Domino that attacks the technology at the professional level, with practical, hands-on assistance to get Domino running in your organization.

Lotus Notes & Domino Essential Reference

By Dave Hatter and
Tim Bankes
1st Edition
700 pages, $45.00
ISBN: 0-7357-0007-9

You're in a bind because you've been asked to design and program a new database in Notes that will keep track of and itemize a myriad of inventory and shipping data for an important client. The client wants a user-friendly interface, without sacrificing speed or functionality. You are experienced (and could develop this app in your sleep), but feel that you need to take your talents to the next level. You need something to facilitate your creative and technical abilities, something to perfect your programming skills. Your answer is waiting for you: *Lotus Notes & Domino Essential Reference.* It's compact and simply designed. It's loaded with information. All of the objects, classes, functions, and methods are listed. It shows you the object hierarchy and the overlaying relationship between each one. It's perfect for you. Problem solved.

Networking Titles

Cisco Router Configuration & Troubleshooting

By Mark Tripod
2nd Edition
450 pages, $39.99
ISBN: 0-7357-0999-8

Want the real story on making your Cisco routers run like a dream? Why not pick up a copy of *Cisco Router Configuration & Troubleshooting* and see what Mark Tripod has to say? His company is the one responsible for making some of the largest sites on the Net scream, like Amazon.com, Hotmail, USAToday, Geocities, and Sony. In this book, he provides advanced configuration issues, sprinkled with advice and preferred practices. You won't see a general overview on TCP/IP—he talks about more meaty issues like security, monitoring, traffic management, and more. In the troubleshooting section, Mark provides a unique methodology and lots of sample problems to illustrate. By providing real-world insight and examples instead of rehashing Cisco's documentation, Mark gives network administrators information they can start using today.

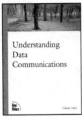

Understanding Data Communications

By Gilbert Held
6th Edition
550 pages, $34.99
ISBN: 0-7357-0036-2

Updated from the highly successful fifth edition, this book explains how data communications systems and their various hardware and software components work. Not an entry-level book, it approaches the material in a textbook format, addressing the complex issues involved in internetworking today. A great reference book for the experienced networking professional, written by noted networking authority, Gilbert Held.

DCE/RPC over SMB

by Luke Leighton
1st Edition
400 pages, $45.00
ISBN: 1-57870-150-3

When Microsoft's systems were locked into offices and chained to small LANs, they were relatively safe. Now, as they've been unleashed onto the Internet, they are more and more vulnerable to attack. Security people, system and network administrators, and the folks writing tools for them all need to be familiar with the packets flowing across their networks. It's the only way to really know how much trouble a system is in. This book describes how Microsoft has taken DCE/RPC (Distributed Computing Environment / Remote Procedure Calls) and implemented it over SMB (Server Message Block) and TCP/IP. SMB itself runs over three transports: TCP/IP, IPX/SPX, and NETBEUI.

Luke Leighton presents Microsoft Developer NT system calls (including what some such calls would be, if they were documented) and shows what they look like over-the-wire by providing example C code to compile and use. This gives administrators and developers insights into how information flows through their network, so that they can improve efficiency, security, and heterogeneous transfers.

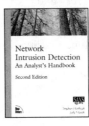

Intrusion Detection: An Analyst's Handbook

by Stephen Northcutt and Judy Novak
2nd Edition
450 pages, $45.00
ISBN: 0-7357-1008-2

Get answers and solutions from someone who has been in the trenches with *Network Intrusion Detection: An Analyst's Handbook*. Author Stephen Northcutt, original developer of the Shadow intrusion detection system and former Director of the United States Navy's Information System Security Office at the Naval Security Warfare Center, lends his expertise to intrusion detection specialists, security analysts, and consultants responsible for setting up and maintaining an effective defense against network security.

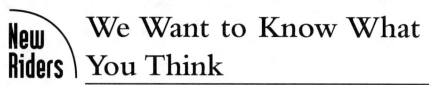

We Want to Know What You Think

To better serve you, we would like your opinion on the content and quality of this book. Please complete this card and mail it to us or fax it to 317-581-4663.

Name _____

Address _____

City _____ State _____ Zip _____

Phone _____

Email Address _____

Occupation _____

Operating System(s) that you use _____

What influenced your purchase of this book?
- ❏ Recommendation   ❏ Cover Design
- ❏ Table of Contents   ❏ Index
- ❏ Magazine Review   ❏ Advertisement
- ❏ New Riders' Reputation ❏ Author Name

How would you rate the contents of this book?
- ❏ Excellent   ❏ Very Good
- ❏ Good   ❏ Fair
- ❏ Below Average   ❏ Poor

How do you plan to use this book?
- ❏ Quick reference   ❏ Self-training
- ❏ Classroom   ❏ Other

What do you like most about this book?
Check all that apply.
- ❏ Content   ❏ Writing Style
- ❏ Accuracy   ❏ Examples
- ❏ Listings   ❏ Design
- ❏ Index   ❏ Page Count
- ❏ Price   ❏ Illustrations

What do you like least about this book?
Check all that apply.
- ❏ Content   ❏ Writing Style
- ❏ Accuracy   ❏ Examples
- ❏ Listings   ❏ Design
- ❏ Index   ❏ Page Count
- ❏ Price   ❏ Illustrations

What would be a useful follow-up book to this one for you? _____

Where did you purchase this book? _____

Can you name a similar book that you like better than this one, or one that is as good? Why?
_____
_____

How many New Riders books do you own? _____

What are your favorite computer books? _____
_____

What other titles would you like to see us develop? _____
_____

Any comments for us? _____
_____
_____
_____

MySQL, 0-7357-0921-1

Fold here and tape to mail

- -

New Riders Publishing
201 W. 103rd St.
Indianapolis, IN 46290

 How to Contact Us

Visit Our Web Site

www.newriders.com

On our Web site you'll find information about our other books, authors, tables of contents, indexes, and book errata.

Email Us

Contact us at this address:

nrfeedback@newriders.com

- If you have comments or questions about this book
- To report errors that you have found in this book
- If you have a book proposal to submit or are interested in writing for New Riders
- If you would like to have an author kit sent to you
- If you are an expert in a computer topic or technology and are interested in being a technical editor who reviews manuscripts for technical accuracy
- To find a distributor in your area, please contact our international department at this address.

nrmedia@newriders.com

- For instructors from educational institutions who want to preview New Riders books for classroom use. Email should include your name, title, school, department, address, phone number, office days/hours, text in use, and enrollment, along with your request for desk/examination copies and/or additional information.
- For members of the media who are interested in reviewing copies of New Riders books. Send your name, mailing address, and email address, along with the name of the publication or Web site you work for.

Bulk Purchases/Corporate Sales

If you are interested in buying 10 or more copies of a title or want to set up an account for your company to purchase directly from the publisher at a substantial discount, contact us at 800-382-3419 or email your contact information to corpsales@pearsontechgroup.com. A sales representative will contact you with more information.

Write to Us

New Riders Publishing

201 W. 103rd St.

Indianapolis, IN 46290-1097

Call Us

Toll-free (800) 571-5840 + 9 + 7477

If outside U.S. (317) 581-3500. Ask for New Riders.

Fax Us

(317) 581-4663

Solutions from experts you know and trust.

www.informit.com

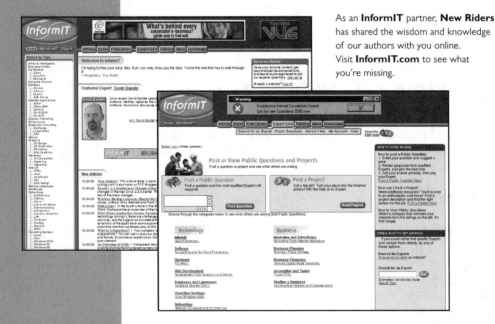
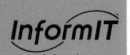

Colophon

The image on the cover is a photograph of the House of the Doves, part of the Mayan ruins at Uxmal.

Uxmal, which means "thrice built," was developed in stages from around 600 AD through 1000 AD. Considered one of the finest examples of Mayan architecture, the ruins at Uxmal are thought to have been mainly a religious center for the surrounding communities. Several of the structures were used for training astronomers, mathematicians, priests, and healers. The ruins are dominated by the Pyramid of the Magician, which, legend has it, was built in one night by the God Itzamna. It actually consists of five pyramids built on top of each other, through several separate stages.

The ruins at Uxmal are some of the most magnificent in the Mayan world. They are brilliantly preserved and amazingly intricate. The buildings are arranged according to the astrological understanding at the time and are adorned with intricate carvings. Chaac, the Mayan Rain God, is one of the most prevalent symbols at the sight.

Chaac was a very important figure in Mayan culture. He was believed to have been part of the creation of the world and humanity and was responsible for bringing the rain that was vital to Mayan crops. Chaac lived in a cenote (a natural well carved out of limestone) at Chichen Itza. When he arose from his cenote, his huge, hooked nose would penetrate the heavens and bring the rain down upon the fields.

Today the ruins at Uxmal are some of the best preserved ruins in the world. They continue to amaze visitors with their beauty and spiritual power. They have stood for over a thousand years, representing one of the greatest cultures the world has ever seen. We can only hope that a thousand years from now, we as a culture have withstood the test of time as well as the Maya.